Criminal Litigation and Sentencing

Authors

Elizabeth Beckerlegge, Barrister, Senior Lecturer, University of the West of England, Bristol

James Griffiths, Barrister, Senior Lecturer, The City Law School

Peter Hungerford-Welch, Barrister, Associate Dean, The City Law School

Robert McPeake, Barrister, Principal Lecturer, The City Law School

Editor

Robert McPeake, Barrister, Principal Lecturer, The City Law School

Series Editor

Julie Browne, Barrister, Senior Lecturer, The City Law School

Criminal Litigation and Sentencing

The City Law School, City University, London

OXFORD
UNIVERSITY PRESS

OXFORD
UNIVERSITY PRESS

Great Clarendon Street, Oxford OX2 6DP

Oxford University Press is a department of the University of Oxford.
It furthers the University's objective of excellence in research, scholarship,
and education by publishing worldwide in

Oxford New York

Auckland Cape Town Dar es Salaam Hong Kong Karachi
Kuala Lumpur Madrid Melbourne Mexico City Nairobi
New Delhi Shanghai Taipei Toronto

With offices in

Argentina Austria Brazil Chile Czech Republic France Greece
Guatemala Hungary Italy Japan Poland Portugal Singapore
South Korea Switzerland Thailand Turkey Ukraine Vietnam

Oxford is a registered trade mark of Oxford University Press
in the UK and in certain other countries

Published in the United States
by Oxford University Press Inc., New York

© City University, 2009

The moral rights of the author have been asserted
Database right Oxford University Press (maker)

Crown copyright material is reproduced under Class Licence
Number C01P0000148 with the permission of OPSI
and the Queen's Printer for Scotland

All rights reserved. No part of this publication may be reproduced,
stored in a retrieval system, or transmitted, in any form or by any means,
without the prior permission in writing of Oxford University Press,
or as expressly permitted by law, or under terms agreed with the appropriate
reprographics rights organization. Enquiries concerning reproduction
outside the scope of the above should be sent to the Rights Department,
Oxford University Press, at the address above

You must not circulate this book in any other binding or cover
and you must impose the same condition on any acquirer

British Library Cataloguing in Publication Data
Data available

Typeset by Laserwords Private Limited, Chennai, India
Printed in Great Britain on acid-free paper by
Ashford Colour Press Ltd, Gosport, Hampshire

ISBN 978–0–19–956850–5

10 9 8 7 6 5 4 3 2 1

FOREWORD

I am delighted to write this Foreword to the manuals which are written by practitioners and staff of the Inns of Court School of Law (ICSL [now The City Law School]).

The manuals are designed primarily to support training on the Bar Vocational Course (BVC). They now cover a wide range, embracing both the compulsory and the optional subjects of the BVC. They provide an outstanding resource for all those concerned to teach and acquire legal skills wherever the BVC is taught.

The manuals for the compulsory subjects are updated and revised annually. The manuals for the optional subjects are revised every two years. To complement the Series, the publishers will maintain a website for the manuals which will be used to keep them up-to-date throughout the academic year.

The manuals, continually updated, exemplify the practical and professional approach that is central to the BVC. I congratulate the staff of The City Law School who have produced them to an excellent standard, and Oxford University Press for its commitment in securing their publication. As my predecessor the Hon. Mr Justice Gross so aptly said in a previous Foreword, the manuals are an important ingredient in the constant drive to raise standards in the public interest.

Lord Justice Etherton
Chairman of the Advisory Board of the Institute of Law
City University, London

PREFACE

It is essential that practitioners in the criminal courts have mastered the rules of criminal procedure and sentencing. However, such rules never stand still and practitioners must frequently update their knowledge of the relevant statutory provisions and case law. This task has grown increasingly onerous over the last two decades, not least because of the constant stream of legislation in this field.

This manual endeavours to provide a clear guide to the law and rules which govern practice in the magistrates' courts, youth courts, the Crown Court and appellate courts. This edition has been updated to include all relevant developments in the law to 30 April 2009. As ever, though, criminal justice does not stand still. Significant developments will be dealt with on the series' companion website, which we hope is a valuable additional resource for readers of the manual. The website is available at <http://www.oxfordtextbooks.co.uk./orc/barmanuals/>.

15 June 2009

OUTLINE CONTENTS

Foreword v
Preface vii
Outline contents ix
Detailed contents xi
Table of cases xv
Table of statutes xxiii
Table of secondary legislation xxxiii

1	Introduction	1
2	Preliminaries	16
3	Bail	57
4	Allocation	97
5	Summary trial	114
6	Youth court trials	130
7	Sending cases to the Crown Court	154
8	Appeals from decisions of magistrates	160
9	Disclosure	171
10	Indictments	183
11	Crown Court trial	194
12	Appeals to the Court of Appeal	238
13	Procedure between conviction and sentence	269
14	The principles of sentencing	291
15	Non-custodial sentences in the magistrates' court	300
16	Custodial sentences in the magistrates' court	316
17	Non-custodial sentences in the youth court	324
18	Custodial sentences in the youth court	329
19	Non-custodial sentences in the Crown Court	331
20	Custodial sentences in the Crown Court	335

APPENDIX 1: Triable either way offences—determining the mode of trial (ss 17A–23, MCA 1980) 341
APPENDIX 2: Victims and other witnesses 344

Index 353

DETAILED CONTENTS

Foreword		v
Preface		vii
Outline contents		ix
Detailed contents		xi
Table of cases		xv
Table of statutes		xxiii
Table of secondary legislation		xxxiii

1 Introduction 1

1.1	Introduction to criminal litigation	1
1.2	Introduction to the criminal justice system	4
1.3	Recent developments	6
1.4	Abbreviations	9
1.5	Criminal Justice Act 2003: what's in force?	10

2 Preliminaries 16

2.1	Preamble	16
2.2	Arrest and charge	21
2.3	Instituting proceedings other than by arrest and charge	43
2.4	Issue of a warrant	45
2.5	Jurisdiction to try offences	46
2.6	Public funding for legal representation and advice	46
2.7	Costs	52
2.8	Reducing delay in the criminal process	54
2.9	Serious organised crime	55

3 Bail 57

3.1	Bail—practice and procedure	57
3.2	Taking a decision on bail—when and how	63
3.3	Applying for bail—what happens in court?	66
3.4	Objections to a release on bail	67
3.5	Refusing to release a defendant on bail	67
3.6	Overcoming objections to bail—the power of imagination	72
3.7	Attaching conditions to release on bail	72
3.8	Changing bail conditions	76
3.9	What happens if the defendant disobeys?	77
3.10	Renewing an application for bail (or 'If at first you don't succeed, try again—but only once!')	83
3.11	Appealing against a bail decision	85
3.12	Representation for bail applications	87
3.13	Juvenile bail	88
3.14	Remands	89
3.15	When will a case be remanded?	89
3.16	Who can remand a case?	92
3.17	Duration of remands	92
3.18	What are the alternatives to remanding a case?	95

4 Allocation 97

4.1	Classification of offences	97
4.2	Procedure for determining allocation	99
4.3	Special cases	105
4.4	Linked summary and indictable offences	107
4.5	Advantages and disadvantages of each mode of trial	108
4.6	Advance information	109
4.7	Allocation Guidelines	110

5 Summary trial 114

5.1	Procedure at trial	114
5.2	The trial	115
5.3	The clerk to the justices and court legal adviser	123
5.4	Committal to the Crown Court for sentence	126

6 Youth court trials 130

6.1	Introduction	130
6.2	Juveniles and criminal responsibility	133
6.3	The youth court	134
6.4	Juveniles in the adult courts	145
6.5	Young adults	148
6.6	Alternatives to prosecution	149

7 Sending cases to the Crown Court 154

7.1	Background	154
7.2	Procedure under s 51	154
7.3	Restrictions on reporting	156
7.4	Effecting the transfer	157
7.5	Applications for dismissal	158
7.6	Voluntary bills of indictment	158

8 Appeals from decisions of magistrates 160

8.1	Appeal to the Crown Court	160
8.2	Appeals to the High Court by way of case stated	162
8.3	Application for judicial review	165
8.4	Appeal to the House of Lords	170

9 Disclosure 171

9.1	The duty of the investigating officer	171
9.2	Prosecution disclosure	172

xii Detailed Contents

9.3	Defence disclosure	173
9.4	Sanctions for non-compliance by the defence	177
9.5	Public interest immunity	178
9.6	Third party disclosure	181

10 Indictments 183

10.1	What is an indictment?	183
10.2	Joinder of counts	186
10.3	Joinder of defendants	187
10.4	Discretion to order separate trials	188
10.5	Misjoinder	189
10.6	Deciding the contents of the indictment	190
10.7	Alternative counts	192
10.8	Amending the indictment	192

11 Crown Court trial 194

11.1	Preliminary hearings	194
11.2	The arraignment	197
11.3	The jury	203
11.4	Change of plea	208
11.5	The prosecution case	209
11.6	Submission of no case to answer	216
11.7	The defence case	218
11.8	Closing speeches	219
11.9	Two or more defendants	219
11.10	Unrepresented defendants	220
11.11	The summing up	220
11.12	Bail	226
11.13	The verdict	227
11.14	Sentence	233
11.15	The effect of the European Convention on Human Rights	233
11.16	Less common pleas	234
11.17	Trial by judge alone	236

12 Appeals to the Court of Appeal 238

12.1	The Criminal Division of the Court of Appeal	238
12.2	The appeal against a ruling	239
12.3	The appeal against conviction	242
12.4	Evidence	252
12.5	Appeal against sentence	255
12.6	Procedure for appeal	256
12.7	Powers of the single judge	258
12.8	Powers of the Court of Appeal	259
12.9	The appeal against acquittal and order for retrial	262
12.10	Other methods of appeal	263
12.11	Appeal to the House of Lords	265
12.12	Reference to the European Court of Justice	265
12.13	The Criminal Cases Review Commission	265

13 Procedure between conviction and sentence 269

13.1	Advance indications of the sentence	269
13.2	Advising on sentence	271
13.3	Adjournments	272
13.4	The facts of the offence	274
13.5	Character and antecedents evidence	279
13.6	Reports	281
13.7	Defence mitigation	284
13.8	Pronouncing sentence	285
13.9	Taking other offences into consideration	286
13.10	Sample offences	288
13.11	Legal representation	289
13.12	Differences between sentencing procedure in the Crown Court and in the magistrates' courts	290

14 The principles of sentencing 291

14.1	Introduction	291
14.2	Sentencing Guidelines Council	291
14.3	Purposes of sentencing	292
14.4	The sentencing process	292
14.5	The concept of seriousness	292
14.6	Credit for guilty plea	295
14.7	Effect of previous convictions	297
14.8	Specimen/sample counts	298
14.9	'TICs' (offences 'taken into consideration')	298

15 Non-custodial sentences in the magistrates' court 300

15.1	Absolute discharge	300
15.2	Conditional discharge	300
15.3	Fines	301
15.4	Community sentences under the Criminal Justice Act 2003	303
15.5	Persistent offenders	307
15.6	Credit for time spent on remand	308
15.7	Breach of community orders under the Criminal Justice Act 2003	308
15.8	Amendment of community orders	310
15.9	Commission of subsequent offences	311
15.10	Disqualification under PCC(S)A 2000, s 146	312
15.11	Surcharges	312
15.12	Anti-social behaviour orders (ASBOs)	312

16 Custodial sentences in the magistrates' court 316

16.1	Introduction	316
16.2	Magistrates' powers of custodial sentencing	316
16.3	Imprisonment	316
16.4	Prison sentences of less than 12 months: 'custody plus'	320
16.5	Suspended sentences	321
16.6	Intermittent custody	323
16.7	Offenders aged 18–20: detention in a young offender institution	323

17 Non-custodial sentences in the youth court 324

| 17.1 | Introduction | 324 |
| 17.2 | Fines and discharges | 325 |

17.3	Referral order	325
17.4	Pre-sentence reports on young offenders	326
17.5	Youth Rehabilitation Order under the Criminal Justice and Immigration Act 2008	326

18 Custodial sentences in the youth court 329

18.1	Introduction	329
18.2	Detention and training orders	329
18.3	More serious offences	330
18.4	Summary: custodial sentences available according to age	330

19 Non-custodial sentences in the Crown Court 331

19.1	Fines	331
19.2	Other non-custodial sentences	331
19.3	Breach of community order imposed by the Crown Court	332
19.4	Revocation of Crown Court community orders other than for breach	333
19.5	Commission of subsequent offences	333

20 Custodial sentences in the Crown Court 335

20.1	Introduction	335
20.2	Sentences over 12 months—release on licence	335
20.3	Life sentences—murder	336
20.4	Mandatory minimum sentences	336
20.5	Dangerous offenders	337
20.6	Young offenders—long-term detention under PCC(S)A 2000, s 91	339

APPENDIX 1: Triable either way offences—determining the mode of trial (ss 17A–23, MCA 1980) 341
APPENDIX 2: Victims and other witnesses 344

Index 353

TABLE OF CASES

A v DPP (2000) 164 JP 3137...114
A and Others [2007] EWCA Crim 2485...248
A and Others [2007] EWCA Crim 2845...249
Abassy v Commissioner of Police of the Metropolis [1990] 1 WLR 385...24
Abdroikov, Green and Wilkinson [2007] UKHL 37...203, 248
Abu Hamza [2006] EWCA Crim 2918; [2007] 3 All ER 451...206
Ahluwalia [1992] 4 All ER 889...254
Ahmed (1984) 80 Cr App R 295...199
Ahmed (1995) *The Times* 9 March...246
Ajodha v The State [1982] AC 204...212
Al-Ali *The Times*, 3 October 2008...241
Alan I [2007] EWCA Crim 2999...203
Alden (2002) 2 Cr App R (S) 326...105
Alladice (1988) 87 Cr App R 380...37
Allen v West Yorkshire Probation Service Community Service Organisation [2001] EWHC Admin 2...163
Altrincham Justices, *ex parte* Pennington [1975] 1 QB 549...167
Andrews [1999] Crim LR 156 (CA)...206
Archer [1994] Crim LR 80...276
Argent [1997] 2 Cr App R 27 (CA)...223
Armsaramah (2000) 164 JP 709 (CA)...319
Ashton [2006] EWCA Crim 794; [2007] 1 WLR 181...243, 249
Assim [1966] 2 QB 249...188
Atlan [2004] EWCA Crim 1798; [2005] Crim LR 63...232
Attorney-General's Reference (No 4 of 1989) [1990] 1 WLR 41 (CA)...264
Attorney-General's References (Nos 3 and 4 of 1996) [1997] 1 Cr App R (S) 29...278
Attorney-General's Reference (No 28 of 1996) (R v Shaw) (1997) *The Times* 27 January...265
Attorney-General's Reference (No 60 of 1996) (R v Harnett) (1997) *The Times* 27 January...265
Attorney-General's Reference (No 2 of 2000) (2001) 165 JP 195 (CA)...217
Attorney-General's Reference (No 110 of 2002) [2003] EWCA Crim 540...265
Attorney-General's Reference (No 80 of 2005) (R v Wedlock-Ward) [2005] EWCA Crim 3367...202
Attorney-General's Reference (No 11 of 2006) [2006] EWCA Crim 856; [2006] 2 Cr App R (S) 108...318
Attorney-General's Reference (No 8 of 2007) (R v Krivec) [2007] EWCA Crim 922; [2008] 1 Cr App R (S) 1...293
Austin [2003] Crim LR 426...231

AWG Group v Morrison (unreported 1 December 2005)...248
Aylesbury Crown Court, *ex parte* Lait [1998] Crim LR 264...166
Azam [2006] EWCA Crim 161...207
Aziz [1996] AC 41...222

B [2003] All ER (D) 67...248
B (Sentence: Detention and training orders) [2005] EWCA Crim 312; [2005] 2 Cr App R (S) 87...340
Baldwin [2002] EWCA Crim 2647; (2002) *The Times* 22 November...318
Bansal [1999] Crim LR 484...250
Banton [2007] EWCA Crim 1847...230
Barber [2002] 1 Cr App R (S) 130 (CA)...295
Barking and Dagenham Justices, *ex parte* DPP (1995) 159 JP 373...120
Barnet Magistrates' Court, *ex parte* DPP (1994) 158 JP 1060...96
Barrell and Wilson (1979) 69 Cr App R 250...186, 187
Barrow v The Queen [1998] 2 WLR 957 (PC)...222
Barton v DPP [2001] EWHC Admin 223; (2001) 165 JP 779...184, 297
Battle Justices, *ex parte* Shepherd (1983) 5 Cr App R (S) 124...167, 169
Beckles (2003) 36 EHRR 13; [2004] EWCA Crim 2766; [2005] 1 WLR 2829...224
Beedie [1998] QB 356 (CA)...235
Belmarsh Magistrates' Court, *ex parte* Gilligan [1998] 1 Cr App R 14...211
Bennett (1980) 2 Cr App R (S) 96...273
Bentley [2001] 1 Cr App R 21...267
Beresford (1971) 56 Cr App R 143...254
Berrada (1989) 91 Cr App R 131...221
Beswick (1996) 160 JP 33 (CA)...277
Betts and Hall [2001] 2 Cr App R 257 (CA)...224
Bevan (1993) 98 Cr App R 354...218
Bezicheri v Italy (1989) 12 EHRR 210...84
Bibby [1972] Crim LR 513...279
Birchall [1999] Crim LR 311 (CA)...223
Birmingham Crown Court, *ex parte* Ali and another [1999] Crim LR 504 (DC)...74
Birmingham Crown Court, *ex parte* Sharma [1988] Crim LR 741...118
Birmingham Justices, *ex parte* Hodgson [1985] QB 1131...104, 105
Birmingham Justices, *ex parte* Wyatt [1976] 1 WLR 260...290

Blackfriars Crown Court, *ex parte* Sunworld Ltd [2000] 1 WLR 2102...164
Blyth Juvenile Court, *ex parte* G [1991] Crim LR 693...84
Bolivar [2003] EWCA Crim 1167...247
Bolton Justices, *ex parte* Scally [1991] 1 QB 537...168
Boness [2005] EWCA Crim 2395; [2006] 1 Cr App R (S) 120...313
Boodram v Trinidad and Tobago [2002] 1 Cr App R 12...247
Booth, Holland and Wood [1999] 1 Cr App R 457...261
Bourne Justices, *ex parte* Cope (1989) 153 JP 161...104
Bournemouth Magistrates' Court, *ex parte* Cross (1989) 89 Cr App R 90...71
Bow Street Magistrates' Court, *ex parte* Welcome (1992) 156 JP 609...118
Bowerman [2002] 2 Cr App R 189...221
Bowers and Others (unreported, 20 June 2006) (CA)...104
Bowker [2007] EWCA Crim 1608...149
Bowles [1996] 2 Cr App R (S) 248...297
Boyle [1993] Crim LR 40...80
Boyle v Criminal Cases Review Commission [2007] EWHC 8 (Admin) (7 March 2007)...267
Braden (1988) 87 Cr App R 289...106
Bradford Justices, *ex parte* Wilkinson [1990] 1 WLR 692...167
Bradshaw [1997] 2 Cr App R (S) 128...289
Bristol Magistrates' Court, *ex parte* Davies [1999] Crim LR 504...83
Britton [2007] 1 Cr App R(S) 121...149
Broadhead [2006] EWCA Crim 1705...246
Brown [2001] EWCA Crim 961; [2002] 1 Cr App R 5...217
Brushett [2001] Crim LR 471...181
Bryant [2005] EWCA Crim 2079...19
Buffery (1993) 14 Cr App R (S) 511...295
Buono (1992) 95 Cr App R 338...232
Burfoot (1990) 12 Cr App R (S) 252...289
Burgess v Governor of Maidstone Prison [2000] All ER (D) 1688...58
Bushell (1980) 2 Cr App R (S) 77...54

C [2004] UKHL 3; [2004] 2 WLR 335...179
C [2005] EWCA Crim 2170...248
Caballero v UK (2000) 30 EHRR 643...61
Cain [1976] Crim LR 464...271
Cain [2006] EWCA Crim 3233 (CA)...291
Cairns [2002] EWCA Crim 2838; [2003] 1 WLR 796...175, 186
Cameron [2001] Crim LR 587 (CA)...246
Campbell (1911) 6 Cr App R 131...279
Campbell [2007] EWCA Crim 1472; [2007] 1 WLR 2798...222
Campbell v DPP [2003] All ER (D) 412...163
Canavan [1998] 1 Cr App R 79; [1998] 1 Cr App R (S) 243...111, 289
Carlton (1994) 15 Cr App R (S) 335...297
Central Criminal Court, *ex parte* Guney [1994] 1 WLR 438; [1995] 1 WLR 376; [1996] AC 616 (CA)...58, 83, 92
Central Criminal Court, *ex parte* Guney [1996] 2 All ER 705 (HL)...226
Chaaban [2003] EWCA Crim 1012; (2003) *The Times* 8 May...197
Chalkley and Jeffries [1998] QB 848...24, 243, 251
Chandler [1964] 2 QB 322...206

Charlton (2000) 164 JP 685...329
Chatterjee [1996] Crim LR 801...246
Chichester Magistrates' Court, *ex parte* DPP (1993) 157 JP 1049...124
Chief Constable of Norfolk v Clayton [1983] 2 AC 473...44
Chief Constable of South Yorkshire [2004] 4 All ER 193...26
Christie v Leachinsky [1947] AC 573 ...21, 24
Clark [1996] 2 Cr App R (S) 351...111, 289, 297
Clarke [2000] 1 Cr App R (S) 224...81
Clarke [2006] EWCA Crim 3427...246
Clarke [2008] UKHL 8; [2008] 1 WLR 338...186
Claydon [2004] 1 Cr App R 36 (CA)...196
Clement (1991) *The Times* 12 December...201
Cliff [2004] EWCA Crim 3139; [2005] 2 Cr App R(S) 22...312
Clinton [1993] 1 WLR 1181...246
Cockley (1984) 79 Cr App R 181...246
Colchester Justices, *ex parte* Abbott (2001) *The Times* 13 March...105, 106
Coles v DPP (1998) 162 JP 687...52, 123
Collins [1947] KB 560...288
Collins [2007] EWCA Crim 854...218
Collison (1980) 71 Cr App R 249...192, 230
Condron [1997] 1 WLR 827 (CA)...223
Condron v United Kingdom [2000] Crim LR 679 (CA)...244, 245
Conley [2005] EWCA Crim 63...243
Connelly v DPP [1964] AC 1254...234
Considine (1980) 70 Cr App R 239...105
Cooper [1969] 1 QB 267...242
Cordingley [2007] EWCA Crim 2174...248
Costen (1989) 11 Cr App R (S) 511...295
Costley (1989) 11 Cr App R (S) 357...276
Coulter v HM Advocate [2001] 2 WLR 779 (PC)...206
Courtie [1984] AC 463...287
Coutts [2006] UKHL 39; [2006] 1 WLR 2154...230
Cowan [1996] QB 373 (CA)...223
Cox [1993] 1 WLR 188; (1993) 96 Cr App R 464...32, 289, 317
Cox and Thomas [1999] 2 Cr App R 6...258
Crabtree [1952] 2 All ER 974...279
Cranston (1993) 14 Cr App R (S) 103 (CA)...277
Criminal Cases Review Commission, *ex parte* Pearson [1999] 3 All ER 498...267
Crompton and Crompton v North Tyneside Metropolitan Borough Council [1991] COD 52...164
Crown Prosecution Service v P [2007] EWHC 946 (Admin)...134, 2008
Crown Prosecution Service v South East Surrey Youth Court and Ghanbari [2005] EWHC 2929 (Admin)...141, 143, 145
Croydon Crown Court, *ex parte* Cox [1997] 1 Cr App R 20...86
Cunnah [1996] 1 Cr App R (S) 393...283
Curry (1998) *The Times* 23 March...211

Dabhade [1993] QB 329...235
Dallison v Caffery [1965] 1 QB 348...24
Davis [1993] 1 WLR 613...179, 180
Davis [2001] 1 Cr App R 115...244
Davis (June 2008) (HL)...8
Davis (Seaton Roy) (1986) 8 Cr App R (S) 64...80
Derby Magistrates' Court, *ex parte* B [1996] AC 487...19

Derby Magistrates' Court, *ex parte* DPP (1999) *The Times* 17 August...129
Dewsbury Magistrates' Court, *ex parte* K (1994) *The Times* 16 March...116
Dhesi v Chief Constable of the West Midlands (2000) *The Times* 9 May...24
Dickinson [1977] Crim LR 303...255
Dimes v Grand Junction Canal (1852) 3 HLC 759...167
Dixon [2000] 1 WLR 782...258
Docherty [1999] 1 Cr App R 274...207
Dodd (1981) 74 Cr App R 50...208
Doherty [1997] 2 Cr App R 218 (CA)...247
Dover and East Kent Justices, *ex parte* Dean [1992] Crim LR 33...84
Dow [2003] EWCA Crim 3621...247
Dowdall (1992) 13 Cr App R (S) 441 (CA)...199, 279
Dowler v Merseyrail [2009] EWHC 558 (Admin)...56
DPP, *ex parte* Horner [2006] EWHC 1607 (Admin)...54
DPP v Blake (1989) 89 Cr App R 179...34
DPP v Gane [1991] Crim LR 711 (DC)...121
DPP v Kirk [1993] COD 99...164
DPP v McCabe [1992] Crim LR 885...184
DPP v Merriman [1973] AC 584...184, 187
DPP v Richards [1988] QB 701...58
DPP v Short (2002) 166 JP 474...45
DPP v T [2006] EWHC 728 (Admin); [2007] 1 WLR 209...314
Drew [1985] 1 WLR 914...208
Druce (1993) 14 Cr App R (S) 691 (CA)...276
Dubarry (1976) 64 Cr App R 7...247
Duggan [1992] Crim LR 513 (CA)...232
Dunlop [2006] EWCA Crim 1354...263
Dunmow Justices, *ex parte* Nash (1993) 157 JP 1153 (DC)...109
Durham Justices, *ex parte* Virgo [1952] 2 QB 1...118
Dyson (1944) 29 Cr App R 104...70

Ealing Magistrates' Court, *ex parte* Sahota (1998) 162 JP 73...123
Easton [1995] 1 WLR 1348...225
Edwards (1983) 77 Cr App R 5...245
Elliott [2002] EWCA Crim 931...32
Ely Justices, *ex parte* Burgess [1992] Crim LR 888...168
Emery (1943) 29 Cr App R 47...118
Ensor [1989] 1 WLR 497 (CA)...246
Epping and Ongar Justices, *ex parte* Breach [1987] RTR 233...117
Essa [2009] EWCA Crim 43...225
Eubank [2002] 1 Cr App R (S) 4; [2001] EWCA Crim 891; [2001] Crim LR 495; [2002] 1 Cr App R (S) 4...199, 276

F [1994] Crim LR 377...232
F [1999] Crim LR 306 (CA); (1998) *The Times* 20 October...243
Fairbanks [1986] 1 WLR 1202 (CA)...229
Farr (1999) 163 JP 193...221
Farrand and Galland [1989] Crim LR 573...165
Farrow (1998) *The Times* 20 October...243
Fennell [2000] 1 WLR 2011 (CA)...105
Ferguson v The Queen [1979] 1 WLR 94...221
Fitzpatrick [1999] Crim LR 832...225
Fletcher (1949) 113 JP 365...70

Follett [1989] QB 338 (CA)...189, 190
Ford [1989] QB 868 (CA)...205
Forde [1923] 2 KB 400...251
Forest of Dean Justices, *ex parte* Farley [1990] RTR 228...235
Foster [2007] EWCA Crim 2869; [2008] 1 WLR 1615...193, 230
Foucher v France (1998) 25 EHRR 234...233
France v Dewsbury Magistrates' Court [1988] Crim LR 295...80
Francom [2001] 1 Cr App R 237...244
Fricker (1999) *The Times* 13 July...207

G [2001] 1 WLR 1727...235
Galandauer v Snaresbrook Crown Court [2006] EWHC 1633 (Admin)...53
Galbraith [1981] 1 WLR 1039...120, 216
Gandy (1989) 11 Cr App R (S) 564...199, 276
Gardener [1994] Crim LR 301...276
Garman v Plaice [1969] 1 WLR 19...45
Garrett [2005] EWCA Crim 1169...246
Gaughan [1990] Crim LR 880...221
Gayle [1999] Crim LR 502...32
GC [2008] EWCA Crim 1033...249
George Maxwell Developments Ltd [1980] 2 All ER 99...274
Ghafoor (Imran) [2003] 1 Cr App R (S) 84...149
Gibbons v DPP (2001) 165 JP 812...121
Gillam (1980) 2 Cr App R (S) 267...255, 291
Gillette (1999) *The Times* 3 December (CA)...319
Gleeson [2003] EWCA Crim 3357; [2004] 1 Cr App R 29...216
Gloucester Crown Court, *ex parte* Chester [1998] COD 365...170
Goodyear [2005] EWCA Crim 888; [2005] 1 WLR 2532...201, 202, 269, 271
Gorman [1987] 1 WLR 545...228
Gough [1993] AC 646 (HL)...44, 167, 206, 233
Gough [1998] Crim LR 148...169
Gray [2004] EWCA Crim 1074; [2004] 2 Cr App R 30...222
Greater Manchester Probation Committee v Bent (1996) 160 JP Rep 297...310
Gregory [1993] Crim LR 623...221
Griffith v Jenkins [1992] AC 76...165
Griffiths (1932) 23 Cr App R 153...288
Grondkowsik and Malinowski [1946] KB 369...189
Guppy (1995) 16 Cr App R (S) 25...254

H [2003] UKHL 1; [2003] 1 All ER 497...234
H [2004] UKHL 3; [2004] 2 WLR 335...179, 180, 181
H (Interlocutory application: Disclosure) [2007] UKHL 7; [2007] 2 AC 270...196
Hall [1989] Crim LR 228...54
Hall [2002] EWCA Crim 1881...247
Hallam [2007] EWCA Crim 1495...228
Hamilton-Johnson v RSPCA [2000] 2 Cr App R (S) 390...54
Hanberry [1977] QB 924...207
Hanratty [2002] EWCA 1141 (CA)...253
Hanson [2005] EWCA Crim 824; [2005] 1 WLR 3169...222
Harnett *see* Attorney-General's Reference (No 60 of 1996)
Harris (1993) *The Times* 22 March...192
Harron [1996] Crim LR 581...225

Harrow Crown Court, *ex parte* Dave [1994] 1 WLR 98 (DC)...161
Hart [2006] EWCA Crim 3239...260
Hartrey (1993) 14 Cr App R (S) 507...275
Harward (1981) 73 Cr App R 168...187
Hastings [2003] EWCA Crim 3730; (2003) *The Times* 12 December...226
Hauschildt v Denmark (1990) 12 EHRR 266...233
Hawkins (1985) 7 Cr App R (S) 351...199, 276
Hazelwood (1984) 6 Cr App R (S) 52...279
Hendon Justices, *ex parte* DPP [1994] QB 167...117, 168
Hereford Magistrates' Court, *ex parte* Rowlands [1998] QB 110...166
Highton [2005] EWCA Crim 1985; [2005] 1 WLR 3472...222
Hobson [1998] 1 Cr App R 31...247
Holgate-Mohammed v Duke [1984] AC 437...24
Horsman [1998] QB 531...260
Horton (1985) 7 Cr App R (S) 299...255
Hourigan [2003] EWCA Crim 2306...80
Howell [2003] EWCA Crim 1...32
Howells [1999] 1 WLR 307 (CA)...317, 319
Huntingdon Crown Court, *ex parte* Jordan [1981] QB 857...118
Huntingdon Magistrates' Court, *ex parte* Percy [1994] COD 323...163
Hussain [2004] EWCA Crim 325...229
Hutchison Reid v UK (2003) 37 EHRR 9...61
Hutton (1990) Crim LR 875...207

Igbebion [2004] EWCA Crim 2724...81
Inner London Crown Court, *ex parte* Barnes (Anthony) [1996] COD 17...147
Inner London Crown Court, *ex parte* London Borough of Lambeth Council [2000] Crim LR 303...161
Inns (1975) 60 Cr App R 231...271
Inskip [2005] EWCA Crim 3372...250
Ipswich Crown Court, *ex parte* Baldwin [1981] 1 All ER 596...170
Ipswich Justices, *ex parte* D (5 December 1994)...170
IRC, *ex parte* Dhesi (1995) *The Independent* 14 August...159

Jackson [1992] Crim LR 214 (CA)...221
Jackson [1996] Crim LR 355...255
Jackson [1999] 1 All ER 572...258
Jacques [2003] All ER (D) 26...253
Jasper v United Kingdom (2000) 30 EHRR 441...179
JJB [2004] EWCA Crim 14...136, 2008
Johal [1973] QB 475...193
Johnson [1988] 1 WLR 1377...178
Johnson [1994] Crim LR 949...218
Johnson [2006] EWCA Crim 2486; [2007] 1 WLR 585...338
Johnson v Leicestershire Constabulary (1998) *The Times* 7 October...168
Jones (1996) *The Times* 23 July...253
Jones [1997] 1 Cr App R 86...254
Jones [1997] Crim LR 598...246
Jones [2001] EWCA Crim 168; [2001] QB 862; [2003] 1 AC 1...197
Jones [2003] AC 1; [2002] 2 All ER 113...82, 95, 116

Jones v Whalley [2006] UKHL 41...41
Jones and Jenkins [2003] EWCA Crim 1966; [2004] 1 Cr App R 5...222

K [2006] EWCA Crim 724; [2006] 2 All ER 552...19, 171, 197
Kaj Raninen v Finland [1998] EHRLR 344...233
Kamar (2002) *The Times* 5 November (CA)...247
Kanaris v Governor of Pentonville Prison [2003] 1 All ER 593; [2003] 1 WLR 443; [2003] UKHL 2...197
Kansal [2001] 3 WLR 751...267
Kefford [2002] EWCA Crim 519; [2002] 2 Cr App R (S) 106...318
Keily [1990] Crim LR 204...271
Kelleher [2003] EWCA 2846...250
Kemp [1995] 1 Cr App R 151 (CA)...217
Kent Justices, *ex parte* Machin [1952] 2 QB 355...104
Kepple [2007] EWCA Crim 1339...198
Kerr (1980) 2 Cr App R (S) 54...276
Kerrigan (1993) 14 Cr App R (S) 179; (1992) 156 JP 889 (CA)...199, 276
Khan [2008] EWCA Crim 531; [2008] 3 All ER 502...203, 249
Khan [2008] EWCA Crim 1112...228
Khela [2006] 1 Cr App R 23 (CA)...230
Kidd [1998] 1 All ER 42...297
Kingston Crown Court, *ex parte* Bell (2000) 164 JP 633...161
Knightsbridge Crown Court, *ex parte* Goonatilleke [1986] QB 1...168
Komsta [1990] 12 Cr App R (S) 63...274
Kray (1969) 53 Cr App R 412...206
Krivec (Attorney-General's Reference No 8 of 2007) [2007] EWCA Crim 922; [2008] 1 Cr App R (S) 1...293
Krivee (2007) *The Times*, 24 April...264

L [2007] EWCA Crim 764...171
L v DPP [2009] EWHC 238 (Admin)...19
L and B v DPP [1998] 2 Cr App R 69...119
Lahaye [2005] EWCA Crim 1209; [2006] 1 Cr App R 11...230
Lake (1976) 64 Cr App R 172...189
Lambert [2006] EWCA Crim 827...243
Lamming (1989) 90 Cr App R 450...252
Landy (1995) 16 Cr App R (S) 908...296
Lang [2005] EWCA Crim 2864; [2006] 2 Cr App R (S) 3...338
Langford (2001) *The Times* 12 January...226
Larkin [1943] KB 174...278
Lashley [2005] EWCA Crim 2016; (2005) *The Times* 28 September...19, 209
Last [2005] EWCA Crim 106; [2005] 2 Cr App R (S) 64...336
Latte (1996) (CA)...254
Lavery [2008] EWCA Crim 2499...299
Lawrence v Same [1968] 2 QB 93...121
Lawson [2005] EWCA Crim 84; [2007] 1 Cr App R 20...207
Lawson v Stafford Magistrates' Court [2007] EWHC 2490...19
Laycock [2003] EWCA Crim 1477; [2003] Crim LR 803...189
Lee [1984] 1 WLR 578...251
Lee [2003] EWCA Crim 1167...247
Lee (Anthony William) (A Minor) [1993] 1 WLR 103...147
Lesley [1996] 1 Cr App R 39...225
Letellier v France (1992) 14 EHRR 83...65
Levantiz [1999] 1 Cr App R 465...185
Lewis (26 April 2001)...250

Lewis (1984) 79 Cr App R 94...332
Leyland Justices, *ex parte* Hawthorn [1979] QB 283 (HC)...168
Lillis [1972] 2 QB 236...228
Lincoln Magistrates' Court, *ex parte* Mawer [1995] Crim LR 878...76
Liverpool City Justices, *ex parte* Topping [1983] 1 WLR 119...44
Liverpool City Magistrates' Court, *ex parte* DPP [1993] QB 233...79
Liverpool Crown Court, *ex parte* Roberts [1986] Crim LR 622...168
Livesey [2006] EWCA Civ 3344; [2007] 1 Cr App R 35...231
LM [2002] EWCA Crim 3047; [2003] Crim LR 205...149
Locabail (UK) Ltd v Bayfield [2000] QB 451...233
Lockley and Sainsbury [1997] Crim LR 455...190
Loi [2003] EWCA 801...248
Lombardi [1989] 1WLR 73 (CA)...191
Lucas [1981] 1 QB 720...225
Ludlow v Metropolitan Police Commissioner [1971] AC 29 (HL)...187, 188

M v Isleworth Crown Court [2005] EWHC 363...86
McFarlane (1995) 16 Cr App R (S) 315...199
McGarry [1999] 1 Cr App R 377...224
McGinlay (1976) 52 Cr App R 156...290
McGrath [2005] EWCA Crim 353; [2005] 2 Cr App R (S) 85...313
McGuinness [1999] Crim LR 318...32
McKendrick [2005] 2 Cr App R (S) 68...81
McKerry v Teesdale and Wear Valley Justices (2000) 164 JP 355...121
McNally [1954] 1 WLR 933...208
McVey [1988] Crim LR 127...221, 222
Maher [1983] QB 784...54
Maidstone Crown Court, *ex parte* Hollstein [1995] 3 All ER 503...63
Maidstone Crown Court, *ex parte* Jodka (1997) 161 JP 638 (DC)...74, 226
Maidstone Crown Court, *ex parte* Lever [1995] 1 WLR 928...83
Makanjuola [1995] 1 WLR 1348...225
Malcolm v Director of Public Prosecutions [2007] EWHC 363...18
Manchester Crown Court, *ex parte* DPP [1993] 2 WLR 846 (HL)...238
Manchester Crown Court, *ex parte* McDonald [1999] 1 WLR 841...62, 63
Manchester Crown Court, *ex parte* Williams (1990) 7 54 JP 589...159
Mandair [1995] 1 AC 208...229
Manzur and Mahmood [1997] 1 Cr App R 414...201
Marr (1989) 90 Cr App R 154...221
Marsh [2002] EWCA 1497...246
Marshall (1995) 159 JP 688...79
Martin [2006] EWCA Crim 1035; [2007] 1 Cr App R (S) 3...293
Marylebone Justices, *ex parte* Farrag [1981] Crim LR 182...167
Matthews and Matthews (1984) 78 Cr App R 23...246
Maxwell [1990] 1 WLR 401 (HL)...229

Mayers [2008] EWCA Crim 2989...215
Mearns [1991] 1 QB 82...108
Medicaments and Related Classes of Goods (No 2), In re [2001] 1 WLR 700...167, 248
Mercer [2001] All ER (D) 187...254
Metropolitan Police Commission v Wilson [1984] AC 242...228
Michael v Gowland [1977] 1 WLR 296...164
Middlesex Crown Court, *ex parte* Okoli [2000] Crim LR 921...87
Mielle [2007] EWCA Crim 3130...263
Miles [2006] EWCA Crim 256 (CA)...288, 298
Mills (1979) 68 Cr App R 154...289
Mills [2008] EWCA Crim 3001...207
Millward [1999] 1 Cr App R 61...250
Mirza (1992) 14 Cr App R (S) 64 (CA)...276
Mirza [2004] 1 AC 1118 (HL)...226
Mitchell v The Queen [1998] AC 695 (PC)...212
Modeste [1983] Crim LR 746...232
Moghal (1977) 65 Cr App R 56...242
Mohun [1992] Crim LR 598; (1993) 14 Cr App R (S) 5...199, 276, 277
Montgomery v HM Advocate [2001] 2 WLR 779 (PC)...206
Morais [1988] 3 All ER 161...186
Moran v DPP [2002] EWHC 89...120
Moringiello [1997] Crim LR 902 (CA)...254
Morris [1991] Crim LR 385...247
Morse [1991] Crim LR 195...34
Moss (1984) 5 Cr App R (S) 209...269, 291
Mottram [1981] 3 Cr App R (S) 123...276
Mountain (1979) 68 Cr App R 41...54
Murphy v DPP [2006] EWHC 1753 (Admin)...178
Murray v Ministry of Defence [1988] 1 WLR 692...24
Mynott [2003] All ER (D) 39...253

Nangle [2001] Crim LR 506 (CA)...247
Nasser (1998) *The Times* 19 February...247
Neill v North Antrim Magistrates' Court [1992] 4 All ER 846...211
Neumeister v Austria (No 1) (1979–80) 1 EHRR 91...84
Neve (1986) 8 Cr App R (S) 270...81
Newbury Justices, *ex parte* Drake [1993] COD 24...168
Newcastle Upon Tyne Magistrates' Court, *ex parte* Poundstretchers Ltd [1998] COD 256...45
Newland [1988] QB 402...188, 189, 190
Newport Justices, *ex parte* Carey (1996) 160 JP 613...123
Newton (1982) 77 Cr App R 13...198, 199, 255, 276, 277, 278
Nicholson [1947] 2 All ER 535...288
Norbrook Laboratories (GB) Ltd v Health and Safety Executive (1998) *The Times* 23 February...121
Norman [2008] EWCA Crim 1810; [2009] 1 Cr App R 13...234
North Shields Justices, *ex parte* Darroll [1991] COD 317...116
North West Suffolk (Mildenhall) Magistrates' Court, *ex parte* Forest Heath DC (1997) 161 JP 401...163
Northallerton Magistrates' Court, *ex parte* Dove [2000] 1 Cr App R (S) 136...53
Northampton Magistrates' Court, *ex parte* CCE [1991] Crim LR 598 (DC)...104

Nottingham Crown Court, *ex parte* DPP [1995] Crim LR 902...276
Nottingham Justices, *ex parte* Davies [1981] QB 38...84
Nottingham Justices, *ex parte* Fohmann (1986) 84 Cr App R 316...53
Nottingham Justices, *ex parte* Fraser (1995) 159 JP 612...168
Nottingham Magistrates' Court, *ex parte* Furnell (1996) 160 JP 201...118
NW and Others [2008] EWCA Crim 2...241

Ofili, Re [1995] Crim LR 880...62
O'Hare [2006] EWCA Crim 471; [2006] Crim LR 950...77, 116, 198
Oladimeji v DPP [2006] EWHC Crim 1100...163
Oldbury Justices, *ex parte* Smith (1995) 159 JP 316...170
Olden [2007] EWCA Crim 726...22
O'Leary (1988) 87 Cr App R 387...242
Oliver [1996] 2 Cr App R 514 (CA)...227
Oliver & Little [1993] 2 All ER 9...297
Ollerenshaw [1999] 1 Cr App R (S) 65...319
Olliver and Olliver (1989) 11 Cr App R (S) 10...53
Olotu v Home Office and another [1997] 1 WLR 328...63
O'Neill [2003] EWCA Crim 411 (unreported)...185
Oni [1992] Crim LR 183...30
Oosthuizen [2005] EWCA Crim 1978; (2005) *The Times* 5 September (CA); [2006] 1 Cr App R (S) 73...295
Osborn [2002] All ER (D) 320 (CA)...246
O'Toole (1971) 55 Cr App R 206...300
Oudkerk [1994] Crim LR 700...277
Owen [1952] 2 QB 362...228
Owens and Another (unreported, 6 September 2006)...249
Oxford City Justices, *ex parte* Smith (1982) 75 Cr App R 200...96

P Foster (Haulage) Ltd v Roberts [1978] 2 All ER 751...118
P (Shane Tony) [2004] EWCA Crim 287; [2004] 2 Cr App R (S) 343...313
Palmer [2002] EWCA Crim 892; *The Times*, 18 April 2002...193
Panayioutou [1989] 11 Cr App R (S) 535...275
Parker and the Barnet Magistrates' Court, *ex parte* DPP (1994) 158 JP 1061...167
Parks [1961] 1 WLR 1484...254
Payne [1950] 1 All ER 102...273
Peace [1976] Crim LR 119...271
Pendleton [2002] 1 WLR 72 (HL)...253
Peterborough Justices, *ex parte* Dowler [1996] 2 Cr App R 561...166
Peterson [1997] Crim LR 339...260
Pinfold [1988] QB 462...252
Pitman [1991] 1 All ER 468 (CA)...271
Plowden v DPP [1991] Crim LR 850...163
Pluck [2002] All ER (D) 281 (CA)...247
Plymouth Justices, *ex parte* Hart [1986] QB 950...119
Podola [1960] 1 QB 325...234
Pointer [1997] Crim LR 676...32
Poole [2002] 1 WLR 1528 (CA)...208
Pople [1951] 1 KB 53...192
Porter v Magill [2002] 2 AC 357 (HL)...44, 203, 206, 233, 248

Portsmouth Crown Court, *ex parte* DPP [1994] COD 13 (DC)...168
Powell [2006] EWCA Crim 685...217
Prestatyn Magistrates' Court [2002] EWCA 1177...106
Pye v Leeds Youth Court [2006] EWHC 2527...329

R v Defendant *see under name of Defendant*
R (C) v Balham Youth Court [2003] EWHC (Admin) 1332; [2004] 1 Cr App R (S) 22...339
R (CPS) v Redbridge Youth Court [2005] EWHC 1390 (Admin); (2005) 169 JP 393...340
R (D) v Camberwell Green Youth Court [2005] 1 WLR 393...137, 2008
R (Davies) v Solihull Justices [2008] EWHC 1157...116
R (DPP) v Acton Youth Court [2001] EWHC Admin 402; [2001] 1 WLR 1828...181
R (Guest) v DPP DC 5 March 2009...43
R (H) v Southampton Youth Court [2004] EWHC 2912 (Admin)...135, 142, 340, 2008
R (Harrington) v Bromley Magistrates' Court [2007] EWCA 2896...126
R (Kelly) v Warley Magistrates' Court [2007] EWHC 1836 (Admin); [2008] 1 Cr App R 195...5, 20
R (M and W) v West London Youth Court [2004] EWHC (Admin) 1144...339
R (McCann) v Crown Court at Manchester [2003] 1 AC 787 (HL)...312
R (McGowan) v Brent Justices (2002) 166 JP 29...121
R (Malik) v Central Criminal Court [2007] 1 WLR 2455...85
R (Merritt) v Peterborough Magistrates' Court [2009] EWHC 467 (Admin)...126
R (P) v Liverpool City Magistrates (2006) 170 JP 453...166
R (R (a juvenile)) v Thames Youth Court (2002) 166 JP 613...116
R (Sullivan) v Maidstone Crown Court [2002] 1 WLR 2747...176
R (W) v Acton Youth Court [2005] EWHC 954 (Admin); (2006) 170 JP 31...312–13
R (on the application of DPP) v Acton Youth Court [2002] Crim LR 75...138
R (on the application of DPP) v Chorley Justices [2006] EWHC 1795 (Admin)...17, 19
R (on the application of DPP) v Havering Magistrates' Court [2001] 3 All ER 997; [2001] 2 Cr App R 2...61, 66, 79
R (on the application of Ellison) v Teesside Magistrates' Court [2001] EWHC Admin 12...72, 79
R (on the application of Jeffrey) v Warwick Crown Court [2002] EWHC 2469...87
R (on the application of O) v Harrow Crown Court [2003] 1 WLR 2756 (QBD, Admin)...61
R (on the application of Ratra) v DPP [2004] EWHC 87...119
R (on the application of Robertson) v South Western Magistrates' Court [2003] EWHC 63...163
R (on the application of TP) v West London Youth Court [2005] EWHC 2583 (Admin)...135, 2008
R (on the application of U) v Commissioner of Police for the Metropolis [2003] 1 Cr App R 29...151
R (on the application of Vickers) v West London Magistrates' Court [2003] EWHC Admin 1809...79
R (on the application of W) v Brent Youth Court and DPP and others [2006] EWHC 95 (Admin) (DC)...142

R (on the application of Westminster City Council) v Middlesex Crown Court [2002] EWHC 1104...165
R (on the application of Wyman) v Chief Constable of Hampshire Constabulary [2006] EWHL 1904 (Admin)...41
Rafferty (1999) 1 Cr App R 235 (CA)...295
Rajcoomar [1999] Crim LR 728...251
Ramstead v The Queen [1999] 2 AC 92 (PC)...228
Redbridge Justices, *ex parte* Ram [1992] QB 384...121
Redfern [2004] EWCA Crim 3291; [2005] 2 Cr App R (S) 44...337
Reid (1999) *The Times* 17 August...221
Reid v DPP [1993] COD 111 (DC)...164
Remice v Governor of Belmarsh Prison [2007] Crim LR 796...95
Revitt and others v DPP [2006] EWHC 2266 (Admin)...118
Reynolds [2007] EWCA Crim 538; [2007] 2 Cr App R (S) 87...338
Roberts [2008] EWCA Crim 1304; [2009] 1 Cr App R 20...187
Roberts v Chief Constable of the Cheshire Constabulary [1999] 1 WLR 662...27
Robinson (1969) 53 Cr App R 314...279
Romsey Justices, *ex parte* Gale [1992] Crim LR 451...167
Ronson [1991] Crim LR 794...54
Rose [1982] AC 822...261
Rosenburg [1999] 1 Cr App R (S) 365...297
Ross (1988) 86 Cr App R 337...92
Rowe and Davis v United Kingdom (2000) 30 EHRR 1...178
Russell-Jones [1995] 1 Cr App R 538...210

S v Recorder of Manchester [1971] AC 481...208
S (an infant) v Recorder of Manchester [1971] AC 481...118
St Albans Crown Court, *ex parte* Cinnamond [1981] QB 480...167
Sampson (unreported, 24 October 2006) (CA)...238
Samuel [1988] 1 WLR 920...37
Sanders v UK [2000] Crim LR 767 (ECtHR)...44
Sandwell Justices, *ex parte* West Midlands Passenger Transport Board [1979] Crim LR 56...45
Savage [1992] 1 AC 714...229
Sawyer (1980) 71 Cr App R 283...207
SC v UK (2004) EHRR 10 (ECtHR)...135, 2008
Scollan [1999] Crim LR 566...247
Scunthorpe Justices, *ex parte* M (1998) *The Times* 10 March...45
Seed [2007] EWCA Crim 254; [2007] 2 Cr App R (S) 69...318
Seelig [1992] 1 WLR 148...21
Sekhon [2002] EWCA Crim 2954...243
Self [1992] 3 All ER 476...23
Sequeira (1982) 4 Cr App R (S) 65...287, 288
Shatwell and Lea [2002] EWCA Crim 215...247
Shaw *see* Attorney-General's Reference (No 28 of 1996)
Shaw v DPP (unreported, 25 January 2007)...45
Sheikh [2004] EWCA Crim 492; [2004] 2 Cr App R 13...208
Shippey [1988] Crim LR 767...216
Simons [1953] 1 WLR 1014...288
Singh (1981) 3 Cr App R (S) 90...289
Singh (1982) 4 Cr App R (S) 38...54
Smith [1990] 1 WLR 1311...271
Smith [1997] QB 836...107, 190
Smith [1999] 2 Cr App R 238 (CA)...246

Smith [1999] 2 Cr App R 444...268
Smith [2000] 1 All ER 263...217
Smith [2002] EWCA Crim 2907...268
Smith [2003] EWCA Crim 283; [2003] 1 WLR 2229...205
Smith [2005] EWCA Crim 530; [2005] 2 Cr App R (S) 100...297
Snaresbrook Crown Court, *ex parte* Input Management Ltd (1999) 163 JP 533...161
Solomon (1984) 6 Cr App R (S) 120...279
Soneji [2005] UKHL 49...243
Southwark Crown Court, *ex parte* Johnson [1992] COD 364 (DC)...238
Southwark Crown Court, *ex parte* Ward [1995] COD 140...238
Speechley [2004] EWCA Crim 3067; [2005] 2 Cr App R (S) 15...217
Spencer [1987] AC 128...207
Spencer [1995] Crim LR 235...221
Spratt [1980] 1 WLR 554...260
Steel v UK [1988] 28 EHRR 602...25
Stephens [2002] EWCA Crim 1529...221
Stephenson [2005] EWCA Crim 3111...246
Stevens [2006] EWCA Crim 255; [2006] 2 Cr App R (S) 68...315
Stockport Justices, *ex parte* Conlon [1997] 2 All ER 204...53
Stockwell (1993) 97 Cr App R 260...225
Stone [1970] 1 WLR 1112...201, 273
Stosiek (1982) 4 Cr App R (S) 205...279
Stroud (1977) 65 Cr App R 150...255
Sunderland Justices, *ex parte* Dryden (1994) *The Times* 18 May...95

T [2008] EWCA Crim 815...134
T v UK (2000) 30 EHRR 121 (ECtHR)...133, 147, 2008
Tang (1995) *The Times* 23 May...265
Tarrant [1998] Crim LR 342...205
Taylor [2003] EWCA Crim 2447; (2003) *The Times* 8 October...220
Teasdale [1993] 4 All ER 290...222
Teeluck v State of Trinidad and Tobago [2005] UKPC 14; [2005] 1 WLR 2421...222
Thakrar [2001] 1 All ER (D) 103 (CA)...247
Thames Magistrates' Court, *ex parte* Polemis [1974] 1 WLR 1371...167
Tharakan [1995] 2 Cr App R 368...227
Thomas [1983] Crim LR 619...192
Thomas [2002] EWCA 941...252
Thompson (1995) 159 JP 568...271
Thongjai v The Queen [1998] AC 54 (PC)...212
Togher [2001] 3 All ER 463...244, 245, 251
Tolera [1999] 1 Cr App R 29; [1999] 1 Cr App R (S) 25 (CA)...199, 277
Tonge (1993) 157 JP 1137 (CA)...227
Tovey [2005] EWCA Crim 530; [2005] 2 Cr App R (S) 100...297
Truro Crown Court, *ex parte* Adair [1997] COD 296...167
Tunbridge Wells Justices, *ex parte* Tunbridge Wells Borough Council [1996] 160 JP 574...166
Turnbull [1977] QB 224...216, 222, 276

Turner [1970] 2 QB 321...201, 202, 269, 270, 271
Turner [1995] 1 WLR 264...178
Twitchell [2000] 1 Cr App R 373...254

Underwood [2004] EWCA Crim 2256; [2005] 1 Cr App R 13...199
Underwood [2005] 1 Cr App R (S) 90...277

Van Pelz [1943] KB 157...279
Vasiliou [2000] Crim LR 845...172
Vehicle and Operator Services Agency v George Jenkins Transport Ltd and others [2003] EWHC 2879...163, 164
Vincent v The Queen [1993] 1 WLR 862 (PC)...168
Vye [1993] 1 WLR 471...223

W v DPP [2005] EWHC 1333; (2005) 169 JP 435...313
W v W (1993) *The Times* 4 June...124
Wadmore [2006] EWCA Crim 686; [2007] 1WLR 339...313
Waldie v DPP (1995) 159 JP 514...164
Wang [2005] UKHL 9; [2005] 1 All ER 782...226
Ward (1982) 4 Cr App R (S) 103...255
Ward [1993] 1 WLR 619...179, 180
Ward (1994) 98 Cr App R 337...32
Warden [1996] 2 Cr App R 269...301
Warley Magistrates' Court, *ex parte* DPP [1998] 2 Cr App R 307...101
Watson [1988] QB 690 (CA)...232
Watton (1978) 68 Cr App R 293...259
Weaver [1968] 1 QB 353...207
Webber [2004] UKHL 1; [2004] 1 WLR 404...217, 224
Wedlock-Ward [2005] EWCA Crim 3367...202
Weekes (1980) 74 Cr App R 161 (CA)...201, 273
Wells (1995) 159 JP 243...159
West Midlands Probation Board v Sutton Coldfield Magistrates' Court [2008] EWHC 15 (Admin)...310
West Yorkshire Probation Board v Boulter [2005] EWHC 2342; [2006] 1 WLR 232...310
Wheeler [1967] 1 WLR 1531...225
Wheeler (2000) 164 JP 565...176
Whelan [1997] Crim LR 659...252
Whitlock (1992) 13 Cr App R (S) 157 (CA)...128
Whybrow (1994) *The Times* 14 February...246
Wilkins (1977) 66 Cr App R 49...279
Williams (1990) 12 Cr App R (S) 415...277
Wilson (1979) 69 Cr App R 83...184, 206
Winzar [2002] EWCA 2950...253
Wood [1991] Crim LR 926; (1991) 13 Cr App R (S) 207...199, 279
Wood Green Crown Court, *ex parte* Taylor [1995] Crim LR 879...161
Worcester Justices, *ex parte* Daniels (1997) 161 JP 121...168
Wright [2000] Crim LR 510...225
Wright v Nicholson [1970] 1 WLR 142...45
Writtle v DPP [2009] EWHC 236 (Admin)...19

X v UK (1978) 5 EHRR 273 (ECtHR)...233

Y [2008] EWCA Crim 10...241
Yeardley [2000] 1 QB 374...200
Young [1995] QB 324...250

TABLE OF STATUTES

Access to Justice Act 1999...87
    s 1(1)...46
    s 12...88
    s 12(1)...47
    s 12(2)...47, 49
    s 13...88
    s 13(1)...48
    s 14...49, 88
    s 15...88
    s 16...51
    Sch 3...49, 88
        para 1...49
        para 2(1)...49
        para 5(1)–(2)...50
Administration of Justice Act 1960
    s 1...170
Administration of Justice (Miscellaneous Provisions) Act 1933...158
    s 2...158, 183
    s 2(2)...190, 191
Anti-Social Behaviour Act 2003...7
Attachment of Earnings Act 1972...302

Bail Act 1976...38, 59, 60, 61, 62, 71, 80, 81, 82, 88, 89
    s 3...40, 71, 75
    s 3(1)...58, 59, 72
    s 3(2)...72
    s 3(3)...72–3
    s 3(4)...73
    s 3(5)...73, 74
    s 3(6)...61, 72, 73, 74
    s 3(6)(d)...272, 283
    s 3(6ZAA)–(6ZAB)...75
    s 3(8)–(8A)...76
    s 3A(2)–(3)...40, 76
    s 3A(4)...40, 77
    s 3A(5)...40, 76
    s 4...57, 58, 59, 60, 64, 66, 67, 71, 77, 233, 272
    s 4(1)...57, 60
    s 4(2)...57
    s 4(2A)...58
    s 4(2B)...58
    s 4(3)–(4)...58, 59
    s 4(8)...63
    s 4(9)...70
    s 5...64, 65
    s 5(1)...64
    s 5(3)...64, 65, 71
    s 5(4)–(5)...65
    s 5(6)...66
    s 5(6A)–(6B)...65, 85
    s 5(9)...74
    s 5B...87
    s 5B(1)...87
    s 6...58, 59, 75, 77, 79, 80, 91
    s 6(1)–(2)...80
    s 6(6)–(7)...80
    s 7...69, 140
    s 7(2)...58
    s 7(3)...79
    s 7(5)...61, 79
    s 8...73
    s 8(4)...73
    s 9A...68
    Sch 1...60, 62, 67, 68, 69, 71, 77
        paras 6A–6C...68
        Part I...68, 71
            para 2A...59
            para 7...272
            para 8...71, 72
            para 9...70
            para 9A...65
            paras 9AA–9AB...71
        Part IA...79
        Part II...71, 72
        Part IIA...65, 66, 83, 84, 85
            paras 1–2...83
            para 3...83, 84
Bail (Amendment) Act 1993...86

Children Act 2004...132
Children and Young Persons Act 1933...130, 148
    s 31...135, 2008
    s 34A...136, 2008
    s 39...139, 147
    s 44...143, 324
    s 47(2)...139, 140
    s 49...138, 139
    s 50...133, 2008
Children and Young Persons Act 1963
    s 29...149
Children and Young Persons Act 1969
    s 23(5A)...89
Contempt of Court Act 1981
    s 4(2)...70
Courts Act 2003...107, 303

s 2...46
s 45...114
Sch 3...114
Sch 5...303
Sch 6...303
Courts and Legal Services Act 1990
    s 119(1)...73
Crime and Disorder Act 1998...54, 107, 108, 146, 150, 162, 312, 350
    s 1...162, 312
    s 1(7)...313
    s 1(10)...315
    s 1C...312
    s 1C(4)...313
    s 2...162
    s 4(2)...162
    s 8...136, 2008
    s 34...133, 134, 2008
    s 37...130
    s 39...131, 150
    s 43...62
    s 45...62
    s 47...149
    s 47(1)–(4)...148
    s 49...55
    s 49(1)–(2)...55
    s 50...55
    s 50(1)–(2)...55
    s 50(3)(a)–(b)...55
    s 51...63, 85, 91, 106, 107, 108, 115, 149, 154, 157, 186, 190
    s 51(1)...103, 104, 155
    s 51(2)–(5)...155
    s 51(6)...155–6
    s 51(7)...146, 156
    s 51(8)–(10)...156
    s 51(11)...107, 156
    s 51(12)–(13)...156
    s 51A...141, 142, 144, 155, 156, 157, 186, 190
    s 51B...144, 155, 157, 236
    s 51C...144, 155
    s 51D(1)–(4)...157
    s 51E(d)...107
    s 52...91
    s 52A...156, 157
    s 52A(1)–(2)...156
    s 52B...157
    s 54(1)...74
    s 55...82
    s 56...61
    s 57...95, 100
    s 65...39, 150, 325
    s 66...150
    s 66(4)...152, 325
    ss 66A–H...153
    ss 97–98...88
    Sch 3
        para 2(1)...158
Crime (Sentences) Act 1997
    s 40...302

Criminal Appeal Act 1968...239, 242, 244, 245, 250, 251, 252, 256, 261
    s 1...266
    s 1(2)...250
    s 2...242, 250
    s 2(1)...243
    s 2(1)(a)...243, 245
    s 3...251, 259, 260
    s 3A...260
    s 4(3)...259, 260
    s 7...260
    s 9...255
    s 10...261
    s 11(3)...254
    s 17...265
    s 19...258
    s 20...260
    s 22(1)...258
    s 23...252, 253, 258
    s 23(1)...252–3
    s 23(1)(c)...254
    s 23(2)...253, 254
    s 23(2)(a)...254
    s 23(3)–(4)...253
    s 29...260
    s 29(1)...260
    s 31...258
    s 31A...259
    s 31A(3)...259
    s 33...265
    s 44A...47, 252
    s 44A(3)–(4)...252
Criminal Appeal Act 1995...123, 239, 242, 245, 252, 266
    s 2...242, 243, 246
    s 2(1)...243
    s 2B(3)...123
    s 2B(5)...123
    s 4...252
    s 6...259
    s 7...252
    s 9...266
    s 11...266
    s 13...266
    s 14(1)–(3)...266
    s 14(4)...267
    s 14(5)...268
    s 19(1)...267
Criminal Damage Act 1971
    s 1...341
Criminal Evidence (Witness Anonymity) Act 2008...8, 215
Criminal Justice Act 1948
    s 37(1)(d)...169
Criminal Justice Act 1967
    s 6...228
    s 9...119, 275, 349
    s 9(2)(a)–(b)...116
    s 10...211
    s 17...200
Criminal Justice Act 1972
    s 36...264

s 36(1)...263
s 36(3)...264
Criminal Justice Act 1982
  s 37(2)...301
Criminal Justice Act 1987...196
  s 4...280
Criminal Justice Act 1988...33, 107, 344
  Part VI...36
  s 35...264
  s 36...271
  s 38...106
  s 40...105, 107, 108, 144, 190, 229
  s 153...65
  s 154...65, 84, 85
  s 156...161
Criminal Justice Act 1991...134, 2008
  s 53...280
  s 56...136, 2008
  s 68...133, 134, 2008
  Sch 8...134, 2008
Criminal Justice Act 2003...6, 8, 10, 25, 26, 28, 43, 58, 68,
    71, 80, 89, 99, 102, 106, 110, 128, 141, 143, 149, 154,
    155, 158, 172, 177, 203, 269, 292, 297, 303, 307, 308,
    316, 317, 319, 320, 326, 333, 335
  Part 3...39
  Part 7...236
  Part 8...214
  Part 10...235
  s 4...60
  s 6...27
  s 8...25
  s 9...26, 263
  s 10...26
  s 11...21
  s 13...61, 73
  s 13(2)...76
  s 14...68
  s 14(2)...71
  s 15...68
  s 15(2)...71
  s 15(3)...79
  s 16...85
  s 17...86
  s 18...43, 86
  s 19...68
  s 22...41
  s 22(2)...42
  s 22(3)...42
  s 22(3A)...43
  s 23...41
  s 24...41, 43
  s 24(1)–(2)...42
  s 25...41
  s 26...41, 42
  s 27...41
  s 28...38
  s 29...39, 43, 80
  s 29(1)...43
  s 29(2)–(3)...44
  s 29(5)...44

s 30(1)...44
s 30(5)...44
s 31...46
s 31(1)...44
s 40...27
s 40(4)...43
s 43...236, 237
s 43(1)(b)...236
s 43(4)–(7)...236
s 44...236, 237
s 44(4)–(6)...236
s 45...237
s 46...237
s 46(4)–(5)...237
s 51...119, 213, 350
s 51(4)...214
s 51(6)–(7)...214
s 54...214
s 56(2)...214
s 57...239
s 57(4)...239
s 58...238, 239, 240, 241
s 58(1)...241
ss 59–61...239, 240
s 62...239, 241
s 62(2)...241
s 62(8)–(9)...241
s 62(11)...241
s 63...239, 241, 242
s 63(1)–(2)...241
s 64...239, 242
s 65...239
s 66...239, 241
ss 67–74...239
s 75...235, 262
s 75(a)–(c)...262
s 75(4)...262
s 76...235, 262
s 77...262
s 78...235, 236, 262, 263
s 78(2)...235, 263
s 78(3)...263
s 79...235, 262, 263
s 79(2)...235
ss 80–97...262
ss 98–99...222
s 100...222, 350
ss 101–112...222
s 116...211, 350
s 116(2)(e)...211
s 137...213, 350
s 137(1)...214
s 137(3)–(4)...214
s 139(1)–(2)...210
s 142...143, 149, 324
s 142(1)...292
s 142A...143, 324
s 142A(1)–(4)...324
s 143(1)...292, 293
s 143(2)...294, 297

s 143(3)...293
s 144(1)...295
s 145...294
s 146(2)...294
s 146(4)–(5)...294
s 148...328
s 148(1)...292, 304
s 148(2)...304
s 148(5)...304
s 149(1)...308
s 150...328
s 150A...304
s 151...307, 309
s 151(2)...304
s 152(2)...292, 317, 319, 333
s 152(3)...317
s 154...122
s 155...122, 316
s 156...304, 319
s 162...301
s 163...331
s 166(2)...304
s 166(3)(b)...319
s 167...291
s 169...291
s 170...293
s 170(5)(a)...291
s 172...293
s 172(1)...291
s 174...286
s 174(1)...286
s 177...132
s 177(1)...303, 304
s 177(3)–(4)...303
s 177(5)...303, 333
s 177(6)...303
s 181(2)...320
s 181(5)–(7)...320
s 182(1)...320
s 183...323
s 183(4)–(5)...323
s 183(7)...323
s 189...321
s 189(1)...323
s 189(1)(b)...321
s 189(3)–(4)...321
ss 190-2...321
s 199...304
s 200...304
s 200(2)...305, 311
s 200(3)...305
ss 201–206...305
s 207...306
ss 209–212...306
ss 213–15...307
s 217...303
s 220...307
s 221(2)...307
s 224...128, 142, 337
s 225...337, 338
s 225(2)...337

s 225(3)...127, 337
s 225(3A)–(3B)...337
s 225(4)...337
s 226...142, 144, 337, 338
s 226(3)...128
s 227...204, 337, 338
s 227(2)...127, 337
s 227(2A)–(2C)...337
s 227(3)–(4)...337
s 227(5)...338
s 228...142, 144, 204, 338, 340
s 228(2)...128
s 229...337
s 229(2)...338
ss 230-6...337
s 240...319
s 240A...319
s 250...336
s 282...316
s 300(2)...302
s 301...302
s 316...260
s 321...248
Sch 2...38, 39, 127
 para 6...39
Sch 3...105, 126, 127, 128, 146, 154, 158
 para 9...135, 2008
Sch 4...241
Sch 5...262
 Part 1...235
Sch 8...308
 Part 2...58
 Part 3...310
 Part 4...310
 Part 5...311
 para 5(1)–(2)...308
 para 6(1)...308
 para 7...308
 para 8(2)...332
 para 8(4)...332
 para 9(1)...308
 para 9(2)–(4)...308, 309
 para 9(6)...309, 332
 para 9(8)...309
 para 10...309
 para 10(1)...332
 para 10(1)(a)–(c)...333
 para 10(2)–(6)...333
 para 13...310
 para 13(3)–(5)...310
 para 14(1)–(4)...333
 para 16...311
 para 17...311
 para 17(1)...311
 para 18...311
 para 20...311
 para 21...311
 para 21(3)–(4)...311
 para 22...311, 334
 para 22(1)...311, 333
 para 23...311, 334

para 23(1)...334
para 23(1)(b)...334
para 23(2)–(3)...334
Sch 12...322
paras 4–5...322
para 8...322
para 8.3...322
Sch 15...128, 139, 142, 337
Parts 1–2...128, 337
Sch 15A...337
Sch 21...336
Sch 25...122
Sch 26...122, 316
Sch 33...248
Sch 37
Part 2...59
Criminal Justice and Court Services Act 2000...26, 70, 88
s 57...71
s 58...70
s 61...323
Sch 6...71
Criminal Justice and Immigration Act 2008...6, 8, 10–15, 69, 132, 143, 153, 324, 326
s 1...326
s 1(2)–(3)...328
s 1(6)...328
s 44...240
s 51...75
s 52...70
s 54...115
Sch 1...327
Sch 2...328
Schs 9–10...153
Sch 11...75
Sch 12...70
Criminal Justice and Public Order Act 1994...30, 61
s 25...59, 61
s 25(2)...61
s 26...59, 61
s 27...40
s 27(3)...40
s 28...39
s 32...225
s 34...30, 217, 223, 224, 225
s 34(2)(c)...217
s 35...218
ss 36–37...30
s 38(3)...223
s 49...138
s 52...239
Sch 3
para 3...40
Sch 5...116
Criminal Law Act 1967
s 6...259
s 6(1)(b)...200
s 6(3)...108, 121, 192, 200, 234
s 6(3A)–(3B)...229
Criminal Procedure (Attendance of Witnesses) Act 1965
s 2...181, 202
ss 3–4...202

Criminal Procedure (Insanity) Act 1964...234
s 4...234
s 4(2)...234
s 4(5)...234
s 4A...234
s 4A(5)...234
s 5...234
Criminal Procedure and Investigations Act 1996...99, 105, 171, 177, 178, 181, 195, 225
s 3...172, 176
s 5...172, 175, 177
s 5(5A)–(5B)...175
s 6...172
s 6A...172
s 6A(1)...173–4
s 6A(2)...174, 177, 218, 219
s 6A(3)...174, 176, 218
s 6B...174, 175
s 6C...174, 175, 177
s 6C(1)–(2)...174
s 6D...175
s 6D(1)...175
s 6E...175
s 6E(1)...176
s 6E(2)...175
s 6E(4)...175
s 6E(5)...176
s 7A...172
s 7A(1)...172
s 7A(2)–(6)...173
s 7A(8)...173
s 8...196
s 11...175, 177, 225
s 11(5)...175, 177, 178
s 11(6)–(7)...177
s 11(8)–(10)...178
s 21A...174
s 21A(2)...174–5
s 23...171
s 29...195, 196, 197, 237
s 29(2)...196
s 31...196
s 31(3)...196
s 35...237
s 40...195
ss 54–57...235
s 58...285
s 58(4)–(5)...285
s 58(8)...285
ss 59–61...285
Customs and Excise Management Act 1979
s 170(2)...176
Domestic Violence, Crime and Victims Act 2004
Chp 2...347
s 17...237
s 17(2)...237
s 18...237
s 18(5)...237
s 19...237
ss 47–53...347

Drug Trafficking Act 1994...33
Drugs Act 2005...29

Extradition Act 1989
 s 9...47
 Sch 1
  para 6...47
Extradition Act 2003...58

Factories Act 1961...98
Firearms Act 1968...142, 189
 s 51A...337
Forgery and Counterfeiting Act 1981...99

Human Rights Act 1998...22, 61, 65, 68, 121, 126, 167, 224, 244, 245, 250, 261
 s 2(1)...124, 125
 s 3(1)...245
 s 4...261
 s 5...261
 s 5(2)...261
 s 22(4)...267
 Sch 1
  art.6...95

Indictments Act 1915...159
 s 3...183
 s 3(1)...183
 s 5...159, 183
 s 5(1)...185, 192, 193
 s 5(3)...188, 189
Interpretation Act 1978
 s 1(a)...97

Juries Act 1974...205
 s 1...203
 s 9(2)...204
 s 9A(1)...204
 s 9B...204
 s 13...227
 s 16...206
 s 17...231
 s 17(3)...231
 Sch 1
  Part 2...204

Legal Aid Act 1988...87
 s 21(3)(c)...87

Magistrates' Courts Act 1980...8, 89, 91, 99, 146, 272
 s 6(1)...62
 s 8(1)...91
 ss 8A–8C...114
 s 9(1)...126
 s 10...91, 156
 s 10(3)...272, 291
 s 10(4)...91
 s 11...82, 91, 116, 117
 s 11(1)...95, 115
 s 12...116, 117
 s 12(5)(c)...117
 s 12A...117
 s 12A(1)–(2)...117
 s 13...91, 96, 140
 s 14...95, 115
 s 14(1)(b)...95
 s 15...117
 s 17...97, 100
 s 17A...99, 100, 126, 341
 s 17A(1)...341
 s 17A(3)–(5)...342
 s 17A(6)...101, 342
 s 17B...99, 126, 341
 s 17B(3)...101
 s 17C...341
 s 17D...127, 341
 s 17E...100, 341
 s 18...341
 s 18(2)...99
 s 18(4)...91
 s 18(5)...341
 s 19...91, 104, 110, 341, 343
 s 19(1)...342
 s 19(2)(a)...102
 s 19(2)(b)...342
 s 19(3)...342
 s 20...91, 341, 342, 343
 s 20(3)(a)–(b)...342
 s 20(7)...126
 s 20(9)(b)...155
 s 20A...103, 269
 s 21...91, 155, 341, 342, 343
 s 22...91, 105, 107, 341, 343
 s 22(1)–(3)...343
 s 22(4)–(5)...106, 343
 s 22(6)...106
 s 22(6)(a)–(b)...343
 s 22(8)...105
 s 22(11)...106, 341
 s 23...91, 341
 s 23(1)(a)–(b)...100
 s 23(4)(b)...155
 s 23(5)...155
 s 24...141
 s 24(1)...135, 2008
 ss 24A–24B...156
 s 25(2D)...155
 s 29(3)–(7)...342
 s 32...122, 301
 s 32(1)...316
 s 33...343
 s 42...70
 s 43B...40, 77
 s 75(1)...302
 s 82(1)...302
 s 82(4)...303
 s 82(4A)...302
 s 83...302
 s 85(1)–(2)...302
 s 85(4)...302
 s 97...181
 s 108...160
 s 111...86

s 111(1)...162
s 111(2)...164
s 111(4)...163
s 113...161, 164
s 115...47
s 120...83
s 122(2)...117
s 123...45
s 128...95
s 128(3A)...94
s 128(6)–(7)...94
s 128A...94, 95
s 131(1)...94
s 133...122
s 133(1)–(2)...316
s 135...82
s 142...52, 116, 123, 160, 286
s 142(1A)...123
s 142(2)–(2A)...123
s 144...44
Sch 1...97, 316
    para 28(c)...111
Sch 2...113, 341
Mental Health Act 1973...346
Mental Health Act 1983...215, 283, 306, 327
  s 1(2)...33
  ss 35–36...272
  s 37...283
  s 54(3)...284
Misuse of Drugs Act 1971...26, 99

Offences Against the Person Act 1861
  s 18...98, 192, 199, 229
  s 20...98, 112, 185, 192, 199, 229
  s 47...112, 229

Police and Criminal Evidence Act 1984...22, 29
  s 24(1)...22
  s 24(2)–(4)...22
  s 24(5)...22–3
  s 24(6)...23
  s 24A...23
  s 24A(1)–(4)...23
  s 28...24
  s 28(1)...24
  s 28(3)–(4)...24
  s 30...59
  s 30(1)–(3)...24
  s 30(10)–(10A)...24
  s 30A...25, 60, 92
  s 30B...25
  s 30D...25
  s 32...24
  s 32(1)...24
  s 34...25
  s 35...25
  s 35(1)...24
  s 36...25
  s 37...25
  s 37(7)...38
  s 37A...38

s 37B...38
s 37B(1)...38
s 37B(2)–(9)...39
ss 37C–37D...39
s 38...25, 62
s 38(1)...39
s 38(1)(a)...39
ss 39–40...25
s 41...25
s 41(9)...28
ss 42–45...25
s 46...25, 40
s 47...41, 92
s 47(1A)...76
s 54(2A)...26
s 56(1)...37
s 58...35, 36
s 58(1)...35
s 58(6)...35, 36
s 58(8)...35
s 61...26
s 63B...26, 69
s 67(8)–(10)...21
s 76...212
s 78...196, 212, 213, 247
s 79...120, 218
s 82...212
Police and Justice Act 2006...138
  s 17...43
Powers of Criminal Courts (Sentencing) Act
  2000...300, 326, 329, 344
  Part III...150
  s 1...92, 349
  s 3...100, 106, 111, 126, 127, 149, 331, 343
  s 3(1)–(2)...126
  s 3(3)–(4)...127
  s 3A...100, 102, 127
  s 3B...127, 128, 141, 144
  s 3B(2)...127
  s 3C...128, 142, 143, 144
  s 4...101, 111, 127
  s 4(4)...127
  s 4A...128, 144
  s 4A(4)...128
  s 5...127, 128
  s 5(1)...126, 127
  s 5A...127, 128
  s 6...128, 144
  s 7...144
  s 8...146
  s 8(2)...332
  s 9...149
  s 11...272
  s 11(3)...283
  s 12(1)(a)–(b)...300
  s 13(5)...300
  s 13(6)...301
  s 13(7)–(8)...300
  ss 16–18...325
  s 17(1)–(2)...325

s 19(4)...326
s 23...326
s 36...282
s 36(5)...282
s 51(1)...280
s 78...122
s 78(1)...316
s 79(2)...281
s 79(2)(a)...283
s 80(2)...281
s 80(2)(a)...289
s 80(2)(b)...277
s 81...282
s 81(1)–(3)...281
s 81(5)–(6)...281
s 83...290
s 83(1)–(2)...289
s 83(3)...290
s 85...340
s 91...127, 141, 142, 144, 149, 289, 330, 339, 340
s 91(1)...146
s 91(3)...127, 339
s 96...323
s 100...329
s 101(1)...329
s 101(2A)...329
s 104(3)...330
s 105...330
s 110...336
s 111...106, 336
s 111(1)...106
s 111(2)...106-7
s 111(4)–(6)...107
s 120...129
s 137...136, 325, 2008
s 139(4)...331
s 146...312
s 150...325
s 152(1)...284
s 152(2)...285
s 155...286
s 156...326
s 156(3)...283
s 156(5)...326
s 161...289
s 162...281
s 162(1)...282, 283
s 162(2)...282
Sch 2...282
Sch 3
 Part 2...58
Sch 6...282
Prevention of Crime Act 1957
s 1...221
Proceeds of Crime Act 2002...8, 251
s 6...128
ss 40–41...251
s 75...288
Prosecution of Offences Act 1985...16, 62
s 6(2)...16

s 16...52
s 17...52, 53
s 18...52, 53
s 18(1)...54
ss 19–21...52
s 22...62, 88
s 22A...88
s 23(9)...235
Public Order Act 1986...112
ss 4–5...43

Rehabilitation of Offenders Act 1974...153, 280
s 7...280
s8A...153
Road Traffic Offenders Act 1988
s 24...229
s 24(3)–(4)...121

Serious Organised Crime and Police Act 2005...23, 55
s 2(1)...55
s 110...22
Sch 7...24
Sexual Offences Act 1956...128
Sexual Offences Act 2003...127, 128, 142
s 3...144
s 13...144
ss 25–26...144
Summary Jurisdiction Act 1857
s 6...165
Supreme Court Act 1981
s 9(1)...239
s 28...165
s 29...86
s 31...169
s 31(5)...166
s 43(1)...166
s 48...161
s 48(2)...54
s 66(3)...165
s 75(1)...157
s 81...85, 92, 161

Terrorism Act 2000...28
s 41...21, 36
Sch 8...21, 37
Theft Act 1968...26, 71, 98
s 1...183
s 8...197
s 9(1)(b)...185
s 12(4)...229
s 22...184
Tribunals, Courts and Enforcement Act 2007
s 62...302

Vulnerable Witnesses (Scotland) Act 2004
s 271F...138

Youth Justice and Criminal Evidence Act 1999...136, 137, 215, 348, 2008
ss 16–18...213
s 19...213
s 19(6)...138

s 20...213
s 21...137, 213, 2008
s 21(1)(b)...213
s 21(3)...137, 2008
ss 22–25...213
s 26...213
s 27...213
s 27(2)...137, 2008
s 28...137, 213, 2008
ss 29–30...213, 214
ss 31–33...213
s 33A...215
s 33A(4)–(5)...215
s 33B...215
s 33B(2)...215
s 34...220
s 35...220, 223
s 38...138
s 41...350
s 45...139
s 46...215
s 55...141
s 58...30
Sch 2...139
Youth Justice and Criminal Evidvence Act 1999...8

Bills in Parliament
Coroners and Justice Bill 2009...8
Policing and Crime Bill 2008–9...8

International and European legislation
European Convention on Human Rights...37, 52, 61, 65, 68, 84, 167, 233, 244, 245, 251, 261
  art 3...133, 134, 2008
  art 5...24, 60, 61
  art 5(1)...60
  art 5(2)...24
  art 5(3)...60, 61
  art 5(4)...84
  art 5(5)...60
  art 6...4, 17, 61, 120, 135, 137, 151, 179, 205, 233, 234, 244, 249, 2008
  art 6(1)...178, 179, 224, 233, 244
  art 6(2)–(3)...233
  art 7...149
  art 8...182
Treaty on European Union
  art 31...262
  art 34...262
United Nations Convention on the Rights of the Child...134, 2008

TABLE OF SECONDARY LEGISLATION

Civil Procedure Rules 1998 (SI 1998/3132)...4
   Part 52...162
   PD 52...162
      paras 18.1–18.20...162
   Part 54...169
   PD 54...169
Criminal Appeal (Amendment) Rules 2000 (SI 2000/2036)...261
Criminal Appeal Rules 1968 (SI 1968/1262)...256, 261
Criminal Defence Service (General) (No. 2) Regulations 2001...88
Criminal Defence Service (Recovery of Defence Costs Orders) Regulations 2001 (SI 2001/856)...53
Criminal Defence Service (Representation Order Appeals) Regulations 2001...88
Criminal Justice Act 1988 (Reviews of Sentencing) Order 1994 (SI 1994/119)...264
Criminal Justice Act 2003 (Surcharge) (No. 2) Order 2007 (SI 2007/1079)
   paras 3–4...312
Criminal Justice (Sentencing) (Licence Conditions) Order 2005 (SI 2005/648)...336
   paras 2–3...336
Criminal Procedure (Amendment) Rules 2007...16
Criminal Procedure and Investigations Act 1996 (Defence Disclosure Time Limits) Regulations 1997 (SI 1997/684)
   reg 2...176
Criminal Procedure Rules 2005 (SI 2005/384)...4, 16, 17, 18, 19, 114, 115, 120, 197, 245
   Part 1
      r 1.1...4
      r 1.1(1)...4, 17
      r 1.1(2)...4–5, 17
      r 1.2...4, 19
      r 1.2(1)...18
      r 1.3...17
   Part 3...5, 194
      r 3...17
      r 3.2...5, 18, 19, 239
      r 3.4(1)–(4)...18
      r 3.5...5, 239
      r 3.5(2)...5
      r 3.5(6)...5
      r 3.8...5, 6
      r 3.9...5
      r 3.9(3)...239
      r 3.10...5, 239
   Part 7
      r 7.3...45
   Part 14...183, 184
      r 14.1...186
      r 14.1(2)...186
      r 14.1(3)(a)...186
      r 14.2...183, 187
      r 14.2(1)...183
      r 14.2(2)...184
      r 14.2(3)...186, 187, 189, 190, 191, 219, 273
      r 14.2(5)...190
   Part 15...195
   Part 16...215
   Part 19...76
      r 19.25...77
   Part 21...99, 171
      r 21...109
      rr 21.4–21.6...109
   Part 24...219
   Part 25...180
   Part 28
      r 28.3...203
      r 28.5(3)...181
      r 28.6(1)–(2)...182
   Part 29...213
      rr 29.4–29.7...213
   Part 37
      r 37.3(3)...122
      r 37.3(3)(a)(i)...120
      r 37.3(5)–(6)...121
   Part 50
      r 50.2(1)–(2)...314
      r 50.3(2)–(3)...314
   Part 63...160
      r 63.2(4)...160
   Part 64...162
   Part 65
      r 65.2(2)...239
   Part 66...240
   Part 74...265
   Part 75...265
Crown Court Rules 1982 (SI 1982/1109)
   s.7...160

Fines (Deductions from Income Support) Regulations 1992 (SI 1992/2182)...302

Indictments (Procedure) Rules 1971 (SI 1971/1253)...158, 159, 184
  r 9...245
  r 14.2(3)...188

Practice Direction (Costs: Criminal Proceedings) [2004] 2 All ER 1070...52, 53
Practice Direction (Criminal: Consolidated) [2002] 3 All ER 904...17, 77, 82, 102, 110, 114, 120, 145, 147, 158, 227, 256, 260, 275, 280
  Part I...257
  para 28...275
  paras 28.1–28.2...275
  para I.6...280
  para I.7.2...319
  para I.8.1...319
  para I.13...79
  para I.13.3...77
  para I.13.7...79
  para I.13.17...116
  paras I.15.1–15.2...257
  para I.16.1...260
  para I.17.1...257
  para I.17.5...257
  paras I.18.1–18.2...257
  para I.18.5...257
  Part II...258
  para III.24...212
  para III.25...58
  para III.25.3...227
  para III.25.4...227
  para III.25.5...227
  para III.27...198, 279
  para III.27.1.4–27.4...280
  para III.27.8...280
  para III.27.10...280
  para III.28...295, 348
  para III.30...147
  para III.30.1...147
  paras III.30.15–30.16...148
  para III.30.3...147
  para III.30.4...145
  para IV.34.2...191
  paras IV.35.2–35.3...158
  paras IV.35.5–35.6...159
  para IV.41...194
  para IV.41.3...194
  para IV.41.5...194
  para IV.41.8...194
  para IV.41.11...194
  para IV.42.1...204
  para IV.42.3...204
  paras IV.42.6–IV.6.9...226
  para IV.44...218
  para IV.45...201
  para IV.46...231
  para IV.46.1...225
  para V.50...250
  para V.50.4...250
  para V.51...110
  paras V.51.1–V.51.2...110
  para V.51.3...110–11
  para V.51.4...111, 112
  para V.51.5...111
  para V.51.6...111
  paras V.51.7–V.51.12...111, 112
  para V.51.13...111, 112
  paras V.51.14–V.51.18...111, 113
  para V.55...124–6
  Part 56...115
  Annex E...115, 194
Practice Direction (Criminal: Consolidated) (Amendment No. 11)...6
Practice Direction (Criminal: Consolidated) (Case Management) 2005
  Part V.56.2...6
  Annex E...6
Practice Direction (Magistrates' Courts: Anti-Social Behaviour Orders: Composition of Benches) (2006) 170 JP 173...315
Practice Direction (Submission of No Case) [1962] 1 WLR 227...119
Prosecution of Offences (Custody Time Limits) Regulations 1987 (SI 1987/299)...62
  r 4A...62

Codes
Code of Conduct of the Bar...176, 285
Code for Crown Prosecutors...151, 152
  paras 8.8–8.9...151
Conditional Cautioning code of Practice...42
Criminal Procedure and Investigations Act 1996, Code of Practice...171
  para 5.4...171
LSC Code of Conduct...51
  para 2.1...51
  para 2.2...52
  paras 5.1–5.2...52
Pace Codes of Practice...21, 25, 32, 38, 213
  Codes A–B...21
  Code C...21, 152
    para 1.1...28
    para 2.4...25
    para 3D...38
    para 3.1...38
    paras 3.6–3.10...29
    para 6...36
    paras 6 4–6.5...35
    para 6.6...35, 36
    para 6.8...35
    para 6.15...35
    para 6A...35
    para 9.13...31
    para 10.1...29
    para 10.4...30
    para 10.5...24
    para 11.1...32
    para 11.1A...31
    para 11.4...32
    para 11.6...32

para 11.18...34
para 15.1B Notes for Guidance...27
para 15.2A...27
para 15.3C...27
para 16.5...39
Annex A...38
Annex B
　para 2...36
Annex C...30
Annex G...31
　para 2...31
　paras 4–5...29
　para 7...29

Notes for Guidance...33
　Note 6D...35
　para 11C...33
　para 1G...33
Code D...21
Code E...21, 32
Code F...21
Code G...21
　para 1.2...22
　para 1.3...22
　para 4.1...23
Code G NfG 3...23
Code H...21, 28

Introduction

1.1 Introduction to criminal litigation

1.1.1 Aims of the course

The main intention of those responsible for designing both the Criminal Litigation element of the Bar Vocational Course, and this manual, has been to make the subject both real and practical. Your Criminal Litigation Course should instil you with a knowledge of how the criminal justice system actually works; then give you the opportunity to demonstrate that you have assimilated such knowledge and are able to make the decisions which a barrister could find himself or herself making in practice.

1.1.2 Objectives and structure of the course

By the end of the course, and having read this manual, you should be:
(a) familiar with the progress of a case through the criminal courts, understanding the various stages and what each stage involves;
(b) able to prepare for a hearing in the magistrates' court or Crown Court, knowing what the procedure will be in court and what matters will need to be covered;
(c) capable of taking informed decisions (and, if necessary, advising your client on how to act) with regard to the various different paths that a case can take, both as to its final resolution and the intermediate hearings;
(d) able to decide whether or not a decision taken in criminal proceedings merits an appeal—whether it be in relation to conviction, sentence or some procedural matter;
(e) able to prepare properly for an appeal and advise your client which is the most suitable method of appeal (where a choice exists).

The Criminal Litigation Course starts at the beginning of the process (eg an individual being charged with an offence) and works its way through to the possible endings—acquittal, conviction and sentence, appeal. This manual reflects that pattern because this seems to be the best way to promote an understanding of the various practices and procedures that govern the passage of a case through the criminal courts. The manual begins with preliminary matters, such as powers of arrest, then the commencement of criminal proceedings against an accused person. Having dealt with the subject of bail, the manual then looks at what happens when an accused person first appears in court and how a decision is made on which court should try the accused. The usual way of disposing of a case is summary trial by magistrates, so that is next on the list. The manual then examines the treatment of juveniles in the criminal justice system, in particular trial venues and procedures. Our focus then shifts to the Crown Court—how a case may get there (sent for trial or sentence or on appeal from a decision of the magistrates) and then pre-trial issues (such as disclosure, drafting an indictment and pleas). This leads us on to consideration of the trial in the Crown Court and then the possibility of further proceedings in the Court of Appeal and House of Lords (which becomes the Supreme Court of the UK from 1 October 2009). Finally, we look at sentencing powers and procedures in each of the three types of trial court—magistrates', youth and Crown Courts.

1.1.3 Sources of information

1.1.3.1 Practitioner works

Throughout the text of this manual, you can find references to other sources, in particular, law reports and statutes, but there are also references to relevant passages in the main practitioner works. These are:

- Archbold, *Criminal Pleading, Evidence and Practice*, 2009 edn, Sweet & Maxwell;
- *Blackstone's Criminal Practice*, 2009 edn, OUP;
- *Stones' Justice's Manual* (annual editions), Butterworths.

Other practitioner works for the criminal barrister include *Wilkinson's Road Traffic Offences* and *Archbold Magistrates' Courts Criminal Practice 2009* (both Sweet & Maxwell).

You are strongly advised to read further about criminal litigation topics in any of these books. In addition, there are excellent books aimed more specifically at readers who are at the vocational stage. These include:

- John Sprack, *A Practical Approach to Criminal Procedure*, 12th edn, OUP;
- Peter Hungerford-Welch, *Criminal Litigation & Sentencing*, 7th edn, Cavendish.

You should also look at journals such as the *Criminal Law Review* which carry both articles and case commentaries. Articles relevant to the criminal practitioner often appear in *Criminal Law and Justice Weekly* (previously *Justice of the Peace*) and *Legal Action* (the magazine of the Legal Action Group), amongst others.

1.1.3.2 Websites

Increasingly, information about the criminal justice system can be found online. There are portals with links to other sources. Examples include:

- <http://www.venables.co.uk>—a portal designed and run by Delia Venables with many useful links;
- <http://www.bailii.org>—the website of the British and Irish Legal Information Institute;
- <http://www.lawborepro.net>—the website of the City Law School, City University, London;
- <http://www.kent.ac.uk/lawlinks>—the website for law at the University of Kent.

There are also many websites where you can access information directly. Examples include, in no particular order:

- <http://www.opsi.gov.uk>—the website of the Office of Public Sector Information, where you can find Acts of Parliament, statutory instruments and their accompanying Explanatory Notes;

- <http://www.lawcom.gov.uk>—the website of the Law Commission (where you can find not simply proposals for law reform but also the research that underpins them);
- <http://www.justice.gov.uk>—the website of the Ministry of Justice (which combines the former roles in the criminal justice system of the Home Office and the department of Constitutional Affairs);
- <http://www.jsboard.co.uk>—the website of the Judicial Studies Board where you can find specimen directions (telling you how a judge ought to direct a jury on a specific legal point) and the Bench Books (which provide, amongst much valuable information, systematic approaches to sentencing);
- <http://www.hmcourts-service.gov.uk>—the website of the Court Service, where you can find the Criminal Procedure Rules (including amendments) and Practice Directions;
- <http://www.sentencing-guidelines.gov.uk>—the website for the Sentencing Guidelines Council, which provides guidance for sentencers;
- <http://www.cjsonline.gov.uk>—the website for the criminal justice system for England and Wales;
- <http://www.cps.gov.uk>—the website of the Crown Prosecution Service, which contains a lot of helpful information, not least the legal guidance that Crown Prosecutors use, as well as statistics on the work of the CPS;
- <http://www.legalservices.gov.uk/criminal.asp>—the website of the Legal Services Commission and, in particular, of the Criminal Defence Service (the source of public funding for those involved in the criminal justice system).

1.1.3.3 The manual (and other BVC manuals)

This manual is designed primarily for use in conjunction with the Criminal Litigation classes on the Bar Vocational Course. It should prepare you to deal with a particular topic as well as supporting specific classes through the material it contains. It is also designed to stand alone as a practical and sensible guide to legal practice in the criminal courts of England and Wales. It contains most of the 'bare bones' of what anyone needs to know when starting on a career in the criminal courts; it devotes rather less space to the remoter world of the Court of Appeal and the House of Lords (or, from 1 October 2009, the Supreme Court of the United Kingdom).

The manual does not contain the totality of information on the criminal justice system and that is not its aim. It is intended to deal primarily with matters of significance to the junior practitioner and supplies the level of information which should be 'at the ready' when that practitioner finds himself or herself in court. It is not intended to supplant the excellent practitioner works mentioned in 1.1.3.1 and we would recommend that you should always regard those sources as the best place to research legal issues (as well as the primary sources—legislation and case law).

Remember that there are other BVC manuals as well, which may contain information and guidance which is relevant to work in the criminal justice system. These include:

- the *Advocacy* manual (with how-to-do-it guides on bail applications, submissions of no case and witness handling, for example);
- the *Drafting* manual (with guidance on writing a skeleton argument to support an application);
- the *Evidence* manual (to check on admissibility points, for example);

- the *Case Preparation* manual (to get tips on how to research the law for your case and manage the facts);
- the *Professional Conduct* manual (to make sure that you don't do something you shouldn't, or vice versa).

You may find it useful to pull together guidance from a number of the manuals to help you see the complete picture.

Note: In some chapters of *Criminal Litigation and Sentencing*, statistical tables are reproduced with the kind permission of the Home Office Statistics Department. Owing to different recording procedures in some areas of the country and some incomplete data, the figures in these tables should be taken only as a guide.

1.2 Introduction to the criminal justice system

1.2.1 The Criminal Procedure Rules 2005

1.2.1.1 Generally

The year 2005 saw the introduction of the first comprehensive collection of rules governing the work of the criminal justice system—the Criminal Procedure Rules 2005. These Rules came into effect on 4 April 2005 and although the first edition was expressly intended to be largely a codification of the existing disparate rules for the various criminal courts, there were already some significant changes and additions.

In particular, the Rules set out case management powers for the magistrates' and Crown Courts (in Part 3) and, perhaps most significantly, an overriding objective for the code. This is an echo of the insertion of an overriding objective into civil litigation via the Civil Procedure Rules in 1998 and is no doubt intended to be equally important for the conduct of criminal litigation.

Rule 1.2 states that those involved in the conduct of a case must act in accordance with the Rules (and Practice Directions) and inform the court at once of any significant non-compliance.

Reference will be made to the Rules, where appropriate, in the manual. The original Rules can be found in SI 2005/384 but there have been several subsequent amendments and the current Rules (and updates) can be found online at <http://www.justice.gov.uk/criminal/procrules_fin/index.htm>.

1.2.1.2 The overriding objective

The overriding objective is set out in r 1.1 and is as follows:

(1) *The overriding objective of this new code is that criminal cases be dealt with justly.*

(2) *Dealing with a criminal case justly includes—*

    (a) *acquitting the innocent and convicting the guilty;*

    (b) *dealing with the prosecution and the defence fairly;*

    (c) *recognising the rights of a defendant, particularly those under Article 6 of the European Convention on Human Rights;*

    (d) *respecting the interests of witnesses, victims and jurors and keeping them informed of the progress of the case;*

    (e) *dealing with the case efficiently and expeditiously;*

    (f) *ensuring that appropriate information is available to the court when bail and sentence are considered; and*

(g) dealing with the case in ways that take into account—
 (i) the gravity of the offence alleged,
 (ii) the complexity of what is in issue,
 (iii) the severity of the consequences for the defendant and others affected, and
 (iv) the needs of other cases.

1.2.1.3 Case management powers

Under Part 3 of the 2005 Rules, courts are given significant new powers to manage cases through the criminal justice system efficiently and effectively. These powers apply to all cases in the magistrates' courts and Crown Courts. The principle behind them is to facilitate the overriding objective through enabling courts to engage in active case management. Appropriate directions are to be given in each case as early as possible and the parties are to actively assist the court, where necessary by applying for directions. This will be promoted through the appointment, for every case, of an individual—the case progression officer (c.p.o.)—to be responsible for progressing the case. Prosecution, defence and court must each have a c.p.o. and their contact details must be exchanged.

In actively managing a case, a number of objectives are identified (in r 3.2):

- identifying the real issues at an early stage;
- identifying the needs of witnesses at an early stage;
- setting a timetable for the progress of the case, and deciding what must be done, by whom and by when;
- monitoring case progress and compliance with any directions;
- ensuring that evidence is presented in the most succinct and clear way;
- avoiding unnecessary hearings;
- encouraging co-operation;
- using technology.

In particular, applications for directions, representations and any resultant hearings may take place via letters, telephone or electronic communications (presumably this includes e-mails). Alternatively, the court may give a direction without a hearing and can specify 'the consequences' of failure to comply with a direction (r 3.5(2)). Directions must be given at every hearing, to enable the case to conclude at the next hearing, if possible, or as soon as is possible thereafter. The punitive sanction alluded to in r 3.5(2) (above) appears again in r 3.8—'where a direction has not been complied with, [the court is to] find out why, identify who was responsible, and take appropriate action'. Each party must ensure that their case is ready for trial and, as part of this process, the court may require a party to identify those witnesses which he intends to call to give oral evidence, the order in which they will be called, any arrangements for facilitating the giving of evidence and to identify what other material he intends to make available to the court (see rr 3.9 and 3.10). Concerns that Part 3 did not provide for any appropriate sanction and thus was toothless led to the amendment of r3.5 (see *R (Kelly) v Warley Magistrates' Court* [2007] EWHC 1836 (Admin.)). r.3.5(6) has been added, to specify that failure to comply with a rule or direction may lead to changes to a hearing (it may be fixed, postponed, extended or cancelled), a costs order may be made to penalise the defaulting party or 'the court may impose such other sanction as may be appropriate'. These changes took effect from April 2008 onwards.

The improvements in case management were also developed in other ways. For example, cases which are tried summarily in the magistrates' court will require completion of a case progression form (set out in Annex E of the Practice Direction; see *Amendment No. 11 to the Consolidated Criminal Practice Direction (Case Management)*). This form, together with its guidance notes, set out a case progression timetable for effective preparation of the case (see Part V.56.2 of the amended Practice Direction). Where a case is sent to Crown Court for trial, a plea and case management hearing (PCMH) will be scheduled; the amended r3.8 specifies that 'in order to prepare for a trial in the Crown Court, the court must conduct a [PCMH] unless the circumstances make it unnecessary'. The PCMH should take place within about 14 weeks after sending the case for trial if the defendant is in custody (or about 17 weeks, if he is on bail). According to the amended Practice Direction, a PCMH 'should reduce the number of ineffective and cracked trials and delays during the trial to resolve legal issues'. Where possible, courts should fix the dates of cases so that the trial advocates are also able to attend the PCMH.

1.2.2 Structure and relationship of the courts

All cases begin in the magistrates' court. A youth court is a type of magistrates' court which deals exclusively with juveniles. The vast majority of cases will be tried in the magistrates' court and will end there (unless the accused is committed to the Crown Court for sentence, or appeals to either the Crown Court or the High Court). The remaining cases will begin in the magistrates' court but be committed for trial to the Crown Court with the possibility of an appeal to the Court of Appeal. From both the Court of Appeal and the High Court it is possible, though rare, to appeal to the House of Lords (which becomes the new Supreme Court of the United Kingdom on 1 October 2009) on matters of law. The inter-relationship of the courts is set out in **Figure 1.1**.

It is appropriate at this stage to note that the magistrates' court has a civil jurisdiction, in addition to its criminal work. Whatever powers the magistrates' court has are given to it by Acts of Parliament—it has no inherent jurisdiction. Numerous Acts establish the jurisdiction of magistrates to deal with a considerable variety of work. Perhaps the most significant aspects of their work, for a barrister, are their jurisdiction over family and domestic proceedings and their role in licensing matters. This may change as more civil matters are determined by magistrates despite their apparently criminal nature, for example, granting anti-social behaviour orders.

1.3 Recent developments

It is not at all unusual for the criminal justice system to undergo significant changes at least once a year. We have not seen a new Criminal Justice Act since 2003 but it does not follow that nothing has happened since then. Some of the more significant changes over the 2008–9 period are described below.

1.3.1 New Acts

1.3.1.1 Criminal Justice and Immigration Act 2008

The Government proposed a number of changes to the criminal justice system in its 2006 paper, 'Rebalancing the criminal justice system in favour of the law-abiding majority'. This Act is intended to implement those proposals. Amongst them are:

Figure 1.1 Structure and relationship of the courts.

```
                              HOUSE OF LORDS*
                                    ↑
                            (Appeals: Chapter 12)

                            COURT OF APPEAL
                            (Criminal Division)
                                   ↗
                      (Appeals: Chapter 12)        (Appeals: Chapter 12)

                         (Appeal by way of case
                         stated and application for
    CROWN COURT  ───→    judicial review on matters  ──→  HIGH COURT
                         not relating to trial on
                         indictment: Chapter 8)

    (Indictments and
    pleas: Chapter 10
    Trial: Chapter 11    (Sending for trial: Chapter 7   (Appeal by way of case stated:
    Sentence: Chapters    Committal for sentence: Chapter 5   Chapter 8
    19 and 20)            Appeals: Chapter 8                  Application for judicial review:
                          Appeal against a refusal of bail:   Chapter 8)
                          Chapter 3)

                         MAGISTRATES' COURT    YOUTH COURT

                         (Remands and bail:    (Trial: Chapter 6
                         Chapter 3             Sentence: Chapters
                         Mode of trial: Chapter 4   17 and 18)
                         Summary trial: Chapter 5)

                         Disclosure: Chapter 9
                         Sentence: Chapters 15 and 16

                         COMMENCEMENT OF PROCEEDINGS
                         (Preliminaries: Chapter 2)
```

*On 1 October 2009, the House of Lords will become the Supreme Court of the United Kingdom.

- the introduction of violent offender orders;
- powers for courts to order the temporary closure of premises associated with serious anti-social behaviour (similar to powers to close premises associated with drug dealing under the Anti-Social Behaviour Act 2003);
- the reinstatement of certain magistrates' powers to commit an offender to Crown Court for sentence, following conviction on a summary trial;

- enhanced powers for a court to proceed to try a case in the absence of the accused — 'may' do so in cases involving juvenile accused and 'shall' do so when the absent accused is an adult unless it would be contrary to the interests of justice;
- the extension of conditional cautions to juvenile offenders;
- further changes to make sentencing decisions clearer; and
- the introduction of a new generic community sentence for juveniles, the Youth Rehabilitation Order.

1.3.1.2 Criminal Evidence (Witness Anonymity) Act 2008

Introduced very rapidly in July 2008, this short Act was intended to empower courts to order that a witness's identity be withheld in a trial. This 'power' had hitherto accreted as a common law power but the decision of the House of Lords in *R v Davis* (in June 2008) to the effect that the courts had no such power at common law meant that Parliament had to act swiftly.

1.3.2 Bills in Parliament

Further changes are in the pipeline, with various Government Bills currently proceeding through Parliament, containing provisions relevant to criminal justice.

1.3.2.1 Coroners and Justice Bill 2009

Although mainly reforming the procedure for inquests, this Bill introduces or amends several crimes (in particular, the defence of diminished responsibility in murder cases), amends the provisions for witness anonymity orders, amends the provisions dealing with special measures directions (see Youth Justice and Criminal Evidence Act 1999) and proposes a new body—the Sentencing Council for England and Wales—to replace both the Sentencing Guidelines Council and the Sentencing Advisory Panel.

1.3.2.2 Policing and Crime Bill 2008–9

Whilst mainly concerned with reforming the rules on police accountability, sex workers and the sale and consumption of alcohol, this Bill also makes significant changes to the statutory scheme for the recovery of criminal assets, set out in the Proceeds of Crime Act 2002.

1.3.3 Updates and the online resource centre

Since the advent of the CJA 2003, this manual has been written on the basis that the provisions of this important Act would soon be brought into effect. However, as time has passed since then, some provisions remain unimplemented and a timetable for the Act to take full effect has remained uncertain. For example, the allocation provisions (see **Chapter 4**) which were intended to replace the committal for trial provisions in the MCA 1980 have not been implemented and are now amended by provisions in the Criminal Justice and Immigration Act 2008. For some years now, a schedule of those CJA provisions mentioned in the manual has been on the online resource centre, showing precisely which ones are in force and from when. This online resource centre will be important for you to refer to when checking that a specific provision of the CJA 2003 is in force or has been repealed or amended. The position on implementation as at 16 April 2009 has been included at **1.5** below, for your ease of reference.

1.4 Abbreviations

Abbreviations are often used in the text. Some are probably familiar, eg *Archbold*, *Stone's*, WLR for Weekly Law Reports. Others will become familiar in time. The following list of common abbreviations should help.

BA 1976 (Bail Act 1976);
CAA 1968 or 1995 (Criminal Appeal Act, either 1968 or 1995);
CDA 1998 (Crime and Disorder Act 1998);
CDSA 2006 (Criminal Defence Service Act 2006);
CICB (Criminal Injuries Compensation Board);
CJA (Criminal Justice Act, various years but most notably 2003);
CJIA (Criminal Justice and Immigration Act 2008);
CJCSA 2000 (Criminal Justice and Court Services Act 2000);
CJPOA 1994 (Criminal Justice and Public Order Act 1994);
CLA (Criminal Law Act, various years);
CPIA 1996 (Criminal Procedure and Investigations Act 1996);
CPS (Crown Prosecution Service);
Cr App R (Criminal Appeal Reports. A specialist series, reporting cases from the Divisional Court of the Queen's Bench Division, Court of Appeal (Criminal Division), and the House of Lords/Supreme Court);
Cr App R (S) (Criminal Appeal Reports (Sentencing). A companion to the Cr App R but concentrating on sentencing decisions);
Crim LR (Criminal Law Review. A monthly publication with brief, up-to-date reports of cases and useful articles);
C(S)A 1997 (Crime (Sentences) Act 1997);
CYPA 1933 or 1969 (Children and Young Persons Act, either 1933 or 1969);
DTO (Detention and Training Orders);
DTTO (Drug Testing and Treatment Orders);
DVCVA 2004 (Domestic Violence, Crime and Victims Act 2004);
EAH (early administrative hearings);
ECHR (European Convention on Human Rights and Fundamental Freedoms);
HRA 1998 (Human Rights Act 1998);
JA 1974 (Juries Act 1974);
MCA 1980 (Magistrates' Courts Act 1980);
MHA 1983 (Mental Health Act 1983);
PACE 1984 (Police and Criminal Evidence Act 1984);
PJA 2006 (Police and Justice Act 2006);
PCC(S)A 2000 (Powers of Criminal Courts (Sentencing) Act 2000);
ROA 1974 (Rehabilitation of Offenders Act 1974);
SCA 1981 (Supreme Court Act 1981);
SOCA (Serious Organised Crime Agency);
SOCPA 2005 (Serious Organised Crime and Police Act 2005);
TIC (taken into consideration);
YJCEA 1999 (Youth Justice and Criminal Evidence Act 1999).

1.5 Criminal Justice Act 2003: what's in force?

As noted above, this manual has for several years been written on the assumption that the CJA 2003 would come into full effect at some point quite proximate to the Act receiving the Royal Assent. This has proved illusory with respect to several topics even now, some six years after the Act entered the statute books. The following table is intended to assist you in following which provisions are now in effect and which of the rest are expected to come into effect at some point. It should be noted that some revisions were made to the CJA 2003 by the Criminal Justice and Immigration Act 2008. These are flagged up in the table and reference is also made in the relevant chapters. You should also refer to the Online Resource Centre of this manual, which can be found at <www.oxfordtextbooks.co.uk/orc/barmanuals/>, for future updates. The table sets out the position as at 16 April 2009.

Criminal Justice Act 2003 Provisions	Page Reference	In force?
6	27	Yes
8	25	Yes
9	26	Yes
10	26	Yes
11	21	Yes
13	61, 73	Yes
13(2)	76	Yes
14	68	Yes, but only where the current offence was committed on or after 1.1.07 AND is punishable by life imprisonment (or the equivalent for a juvenile offender)
14(2)	71	Yes (see above)
15	68	Yes for (3). Yes for (1) and (2) but only where the failure to surrender occurred on or after 1.1.07 AND the offence is punishable by life imprisonment (or the equivalent for a juvenile offender)
15(2)	71	Yes (see above)
15(3)	79	Yes
16	86	Yes
17	86	Yes
18	86	Yes
19	68	Yes
22	41	Yes
22(2)	42	Yes
22(3)	42	Yes
23	42	Yes
24	42	Yes
24(1), (2)	42	Yes
25	42	Yes
26	42	Yes
27	42	Largely in force now; exceptions basically restrict the people who may give conditional cautions (see ss 22–24) to police constables and investigating officers
28	38	See Sch 2 for details

29	43, 80	Yes, but only where proceedings are initiated by a police force or someone authorised by such force and only in the specified locations of magistrates' courts (mainly in and around London, and more recently in Cheshire). See SI 2007/1999; SI 2008/1424
29(5)	44	Yes, see above
30(1)	44	Yes, see s 29
30(5)	44	Yes, see s 29
31	46	Yes
31(1)	44	Yes
40	27	Yes
40(4)	43	Yes
Part 7	236, 350	Basic provisions on judge-only trials where jury tampering has occurred or may occur are now in force: see SI 2006/1835
43	236	No
43(1)(b)	236	No
43(4)–(7)	236	No
44	236	Yes
44(4)	236	Yes
44(5), (6)	236	Yes
45, 46	237	Yes (45 only so far as it covers applications under s 44)
46(4), (5)	237	Yes
Part 8	213	Not in force except that rules of court may be made: s 55
51	119, 213, 350	Yes but only in relation to trials at Crown Court locations where live link facilities are available AND ONLY when the charges include one of those listed in the SI (basically specific sexual offences – rape, burglary with intent to rape, sexual assault, etc): see SI 2007/3451.
51(4)	214	Yes, but see above
51(6), (7)	214	Yes, but see above
54	214	Yes, but see above
56(2)	214	Yes, but see above
57	239	Yes
57(4)	239	Yes
58	238, 241	Yes
58–61	240	Yes
62	241	No
62(2)	241	No
62(8), (9)	241	No
62(11)	241	No
63	241, 242	No
63(1)		No
63(2)	241	No
64–74	239, 241, 242	Yes, except ss 65–66
Part 10	235	Yes
75	235, 262	Yes
75(2)(a)–(c)	262	Yes

75(4)	262	Yes
76	235, 262	Yes
77		Yes
78	263	Yes
78(2)	263	Yes
78(3)	263	Yes
79	263	Yes
79(2)	236	Yes
80	262	Yes
81–97	262	Yes
98, 99		Yes
100	350	Yes
101–112		Yes
116	211, 350	Yes
116(2)(e)		Yes
137	213, 350	No
137(1)	214	No
137(3), (4)	214	No
139(1), (2)	210	Yes
142(1)	143, 149, 292	Yes
143(1)	293	Yes
143(2)	294, 297	Yes
143(3)	293, 294	Yes
144(1)	295	Yes
145	294	Yes
146(2)	294	Yes
146(4), (5)	294	Yes
148	304	Yes
148(1)	292, 304	Yes
148(2)	304	Yes
149(1)	308	Yes
151	304, 307, 309	No
152(2)	292, 317, 318, 333	Yes
152(3)	318, 319	Yes
153(2)	319	Yes
154	122	No
155	122, 316	No
156	304, 319, 326	Yes
161	289	No
161A, 161B	312	Yes, if offence committed on or after 1/4/07
162	301	Yes
163	331	Yes
164(4A)		Yes
166(2)	304	Yes
166(3)(b)	319	Yes
167	291	Yes
169	291	Yes
170(5)(a)	291	Yes
170(7)		Yes
172(1)	291	Yes
174	286	Yes

177	132	Yes, except for those aged 16 or 17 when convicted of an offence (for this group implementation has been postponed until 4 April 2010 when the expectation is that it will be replaced by the youth rehabilitation order; see CJIA 2008, s 1)
177(1)	303, 304	Yes, subject to the above caveat
177(3), (4)	303	Yes, subject to the above caveat
177(5)	303, 333	Yes, subject to the above caveat
177(6)	303	Yes, subject to the above caveat
177(7)		Yes, subject to the above caveat
178		Yes
179		Yes, subject to the same caveat as s 177
181(2)	320	No
181(5), (6)	320	No
181(7)	320	No
182(1)	320	Yes but only for the purposes of the passing of a prison sentence subject to intermittent custody and licence
183	323	Yes but limited as with s 182 above
183(4), (5)	323	Yes but limited as with s 182 above
183(7)	323	Yes but limited as with s 182 above
185		Yes but limited as with s 182 above
189	321, 323	Yes
189(1)(b)	321	Yes
189(3), (4)	321	Yes
190	321	Yes
191, 192	321	Yes
199	304	Yes
200	304	Yes
200(1)		Yes
200(2)	305, 311	Yes
200(3)		Yes
201	305	Yes
201(1)(a)		Yes
202–207	305	Yes (with very limited exceptions in s 204(4) and (5))
209	306	Yes
210	306	Yes
211	306	Yes
212, 213	306	Yes (with the exception of s 213(3)(b))
214	307	Yes
215	307	Yes
217(1), (2)	303	Yes
220	307	Yes
221(2)	307	Yes
224	128, 142, 337	Yes
225	337	Yes
225(1)		Yes
225(2)	337	Yes
225(3)	337	Yes
225(4)	337	Yes
226	142, 144, 337	Yes

226(1)		Yes
226(3)	128	Yes
227	204, 337, 338	Yes
227(2)	127, 337	Yes
227(3), (4)	337	Yes
228	142, 144, 204, 337, 338, 340	Yes
229	337, 338	Yes
229(3)	338	Yes
230–236	337	Yes
240	319	Yes
250	336	Yes
264A		Yes
264A(2)–(4)		Yes
282	316	No
287		Yes
300, 301	302	The substantive provisions are not yet in force
306		Yes
309		Yes
310(4), (5)		Yes
316	260	Yes
Sch 2	38, 39, 127	Yes, except limited implementation of para 3
Sch 2, para 6	39	Yes
Sch 3	105, 126, 127, 128, 146, 154, 158	CDA 1998 s 51, 51b, 51C not in force, s 51A mostly in force, s 51D, s 51E in force only for crimes sent for trial under CDA 1998, s 51A(3)(d); PCC(S)A 2000 ss 3, 3A and 3B are not yet in force and CJIA 2008 repeals some of the changes, s 3C is in force. Further reference should be made to *Halsbury's Is It In Force?*
Sch 3, para 9	135	No
Sch 4	241	No
Sch 5	262	Yes
Sch 5, Part 1	235	Yes
Sch 8	308	Yes, but where a 16/17 year old is convicted the date of commencement has been deferred to 4 April 2010 but is expected to be replaced at that date by the new youth rehabilitation order in the CJIA 2008
Sch 8, para 5	308	Yes, subject to the caveat above
Sch 8, para 5(1), (2)	308	Yes, subject to the caveat above
Sch 8, para 6(1)	308	Yes, subject to the caveat above
Sch 8, para 7	308	Yes, subject to the caveat above
Sch 8, para 8(2)	332	Yes, subject to the caveat above
Sch 8, para 8(4)	332	Yes, subject to the caveat above
Sch 8, para 9(1)	308	Yes, subject to the caveat above
Sch 8, para 9(2)–(4)	304	Yes, subject to the caveat above
Sch 8, para 9(6)	309, 332	Yes, subject to the caveat above
Sch 8, para 9(8)	309	Yes, subject to the caveat above
Sch 8, para 10(1)	309, 332	Yes, subject to the caveat above
Sch 8, para 10(1)(a)–(c)	333	Yes, subject to the caveat above
Sch 8, para 10(2)–(6)	333	Yes, subject to the caveat above
Sch 8, para 11(1)		Yes, subject to the caveat above

Sch 8, para 12		Yes, subject to the caveat above
Sch 8, para 13		Yes, subject to the caveat above
Sch 8, para 13(3)–(5)		Yes, subject to the caveat above
Sch 8, para 14(1)	333	Yes, subject to the caveat above
Sch 8, para 14(2), (3)	333	Yes, subject to the caveat above
Sch 8, para 16, 17		Yes, subject to the caveat above
Sch 8, para 17(1)		Yes, subject to the caveat above
Sch 8, para 18–21		Yes, subject to the caveat above
Sch 8, para 21(1)		Yes, subject to the caveat above
Sch 8, para 21(3), (4)		Yes, subject to the caveat above
Sch 8, para 22	333	Yes, subject to the caveat above
Sch 8, para 22(1)	333	Yes, subject to the caveat above
Sch 8, para 23		Yes, subject to the caveat above
Sch 8, para 23(1)		Yes, subject to the caveat above
Sch 8, para 23(1)(b)		Yes, subject to the caveat above
Sch 8, para 23(2)		Yes, subject to the caveat above
Sch 8 Part 3		Yes, subject to the caveat above
Sch 8 Parts 4, 5		Yes, subject to the caveat above
Sch 12	322	Yes
Sch 15	128, 139, 142, 337	Yes
Sch 15, Parts 1, 2	337	Yes
Sch 21	336	Yes
Sch 25	122	No
Sch 26	122, 316	No
Sch 33		Yes
Sch 37, Part 2	59	No

2

Preliminaries

2.1 Preamble

There are essentially two methods of commencing prosecutions, namely the arrest and charge of the suspect, described at **2.2** below, and the issue of process, described at **2.3** below. Two matters may be conveniently dealt with now by way of preamble.

2.1.1 Jurisdiction and immunity

English courts accept jurisdiction to try an accused for an offence committed in England and Wales, regardless of the nationality of the offender. In addition, English courts have jurisdiction over some offences committed abroad in certain circumstances, such as offences of murder and manslaughter where the accused is a British subject, and offences of hijacking regardless of the nationality of the accused. For a complete list of such offences, see *Archbold* (2009 edn), para 2–33 ff. and *Blackstone's Criminal Practice* (2009 edn), para A8.1 ff. For the limited jurisdiction of magistrates' courts, see **2.5** below.

Certain persons are entitled to immunity from prosecution. The Queen is immune, as are foreign sovereigns and heads of state, their families and personal servants. Diplomatic agents, their staff and families are also immune. For a complete list of those immune from prosecution, see *Archbold* (2009 edn), para 1–82 ff., *Blackstone's Criminal Practice* (2009 edn), para D1.76.

2.1.2 The right to prosecute

The Crown Prosecution Service (CPS) was created by the Prosecution of Offences Act 1985, and is a single, national, prosecution service, with the Director of Public Prosecutions (DPP) at its head, and under the 'superintendence' of the Attorney-General. The main duty of the CPS is to take over and conduct all criminal proceedings commenced by the police, which includes the power to discontinue proceedings or to change or amend any charges originally preferred.

The right of an individual, and of certain statutory bodies such as the Inland Revenue, to institute and conduct criminal proceedings, is expressly preserved by the Act. However, under s 6(2), the DPP has an unfettered discretion to intervene in any proceedings, and conduct them on his or her own behalf.

2.1.3 The Criminal Procedure Rules

The vast majority of the rules of procedure are to be found in the Criminal Procedure Rules (as amended by the Criminal Procedure (Amendment Rules) 2007 and the Criminal Procedure (Amendment No 2) Rules 2008) which came into effect in April 2005. The amended rules came into effect on 6 April 2009. The rules are supplemented by the *Consolidated Criminal Practice Direction*. Both rules and Practice Direction can be found at <http://www.justice.gov.uk>. Students should be familiar with both the Rules and the Practice Direction, which underpin the whole litigation process.

The overriding objective of the rules, according to r 1.1(1), is that 'criminal cases be dealt with justly'.

Dealing with criminal cases justly includes, according to r 1.1(2):

(a) *acquitting the innocent and convicting the guilty;*

(b) *dealing with the prosecution and the defence fairly;*

(c) *recognizing the rights of a defendant, particularly those under Article 6 of the European Convention on Human Rights;*

(d) *respecting the interests of witnesses, victims and jurors and keeping them informed of the progress of the case;*

(e) *dealing with the case efficiently and expeditiously;*

(f) *ensuring that appropriate information is available to the court when bail and sentence are considered; and*

(g) *dealing with the case in ways that take into account:*

   (i) *the gravity of the offence alleged;*

   (ii) *the complexity of what is in issue;*

   (iii) *the severity of the consequences for the defendant and others affected; and*

   (iv) *the needs of other cases.*

The court must further the overriding objective, in particular, under r 1.3, when:

(a) *exercising any power given to it by legislation (including these Rules);*

(b) *applying any practice direction; or*

(c) *interpreting any rule or practice direction.*

2.1.3.1 Active case management

Rule 3 imposes a duty on the court to further the overriding objective by active case management. This includes:

(a) *the early identification of the real issues;*

(b) *the early identification of the needs of witnesses;*

(c) *achieving certainty as to what must be done, by whom, and when, in particular by the early setting of a timetable for the progress of the case;*

(d) *monitoring the progress of the case and compliance with directions;*

(e) *ensuring that evidence, whether disputed or not, is presented in the shortest and clearest way;*

(f) *discouraging delay, dealing with as many aspects of the case as possible on the same occasion, and avoiding unnecessary hearings;*

(g) *encouraging the participants to co-operate in the progression of the case; and*

(h) *making use of technology.*

In addition, the court must actively manage the case by giving any direction appropriate to the needs of that case as early as possible.

Advice was given to magistrates on the robust management of cases in *R (on the application of the DPP) v Chorley Justices* [2006] EWHC 1759 (Admin.):

The duty of the court is to see that justice is done. That does not involve allowing people to escape on technical points or by attempting, as happened here, an ambush. It involves the courts in looking at the real justice of the case and seeing whether the rules have been complied with by 'cards being put on the table' at the outset and the issues being clearly identified. . . . for the future, no solicitor should expect that his client will be able to rely on this sort of technical point or this type of ambush. The days for that tactic to succeed are over.

2.1.3.2 Duties of participants

Under r 1.2(1) the duties of the participants in a criminal case are set out. For the purposes of this rule, anyone involved in any way with a criminal case is a participant in its conduct. The duties of the participants in a criminal case include:

(a) prepare and conduct the case in accordance with the overriding objective;

(b) comply with these Rules, practice directions and directions made by the court; and

(c) at once inform the court and all parties of any significant failure (whether or not that participant is responsible for that failure) to take any procedural step required by these Rules, any practice direction or any direction of the court. A failure is significant if it might hinder the court in furthering the overriding objective.

2.1.3.3 Progressing the case

In addition, all parties must be accountable for the progression of the case. Rule 3.4 provides:

(1) At the beginning of the case each party must, unless the court otherwise directs—

   (a) nominate an individual responsible for progressing that case; and

   (b) tell other parties and the court who he is and how to contact him.

(2) In fulfilling its duty under rule 3.2, the court must where appropriate—

   (a) nominate a court officer responsible for progressing the case; and

   (b) make sure the parties know who he is and how to contact him.

(3) In this Part a person nominated under this rule is called a case progression officer.

(4) A case progression officer must—

   (a) monitor compliance with directions;

   (b) make sure that the court is kept informed of events that may affect the progress of that case;

   (c) make sure that he can be contacted promptly about the case during ordinary business hours;

   (d) act promptly and reasonably in response to communications about the case; and

   (e) if he will be unavailable, appoint a substitute to fulfill his duties and inform the other case progression officers.

EXAMPLE

An example of the new approach under the Criminal Procedure Rules can be found in *Malcolm v Director of Public Prosecutions* [2007] EWHC 363, a case on whether the magistrates could receive further evidence after they had retired to consider their verdict. The court stated:

In my judgment, Miss Calder's submissions, which emphasized the obligation of the prosecution to prove its case in its entirety before closing its case, and certainly before end of the final speech for the defence, had an anachronistic, and obsolete, ring. Criminal trials are no longer to be treated as a game, in which each move is final and any omission by the prosecution leads to its failure. It is the duty of the defence to make its defence and the issues it raises clear to the prosecution and to the court at an early stage. That duty is implicit in rule 3.3 of the Criminal Procedure Rules, which requires the parties actively to assist the exercise by the court of its case management powers, the exercise of which requires early identification of the real issues. Even in a relatively straightforward trial such as the present, in the magistrates' court (where there is not yet any requirement of a defence statement or a pre-trial review), it is the duty of the defence to make the real issues clear at the latest before the prosecution closes its case.

See also *R v Bryant* [2005] EWCA Crim 2079; *R v B* [2005] EWCA Crim 805; *R v K* [2006] 2All ER 552; and *R v Lashley* [2005] EWCA Crim 2016.

In *R (on the application of the DPP) v Chorley Justices* [2006] EWHC 1795 (Admin.), Andrew Forrest was charged with driving with excess alcohol. The magistrates upheld a submission of no case to answer due to technical errors in the way that the case was brought. The prosecution asked them to state a case for the consideration of the High Court and when they refused to do so, the prosecution applied to the High Court for an order that they do so. The High Court did make that order, and in the course of consideration Thomas LJ said:

24 . . . . *[T]he Criminal Procedure Rules . . . have effected a sea change in the way in which cases should be conducted, but it appears from what has happened in this case that not everyone has appreciated the fundamental change to the conduct of cases in the Magistrates' Courts that has been brought about by the rules. The rules make clear that the overriding objective is that criminal cases be dealt with justly; that includes acquitting the innocent and convicting the guilty, dealing with the prosecution and the defence fairly, respecting the interests of witnesses, dealing with the case efficiently and expeditiously, and also, of great importance, dealing with the case in a way that takes into account the gravity of the offence, the complexity of what is in issue, the severity of the consequences to the defendant and others affected and the needs of other cases. Rule 1.2 imposes upon the duty of participants in a criminal case to prepare and conduct the case in accordance with the overriding objective, to comply with the rules and, importantly, to inform the court and all parties of any significant failure, whether or not the participant is responsible for that failure, to take any procedural step required by the rules.*

25 *Rule 3.2 imposes upon the court a duty to further that overriding objective by actively managing the case.*

26 *The pertinent part relevant to what happened in this case is the early identification of the real issues. It is, it seems to us, clear that what should have happened is that at the first hearing of a case of this kind, after the entry of the plea of not guilty, the defendant should have been asked first what was in issue. At that stage and at the first hearing, he should then have been asked what witnesses did he need. . . . Mr Forrest should, thirdly, have been asked what issues were taken by the defence. In our experience, it is very rare in a court, when such a question is asked, that parties do not reply. Most people approach a case on the basis that they want justice done as they wish to be acquitted if they are innocent; it is our experience that the case where a defendant refuses to identify the issue is rare indeed. If a defendant refuses to identify what the issues are, one thing is clear: he can derive no advantage from that or seek, as appears to have happened in this case, to attempt an ambush at trial. The days of ambushing and taking last-minute technical points are gone. They are not consistent with the overriding objective of deciding cases justly, acquitting the innocent and convicting the guilty.*

28 . . . *[H]owever, for the future, no solicitor should expect that his client will be able to rely on this sort of technical point or this type of ambush. The days for that tactic to succeed are over. If a solicitor is instructed late and the points have not been identified that the defendant wishes to take, then the solicitor has a duty to ensure that they are brought to the attention of the Crown Prosecution Service and the court well in advance of the trial.* Note that the CPS brought these proceedings in the High Court against the Magistrates' Court. The costs were paid by Andrew Forrest.

There are a growing number of cases on the effect of the Criminal Procedure Rules. See for example, *Lawson v Stafford Magistrates' Court* [2007 EWHC 2490; *L v DPP* [2009] EWHC 238 (Admin) and *Writtle v DPP* [2009] EWHC 236 (Admin).

The Rules have implications as to the operation of litigation privilege and legal professional privilege. In *R v Derby Magistrates' Court, Ex p B* [1996] AC 487, the court said:

The principle which runs through all these cases, and the many other cases which were cited, is that a man must be able to consult his lawyer in confidence, since otherwise he might hold back half the truth. The client must be sure that what he tells his lawyer in confidence will never be revealed without his consent. Legal professional privilege is thus much more than an ordinary rule of evidence, limited in its application to the facts of a particular case. It is a fundamental condition on which the administration of justice as a whole rests.

> In *R (Kelly) v Warley Magistrates' Court* [2007] EWHC 1867(Admin), a case management order was made requiring disclosure of details of defence witnesses. The Court held that litigation privilege attaches to the identity and other details of witnesses intended to be called in adversarial litigation, civil or criminal, whether or not their identity is the fruit of legal advice. The Rules cannot extract the litigant's historic right not to disclose his case until he presents it from the categories of protection, litigation privilege and where it applies legal professional privilege.
>
> For a further discussion of this area in connection with procedural failures at trial, see **Chapter 12**.

2.1.3.4 Sanctions

Sanctions for non-compliance have not yet been clarified. Lawyers may be placed in difficulty if, for example, the rules are not complied with because of the client, e.g. a late change of instructions. The difficulty is that it may be in breach of the duty of confidentiality or of legal professional privilege to explain the breach of the rules to the court.

2.1.4 Criminal Justice: Simple, Speedy, Summary: CJSSS

Students should also be aware of CJSSS, which was rolled out in every Magistrates' Court in England and Wales between April and December 2007 and is now being implemented in Youth Courts. CJSSS is primarily about improving the speed and effectiveness of Magistrates' and Youth Courts and has two main aims:

- to reduce the number of hearings from an average of five or six to just one for guilty pleas and two for contested cases and
- to reduce the average time taken from charge to disposal to six weeks or less.

The CJSSS initiative is based on the following principles:

(i) Pre-court – the aim is to ensure:
   1. The prosecution case is sufficiently ready to help ensure the first hearing is effective and proportionate to that end;
   2. That the level of information is appropriate and sufficient for the type of charge, expectation of plea and decisions required by the court; and
   3. That all appropriate information has been provided to the defence and court, the defence to ensure that the defence case is sufficiently ready to help ensure the first hearing is effective.

(ii) At first hearing:
   1. Court is to ensure that issues are identified;
   2. Defendant to enter a plea;
   3. Where a guilty plea is entered, sentence will take place on the same day where possible; where a not guilty plea is entered, an effective trial date will be fixed within 6 weeks, where possible.

(iii) From first hearing to trial – to ensure:
   1. The case management regime is appropriate to the seriousness of the case;
   2. Pre-trial reviews to be by exception;
   3. Case progression to take place outside of the courtroom—interim hearings only to take place where necessary;
   4. Trials proceed where appropriate on the appointed day in the absence of the defendant where there is a failure to appear.

2.2 Arrest and charge

Most police powers of arrest, interviewing and charging a suspect are contained in the Police and Criminal Evidence Act 1984 (PACE 1984) and the Codes of Practice created thereunder. In general terms, the Act provides the overall framework, and the Codes provide the fine detail. There are eight major Codes of Practice, namely:

- Code A: Code of Practice for the Exercise by Police Officers of Statutory Powers of Stop and Search.
- Code B: Code of Practice for the Searching of Premises by Police Officers and the Seizure of Property found by Police Officers on Persons and Premises.
- Code C: Code of Practice for the Detention, Treatment and Questioning of Persons by Police Officers.
- Code D: Code of Practice for the Identification of Persons by Police Officers.
- Code E: Code of Practice on Tape Recording.
- Code F: Code of Practice for the Visual Recording with Sound of Interviews with Suspects.
- Code G: Code of Practice for the Statutory Power of Arrest by Police Officers.
- Code H: Code of Practice in connection with the detention and questioning by police officers if persons under s41 and Sch 8 of the Terrorism Act 2000.

The Codes contain detailed regulations on the exercise of police powers, and 'notes for guidance'. The notes for guidance are not provisions of the Codes, but are guidance to police officers and others about their application and interpretation.

The Codes of Practice apply to:

- police officers (PACE 1984, ss 67(8) and (10)); and
- persons 'other than police officers who are charged with the duty of investigating offences or charging offenders' (PACE 1984, s 67(9)). This includes local authority officials, post office investigators, officers of the Serious Fraud Office, customs officers and store detectives. Whether a body or person conducting an enquiry is subject to s 67(9) is a question of fact in each case (*R v Seelig* [1992] 1 WLR 148).

Revised Codes of Practice came into effect on 1 January 2006. Codes A–F were further updated on 1 February 2008. By the CJA 2003, s 11, any further revisions may be brought into effect by the Home Secretary without the requirement to publish a draft code for consultation. Students are advised to consult the Codes in detail for their full terms and effect.

While students should be familiar with all Codes, this manual is mainly concerned with Code C, and any reference to 'The Code' should be understood accordingly. Students should consult practitioner texts for a full discussion of this area (note: Code H applies only to terrorism cases).

2.2.1 Powers of arrest without warrant

The term 'arrest' is not defined by statute. In *Christie v Leachinsky* [1947] AC 573, it was referred to as 'the beginning of imprisonment'. It is a restraint on the liberty of the person within the law. There must be:

(a) a power of arrest; and

(b) a properly carried out arrest.

A police officer has a number of powers of arrest, the most important of which are contained in PACE 1984, as substituted by the Serious Organised Crime and Police Act (SOCPA) 2005, s 110:

Essentially there are two elements:

(a) there must be actual, suspected or attempted involvement in a criminal offence by the person; and

(b) *reasonable* grounds for believing that the arrest is *necessary*.

Arrest by a police officer is covered by PACE Code G for the Statutory Powers of Arrest by Police Officers. Note in particular:

1.2 The right to liberty is a key principle of the Human Rights Act 1998. The exercise of the power of arrest represents an obvious and significant interference with that right.

1.3 The use of the power must be fully justified and officers exercising the power should consider if the necessary objectives can be met by other, less intrusive means. Arrest must never be used simply because it can be used. Absence of justification for exercising the powers of arrest may lead to challenges should the case proceed to court. When the power of arrest is exercised it is essential that it is exercised in a non-discriminatory and proportionate manner.

24 Arrest without warrant: constables

(1) A constable may arrest without a warrant:

    (a) anyone who is about to commit an offence;

    (b) anyone who is in the act of committing an offence;

    (c) anyone whom he has reasonable grounds for suspecting to be about to commit an offence;

    (d) anyone whom he has reasonable grounds for suspecting to be committing an offence.

(2) If a constable has reasonable grounds for suspecting that an offence has been committed, he may arrest without a warrant anyone whom he has reasonable grounds to suspect of being guilty of it.

(3) If an offence has been committed, a constable may arrest without a warrant:

    (a) anyone who is guilty of the offence;

    (b) anyone whom he has reasonable grounds for suspecting to be guilty of it.

See *R v Olden* [2007] EWCA Crim 726 as to the arresting officer's reasonable belief.

(4) But the power of summary arrest conferred by subsection (1), (2), or (3) is exercisable only if the constable has reasonable grounds for believing that for any of the reasons mentioned in subsection (5) it is necessary to arrest the person in question.

(5) The reasons are:

    (a) to enable the name of the person in question to be ascertained (in the case where the constable does not know, and cannot readily ascertain, the person's name, or has reasonable grounds for doubting whether a name given by the person as his name is his real name);

    (b) correspondingly as regards the person's address;

    (c) to prevent the person in question:

        (i) causing physical injury to himself or any other person;

        (ii) suffering physical injury;

> (iii) causing loss of or damage to property;
>
> (iv) committing an offence against public decency (subject to subsection (6)); or
>
> (v) causing an unlawful obstruction of the highway;
>
> (d) to protect a child or other vulnerable person from the person in question;
>
> (e) to allow the prompt and effective investigation of the offence or of the conduct of the person in question;
>
> (f) to prevent any prosecution for the offence from being hindered by the disappearance of the person in question.

The arrested person, on being told the reason for the arrest, must also be told why the arrest is considered necessary, and this must be recorded in the officer's notebook: Code G Note for Guidance 3 and Code G para 4.1 respectively.

> (6) Subsection (5)(c)(iv) applies only where members of the public going about their normal business cannot reasonably be expected to avoid the person in question.

Section 24A provides for the arrest of a person by another—a citizen's arrest. For this to be lawful, the offence must be an indictable offence and there is no provision for arresting on suspicion. How a member of the public is expected to know whether or not the offence is indictable is not explained. See *R v Self* [1992] 3 All ER 476 for an example of a citizen's arrest.

Section 24A provides as follows:

24A Arrest without warrant: other persons

> (1) A person other than a constable may arrest without a warrant:
>
> (a) anyone who is in the act of committing an indictable offence;
>
> (b) anyone whom he has reasonable grounds for suspecting to be committing an indictable offence.
>
> (2) Where an indictable offence has been committed, a person other than a constable may arrest without a warrant:
>
> (a) anyone who is guilty of the offence;
>
> (b) anyone whom he has reasonable grounds for suspecting to be guilty of it.
>
> (3) But the power of summary arrest conferred by subsection (1) or (2) is exercisable only if:
>
> (a) the person making the arrest has reasonable grounds for believing that for any of the reasons mentioned in subsection (4) it is necessary to arrest the person in question; and
>
> (b) it appears to the person making the arrest that it is not reasonably practicable for a constable to make it instead.
>
> (4) The reasons are to prevent the person in question:
>
> (a) causing physical injury to himself or any other person;
>
> (b) suffering physical injury;
>
> (c) causing loss of or damage to property; or
>
> (d) making off before a constable can assume responsibility for him.

2.2.2 'Indictable' offences

Prior to the Serious Organised Crime and Police Act 2005, offences were categorised as 'arrestable' or 'serious arrestable'. This categorisation in fact gave no greater powers of arrest and has now been abandoned under the SOCPA 2005, Sch 7. Such offences are now referred to simply as 'indictable offences'.

2.2.3 Effecting the arrest

A person is arrested by:

- being informed by a police officer that he or she is under arrest; or
- being physically seized by a police officer, in which case he or she must be informed that he or she is under arrest as soon as is practicable after the arrest (PACE 1984, s 28(1)); or
- a combination of words and conduct which makes it clear that the officer will, if necessary, use force to prevent the person from leaving (*Murray v Ministry of Defence* [1988] 1 WLR 692).

The arrested person must be told the reason for the arrest, even if it is obvious (ss 28(3) and (4)). ECHR, Article 5(2) also provides that an arrested person should be told promptly and in language which he understands of the reason for his arrest and any charge against him.

If the reason given renders the arrest unlawful, it is irrelevant that there was a valid reason for the arrest if it was not communicated to the arrested person at the time (*Christie v Leachinsky* [1947] AC 573; *Abassy v Commissioner of Police of the Metropolis* [1990] 1 WLR 385).

It is not a requirement of s 28 that the arresting officer supply the reason for the arrest, as long as a reason is provided as soon as practicable thereafter (*Dhesi v Chief Constable of the West Midlands, The Times,* 9 May 2000, where the defendant was arrested by one officer and directed towards another nearby who supplied the reason). By virtue of Code C, para 10.5, the person who is arrested should also be cautioned. See **2.2.7** for a discussion of the caution.

A police officer effecting the arrest of a person may search him or her, if he has reasonable grounds for believing that the person may present a danger to himself or to others, by virtue of PACE 1984 s32(1). Other powers of search after arrest are also contained in s32.

The arrested person must be taken to a police station as soon as is practicable, unless it is reasonable to carry out other investigations first, for example, search of the arrested person and/or certain premises (PACE 1984, ss 30(1), (10) and (10A) and *Dallison v Caffery* [1965] 1 QB 348), or released on street bail (see **2.2.4**).

In each police area, certain police stations are designated as being suitable for the detention of arrested persons (PACE 1984, s 35(1)). If it is anticipated that the detention will exceed six hours, the arrested person must be detained in a designated police station (ss 30(2) and (3)).

There is nothing improper in arresting a suspect on a holding charge provided there are reasonable grounds for arresting that person on that charge. It makes no difference, if the arrest is proper, that the motive is to investigate other and more serious offences (*R v Chalkley and Jeffries* [1998] QB 848). But if the arresting officer knows that there is no possibility of a charge being brought, the arrest will be improper even if there are in fact reasonable grounds for suspecting that an offence has been committed (*Holgate-Mohammed v Duke* [1984] AC 437).

Powers of arrest are also governed by ECHR, Article 5, to which students are referred. Article 5 is construed narrowly, and sets out an exhaustive list of the circumstances in which a person may properly be detained. UK domestic law has been held to be formulated with 'the degree of precision required by the Convention' in *Steel v UK* [1988] 28 EHRR 602.

2.2.4 Street bail

By virtue of PACE 1984, s 30A, as inserted by the CJA 2003, the police officer has the power to release the arrested person on bail, even before he is taken to the police station. The only condition which the police may impose on street bail is to attend a police station. There is no restriction on which police station. However, the police officer must give the bailed person a notice, specifying the offence for which he was arrested, the ground on which he was arrested and certain other practical matters (s 30B). If the bailed person fails to attend as required, he may be arrested (s 30D).

2.2.5 At the police station

The following, rather complicated, timetable for the detention of the arrested person (hereafter called the 'suspect') is contained in PACE 1984, ss 34–46.

Note that a volunteer, that is, a person who attends a police station voluntarily, is entitled to leave at any time. To prevent him or her leaving, he or she must be arrested. The timetable for detention, set out below, begins to run at the moment of arrest.

Stage 1: At the police station, the suspect is taken to the custody officer. Each designated police station has one or more officers, of at least the rank of sergeant, appointed as custody officers. The custody officer must not, except in exceptional circumstances, be an officer involved in the investigation.

As regards the suspect, the custody officer has several duties, including, under the revised Code, specific duties in relation to vulnerable suspects. The most important duties are:

(a) To inform the suspect of his or her rights to consult a solicitor, to have someone informed, and to examine the Codes of Practice (see **2.2.10** below).

(b) To determine whether the suspect:

(i) is in need of medical treatment or attention (see **2.2.6** below);

(ii) requires either an appropriate adult, help to check documentation, or an interpreter;

and to record the decision.

(c) To maintain a custody record, being a complete record of the suspect's detention, including such matters as times of meals, interviews, the caution, if given, and the charge. A solicitor or appropriate adult must be permitted to consult a suspect's custody record as soon as practicable after the suspect's arrival at the police station and at any other time during the suspect's detention (Code C, para 2.4).

(d) To ascertain and record everything which the suspect has with him when detaining him. Prior to the CJA 2003, every item in the suspect's possession was individually recorded. This was useful to the defence solicitor in that it may reveal other reasons behind the suspect's arrest. It also protected the police themselves from allegations of tampering with the possessions. Recording possessions, however, was also seen as time-consuming and unnecessary. The CJA 2003, s 8 therefore provides that though the custody officer will still have to ascertain everything that the detained person has with him, he will no longer have to record it on the custody record. Any record that is made does not have to be part of the custody record under s 54(2A), but the suspect must be allowed the opportunity to check and sign it as correct. There is no provision that the suspect's solicitor is given the opportunity to examine the record if not in the custody record.

It is a matter for the custody officer to decide whether a record should be made and that if the record is not on the custody record, the custody officer should record where the record exists. Home Office Circular 60/2003, para 5.3 indicates in deciding whether to record property, the custody officer should have regard to:

- the circumstances of the case, eg whether the property could be the proceeds of crime, could have been used in the commission of crime or could be relevant evidence;
- the nature and volume of the property—drugs, money and property of substantial value should always be recorded;
- the wishes of the suspect—he should be asked if there are any items he wants to be recorded and his wishes should, 'within reason and if practicable', be complied with;
- the facilities for securing property—detailed records may not be necessary if placed in a sealed bag in the presence of the suspect.

(e) To oversee the whole of the suspect's detention. As the custody officer is unconnected with the investigation, he or she can take a more detached view when assessing whether the suspect should be released or detained, or whether there is sufficient evidence to charge the suspect.

(f) To order the release of the suspect, or his or her charge, unless continued detention without charge is necessary:
   (i) to secure or preserve evidence relating to the offence; or
   (ii) to obtain such evidence by questioning the suspect.

The CJA 2003, ss 9 and 10 amend PACE 1984, s 61 and abolish previous requirements that the taking of fingerprints and non-intimate samples be subject to the suspect's consent. This change now allows them to be taken by the police as a matter of routine, where the suspect has been arrested for a recordable offence.

The CJA 2003 also provides that the fingerprints and samples may be kept indefinitely. This was challenged in *R (on the application of S) v Chief Constable of South Yorkshire; R (on the application of Marper) v Chief Constable of South Yorkshire* [2004] 4 All ER 193 where the right to retain such data for ever was challenged but upheld.

Under PACE 1984, s 63B, the police may test detained persons over the age of 18 for drugs. This power applies to certain trigger offences only, listed in the Criminal Justice and Court Services Act 2000, and includes certain offences under the Theft Act 1968 and under the Misuse of Drugs Act 1971. The police must first have reasonable grounds to suspect that the offender's offending is contributed to or caused by his drug habit. Once a sample has been taken, it can be used to inform decisions in relation to bail and sentencing, and guides supervision while in detention.

Stage 2: If the custody officer authorises detention, periodic reviews of the detention must be made by a review officer to determine whether that detention is still necessary. The review officer must give the opportunity to the suspect, his solicitor (if available) or an appropriate adult (if available) to make representations about the detention. If the suspect has not yet been charged, the review officer must be:

- an officer of at least the rank of inspector; and
- not directly involved in the investigation.

The first review must be held within six hours of the original decision to detain. Note that, in any event, a suspect who is detained in a cell should be visited at least every hour.

Note: there are a number of persons who are not subject to statutory review, eg those who attend the police station voluntarily. The Notes for Guidance, para 151B of the Code, however, states that those persons should nevertheless still have their detention reviewed as a matter of good practice.

Stage 3: A second review of the detention must be held within nine hours of the first review. Reviews must thereafter be held at no more than nine-hourly intervals. According to *Roberts v Chief Constable of the Cheshire Constabulary* [1999] 1 WLR 662, failure to review renders a previously lawful detention unlawful, and amounts to the tort of false imprisonment.

Generally the review officer must be present at the police station holding the suspect. CJA 2003, s 6 however, permits the reviews of detention under s 40 to be conducted by telephone without any pre-conditions. In other words, reviews by telephone may take place as a matter of course, and there is no requirement of, for example, practicability or impracticability of reviews on site.

The revised Code C, para 15.3C states that the decision on the type of review 'must always take full account of the needs of the person in custody'. The benefits of carrying out a review in person should always be considered, based on the individual circumstances of each case with specific additional consideration being given if the person is a juvenile, mentally vulnerable, has been subject to medical attention other than routine minor ailments or there are presentational or community issues around the person's detention.

Even though the review may be conducted by telephone, the review officer must still give the suspect or his/her solicitor the opportunity to make representations, which may be made orally or by fax, if fax facilities are available.

Telephone reviews are not permitted where video-conferencing facilities are available and practicable to use. At present, video-conferencing facilities are not available.

Stage 4: After a maximum of 24 hours after arrival at the police station, the suspect must be released or charged, unless the following conditions are satisfied:

(a) The continued detention is authorised by an officer of at least the rank of superintendent.

(b) The suspect is under arrest in connection with an indictable offence.

(c) The authorising officer has reasonable grounds for believing that the suspect's continued detention is necessary to:

   (i) secure or preserve evidence relating to the offence; or

   (ii) obtain such evidence by questioning the suspect.

(d) The authorising officer has reasonable grounds for believing that the investigation is being conducted diligently and expeditiously.

At para 15.2A, the Code states that in the case of a juvenile or mentally vulnerable person detention beyond 24 hours will be dependent upon the circumstances of the case and with regard to the person's:

(a) special vulnerability;

(b) the legal obligation to provide an opportunity for representations to be made prior to a decision about extending detention;

(c) the need to consult and consider the views of any appropriate adult; and

(d) any alternatives to police custody.

Home Office Circular 60/2003 provides that the power to detain beyond 24 hours:

- should be used sparingly and only where there is full justification;
- should only be used where the authorising officer is satisfied that alternatives to continued detention, such as bail or restorative justice, have been considered and determined to be inappropriate;
- in the case of a juvenile or mentally vulnerable person, should normally be used only where he or she is detained in respect of an indictable offence.

Stage 5: After a maximum of 36 hours, the suspect must be released or charged unless a warrant of further detention is issued by a magistrates' court. A court may authorise detention for a further 36 hours if:

(a) the court comprises at least two magistrates;

(b) the application for the warrant is made on oath and supported by written information which is also supplied to the suspect;

(c) the suspect is present in court;

(d) the suspect is detained in connection with an indictable offence (amended by the CJA 2003);

(e) the court is satisfied of the matters in paras (c) and (d) of **Stage 4** above.

Stage 6: After a maximum of 72 hours the court may authorise further detention if all the conditions of Stage 5 above are satisfied. This further detention is for a maximum of 36 hours, and, in any event, the court may not authorise detention for a period of more than 96 hours.

Stage 7: No detention without charge is permitted after 96 hours. Thereafter the suspect must be charged and/or released.

Time	Offence	Authorisation
Up to 24 hours	Any	Custody sergeant
Up to 36 hours	Indictable offences	An officer of at least the rank of superintendent
Up to 72 hours	Indictable offences	Magistrates' court
Up to 96 hours	Indictable offences	Magistrates' court

Figure 2.1 Detention periods.

Notes:

1. Code C, para 1.1 provides: 'All persons in custody must be dealt with expeditiously, and released as soon as the need for detention no longer applies.'

2. A person who has been released may not be re-arrested without a warrant for the offence for which he was originally arrested unless new evidence justifying a further arrest has come to light (PACE 1984, s 41(9)).

3. These time limits do not apply to those who are detained under the Terrorism Act 2000. See further Code H.

4. In appropriate cases, an identification procedure will be held. You are advised to consult *Blackstone's Criminal Practice*, section F18 and the **Evidence** manual for details.

2.2.6 The risk assessment

Paragraphs 3.6–3.10 of the Code require the custody officer to initiate a structured risk assessment of whether the suspect is likely to present a specific risk to custody staff or to him or herself, and to make an appropriate response if such risks are identified. Guidance as to risk assessments is set out in HO Circular 32/2000, and includes the following points:

(a) The requirement to carry out a risk assessment applies to all persons entering into police custody, and all persons must be asked the questions set out in (b) below.

(b) The questions include whether the suspect has any injury or illness, whether they are taking any medication, whether they are suffering from any mental health problems or depression, and whether they have ever tried to harm themselves.

(c) The result of the risk assessment must be entered into the custody record, indicating whether any risks have been identified and the answers to the questions.

(d) Risk assessment is an ongoing process and must be reviewed if circumstances change.

(e) Risk categories include medical or mental conditions, medication issued, special needs, violence, escape risk, suicide or self-harm, injuries, vulnerability and any force, restraint or spray used.

(f) It is the responsibility of the custody officer to decide on the appropriate response to any risk identified.

(g) If the suspect is to be transferred from a police station, a Prisoner Escort Record must be completed setting out the details of the risk assessment.

It is essential that health care professionals who are consulted consider the functional ability of the suspect, rather than simply relying on a medical diagnosis, eg is it possible for a person with a severe mental illness to be fit for interview? (See Annex G, para 4 and see above.)

Health care professionals should also advise on the need for an appropriate adult to be present, whether a reassessment of the suspect's fitness for interview may be necessary if the interview lasts beyond a specified time, and whether a further specialist opinion may be required (Annex G, para 5).

The role of the health care professional is to consider the risks and advise the custody officer as to the outcome of that consideration. The health care professional's determination and any advice or recommendations should be made in writing and form part of the custody record (Annex G, para 7). This leaves open the issue of whether all the symptoms of which the suspect complains are to be included, and also the question of just how much of the suspect's medical history may be available to the police.

Note also that the power to test a person detained for drugs was introduced into PACE 1984 by the Drugs Act 2005.

2.2.7 The caution

Under para 10.1 of the Code, where there are 'grounds to suspect' a person of an offence, he or she must be cautioned before questioning if either the suspect's answers or silence may be put before a court in a prosecution. There must be some reasonable, objective grounds for suspicion, based on known facts or information relevant to the likelihood that the person to be questioned has committed the offence.

Because a caution is required only where there are 'grounds to suspect' the person of an offence, it need not be given where the questions are merely general, preliminary questions, to establish, for example, identity or ownership, in furtherance of a proper and effective search, or to obtain verification of any written record of comments made outside the context of an interview.

In addition, para 10.4 provides that the caution must be given on arrest unless the suspect has already been cautioned immediately prior to arrest, or because it is impracticable to administer the caution by reason of the suspect's behaviour at the time.

The caution should be re-administered after a break in questioning, but see *R v Oni* [1992] Crim LR 183, where it was held to be unnecessary after a break of only two minutes. It should always be re-administered, however, if there is any doubt as to whether or not it is necessary.

The wording of the caution arises from the provisions of the CJPOA 1994, s 34. Section 34 provides that a court 'may draw such inferences as appear proper' if evidence is given that the suspect:

(a) *at any time before he was charged with the offence, on being questioned under caution by a constable trying to discover whether or by whom the offence had been committed, failed to mention any fact relied on in his defence in those proceedings; or*

(b) *on being charged with the offence or officially informed that he might be prosecuted for it, failed to mention any such fact, being a fact which, in the circumstances existing at the time, the accused could reasonably have been expected to mention when so questioned, charged or informed, as the case may be.*

The caution is in the following terms:

You do not have to say anything. But it may harm your defence if you do not mention, when questioned, something which you later rely on in court. Anything you do say may be given in evidence.

Provided that the sense of the caution is preserved, minor deviations from the stated form do not constitute a breach of the Code.

This caution will be used in the majority of cases. However, s 58 of the Youth Justice and Criminal Evidence Act 1999 (YJCEA 1999) amends the CJPOA 1994 by providing that no inferences may be drawn where the suspect has not been given the opportunity to obtain legal advice. In these circumstances, the above caution is not to be used. In these circumstances, the appropriate caution is:

You do not have to say anything, but anything you do say may be given in evidence.

Note that this is the same caution which is used in the exceptional cases where the suspect is questioned after charge.

The circumstances in which the latter form of caution should be used instead of the former are set out in Annex C as follows:

1. *The Criminal Justice and Public Order Act 1994 sections 34, 36 and 37 as amended by the Youth Justice and Criminal Evidence Act 1999 section 58 describe the conditions under which adverse inferences may be drawn from a person's failure or refusal to say anything about their involvement in the offence when interviewed [note that this does not accurately reflect the wording of ss 34, 36 or 37], after being charged or informed they may be prosecuted. These provisions are subject to an overriding restriction on the ability of a court or jury to draw adverse inferences from a person's silence. This restriction applies:*

(a) *to any detainee at a police station (see Note 1OC) who, before being interviewed (see section 11) or being charged or informed they may be prosecuted (see section 16) has:*

　(i) *asked for legal advice (see section 6, paragraph 6.1);*

　(ii) *not been allowed an opportunity to consult a solicitor, including the duty solicitor, as in this Code; and*

　(iii) *not changed their mind about wanting legal advice (see section 6, paragraph 6.6(d)).*

Note that the condition in (ii) will:

- *apply when a detainee who has asked for legal advice is interviewed before speaking to a solicitor (as in section 6, paragraph 6.6(a) or (b));*

- *not apply if the detained person declines to ask for the duty solicitor (see section 6, paragraph 6.6(c) and (d)).*

(b) *to any person charged with, or informed they may be prosecuted for, an offence who:*

　(i) *has had brought to their notice a written statement made by another person or the content of an interview with another person which relates to that offence (see section 16, paragraph 16.4);*

　(ii) *is to be interviewed about that offence (see section 16, paragraph 16.5); or*

　(iii) *makes a written statement about that offence (see Annex D, paragraphs 4 and 9).*

Note that it would be possible for a suspect to be given both cautions at different times, eg where the usual caution is given on arrest, but the shorter caution is administered later when a decision to delay access to a solicitor is made at the police station by an officer of not less than superintendent rank. Further, the usual caution would need to be administered if and when legal advice is obtained, and then the shorter caution once again if the suspect is, unusually, questioned after charge.

2.2.8 Interviews

An interview is defined by Code C, para 11.1A as:

the questioning of a person regarding their involvement or suspected involvement in a criminal offence or offences which . . . must be carried out under caution.

An interview should not be held in relation to a person who appears to be unable to:

(a) appreciate the significance of questions put to him or her, or their answers;

(b) understand what is happening because of drink, drugs, any illness, ailment or condition.

Many defence solicitors found that there was confusion between deciding whether a suspect was fit to be *detained* and whether he or she was fit to be *interviewed*. Paragraph 9.13 of the revised Code requires a custody officer to ask a health care professional called to see a suspect, both about the risks or problems associated with continued detention and about 'when to carry out an interview' as well as any safeguards that are required.

Further, the revised Code includes Annex G, 'Fitness to be Interviewed', which provides guidance as to whether a detainee might be at risk in an interview. 'Risk' here means, according to Annex G, para 2, that:

- conducting the interview could significantly harm the detainee's physical or mental state;
- anything the detainee says in the interview about his or her involvement or suspected involvement in the offence about which he or she is being interviewed might be considered unreliable in subsequent court proceedings because of his or her physical or mental state.

The arrested person must not be interviewed except at a police station, unless any delay would be likely to lead to interference with evidence, harm to persons, the alerting of suspects or the hindering of the recovery of property (para 11.1).

Any interview at a police station should take place in an adequately lit, heated and ventilated interview room. At the beginning of the interview, the interviewing officer must identify himself or herself and any other officer present. The suspect must not be required to stand during the interview, and should be given breaks at recognised mealtimes. In addition, there should be short breaks for refreshment every two hours. The Code specifically provides that in any period of 24 hours, the suspect should be allowed a continuous period of eight hours' sleep without interruption, normally at night.

All interviews with persons cautioned in respect of an indictable offence, or where questions are put to, or a statement of another person is shown to, a person who has been charged, should be tape-recorded. Tapes need not be made if it is not reasonably practicable to do so for reasons such as the failure of the equipment, and the custody officer considers that the interview should not be delayed. For detailed provisions relating to tape-recording, see Code E.

Problems occasionally arise where a brief conversation or 'exchange' takes place between police officers and a suspect outside a police station, for example, after a speeding or stolen car has been stopped. If the exchange goes beyond a mere request for information and the suspect is, in effect, questioned about his or her involvement in an offence, then the exchange has become an interview. It is the nature of the questioning rather than the length which is relevant (*R v Ward* (1994) 98 Crim App R 337). If the questioning has become an interview, then the defendant is immediately protected by the provisions of the Code, including the requirement to caution, and any breaches will be taken into account by the court at any subsequent trial in determining the reliability of any confession that may have been made (see for example *R v Cox* (1993) 96 Cr App R 464). For a full discussion of the law relating to confessions, see *Blackstone's Criminal Practice* (2008 edn) F17, etc.

A problem unresolved under the 1995 Code was the point at which an interview must cease. Paragraph 11.4 of the 1995 Code provided that as soon as the officer believed that a prosecution should be brought against the suspect, and there was sufficient evidence for a prosecution to succeed, the officer should ask the suspect if he or she had anything further to say and, if not, the officer should stop the interview. It has consequently been held that anything said after that moment should not be admissible as evidence (*R v Pointer* [1997] Crim LR 676; *R v Gayle* [1999] Crim LR 502). Other cases, however, have held that the term 'sufficient evidence to prosecute' must involve some consideration of any explanation given by the suspect (*R v McGuinness* [1999] Crim LR 318; *R v Elliott* [2002] EWCA Crim 931; *R v Howell* [2003] EWCA Crim 1).

Paragraph 11.6 of the revised Code seeks to resolve this issue and provide the police with some leeway. Paragraph 11.6 provides as follows:

The interview or further interview of a person about an offence with which that person has not been charged or for which they have not been informed they may be prosecuted, must cease when:

(a) the officer in charge of the investigation is satisfied all the questions they consider relevant to obtaining accurate and reliable information about the offence have been put to the suspect, this includes allowing the suspect an opportunity to give an innocent explanation, and asking questions to test if the explanation is accurate and reliable eg to clear up ambiguities or clarify what the suspect said;

(b) the officer in charge of the investigation has taken account of any other available evidence; and

(c) the officer in charge of the investigation, or in the case of a detained suspect, the custody officer . . . reasonably believes there is sufficient evidence to provide a realistic prospect of conviction for that offence.

This paragraph does not prevent officers in revenue cases or acting under the confiscation provisions of the Criminal Justice Act 1988 or the Drug Trafficking Act 1994 from inviting suspects to complete a formal question and answer record after the interview is concluded.

2.2.9 Persons at risk

Special rules apply when the police are dealing with persons at risk, that is, juveniles, the mentally disordered or otherwise mentally vulnerable persons. The reason, according to the Notes for Guidance, is that, although such persons are often capable of providing reliable evidence, they may, without knowing or wishing to do so, be particularly prone in certain circumstances to provide information that may be unreliable, misleading or self-incriminating. Special care should always be taken when questioning such a person and, because of the risk of unreliable evidence, corroboration should be obtained wherever possible.

Paragraph 1G of the Code (Notes for Guidance) provides that the term 'mentally vulnerable' applies to those who 'because of their mental state or capacity, may not understand the significance of what is said, of questions or of their replies'. This would appear to be a much wider definition than under the 1995 Code and would appear to include those whose mental state is adversely affected by drink or drugs, as the term is not restricted to those whose mental state is affected by some kind of mental disorder.

'Mental disorder' is defined by the Mental Health Act 1983, s 1(2) as 'mental illness, arrested or incomplete development of mind, psychopathic disorder and any other disorder or disability of mind'. When a custody officer has any doubt as to the mental state or capacity of any detainee, the officer should treat the detainee as mentally vulnerable and call an appropriate adult.

A juvenile or person who is mentally disordered or otherwise mentally vulnerable should not be interviewed regarding their involvement or suspected involvement in a criminal offence or asked to provide a statement under caution except in the presence of an appropriate adult.

The role of an appropriate adult is set out in Notes for Guidance, Code C, para 11C, which provides:

Although juveniles or people who are mentally disordered or otherwise mentally vulnerable are often capable of providing reliable evidence, they may, without knowing or wishing to do so, be particularly prone in certain circumstances to provide information that may be unreliable, misleading or self-incriminating. Special care should always be taken when questioning such a person, and the appropriate adult should be involved if there is any doubt about a person's age, mental state or capacity. Because of the risk of unreliable evidence it is also important to obtain corroboration of any facts admitted whenever possible.

If an appropriate adult is present at the interview, he or she should be informed that:

- he or she is not expected to act simply as an observer; and
- the purpose of his or her presence is to:
  — advise the person being interviewed;
  — observe whether the interview is being conducted properly and fairly; and
  — facilitate communication with the person being interviewed.

An appropriate adult must be 'appropriate' both in the sense of being capable of understanding what is happening and in the sense of being someone the person at risk wishes to have present. The hierarchy for contacting the appropriate adult is as follows:

(i) the parent or guardian of a juvenile, or the guardian of the person who is mentally disordered. An estranged parent, however, is not a suitable appropriate adult, where the juvenile specifically objects to their presence: see *R v Morse* [1991] Crim LR 195 and *DPP v Blake* (1989) 89 Cr App R 179.

(ii) If no-one in the above category is available, then the police will ask a social worker from the local authority to act;

(iii) If no-one in either category is available, then the police will contact another responsible adult who is aged 18 or over who is not connected with the police.

Police officers, persons connected to the victim or anyone to whom the suspect has made admissions prior to his attending as an appropriate adult should not act as appropriate adults. In particular, a solicitor should never act as an appropriate adult. The support and assistance that the suspect receives from the appropriate adult is in addition to the legal advice he or she receives from the solicitor.

In an emergency, however, a person at risk may be interviewed without delay under para 11.18 of the Code if an officer of not less than the rank of superintendent is satisfied that the interview would not significantly harm the person's physical or mental state, and considers that delay would be likely to:

- lead to interference with or harm to evidence connected with an offence;
- lead to interference with or physical harm to other people or serious loss or damage to property;
- lead to the alerting of other people suspected of committing an offence but not yet arrested for it; or
- hinder the recovery of property obtained in consequence of the commission of an offence.

This provision also applies to:

- any person other than persons at risk who at the time of the interview appears to be unable to:
  — appreciate the significance of questions and their answers; or
  — understand what is happening because of the effects of drink, drugs or any illness, ailment or condition;
- a person who has difficulty understanding English or has a hearing disability if at the time of the interview an interpreter is not present.

An appropriate adult should always be involved if there is any doubt about a person's age, mental state or capacity.

2.2.10 The rights of the suspect

The suspect has three important rights in the police station.

2.2.10.1 The right to see a solicitor

PACE 1984, s 58(1) provides that a person who has been arrested and is being held in custody is entitled, upon request, to consult privately with a solicitor at any time, whether in person, in writing or by telephone. The suspect must be informed of this right by the custody officer on arrival at the police station and, if he or she declines legal advice, the suspect must be asked why, and any reasons should be recorded on the custody or interview record as appropriate. The request must be complied with as soon as is practicable.

Note that s 58 gives the suspect the right to consult a solicitor but not specifically the right to have the solicitor present during the interview. Paragraph 6.8 of the Code provides that a detainee who has been permitted to consult a solicitor shall be entitled on request to have the solicitor present when they are interviewed unless one of the exceptions in para 6.6 applies.

Additionally, the Code provides that:

- Nothing must be said or done by police officers with the intention of dissuading a suspect from obtaining legal advice (para 6.4).

- If a suspect declines to consult a solicitor, it must be explained to him or her that he or she has the right to speak to the solicitor on the telephone and, if he or she continues to decline, he or she should be asked why and the reasons recorded on the custody record (para 6.5).

- When the solicitor arrives at the police station to see the suspect, the suspect should be informed, even if he or she has previously declined legal advice (para 6.15).

- If the suspect has requested legal advice, and the solicitor is on his or her way or about to set off, the interview should normally await his or her arrival (para 6A).

- If the suspect commences the interview having declined legal advice, but asks for it during the interview, there should be no further questioning until he has had the opportunity to speak with the solicitor (para 6.6).

Code C, Note 6D sets out the duty of the solicitor:

The solicitor's only role in the police station is to protect and advance the legal rights of their client. On occasions this may require the solicitor to give advice which has the effect of their client avoiding giving evidence which strengthens a prosecution case. The solicitor may intervene in order to seek clarification or to challenge an improper question to their client or the manner in which it is put, or to advise their client not to reply to particular questions, or if they wish to give their client further legal advice.

The right must not be denied, and may not be delayed for more than 36 hours after the suspect's arrival at the police station. Access to legal advice may be delayed only if, under PACE, ss 58(6) and (8):

(a) the suspect is in police detention in connection with an indictable offence, and has not yet been charged with an offence;

(b) an officer of not less than the rank of superintendent authorises the delay; and

(c) that officer has reasonable grounds for believing that the exercise of the right at the present time will lead to:

— interference with, or harm to, evidence connected with an indictable offence; or

— interference with, or physical harm to, other people; or

— lead to the alerting of other people suspected of having committed an indictable offence but not yet arrested for it; or

— hinder the recovery of property obtained in consequence of the commission of such an offence.

Code C, Annex B, para 2 further provides that access to legal advice may also be delayed if the indictable offence is a drug trafficking offence or an offence to which the Criminal Justice Act 1988, Pt VI (confiscation orders) applies, and certain other conditions are satisfied.

Once a suspect has requested legal advice, he or she may not be interviewed (or an interview continued) unless:

(a) PACE 1984, s 58(6) applies (see above); or

(b) an officer of superintendent rank or above has reasonable grounds for believing that:

  (i) the consequent delay might (note that the earlier version of the Code used the word will):

  — lead to interference with, or harm to, evidence connected with an offence,

  — lead to interference with, or physical harm to, other people;

  — lead to serious loss of, or damage to, property;

  — lead to the alerting of other people suspected of having committed an offence but not yet arrested for it;

  — hinder the recovery of property obtained in consequence of the commission of an offence; or

  (ii) when a solicitor, including a duty solicitor, has been contacted and has agreed to attend, awaiting their arrival would cause unreasonable delay to the process of investigation; or

(c) the solicitor that the suspect has nominated or selected from a list cannot be contacted, has previously indicated that he or she does not wish to be contacted, or declines to attend and the suspect has declined to ask for the duty solicitor having been advised about the Duty Solicitor Scheme; or

(d) the detainee has changed his or her mind about wanting legal advice and consented to the interview beginning (or continuing).

See Code C, para 6.6.

The rights may be delayed only for as long as the grounds exist, and in no case for longer than 36 hours.

The suspect must be told why access to a solicitor has been delayed, and that reason must be entered in the custody record.

Both PACE 1984, s 58 and para 6 of the Code provide for the right of the suspect to consult *privately* with a solicitor at any time. The only exception to this is under s 41 and

Sch 8 of the Terrorism Act 2000, which provide that, if certain conditions are met, an Assistant Chief Constable may direct that any consultation take place in the sight and hearing of a qualified officer. Defence solicitors, however, have long been concerned that consultations between a suspect and his or her solicitor have on occasion been the subject of covert surveillance. No provisions are included in the Code to prevent or control such surveillance.

Wrongful denial of access to a solicitor may lead to a confession made without having taken legal advice being excluded at any subsequent trial. See for example *R v Samuel* [1988] 1 WLR 920 and *R v Alladice* (1988) 87 Cr App R 380. For a full discussion of the cases where a confession has been obtained in such circumstances, students should refer to *Blackstone's Criminal Practice* (2009 edn), F17.11–17.18.

A further limitation on access to legal advice stems from the changes to the legal aid system as a result of the introduction of Criminal Defence Service Direct (CDS Direct). As a result, in all cases where legal advice is sought—even when the suspect has asked for a named solicitor or firm—the police must contact the Defence Solicitor Call Centre (DSCC). The only exception is when the suspect pays for the advice himself. The DSCC will determine whether the advice may be given over the phone or whether a solicitor should attend. If telephone advice is appropriate, it will be free through CDS Direct. If the suspect wishes to talk to his own solicitor, he will have to pay for the call. A solicitor will only attend in person if deemed necessary by CDS Direct.

In *CDS Direct: Flying in the Face of the Evidence*, published on 6 October 2008, Professors Lee Bridges and Ed Cape claimed that the universal right of all suspects to consult a solicitor of their choice has been undermined by these changes. The authors argue that the new services:

1 were never properly evaluated;
2 were forced through after a rushed and inadequate consultation and botched parliamentary procedure;
3 are of questionable legality under PACE; 1984
4 may contravene the European Convention on Human Rights;
5 fly in the face of a substantial and accumulated evidence base on access to legal services at police stations.

Professor Cape said: 'Previously when a person arrested in a police station asked for a lawyer, the police were obliged to contact that lawyer directly as soon as possible. Now, even in a straightforward. . . case [the suspect] will have to go through six stages of referral before they can speak to their lawyer. More worrying is the fact that this can also be the case for a suspect who is mentally ill. The schemes may save a small proportion of the legal aid budget, but at what cost to access to justice?'

Finally, it is important to remember that the role of the solicitor and that of the appropriate adult are quite different. This means that the solicitor will never act as an appropriate adult.

2.2.10.2 The right to have someone informed

Under PACE 1984, s 56(1) the suspect has the right to have a friend or relative, or some other person who is known to him or her, or who is likely to take an interest in his or her welfare, told of the arrest. The request must be complied with as soon as is practicable.

This right may be delayed in circumstances similar to the circumstances permitting the delay of access to legal advice.

In addition, the suspect must be given writing materials on request and allowed to make one phone call for a reasonable time, unless the above circumstances apply.

2.2.10.3 The right to consult the Codes

The suspect has the right to consult all the Codes of Practice. This does not entitle him or her to delay unreasonably any investigation or administrative action while this is done (Code C, paras 3.1 and 3D).

2.2.11 The charge

Except for routine cases or where the police need to make a holding charge, the decision as to which offence the suspect is charged with is a matter for the CPS rather than the police. This is known as statutory charging. Statutory charging is now operational in all 42 CPS areas and covers about 30% of all cases. These are all indictable and most triable either way offences and certain specified summary offences. The police retain the responsibility for the charging decision in the remaining 70% of cases.

PACE 1984, s 37(7) as amended by the CJA 2003, s 28 and Sch 2, provides that once the custody officer has sufficient evidence upon which to charge, he has the following options:

(a) to release the suspect without charge, and on bail for the purpose of enabling the DPP to make a decision as to the charge. The suspect must be informed that there will be a consultation with the DPP as to the charge. Consultation with the DPP should take place as soon as is reasonably practicable.

The ultimate aim is that the CPS will decide on charge in all indictable only, triable either way and summary only offences where the custody officer has decided that there is sufficient evidence to charge, except for specified offences. The specified offences include most road traffic offences, absconding under the Bail Act 1976 and various other summary only offences. The custody officer has to have regard to the decision of the DPP.

In the interim, except for certain specified offences, listed in Annex A of the Notes of Guidance to the Code (which include serious offences of violence and certain public order offences), the police may decide on charge:

- in any summary or either way offence;
- where it appears to the custody officer that a guilty plea is likely; and
- where the case is suitable for sentencing in the magistrates' court.

Under PACE 1984, s 37A (inserted by the CJA 2003, Sch 2) the DPP may issue guidance for the purposes of enabling custody officers to decide how to deal with persons under s 37(7) and what information should be forwarded to the DPP.

The CPS will apply a two-part test to decide whether or not a person should be charged. They will consider:

(i) if there is sufficient evidence to charge the suspect, and
(ii) if so, is it in the public interest to charge the suspect, or whether the matter should be dealt with any other way.

Section 37B provides details as to the consultation with the DPP. It provides as follows:

(1) *Where a person is released on bail under section 37(7)(a) above, an officer involved in the investigation of the offence shall, as soon as reasonably practicable, send to the Director of Public Prosecutions such information as may be specified in guidance under section 37A above.*

(2) The Director of Public Prosecutions shall decide whether there is sufficient evidence to charge the person with the offence.

(3) If he decides that there is sufficient evidence to charge the person with an offence, he shall decide—

   (a) whether or not the person should be charged and, if so, the offence with which he should be charged, and

   (b) whether or not the person should be given a caution and, if so, the offence in respect of which he should be given a caution.

(4) The DPP shall give written notice of his decision to an officer involved in the investigation of the offence.

(5) If his decision is—

   (a) that there is not sufficient evidence to charge the person with an offence

   (b) that there is sufficient evidence to charge the person with an offence but that the person should not be charged with an offence or given a caution in respect of the offence,

   a custody officer shall give the person notice in writing that he is not to be prosecuted.

(6) If the decision of the Director of Public Prosecutions is that the person should be charged with an offence or given a caution, in respect of the offence, the person shall be charged or cautioned accordingly.

(7) But if his decision is that the person should be given a caution in respect of the offence and it proves not to be possible to give the person such a caution, he shall instead be charged with the offence.

(8) For the purposes of this section, a person is to be charged with an offence either—

   (a) when he is in police detention after returning to a police station to answer bail or is otherwise in police detention at a police station, or

   (b) in accordance with section 29 of the Criminal Justice Act 2003.

(9) In this section 'caution' means—

   (a) a conditional caution within the meaning of Part 3 of the Criminal Justice Act 2003, and

   (b) a warning or reprimand under section 65 of the Crime and Disorder Act 1998.

Sections 37C and 37D, inserted by the CJA 2003, Sch 2 contain further provisions about the release of the suspect on bail.

(b) to release the suspect without charge and on bail but not for the purpose of deciding on charge, e.g. to enable further enquiries to be made. The suspect may apply to court for the conditions of bail to be varied under the CJA 2003, Sch 2, para 6;

(c) to release the suspect without charge and without bail, e.g. where there is no immediate prospect of further proceedings being taken;

(d) to charge the suspect.

Once the suspect has been charged with the offence, he or she should not be asked any further questions, except in exceptional circumstances as provided by Code C, para 16.5. This includes:

- to prevent harm or loss to some other person or to the public;
- to clear up an ambiguity in a previous statement or answer;
- in the interests of justice for the suspect to have put to him or her an opportunity to comment on information about the offence that has come to light since he or she was charged, or informed that he or she may be prosecuted.

2.2.12 The decision to release

After the charge the custody officer must order the suspect's release from custody under PACE 1984, s 38(1) unless one of the situations contained in s 38(1)(a), as amended by s 28 of the CJPOA 1994, applies:

(a) The suspect's name or address cannot be ascertained.

(b) The custody officer has reasonable grounds for doubting whether the name and address supplied are genuine.

(c) The custody officer has reasonable grounds for believing that:

   (i) the suspect will not surrender to bail; or

   (ii) (imprisonable offences) the detention is necessary to prevent the suspect from committing an offence; or

   (iii) where the person has attained the age of 18, the detention is necessary for a sample to be taken;

   (iv) (non-imprisonable offences) the detention is necessary to prevent the suspect from causing physical injury to any other person or loss or damage to property; or

   (v) the detention is necessary to prevent the suspect from interfering with the administration of justice or with the investigation of any offence or offences; or

   (vi) the detention is necessary for the suspect's own protection.

If the suspect is to be released after charge, he or she is likely to be bailed to attend at the appropriate magistrates' court to answer to the charge on a specified day. The CJPOA 1994, s 27 provides that s 3 of the Bail Act 1976 (BA 1976) (power of the court to impose conditions on bail) shall apply with certain modifications (see below) to bail granted by the police.

The bail decision is taken by the custody officer, who may not impose conditions on the grant of bail unless it appears, under s 3A(5) of the BA 1976 (inserted by s 27 of the CJPOA 1994) that it is necessary to do so for the purposes of preventing the bailed person from:

- failing to surrender to custody; or
- committing an offence while on bail; or
- interfering with witnesses or otherwise obstructing the course of justice, whether in relation to the bailed person or any other person.

The main differences between conditions imposed by police and those imposed by the court are as follows:

(a) The court, but not the police, has the power to order that reports be compiled on the bailed person (BA 1976, s 3A(3), as inserted by the CJPOA 1994, s 27(3)).

(b) The court, but not the police, may require the bailed person to reside in a bail hostel (BA 1976, s 3A(2), as inserted by the CJPOA 1994, s 27(3)).

(c) Where the custody officer has granted bail, either the custody officer or another officer serving at the same police station may vary the conditions of bail, at the request of the bailed person (BA 1976, s 3A(4), inserted by the CJPOA 1994, s 27(3)). Further, the bailed person may apply to a magistrates' court to have conditions of bail varied, but should bear in mind that the court has the power to impose more onerous conditions (MCA 1980, s 43B, inserted by the CJPOA 1994, Sch 3, para 3).

If the suspect is detained after charge, he or she must be brought before a magistrates' court as soon as is practicable, and in any event not later than the first sitting after he or she has been charged with an offence. If no suitable court is sitting, the clerk of the court must be informed, and a special sitting will be arranged. See generally PACE 1984, s 46.

If release is authorised, the suspect is bailed to appear before the magistrates' court on a specified day to answer the charge (see PACE 1984, s 47).

A useful article is 'Detention in a police station and false imprisonment' by J Mackenzie, 142 NLJ 534.

2.2.13 Alternatives to charge

As an alternative to charge and prosecution of the suspect or his or her release without charge, the suspect may be dealt with in one of the following ways.

2.2.13.1 An informal warning

Such informal warnings may be appropriate for minor matters, particularly minor public order matters. Such a warning will not appear on the person's list of previous convictions.

2.2.13.2 A formal caution

Though the formal caution was introduced for juveniles, it is now available for all offenders. It is a very common way of dealing with offenders, particularly first-time offenders and in particular it may be given to offenders who are elderly, the ill or those suffering from acute distress.

The caution is usually administered by an officer of at least the rank of inspector and the offender must sign a form acknowledging the offence and his or her guilt.

The caution may only be given if the following conditions are fulfilled:

(a) there is sufficient evidence to justify a prosecution;

(b) the offender must admit his or her guilt; note that the offender must admit guilt to **all** the requisite elements of the offence: *R (on the application of Wyman) v Chief Constable of Hampshire Constabulary* [2006] EWHC 1904 (Admin.);

(c) the offender agrees to the caution, knowing that the caution may be referred to in court in the event of a future conviction.

In fact, it would be unusual for the caution to be subsequently referred to, unless the offender is now convicted of the same type of offence for which he or she was cautioned.

Two recent cases illustrate the use of the formal caution. In the first, *R v Chief Constable of Hampshire Constabulary* [2006] EWHC 1904 (Admin), the defendant agreed to a formal caution but he successfully applied for the caution to be quashed on the grounds that the proper procedure had not been followed and he could not properly be said to have admitted all elements of the offence.

In *Jones v Whalley* [2006] UKHL 41, the defendant accepted a formal caution, on the express assurance by the police officer that he would not have to go before a criminal court in connection with the offence. The complainant, however, brought a private prosecution. The House of Lords decided that, in view of the formal caution, the private prosecution was an abuse of process but did not decide whether a private prosecution could or should survive the implementation of a formal caution.

Guidance as to the use of informal and formal cautions was given in HO Circular 16/2008.

2.2.13.3 Conditional cautions

CJA 2003, ss 22–27 introduce the conditional caution. These sections allow an adult offender to be released subject to being cautioned, but unlike other cautions, the conditional caution is 'a caution which is given in respect of an offence committed by the offender and which has conditions attached to it with which the offender must comply' (s 22(2)). Failure to comply may result in the offender being prosecuted for the offence.

Guidance on the giving of conditional cautions states that:

> A conditional caution may be appropriate where a Crown Prosecutor considers that while the public interest justifies a prosecution, the interests of the person, victim or community may be better served by the person complying with certain conditions aimed at rehabilitation or reparation which may include restorative processes.

The person giving the conditional caution is known as the 'authorised person' and is either a constable, an investigating officer or a person authorised by a relevant prosecutor, a group of people including the Attorney-General, the Director of Public Prosecutions, the director of the Serious Fraud Office and the Commissioners of Customs and Excise.

Before the conditional caution may be given, five conditions must be complied with, namely:

(a) the authorised person has evidence that the offender committed an offence;

(b) the authorised person decides that there is sufficient evidence to charge the offender and that a conditional caution should be given;

(c) the offender admits the offence;

(d) the authorised person explains the effect of the conditional caution to the offender and warns him that failure to comply with the conditions may result in his prosecution for the offence;

(e) the offender signs a document setting out:

   (i) the details of the offence;

   (ii) an admission by him that he committed the offence;

   (iii) his consent to the giving of a conditional caution;

   (iv) the conditions attached to the caution.

The conditions which are imposed have the following objects, under s 22(3):

(a) facilitating the rehabilitation of the offender;

(b) ensuring that he makes reparation for the offence;

(c) punishing the offender (inserted by the Police and Justice Act 2006 s 17.

The Conditional Cautioning Code of Practice states that the conditions must be:

- *Proportionate* to the offence—it should not be more onerous than the punishment that would be likely to be imposed if the offender were prosecuted.

- *Achievable* within a reasonable time—having particular regard to any limitations on prosecution if the offender breaches the conditions.

- *Appropriate*—any conditions should be relevant to the offence or the offender.

Failure without reasonable cause to comply with any of the conditions renders the person liable to prosecution for the offence and the document referred to above is admissible as evidence: s 24(1)and (2).

The authorised person may seek the advice and assistance of the National Probation Service in deciding whether a conditional caution should be given and, if one is given, the conditions that should be attached (s 26).

If the offender fails to comply with the conditions he may be prosecuted for the original offence. In such proceedings, the notice which the offender signed is admissible (s 24). Examples of offences for which conditional cautions have been given include:

- Criminal damage
- Offences contrary to the Public Order Act 1986, s 4 and s 5
- Affray
- Common assault
- Theft
- Burglary
- Possessing controlled drugs.

Examples of conditions which have been attached as part of a conditional caution include:

- Compensation
- Taking part in a restorative justice programme
- Providing a face-to-face apology to the victim
- Attending alcohol intervention sessions.

S22(3A) as inserted by the Police and Justice Act 2006 s17, will permit the payment of a financial penalty, limited to one-quarter of the maximum fine that could be ordered, and/or a condition that the offender attend at a specified place at specified times for up to 20 hours.

There are a number of disadvantages to the offender of accepting a conditional caution. The caution is an admission of guilt which will stay on his record, and be disclosable should he subsequently apply for certain types of employment. Further, a subsequent caution for an offence is very unlikely, any fingerprints taken will be retained and if the caution was given for a sexual offence, the offender will be placed on the sex offenders register.

Where a conditional caution is quashed, it will not ordinarily amount to an abuse of process to prosecute for the offence in question. Such a course of action will generally be in the public interest: *R (Guest) v DPP* (Divisional Court, unreported, 5 March 2009).

2.3 Instituting proceedings other than by arrest and charge

2.3.1 Written charge and requisition

The CJA 2003 provides a simple system of charge and requisition: s 29. This does not replace or alter the system for charging a suspect in custody: s 18 (and see **2.2**).

The old method of laying an information and issue of summons is abolished except for prosecutions brought by private individuals, and where the public prosecutor is required to lay an information for the purposes of obtaining the issue of a warrant: s 40(4).

Under s 29, the proceedings are started by issuing a document, called a 'written charge', charging the suspect with an offence. At the same time a document called a 'requisition' is issued requiring the suspect to appear before the magistrates' court to answer the written charge. These documents are issued by a person referred to as a 'public prosecutor' (defined below), and served on the person charged and on the court.

See the CJA 2003, s 29:

> *(1) A public prosecutor may institute criminal proceedings against a person by issuing a document (a 'written charge') which charges the person with an offence.*

(2) Where a public prosecutor issues a written charge, it must at the same time issue a document ('a requisition') which requires the person to appear before a magistrates' court to answer the written charge.

(3) The written charge and the requisition must be served on the person concerned and a copy of both must be served on the court named in the requisition.

The 'public prosecutor' is defined in the CJA 2003, s 29(5) as:

(a) A police force or person authorised by a police force to institute criminal proceedings.

(b) The director of the Serious Fraud Office, the Director of Public Prosecutions, the Attorney-General, or a Secretary of State or any person authorised by any one of them to institute criminal proceedings.

(c) The Commissioners of the Inland Revenue or of Customs and Excise, or any person authorised by either of them to institute criminal proceedings.

(d) A person specified in an order made by the Secretary of State for the purposes of this section, or a person authorised by such a person to institute criminal proceedings.

Rules of court made under the MCA 1980, s 144 provide for the form, content, recording authentication and service of written charges and requisitions: s 30(1).

There is no requirement that either the written charge or the requisition should be substantiated on oath: s 31(1).

Under s 30(5) all references in previous statutes referring to informations and summonses are to be interpreted as referring to written charges and requisitions.

2.3.2 Trying two or more written charges

If the accused stands before the court charged with more than one offence, or if several accused stand before the court together, the question arises whether all outstanding matters can be dealt with at once.

Where several accused are jointly charged with an offence, they will almost always be automatically tried together, despite any objection they may make.

Where one accused stands charged with several matters, or several accused stand charged of related offences, then they may be tried together as long as no objection is made. If objection is made, the magistrates will order separate trials unless they are of the opinion that the offences are so connected that the interests of justice would be best served by a single trial. See *Chief Constable of Norfolk v Clayton* [1983] 2 AC 473.

If the magistrates decide against a single trial, it would seem those magistrates are debarred from hearing the case at all, as they are supposed to be unaware of any charges outstanding against an accused (see *R v Liverpool City justices, ex p Topping* [1983] 1 WLR 119). In these circumstances, each case may have to be heard by a different bench. In *R v Gough* [1993] AC 646, the House of Lords held that the test in all cases of apparent bias is: Was there a real danger of bias?

See also *Porter v Magill* [2002] AC 357: the proper formulation was held to be: Would a fair-minded and informed observer conclude that there was a real possibility, or real danger (the two being the same) that the tribunal was biased? This formulation is consistent with the approach of the ECHR in *Sanders v UK* [2000] Crim LR 767.

2.3.3 Amendment

The court has wide powers to amend the charge as originally laid. Further, the MCA 1980, s 123 provides that defects in the information, or any variations between the information and the evidence subsequently adduced, are not grounds upon which objection may be taken.

The discretion to amend should ordinarily be exercised in favour of amendment, unless to do so would result in injustice (*DPP v Short* (2002) 166 JP 474).

It has been held that if the defect or variation was trivial, and the accused was not in fact misled, any subsequent conviction will be upheld. See, for example, *R v Sandwell Justices, ex p West Midlands Passenger Transport Board* [1979] Crim LR 56. On the other hand, if the defect or variation is substantial, the prosecution should seek to amend the information. The magistrates will then consider whether the accused has been misled by the defect, and if so, offer an adjournment so that he or she can prepare for and meet the case now put forward by the prosecution. Failure either to amend, or adjourn, in these circumstances is likely to lead to any subsequent conviction being quashed. See, for example, *Wright v Nicholson* [1970] 1 WLR 142.

It is assumed that these cases will still apply under the new system.

An information could be amended, even to allege a different offence, including a purely summary offence, more than six months after it was laid, provided that the offence arose from the same incident as the offence originally charged, and the amendment was in the interests of justice, and it is assumed that the same will apply to the written charge. See *R v Scunthorpe Justices, ex p M*, *The Times*, 10 March 1998, where an information alleging robbery was amended to common assault, a purely summary offence. A similar point was made in *R v Newcastle Upon Tyne Magistrates' Court, ex p Poundstretcher Ltd* [1998] COD 256 and *Shaw v DPP* (unreported, 25 January 2007).

Late amendments cannot cure an information or charge which discloses no offence known to law (*Garman v Plaice* [1969] 1 WLR 19).

2.3.4 Duplicity

A written charge is said to be duplicitous when two offences are charged within it. In such a situation, the prosecution may elect which charge to proceed with (see the Criminal Procedure Rules 2005, r 7.3, although currently this still refers to 'informations').

Students are referred to **Chapter 10** or *Blackstone's Criminal Practice* (2009 edn), D11.41–11.55, for a full discussion of duplicity.

2.4 Issue of a warrant

2.4.1 Information in a warrant

Instead of issuing a requisition, application may be made to a magistrate to issue a warrant for the arrest of the person named therein. A warrant should contain the following information:

- the name of the court;
- the name and address of the accused; the offence alleged;

- the signature of the magistrate (the signature of the clerk is insufficient);
- if the warrant is to be backed for bail, any conditions of bail imposed by the magistrate (see **3.7**).

2.4.2 Conditions for the issue of a warrant

Before the warrant can be issued the following conditions must be met:

- The information must be in writing. The former condition that the information should be supported by sworn evidence was removed by the CJA 2003, s 31.
- The offence must be imprisonable (or the accused is a juvenile or resides at an unknown address).
- The proceedings must take place before a magistrate, not a clerk.

2.4.3 Warrants 'backed for bail'

In most cases a warrant will not be necessary. A less serious offence is likely to be commenced by the issue of a charge and requisition, and more serious offences are arrestable in any event. However, the warrant is important where the accused fails to appear in answer to the summons, or fails to surrender to bail. A warrant issued in these circumstances is often referred to as a 'bench warrant'.

If the magistrates think that the accused's absence is due to an error, they may order that the warrant be 'backed for bail', that is, the conditions of bail upon which the accused may be released once arrested are endorsed on the back of the warrant. After arrest, the accused must be released once the conditions are complied with (see also **Chapter 3**).

2.5 Jurisdiction to try offences

All magistrates' courts have jurisdiction to try any offence committed in England and Wales: Courts Act 2003, s 2. This replaces the complex jurisdictional rules which had previously applied.

2.6 Public funding for legal representation and advice

2.6.1 The Criminal Defence Service

Most defendants in criminal proceedings do not pay for their own defence. Instead, their solicitors will apply for their defence to be publicly funded by the Legal Services Commission.

The Access to Justice Act 1999 (AJA 1999), s 1(1) created the Legal Services Commission (LSC). It is an executive, non-departmental body, responsible for administration of two separate schemes in England and Wales:

- The Community Legal Service. As from 1 April 2001, the Community Legal Service replaced the old civil scheme of legal aid. See the *Civil Litigation* manual for details.

- The Criminal Defence Service. As from 2 April 2001, the Criminal Defence Service (CDS) replaced the old criminal scheme of legal aid.

A full discussion of either the LSC or the CDS is beyond the scope of this manual and the following points are intended as an introduction only. See <www.official-documents.gov.uk/document/cm69/6993/6993.pdf> for a complete review of the new law and for a discussion of the future shape of the service in a document entitled 'Legal Aid Reform, the Way ahead'.

The CDS is created by the AJA 1999, s 12(1), which provides that the service is created:

For the purpose of securing that individuals involved in criminal investigations or criminal proceedings have access to such advice, assistance and representation as the interests of justice require.

The AJA 1999, s 12(2) provides that, in this part of the Act, 'criminal proceedings' means:

(a) proceedings before any court for dealing with an individual accused of an offence;

(b) proceedings before any court for dealing with an individual convicted of an offence (including proceedings in respect of a sentence or order);

(c) proceedings for dealing with an individual under section 9 of, or paragraph 6 of Schedule 1 to the Extradition Act 1989;

(d) proceedings for binding an individual over to keep the peace or to be of good behaviour under section 115 of the Magistrates' Courts Act 1980 and for dealing with an individual who fails to comply with an order under that section;

(e) proceedings on appeal brought by an individual under section 44A of the Criminal Appeal Act 1968;

(f) proceedings for contempt committed, or alleged to have been committed, by an individual in the face of the court; and

(g) such other proceedings concerning an individual, before any such court or other body, as may be prescribed.

The overview of the General Criminal Contract provided by the LSC (see **2.6.9**) provides as follows:

Objective

1 We want to encourage committed, high quality providers of criminal defence services to become contracted providers. We want to establish and develop long-term relationships with these providers to ensure that those eligible to receive publicly funded criminal defence services have access to competent, appropriate, quality assured and value for money services that meet their needs.

2 The objective of this Contract, therefore, is to secure the provision of competent quality assured, best value Contract work from specified offices.

Criminal Defence Service—Purpose and Objectives

1 The purpose of the CDS is to ensure access for individuals involved in Criminal Investigations or Criminal Proceedings to such Advice, Assistance and Representation as the interests of justice require.

2 The objectives of the CDS within the legal framework established for it are to:

   (a) ensure that the Government meets its statutory and international obligations which provide that:

(i) people arrested and held in custody have the right to consult a solicitor privately at any time; and

(ii) defendants have a right to defend themselves in person, or through legal assistance of their own choosing, or, if they have insufficient means to pay for legal assistance, to be given it free when the interests of justice so require;

(b) *help to ensure that suspects and defendants receive a fair hearing at each stage in the criminal justice process, and in particular that they can state their case on an equal footing with the prosecution;*

(c) *protect the interests of the suspect or defendant, for example by making the prosecution prove its case or advising the defendant to enter an early guilty plea, if that is appropriate;*

(d) *maintain the suspect's or defendant's confidence in the system and facilitate his or her effective participation in the process.*

The Lord Chancellor has set objectives for the Commission regarding the CDS. These are:

(a) to ensure that eligible individuals have access to appropriate CDS services—including at police stations and in magistrates' courts;

(b) to ensure that the services provided on its behalf—whether by contracted private practice suppliers or salaried defenders—are of appropriate quality, and that their quality improves over time;

(c) to ensure effective control over CDS expenditure, and progressively improve the value for money of the criminal defence services it provides and purchases;

(d) to ensure that the CDS contributes fully to achieving the overall Criminal Justice System (CJS) strategic plan, including by working with the other CDS agencies.

2.6.2 Advice and assistance

There are two ways in which an individual may be helped. These are (a) Advice and Assistance, and (b) Representation.

The Commission funds advice and assistance, under the AJA 1999, s 13(1), as it considers appropriate to the following persons:

(a) for individuals who are arrested and held in custody at a police station or other premises, and

(b) in prescribed circumstances, for individuals who are [otherwise] involved in investigations which may lead to criminal proceedings or are before a court in such proceedings or have been the subject of such proceedings.

Advice and assistance also covers help from a solicitor including giving general advice, writing letters, negotiating, obtaining counsel's opinion and preparing a written case. It thus enables people of small means to obtain help from a solicitor.

In order to receive advice and assistance, the applicant must pass the merits test, ie establish that the case has sufficient merit to justify the grant of publicly funded assistance. In order to pass the merits test, the solicitor must be satisfied that the advice required involves a legal issue concerning English law, and there is sufficient benefit to the client, having regard to the matter and the client's personal circumstances, to justify the work being carried out. The sufficient benefit test will be satisfied automatically for the purposes of initial advice given in a police station.

There is no means test for advice and assistance given to a person who is questioned by the police whether or not he or she has been arrested, and whether or not he or she is questioned at a police station. The Commission will only fund other advice and assistance if the individual's capital and income are within the current financial limits (not included in this manual). The individual will not be asked to pay a contribution.

Children may be given advice and assistance, and may be advised directly in some circumstances. Where the child is under 17 years of age and requires the help of a solicitor, a parent or guardian should apply on the child's behalf.

Advice and assistance does not cover representation in court, except in certain limited circumstances, in which case the individual should apply for Advocacy Assistance.

2.6.3 Advocacy Assistance

Advocacy Assistance is defined in the CDS Solicitor Arrangements 2001 as 'advice and assistance by way of advocacy before a court or tribunal together with any necessary preparatory work'. It thus covers the cost of a solicitor preparing the case and initial representation in certain proceedings in both the magistrates' court and Crown Court. It also covers representation for those who fail to pay a fine or obey a magistrates' court order, and are at risk of imprisonment.

Under para 6.3(18) of the General Criminal Contract, in deciding whether the client is entitled to Advocacy Assistance, the solicitor should ask himself or herself the following questions:

(a) Is the applicant before the court as a result of a failure
   (i) to pay a fine or other sum which he or she was ordered to pay; or
   (ii) to obey an order of the court
   where the failure is likely to lead to the applicant being at risk of imprisonment?

If the answer to this is no, or a duty solicitor is available and could deal with the case, Advocacy Assistance should be refused. If the case is not suitable for the duty solicitor because either it is unusual (particularly in that it raises complicated issues of fact, law or procedure), or the applicant's finances are complex, then the next question is whether it is in the interests of justice that Advocacy Assistance be granted. This involves the same issues as set out in Sch 3 (see **2.6.4**) with the additional factor of whether there is a real risk of an order being made which if breached could deprive an individual of his or her liberty. The final question is whether it is reasonable in the circumstances for Advocacy Assistance to be granted. If it is in the interests of justice for Advocacy Assistance to be granted, then it will almost always be reasonable.

If Advocacy Assistance is granted, an application should be made for a Representation Order at the earliest opportunity, if appropriate, and all work should be done under that order. If the Representation Order is refused, the Advocacy Assistance ceases unless the client continues to meet the qualifying criteria.

There is no means test for advice and assistance for a person who is granted Advocacy Assistance.

2.6.4 Representation orders

The Commission funds individuals who have a 'Right to Representation' under the AJA 1999, s 14 and Sch 3. Schedule 3, para 1 provides that the right may be granted to an individual who is before the court for any of the matters mentioned in s 12(2), and to enable him or her to resist an appeal to the Crown Court otherwise than in an official capacity.

The court before which any proceedings take place, or are about to take place, has the power to grant a right of representation (Sch 3, para 2(1)). Where any such right is granted, it includes the right to representation for the purposes of any related bail proceedings and any preliminary or incidental proceedings.

Under Sch 3, para 5(1) the right to representation is granted 'according to the interests of justice'. The court, under para 5(2), will take into account the following factors in deciding what the interests of justice consist of in relation to any individual:

(a) *whether the individual would, if any matter arising in the proceedings is decided against him, be likely to lose his liberty or livelihood or suffer serious damage to his reputation,*

(b) *whether the determination of any matter arising in the proceedings may involve consideration of a substantial question of law,*

(c) *whether the individual may be unable to understand the proceedings or to state his own case,*

(d) *whether the proceedings may involve the tracing, interviewing or expert cross-examination of witnesses on behalf of the individual, and*

(e) *whether it is in the interests of another person that the individual be represented.*

These factors may be amended or added to by the Lord Chancellor by order.

A 'case', according to the General Criminal Contract, means work carried out in criminal proceedings in respect of:

- one offence (that is an offence for which the client is charged or summoned or otherwise required to appear in court); or
- more than one offence, where one or more charges or informations are preferred or laid at the same time, or where the offences are allegedly founded on the same facts or form part of a series of offences (these are further defined in para 5.8 of the General Criminal Contract).

A number of reforms relating to the funding of criminal cases were proposed by Lord Carter in his report entitled 'Procurement of Legal Defence Services', also known as the Carter Report. These reforms are beyond the scope of this work.

2.6.5 The duty solicitor schemes

The Legal Services Commission operates two duty solicitor schemes as part of the CDS. These are:

- the Police Station Duty Solicitor Scheme; and
- the Magistrates' Court Duty Solicitor Scheme.

The primary object of these schemes, according to the CDS Solicitor Arrangements 2001, is:

> ... to ensure that individuals requiring advice and assistance (including advocacy assistance) at a police station, or at a magistrates' court and who choose not to, or are not able to, obtain such help from an Own Solicitor [ie a solicitor who provides advice and assistance to a client other than as a duty solicitor] may have access to the services of a duty solicitor.

The duty solicitor schemes are not means tested.

2.6.6 Appeals against the refusal of Advice, Assistance or Representation

If the defendant is refused Advice and Assistance otherwise than on the ground of means, a further application may be made to another court.

If the Right to Representation is refused, the court will write to the individual giving the reasons for refusal. If the refusal is on the ground of means, there is no appeal, but if it is on the ground of the interests of justice, an application may be made to another court to review the case. If the individual is refused representation in a magistrates' court in relation to a case which is going to be dealt with by the Crown Court, a further application may be made to the Crown Court.

2.6.7 Appeals against conviction or sentence

The Representation Order, if granted, covers obtaining advice on appeal and the preparation of any application for leave or giving notice of appeal against conviction or sentence, and no separate Advice and Assistance would be required.

If no Representation Order has been granted, then the applicant may apply for Advice and Assistance for those purposes.

Advice and Assistance is also available for an application to the Criminal Cases Review Commission.

Advice, Assistance and Representation themselves are included in the definition of 'criminal proceedings' (see **2.6.1**).

2.6.8 Use of counsel

Under the contract, solicitors may generally instruct counsel to undertake contract work on their behalf (other than in certain specific cases) and such instructions are generally a matter for the solicitor and counsel concerned.

Payment for the work done by counsel will be paid either directly to him or her by the LSC or by the instructing solicitor.

2.6.9 The General Criminal Contract

From 2 April 2001, solicitors in private practice have only been able to carry out criminal defence work funded by the Commission if they have a General Criminal Contract (GCC). There are three basic types of GCC, namely the 'All Classes' contract, the Prison Law contract and the Criminal Cases Review Commission contract. Most contracts will be 'All Classes', as the other contracts are designed to allow a small number of specialist firms to continue to provide services in their specialist area.

The LSC audits applicant firms of solicitors, and firms which pass that audit are awarded a Crime category franchise. Firms with a franchise are eligible for a contract, and, if eligible, will usually receive a three-year contract.

Firms with a GCC are audited to ensure that they meet the quality assurance standards set out by the contract.

Under the AJA 1999, s 16, the LSC has prepared a Code of Conduct to be observed by employees of the Commission who provide services as part of the CDS.

The Code sets out a number of duties imposed on such employees, such as the Duty to Act with Integrity and Independence, and the Duty to Act Impartially and to avoid Discrimination. Two duties require closer examination.

2.6.9.1 The duty to protect the interests of the client

Paragraph 2 of the Code provides as follows:

> 2.1 *The primary duty of a professional employee is to protect the interests of the client so far as consistent with any duties owed to the court and any other rules of professional conduct. Subject to this, a professional employee shall do his or her utmost to promote and work for the best interests of the*

client and to ensure that the client receives a fair hearing. A professional employee shall provide the client with fearless, vigorous and effective defence and may use all proper and lawful means to secure the best outcome for the client.

2.2 A professional employee shall not put a client under pressure to plead guilty, and in particular, shall not advise a client that it is in his or her best interests to plead guilty unless satisfied that the prosecution is able to discharge the burden of proof.

2.6.9.2 The duty of confidentiality

Paragraph 5 of the Code provides as follows:

5.1 Subject to paragraph 5.2, an employee shall keep all information about a client confidential within the salaried service. This is an ongoing duty that does not cease once employment has terminated, and can be enforced in a court by the Commission or the client.

5.2 The duty of confidence to a client is subject to any statutory provision, any court order and any relevant rules of professional conduct or otherwise setting out circumstances where the duty of confidentiality may be overridden.

See the General Criminal Contract for full details (at <http://www.legalservices.gov.uk>).

2.7 Costs

Under the Prosecution of Offences Act 1985, ss 16–21, the court finally disposing of a case has the power to make various orders as to costs, of which the most important are set out below.

2.7.1 Defendant's costs order

Under s 16, a defendant who has been acquitted may have an order made in his or her favour for the payment of sums out of central funds (ie the Government) for expenses properly incurred by him or her in the proceedings. This may, but need not, be the full amount which the defendant claims.

The making of an order for costs is discretionary, but the court will normally make an order for costs in the defendant's favour, unless there are positive reasons for not doing so. For example, where the defendant's own conduct has brought suspicion on himself or herself *and* has misled the prosecution into thinking the case against him or her was stronger than it was (*Practice Direction (Costs: Criminal Proceedings)* [2004] 2 All ER 1070). See also update on p 56.

The order may be made where a person:

- is not tried on an indictment for which he or she has been indicted or sent for trial; or
- has been acquitted on any count on the indictment.

The defendant's costs order cannot be rescinded under the MCA 1980, s 142, as the power under that section only applies where the defendant has been found guilty (*Coles v DPP* (1998) 162 JP 687; and see **5.2.13**).

A number of decisions have held that there is no absolute right to costs under the ECHR, but the cases indicate that as a general rule, costs should be awarded in favour of an acquitted defendant. Where the defendant has been acquitted or the case against him has been dismissed or discontinued, a refusal to award costs could amount to a violation of the presumption of innocence if such a refusal amounts to a finding of guilt.

See, as an example of the operation of these sections, *Galandauer v Snaresbrook Crown Court* [2006] EWHC 1633 (Admin).

2.7.2 Prosecution costs

Where the offence is indictable, under s 17, a private prosecutor (but not the CPS or other prosecuting authority) may be awarded, out of central funds, an amount which the court thinks reasonably sufficient to compensate him or her for expenses properly incurred. The prosecution does not have to be successful for such an order to be made. Again, this need not be the full amount.

2.7.3 Costs against the defendant

Under s 18, if the defendant is convicted, he or she may be ordered to pay to the prosecution such a sum as is just and reasonable. For defendants who are tried at the Crown Court, the Criminal Defence Service (Recovery of Defence Costs Orders) Regulations 2001 (SI 2001/856) as amended require the court to impose an order requiring the offender to pay some or all of his or her legal costs. The defendant's means are taken into account in making the order.

Practice Direction (Costs: Criminal Proceedings) [2004] 2 All ER 1070 provides that the order may be made where the court is satisfied that the defendant or appellant has the means and ability to pay. This direction reflects the pre-existing case law. For example, in *R v Nottingham Justices, ex p Fohmann* (1986) 84 Cr App R 316, it was said that justices should not make an order for costs against a convicted person in such a sum that, through lack of means, he or she would be unable to pay that sum within a reasonable period of about a year. However, it has been held, in relation to the payment of fines, that a period of two years would seldom be too long, and that three years may be acceptable in appropriate cases (*R v Olliver and Olliver* (1989) 11 Cr App R (S) 10). However, in *R v Stockport Justices, ex p Conlon* [1997] 2 All ER 204 the court held that where fines were imposed on those of limited means, they should be lesser in amount so that they could be paid 'in a matter of weeks'.

Guidelines for the court in making an order for costs against a defendant, derived from the authorities, were set out in *R v Northallerton Magistrates' Court, ex p Dove* [2000] 1 Cr App R(S) 136:

(a) The defendant's means and any other financial order should be ascertained so that the costs order does not exceed a reasonable sum that the defendant is able to pay.

(b) The sum should never be more than the costs actually incurred.

(c) It is clear from the fact that there is no right of appeal from the making of a costs order that the policy is to compensate the prosecutor and not to further penalise the defendant.

(d) A costs order should be proportionate to the level of the fine and where the total of fine and costs are excessive, the costs should be reduced accordingly. (On the facts, the defendant had been fined £1,000, where the maximum was £5,000, but ordered to pay over £4,600 in costs. It was held that the amount of costs was grossly disproportionate.)

(e) The onus is on the defendant to provide details of his or her means and in default, magistrates are entitled to deduce his or her financial circumstances from the available evidence.

(f) The defendant must be allowed the opportunity to produce information as to his or her means and should be given notice of any unusual application for costs that is to be made.

The courts have also taken the following matters into consideration when making an order for costs against a defendant:

(a) The choice of court of trial: the defendant should not be 'punished' for electing a trial on indictment by an excessive order for costs (*R v Bushell* (1980) 2 Cr App R (S) 77, where the order was, in fact, upheld). On the other hand, nor should he or she be punished for an election made by the prosecution (*R v Hall* [1989] Crim LR 228).

(b) The plea: if the defendant pleads guilty, an order for costs may still be made, although, taking into account any other relevant matters, the court may be persuaded not to make the order as great as it may otherwise have been. If, on the other hand, the defendant pleads not guilty in the face of an overwhelmingly strong prosecution case when he or she must have known he or she was guilty, an order for costs would be appropriate (*R v Singh* (1982) 4 Cr App R (S) 38; *R v Mountain* (1979) 68 Cr App R 41).

(c) The rest of the sentence: if the defendant is sentenced to a custodial sentence, an order for costs is unusual, as he or she will have no income with which to pay such costs. If the court, however, considers that the defendant has sufficient funds, it may make the order nevertheless (*R v Maher* [1983] QB 784).

(d) If the sentence is non-custodial, the defendant is responsible for his own costs. If there is more than one defendant, the amount of costs should be apportioned between them (*R v Ronson* [1991] Crim LR 794).

In *Hamilton-Johnson v RSPCA* [2000] 2 Cr App R (S) 390 the court observed that, in dealing with an unsuccessful appeal, the Crown Court should hesitate before interfering with a costs order made by the magistrates, but that the Crown Court has the power to do so under the Prosecution of Offences Act 1985, s 18(1) (the power to make such orders for costs as seems 'just and reasonable') or under the Supreme Court Act 1981, s 48(2) (the power to alter any part of the decision appealed against including elements which had not been appealed). In this case the Crown Court increased the costs awarded against the defendant, on her unsuccessful appeal, from £260 to £28,500. See, for example, *R v DPP, ex parte Horner* [2006] EWHC 1607 (Admin).

In July 2006 the CPS introduced the Very High Cost Cases scheme to ensure that the CPS lawyers, caseworkers and case auditors effectively manage counsel's fees in such cases. Students should be aware of the scheme but the details are beyond the scope of this work.

2.8 Reducing delay in the criminal process

The Crime and Disorder Act 1998 (CDA 1998) contains a number of provisions designed to reduce delay in the criminal process. Two measures will be dealt with here.

2.8.1 Powers of magistrates' courts exercisable by a single justice

Section 49 of the CDA 1998 empowers a single justice of the peace for a particular area to exercise the powers of a magistrates' court, such as extending bail or imposing or varying conditions of bail, and dismissing an information where no evidence has been adduced by the prosecution. Further, under s 49(2), rules of court are to be developed to enable a justices' clerk to make a number of administrative (as opposed to judicial) decisions. Students should consult s 49 for a full list of these powers and the restrictions placed upon the decisions of a justices' clerk. The purpose of this section is to reduce the delays inherent in a system which requires the decision of three people, and to attempt to achieve continuity in the handling of a case, particularly prior to trial.

2.8.2 Early administrative hearings

The early administrative hearing (EAH) is designed to take place very early in the proceedings with the purpose of dealing with the issue of legal representation. See the CDA 1998, s 50.

Under s 50, the first appearance after charge (other than indictable only and related offences) shall be before a court consisting of a single justice. At this hearing, under s 50(2):

- the accused shall be asked if he or she wishes to receive legal representation; and
- if he or she does, his or her eligibility for it shall be determined; and
- if it is determined that he or she is eligible, the necessary arrangements or grant to him or her shall be made.

In addition, the single justice may exercise any of the powers of the single justice contained in s 49(1) as he or she thinks fit (s 50(3)(a)). Section 50(3)(b) specifically provides that the single justice may remand the accused in custody or on bail.

As the EAH deals mainly with administrative matters only, the powers of the single justice under s 50(1) may be exercised by a justices' clerk. The only exception is that the justices' clerk has no power to remand the accused in custody or remand the accused on bail on conditions other than any previously imposed.

2.9 Serious organised crime

Under the Serious Organised Crime and Police Act 2005, a new agency known as the Serious Organised Crime Agency (SOCA) is created. The Agency has the functions of, under s 2(1):

(a) preventing and detecting serious organised crime; and

(b) contributing to the reduction of such crime in other ways and to the mitigation of its consequences.

The Act further makes provisions about investigations, prosecutions, offenders, and witnesses in criminal proceedings and the protection of persons involved in investigations or proceedings. It also provides for the implementation of certain international obligations relating to criminal matters and makes further provision for combating crime and disorder. Also included are further provisions about the police and policing and persons supporting the police, and other and connected purposes.

The Agency has been criticised as falling outside the realm of normal policing, and is beyond the scope of this work.

2.9.1 Defendant's costs order

Dowler v Merseyrail, [2009] EWHC 558 (Admin.). *Held*: A court could not refuse a defendant's costs order merely because he had brought suspicion upon himself. If a court refuses costs it should give reasons contemporaneously with that decision.

3

Bail

3.1 Bail—practice and procedure

3.1.1 Introduction to bail

Bail is an enormously important issue for many defendants within the criminal justice system. The potential loss of liberty may have serious effects on them, regardless of the outcome of the proceedings. A period remanded in custody may feel like a prison sentence, especially for someone of good character or someone who has never spent any time in custody before. Time spent as a remand prisoner may exceed the length of any custodial sentence passed on the defendant; indeed, the eventual sentence may be non-custodial. The defendant will be prevented from doing his or her job, if he or she has one, resulting in almost certain loss of income and perhaps loss of the job itself. The financial consequences may spill over into, for example, an inability to pay rent or mortgage and so the loss of one's home.

The National Criminal Statistics 2007 show for that year, some 52,000 people were remanded in custody by magistrates, the lowest number for ten years. 56% of those who were sent to the Crown Court for trial and were remanded in custody for at least a part of the time that their case passed through the system were eventually acquitted or their case was not proceeded with. Again, the statistics show that roughly one in four of all defendants who were remanded in custody eventually had an immediate or suspended custodial sentence passed upon them by a magistrates' court. Although, as the rest of this chapter will show, the reasons for deciding to remand a defendant in custody are quite separate from issues of guilt or innocence, or the appropriate sentence for the crime, the possible consequences of this decision (particularly for an unconvicted defendant) require courts to exercise great care before taking it.

3.1.2 Bail Act 1976, s 4—the general right to bail

4.—(1) A person to whom this section applies shall be granted bail except as provided in Schedule 1 to this Act.

    (2) This section applies to a person who is accused of an offence when—

        (a) he appears or is brought before a magistrates' court or the Crown Court in the course of or in connection with proceedings for the offence, or

        (b) he applies to a court for bail in connection with the proceedings.

        This subsection does not apply as respects proceedings on or against a person's conviction of the offence.

> *(2A) This section also applies to a person whose extradition is sought in respect of an offence, when—*
>
> *(a) he appears or is brought before a court in the course of or in connection with extradition proceedings in respect of the offence, or*
>
> *(b) he applies to a court for bail or for a variation of the conditions of bail in connection with the proceedings.*
>
> *(2B) But subsection (2A) above does not apply if the person is alleged to be unlawfully at large after conviction of the offence.*
>
> *(3) This section also applies to a person who, having been convicted of an offence, appears or is brought before a magistrates' court or the Crown Court to be dealt with under—*
>
> *(a) Part 2 of Schedule 3 to the Powers of Criminal Courts (Sentencing) Act 2000 (breach of certain youth community orders), or*
>
> *(b) Part 2 of Schedule 8 to the Criminal Justice Act 2003 (breach of requirement of community order).*
>
> *(4) This section also applies to a person who has been convicted of an offence and whose case is adjourned by the court for the purpose of enabling inquiries or a report to be made to assist the court in dealing with him for the offence.*

As amended by the Extradition Act 2003 and the CJA 2003.

Any question of bail being granted which is not governed by s 4 of the BA 1976 (or some other statutory provision) is at the discretion of the court. See, for example, *Burgess v Governor of Maidstone Prison* [2000] All ER (D) 1688; *Archbold*, 2008 edn, para 3-170; *Practice Direction (Criminal: Consolidated)* [2002] 3 All ER 904, para 111.25.

3.1.3 'Unconditional' bail—the duty to surrender to custody

The question of whether to release a defendant on bail or keep him or her in custody arises whenever a case is remanded (see **3.15** below). If a defendant is granted bail, this means that he or she is released from court subject to a primary duty to attend the next court hearing in the case. This is known as the duty to surrender to custody. (See BA 1976, s 3(1).) Failure to appear at the appointed place, time and date is itself a criminal offence leading to a fine or imprisonment (BA 1976, s 6—see **3.9** below).

It appears that a defendant surrenders to custody by:

- turning up at the court where he or she was due to appear;
- on the due date;
- at the appointed time (usually 10 am); and
- reporting to the appropriate person.

See *DPP v Richards* [1988] QB 701.

The defendant is then allowed to remain *apparently* at liberty, by staying in the public areas of the court building. Strictly, though, he or she is in custody until the case comes up in court. It follows that the defendant is under an implied obligation not to leave the building without first obtaining permission to do so. (Permission should be sought from the court or someone acting on its behalf.) If the defendant leaves without consent, the court may issue a warrant for his or her arrest. See BA 1976, s 7(2); *DPP v Richards* above; confirmed in *R v Central Criminal Court, ex p Guney* [1995] 1 WLR 376; but cf *Burgess v Governor of Maidstone Prison* [2000] All ER (D) 1688.

Remember that some defendants are released on police bail subject to a duty to surrender to custody at a police station. This occurs, typically, where enquiries are being pursued and the individual has not been charged with an offence.

The primary duty may be accompanied by secondary duties imposed on the defendant—for example, to keep a curfew within certain hours; to report to the local police station once a week; to surrender one's passport. These secondary duties are often described as 'conditions of bail' (see **3.7** below). A defendant who is released on bail, subject only to the primary duty to surrender to bail at the next court hearing, is often described as being released on 'unconditional' bail.

The text of the BA 1976, s 3(1), is as follows:

Incidents of bail in criminal proceedings

3.—(1) A person granted bail in criminal proceedings shall be under a duty to surrender to custody, and that duty is enforceable in accordance with section 6 of this Act.

3.1.4 Where there is no right to bail

3.1.4.1 Generally

It is important to realise that the 'right' to bail under the BA 1976 *usually* applies only prior to conviction. It also only applies when a defendant appears in court (see BA 1976, s 4). So there is **no** right to bail in the following situations:

(a) when being arrested;

(b) when being charged with an offence;

(c) when a warrant for the arrest of an accused person is issued;

(d) after conviction for an offence **unless**:

   (i) the case is adjourned so that inquiries or reports can be made to assist the court when passing sentence (BA 1976, s 4(4)); or

   (ii) the defendant is subsequently brought before a court to be dealt with for breach of certain youth community orders, or breach of a requirement of a community order (BA 1976, s 4(3) as amended);

(e) if the accused is charged with murder, manslaughter, rape or a number of other serious sexual offences (or an attempt to commit the offence, where appropriate), and he or she has a previous conviction for one of these offences (it is immaterial which one), the court may only grant bail if there are 'exceptional circumstances which justify it'. (See the Criminal Justice and Public Order Act 1994 (CJPOA), s 25, as amended; and **3.1.5** below.) A previous conviction for manslaughter will only qualify if the accused was sentenced to custody for it;

(f) if the accused appears in court charged with an indictable offence, or one triable either way, and it appears to the court that he or she was already on bail at the time of the present offence, the court need not grant bail under the BA 1976, s 4. The court continues to have discretion to release such a 'bail bandit' on bail once more. (See CJPOA 1994, s 26; BA 1976, Sch 1, Pt I, para 2A. The CJA 2003 *repeals* s26 CJPOA but the repealing provision – Sch 37, Part 2 – has not yet been brought into force.)

3.1.4.2 Street bail

As noted in **3.1.4.1(a)**, there is no right to bail when arrested without a warrant. Under PACE 1984, s 30, an arresting officer is required to take the person arrested 'to a police station as soon as practicable after the arrest'. That requirement is now subject to two exceptions.

The first is where, on the way to a police station, the arresting officer is satisfied that there are no grounds for either keeping the person under arrest or releasing him on bail; in this situation (probably quite unlikely), the person must be released.

The second, and much more significant, exception is the introduction of 'street bail', pursuant to the CJA 2003, s 4. This introduced a new provision—PACE 1984, s 30A—enabling a police officer to release a person on bail following their arrest but prior to their arrival at a police station. The person so bailed is then under the duty to attend at a police station. The location, date and time of that attendance ought to be specified in a notice given by the officer using street bail to the person released on bail. Failure to attend is enforceable by arrest without warrant. For an interesting critique of 'street bail', see article by Anthea Hucklesby [2004] Crim LR 803.

3.1.5 The right to bail—a human right?

The Bail Act 1976, s 4 gives a 'general right to bail' (sic) for defendants in criminal litigation. However, s 4 does not apply to all defendants in the criminal justice system nor at all stages of the system (see **3.1.2** and **3.1.4**). Furthermore, even those defendants to whom BA 1976, s 4 applies cannot demand to be released on bail automatically. There is a presumption, but no more, that such a defendant will be released on bail if a case is remanded. Section 4(1) says that a person to whom s 4 applies shall be granted bail (this is the 'right'), *except* as provided in the BA 1976, Sch 1. When Sch 1 applies, bail will be denied, and he or she will be remanded in custody (see **3.4** below). For the views of one experienced practitioner on how the right to bail works in practice, see Michael Mansfield QC, *Presumed Guilty*, Mandarin, 1993, ch 12.

In addition to the 'general right' to bail in the BA 1976, s 4, Article 5 of the European Convention on Human Rights provides a right to liberty and security. This is clearly relevant to bail.

Relevant provisions in Article 5 include:

1. *Everyone has the right to liberty and security of person. No one shall be deprived of his liberty save in the following cases and in accordance with a procedure prescribed by law:*

   . . .

   (c) *the lawful arrest or detention of a person effected for the purpose of bringing him before the competent legal authority on reasonable suspicion of having committed an offence or when it is reasonably considered necessary to prevent his committing an offence or fleeing after having done so;*

   (d) *the [lawful] detention of a minor . . . for the purpose of bringing him before the competent legal authority;*

3. *Everyone arrested or detained in accordance with the provisions of paragraph 1.c of this article shall be brought properly before a judge or other officer authorised by law to exercise judicial power and shall be entitled to trial within a reasonable time or to release pending trial. Release may be conditioned by guarantees to appear at trial.*

5. *Everyone who has been the victim of arrest or detention in contravention of the provisions of this article shall have an enforceable right to compensation.*

The significance of human rights generally to bail (and Article 5 in particular) can be seen in the publication by the Law Commission of a report (No 269) in 2001, entitled *Bail and the Human Rights Act 1998.* Following on from its very thorough review of the bail laws and procedures in England and Wales (Consultation Paper No 157, 1999), this report made several recommendations about legislative changes. Both documents are available on the Law Commission's website, <http://www.lawcom.gov.uk>.

Article 5 has already been used to assess the legality of an English bail provision—CJPOA 1994, s 25. In its original form, this provision required courts to deny bail to a defendant accused of a serious offence (listed in s25(2)) if he or she had previously been convicted of such an offence. In several cases, notably *Caballero v UK* (2000) 30 EHRR 643, the European Commission found s 25 to contravene Article 5. In consequence, s 25 was amended by the Crime and Disorder Act 1998, s 56. Courts are now allowed to release a defendant who is accused of his second serious offence if there are 'exceptional circumstances which justify it'.

One of the offences covered by s 25 is murder. The grant of bail for this offence has been the subject of separate consideration by the Ministry of Justice during 2008–9. In part, this review was stimulated by the killing of a woman by her son-in-law, a police officer who had been charged with murdering his wife but who had been released on bail by a Crown Court judge. The consultation paper (CP11/08) disclosed the quite surprising information that in January 2008, 13% of defendants charged with murder were on bail (60 people), while 85% of those charged with manslaughter were on bail (35 people). As a result of the consultation, the Government is proposing to amend the law so that a defendant accused of murder may not be granted bail unless the court is of the opinion that there is no significant risk that he would commit an offence that would cause an injury. The onus would be on the Prosecution to show that the risk existed. Any decision to grant bail to a defendant charged with murder would be taken only by a judge of the Crown Court. These proposed changes are contained in the Coroners and Justice Bill which is proceeding through Parliament at the time of writing (April 2009).

In addition, other provisions of the ECHR have been used to attack English bail law in the courts, although not always successfully. For example, Article 6 (right to a fair trial) has been held not relevant to decisions taken under BA 1976, s 7(5) (see **3.9.2**). See *R (on the application of the DPP) v Havering Magistrates' Court* [2001] 3 All ER 997.

The CJPOA 1994, ss 25 and 26 may require further amendment in light of the HRA 1998. As noted above, s 25 was amended, following decisions of the European Court of Human Rights. In 2001, the Law Commission's report (No 269) concluded that there were no provisions either in the BA 1976 or the CJPOA 1994 which were *incapable* of being interpreted and applied compatibly with Convention rights. The Report nevertheless recommended reform of some legislative provisions. Subsequent changes to the BA 1976, s 3(6), reflect this sort of concern (see CJA 2003, s 13, for example; *Blackstone's Criminal Practice* (2009 edn), para D7.20). The amended version of s 25 was considered by the Administrative Court of the QBD in *R (on the application of O) v Harrow Crown Court* [2003] 1 WLR 2756. Kennedy LJ thought that 'exceptional circumstances' should not be construed too narrowly as to do so would risk (further) non-compliance with Article 5(3). He advised that s 25 should be regarded as establishing a norm: look at the circumstances of a particular offence and the alleged perpetrator; if there is not an unacceptable risk, then he is an exception to that norm and should be released on bail. The court went on to consider the burden of proof under s 25—Kennedy LJ felt that 'little is achieved by dwelling on who has the burden of proof . . . what matters is whether the court is satisfied that there are exceptional circumstances'. However, Hooper J felt that s 25 (if read literally) clearly imposed the burden of proof on the defendant to show exceptional circumstances. This was contrary to Article 5(3) (and see *Hutchison Reid v UK* (2003) 37 EHRR 9) and therefore s 25 should be read down to impose only an evidential burden on the defendant—'the burden remains upon the prosecution to satisfy the court that bail should not be granted'.

In situations where there is no right to bail, the defendant may still be released on bail. The court, if it remands such a case, usually has a *discretion* to grant bail. This discretion

62 Bail

is unfettered by the need to satisfy the BA 1976, Sch 1, if bail is to be refused—in other words, the court has more freedom to refuse bail in such circumstances. On the grant of bail at the police station following charge, see PACE 1984, s 38 (see **2.2.12** above).

3.1.6 Custody time limits

There are certain limits on the length of time that a defendant can be kept on remand in custody, under the Prosecution of Offences Act 1985. See the Prosecution of Offences (Custody Time Limits) Regulations 1987, SI 1987/299, as amended. That there should be limits on the time to be spent in custody awaiting trial cannot be doubted. As Lord Bingham CJ declared in *R v Manchester Crown Court, ex p McDonald* [1999] 1 WLR 841, to proceed without time limits:

> ... would manifestly afford inadequate protection to unconvicted defendants, since a person could, if the Bail Act conditions were satisfied, be held in prison awaiting trial indefinitely, and there would be no obligation on the prosecuting authority to bring him to trial as soon as reasonably possible.

The regulations impose deadlines within which the proceedings must reach a specified stage. For example, a defendant who is kept in custody on an indictable offence which is going to the Crown Court must usually be sent for trial within 70 days of his or her first appearance in court. If the deadline is not met, the defendant *must* be released on bail. There are also deadlines which apply generally, regardless of whether or not the defendant is in custody. These are sometimes referred to as *statutory time limits*. They were introduced in the Prosecution of Offences Act 1985, s 22. In their original form, the result of non-compliance was that the defendant was acquitted of the charge. This provision has now been amended so that non-compliance results in the proceedings merely being stayed. In certain circumstances, the case may be re-started later. See also the CDA 1998, ss 43 and 45, on statutory time limits. The prosecution can apply for a deadline to be extended. It must show (on a balance of probabilities) that there is good and sufficient cause for the extension and that it has acted with all due expedition.

When a defendant is freed on bail due to the expiry of a custody time limit, his or her bail should only have conditions attached to it that he or she can comply with *after* his or her release (eg reporting to a police station or a condition to reside at a specified address). Conditions which must be complied with *prior* to release (eg providing a financial surety) cannot be imposed. The significance of this can be seen in *Re Ofili* [1995] Crim LR 880, where O was originally granted bail, subject to providing a surety of £4,000. O could find no one to stand surety in that sum, so he remained in custody. When O challenged this, the Divisional Court held that on the expiry of the custody time limit, he was entitled to be freed on bail, subject only to reporting or residence conditions.

In a magistrates' court the maximum length of time that a defendant should spend in custody where he is charged with an indictable offence is 70 days. This period should be calculated as follows:

- 70 days from first court appearance to the start of summary trial (for either way offences);
- 70 days from first court appearance to a decision on committal for trial (for either way offences and offences which must be tried on indictment).

Where the defendant is charged with a summary offence, the custody time limit becomes 56 (not 70) days, starting with the first appearance and ending with the summary trial; see r.4A of the 1987 Regulations. Note that, in the second point above, if the committal proceedings are held pursuant to the MCA 1980, s 6(1) (ie with consideration of the evidence), then the 70-day limit is satisfied if the magistrates start to hear the prosecution's evidence within that period: they need not reach a decision on whether to commit the accused for trial within that period.

Once the case goes to the Crown Court, the maximum length of time that a defendant should spend in custody prior to his or her trial is 112 days, beginning with the date that he or she was sent for trial by the magistrates and expiring with the date of his or her arraignment (ie being asked in Crown Court to plead either guilty or not guilty).

This period can be extended, but any use of a 'sham' arraignment simply to defeat the purpose of the custody time limit will be struck down. See, for example, *R v Maidstone Crown Court, ex p Hollstein* [1995] 3 All ER 503—H was sent for trial on 24 March 1994, his custody time limit should have expired on 14 July 1994 but was extended to 22 July 1994. He should then have been released on bail but was kept in custody and produced in court on 27 July 1994 when he was arraigned on the indictment and further remanded in custody. He was still remanded in custody on 13 October 1994 (some three months after the expiry of the original time limit) when the Queen's Bench Divisional Court granted his application to quash the decision of 27 July 1994 to remand him in custody—no date for his trial had been fixed and the arraignment was an artificially created situation. The 112-day limit does not apply to defendants who are awaiting trial for offences of homicide and rape (see BA 1976, s 4(8) (as amended)).

If the 112-day period expires, the CPS should either apply for an extension or bring the defendant back to court to be released on bail. A prison governor has no power to release the defendant without an order from the court. If the defendant continues to be detained in the absence of a court order for release, the appropriate remedies are either to apply to the Crown Court for bail or to seek *habeas corpus* or judicial review. No action will lie against the Home Office for false imprisonment, nor will the CPS be liable for breach of statutory duty if it fails to return the defendant to court after expiry of a custody time limit. See *Olotu v Home Office and another* [1997] 1 WLR 328.

Where an **indictable-only** case is sent straight to the Crown Court (under the CDA 1998, s 51), the maximum length of the custody time limit is 182 days. Time runs from the date the case is sent up by the magistrates, less any time already spent in custody.

The precise length of the custody time limits is subject to the HRA 1998 and Article 5(3) of the ECHR which provides that everyone detained 'shall be entitled to trial within a reasonable time or to release pending trial'. However, the relationship between them was considered by Lord Bingham CJ in *R v Manchester Crown Court, ex p McDonald* [1999] 1 WLR 841. After reviewing the ECHR case law on the subject, he stated that:

> We do not . . . find anything in these European cases which in any way throws doubt on the English law . . . It would indeed appear that the term of 112 days prescribed by the regulations imposes what is, by international standards, an exacting standard.

See *Archbold*, 2008 edn, para 3-56; *Blackstone's Criminal Practice*, 2009 edn, para D14.14.

3.2 Taking a decision on bail—when and how

3.2.1 When is the decision taken?

Usually, the question of bail or custody is decided at the end of each day's proceedings in the case, immediately prior to adjourning it to another day. If a case is being heard in court in the morning, and will continue in the afternoon, the court should determine whether the accused will take lunch in the cells (custody) or in the restaurant of his or her choice (bail), immediately before breaking for lunch. Sometimes, though, the question of bail is the sole reason for a case appearing in court. Examples are:

- The defendant, sent in custody to the Crown Court for trial or sentence, who applies to the Crown Court for bail pending the anticipated appearance in the Crown Court (see **3.11.1** below).
- The defendant who has been refused bail by magistrates and appeals to a Crown Court judge (see **3.11.1** below).

3.2.2 How is the decision taken?

The court must decide for itself whether or not to grant bail. It may be addressed by representatives of both prosecution and defence if the grant of bail is opposed, but the decision is one for the court. Lay magistrates will often retire briefly to consider whether to grant bail if release on bail is opposed by the prosecution. District and Crown Court judges will normally decide in court, straight after counsel have finished their submissions. If the release of the defendant on bail is unopposed by the prosecution (and especially if the defendant is already on bail in the current proceedings), the decision to grant bail is usually a formality.

3.2.3 Records, reasons, certificates and rights

3.2.3.1 Records

There are two common situations when a record must be kept of a decision on bail. Pursuant to the BA 1976, s 5(1), these are:

- whenever bail is granted (either by the police or a court);
- whenever a defendant with the right to bail under the BA 1976, s 4 is remanded in custody by a court.

Also, if an application is made to a court either:

- to attach conditions to a grant of bail which was hitherto unconditional; or
- to vary any extant conditions of bail,

the court must make a record of its decision.

If the defendant asks for a copy of the record, he or she must be given one (BA 1976, s 5). In some of the situations set out below, the defendant must be given a copy of the record even if one is not requested.

3.2.3.2 Reasons

Reasons for refusing to grant bail, etc. If a defendant has a right to bail under the BA 1976, s 4, then if a court:

- refuses to grant bail; or
- grants bail subject to conditions; or
- on application for the purpose, imposes or varies conditions in respect of bail,

the court shall give reasons for its decision (BA 1976, s 5(3)).

These reasons shall be entered on the s 5 record and a copy must be given to the defendant (s 5(4)). However, if the decision is taken by the Crown Court, the defendant is legally represented in court, and the representative does not request a copy, a copy need not be given (BA 1976, s 5(5)). The purpose of giving reasons in these situations is to enable the defendant to make an informed decision about applying to another court about bail.

As well as the specific obligations imposed by the BA 1976, s 5(3), there is a more general obligation to provide reasons when refusing bail. Case law decided under the ECHR establishes that a court must:

> ... examine all the facts arguing for or against the existence of a genuine requirement of public interest justifying, with due regard to the principle of the presumption of innocence, a departure from the rule of respect for individual liberty and set them out in their decisions on applications for release.

See *Letellier v France* (1992) 14 EHRR 83.

In its Consultation Paper on Bail and the HRA 1998 (No 157, 1999), the Law Commission proposed that:

> ... magistrates and judges should be provided with appropriate guidance and training on making bail decisions in a way which is compliant with Article 5, and recording those decisions in such a way as to indicate clearly how they have been reached; and that magistrates' courts should be required to use forms which encourage compliant decision-making and the recording of decisions in a compliant way.

Such guidance was subsequently offered by the Law Commission itself. In its Report on Bail and the Human Rights Act 1998 (No 269, 2001), it compiled 'Guidance for bail decision-takers and their advisers'. This is set out in Pt XIII of the Report and also as a separate document on the Law Commission website (see <http://www.lawcom.gov.uk>).

Reasons for granting bail. If a defendant is charged with any one of five specific offences, then, if a court grants bail notwithstanding that the prosecution has made certain representations, the court must state its reasons for granting bail, and these should be entered on the s 5 record. The offences are: murder (including attempts); manslaughter; and rape (including attempts).

The prosecution must have made representations that, if the defendant was granted bail, he or she would either fail to surrender to custody, or commit an offence whilst on bail; or interfere with witnesses or otherwise obstruct the course of justice.

The requirement to state reasons in this situation is imposed on the court by the BA 1976, Sch 1, Pt I, para 9A (inserted by the CJA 1988, s 153).

3.2.3.3 Certificates of full argument

Under the BA 1976, s 5(6A), if magistrates withhold bail after hearing a fully argued application for bail, they must issue a certificate stating that they heard full argument. After two unsuccessful bail applications in a case, if the magistrates allow the defendant a third application (which is unsuccessful), they should issue a certificate indicating the change in circumstances or new consideration that persuaded them to hear the third application. See BA 1976, s 5(6A) and (6B); also BA 1976, Sch 1, Pt IIA (inserted by the CJA 1988, s 154). See further **3.10** and **3.11** below.

3.2.3.4 Right to appeal a refusal of bail

If the magistrates have issued a certificate of 'full argument', they must tell the defendant that he or she may now apply to a Crown Court judge for bail; the position is the same when magistrates send a case to Crown Court for trial. See BA 1976, s 5(6). On appeals generally, see **3.11** below.

3.3 Applying for bail—what happens in court?

The procedure for determining whether a defendant is to be released on bail does not really vary from court to court, either between courts on the same level of the court system or between courts on different levels. Some defendants have a right to bail under the BA 1976, s 4. Others can only seek the exercise of the court's discretion in their favour. In practice it is always incumbent on the defendant to apply for bail notwithstanding the duty of the court to consider it (BA 1976, Sch 1, Pt 11A). See [1988] Crim LR 397 for a contrary view.

3.3.1 The first step—dealing with the opposition

When a court hearing is adjourned and the defendant is to be remanded, the defendant (or defence counsel) is asked whether he or she seeks release on bail. If the answer is yes, the prosecution will be asked if there are any objections to bail (see **3.4** and **3.5** below).

Usually, defence counsel will seek out the prosecution *before* the case is called into court and ask whether there are any objections to bail. If there are none, the application will be unopposed and is likely to succeed (see **3.3.2**). If there are objections, defence counsel may ask what these are and then think about what bail conditions might overcome them. If defence counsel can get the defendant's agreement to such conditions, the approval of the prosecution may then be sought. If this is obtained, the defence can apply to the court for bail and offer the 'agreed' terms. As the application is now unopposed in effect, success (with the agreed conditions) is likely.

3.3.2 The unopposed application for bail

In this situation, the defence having indicated that bail is sought, the prosecution offer no objection. Although the court could try to investigate whether there are reasons why it should withhold bail from the accused, it is unlikely to do so—largely because the prosecution is its normal source of information which is critical of the accused. If prosecuting counsel sees no reason to object, the court is unlikely to discover such a reason from that source for itself.

3.3.3 The bail application which is opposed

If no agreement on bail has been reached between defence and prosecution prior to coming into court (see **3.3.1**) the prosecution objections are set before the court. The strict rules of evidence do not apply to bail applications but the defence is entitled to cross-examine any witness that the prosecution calls. The defendant may also testify. See *R (on the application of DPP) v Havering Magistrates' Court* [2001] 3 All ER 997. Defence counsel then makes oral submissions dealing with the objections to bail. Counsel may suggest that the objections are groundless and/or propose any conditions which might be attached to bail to overcome the objections (see further **3.6** and **3.7.5** below). The defence may call potential sureties into the witness box in an attempt to persuade the court that the defendant is unlikely to abscond. Finally, the court takes its decision to remand either on bail or in custody.

(See further **Chapter 38** in the *Advocacy* manual for a checklist and flow chart on bail applications.)

3.4 Objections to a release on bail

As mentioned above, the prosecution may object to the defendant being freed on bail. In practice, any objections will correspond to one or more of the reasons for refusing bail to a 's 4' defendant, found in the BA 1976, Sch 1. These will be substantiated with information provided to the court by the prosecutor. Examples are:

[margin note: Objections by prosecution will be based on reasons in Sch. 1 (BA 1976)]

(a) 'The accused is likely to fail to surrender to bail': he failed to turn up last time and we had to get a warrant; he has three convictions for this sort of thing already and faces a long spell in prison; he has no permanent address.

(b) 'The accused is likely to commit offences if freed': he was already on bail for an offence when he was arrested for this lot; he's done it in the past; he makes his living from crime.

(c) 'The accused must be remanded in custody for his own protection': he is on 12 charges of burglary, all from houses on the estate where he lives. Some of the residents have told the police that he's a dead man if he shows his face round there.

3.5 Refusing to release a defendant on bail

3.5.1 If the offence is imprisonable

3.5.1.1 The general principle

If a defendant has the right to bail under the BA 1976, s 4, and asks to be released, then the court can only withhold bail where the offence is imprisonable if one (or more) of the following criteria is present in the case:

(a) The court is satisfied that there are substantial grounds for believing that the defendant would:

　(i)　fail to surrender to custody;

　(ii)　commit an offence whilst on bail;

　(iii)　interfere with witnesses or otherwise obstruct the course of justice.

(b) The defendant is charged with an offence triable either way and it appears to the court that he or she was already on bail at the time of the present offence.

[margin note: Concerns about → HRA compatibility ↓]

(c) The court is satisfied that the accused must be kept in custody for his or her own protection (or welfare, if the accused is a child or young person—see **Chapter 6** for definitions of these terms).

(d) The accused is currently serving a custodial sentence imposed for a previous offence.

(e) If this is the first time that the case has been in the court and the court is satisfied it has not been practicable to obtain all the information necessary for a proper decision on bail to be made.

(f) If the accused has already failed to surrender to bail in the current case (or has broken the conditions attached to the grant of bail) and has been arrested for this.

(g) If, after conviction, the case is adjourned for inquiries or reports and it appears to the court that it would be impracticable to complete the inquiries or report without keeping the accused in custody.

(See BA 1976, Sch 1, Pt I.)

It remains to be seen exactly how the list set out in the BA 1976, Sch 1, is compatible with the HRA 1998 and the ECHR. The ECHR does not explicitly identify the grounds on which bail may be refused prior to trial but the matter has been considered by the European Court and the Commission. Four grounds have been recognised:

- fear of absconding (reflected in Sch 1; see (a)(i) above);
- prevention of crime (see (a)(ii) above);
- interference with the course of justice (see (a)(iii) above);
- preservation of public order (not explicitly within Sch 1; debatable which of grounds (b)–(g) would be covered).

The Law Commission has said that grounds (a)(ii) and (c) above are compatible with the ECHR but those responsible for taking bail decisions may require further guidance on their application. Ground (b) was felt to be highly likely to be applied in a manner incompatible with the ECHR. Similarly, the Law Commission described ground (f) as an automatic inference of a kind not permitted by the ECHR (namely, 'that a person who has done a given thing in the past is likely, given the chance, to do it again'). Grounds (b) and (f) have since been modified by the CJA 2003—see below; it remains to be seen whether the modifications go far enough.

Grounds (b) and (f) were modified by the CJA 2003, ss 14 and 15. The amendments were designed to impact on all defendants, with the only distinction being between the effect on adult and juvenile defendants – see further on this **3.5.1.2** below.

3.5.1.2 Exceptions to the general principle

(a) On 1 January 2007, the CJA 2003, ss 14 and 15 came into **limited** effect. The result is that a court is required to **refuse** bail to a person accused of an offence which is punishable with life imprisonment (such as rape or robbery) in two situations:

- If he or she was already on bail in a different case at the date of the new offence. The new offence must have been committed on or after 1 January 2007. This requirement may be defeated if the court can be satisfied that there is no significant risk of the accused committing an offence if released;

- If he or she has previously failed to surrender to custody in the present proceedings. The failure to surrender must have occurred on or after 1 January 2007. Again, the requirement to refuse bail may be overcome by satisfying the court that there is no significant risk that the accused will abscond again if released now.

If the accused is aged under 18, these requirements are relaxed slightly, so that the factors which 'trigger' the refusal 'shall be given particular weight' when deciding whether there are substantial grounds for believing that he would commit offences or abscond, if released.

(b) We should also note that a new ground for refusing bail was inserted into the BA 1976, Sch 1, Pt I (by the CJA 2003, s 19, in force 5 April 2004). Under new paras 6A–6C, in certain areas of the country the courts may deny bail to a defendant who is a Class A drug user. It is a little more complicated than that, of course. There are several criteria to consider:

- the defendant must be aged 18 or over; and
- he or she must have tested positive for the presence of Class A drugs in his or her system (such testing is now permitted after arrest, under PACE 1984, s 63B); and
- either:
  — the current proceedings relate to possession or the supply of Class A drugs; or
  — the court believes that the defendant's misuse of a Class A drug caused or contributed to the current offence; or
  — the court believes that the current offence was motivated by the defendant's intended misuse of a Class A drug; and
- either:
  — the defendant has refused to undergo an assessment of his or her dependency on (or propensity to misuse) Class A drugs; or
  — the defendant has had a positive assessment and refused the offer of such further assessment or assistance or treatment as the original assessor considered appropriate.

    If, in the case of such a defendant, he or she is willing to undergo an assessment, or have the suggested follow-up, and the court decides to release the defendant on bail, it must make it a condition of bail that the defendant has the assessment or participates in the follow-up.

(c) The Criminal Justice and Immigration Act 2008 amends BA 1976, Sch 1, by restricting the grounds on which bail may be refused to a defendant charged with either a **summary** imprisonable offence or with 'summary only' **low-value criminal damage** offence. Both of these changes came into force during 2008. A defendant facing one of these charges need not be granted bail if one of seven grounds is satisfied:

(i) It appears to the court that he has previously failed to surrender to custody (in any criminal proceedings) and the court believes that, taking account of that failure, he would not surrender if released now.

(ii) He was already on bail at the time of the current offence and the court is satisfied that substantial grounds exist to believe that he would commit an offence if released now.

(iii) The court is satisfied that there are substantial grounds to believe that he would commit an offence by engaging in conduct which would, or would be likely to, cause physical or mental injury to any other person, or would cause a person to fear such injury.

(iv) The court is satisfied that the defendant should be kept in custody for his own protection (or welfare, if he is a juvenile).

(v) The defendant is already in custody, serving a sentence.

(vi) The defendant has been released on bail in the current proceedings but has now been arrested under BA 1976, s7, and the court is satisfied that there are substantial grounds to believe that he would fail to surrender, commit an offence, interfere with witnesses or otherwise obstruct the course of justice, if released on bail again.

(vii) There has been insufficient time to obtain the information needed to make a proper decision on bail.

See BA 1976, Sch.1, Part 1A (inserted by CJIA 2008, s52 and Sch 12).

Sch 1, Part 1A will also apply to juvenile defendants. In the case of a juvenile charged with a low-value criminal damage offence, this is achieved by the inclusion of a new section, s9A, into the BA 1976. The usual mode of trial provisions do not apply to juveniles, so s9A empowers magistrates to make an assessment of the value of criminal damage, in order to determine whether an application for bail by the juvenile should be determined under Sch 1, Part 1 or Part 1A.

3.5.2 Considerations for the court

Schedule 1 to the BA 1976 (at Pt I, para 9) says that when a court is considering whether one of the reasons for refusing bail referred to in (a) (in **3.5.1**) exists, it should take account of:

(a) The nature and seriousness of the offence (and probable sentence).
(b) The character, antecedents, associations and community ties of the accused.
(c) The defendant's record of fulfilling bail requirements in the past.
(d) The strength of the case against the accused (unless adjourning for reports or inquiries before passing sentence).
(e) Any other considerations as appear relevant.

With regard to (b), the disclosure of D's *antecedents* means that the magistrates learn of his or her criminal record, if any. There are several points to note about this:

- evidence of any criminal record should be tendered in writing, not orally (*R v Dyson* (1944) 29 Cr App R 104);
- the press *should not* report any convictions which are publicised, at that time (*R v Fletcher* (1949) 113 JP 365) (note that there is no direct power to coerce the media, although note the Contempt of Court Act 1981, s 4(2));
- any magistrate who sits on a bail application hearing and learns of previous convictions is disqualified from subsequently trying D's guilt/innocence in that case (MCA 1980, s 42).

Also on 'associations and community ties', see the suggestions in *Stone's Justices' Manual*, 2008 edn, para 1–481. The phrase covers:

- name, age, nationality and (if applicable) length of residence in the UK;
- family circumstances (married? dependent children? does he or she live with wife/parents/other relatives?);
- residence (type of accommodation; recent addresses and length of stay);
- employment (recent record; present job—location and income);
- possible sureties, any relative, friend, employer in court . . .;
- anything else that the defendant wants to put forward, eg medical problems, difficulties with job or home if remanded in custody.

With regard to (e) above (any other relevant considerations), one should note the **BA 1976, s 4(9)**, which states that a court may have regard to any misuse of controlled drugs by the defendant, where it is relevant to the court's decision on bail. Section 4(9) was inserted by the Criminal Justice and Court Services Act 2000 (CJCSA), s 58; to support this move, the CJCSA 2000 provides that samples of urine or a non-intimate sample may be taken from an adult defendant charged with a 'trigger offence' (as well as in some other circumstances) for the purpose of ascertaining whether he or she has any specified Class A drug in his or her body (see s 57). Failure to provide a sample is an imprisonable offence; information obtained from a sample may be disclosed for the purpose of informing any decision about granting bail in criminal proceedings to that defendant. Trigger offences include typical drug crimes (possession and possession with intent to supply); also most of the offences in the Theft Act 1968 (see CJCSA 2000, Sch 6).

Special considerations will apply to bail decisions concerning *juvenile* defendants, when the relevant provisions of the CJA 2003 come fully into force:

(a) when deciding whether it is satisfied that there are substantial grounds for believing that the defendant would commit offences if released on bail, the court shall give particular weight to the fact that he was already on bail at the date of the present offence (BA 1976, Sch 1, Pt 1, para 9AA, inserted by the CJA 2003, s 14(2));

(b) when deciding whether it is satisfied that there are substantial grounds for believing that the defendant would fail to surrender to custody if released, the court shall give particular weight to the fact that, having been released on bail in the present proceedings, he subsequently failed to surrender to custody without reasonable cause (BA 1976, Sch 1, Pt 1, para 9AB, inserted by the CJA 2003, s 15(2)).

Finally, remember, if a court withholds bail from a 's 4' defendant, it must give its *reasons* in open court and on the record (BA 1976, s 5(3); see **3.2.3** above).

3.5.3 If the offence is non-imprisonable

The grounds for refusing bail set out in **3.5.1** are applied only to defendants charged with crimes for which they can be sent to prison, if convicted. The Bail Act 1976, Sch 1 also covers bail for non-imprisonable offences and is more liberal in allowing bail. The grounds for withholding bail now are:

- for the protection of the defendant;
- where the defendant is already serving a custodial sentence;
- where the defendant has been arrested for a bail offence in connection with this case (see **3.9** below);
- where the defendant has previously failed to surrender to bail and, in the light of that failure, the court is satisfied he or she would not surrender to bail if released now.

There is no power to remand a defendant in custody for the purpose of preparing medical/psychiatric reports if the offence is non-imprisonable.

The detailed provisions which govern the imposition of bail conditions are to be found in the BA 1976, Sch 1, Pt I, para 8. Part I applies to defendants 'accused or convicted of *imprisonable* offences' (emphasis added). There is no corresponding text in Sch 1, Pt II, which deals with *non-imprisonable* offences. It might be thought, then, that the BA 1976 makes no provision for attaching conditions to a grant of bail where a defendant is accused or convicted of a non-imprisonable offence. In fact, it has been decided that the basic power to attach conditions to a grant of bail (BA 1976, s 3) applies to both imprisonable and non-imprisonable offences (see *R v Bournemouth Magistrates' Court, ex p Cross* (1989) 89 Cr App R 90).

This decision can produce a rather odd result by virtue of the different criteria which now apply to non-imprisonable offences when (a) refusing bail and (b) imposing conditions. The BA 1976, s 3(6) and Sch 1, Pt I, para 8 both allow a court to attach conditions to a grant of bail if it appears necessary to do so in order to ensure that the defendant surrenders to custody; but Sch 1, Pt II, does not allow a court to withhold bail on the grounds that it believes the defendant will not surrender to custody. So if the court fears that a defendant will abscond, it may attach conditions to his or her bail but if there are no conditions that will allay such fears, they must release on bail anyway.

3.6 Overcoming objections to bail—the power of imagination

It was mentioned earlier (in **3.3.3** above) that if the prosecution is objecting to the release of the defendant on bail, defence counsel can suggest that certain conditions be attached to the grant of bail. These suggestions can be made to the prosecutor before going into court or once the prosecutor states the objections in court. Additionally, defence counsel can make (or repeat) these suggestions in his or her final submissions to the court. Apart from some qualifications on the power of the courts to attach conditions to a grant of bail, **the conditions which can be used to overcome the fears of the prosecution or court are almost limitless.** See, for example, *R (on the application of Ellison) v Teesside Magistrates' Court* [2001] EWHC Admin 12 which records that a defendant charged with attempted rape was released on bail by a Crown Court judge subject to a number of conditions, one of which was that he was not to consume alcohol.

3.6.1 Keeping one's imagination within reasonable bounds

There are some very common conditions (see **3.7** below) which will be suggested by the defence almost as an automatic reaction to certain objections. Nevertheless, one should not be afraid to put forward novel solutions to allay any objections, subject only to two observations. First, that one should always get the defendant's consent before putting a suggestion forward. Apart from the ethical problem of arguing a case with no instructions from the lay client to do so, there is a practical problem—to get your client released on bail, subject to conditions which he or she will not or cannot accept, is effectively not getting bail. Secondly, remember that the everyday bail conditions are used so often because they are workable and answer a particular objection sensibly. Do not invent new ones which fail to satisfy those criteria. One should seek only to improve the commonplace conditions to deal with novel situations when they arise.

[Handwritten margin note: Never suggest a condition without prior consent from def.]

3.7 Attaching conditions to release on bail

3.7.1 Generally

As regards a person granted bail, the BA 1976, s 3, provides that:

Incidents of bail in criminal proceedings

3.—(1) A person granted bail in criminal proceedings shall be under a duty to surrender to custody, and that duty is enforceable in accordance with section 6 of this Act.

(2) No recognizance for his surrender to custody shall be taken from him.

(3) Except as provided by this section—

   (a) no security for his surrender to custody shall be taken from him,

>   (b) he shall not be required to provide a surety or sureties for his surrender to custody, and
>
>   (c) no other requirement shall be imposed on him as a condition of bail.
>
> (4) He may be required, before release on bail, to provide a surety or sureties to secure his surrender to custody.
>
> (5) He may be required, before release on bail, to give security for his surrender to custody. The security may be given by him or on his behalf.
>
> (6) He may be required to comply, before release on bail or later, with such requirements as appear to the court to be necessary—
>
>   (a) to secure that he surrenders to custody,
>
>   (b) to secure that he does not commit an offence while on bail,
>
>   (c) to secure that he does not interfere with witnesses or otherwise obstruct the course of justice whether in relation to himself or any other person,
>
>   (ca) for his own protection or, if he is a child or young person, for his own welfare or in his own interests,
>
>   (d) to secure that he makes himself available for the purpose of enabling inquiries or a report to be made to assist the court in dealing with him for the offence, and, in any Act, 'the normal powers to impose conditions of bail' means the powers to impose conditions under paragraph (a), (b) (c) or (ca) above,
>
>   (e) to secure that before the time appointed for him to surrender to custody, he attends an interview with an authorised advocate or authorised litigator, as defined by section 119(1) of the Courts and Legal Services Act 1990.

Note that the BA 1976, s 3(6) is shown as amended by the CJA 2003, s 13, which came into force on 5 April 2004.

In **3.1.3** above, it was said that any grant of bail was subject to a primary duty—to surrender to bail at the appointed time, date and place—but also that secondary duties (known as 'conditions of bail') could sometimes be imposed on a defendant. The BA 1976 originally specified two forms of bail condition—the surety and security (see the BA 1976, s 3(3) and (4)). The police were originally limited to these two conditions (but see now **3.7.7**), while the courts had more choice due to the BA 1976, s 3(6), which allowed a court to impose any condition that they thought necessary to secure certain objectives.

3.7.2 The surety

If the court (or police, following an arrest or charge) considers it is necessary to ensure that the defendant surrenders to custody, the defendant may be required to provide sureties to guarantee his or her surrender (BA 1976, s 8). If no sureties are forthcoming, the defendant stays in custody, although technically bail has been granted. A surety is a person—usually a friend, relative or employer—who agrees to ensure that the defendant attends court at the next hearing. The surety acknowledges that, should the defendant fail to surrender, the surety is liable to forfeit a specified sum of money to the court. See also **3.9.6** below on forfeiture. A person may stand as a surety either in the courtroom or in any of the situations covered by the BA 1976, s 8(4) (for example, at the police station after the accused is charged; by the gaoler at court if the surety arrived too late to appear in court; at the prison holding the defendant).

3.7.3 The surety in court

Before starting the final submissions to the court, defence counsel should call any proposed sureties into the witness box. The 'surety' will take an oath and defence counsel should then explain the obligation to ensure the defendant's surrender to bail and the possibility of the surety losing money should this not happen. He or she should then be asked if he or she is still willing to be a surety. If so, counsel will enquire what sum of money he or she is prepared to run the risk of forfeiting and how this will be paid if required by the court to do so. The court will examine the surety's financial resources, character and any criminal record, and relationship to the defendant (kinship, geographical, etc).

If the procedure outlined above is followed, there should be no problems about lack of resources if the surety is subsequently called on to forfeit his or her recognisance. The issue of the surety's ability to pay was considered by the Divisional Court in *R v Birmingham Crown Court, ex p Ali and another* [1999] Crim LR 504. The court declared that a qualified lawyer, or legal executive, should not put someone forward as a possible surety unless he or she has reasonable grounds for believing that the surety would, if necessary, be able to meet the financial undertaking. Failure to observe this requirement is irresponsible and possibly a matter for consideration by a professional disciplinary body. Furthermore, a court should conduct appropriate enquiries with an individual before accepting that person as a surety. It might be necessary to require evidence of the assets that the would-be surety claims to have. How far that enquiry would go depends upon all of the circumstances, the most important of which is the amount of money at stake. (See **3.9.6** below; also the *Advocacy* manual, Chapter 38.)

3.7.4 Security

The defendant may be required to provide security for his or her surrender (BA 1976, s 3(5) as amended by the CDA 1998, s 54(1)). This may take the form of money or other valuables (BA 1976, s 5(9)) and may be demanded from the defendant personally, unlike a surety. It will be deposited with the court and, if the defendant fails to surrender to custody, it may be forfeited by court order, either totally or in part.

The obligation to pay a security, if it is held forfeit, is that of the defendant alone. If a third party actually supplies the funds to deposit with the court, he or she should note that the court is under no obligation to ascertain his or her ability to pay the money. Further, the third party's position need not be considered by the court when it imposes (or varies) bail conditions. Such a third party has far less protection here than when standing as a surety for a defendant: see *R v Maidstone Crown Court, ex p Jodka* (1997) 161JP 638.

3.7.5 Other bail conditions

A court can impose any conditions it (or defence counsel) can think of, but they must be considered to be necessary to ensure that the defendant either:
- surrenders to custody; or
- does not commit offences while on bail; or
- does not interfere with witnesses; or
- does not obstruct the course of justice; or
- is for his own protection (or for his own welfare or in his own interests, if he is a juvenile); or
- is available for inquiries or reports to be completed; or
- attends an interview with a legal representative.

(See BA 1976, s 3(6).)
See *Stone's Justices' Manual*, 2008 edn at para 1–468.

3.7.6 Common conditions

3.7.6.1 Reporting to a police station

A defendant may be ordered to do this in order to ensure that he or she stays within the vicinity. This may be strictly enforced—for example, 'daily at 7 am and 7 pm'—or be a quite loose check—for example, 'every Thursday'. The purpose of this is to ensure the defendant is around to surrender to custody on the appointed date.

Now that the police are able to be more creative in attaching conditions to bail, there is room for confusion here. The police could always release a suspect on bail, subject to a requirement that he attend subsequently at the police station for further inquiries—that was not conditional bail as the attendance was a primary obligation on the accused. Nowadays, the police may also require a suspect to report to the police station if they are concerned that he or she may abscond—this would be a secondary obligation (he or she is not being required to surrender to custody) and if the suspect failed to report as required he or she would only be in breach of a bail condition; he or she would not have committed an offence under the BA 1976, s 6 (see **3.9.1** below).

[handwritten annotation: Breach of primary obligation to surrender to custody]

3.7.6.2 Keeping curfew

Originally a medieval rule requiring fires to be extinguished at a certain hour at night, this now means the obligation to stay indoors between certain hours (usually at night). This condition is often used where a number of crimes have allegedly occurred at roughly the same time of day—for example, five houses have been burgled in the early hours of the morning: curfew to be kept between 11 pm and 6 am. It is commonly used for juvenile defendants.

3.7.6.3 Staying out of/in a certain area

These are separate conditions. The first aims to separate the accused from temptation—the woman who has been charged with shoplifting from four West End stores in London may be ordered not to go within a two-mile radius of Oxford Circus. (As precise measurement of this is virtually impossible for the average citizen, it is wiser not to tempt fate!) The second condition is intended to prevent the defendant either absconding or, occasionally, from contacting prosecution witnesses. Compliance with both conditions may be very difficult to check but, if a breach does come to the attention of a police officer, the defendant may be re-arrested. In a novel twist on this common condition, it was reported in the press in May 1994 that the Marquis of Blandford had a bail condition that he must not use taxi-cabs unless accompanied by his solicitor; at the time, he was charged with, *inter alia*, using taxis and dishonestly not paying the fares.

3.7.6.4 Electronic monitoring

BA 1976, s3 now makes it clear that a court can impose a condition of electronic monitoring of the defendant's compliance with bail conditions, or 'tagging'; see BA 1976, s3(6ZAA) and (6ZAB), inserted by CJIA 2008, s51 and Sch 11. Electronic tagging can be used for juveniles and for adult defendants, although slightly different requirements apply depending on whether or not the defendant is aged under seventeen.

3.7.6.5 Contact details

In order to ensure that cases go ahead as planned whenever possible, magistrates' courts are now often requiring defendants to supply their mobile telephone number or email address so that the court can remind them of an up-coming court appearance. Reluctance to give this information may result in the magistrates making it a condition of bail.

3.7.7 Conditional police bail

In 1993, the Royal Commission on Criminal Justice recommended that the police be given greater powers to attach conditions, when deciding whether to release a detainee on bail from a police station. Originally, the police were limited to requiring just a surety or security. Subsequent changes mean that 'the normal powers to impose conditions of bail' are available to a custody officer at a police station (see PACE 1984, s 47(1A)). The main limitations now are that any conditions must appear to be necessary to ensure that the defendant

- surrenders to custody; or
- does not offend whilst on bail; or
- does not interfere with witnesses or otherwise obstruct the course of justice; or
- is for his own protection (or welfare or otherwise in his own interests, if he is a juvenile).

See the BA 1976, s 3A(5), as amended by the CJA 2003, s 13(2). In addition, the police cannot use some specific bail conditions—residence in a bail hostel (see the BA 1976, s 3A(2)) or in connection with medical reports for defendants accused of murder (see the BA 1976, s 3A(3)).

When considering the use of bail conditions, the police are unlikely to be influenced by representations from defence counsel since barristers do not usually attend a police station. The ability of either a duty solicitor or the defendant's own choice of solicitor to suggest or influence bail conditions at the police station remains the subject of speculation. See further on this, Ede and Edwards, *Criminal Defence* (2002 2nd edn), Law Society.

3.8 Changing bail conditions

If circumstances change, so that the original conditions are no longer appropriate, the defence can apply to the court to alter or remove them. In exceptional situations, the prosecution can apply for existing conditions to be altered (presumably to strengthen them), or for conditions to be attached to an unconditional grant of bail.

Such application is made under the BA 1976, s 3(8), either to the magistrates' court which is dealing with the case or, if the case has been sent to the Crown Court, to a Crown Court judge. Where a defendant has been sent to Crown Court for trial but has not yet been required to surrender to custody at the Crown Court, then the magistrates' court which sent him for trial has concurrent jurisdiction with the Crown Court to hear any application for variation of bail conditions (see *R v Lincoln Magistrates' Court, ex p Mawer* [1995] Crim LR 878). Once the defendant has surrendered to custody at the Crown Court, the magistrates cease to have any jurisdiction over the matter. See also the BA 1976, s 3(8A)—this extends the Crown Court's jurisdiction to cover applications made in serious fraud cases which go to Crown Court on a notice of transfer. (For notices of transfer, see **Chapter 11**.) See *Blackstone's Criminal Practice*, 2009 edn, paras D7.47 and D7.61 for the basic procedure on bail applications to the Magistrates' Court and Crown Court respectively.

The Criminal Procedure Rules 2005 deal with applications for bail in Part 19. Two amendments were made to Part 19 which came into effect in April 2009 (see SI 2008/3269). First, there is now a requirement for a defendant to give advance notice of an application to vary bail conditions in the magistrates' court (this requirement existed already for applications in the Crown Court). Notice must be given not less than 24 hours in advance of the application; it should specify the variation sought and the reasons for it. The second change is where it is proposed that a defendant be released subject to a condition of residence at a specified address. CPR, r 19.25 now requires such a defendant to notify the prosecution of that address as soon as practicable after proceedings have begun against him. The prosecution is placed under an obligation to help the court to assess the suitability of that address. This change flows from concerns about the lack of information available to magistrates when assessing the suitability of an address proposed for a residence requirement, in the aftermath of a murder committed by Anthony Leon Peart on a London bus in 2005, when on bail.

It should be noted that if a defendant is released by the police on conditional bail, he or she may apply to a custody officer to vary those conditions (see the BA 1976, s 3A(4)). The custody officer may impose different conditions and may even make them more onerous than before. Counsel is very unlikely to be involved in such an application. However, the defendant may choose to apply to the magistrates' court and counsel may then be briefed (see the MCA 1980, s 43B).

3.9 What happens if the defendant disobeys?

3.9.1 Failure to surrender to custody

It seems that around 10–15% of all defendants who are remanded on bail by magistrates subsequently fail to surrender to custody. The proportion does not vary much whether one looks at indictable offences or summary offences; see **Figure 3.1**. The court will usually issue a warrant for the arrest of the accused unless, perhaps, defence counsel is able to offer an explanation for the absence. Such warrants are known as *bench warrants*. When the warrant is executed and the accused is brought before the court, the court is very likely to remand the accused into custody. Note that, even though the accused may have had a general right to bail hitherto (under BA 1976, s 4), they have it no longer (BA 1976, Sch 1). As the *Consolidated Criminal Practice Direction* puts it (at 1.13.3), there are at least three possible courses of action that the court may take following a non-appearance by the defendant:

- punish the defendant for the s 6 offence;
- remand the defendant in custody or release subject to more severe conditions;
- try the defendant in his absence.

Clearly, these are not mutually exclusive and a defendant may eventually find that all three actions have been taken in his or her case.

It is becoming the norm in both magistrates' courts and Crown Court, when granting bail, to give the defendant both an oral warning and a printed card to the effect that if he or she does not attend the trial, the court may well proceed in his or her absence. If a defendant has had adequate notice of this sort, the courts are unlikely to be reluctant to proceed in his or her absence even where the charge is a very serious one (see *O'Hare* [2006] EWCA Crim 471).

If the defence counsel is able to put before the court some prima facie good reason for the absence of their client, the bench warrant may be *backed for bail*. In this situation,

England and Wales		Number of persons (thousands)		
		Outcome		
How directed to appear	Total	Dealt with by magistrates[2]	Committed for trial	Failed to appear[3]
Indictable offences				
Summoned	48	35	4	9
Arrested and bailed	351	239	56	56
Arrested and held in custody	76	47	24	5
Total	474	321	83	69
Summary offences (other than motoring)				
Summoned	387	380	*[4]	6
Arrested and bailed	215	195	*[4]	20
Arrested and held in custody	25	23	*[4]	1
Total	626	599	*[4]	27
Summary motoring offences				
Summoned	615	590	*[4]	25
Arrested and bailed	139	130	*[4]	9
Arrested and held in custody	9	9	*[4]	0
Total	763	728	*[4]	35
All offences				
Summoned	1,049	1,005	4	40
Arrested and bailed	705	564	56	85
Arrested and held in custody	110	79	24	6
Total	1,864	1,648	83	131

(1) The number of persons directed to appear includes those who failed to appear to a summons or to bail, who are excluded from the proceedings figures given in other chapters of this volume.
(2) Including those committed to the Crown Court for sentence.
(3) At any stage before final disposal by magistrates' court.
(4) Not applicable, because summary offences committed for trial will not be counted as principal offences as they must accompany an indictable only or triable-either-way offence.

Figure 3.1 Persons directed to appear at magistrates' courts[1] by type of offence, how directed to appear and outcome, 2007.

the warrant is executed by arresting the defendant and taking them to a police station. The defendant will then be re-released from the police station on (court) bail, subject to whatever conditions have been endorsed on the bench warrant, and will not then be produced in court but be under a duty to surrender to the court on a date to be notified. For obvious reasons, it is unusual for a bench warrant to be backed for bail. Indeed, in 2006–7 the Government looked into the possibility of making legislative changes to the scheme for such warrants, including their possible abolition. However, the majority view of respondents to a consultation process did not favour that option and the Government announced in July 2007 that it would proceed instead by publishing guidance on good practice with its 'criminal justice partners'.

3.9.2 Non-compliance with other conditions

No separate offence is committed in this situation but the accused is at risk of arrest (without warrant) by a police officer who has reasonable grounds for believing that a bail condition has been broken. Indeed, a police officer can arrest a defendant when he or she has reasonable grounds for believing that the defendant is likely to break a bail condition (see the BA 1976, s 7(3)). Once arrested, the defendant must be produced in the magistrates' court within 24 hours. The defendant should not be produced in the Crown Court, even if on Crown Court bail, nor may the magistrates commit the defendant to the Crown Court for a decision to be made on bail. See *R v Marshall* (1995) 159 JP 688; *R (on the application of Ellison) v Teesside Magistrates' Court* [2001] EWHC Admin 12.

When the defendant is produced in the magistrates' court, the magistrates have to make a two-stage determination (see the BA 1976, s 7(5); *R (on the application of DPP) v Havering Magistrates' Court* [2001] 2 Cr App R 2). The first stage is to decide whether the defendant has broken (or is likely to break) a condition of his or her bail. The hearing is quite informal; usually, a police officer attends the court and states the grounds for his or her belief that a bail condition has been (or was likely to be) broken. In so doing, the officer may rely on hearsay evidence. There is no need to call other witnesses to testify for the prosecution but the defendant may cross-examine any who are called. The defendant is then entitled to give evidence, if he or she wishes to do so. The defendant must be given a full and fair opportunity to comment on, and respond to, the material put forward by the prosecution but where the defendant asserts that a reasonable excuse existed for a breach, that matter is irrelevant at this stage (see *R (on the application of Vickers) v West London Magistrates' Court* [2003] EWHC Admin 1809).

If the magistrates determine that the defendant has broken a bail condition, the second stage is to consider bail for the future of this case. The defendant may be remanded into custody, or released on bail again. Bail may be subject to the same or different conditions. The breach of bail that was established in stage one is one factor relevant to the magistrates' decision now; another relevant factor would be any suggestion by the defendant that there was a reasonable excuse for the breach. See also *R v Liverpool City Magistrates' Court, ex parte DPP* [1993] QB 233; and the commentary at [2004] Crim LR 64.

3.9.3 Prosecutions for failure to surrender

Under the BA 1976, s 6, it is an offence for a defendant to fail to surrender to custody at the appointed time and place. This offence is often referred to by courts, and counsel, as 'absconding'. It is otherwise commonly referred to, particularly by defendants, as 'doing a runner'. It is punishable by imprisonment or a fine (see **3.9.5**) and any security or sureties will be liable to forfeiture by order of the court (see **3.9.6**). Although the BA 1976, s 6, creates a single offence of failure to surrender to custody, there are some distinctions to observe in the commencement of proceedings (this is an area that is currently dealt with in the *Practice Direction (Criminal: Consolidated)* [2002] 3 All ER 904 at section 1.13):

(a) *Where the defendant fails to surrender to court, having been bailed by police*

It is for the police or prosecutor to decide whether to initiate proceedings for the s 6 offence. If proceedings do go ahead, they should be dealt with on the defendant's first court appearance following arrest. The offence is summary and generally there is a six-month time limit on the commencement of proceedings, starting with the date of absence. However, if the defendant remains undiscovered for a longer period, that will not now defeat proceedings under s 6. The CJA 2003, s 15(3) (in force 5 April 2004), provides that proceedings may be instituted within three months of the date when the defendant eventually surrenders to custody, is arrested in connection with the offence for which bail was granted, or appears in court in respect of that offence (and you should thus read the *Practice Direction (Criminal: Consolidated)* part 1.13.7, with caution). Proceedings will be commenced by the laying of an information, until the new procedure of written charge and requisition comes into full operation (CJA 2003, s 29).

(b) *Where the defendant fails to surrender, having been bailed by a court*

It is for the court to initiate proceedings, at the invitation of the prosecutor. If the defendant is arrested in connection with a new offence, committed outside the jurisdiction of the court which granted bail, the Bail Act offence should be dealt with by the court dealing with the new offence, if practicable. Otherwise, the defendant should be produced at the court dealing with the proceedings for which bail was granted previously—that may be the Crown Court, of course, if the defendant had been sent there for trial or sentence.

In either situation, the bail offence should be dealt with as soon as practicable. It should no longer be the practice to postpone its consideration until the conclusion of the proceedings for the main offence.

3.9.4 The hearing of a s 6 offence

The court is entitled to adopt a relatively informal procedure (*R v Hourigan* [2003] EWCA Crim 2306). The hearing usually begins with the court asking the defendant if he admits the breach of bail. The defendant should always be given the opportunity to explain his absence, and defence counsel should be invited to address the court, if appropriate (see *R v Davis (Seaton Roy)* (1986) 8 Cr App R (S) 64; *R v Boyle* [1993] Crim LR 40; *Hourigan*). The defendant bears the burden of proving a reasonable excuse for non-attendance, on the balance of probabilities. A court should be careful not to tie the hands of a later court (which might deal with the s 6 offence) or the Crown Prosecution Service by expressing a premature view of leniency or indicating that no proceedings need be taken—see *France v Dewsbury Magistrates' Court* [1988] Crim LR 295.

3.9.5 Penalties for failure to surrender

Following conviction by magistrates for absconding, there is a maximum penalty of three months' imprisonment and/or a fine of up to £5,000 (increased to £15,000 when the amendment made by the CJA 2003 to Level 5 on the standard scale of fines takes effect; see BA 1976, s 6(7)). However, the magistrates may instead commit the defendant to the Crown Court for sentence if they think greater punishment is required or if they are sending him to the Crown Court for trial on another offence and feel that it is appropriate for the Crown Court to deal with him for both offences (see BA 1976 s 6(6)). In the Crown Court, the absconder faces a maximum term of 12 months' imprisonment and/or an unlimited fine.

In November 2007, the Sentencing Guidelines Council published definitive guidelines for punishing a failure to surrender to bail. The guidelines address both the defendant's culpability and the harm which resulted from the absence. The guidelines state that the same principles should apply whether the offence is contrary to BA 1976, s 6(1) (no excuse for failure) or s 6(2) (initial reasonable excuse then a failure to surrender as soon as possible thereafter). However, the degree of harm is likely to be less in the latter situation and so it will normally be seen as a less serious offence. Where the failure is to surrender to a police station, the degree of harm is likely to be less (compared to a court) and it may be seen as a less serious offence in the circumstances.

The punishment may be severe if it is thought necessary to deter others. Sentences of six or nine months are not unknown although an absence of 22 years only resulted in a ten-month sentence, in a case described by the Court of Appeal as meriting a sentence 'very much at the top end of the bracket' (see *Clarke* [2000] 1 Cr App R (S) 224, *Igbebion* [2004] EWCA Crim 2724 and *McKendrick* [2005] 2 Cr App R (S) 68, respectively). Where the defendant receives custodial sentences for both the original offence and the BA offence, the sentences should usually be consecutive, subject to the aggregate sentence remaining proportionate to the combined seriousness of the offences (see SGC guidelines, para 33). It has been said that the responsibility for their absence is unaffected by whether or not they were eventually acquitted or convicted of the original offence (see *Clarke* again). For example, in *R v Neve* (1986) 8 Cr App R (S) 270, the defendant had been acquitted at his eventual trial for the main offence but was nevertheless sentenced to six months' imprisonment and ordered to forfeit a security of £10,000 for going to Spain in an attempt to avoid trial. This principle has been confirmed in the SGC guidelines—see para 13: the culpability and harm are the same, regardless of the outcome of the original charge.

It is perhaps necessary to balance these cases with some statistics drawn from the consultation paper on punishing Bail Act offences which was published by the Sentencing Advisory Panel in 2006. In 2004, some 98 per cent of all defendants who were sentenced for a *principal* Bail Act offence were dealt with by magistrates. Of these, the majority were fined and only 10 per cent received a custodial sentence for their failure to surrender. Conversely, in the Crown Court only 600 defendants were sentenced for a principal Bail Act offence but just under 50 per cent of them were sentenced to immediate custody for it. The most common length of custodial sentence was less than 15 days (magistrates' courts) and 15 days to 1 month (Crown Court). Whilst there is no clear trend in the Crown Court, it is clear that from 1999 to 2004, the size of fines increased whilst custodial sentences shrank in the magistrates' courts. Where the Bail Act offence was a *subsidiary* one (approximately two in every three such cases), again the overwhelming majority were disposed of by magistrates (96 per cent). There was a three-way tie between fines, community orders and custody as punishments. In the Crown Court, 58 per cent of these offenders were sentenced to custody whilst only 1 per cent were fined. In these statistics, 'principal offence' meant that either the BA offence was the only one being sentenced or was the offence which attracted the greater sentence. For further research on this important subject, see <http://www.sentencing-guidelines.gov.uk>.

The SGC guidelines identify aggravating and mitigating factors:

1. Aggravating factors include:
    - Leaving the jurisdiction
    - Repeat offending
    - Causing a lengthy delay to the administration of justice
    - Making a determined effort to avoid the court proceedings

2. Mitigating factors include:
    - Prompt voluntary surrender where it is initiated by D
    - Misunderstanding, where it does not amount to a defence (the SGC distinguishes this from a mistake by D, for which D must take responsibility); for example, where D has literacy or language difficulties which were not identified or addressed satisfactorily when bail was granted
    - Being the sole or primary carer of dependent relatives, if this is the reason for the failure to surrender.

The guidelines state that the fact that a defendant has a 'disorganised or chaotic lifestyle', possibly due to a dependency on drink or drugs, will not reduce the seriousness of the offence. This description may apply to many defendants, of course. However, it may be seen as personal mitigation.

The SGC say that it is a key principle that a Bail Act offender should be dealt with as soon as is practicable. A decision on whether a Bail Act offence has been committed is important when deciding whether to grant bail again and, if so, on what conditions. Once the D's guilt is determined, the sentence is to be imposed as soon as is practicable. As the guidelines make clear, a crucial factor in determining the appropriate sentence is whether proceedings for the original offence are being adjourned and, if so, whether the remand is on bail or in custody. In the latter situation, there is little possibility of a non-custodial sentence for the BA offence. Where the D is released on bail, however, the court may wish to consider a community order, possibly with an electronically monitored curfew requirement and a supervision requirement. In more serious situations which cross the custody threshold, a suspended sentence order may have the same impact.

The SGC guidelines indicate that for a first-time offender who pleads not guilty, the worst cases could fall into the range of community order (medium) to 40 weeks' custody in the Crown Court or community order (low) to 10 weeks' custody in the magistrates' court. Where a defendant surrenders late but on the correct day and the proceedings can go ahead as planned, a fine is appropriate; however, the guidelines note that magistrates' courts retain the power to impose a penalty of one day's detention where appropriate (see MCA 1980, s 135).

One of the less obvious possible penalties for absconding is when the court decides to try the defendant for the original offence, in his absence. This can happen in the magistrates' court (see MCA 1980, s 11 and **5.1.1** below) but it can also happen in the Crown Court once the defendant has been arraigned on the indictment (for guidance on when to proceed in the absence of the defendant, see the speech of Lord Bingham in *R v Jones* [2003] AC 1). Whilst any such trial must be fair, the SGC guidelines note the 'encouragement' given to such action in the *Consolidated Criminal Practice Direction* and reflect that taking this action may reduce the harm occasioned by the absence, although not the culpability of the defendant.

3.9.6 Forfeiture of a surety

If a defendant was granted bail subject to providing a surety, then a failure by the defendant to surrender to custody puts the surety in jeopardy of losing the sum which he or she guaranteed by his or her oath to the court.

In the past, forfeiture was likely to occur, usually for the whole sum. The test was that the whole sum would fall to be paid, unless it was fair and just to forfeit a lesser amount or nothing at all. Forfeiture provisions were tightened by the CDA 1998, s 55. When a defendant fails to surrender, the court is required to declare any surety to be forfeit *automatically*. It shall then require the surety (if present in court) to explain why he or she should not have to pay the whole sum. The court retains its discretion to demand payment of a lesser sum. If the surety is absent from court, or the court allows him or her time to produce evidence of his or her lack of culpability, it will issue a summons requiring his or her appearance at a later date.

There is a heavy onus on the surety to prove why he or she should not forfeit the full amount. This should be done either by showing a lack of means to meet the forfeiture or by establishing that he or she acted responsibly. The surety has a duty to maintain contact with the defendant and to keep informed as to the conditions of bail in order to ensure the defendant's surrender to custody. It has recently been pointed out by the Court of Appeal that any reduction in the amount ordered to be forfeited, following a

Bail 83

Any reduction in the amount ordered to be forfeited....

defendant absconding, 'must be the exception not the rule and be granted only in really deserving cases'. Hoffmann LJ observed that 'in one sense the system has unfairness built into it. It may result in persons entirely innocent having to suffer on account of the wrongdoing of another.' Lack of culpability by a surety is a factor to consider but in *R v Maidstone Crown Court, ex p Lever* [1995] 1 WLR 928, two sureties who were found to be blameless for the absconding nevertheless were ordered to forfeit 85% of their total surety of £59,000.

If surety cannot pay amount due then a lesser sum should be ordered.

If the initial enquiry into the surety's means was conducted properly (see **3.7.3**), the surety should have no problem finding the money to pay the forfeit. However, where the enquiry was inadequate, or the surety's means have changed, the sum which the surety is ordered to forfeit should be such as is within his or her actual means. So, in a case where a surety of £25,000 was forfeited but the surety had originally provided an extremely exaggerated account of his assets, the magistrates' court ordered him to pay the forfeit at £12 per fortnight. The matter was then considered by the Divisional Court who observed that it would be correct in any normal case for the court to think of a sum which the surety could be reasonably expected to pay in full within two or three years (not 80 years as here). The matter was remitted to the magistrates for a rehearing. See *R v Bristol Magistrates' Court, ex p Davies* [1999] Crim LR 504.

Usually, the obligation of a surety will end when the defendant is arraigned on the charges as this is when trial normally commences. At this moment, the defendant is understood to have surrendered to the custody of the court and the surety has done all that the court required. This is subject to exceptions, though, and a surety should remain well-informed as to the exact status of the defendant and the view of the court as to whether the surety's obligation is at an end or continues. The penalty for being ill-informed is seen in *R v Central Criminal Court, ex p Guney* [1994] 1 WLR 438, where a surety for Asil Nadir was ordered to forfeit £650,000 following Mr Nadir's departure to Northern Cyprus. It could have been worse, as originally he stood surety for £1 million; in fact, it got even better for Mr Guney, as the Court of Appeal later quashed the forfeiture completely (see [1995] 1 WLR 376 and [1996] AC 616).

See also MCA 1980, s 120; *Archbold*, 2008 edn, para 3–143/145; *Blackstone's Criminal Practice*, 2009 edn, para D7.88-91.

3.10 Renewing an application for bail (or 'If at first you don't succeed, try again—but only once!')

3.10.1 Obligation to consider bail

See the BA 1976, Sch 1, Pt IIA:

1. If the court decides not to grant the defendant bail, it is the court's duty to consider, at each subsequent hearing while the defendant is a person to whom s 4 above applies and remains in custody, whether he ought to be granted bail.

2. At the first hearing after that at which the court decided not to grant the defendant bail, he may support an application for bail with any argument as to fact or law that he desires (whether or not advanced previously).

3. At subsequent hearings the court need not hear arguments as to fact or law which it has heard previously.

According to the BA 1976, Sch 1, Pt IIA (inserted by the CJA 1988, s 154), at every hearing of a case (when the defendant is in custody) the magistrates' court is obliged to consider whether he or she should be released on bail. The defence is allowed to make up to two applications for bail at which the same arguments may be used. If the accused is still in custody after this, the court may consider the matter of bail no longer open to argument from the defence.

Although the court is under a duty (CJA 1988, s 154) to consider bail at subsequent hearings in the case, these will be formalities. The defence may only reopen the issue of bail by raising fresh circumstances or arguments. Section 154 represents the statutory embodiment of a common law rule which was first reported in *R v Nottingham Justices, ex p Davies* [1981] QB 38.

Several cases have considered what constitutes a 'change in circumstances'. It seems to be a question of fact in each case, although the Queen's Bench Divisional Court has stated that the change need not be major. *R v Blyth Juvenile Court, ex p G* [1991] Crim LR 693 offers an illustration. Where there has been no application for bail by a defendant on the first appearance of a case at court and he or she has been remanded in custody, it seems that he or she has a right to apply for bail at a later hearing of the case (see *R v Dover and East Kent Justices, ex p Dean* [1992] Crim LR 33).

It seems possible that, with the advent of the HRA 1998 and the need to comply with decisions already made under the ECHR, a slight amendment to English law may be needed. It has usually been the position in English case law that simple effluxion of time does not give rise to a change in circumstances. However, in *Neumeister v Austria (No 1)* (1979–80) 1 EHRR 91, the European Court declared that a person should be released at the point when it is no longer reasonable to continue his or her detention. So, as time passes, the prisoner who is held in custody on remand should be able to seek review by the court of the decision to detain. This is clearly relevant to a prisoner held on remand under lengthy custody time limits. According to the European Court of Human Rights:

> . . . the nature of detention on remand calls for short intervals [between bail reviews]; there is an assumption in the Convention that detention on remand is to be of strictly limited duration . . . because its raison d'être is essentially related to the requirements of an investigation which is to be conducted with expedition. In the present case an interval of one month is not unreasonable.

See *Bezicheri v Italy* (1989) 12 EHRR 210.

The matter was considered by the Law Commission of England and Wales (in its Consultation Paper No 157, 1999). The Law Commission felt that it was adequate that bail should be reconsidered by magistrates at least every 28 days (see **3.17.2**) but was concerned that the possibility of a renewed application for bail might be denied by operation of Sch 1, Pt IIA. It pointed out that para 3 only says the court '*need not* hear arguments as to fact or law which it has heard previously' and thus has a discretion to hear such arguments. However, in practice courts seem to be reluctant to do so and also rarely accept that there has been a change in circumstances. The Law Commission noted reports asserting that if the accused found a job, sureties or a fixed address, these were seldom sufficient to show a change in circumstances. The Law Commission suggests that Sch 1, Pt IIA, can be interpreted and applied consistently with the ECHR, Article 5(4), but that guidance should be given to courts to the effect that 'the lapse of 28 days since the last fully-argued bail application should itself be treated as an argument which the court has not previously heard'. In its final Report on the subject (No 269, 2001), the Law Commission modified its position slightly. It maintained that a review of bail at least every 28 days complies with Article 5(4), but felt that courts should only have to consider whether the lapse of time has resulted in a change of circumstances. A defendant should not be able to insist on a full re-hearing of bail arguments every 28 days even though there had been no material change in the circumstances. See paras 12.9–12.24 of the Report.

3.10.2 The magistrates' certificate

Under the BA 1976, s 5(6A), if magistrates withhold bail after hearing a fully argued application for bail, they must issue a certificate stating that they heard full argument. After two unsuccessful bail applications in a case, if the magistrates allow the defendant a third application (which is unsuccessful), they should issue a certificate indicating the change in circumstances or new consideration that persuaded them to hear that third application. See BA 1976, s 5(6A) and (6B); also BA 1976, Sch 1, Pt IIA (inserted by the CJA 1988, s 154).

3.11 Appealing against a bail decision

3.11.1 Appeals to a Crown Court judge by a defendant

A defendant can apply to the Crown Court for bail, as provided for in the Supreme Court Act 1981, s 81 (as amended), in particular:

- where a magistrates' court has committed the defendant to the Crown Court in custody on an offence triable either way (either for trial or sentence); or
- where a magistrates' court has sent the defendant to the Crown Court for trial on an indictment-only offence (under the CDA 1998, s 51); or
- where the defendant has been convicted by a magistrates' court, given a custodial sentence, and been refused bail pending an appeal to the Crown Court (against either conviction or sentence); or
- where a case is proceeding in a magistrates' court, the magistrates have heard a fully argued application for bail and refused it.

In this last instance, the defendant can appeal against the refusal to release on bail by producing a certificate issued under the BA 1976, s 5(6A) (see **3.2.3** and **3.10.2**). This appeal will be heard at the nearest location of the Crown Court dealing with Class 4 (low-grade) crimes. The appeal will usually be heard by a judge sitting 'in chambers'. This means that counsel need not wear a wig or gown, even though the hearing often takes place in a courtroom. This is not the same as a hearing in open court. If a defendant wishes to have the hearing in open court with the public able to attend, then that should happen unless the judge finds that the interests of justice require the application to be heard 'in chambers': see *R (Malik) v Central; Criminal Court* [2007] 1 WLR 2455. The defendant will not usually be present at the hearing, although the Crown Court has the power to permit this.

The SCA 1981, s 81 only deals with defendants who are in custody. The CJA 2003, s 16 makes provision for defendants who wish to appeal against the conditions subject to which they have been released. The CJA 2003, s 16 only allows appeals against certain conditions:

- residence (either at a specified address, other than a bail hostel, or *not* at a specified address or area);
- any surety;

- provision of a security;
- curfew;
- electronic tagging;
- not to contact a specific person.

Furthermore, there must already have been a hearing at which the magistrates were asked to vary the bail conditions (see **3.8** above).

3.11.2 Appeal to the High Court by a defendant

The powers of the High Court in respect of bail were significantly amended by the CJA 2003, s 17. Hitherto, a defendant who was refused bail in the magistrates' court could appeal that refusal by going to a High Court judge in chambers (in addition to the possibility of an appeal to a Crown Court judge). That route has now gone. The High Court can only hear bail appeals:

- where a magistrates' court has stated a case for the opinion of the High Court (under the MCA 1980, s 111) and has refused bail; or
- where a defendant seeks judicial review of his conviction or sentence imposed in the magistrates' court and wants to be released on bail; or
- where a Crown Court judge has refused bail to a defendant in the course of proceedings there.

Therefore, a defendant who has been refused bail by magistrates should usually appeal to the Crown Court and no alternative or further appeal to the High Court is possible except as indicated above. A defendant who is denied bail during Crown Court proceedings will find it tough to appeal that refusal. A refusal of bail, at least at an early stage of proceedings, does not 'relate to a trial on indictment' and thus the High Court will have a supervisory role (cf. Supreme Court Act 1981, s 29 and **8.3**). Historically, however, the High Court withheld the chance of judicial review over such refusals because of the alternative appeal route of going to a High Court judge in chambers (see, for example, *R v Croydon Crown Court, ex parte Cox* [1997] 1 Cr App R 20). Now that this route has gone (courtesy of the CJA 2003, s 17), it seems that the option of judicial review has become available. This change was recognised in *M v Isleworth Crown Court* [2005] EWHC 363, although Maurice Kay LJ observed there that this is a jurisdiction that should be exercised 'very sparingly indeed. It would be ironic and retrograde if, having abolished a relatively short and simple remedy on the basis that it amounted to wasteful duplication, Parliament has, by a side wind, created a more protracted and expensive remedy of common application.' During 2005, there were at least ten such applications, some of which succeeded. The test is one of *Wednesbury* unreasonableness.

3.11.3 Appeals by the Crown Prosecution Service

3.11.3.1 Appeal to the Crown Court

Under the Bail (Amendment) Act 1993, as amended by the CJA 2003, s 18, with effect from 4 April 2005, the prosecution has a general right to appeal when a defendant—charged with (or convicted of) any imprisonable offence—is released on bail. This replaces a previous, more limited, right to appeal.

If such a person was granted bail despite objections from the prosecution, and the prosecution is being conducted by the Crown Prosecution Service, an appeal may be made. If the CPS decides to appeal, it must say so (give oral notice of appeal) *before* the defendant is released from custody. Written notice of appeal must follow, within two hours, and must be served on the court and the defendant. Non-compliance with this two-hour period *may* be fatal to the appeal. That was the decision in *R v Middlesex Crown Court, ex parte Okoli* [2000] Crim LR 921 but it has since been held that as long as the prosecutor uses due diligence in service, a few minutes' lateness in serving the defendant may be excused (see *R (on the application of Jeffrey) v Warwick Crown Court* [2002] EWHC 2469).

The appeal must be heard within 48 hours (excluding weekends and bank holidays). The defendant will be kept in custody until the appeal is determined. If the appeal succeeds, the Crown Court judge may remand the defendant in custody or release him or her on bail with conditions.

3.11.3.2 Reconsideration by the magistrates' court

The prosecution now has a limited ability to ask for 'reconsideration' of a decision to release a defendant on bail. The BA 1976, s 5B, enables a prosecutor to apply to a magistrates' court to reconsider such a decision, whether it was originally taken by the court or by a custody officer. Having reconsidered, the magistrates may attach conditions to unconditional bail, vary the current conditions, or withhold bail (BA 1976, s 5B(1)) or, presumably, preserve the status quo. Reconsiderations may only be sought where the defendant is on bail for an offence which must or may be tried on indictment; the application must be based upon information which was not available to the magistrates (or custody officer) when the original decision was taken.

3.12 Representation for bail applications

On the initial appearance before a magistrates' court, a defendant is likely to be represented by a solicitor, under the duty solicitor scheme. If the case is not concluded on that first appearance, the defendant may need further legal representation. State-funded representation can be provided under provisions in the Access to Justice Act 1999.

An application for a representation order may be made to the court, either orally or on the prescribed application form. When the defendant is granted a right to representation in criminal proceedings, that right covers representation for the purposes of any related bail proceedings. The court must determine whether a right to representation should be granted, according to the interests of justice. Various factors may be relevant but, so far as bail is concerned, one would look in particular at 'whether the individual would, if any matter arising in the proceedings is decided against him, be likely to lose his liberty or livelihood . . .'.

It appears that the decision to grant a right of representation is simply one for the magistrates' judgement. However, under the Access to Justice Act 1999 circumstances may be prescribed where a right to representation shall always be granted. Under the Legal Aid Act 1988, there were several such circumstances. One was where the defendant had previously been remanded in custody by the court; was not legally represented then; was in danger of being remanded in custody again (or committed to Crown Court for trial in custody); and wished to be legally represented (Legal Aid Act 1988, s 21(3)(c)). Secondary legislation under the 1999 Act was thought likely to provide for representation in this situation, but has not yet done so.

As the right to representation includes representation at 'any preliminary or incidental proceedings', it should cover representation at a bail application in the Crown Court, after a case has been committed there by magistrates for trial or sentence; also, when the defendant is appealing against conviction or sentence, or after the magistrates have issued a certificate of full argument. See further the Access to Justice Act 1999, ss 12 to 15 and Sch 3; the Criminal Defence Service (General) (No 2) Regulations 2001; and the Criminal Defence Service (Representation Order Appeals) Regulations 2001.

3.13 Juvenile bail

Present government policy is that juveniles should spend as little time as possible awaiting final disposal of their cases. Overall time limits for specified stages of preliminary proceedings are being introduced for all cases but they will be 'tougher' for juvenile cases, and even more strict in cases involving persistent young offenders (see Prosecution of Offences Act 1985, ss 22 and 22A).

While awaiting disposal of their cases, most juveniles will be on bail. There is concern that, in this period, juveniles may commit further offences. Steps are being taken to discourage such re-offending or 'spree' activity. In particular, the government is encouraging the involvement of the voluntary sector in bail support schemes, eg the 'Youth Bail Support Scheme' in Manchester, run by Manchester Children's Society. Youngsters on the Manchester scheme have an individual programme of activities; this is designed to create constructive leisure time, to institute weekly meetings with volunteers, and to provide accompaniment on court appearances. The scheme can also provide support in tackling difficulties at home, at school or in the workplace.

Fast-track procedures have been introduced nationally to cope with persistent young offenders. By this, the Home Office means young offenders who have been dealt with by a court on three or more occasions and who re-offend within three years of their previous court appearance (see eg Home Office Research Findings, No 74, 1998). A variety of reasons exist for the fast-track procedures which were devised by different courts around the country but the government has set a target that all courts should aim to complete at least 50 per cent of their persistent young offender cases within 71 days. Fast-track procedures may also be used for other categories of offender, such as those engaged on 'spree' offending. The procedures work by, for example, being tough on adjournments. There will be resistance to granting an adjournment and the first hearing at court should deal with substantive business. Pre-sentence reports may be required within 15 working days; courts may keep copies of these reports and simply have them updated orally if necessary. In addition to these steps, the government has set guidelines for the length of time which each stage in the youth court should take, in a case involving a persistent young offender. So, no more than two days from arrest to charge; seven days from charge to first appearance in court; no more than 28 days from first appearance in a youth court to commencement of a trial there; and no more than 14 days thereafter to reach the stage of verdict and sentence.

The provisions of the BA 1976 apply to juveniles in basically the same manner as they do to adult defendants. That is, juveniles may be remanded on bail or in custody when proceedings in court are adjourned. If a young person is not released on bail, he or she may be remanded to local authority accommodation. Such accommodation is not necessarily secure, however.

The government has enabled courts to remand juveniles direct to secure local authority accommodation. See the CDA 1998, ss 97–98, although these provisions will be amended when relevant provisions in the Criminal Justice and Court Services Act 2000 come into force. These provisions apply to all children aged 12–14 and girls aged 15 or 16. Boys aged 15 or 16 will continue to be remanded to Prison Service accommodation (either a remand centre or a prison) unless they are considered to be 'vulnerable'. A youth is vulnerable if the court forms the opinion that a remand to Prison Service accommodation would be undesirable due to his 'physical or emotional immaturity or a propensity of his to harm himself' (see the Children and Young Persons Act 1969, s 23(5A)).

3.14 Remands

Put in very simple terms, a remand is the name for the decision taken whenever criminal proceedings are left unconcluded and the court has to take a decision whether to release the defendant on bail or remand in custody until the next hearing in those proceedings. The case itself is adjourned. That adjournment may be to an open date (or date to be fixed), or it may be to a specific date. Thus, the parties to the proceedings may know when they are due back in court when they leave the courtroom today or they may need to wait for notification from the court of the next hearing date. Any time that a case has to be put off to another court session (either on the same day or a different day), it can be said to be adjourned. It is only in certain circumstances that the court will need to take a decision about remanding the defendant at the same time. See **3.15** below.

The main Acts of Parliament referred to in this part of the chapter are:

- the Magistrates' Courts Act 1980 (MCA 1980);
- the Bail Act 1976 (BA 1976);
- the Criminal Justice Act 2003 (CJA 2003).

Remands and bail are dealt with in the main practitioner works at *Archbold* (2008 edn), paras 3.2–3.195 and *Blackstone's Criminal Practice* (2009 edn), at D5 and D7.

3.15 When will a case be remanded?

If a criminal case before a court in England and Wales is not disposed of conclusively on one day, it will have to carry over into another day. For an analysis of how many cases are concluded on the first appearance in court, see **Figure 3.2**, Column 5.

Examples of such 'carry over' are:

(a) a trial which is too long to finish in a single day;

(b) a trial which has finished in a single day but the court wants more information on the offender before passing sentence (eg getting a pre-sentence report);

(c) a case which has been listed for a preliminary matter only to be determined (eg which court will try a defendant charged with an offence triable either way);

(d) a case which has been listed for trial but either party (or perhaps the court, if it has insufficient time that day) is unable to proceed with the case there and then;

(e) a case which has finished in one court but is going to another—on appeal or committal.

Note that, with regard to (a) above, a part-heard trial in the Crown Court continues on

England and Wales

Offence type	From offence to completion	From offence to charge or laying of information	From charge or laying of information to first listing	From first listing to completion	Percentage of defendants dealt with on first court appearance	Average number of times case listed in court	Average length of adjournments in days	Guilty[2]	Not guilty[2]	Number of defendants in sample (thousands)
Indictable offences (including triable either way)										
2003	111	47	8	56	30	3.2	26	55	23	33.1
2004	118	54	9	55	30	3.1	26	55	23	28.5
2005	122	59	10	54	31	3.1	26	56	22	28.1
2006[3]	123	61	10	52	30	3.1	25	58	22	27.7
2007[4]	118	61	10	47	32	3.0	23	59	22	28.8
Summary non-motoring offences										
2003	142	88	33	21	72	1.7	29	35	13	18.5
2004	140	82	33	26	69	1.8	30	39	14	17.5
2005	148	90	34	24	70	1.8	31	38	13	18.8
2006[3]	146	85	37	24	71	1.8	31	37	16	19.0
2007[4]	144	83	37	24	70	1.8	28	38	16	18.2
Summary motoring offences										
2003	162	97	39	26	61	1.8	31	52	8	31.1
2004	166	101	39	26	62	1.8	31	54	9	32.1
2005	162	99	39	24	63	1.8	31	56	9	29.5
2006[3]	160	94	41	25	63	1.8	33	57	10	26.7
2007[4]	162	96	41	25	65	1.8	33	57	10	26.4

Source: Time Intervals Surveys for Criminal Proceedings in magistrates' courts—Ministry of Justice
(1) Results based on proceedings in one sample week in March, June, September, and December for indictable offences and March and September only for summary offences.
(2) Defendants entering an initial guilty or not guilty plea, as a proportion of those proceeded against in sample weeks.
(3) In the June 06 survey—North Yorkshire are data were unavailable.
(4) From June 2007, changes were made to the way adult data were collected. As a consequence, any changes in results could be due to the changed data collection process, and care should be taken when interpreting the results.

Figure 3.2 Defendants proceeded against at magistrates' courts—average time for criminal cases by offence type and stage of proceedings, percentage dealt with on first appearance, average number of times case listed and average length of adjournments[1], 2003–2007.

the next day. A part-heard case in the magistrates' court may continue the next day or may resume in several weeks' time (depending upon the availability of the courtroom and of the district judge or justices of the peace who are trying the case).

Whenever magistrates adjourn a case, they may remand the defendant. The MCA 1980 provides several situations where, on an adjournment, a magistrates' court *must* remand a defendant and then consider the alternatives of bail and custody. See **Figure 3.3**, which is based upon the MCA 1980, s 10.

If the defendant is remanded, he or she will either:

- be kept in custody—ie stay locked up until produced by the (police, prison or other) authorities for the next court appearance; or
- be freed on bail. Being released on bail imposes a duty on a defendant to return to court at the appointed date, place and time (often called 'surrendering to custody'). Failure to attend the next hearing is itself a crime (BA 1976, s 6; see also **3.9** above).

---

1. When D first appeared in the court, was he on bail or in custody?
   If YES—he must now be remanded (on bail or in custody).
   If NO—
2. Has D been remanded at any time during the proceedings for this offence?
   If YES—he must now be remanded (on bail or in custody).
   If NO—
3. The magistrates have a choice to remand or simply adjourn the case.

Figure 3.3 Will the adjournment be a remand?

3.15.1 Situations where remand is required

(a) *Magistrates dealing with an offence triable either way.* If, before or during the summary trial of such an offence, an adjournment is needed, then usually the defendant must be remanded on bail or in custody. See **Figure 3.3**.

(b) *Magistrates determining which court will try an 'either way' offence.* If the magistrates adjourn a case while determining whether the defendant will be tried by the magistrates or a jury (MCA 1980, ss 19–23), they must usually remand the defendant on bail or in custody (MCA 1980, s 18(4)). See **Figure 3.3**.

(c) *Magistrates sending a defendant to the Crown Court for trial.* Following a decision to send the defendant to the Crown Court for trial, if the defendant is currently remanded in custody, the magistrates may either order that he or she be kept in custody pending his or her trial or release him or her on bail with a direction that he or she appear before the Crown Court for trial (MCA 1980, s 8(1); CDA 1998, ss 51 and 52).

There are two other situations to be aware of:

(d) *Magistrates dealing with a summary offence.* Prior to deciding whether a defendant is guilty or innocent in such a case, the magistrates may have to adjourn the proceedings. If they do so, they have a choice—either to remand the defendant or simply to adjourn (MCA 1980, s 10(4)). If the defendant fails to appear at court on the next appointed date, the magistrates may proceed to try the case in the absence of the defendant or, in some circumstances, issue a warrant for arrest (MCA 1980, ss 11 and 13). See **Chapter 5**.

(e) *Magistrates deferring sentence.* Where a magistrates' court defers sentence on a convicted defendant (for up to six months) under the PCC(S)A 2000, s 1, this is not a remand, and the defendant, although released subject to a duty to return to court, is not on bail. (See *R v Ross* (1988) 86 Cr App R 337.)

3.15.2 The use of remands and adjournments by magistrates

For an analysis of the use of remands and adjournments by magistrates, see **Figure 3.4**.

3.16 Who can remand a case?

3.16.1 Remands in the magistrates' court

It might seem, from what you have just read, that only magistrates can remand a criminal case. This is not the whole story. The vast majority of remands occur in the magistrates' court simply because that is where the bulk of criminal litigation takes place, particularly when you realise that almost all hearings in a case prior to trial occur in the magistrates' court.

3.16.2 Remands in the Crown Court

The question of a simple adjournment never seems to arise in the Crown Court. A defendant who is committed to the Crown Court (whether for trial or sentence) will be remanded either on bail or in custody. Once there, the Crown Court judge has the power to grant bail for the period before the matter is dealt with (see the Supreme Court Act 1981, s 81, as amended).

Once a Crown Court trial has started, the judge will remand the defendant either in custody or on bail during any lunch or overnight breaks in the trial. Whether or not to release on bail is usually regarded as a matter solely within the power and discretion of the trial judge; see the observation by Peter Gibson LJ in *R v Central Criminal Court, ex p Guney* [1995] 1 WLR 376 that from 'the commencement of a [Crown Court] trial it is for the court conducting the trial to decide whether the defendant should be in custody or on bail'.

3.16.3 Police bail

This chapter concentrates on bail in court, as that is where barristers will usually be involved in bail decisions. We should, however, note that the police may also release people on bail. This will usually follow detention at a police station, under PACE 1984, s 47 (and see **2.2.12**), or away from the police station, using 'street bail' under PACE 1984, s 30A (see further **3.1.4.2** above).

3.17 Duration of remands

3.17.1 General examples

There are various maximum periods for a remand by magistrates in different circumstances.

Bail 93

England and Wales				Thousands of persons and percentages		
	All persons charged or summoned			Total		
Outcome	Not remanded by magistrates	Bailed by magistrates	Remanded in custody by magistrates[2]	2007	2006	2005
	Number of persons (thousands)					
Acquitted or not proceeded etc.	197.5	92.2	7.3	297.0	336.9	388.0
Convicted:						
Discharge	60.1	40.3	2.0	102.5	97.0	103.4
Fine	866.4	70.1	2.5	939.0	959.4	1,022.0
Community sentence[4]	63.3	111.9	6.4	181.6	173.6	181.8
Fully suspended sentence	5.9	17.5	2.1	25.5	23.3	7.8
Immediate custody[5]	18.3	21.2	11.7	51.2	53.4	57.3
Otherwise dealt with[6]	21.1	10.4	1.9	33.4	37.3	34.4
Total number sentenced	1,035.1	271.5	26.6	1,333.2	1,344.0	1,406.7
Committed for sentence:						
on bail	3.0	6.5	0.4	10.0	9.7	9.8
in custody	3.0	0.7	4.1	7.9	9.2	9.6
Committed for trial:						
on bail	18.8	37.1	1.7	57.7	54.9[3]	56.2
in custody	16.1	1.6	9.0	26.7	24.6[3]	24.6
Failed to appear to a summons[7]	71.4	-	-	71.4	79.3	95.9
Failed to appear to bail[8]	-	56.9	2.7	59.6	64.2	69.0
Total	1,345.0	466.7	51.9	1,863.5	1922.8	2,059.9
Of these						
Prosecutions						
for failing to surrender to bail[9]	*	*	*	138.2	141.7	156.9
	Percentage of persons					
Acquitted or not proceeded etc.	15	20	14	16	18	19
Convicted:						
Discharge	4	9	4	6	5	5
Fine	64	15	5	50	50	50
Community sentence[4]	5	24	12	10	9	9
Fully suspended sentence	0	4	4	1	1	0
Immediate custody[5]	1	5	23	3	3	3
Otherwise dealt with[6]	2	2	4	2	2	2
Total percentage sentenced	77	58	51	72	70	68
Committed for sentence:						
on bail	0	1	1	1	1	0
in custody	0	0	8	0	0	0
Committed for trial:						
on bail	1	8	3	3	3	3
in custody	1	0	17	1	1	1
Failed to appear to a summons[7]	5	0	0	4	4	5
Failed to appear to bail[8]	0	12	5	3	3	3
Total	100	100	100	100	100	100

(1) Includes estimates for those offences omitted from data supplied (see paragraph 8, Appendix 2).
(2) Includes those remanded for part of the time in custody and part on bail.
(3) Differ from figures in Table 4.8 which shows cases completed at the Crown Court in 2007.
(4) Includes community rehabilitation orders, supervision orders, community punishment orders, attendance centre orders, community punishment and rehabilitation orders, curfew orders, reparation orders, action plan orders and detention and training orders.
(5) Includes detention and training orders and unsuspended imprisonment.
(6) Includes one day in police cells, disqualification order, restraining order, confiscation order, travel restriction order, disqualification from driving, ASBO and recommendation for deportation and other disposals.
(7) May include some cases initiated by a summons but where the defendant was subsequently remanded on bail.
(8) It is not known whether the persons prosecuted were remanded partly in custody as well as on bail.
(9) Prosecutions arise from failure to surrender to bail at both magistrates' and Crown Courts; they may not be completed in the same year in which the bail was breached. Figures shown are for all occurrences of this offence and include both principal and non-principal offences.

Figure 3.4 Persons proceeded against at magistrates' courts by type of court remand and outcome of proceedings[1], 2007.

Before conviction
  (a) Three clear days in police custody (MCA 1980, s 128(7)).
  (b) Eight clear days in prison custody (MCA 1980, s 128(6)). (Exception: if an 'either way' offence is to be tried by the magistrates but they cannot convene in time, remand to whenever they can convene the court.)
  (c) Twenty-eight clear days in prison custody if the defendant is in court, and has previously been remanded in custody for this offence. (See **3.17.2** below.)
  (d) Twenty-eight clear days in prison custody if the defendant has at least that long still to serve on a current custodial sentence (MCA 1980, s 131(1)).
  (e) Any period to which both the prosecution and defence agree on bail (MCA 1980, s 128(6)).

After conviction
  (f) Three weeks in custody for inquiries or reports for sentencing.
  (g) Four weeks on bail for inquiries, etc.

Each of these periods is the maximum duration for a *single* remand. At its conclusion, the defendant will be produced before the magistrates once more. At that time, and subject to the custody time limits (see **3.1.6** above), the magistrates may again remand him or her either on bail or in custody for a further period. Once a defendant is sent to the Crown Court, either for trial or sentence to be passed, he or she is remanded on bail or in custody until such time as the case is listed for hearing (again, subject to the custody time limits).

3.17.2 Avoiding weekly remands

A very large number of prisoners is held on remand in custody at any time in England and Wales. Typically, the prisoner has been remanded in custody by a court, prior to his or her trial, and is therefore usually subject to eight-day remands (see **3.17.1(b)** above). The need to produce all of these prisoners at court, every week, would impose a tremendous burden on the Prison Service and its subcontractors, in terms of both administration and logistical arrangements. This effort would in large measure be wasted if the only reason for the court appearance was that eight days had passed. In order to minimise wasted costs, magistrates' courts have the power either to remand prisoners in their absence or to extend the remand period beyond the eight-day norm.

A magistrates' court can remand a defendant in custody, in his or her absence, on up to three occasions. To do so, the defendant must have legal representation and have consented to this procedure. (See the MCA 1980, s 128(3A).) This can effectively extend the remand period up to four weeks, although the case is still listed every eight days and the defendant is formerly remanded in his or her absence.

An alternative procedure is simply to remand the defendant for up to 28 clear days. Magistrates' courts are able to do this if:

  (a) the accused has been remanded in custody already in the case; and
  (b) the accused is present in court when the extended remand is ordered; and
  (c) the court has fixed a date when the next stage in the proceedings will take place.

The power to do so derives from the MCA 1980, s 128A. Clearly, it is more straightforward than the alternative under the MCA 1980, s 128(3A) and is the usual method of remanding a prisoner in custody for periods exceeding eight days.

In addition to the above powers, there may also be the opportunity to conduct proceedings via a live television link between the magistrates' court and the prison where a defendant is being held. This power derives from the Crime and Disorder Act 1998, s 57, which provides that a court may treat the defendant as being present for pre-trial hearings where he or she is in custody but is able to see and hear the court (and be seen and heard by the court) via a live television link or other means. This procedure has been piloted in certain magistrates' courts and will be applied nationally to both magistrates' and Crown Courts in due course. See *Blackstone's Criminal Practice* (2008 edn), para D5.23.

3.17.3 Remands in the Crown Court

Neither s 128 nor s 128A MCA 1980 apply to the Crown Court. However, where the Crown Court hears an appeal against a bail decision made by magistrates, any consequent remand in custody ought to be made in a manner consistent with those provisions. Thus, a defendant ought not to be remanded in custody to re-appear in the magistrates' court more than eight days later unless the requirements of s 128A are satisfied. See *Remice v Governor of Belmarsh Prison* [2007] Crim LR 796.

3.18 What are the alternatives to remanding a case?

Alternatives to remanding a case have been mentioned already but, in brief, the court may:

(a) *Try the case anyway.* If a case is ready for summary trial and the defendant does not appear, the magistrates may go ahead and try the case in his or her absence, having entered a formal plea of not guilty. (See **5.1.1** below and the MCA 1980, s 11(1).) This power to try absent defendants does not exist in the Crown Court—the accused must be present at the start of a jury trial to enter a plea to the indictment personally. However, once the plea has been entered, typically at a plea and case management hearing, if the accused chooses to absent himself from subsequent proceedings, the court *may* try him in his absence. See the guidance on this subject given by Lord Bingham in *R v Jones* [2003] AC 1. The power to hold a summary trial in the absence of the accused is used sparingly. One reason for reluctance is the 'statutory declaration' (see MCA 1980, s 14). This refers to the ability of a person convicted in his or her absence to declare that he or she did not know of the proceedings or summons which resulted in his or her conviction. Once the declaration is made, and served on the clerk to the justices, then the summons and all subsequent proceedings (such as a summary trial and guilty verdict) are void (see the MCA 1980, s 14(1)(b)). There may also be concerns about ensuring the defendant has a fair trial; see further the Human Rights Act 1998, Sch 1, Art 6.

(b) *Adjourn to another date.* A case may be simply adjourned to another date and the prosecution and accused told to be at court on that date. No penal sanction exists in this situation to compel attendance at the adjourned hearing. The defence may seek an adjournment in order, for example, to instruct an expert witness to appear as a witness for the defendant. (See *R v Sunderland Justices, ex p Dryden, The Times*, 18 May 1994.)

(c) *Adjourn indefinitely and issue a warrant for arrest.* If the defendant does not appear at court, the outcome will often be the issue of a warrant for his or her arrest (sometimes called a 'bench' warrant) (see the MCA 1980, s 13). When the defendant is arrested on a bench warrant, he or she will usually stay in custody until a court hearing can be arranged. Sometimes, if the magistrates suspect there might be a reasonable excuse for the defendant's non-attendance, they can issue the warrant *and* release the defendant on bail without requiring a court hearing upon arrest. The effect of this combination is that the defendant will be arrested and taken to a police station (this constitutes execution of the warrant); at the police station, he or she is then released on bail to attend the magistrates' court at a later date. Such a warrant is usually described as being 'backed for bail'. Crown Court judges can also issue such warrants if a defendant is absent from court without permission. (See also **2.4** and **3.9** above.) The warrant may be issued once the court is satisfied that the information against the accused has been supported on oath, that the accused is aware of the hearing and the offence is imprisonable. Warrants may be issued for non-imprisonable offences if the first two criteria are satisfied *and* the court proposes to impose a disqualification on the defendant.

(d) *Dismiss the case.* If the prosecution is not ready to proceed with a summary trial, it is possible that the magistrates will dismiss the charge if there has been a long delay between the commission of the alleged offence and the court hearing. See, for example, *R v Oxford City Justices, ex p Smith* (1982) 75 Cr App R 200; cf *R v Barnet Magistrates' Court, ex p DPP* (1994) 158 JP 1060. See also **2.3.1** above.

Allocation

4.1 Classification of offences

All offences fall into one of the following categories:

- **summary offences**, ie those which must be tried in the magistrates' court;
- **offences triable only on indictment**, ie those which must be tried in the Crown Court;
- **offences which are triable either way**, ie those which may be tried in either the magistrates' court or the Crown Court.

"Indictable offence"

Note that the term 'indictable offence' means an offence which 'is triable on indictment, whether it is exclusively so triable or triable either way' (Interpretation Act 1978, s 1(a)).

4.1.1 Summary offences

Summary trial, ie trial by magistrates, is a creature of statute, and all summary offences, similarly, are created by statute. The statute usually does this by providing a maximum penalty for summary conviction, with no alternative penalty for conviction on indictment. A huge number of offences are summary. See **Figure 4.1** for examples.

4.1.2 Offences triable only on indictment

All common law offences are triable only on indictment, ie by a judge and jury in the Crown Court, such as murder and manslaughter. Other offences in this category are created by statute which provides for a maximum penalty for conviction on indictment, with no alternative penalty on summary conviction. See **Figure 4.1** for examples.

4.1.3 Offences which are triable either way

Offences which are triable either way are technically indictable but may be tried in the magistrates' court if both the magistrates and the defendant agree. See **4.2** for details. Offences are shown to be triable either way by either:

- the statute which created them providing for alternative penalties on summary conviction or conviction on indictment; or
- re-classification by statute, in particular the Magistrates' Courts Act 1980 (MCA), s 17, which downgrades to triable either way many offences which were formerly triable only on indictment: see the list in Sch 1 to the Act.

Type of offence	Triable only on indictment	Triable-either-way	Triable only summarily
1. Offences against the person	Murder Manslaughter Attempt to procure an abortion Causing grievous bodily harm with intent under s 18 OAPA 1861	Inflicting grievous bodily harm under s 20 OAPA 1861 Unlawful wounding Assault occasioning actual bodily harm Assault with intent to resist arrest	Common assault Assault on a police constable in the execution of his duty
2. Sexual offences	Rape Buggery Incest	Indecent assault Living on the earnings of a prostitute	Soliciting
3. Theft Act offences	Robbery Aggravated burglary Blackmail Assault with intent to rob Burglary comprising commission of, or intention to commit, an offence only triable on indictment Burglary of a dwelling with threats to occupants	All Theft Act offences not being in the other two categories	Taking a motor vehicle without consent Taking a pedal cycle without consent
4. Criminal damage	Damage or arson with intent to endanger life	Damage where the value involved is over £5,000	Damage where the value involved is £5,000 or less
5. Road traffic	Causing death by dangerous driving	Dangerous driving	Most other traffic offences, eg: Speeding Failing to report an accident Driving while disqualified Driving without insurance Drunk in charge of a motor Vehicle Failing to stop at a red traffic light Aggravated TWOC where only damage is caused and of value less than £5,000
6. Miscellaneous	Perjury Attempt to pervert the course of justice Possessing a firearm with intent to endanger life Using a firearm to resist arrest Carrying a firearm to commit an indictable offence Collecting, communicating etc information intended to be useful to an enemy Riot	Making false statements on oath not being in judicial proceedings Carrying a loaded firearm in a public place Shortening a shotgun Having an offensive weapon in a public place Using, communicating, etc information entrusted in confidence to a person holding office under the Crown	Interference with vehicles Being drunk and disorderly Obstructing police Using threatening words or behaviour Dropping litter Failure to pay TV licence All offences under the Factories Act 1961

Type of offence	Triable only on indictment	Triable-either-way	Triable only summarily
		Violent disorder	
		Affray	
		Stirring up racial hatred	
		All offences under the Forgery and Counterfeiting Act 1981	
		Offences under the Misuse of Drugs Act 1971	

Figure 4.1 Classification of offences.

4.2 Procedure for determining allocation

Where the offence is triable either way, and may be tried in *either* the magistrates' court or the Crown Court, it must first be determined which court should try the case.

The procedure is governed by the MCA 1980, as amended by the Criminal Procedure and Investigations Act 1996 (CPIA) and further amended by the Criminal Justice Act 2003. The amendments were intended to reduce the workload of the Crown Court, by ensuring that cases in which the defendant intends to plead guilty are dealt with summarily unless the case is serious. To achieve this, the defendant is asked, before a mode of trial decision is made, to indicate his or her plea. Students should also refer to the Criminal Procedure Rules Part 21.

The National Allocation Guidelines set out the objectives as:

(a) to ensure that (subject to exceptions) the court that determines guilt also imposes sentence, and

(b) where the determination is that trial on indictment is appropriate the case reaches the Crown Court as soon as possible.

4.2.1 Absence of the defendant

The MCA 1980, s 18(2) provides that the defendant must be present during the proceedings in which he or she is asked to indicate his or her plea. There are three exceptions to this:

(a) Section 17B provides for the proceedings to continue in the defendant's absence due to his or her unruly behaviour. In order for the proceedings to continue in the defendant's absence, the following conditions must be satisfied:

  (i) the defendant is legally represented; and

  (ii) the court considers that by reason of the defendant's disorderly conduct before the court it is not practicable for proceedings under s 17A above to be conducted in his or her presence; and

  (iii) the court considers that it should proceed in the absence of the defendant.

In these circumstances, the procedure contained in s 17A and described in **4.2.2** is followed, except that all the indications as to plea are provided by the defendant's legal representative on the defendant's behalf, rather than by the defendant.

(b) Where the defendant is legally represented and consents to the case continuing in his or her absence (such consent being indicated by the representative), and the court is satisfied that there is a good reason (such as illness) for that absence (MCA 1980, ss 23(1)(a) and (b)).

(c) The defendant is in custody and the court has decided to use a live TV link, having been satisfied that appropriate facilities exist (Crime and Disorder Act 1998, s 57).

4.2.2 The standard procedure

The MCA 1980, s 17 as amended applies where a defendant who has attained the age of 18 is charged with a triable either way offence whether or not he or she is legally represented. The defendant must be present in court for this stage of the proceedings, unless one of the exceptions set out in **4.2.1** applies.

The procedure may be presided over by a lay justice sitting alone under the MCA 1980, s 17E, though it is more usual to have two or more lay magistrates.

The procedure is in two stages. The first stage is to ascertain the defence's likely plea, if the matter were to proceed to trial. This is known as plea before venue. If the defendant then pleads guilty the court can move into the sentencing procedure. If the defendant indicates a not guilty plea, the court will then move to the second stage, known as allocation, to determine the court of trial.

The standard procedure is as follows:

Plea before venue

(a) The charge is written down, if it has not already been written down, and read to the defendant.

(b) The court explains to the defendant in ordinary language that he or she may indicate whether he or she would plead guilty should the case proceed to trial. The court should further explain to the defendant that if he or she indicates a plea of guilty, the court will:

   (i) proceed as if the proceedings had constituted a summary trial from the outset;

   (ii) proceed as if the defendant had in fact pleaded guilty to the charge;

   (iii) warn the defendant of the possibility of committal for sentence under the Powers of Criminal Court (Sentencing) Act 2000, s 3 or s 3A.

(c) The court then asks the defendant whether, if the case were to proceed to trial, he or she would plead guilty or not guilty.

There is no set form of words to follow and some courts have developed their own. A suggested form of words to be used by the court has been devised by the Judicial Studies Board, however, and is as follows:

For this charge you may be tried in either the magistrates' court or by a jury in the Crown Court. First however this court must ask you whether, if the case proceeds to trial, you would plead guilty or not guilty. Before you answer that, I want to explain what will happen then. If you say that you would plead guilty, the court will hear the prosecution case against you, listen to your mitigation, and formally find you guilty. The court will then decide that sentence it thinks you should receive. Do you understand?

(Unless repeated or further explanation is required, say) then if the charge against you was to go to trial, would you plead guilty or not guilty?

A fuller form of wording was set out in an annex to a HO circular 45/1997 as follows:

This offence may be tried either by this court or by the Crown Court before a judge and jury.

Whether or not this court can deal with your case today will depend upon your answers to the questions which I am going to put to you. Do you understand?

You will shortly be asked to tell the court whether you intend to plead guilty or not guilty to (certain of) the offence(s) with which you are charged. Do you understand?

If you tell us that you intend to plead guilty, you will be convicted of the offence. We may then be able to deal with (part of) your case at this hearing. The prosecutor will tell us about the facts of the case, you (your representative) will have the opportunity to respond (on your behalf) and we shall then go on to consider how to sentence you. Do you understand?

We may be able to sentence you today or we may need to adjourn the proceedings until a later date for the preparation of a pre-sentence report by the Probation Service. If we believe that you deserve a greater sentence than we have the power to give you in this court, we may decide to send you to the Crown Court, either on bail or in custody, and you will be sentenced by that court which has greater sentencing powers. Do you understand?

[In cases where s4 of the PCC(S)A 2000 applies:] If you indicate a guilty plea for this/these offence(s), even if we believe that our own sentencing powers are great enough to deal with you here, we may still send you to the Crown Court to be sentenced there for this/these offence(s) because you have also been charged with a related offence(s) [for which you have already been committed for trial in that court] [for which you will be committed for trial in that court]. Do you understand?

If, on the other hand, you tell us that you intend to plead not guilty, or if you do not tell us what you intend to do, we shall go on to consider whether you should be tried by this court or by the Crown Court on some future date. If we decide that it would be appropriate to deal with your case in this court, we shall ask whether you are content for us to do so or whether you wish your case to be tried in the Crown Court.

Before I ask you how you intend to plead, do you understand everything I have said or is there any part of what I have said which you would like me to repeat or explain?

(d) The defendant indicates a plea of guilty, a plea of not guilty or fails to indicate a plea.

  (i) *Indication of a plea of guilty.* This allows the defendant the earliest opportunity to record a plea of guilty, and gain the credit from having done so, and also to ensure that cases which could properly be dealt with in the magistrates' court remain there: *R v Warley Magistrates' Court ex p DPP [1998] 2 Cr App R 307.* It should be noted that this is not the plea itself, but an indication of what the plea would be in the event of a trial. By virtue of MCA 1980, s 17A(6) however, the court proceeds as if the proceedings had constituted a summary trial from the beginning, and treats the indication of plea as if it were, in fact, a plea of guilty. No further pleas are taken. The court proceeds on to the sentencing stage.

  (ii) *Indication of a plea of not guilty.* Where the defendant indicates that he or she will plead not guilty, the court proceeds to determine the allocation as set out in (e)–(l) below.

  (iii) *No indication of plea.* Where the defendant fails to indicate a plea, he or she is taken to have indicated a plea of not guilty (MCA 1980, s 17B(3) as amended).

Allocation

(e) The prosecution has the opportunity to inform the court of the accused's previous convictions, if any. Note that the reference to convictions refers to both convictions in the UK and findings of Court Martials.

(f) The prosecution and defence have the opportunity to make representations as to whether summary trial or trial on indictment would be more suitable.

According to the Sentencing Guidelines Council draft National Allocation Guidelines, guideline 3.8, the assessment of the seriousness of the case for the allocation decision is based on the prosecution case at its highest and, under 3.3, the adequacy of the court's sentencing powers will be based on the assumption that the prosecution version of events is correct.

Guideline 3.8 further provides that the defence representations should normally be directed to identifying inaccuracies in the factual outline of the case, assessing the adequacy of the court's sentencing powers and determining the relevance of an offender's previous convictions.

(g) The court makes the decision as to whether summary trial or trial on indictment is more suitable, taking into account:

   (i) whether the sentence which the magistrates' court would have power to impose for the offence would be adequate; and

   (ii) any representations advanced by the prosecution or the defence; and

   (iii) whether the nature and circumstances of the case make it of serious character having regard to the allocation guidelines issued under the CJA 2003 as definitive guidelines. You are referred to the Sentencing Guidelines Council National Allocation Guidelines 2006 for full details. The principal guidelines and the Mode of Trial Guidelines under the *Consolidated Criminal Practice Direction* are set out in **4.7** for reference. New guidelines are likely, given the intended increase in the magistrates' sentencing powers under the CJA.

   (iv) the defendant's previous convictions (under s 19(2)(a) inserted by the CJA 2003).

(h) if the defendant is charged with more than one offence, such offences being offences that could be tried together, or arise out of the same or connected circumstances, the reference to 'sentence' is to the aggregate sentence which the magistrates' court would have power to impose for all the offences taken together.

Where summary trial appears more suitable

(i) If the court decides that summary trial is more suitable, the court shall explain to the defendant in ordinary language that:

   (i) it appears to the court more suitable for him to be tried summarily; and

   (ii) that he can consent to be so tried or, if he wishes, be tried on indictment; and;

   (iii) that in the case of a specified offence, that if he is tried in the magistrates' court and convicted, he may be committed to the Crown Court for sentence under PCC(S)A 2000, s 3A.

See **5.4** below.

Indication of sentence

(j) The defendant may request an indication of sentence, that is, whether a custodial or non-custodial sentence would be more likely to be imposed if he were to be tried summarily. Such an indication may but need not be given. The statute refers to this as an 'indication' and whether the custodial or non-custodial sentence would be 'more likely'. This is not quite the same as saying that the indicated sentence will inevitably be given, but the section does have that effect. Section 20A of the MCA 1980 says that where a plea has been taken following a sentence indication *'no court may impose a custodial sentence for the offence unless such a sentence was indicated'*. The Sentencing Guidelines Council sets out the key elements of giving a sentence indication in the National Allocation Guidelines:

(i) A court should assess the type of sentence realistically possible in the light of the facts as presented by the prosecution, with the additional element of a guilty plea tendered at this stage in the proceedings, and subject to defence representations as to the accuracy of the factual outline of the case. Wherever possible, the key elements of the basis upon which the indication is given should be recorded in writing.

(ii) A court should proceed with caution where an offender is unrepresented. The offender should be advised of the availability of independent legal advice. The Justices' Clerk [. . .] present in court has a duty to assist the unrepresented party, and this will include drawing to the attention of an unrepresented defendant that there is an entitlement to request an indication of sentence.

(iii) A court should not give an indication of sentence where there are alternative charges unless the prosecution has indicated that an agreement as to acceptable pleas has been established following discussions with the defence, and there is an appropriate factual basis upon which an indication could be given.

(iv) The prosecution must ensure that the court is fully informed of the facts of the case and any relevant background.

(v) The court is entitled to expect that the Justices' Clerk [. . .] present in court, and the prosecution and defence advocates, will ensure that the court considers any relevant guidelines or other authorities affecting sentence.

(vi) The information presented to the court will not include personal mitigation except in so far as it has influenced the facts of the case presented to the court or it is actively agreed by the prosecution advocate.

(vii) Any indication given must be recorded in writing and entered onto the court register.

(k) If an indication of sentence is given, the court must ask the defendant whether he or she wishes, on the basis of the indication, to reconsider the plea given or taken to have been given. If he or she does wish to reconsider, the question shall be put to him again. If he or she indicates that he would plead guilty, the court proceeds as if the proceedings had constituted a summary trial from the beginning, and he had pleaded guilty.

(l) Where the court does not give an indication of sentence (either because it has declined to do so or because it was not asked) and the defendant does not wish to reconsider the indication of plea, and does not indicate that he or she would plead guilty:

 (i) the defendant is asked if he or she consents to be tried summarily, and, if he or she consents, the court proceeds to summary trial; or

 (ii) if he or she does not consent, the court proceeds to send him or her to Crown Court for trial, under the Crime and Disorder Act 1998, s 51(1).

The Sentencing Guidelines Council suggests that it would not be appropriate to give an indication of sentence in certain circumstances, for example:

- where the court considers that the defendant is already under pressure to plead guilty and the indication would add to that pressure;
- where the case is borderline between a custodial and a non-custodial sentence and it is not reasonable for the court to indicate which is likely;
- where the request for an indication appears to be a tactical measure.

In *R v Bowers and Others* CA (unreported, 20 June 2006), the trial judge gave an indication of sentence but not in accordance with procedure. The Court of Appeal held that, as the defendants knew of the irregularity and of the risks attached and decided to take them, then in these circumstances they could have no cause for complaint.

Where trial on indictment appears more suitable

(m) If the court decides, under s 19, that the offence appears more suitable for trial on indictment, nothing is explained to, or asked of, the defendant as described above. The court simply tells the defendant of its decision and proceeds in accordance with the Crime and Disorder Act 1998, s 51(1). The defendant's consent is not required.

4.2.3 Failure to comply with the procedure

The procedure outlined above is obligatory, and any deviation from it is likely to render the whole proceedings null and void. The defendant then has the option of applying for judicial review to quash any eventual conviction. For example, in *R v Kent Justices, ex p Machin* [1952] 2 QB 355, under the pre-CJA law, the magistrates failed to tell the defendant of the possibility of a committal for sentence, and the conviction and subsequent committal were quashed.

It is open to the prosecution to seek judicial review of the magistrates' decision, although such proceedings are rare, and are unlikely to be successful. However, for a case where the Divisional Court did overrule the magistrates, see *R v Northampton Magistrates' Court, ex p CCE* [1991] Crim LR 598.

4.2.4 Changing the mode of trial

4.2.4.1 The defendant

The defendant may change his or her election from summary trial to trial on indictment, or vice versa, if the magistrates consent. The typical situation is that the defendant has elected summary trial without taking proper advice and then sought legal representation for the purposes of trial or sentence. In these circumstances the magistrates are likely to allow the change, but it is a matter within their discretion. The test is whether the defendant understood the nature and significance of the choice which he or she was being asked to make (*R v Birmingham Justices, ex p Hodgson* [1985] QB 1131).

According to *R v Bourne Justices, ex p Cope* (1989) 153 JP 161, the essential issue is whether the defendant realised that by his or her election he or she was depriving himself or herself of the right to a jury. The fact that the prosecution witnesses were present and ready to give evidence, and that it would not be desirable to delay the case further was not relevant to the defendant's understanding. However, once it was established that he or she did understand the decision he or she was being asked to make, these matters were ones which the justices could take into account in exercising their discretion to allow a change of election.

If the magistrates allow a change of election, they should also allow a change of plea, if one has been given, as the plea has a major influence on where the defendant should be tried (*R v Birmingham Justices, ex p Hodgson* [1985] QB 1131).

The principles outlined above pre-date the CPIA 1996, but do not appear to be affected by the passing of that Act.

4.2.4.2 The magistrates

The magistrates may change their minds in one situation only under the CJA 2003, Sch 3. This is where the magistrates have accepted summary trial and the defendant has consented, but the prosecution apply to the court for the offence to be tried on indictment instead. Such an application must be made before the start of the summary trial and may be granted if the magistrates are satisfied that the sentence which they would have the power to impose would be inadequate. If the accused faces two or more offences in the same proceedings, and the magistrates consider they form a series of offences of the same or a similar character, they may consider the maximum aggregate sentence which they would have the power to impose if the accused were to be convicted of all the offences.

4.3 Special cases

4.3.1 Criminal damage

Under the MCA 1980, s 22, where the defendant is charged with criminal damage (other than where the damage was caused by fire) the magistrates must proceed as if the offence were summary only when the value of the damage is less than £5,000. The court is only proceeding *as if* the offence is summary, but it is not summary for all purposes (*R v Considine* (1980) 70 Cr App R 239 and *R v Fennell* [2000] 1 WLR 2011).

See also *R v Alden* (2002) 2 Cr App R (S) 326, which confirmed that if the Crown Court is dealing with criminal damage (other than under a provision such as CJA 1988, s 40), the maximum sentence of 10 years is available.

4.3.2 Special procedure in criminal damage cases

Under s 22, before embarking on the normal procedure for determining the mode of trial as set out in **4.2** above, the procedure set out below must be followed:

(a) The court shall, having regard to any representations made by the prosecution or defence, consider the value of the thing involved. There is no appeal on the basis that the value was mistaken (s 22(8)).

When determining the value of the damage where the property is damaged beyond repair, the value is the market value of the property at the material time. The court is not concerned with determining consequential loss. See *R v Colchester Justices, ex p Abbott*, *The Times*, 13 March 2001, where the value of damaged genetically modified crops was the market value, and not the consequential loss of lost research.

(b) If the value is:
   (i) £5,000 or less, the court proceeds to summary trial. The defendant has no right to trial on indictment, nor may he or she be committed for sentence under PCC(S)A 2000, s 3. Under the CJA 2003, the maximum penalty is increased from three months' imprisonment to 51 weeks or a fine up to Level 4 on the Standard Scale (currently £2,500).
   (ii) more than £5,000, the offence is triable either way, and the court follows the procedure to determine the mode of trial set out in **4.2** above. If the offence is tried summarily the maximum penalty is six months' imprisonment and a £5,000 fine;
   (iii) uncertain, the court will ask the defendant if he or she consents to summary trial, after the lower penalty and absence of any power to commit for sentence have been explained. If consent is given then the court proceeds to summary trial. If not, the court will follow the procedure for determining the mode of trial set out in **4.2** above. See ss 22(4)–(6). See, for example, *R v Prestatyn Magistrates' Court* [2002] EWCA 1177, where the defendants were charged with criminal damage to an experimental crop of genetically modified maize, which had been grown as a development measure with significant investment. It was grown for research rather than sale. The court held that to view it as an ordinary crop was artificial. In the circumstances, the value of the crop was uncertain. This appears to conflict with *Ex p Abbott* (above).

4.3.3 A series of offences

If the defendant is charged with two or more offences which appear to the court to be a series of offences of the same or a similar character, then the court has regard to the aggregate value in determining the mode of trial. Thus, if the value of all items damaged totals £5,000 or less, then the magistrates proceed as if the offences are all summary, regardless of the number of offences. See s 22(11), inserted by the CJA 1988, s 38. For an example of the operation of s 22(11), see *R v Braden* (1988) 87 Cr App R 289.

4.3.4 Burglary

Where the defendant has been convicted of a third offence of burglary since 1999, the Powers of Criminal Court (Sentencing) Act 2000, s 111, requires him or her to be given a custodial sentence of three years, unless there are circumstances which do not justify imposing such a sentence. This sentence is in excess of the magistrates' sentencing powers, and the magistrates have no alternative but to treat the offence as triable only on indictment and send the matter to the Crown Court under the Crime and Disorder Act 1998, s 51.

Section 111 provides as follows:

(1) This section applies where:
   (a) a person is convicted of a domestic burglary committed after 30 November 1999;
   (b) at the time when that burglary was committed, he was 18 or over and had been convicted in England and Wales of two other domestic burglaries; and
   (c) one of those other burglaries was committed after he had been convicted of the other, and both of them were committed after 30 November 1999.

(2) The court shall impose an appropriate custodial sentence for a term of at least three years except where the court is of the opinion that there are particular circumstances which:

(a) relate to any of the offences or to the offender; and
(b) would make it unjust to do so in all the circumstances.

(4) Where:
(a) a person is charged with a domestic burglary which, apart from this subsection, would be triable either way; and
(b) the circumstances are such that, if he or she were convicted of the burglary, he could be sentenced for it under subsection (2) above, the burglary shall be triable only on indictment.

(5) In this section 'domestic burglary' means a burglary committed in respect of a building or part of a building which is a dwelling.

(6) In this section 'an appropriate custodial sentence' means:
(a) in relation to a person who is 21 or over when convicted of the offence mentioned in subsection (1)(a) above, a sentence of imprisonment;
(b) in relation to a person who is under 21 at that time, a sentence of detention in a young offender institution.

4.4 Linked summary and indictable offences

The CJA 1988 and the Crime and Disorder Act 1998 provide two exceptions to the otherwise inflexible rule that summary offences are only triable summarily.

4.4.1 Sending summary offences to the Crown Court

Under the Crime and Disorder Act 1998 s 51, as amended by the Courts Act 2003, a related summary offence may be sent to the Crown Court for trial with the indictable offence to which it is related. There are two conditions:

(i) The summary offence is related if it *'arises out of circumstances which are the same as or connected with those giving rise to the indictable offence'* (s 51E(d)).

(ii) The summary offence must be an offence which is punishable with imprisonment or involves obligatory or discretionary disqualification from driving (s 51(11)).

4.4.2 Including a summary offence on the indictment

Similar to the power contained in s 51 is the power in the CJA 1988 s 40. This allows a summary offence to be included in an indictment, but in this case the initiative for including the summary offence comes from the prosecution and the magistrates are not involved.

Under s 40, there are three conditions that must be fulfilled:

(i) the summary offence is common assault, taking a motor vehicle without consent, driving whilst disqualified, criminal damage within the MCA 1980 s 22, assaulting a prison custody officer or secure training officer or is punishable by imprisonment or disqualification and is specified by the Home Secretary as being suitable for inclusion; and

(ii) the summary offence is either founded on the same facts as an offence on the indictment or is, or forms part of, a series of offences of the same or a similar character. See for example, *R v Smith* [1997] QB 836, where the defendant was charged on indictment with dangerous driving. Counts for taking a motor vehicle without authority, driving whilst disqualified were added under s 40. The Court of Appeal held that, as the latter two offences were not founded on the same facts as the first, they were improperly joined and the convictions in relation to them were quashed (note that the counts alleging indictable offences were unaffected); and

(iii) the evidence was disclosed by material pursuant to the Crime and Disorder Act 1998 and has been served on the person charged.

The effect of s 40, taken together with the Criminal Law Act 1967 s 6(3), is that if a person is indicted in a count charging assault occasioning actual bodily harm, he or she can only be found guilty of common assault if that offence is specifically included in the indictment. This also applies to other offences included under s 40 (*R v Mearns* [1991] 1 QB 82) and may also apply to summary offences sent to the Crown Court under s 51. See **Chapter 10** for the CLA 1967, s 6(3).

4.4.3 At the Crown Court

At the Crown Court, under both s 51 and s 40, the defendant may plead not guilty and be tried in relation to the summary offence in exactly the same way in which he or she is tried for the indictable offence, set out in **Chapter 11**. If the defendant is convicted, the powers of the Crown Court in relation to sentence for the summary offence are limited to those of the magistrates.

4.5 Advantages and disadvantages of each mode of trial

There are many matters to be taken into account in advising on the most appropriate forum:

(a) *Speed.* Whether a case in the magistrates' court is likely to be heard more quickly than if it had been listed for hearing in the Crown Court depends on local waiting lists. However, the case itself is likely to take less time in the magistrates' court.

(b) *Expense.* Proceedings in the magistrates' court are much less expensive than in the Crown Court—a very important consideration if the defendant is not legally aided.

(c) *Informality.* Proceedings in the magistrates' court are much more informal than in the Crown Court, as fewer people are involved, and counsel do not wear wig and gown. The Crown Court can be daunting to someone who has little experience of criminal courts.

(d) *Disclosure.* In the Crown Court, the defendant must serve a defence statement setting out the basic nature of the defence case. Such a statement is voluntary in the magistrates' courts but not obligatory.

(e) *Sentence.* The magistrates' powers of sentence are very much less than those of the Crown Court, though they do have the power to commit to the Crown Court for sentence. However, if the defendant intends to plead guilty, he or she is likely to opt for a hearing in the magistrates' court in the hope that the magistrates do not commit him or her to Crown Court for sentence. See **Chapters 15–16** for details of the magistrates' powers of sentence.

(f) *Division between the tribunals of fact and law.* In the magistrates' court, the tribunals of fact and law are the same, so that they will first have to hear evidence before deciding on any question of admissibility, and then, if inadmissible, endeavour to forget it. In the Crown Court this problem simply does not arise. The judge alone will decide on admissibility, and evidence will only go before the jury if it is admissible.

(g) *Legal submissions.* Despite the fact that lay magistrates are advised by a clerk, any submissions on the law are made to laymen. (The case may be heard by a district judge, but this would not be known when determining the mode of trial.) In the Crown Court, the same submission would be made to a professional lawyer.

(h) *Appeals.* Appeals from the magistrates' court may be made without leave, (see **Chapter 8**). Appeals from the Crown Court always require leave, and the procedure generally is much more complicated (see **Chapter 12**).

(i) *The benefit of the doubt.* It is generally assumed that a jury is more likely to give the defendant the benefit of the doubt than magistrates. In any event, if the case involves a substantial attack on the police evidence, the defendant is likely to find a jury more sympathetic than magistrates.

You are referred to Home Office Research Study No 125, entitled *Magistrates' Courts or the Crown Court? Mode of Trial Decisions and Sentencing* (London: HMSO, 1992).

4.6 Advance information

The prosecution has a duty to provide the defence with the evidence upon which it will rely at trial on indictment, and with undisclosed material in certain circumstances. See **Chapter 9** for a full discussion of the rules relating to disclosure.

The Criminal Procedure Rules 2005, r 21, provides that where the accused is charged with a triable either way offence, the prosecution must provide the defence with copies of its witness statements, *or* a summary of the evidence upon which it proposes to rely, at or before the beginning of the day of the first hearing. The purpose of obtaining advance information is to facilitate a mode of trial decision.

The prosecution is entitled to refuse a request, but, under r 21.4 only where it thinks that compliance would lead to the intimidation of witnesses or some other interference with the course of justice. Failure to comply for any other reason will lead to an adjournment, unless the court considers that the defendant has not been prejudiced. See generally r 21.6.

The request for information should be made *before* mode of trial proceedings have been held, and the information should be provided as soon as practicable. Thus, the defendant is able to make his or her decision as to the mode of trial with full knowledge of all the circumstances.

Obtaining advance information is now very common, but the defence may decide against a request if clearly one mode of trial is preferable. However, it is the duty of the court under r 21.5 to satisfy itself that the defendant is aware of his or her right to advance informaiton.

Note that the magistrates have no power to *order* disclosure under these rules (*R v Dunmow Justices, ex p Nash* (1993) 157 JP 1153, DC). See further the Protocol for the Provision of Advance Information (etc.) in the Magistrates' Courts (draft issued 12 May 2006).

4.7 Allocation Guidelines

The Sentencing Guidelines Council's National Allocation Guidelines set out the following principles for consideration:

3.3 Adequacy of sentencing powers to be based on an assumption that the prosecution version of the facts is correct.

3.4 The charges and range of conduct to be considered. This means that where, for example, a defendant is alleged to have acted criminally over a long period, the charges need to be constructed with care as the court is not entitled to make assumptions about the extent of criminality where offences are neither admitted nor proved.

3.5 The need for a separate tribunal to determine fact. Procedures are likely to be generally adequate in the magistrates' court, but there may be a few exceptional cases where it will be especially important to have the separation between the judge and the jury that is possible in the Crown Court.

3.6 Presumption in favour of summary trial. As many cases as possible should be dealt with in a magistrates' court.

3.7 Linked cases. As a general rule, it is preferable for all issues to be dealt with in a single trial.

3.8 Any representations of the prosecution or defence should be considered.

The following Mode of Trial Guidelines were introduced in order to assist magistrates make a mode of trial decision prior to the CJA 2003. They are now included in the *Consolidated Criminal Practice Direction*.

Practice Direction (criminal: consolidated) [2002] 3 All ER 904,
para V.51, *Mode of Trial*

V.51.1 The purpose of these guidelines is to help magistrates decide whether or not to commit 'either way' offences for trial in the Crown Court. Their object is to provide guidance not direction. They are not intended to impinge upon a magistrate's duty to consider each case individually and on its own particular facts. These guidelines apply to all defendants aged 18 and above.

General mode of trial considerations

V.51.2 Section 19 of the Magistrates' Courts Act 1980 requires magistrates to have regard to the following matters in deciding whether an offence is more suitable for summary trial or trial on indictment:

(a) *the nature of the case;*

(b) *whether the circumstances make the offence one of a serious character;*

(c) *whether the punishment which a magistrates' court would have power to inflict for it would be adequate;*

(d) *any other circumstances which appear to the court to make it more suitable for the offence to be tried in one way rather than the other;*

(e) *any representations made by the prosecution or the defence.*

V.51.3 Certain general observations can be made:

(a) *the court should never make its decision on the grounds of convenience or expedition;*

(b) *the court should assume for the purpose of deciding mode of trial that the prosecution version of the facts is correct;*

(c) the fact that the offences are alleged to be specimens is a relevant consideration (although, it has to be borne in mind that difficulties can arise in sentencing in relation to specimen counts, see Clark [1996] 2 Cr App R (S) 351 and Canavan [1998] 1 Cr App R (S) 243); the fact that the defendant will be asking for other offences to be taken into consideration, if convicted, is not;

(d) where cases involve complex questions of fact or difficult questions of law, including difficult issues of disclosure of sensitive material the court should consider committal for trial;

(e) where two or more defendants are jointly charged with an offence each has an individual right to elect his mode of trial;

(f) in general, except where otherwise stated, either-way offences should be tried summarily unless the court considers that the particular case has one or more of the features set out in paras 51.4–51.18 and that its sentencing powers are insufficient;

(g) the court should also consider its powers to commit an offender for sentence, under [PCC(S)A 2000, ss 3 and 4], if information emerges during the course of the hearing which leads them to conclude that the offence is so serious, or the offender such a risk to the public, that their powers to sentence him are inadequate. This means that committal for sentence is no longer determined by reference to the character and antecedents of the defendant.

Features relevant to individual offences

V.51.4 Where reference is made in these guidelines to property or damage of 'high value' it means a figure equal to at least twice the amount of the limit (currently £5,000) imposed by statute on a magistrates' court when making a compensation order.

[**Note:** *Each of the guidelines in respect of the individual offences set out below (except those relating to drugs offences) are prefaced by a reminder in the following terms 'Cases should be tried summarily unless the court considers that one or more of the following features is present in the case and that its sentencing powers are insufficient. Magistrates should take account of their powers under [PCC(S)A 2000, ss 3 and 4] to commit for sentence', see para V.51.3(g).*]

V.51.5 Burglary: dwelling-house

    (a) Entry in the daytime when the occupier (or another) is present.

    (b) Entry at night of a house which is normally occupied, whether or not the occupier (or another) is present.

    (c) The offence is alleged to be one of a series of similar offences.

    (d) When soiling, ransacking, damage or vandalism occurs.

    (e) The offence has professional hallmarks.

    (f) The unrecovered property is of high value: see para 51.4 for definition of 'high value'.

    (g) The offence is racially motivated.

Note: *Attention is drawn to para 28(c) of schedule 1 to the [MCA 1980], by which offences of burglary in a dwelling cannot be tried summarily if any person in the dwelling was subjected to violence or the threat of violence.*

V.51.6 Burglary: non-dwellings

    (a) Entry of a pharmacy or doctor's surgery.

    (b) Fear is caused or violence is done to anyone lawfully on the premises (eg nightwatchman, security guard).

    (c) The offence has professional hallmarks.

    (d) Vandalism on a substantial scale.

    (e) The unrecovered property is of high value: see para 51.4 for definition of 'high value'.

    (f) The offence is racially motivated.

V.51.7 *Theft and fraud*

> (a) *Breach of trust by a person in a position of substantial authority, or in whom a high degree of trust is placed.*
>
> (b) *Theft or fraud which has been committed or disguised in a sophisticated manner.*
>
> (c) *Theft or fraud committed by an organised gang.*
>
> (d) *The victim is particularly vulnerable to theft or fraud (eg the elderly or infirm).*
>
> (e) *The unrecovered property is of high value: see para 51.4 for definition of 'high value'.*

V.51.8 *Handling*

> (a) *Dishonest handling of stolen property by a receiver who has commissioned the theft.*
>
> (b) *The offence has professional hallmarks.*
>
> (c) *The property is of high value: see para V.51.4 for definition of 'high value'.*

V.51.9 *Social security frauds*

> (a) *Organised fraud on a large scale.*
>
> (b) *The frauds are substantial and carried out over a long period of time.*

V.51.10 *Violence (ss 20 and 47 of the Offences against the Person Act 1861)*

> (a) *The use of a weapon of a kind likely to cause serious injury.*
>
> (b) *A weapon is used and serious injury is caused.*
>
> (c) *More than minor injury is caused by kicking or head-butting.*
>
> (d) *Serious violence is caused to those whose work has to be done in contact with the public or who are likely to face violence in the course of their work.*
>
> (e) *Violence to vulnerable people (eg the elderly and infirm).*
>
> (f) *The offence has clear racial motivation.*

Note: The same considerations apply to cases of domestic violence.

V.51.11 *Public Order Act offences*

> (a) *Cases of violent disorder should generally be committed for trial.*
>
> (b) *Affray.*
>
> (i) *Organised violence or use of weapons.*
>
> (ii) *Significant injury or substantial damage.*
>
> (iii) *The offence has clear racial motivation.*
>
> (iv) *An attack on police officers, ambulance staff, fire-fighters and the like.*

V.51.12 *Violence to and neglect of children*

> (a) *Substantial injury.*
>
> (b) *Repeated violence or serious neglect, even if the physical harm is slight.*
>
> (c) *Sadistic violence (eg deliberate burning or scalding).*

V.51.13 *Indecent assault*

> (a) *Substantial disparity in age between victim and defendant, and a more serious assault.*
>
> (b) *Violence or threats of violence.*
>
> (c) *Relationship of trust or responsibility between defendant and victim.*
>
> (d) *Several more serious similar offences.*
>
> (e) *The victim is particularly vulnerable.*
>
> (f) *Serious nature of the assault.*

V.51.14 *Unlawful sexual intercourse*

   (a) *Wide disparity of age.*
   (b) *Breach of position of trust.*
   (c) *The victim is particularly vulnerable.*

Note: Unlawful sexual intercourse with a girl under 13 is triable only on indictment.

Drugs

V.51.15 Class A

   (a) *Supply; possession with intent to supply: these cases should be committed for trial.*
   (b) *Possession: should be committed for trial unless the amount is consistent only with personal use.*

V.51.16 Class B

   (a) *Supply; possession with intent to supply: should be committed for trial unless there is only small scale supply for no payment.*
   (b) *Possession: should be committed for trial when the quantity is substantial and not consistent only with personal use.*

V.51.17 *Dangerous driving and aggravated vehicle taking*

   (a) *Alcohol or drugs contributing to dangerousness.*
   (b) *Grossly excessive speed.*
   (c) *Racing.*
   (d) *Prolonged course of dangerous driving.*
   (e) *Other related offences.*
   (f) *Significant injury or damage sustained.*

V.51.18 *Criminal damage*

   (a) *Deliberate fire-raising.*
   (b) *Committed by a group.*
   (c) *Damage of a high value.*
   (d) *The offence has clear racial motivation.*

Note: *Offences set out in Sch 2 to the MCA 1980 (which includes offences of criminal damage which do not amount to arson) must be tried summarily if the value of the property damaged or destroyed is £5,000 or less.*

5

Summary trial

5.1 Procedure at trial

Some 96 per cent of all criminal cases are tried in magistrates' courts. The procedure is the same, whether the offence is triable only summarily, or triable either way, though if the offence is triable either way, the magistrates must first determine the mode of trial (see **Chapter 4**).

See generally *Stone's Justices' Manual* (2009 edn) at para 1–589 ff. and *Blackstone's Criminal Practice* (2009 edn), at paras D20 and D21.

5.1.1 Case management hearings (sometimes known as pre-trial reviews)

Pre-trial hearings have been held from time to time where magistrates have felt such a court to be appropriate. See, for example, *A v DPP* (2000) 164 JP 3137. This system has now been placed on a formal footing by the Courts Act 2003 s 45 and Sch 3, which inserts new sections 8A–C into the MCA 1980 and the Criminal Procedure Rules Part 3.

A case management hearing is one which is held any time before the court begins to hear evidence from the prosecution at the trial. The objective is to achieve an effective first hearing in compliance with the Criminal Procedure Rules. In particular, the objective is to ensure that at the first hearing:

1. The plea can be taken.
2. The appropriate venue is determined.
3. The real issue(s) are identified.
4. The case (including sentence) can be concluded there and then. If it cannot be concluded, directions can be given so that it can be concluded at the next hearing or as soon as possible afterwards.

It is a further objective to enable directions to be given so that appropriate cases may be committed, sent, or transferred to the Crown Court as soon as possible, and so that such cases may be concluded there without undue delay.

In order to achieve this:

1. If he has not already done so and wishes to do so, the defendant should seek representation as soon as possible or see the duty solicitor on the day. Further, the court administration should determine all applications for legal representation within 48 hours of receipt.

2   If the defendant does not attend, the prosecution advocate will generally apply for a warrant not backed for bail. The overriding objective and the case management obligations prescribed by the Criminal Procedure Rules apply whether the defendant is present or not. The parties' advocates should therefore prepare for the hearing accordingly and, at the hearing, actively assist the court even if the defendant is absent.

3   In indictable-only cases to which the Crime and Disorder Act 1998 s51 applies, the defence must expect to be required to indicate a likely plea and prepare accordingly. Whatever the plea, the court will give directions to facilitate the hearing at the Crown Court. See generally **Chapter 4** on allocation.

4   In 'either way' cases, the defendant must expect that the court will take the plea and move on to determine the mode of trial. See generally **Chapter 4** on allocation.

The rules also set out the obligations of the parties to achieve these objectives, and a standard set of written directions. The standard directions can be found in the Consolidated Criminal Practice Direction Part 56 and Annex E.

5.2 The trial

5.2.1 The absence of the defendant

Although the defendant will in fact often be present in court for the hearing, the magistrates have the power to proceed in his absence. There are three situations in which this may arise.

5.2.1.1 Where the defendant fails to attend

Under the Magistrates' Courts Act 1980 (MCA), s 11(1), (as amended by the Criminal Justice and Immigration Act 2008 s54) the magistrates must hear the case in the defendant's absence if he or she fails to attend court in answer to a summons, if the defendant is over the age of 18 (and may do so if he or she is under that age), unless it appears to the court to be contrary to the interests of justice. If the offence is triable either way, the prosecution must first establish that the defendant actually knew of the summons, for example through attending an earlier hearing.

If the offence is triable only summarily, then the prosecution may prove that the summons was served simply by establishing that, for example, it was sent by registered post to the defendant's last known address, but the prosecution does not have to prove that the defendant received it.

Once service of the summons has been proved, a plea of not guilty will be entered on the defendant's behalf and the prosecution evidence will be called. Such hearings often end in the conviction of the defendant, as none of the prosecution evidence will have been tested by cross-examination, and the magistrates will not have heard the defence case.

If the defendant did not, in fact, know of the proceedings, he or she may make a 'statutory declaration' of this under the MCA 1980, s 14, within 21 days of finding out about them. If the declaration is made, the summons, trial and conviction are rendered void. However, the information remains valid, so that the prosecution can start again.

The *Consolidated Criminal Practice Direction* provides that the court must exercise its discretion to proceed in the absence of the defendant with the utmost care and caution.

The overriding concern must be to ensure that such a trial is as fair as circumstances permit and leads to a just outcome.

Paragraph 1.13.17 provides that due regard should be had to the judgment of Lord Bingham in *R v Jones* [2003] AC 1; [2002] 2 All ER 113 in which Lord Bingham identified circumstances to be taken into account before proceeding, which include: the conduct of the defendant, the disadvantage to the defendant, public interest, the effect of any delay and whether the attendance of the defendant could be secured at a later hearing. Other relevant considerations are the seriousness of the offence and likely outcome if the defendant is found guilty. If the defendant is only likely to be fined for a summary offence this can be relevant since the costs that a defendant might otherwise be ordered to pay as a result of an adjournment could be disproportionate. In the case of summary proceedings the fact that there can be an appeal that is a complete rehearing is also relevant, as is the power to re-open the case under s 142 of the MCA 1980. *R v Jones* was relied on in *R (R (a juvenile)) v Thames Youth Court* (2002) 166 JP 613, where the defendant was unable to attend court because on the day of his trial he was arrested in connection with an unrelated offence. It was held that in cases where the defendant had not absented himself voluntarily, but intended to be present and was prevented from attending, the threshold of prejudice and fairness that he had to demonstrate is a comparatively low one. See also *R (Davies) v Solihull Justices* [2008] EWHC 1157.

Whether the defendant's absence should lead to a rehearing of the case was a matter within the justices' discretion, and as long as this was based on facts the justices were entitled to find, the divisional court would not overturn it (*R v North Shields Justices, ex p Darroll* [1991] COD 317).

See also *R v O'Hare* [2006] Crim LR 950 setting out the factors for the advocate to consider in deciding whether to continue to act, including the presence or absence of prosecution witnesses and the ability to conduct the trial in the absence of the client.

The s 11 procedure tends to be used only for the less serious offences. In any event, if the defendant is charged with a triable either way offence, the defendant normally has to be present during mode of trial proceedings.

Note that the court ought to be reluctant to try, in his absence, an offender who is young, has not been placed on bail and/or has no record of failing to appear (*R v Dewsbury Magistrates' Court, ex p K, The Times*, 16 March 1994).

5.2.1.2 Pleading guilty by post

Under the MCA 1980, s 12 as substituted by Sch 5 to the Criminal Justice and Public Order Act 1994 (CJPOA), a defendant may plead guilty by sending a letter to court. This can be done if:

- the offence is summary; and
- proceedings have been started by the service of a summons.

In such circumstances the procedure is as follows:

(a) The prosecution serves on the defendant:

    (i) the summons;

    (ii) a brief statement of the facts upon which the prosecution proposes to rely or a copy of such written statements as comply with the Criminal Justice Act 1967 (CJA), ss 9(2)(a) and (b);

    (iii) any information relating to the accused which will or may be placed before the court; and

    (iv) a notice explaining the procedure.

(b) If he or she wishes to plead guilty, the defendant notifies the court and may enclose a statement of his or her mitigation. Subsequently, the defendant may withdraw this plea, and the case then proceeds as if it were a not guilty plea.

(c) Neither the prosecution nor the defence is represented or appears at court, and the court proceeds on the basis of the statements which are read out in court. Failure to do so will lead to the conviction being quashed, as in *R v Epping and Ongar Justices, ex p Breach* [1987] RTR 233 where the defendant's statement in mitigation was not read out. The magistrates may refuse to accept the plea of guilty if the statement in mitigation discloses information which amounts to a defence.

(d) The magistrates, if content to accept the plea, may sentence, or adjourn for the accused to be present. The magistrates may only sentence the defendant in his or her absence if he or she is to be fined, absolutely discharged, or have his or her driving licence endorsed.

Section 12A of the MCA 1980 deals with the situation where the defendant actually appears in court. Two situations may occur:

- The defendant has informed the court that he or she wishes the case to proceed under s 12, but he or she nevertheless appears in court at the appointed time. The court may proceed to deal with the matter as if he or she were absent, if he or she consents to such a course: s 12A(1).
- The defendant has not notified the court that he or she wishes the case to proceed under s 12, and appears at the appointed time. If he or she indicates that he or she wishes to plead guilty, and consents, the court may proceed to deal with the matter as if he or she were absent (s 12A(2)).

In either case, the court must afford the defendant an opportunity to make oral submissions with a view to mitigation of sentence (s 12(5)(c)).

5.2.1.3 The disorderly defendant

If the defendant's behaviour is so disruptive that the proceedings cannot continue, he or she may be removed, and the court may proceed in his or her absence under MCA 1980, s 11.

Note: If the defendant is represented, he or she is deemed to be present unless his or her presence is expressly required by statute (MCA 1980, s 122(2)).

5.2.2 Absence of the prosecution

Under the MCA 1980, s 15, if the prosecution fails to appear at the time and place fixed for the summary trial, the magistrates may adjourn the case or dismiss the information. Where the magistrates act unreasonably in dismissing a case, their decision is a nullity, and a mandatory order would issue (*R v Hendon Justices, ex p DPP* [1994] QB 167) (see **8.3.1.1**).

If the case is adjourned part-heard, then the magistrates may proceed in the absence of the prosecution, the evidence given on the earlier occasion being treated as the entirety of the prosecution case. In these circumstances, the defendant will not face cross-examination of his or her evidence by the prosecution.

5.2.3 Representations in private

A decision to hear representations in private is within the magistrates' discretion, but careful consideration should always be given to whether such a step is appropriate, given the magistrates' role as fact-finder. In order to guard against injustice, steps must be taken to ensure that all parties are notified of the hearing and are represented, with a contemporaneous note being taken, normally by the clerk (see *R v Nottingham Magistrates' Court, ex p Furnell* (1996) 160 JP 201).

5.2.4 Taking the plea

The defendant must plead unequivocally guilty or not guilty. Remember that in relation to a triable either way offence, the plea will have been taken at the mode of trial stage. In practice, this often throws up two separate problems:

(a) *The defendant who wishes to change his plea*. The court may consider an application made by a defendant who has unequivocally pleaded guilty to change his or her plea, at any time before sentence (see *S (an infant) v Recorder of Manchester* [1971] AC 481). Whether he or she will be allowed to change the plea is entirely within the discretion of the magistrates. If they take the view that the defendant understood the charge, the consequence of his or her plea, and had intended to make it, they will be unlikely to allow a change. See generally, *R v McNally* [1954] 1 WLR 933 and *Revitt and others v DPP* [2006] EWHC 2266 (Admin).

Where the magistrates have allowed the defendant to change his plea from guilty to not guilty, they should also allow him to reconsider his consent to summary trial (*R v Bow Street Magistrates' Court, ex p Welcome* (1992) 156 JP 609).

Where the defendant has pleaded not guilty, and wishes to change his or her plea to guilty, he or she may do so with leave of the court (which for obvious reasons is likely to be granted) any time before the court retires to consider the verdict.

(b) *The defendant's plea is equivocal*. This covers three situations:

(i) The defendant, when pleading guilty, explains his or her plea in words amounting to a defence. See *R v Emery* (1943) 29 Cr App R 47, where the defendant said 'Plead guilty in self-defence'. The magistrates should then explain the law and the defendant is asked to plead again. If the plea is still equivocal, the magistrates must record a plea of not guilty and proceed to trial. If they make no enquiry into the plea, the defendant may later challenge the validity of the plea on appeal.

(ii) The defendant unequivocally pleads guilty, but the plea is rendered equivocal by information given to the magistrates before sentence (see *R v Durham Justices, ex p Virgo* [1952] 2 QB 1 contrasted with *R v Birmingham Crown Court, ex p Sharma* [1988] Crim LR 741). In *P Foster (Haulage) Ltd v Roberts* [1978] 2 All ER 751, it was said that this should not be termed an equivocal plea, and is merely a situation in which the magistrates have a discretion to allow a change of plea.

(iii) The defendant unequivocally pleads guilty and no further information is given to the court casting doubt on the correctness of the plea. However, if the defendant argues that the plea was made under duress, the Crown Court may treat it as an equivocal plea. See *R v Huntingdon Crown Court, ex p Jordan* [1981] QB 857.

In any event, the magistrates should always ensure that the defendant, particularly an unrepresented defendant, understands the offence, the consequences of the plea, and intends to make that plea. The proper forum for any dispute is the Crown Court, which may review the case, and, if it decides that the plea was equivocal, it should remit it to the magistrates with an order that they enter a plea of not guilty and proceed to trial. Before making any such order, the Crown Court should read affidavits from the magistrates and the clerk as to what happened, and magistrates and clerks should cooperate by swearing such affidavits. See *R v Plymouth Justices, ex p Hart* [1986] QB 950.

5.2.5 The prosecution opening speech

Magistrates will be familiar with the cases that frequently come before them, so that, although the prosecution has the right to an opening speech, it is usually brief and is often not made.

In *L and B v DPP* [1998] 2 Cr App R 69, the case was adjourned for a month after hearing the prosecution witnesses. The defendants appealed against their convictions as the prosecution had made a second speech on the resumed hearing, at the magistrates' request, to remind them of the evidence given at the earlier hearing. It was held that there was nothing unfair in that, subject to the safeguard that the defence should always be asked to address the court in reply to correct any errors or draw attention in differences of recollection.

5.2.6 The prosecution evidence

The prosecution calls the evidence upon which it relies. This will take the form of witnesses and written statements, if admissible and appropriate.

As to the defence knowledge of the prosecution case, see **4.6 and Chapter 9.**

In the Crown Court, the trial judge is the tribunal of law whereas the jury is the tribunal of fact. In the magistrates' court, however, the magistrates are both tribunal of law and tribunal of fact. The question as to whether the magistrates, having heard evidence and decided that it is inadmissible, should then recuse themselves was discussed in *R (on the application of Ratra) v DPP* [2004] EWHC 87. Whether it should do so would depend on the principles derived from previous authority, namely, first, whether all the circumstances that had a bearing on the suggestion that the judge was biased would lead a fair-minded and informed observer to conclude that there was a real possibility, or a real danger, the two being the same, that the tribunal was biased; secondly, interlocutory rulings did not in the ordinary way (unless there was special reason) deprive the district judge or the justices from continuing with the hearing; and thirdly, even when justices had ruled evidence inadmissible there could, in exceptional cases, be circumstances in which the inadmissible evidence was so highly prejudicial that, as a matter of fairness and appearance of fairness, a differently constituted bench ought properly to conduct the trial.

The prosecution evidence will consist of live witnesses, statements admitted under CJA 1967 s9 and evidence by way of video link under the CJA 2003, s 51. It must be in the interests of the efficient or effective administration of justice, taking into account a number of factors, for video link evidence to be admitted. You are advised to see *Blackstone's Criminal Practice*, section D14 and the **Evidence** manual for details.

5.2.7 The submission of no case to answer

At the end of the prosecution evidence, the defence may make a submission of no case to answer. According to Lord Parker CJ, in *Practice Direction (Submission of No Case)* [1962] 1 WLR 227, a submission that there is no case to answer may properly be made and upheld:

- when there has been no evidence to prove an essential element in the alleged offence; or
- when the evidence adduced by the prosecution has been so discredited as a result of cross-examination or is so manifestly unreliable that no reasonable tribunal could safely convict on it.

The Practice Direction was revoked by *Practice Direction (criminal: consolidated)* [2002] 3 All ER 904. No alternative direction was given, however, leaving justices with no revised guidance as to the test to be applied.

In the Crown Court, the test which the trial judge will apply, in deciding on a submission of no case to answer, is set out in *R v Galbraith* [1981] 1 WLR 1039 (see **11.6**). In applying the test, the trial judge does not consider the credibility of the witnesses, as this is a matter for the jury. Similarly, when deciding the issue in the magistrates' court, the magistrates will not normally take into account the credibility of the witnesses (*R v Barking and Dagenham Justices, ex p DPP* (1995) 159 JP 373).

New guidance is given in the Criminal Procedure Rules, Part 37.3(3)(a)(i) as follows: on the defendant's application or the court's own motion, the court may acquit *'on the ground that the prosecution evidence is insufficient for any reasonable court to properly convict'*.

Note that, though it is now usual for magistrates to give reasons following a finding of guilt, Article 6 of the European Convention on Human Rights imposes no obligation to provide reasons for refusing to accede to a submission of no case to answer. Given the highly specific nature of summary procedure, the interests of justice would not be served by imposing such a requirement (*Moran v DPP* [2002] EWHC 89).

5.2.8 The defence case

Assuming no submission of no case to answer is made, or is made and fails, the defence may present its case. The right of the defence to make an opening speech is rarely exercised (see **5.2.9**) and the defence usually begins to call its evidence straight away. The defendant should give evidence before any other witnesses he intends to call (PACE 1984, s 79). Evidence may be produced as discussed above in relation to the prosecution.

5.2.9 Closing speeches

Traditionally the defence has the right to either an opening or a closing speech, and invariably elects a closing speech, thus having the benefit of the last word. That right does not appear in the Criminal Procedure Rules, though he does have a right to address the court at the close of the case.

Similarly, the prosecution has not had the right to a closing speech. However, if either party wished to make a second speech, they may have done so with the leave of the court; but if the court was going to allow one party to make a second speech, it must allow the other party a second speech also. If both parties are allowed a second speech, the prosecution must go first, thus allowing the defence the benefit of the last word.

The Criminal Procedure Rules provide that the prosecution has – not the right to a closing speech, but the right to make representations to the court on the relevant **law**. Any representations made on the law on behalf of the prosecution may be responded to by the defence.

5.2.10 The verdict

Lay magistrates usually retire to consider their verdict, and no one must retire with them as this may create the impression that they have somehow influenced the decision. As to the position of the clerk to the justices, see **5.3** below. The verdict is a majority decision, and the chairman has no casting vote. Therefore, if an evenly numbered court is equally divided, it must adjourn for a fresh hearing before a new bench (*R v Redbridge Justices, ex p Ram* [1992] QB 384).

District judges rarely retire, and usually announce their decision immediately after the defence's closing speech.

In reaching their decision, the magistrates may rely on any local knowledge that they have, but both prosecution and defence should have been informed of this during the trial so that they might be afforded an opportunity to comment upon that knowledge (*Norbrook Laboratories (GB) Ltd v Health and Safety Executive, The Times*, 23 February 1998).

See also *Gibbons v DPP* (2001) 165 JP 812, where the district judge hearing a trial visited the place of the offence after closing speeches and checked, inter alia, whether an eyewitness's view could have been obstructed. The Divisional Court held that, given the importance of such matters, the district judge should, at the very least, have informed the parties beforehand so that they could make submissions, if they chose, as to the witness's actual position. The convictions were quashed and a retrial ordered.

Traditionally magistrates have not given reasons for their decisions. They should indicate the basis of their decision, but not in any form of judgment or elaborate form. Following the Human Rights Act 1998, they must now show that they have considered the ingredients of the offence so that the accused knows he has been found guilty. This can be done in a few sentences. See generally *R (McGowan) v Brent Justices* (2002) 166 JP 29 and *McKerry v Teesdale and Wear Valley Justices* (2000) 164 JP 355.

The Criminal Procedure Rules Part 37.3(5) and (6) provide:

(5) *If the court—*
   (a) *convicts the defendant; or*
   (b) *makes a hospital order instead of doing so,*

   it must give sufficient reasons to explain its decision.

(6) *If the court acquits the defendant, it may—*
   (a) *give an explanation of its decision; and*
   (b) *exercise any power it has to make—*
      (i) *a civil behaviour order,*
      (ii) *a costs order.*

It should be noted that the provisions of the Criminal Law Act 1967 (CLA), s 6(3), do not apply in magistrates' courts. Thus the magistrates have no power to find the defendant guilty of an alternative offence not specifically charged (except under ss 24(3) and (4) of the Road Traffic Offenders Act 1988, under which a defendant charged with dangerous driving may be found guilty of careless driving). See generally *Lawrence v Same* [1968] 2 QB 93. However, it would be open to the magistrates to ask for a summons for the alternative offence to be preferred immediately and proceed to deal with it at once. As to where the magistrates convict on a more serious charge and dismiss others because further convictions would be oppressive, see *DPP v Gane* [1991] Crim LR 711, DC.

For a discussion of the CLA 1967, s 6(3), see **Chapter 11**.

5.2.11 Sentence

If the magistrates find the case proved, they will proceed to sentence, after an adjournment if necessary. A detailed analysis of the procedure prior to sentence is found in **Chapter 13**, but in brief is as follows:

- the prosecution gives details of the defendant's character and antecedents;
- any pre-sentence or other reports are placed before the court;
- the defence enters a plea in mitigation;
- the court passes sentence.

The magistrates' sentencing powers are discussed in full in **Chapters 15** and **16**. However, in brief, the magistrates may sentence a person over the age of 21 to a maximum period of twelve months' imprisonment on each offence, or the statutory maximum, whichever is the less. Where the person is convicted of two or more offences, the sentences may be made to run consecutively to a maximum of 65 weeks, see the CJA 2003, ss 154–155, Schs 25 and 26. In addition to any period of imprisonment the magistrates may fine an offender up to £5,000 per offence. See generally the Powers of Criminal Courts (Sentencing) Act 2000 (PCC(S)A), s 78 and the MCA 1980, ss 32 and 133.

5.2.12 The Criminal Procedure Rules

The outline of the procedure at trial is summarised in the Criminal Procedure Rules at Part 37.3(3) as follows:

(a) *the prosecutor may summarise the prosecution case, identifying the relevant law and facts;*

(b) *the prosecutor must introduce the evidence on which the prosecution case relies;*

(c) *at the conclusion of the prosecution case, on the defendant's application or on its on initiative, the court—*

   (i) *may acquit on the ground that the prosecution evidence is insufficient for any reasonable court properly to convict, but*

   (ii) *must not do so unless the prosecution has had an opportunity to make representations;*

(d) *the justices' legal adviser or the court must explain, in terms the defendant can understand (with help if necessary)—*

   (i) *the right to give evidence, and*

   (ii) *the potential effect of not doing so at all, or of refusing to answer a question while doing so;*

(e) *the defendant may introduce evidence*

(f) *a party may introduce further evidence if it is then admissible (for example because it is in rebuttal of evidence already introduced);*

(g) *the defendant may make representations about the case; and*

(h) *the prosecutor may make representations about the relevant law and the defendant may respond.*

5.2.13 Power to rectify mistakes

Under the MCA 1980, s 142 as amended by the Criminal Appeal Act 1995, a magistrates' court may vary or rescind a sentence or other order imposed or made by it, if it appears to the court to be in the interests of justice to do so. The purpose of this provision is to prevent the judicial review of proceedings which clearly should be re-heard.

The following points should be noted:

(a) The magistrates may re-open the case regardless of whether the defendant pleaded guilty or not guilty.

(b) There is no time limit to the re-opening of the case. The original 28-day time limit (abolished in 1995) is still a useful guideline, but delay is not the only factor to be taken into account by the magistrates in exercising their discretion under s 142 (*R v Ealing Magistrates' Court, ex p Sahota* (1998) 162 JP 73).

(c) The magistrates re-opening the case need not be the same magistrates who dealt with the case originally.

These three points were introduced by the Criminal Appeal Act 1995, and considerably widen the magistrates' powers under s 142. It may be that many matters which could previously have been dealt with only by way of appeal may now be dealt with under s 142. For this reason, students should always consider s 142 when dealing with any error made by the magistrates.

In exercising their discretion, the magistrates were entitled to consider the inconvenience to witnesses if defendants did not appear for their trial through their own fault. They were also able to take into account the apparent strength of the prosecution case, though they should attach little weight to that factor (*R v Newport Justices, ex p Carey* (1996) 160 JP 613).

Three further points should be made:

(a) The power to rescind under s 142 only applies where the defendant has been found guilty. See, for example, *Coles v DPP* (1998) 162 JP 687.

(b) When a person is convicted by a magistrates' court, and it appears in the interest of justice that the case should be re-heard by a different bench, the court may so direct (s 142(2), as amended). In this situation the case is treated as if it has simply been adjourned.

(c) The court's right to exercise its powers under s 142 are lost after the case has been appealed to the Crown Court or the High Court by way of case stated, and the court has determined the appeal (s 142(1A) and (2A) inserted by the Criminal Appeal Act 1995, ss 2B(3) and (5)).

5.3 The clerk to the justices and court legal adviser

The clerk to the justices is a barrister or solicitor of at least five years' standing. He or she is usually supported by assistant clerks who often are, but need not be, legally qualified.

The clerk has a wide administrative function. This derives from the magistrates' jurisdiction over both domestic and licensing matters in addition to their criminal jurisdiction. Here the clerk is involved in a number of areas, such as the taking of informations and the grant of public funding for defence representation.

By virtue of the Consolidated Criminal Practice Direction para V.55.1, the justices' clerk or legal adviser is responsible for:

(a) the legal advice tendered to the justices within the area;

(b) the performance of any of the functions set out below by any member of his staff acting as legal adviser;

(c) ensuring that competent advice is available to justices when the justices' clerk is not personally present in court; and

(d) the effective delivery of case management and the reduction of unnecessary delay.

Under para V.55.3 the clerk or legal adviser has the responsibility of providing the justices with any advice they require properly to perform their functions, whether or not the justices have requested that advice, on:

(a) questions of law (including European Court of Human Rights jurisprudence and those matters set out in section 2(1) of the Human Rights Act 1998). The following cases were decided under the previous law but would still seem to have importance. In *R v Chichester Magistrates' Court, ex p DPP* (1993) 157 JP 1049, it was stated that where the justices wish their clerk to advise them on matters of law, it is essential that the clerk is present in court during the submissions of the parties. In *W v W, The Times*, 4 June 1993, it was held that where the clerk wishes to refer the justices to an authority not previously cited, the advocates in the case should be informed and given the opportunity to comment. See also para V.55.7;

(b) questions of mixed law and fact;

(c) matters of practice and procedure;

(d) the range of penalties available;

(e) any relevant decisions of the superior courts or other guidelines;

(f) other issues relevant to the matter before the court; and

(g) the appropriate decision-making structure to be applied in any given case.

In addition, the legal adviser should assist the court, where appropriate, by reminding them of the evidence and as to the formulation of reasons and the recording of those reasons. He or she must not, however, play any part in the findings of fact: para V.55.4.

During the trial, the justices' clerk or legal adviser may ask questions of witnesses and the parties in order to clarify the evidence and any issues in the case. A legal adviser has a duty to ensure that every case is conducted fairly: V.55.5. Further, he or she is under a duty to assist unrepresented parties to present their case, but must do so without appearing to become an advocate for the party: V.55.9.

See the Consolidated Criminal Practice Direction para 55 as to the role of the clerk:

55.1 A justices' clerk is responsible for:

(a) the legal advice tendered to the justices within the area;

(b) the performance of any of the functions set out below by any member of his/her staff acting as legal adviser;

(c) ensuring that competent advice is available to justices when the justices' clerk is not personally present in court; and

(d) the effective delivery of case management and the reduction of unnecessary delay.

55.2 *Where a person other than the justices' clerk (a 'legal adviser'), who is authorised to do so, performs any of the functions referred to in this direction he will have the same responsibilities as the justices' clerk. The legal adviser may consult the justices' clerk or other person authorised by the justices' clerk for that purpose before tendering advice to the bench. If the justices' clerk or that person gives any advice directly to the bench, he should give the parties or their advocates an opportunity of repeating any relevant submissions prior to the advice being given.*

55.3 *It shall be the responsibility of the legal adviser to provide the justices with any advice they require to properly perform their functions whether or not the justices have requested that advice, on:*

(a) *questions of law (including ECHR jurisprudence and those matters set out in s 2(1) of the Human Rights Act 1998);*

(b) *questions of mixed law and fact;*

(c) *matters of practice and procedure;*

(d) *the range of penalties available;*

(e) *any relevant decisions of the superior courts or other guidelines;*

(f) *other issues relevant to the matter before the court; and*

(g) *the appropriate decision making structure to be applied in any given case.*

In addition to advising the justices it shall be the legal adviser's responsibility to assist the court, where appropriate, as to the formulation of reasons and the recording of those reasons.

55.4 *A justices' clerk or legal adviser must not play any part in making findings of fact, but may assist the bench by reminding them of the evidence, using any notes of the proceedings for this purpose.*

55.5 *A justices' clerk or legal adviser may ask questions of witnesses and the parties in order to clarify the evidence and any issues in the case. A legal adviser has a duty to ensure that every case is conducted fairly.*

55.6 *When advising the justices, the justices' clerk or legal adviser, whether or not previously in court, should:*

(a) *ensure that he is aware of the relevant facts; and*

(b) *provide the parties with the information necessary to enable the parties to make any representations they wish as to the advice before it is given.*

55.7 *At any time justices are entitled to receive advice to assist them in discharging their responsibilities. If they are in any doubt as to the evidence which has been given, they should seek the aid of their legal adviser, referring to his notes as appropriate. This should ordinarily be done in open court. Where the justices request their adviser to join them in the retiring room, this request should be made in the presence of the parties in court. Any legal advice given to the justices other than in open court should be clearly stated to be provisional and the adviser should subsequently repeat the substance of the advice in open court and give the parties an opportunity to make any representations they wish on that provisional advice. The legal adviser should then state in open court whether the provisional advice is confirmed or if it is varied the nature of the variation.*

55.8 [Appraisal of performance.]

55.9 *The legal adviser is under a duty to assist unrepresented parties to present their case, but must do so without appearing to become an advocate for the party concerned.*

55.10 *The role of legal advisers in fine default proceedings or any other proceedings for the enforcement of financial orders, obligations or penalties is to assist the court. They must not act in an adversarial or partisan manner. With the agreement of the justices a legal adviser may ask questions of the defaulter to elicit information which the justices will require to make an adjudication, for example to facilitate his explanation for the default. A legal adviser may also advise the justices in the normal way as to the options open to them in dealing with the case. It would be inappropriate for the legal adviser to set out to establish wilful refusal or neglect or any other type of culpable behaviour, to offer an opinion on the facts, or to urge a particular course of action upon the justices. The duty of impartiality is the paramount consideration for the legal adviser at all times, and this takes precedence over any role he or she may have as a collecting officer. The appointment of other staff to 'prosecute' the case for the collecting officer is not essential to ensure compliance with the law, including the Human Rights Act 1998. Whether to make such appointments is a matter for the justices' chief executive.*

5.4 Committal to the Crown Court for sentence

In certain circumstances the magistrates, having found the defendant guilty of an offence or if the defendant pleads guilty, may commit the defendant to the Crown Court for sentence. The most important powers of committal are as follows.

5.4.1 Committal for sentence

Where an adult defendant indicates a guilty plea at the plea before venue stage, the magistrates' court must decide if their sentencing powers are sufficient, or whether the defendant should be committed to the Crown Court for sentence. If the court decides that their powers are sufficient, they may not subsequently commit the case for sentence in the Crown Court, except in the case of dangerous offenders or where a case is committed to the Crown Court because the offender is already being sent there for other matters. See, for example, *R (Harrington) v Bromley Magistrates' Court* [2007] EWCA 2896 where the magistrates adjourned for reports, with all options open, except committal to the Crown Court. The defendant's subsequent committal was quashed. A similar conclusion was reached in *R (Merritt) v Peterborough Magistrates' Court* [2009] EWHC 467 (Admin).

See s 3 of the Powers of Criminal Courts (Sentencing) Act 2000, as amended by the CJA 2003, Sch 3, which provides as follows:

(1) Subject to subsection 4 below, this section applies where—

(a) a person aged 18 or over appears or is brought before a magistrates' court ('the court') on an information charging him with an offence triable either way ('the offence');

(b) he or his representative indicates under section 17A or (as the case may be) 17B of the Magistrates' Courts Act 1980 (initial procedure: accused to indicate intention as to plea), but not section 20(7) of the Act, that he would plead guilty if the offence were to proceed to trial; and

(c) proceeding as if section 9(1) of the Act were complied with and he pleaded guilty under it, the court convicts him of the offence,

(2) If the court is of the opinion that—

(a) the offence; or

(b) the combination of the offence and one or more offences associated with it,

was so serious that the Crown Court should, in the court's opinion, have the power to deal with the offender in any way it could deal with him if he had been convicted on indictment, the court may commit him in custody or on bail to the Crown Court for sentence in accordance with section 5(1) below.

(3) Where the court commits a person under subsection (2) above, section 6 below (which enables a magistrates' court, where it commits a person under this section in respect of an offence, also to commit him to the Crown Court to be dealt with in respect of certain other offences) shall apply accordingly.

(4) This section does not apply in relation to an offence as regards which this section is excluded by section 17D of the Magistrates Courts Act 1980 (certain offences where value involved is small).

Under the PCC(S)A 2000, s 3A as inserted by the CJA 2003, Sch 2, where the court is dealing with a dangerous adult defendant, and the court is of the opinion that the criteria are met for imposition of a sentence under s 225(3) (where the court considers that the offence is such as to justify the imposition of imprisonment for life) or the CJA 2003, s 227(2) (the imposition of an extended sentence), the court may commit the defendant to the Crown Court for sentence. In these circumstances, the court is not bound by any indication of sentence that may have been given, and no appeal may be brought on that basis. See generally the PCC(S)A 2000, s 3 as amended by the CJA 2003, Sch 3.

Where the defendant is committed under s 3 or s 3A, the Crown Court may 'inquire into the circumstances of the case and may deal with the offender in any way in which it could deal with him if he had just been convicted of the offence on indictment before the court': PCC(S)A 2000, s 5 as inserted by the CJA 2003, Sch 3.

Once a defendant has been committed for *trial* on an indictable offence, magistrates may then also commit that defendant for *sentence* on other, related, indictable offences to which he or she has indicated a guilty plea (see PCC(S)A 2000, s 4). In this situation, the Crown Court may sentence the defendant for a 's 4' offence as if he or she had just been convicted of the offence on indictment (see PCC(S)A 2000, s 5(1)). There is an exception—if the defendant is not convicted of the offence for which he or she was sent for trial *and* the magistrates have not stated that the 's 4' offence is one that they would have committed for sentence anyway under s 3 or 3A, the Crown Court is limited to the sentencing powers of the magistrates' court (see PCC(S)A 2000, ss 4(4) and 5).

5.4.2 Committal for sentence on indication of guilty plea by child or young person

Where a child or young person indicates a plea of guilty to one of a number of grave crimes, as defined by the PCC(S)A 2000, s 91, he or she may be committed to the Crown Court for sentence under the PCC(S)A 2000, s 3B as inserted by the CJA 2003, Sch 3. These crimes are any offence which is punishable with 14 years or more imprisonment for adult offenders, and various offences under the Sexual Offences Act 2003.

The committal may be made, under s 3B(2):

'If the court is of the opinion that—

(a) the offence; or

(b) the combination of the offence and one or more offences associated with it,

was such that the Crown Court should, in the court's opinion, have power to deal with the offender as if the provisions of section 91(3) below applied . . .'

Where the defendant is committed under s 3B, the Crown Court may 'inquire into the circumstances of the case and may deal with the offender in any way in which it could deal with him if he had just been convicted of the offence on indictment before the court' PCC(S)A 2000, s 5A as inserted by the CJA 2003, Sch 3.

Where the defendant is under 18 and is tried summarily for a *specified offence* in the magistrates' court he or she may be committed for sentence as described above under the PCC(S)A 2000, s 3C as inserted by the CJA 2003. A *specified offence* is defined in the

CJA 2003, s 224 and Sch 15. Specified violent offences are set out in Part 1 of Sch 15 and comprise 65 separate offences, including manslaughter, kidnapping, false imprisonment, and grievous bodily harm. Specified sexual offences are set out in Part 2 of Sch 15 and comprise a further 88 offences being many of those under the Sexual Offences Acts 1956 and 2003.

Section 3C provides that the young offender must be committed for sentence to the Crown Court where 'it appears to the court that the criteria for the imposition of a sentence under section 226(3) [a sentence of detention for public protection] or section 228(2) (an extended sentence of detention) would be met'.

5.4.3 Committal for sentence on the indication of a guilty plea by a child or young person with related offences

The PCC(S)A 2000, s 4A (as amended by the CJA 2003, Sch 3) states that where a child or young person indicates that he or she would plead guilty to a grave offence (see **5.4.2**), the magistrates' court may commit him or her to the Crown Court for sentence if it has already sent him to Crown Court for *trial* on one or more related offences. The Crown Court 'shall inquire into the circumstances of the offence and may deal with the offender in any way in which it could deal with him if he had just been convicted of the offence on indictment before the court' (see the PCC(S)A 2000, s 5A, inserted by the CJA 2003, Sch 3). A similar caveat applies here as for adult offenders being sentenced under the PCC(S)A 2000, s 5—namely:

- if the magistrates do not indicate that the 's 4A' offence is one which they would also have committed for sentence under s 3B or 3C; and
- the child or young person is not convicted of at least one of the related offences; then
- the Crown Court is restricted to the sentencing powers of the Youth Court (see **5.4.1** and PCC(S)A 2000, s 4A(4)).

5.4.4 Committal under the Powers of Criminal Courts (Sentencing) Act 2000, s 6

Section 6 provides that where the magistrates are committing a defendant to the Crown Court in any of the circumstances outlined in **5.4.1** or **5.4.5**, they may also commit for any other offences of which the defendant has been convicted.

The effect is that the magistrates may commit to the Crown Court summary offences which could not otherwise be committed. Thus, a single court can deal with the defendant for all outstanding offences, and this avoids the otherwise inconvenient result of the magistrates' court dealing with the summary offences and the Crown Court dealing with everything else.

The purpose of the section is convenience, and to ensure consistency of sentencing. In these circumstances it would be unfair to the defendant if he or she incurred any greater penalty as regards the summary offences, and therefore the powers of the Crown Court when dealing with a defendant on a committal under s 6 are limited to those of the magistrates. For example, see *R v Whitlock* (1992) 13 Cr App R (S) 157, CA.

Note the power to commit a defendant under the Proceeds of Crime Act 2002 s 6 for a confiscation order to be made.

5.4.5 Breach of a Crown Court order

Where the defendant is convicted of an offence which constitutes a breach of a Crown Court order, the magistrates may commit the offender to the Crown Court (see **19.3** for further details). The most important orders are:

(a) A suspended sentence. If the defendant is convicted of an imprisonable offence committed while subject to a suspended sentence, the magistrates may either commit for sentence or simply notify the Crown Court of the breach (PCC(S)A 2000, s 120).

(b) A community order or conditional discharge. If the defendant is in breach of either order, the magistrates may commit him or her in custody or on bail or deal with him or her themselves. If it is a breach of a conditional discharge, the committal is likely to be on bail.

5.4.6 Appeals

If the defendant wishes to appeal against committal, he or she must apply for judicial review (see **8.3**). He or she cannot appeal to the Crown Court as a committal is neither a conviction nor a sentence (see **8.1**). Nor can he or she appeal by way of case stated as the case has not yet finished (see **8.2.1**).

Similarly, the prosecution may apply for judicial review of the magistrates' refusal to commit. For an example, see *R v Derby Magistrates' Court, ex p DPP, The Times*, 17 August 1999, where the defendant assaulted his partner by banging her head against a glass door, causing permanent scarring. The prosecution argued that the decision to accept jurisdiction to sentence in these circumstances was irrational, and further argued that the door constituted a 'weapon' within the National Mode of Trial Guidelines (see **4.7**). The High Court rejected this argument, saying that to describe a door as a weapon was an abuse of language. The court accepted that the maximum sentence which the magistrates could impose would be a lenient one, but it could not be characterised as one that no reasonable bench could properly impose. The application was rejected.

6

Youth court trials

6.1 Introduction

For most people charged with a criminal offence, there are only two courts that they need to know about. These are the magistrates' court and Crown Court. (Although remember that cases can go *on appeal* to the Divisional Court or Court of Appeal and then to the House of Lords.)

For juveniles there is another court—the youth court. This court is a special type of magistrates' court. To avoid confusion, the ordinary magistrates' court will be referred to in this chapter as the *adult* magistrates' court.

Since Parliament passed the Children and Young Persons Act 1933 (CYPA), courts have been under a statutory duty to have regard to the welfare of juveniles when dealing with them. The youth justice system of England and Wales has been subjected to considerable scrutiny over recent years and has recently undergone major changes. It may be helpful to review, briefly, some of the history and objectives that lay behind the root and branch reforms that began in 1998 and have continued up to the present. For a longer-term look back, one can refer to 'Youth justice? Half a century of responses to youth offending' by Caroline Ball [2004] Crim LR 167.

In a 1996 report, *Misspent Youth*, the Audit Commission said that:

> The current system for dealing with youth crime is inefficient and expensive, while little is done to deal effectively with juvenile nuisance. The present arrangements are failing the young people who are not being guided away from offending to constructive activities. They are also failing victims . . . and they lead to waste in a variety of forms, including lost time, as public servants process the same young offenders through the courts time and again . . .

Prior to this, in 1997, the Home Office had published a seminal White Paper on youth justice—*No More Excuses—A New Approach to Tackling Youth Crime in England and Wales*. It expressed concern that too much effort went into merely 'processing' juveniles and very little was directed to the prevention of crime or providing a service to victims, offenders and witnesses. Earlier intervention—nipping crime in the bud—was the preferred option. A 'fundamental change of approach' was required for the youth courts, looking beyond simple questions of 'guilt or innocence'. Courts were to enquire more widely into the circumstances of the offending behaviour, leading on to action being taken to change that behaviour.

One apparent problem was the confusion caused by the conflict between the statutory duty imposed by the CYPA 1933 to look to the welfare of a juvenile offender and the aims of protecting the public and preventing offending. An attempt to clarify the correct approach came in the Crime and Disorder Act 1998, s 37:

> (a) It shall be the principal aim of the youth justice system to prevent offending by children and young persons.

(b) In addition to any other duty to which they are subject, it shall be the duty of all persons and bodies carrying out functions in relation to the youth justice system to have regard to that aim.

So, to consider how best to prevent offending, it would be sensible to identify the most common factors associated with criminal behaviour and address them. Research quoted in the White Paper, *No More Excuses*, identified the following key factors as relevant to youth criminality:

- being male;
- being brought up by a criminal parent or parents;
- living in a family with multiple problems;
- experiencing poor parenting and lack of supervision;
- poor discipline in the family and at school;
- playing truant or being excluded from school;
- associating with delinquent friends; and
- having siblings who offend.

The 'single most important factor in explaining criminality is the quality of a young person's home life, including parental supervision' (White Paper, ch 1). So, youth courts now have the power to refer first-time offenders, who show contrition, to youth offender panels who will draw up a contract, regulating the juvenile's future behaviour. The police now have the power to give a warning to a juvenile (ie rather than prosecute) and to refer the juvenile to rehabilitation programmes, run by youth offending teams (YOTs). YOTs are multi-agency bodies, created by local authorities, in cooperation with the local chief officer of police, probation service and health authority, under powers given by the CDA 1998, s 39. The Home Office says that these YOTs are at the cutting edge of the government's reforms for youth justice. Amongst their tasks, they are to:

tackle the issues identified in the White Paper—from poor parental supervision and domestic violence or abuse to peer group pressure, from truancy and school exclusion to substance misuse or mental health problems—which can place young people at risk of becoming involved in crime.

Sentences introduced in 1998 as part of the reform programme include reparation orders, detention and training orders, action plan orders and parenting orders. Juvenile offenders may be confronted by the victims of their crimes and required to make a direct apology (reparation orders); children and parents may have to attend family counselling sessions (parenting orders). In an attempt to stop offending before it starts ('nipping crime in the bud') powers were given to courts and local authorities to make child safety orders and impose local child curfews on children under ten years. The former are targeted at individual children who are seen to be at risk of being drawn into crime; a court can require a child to be at home at specific times or stay away from specific places or people, and specific conduct may be forbidden (for example, truanting from school). The latter aim to minimise the risk that peer pressure and the absence of responsible adult role models in a community will foster anti-social behaviour; local authorities are empowered to bar all children under ten years from a specified public area after a certain time (not to be earlier than 9 pm).

As noted above, the Audit Commission's 1996 report was very useful in encouraging the recent changes. In 2004, the Commission reviewed the results (see *2004 Youth Justice*). Its bottom line conclusion was that 'the new system is a considerable improvement on the old one'. For example, young offenders were being dealt with faster (on average, twice as quickly compared to 1997). Young offenders were more likely to make amends for their actions (in 2002–3, nearly one in three young offenders received either a referral order or reparation order as their sentence). Reconviction rates, where the young offender had received a final warning or reprimand, were between 7 and 10 per cent lower than had been predicted. Nevertheless, the report identified some continuing problems—for example, low public confidence in the youth justice system (apparently, three out of four people had not heard of YOTs); also, young offenders from black and ethnic minority backgrounds were much more likely to be remanded in custody or receive a custodial sentence than those from white backgrounds (1 in 12 and 1 in 10 given custodial sentences, compared to 1 in 40). Perhaps the most significant observation in the Report is this:

Many young offenders who end up in custody have a history of professionals failing to listen, assessments not being followed by action and nobody being in charge. If effective early intervention had been provided for just one-in-ten of these young people, annual savings in excess of £100 million could have been made . . . [E]arly intervention programmes can be effective if they are properly co-ordinated . . . [B]etter still, mainstream agencies, such as schools and health services, should take full responsibility for preventing offending by young people.

The Government responded to the Audit Commission's report in December 2004. The Government accepted the point about early and effective intervention, noting that it aims to establish 2,500 Children's Centres by 2008 and highlighting its reforms evolving from its 2003 Green Paper, *Every Child Matters* and the Children Act 2004 (further information is available on the website <http://www.everychildmatters.gov.uk>; a report relating specifically to children in the criminal justice system was published in December 2004). The response also indicated that the Government aimed to make much greater use of Final Warnings and reprimands (revised guidelines on the Final Warning Scheme were published in March 2005). This should allow courts to focus on the more serious offences and persistent young offenders.

In 2003, the Government introduced a youth community sentence. This was intended to have a 'menu of interventions', operating in a similar fashion to the adult community order which was introduced in the CJA 2003, s 177, and replace the eight existing community sentences for juveniles. In 2007, its implementation was then postponed until April 2009. It now seems unlikely that it will come into force— in 2009, its implementation date was deferred once more, to 2010, and the Criminal Justice and Immigration Act 2008 introduced the Youth Rehabilitation Order. As this Act's Explanatory Notes state—the YRO is a

new generic community sentence for children and young people. It sets out the requirements that may be attached to a YRO, makes provision for their enforcement . . . and abolishes certain existing community sentences which are to be replaced by the YRO . . . When imposing a YRO, the court will be able to choose from a 'menu' of different requirements that the offender must comply with.

The sentences which are abolished (or 'combined' in the new YRO) are – curfew orders, attendance centre orders, exclusion orders, supervision orders and action plan orders.

See further, **Chapter 17** below.

In its 2004 report, *Youth Justice*, the Audit Commission observed that

given the scope of the reforms and the relatively short space of time in which they have been up and running, it would be unwise to embark on further wholesale change.

(See <http://www.audit-commission.gov.uk>). This suggestion seems to have gone unheeded.

6.2 Juveniles and criminal responsibility

6.2.1 What do we mean by 'juvenile'?

A juvenile is basically anyone under the age of 18 (Criminal Justice Act 1991 (CJA), s 68). Once an individual has reached his or her eighteenth birthday, he or she must be treated like any other adult defendant. This could lead to problems if the defendant's eighteenth birthday occurs while a case is pending at court (see **6.5.2** below). Thus, while for the layman the term 'juvenile' generally means a youth or young person, for the criminal justice system one's youth ends on the eighteenth birthday. However, we must continue to divide this population into different age groups, as we shall see below.

6.2.2 The under 10s

Currently, children aged under 10 years are irrebuttably presumed to be incapable of committing any crime. Therefore, they do not fall within the criminal jurisdiction of any court (CYPA 1933, s 50). The abolition of the presumption of innocence for children aged 10–13, coupled with the introduction of child safety orders and local child curfews for the under-10s, has led to concern in some places that some under-10s may soon feel criminalised, even if they are not strictly covered by the criminal justice system. We noted in **6.1** the power to impose local child curfews and child safety orders.

Finally, it should be noted that older children and adults sometimes use children under 10 to carry out crimes, knowing that no criminal action can be taken against such innocent pawns. It may result in the conviction of the 'manipulator', usually as the principal offender, with the child being regarded as merely an innocent agent of the other. See also *Archbold*, 2008 edn, paras 1-90/91 and 18-7; *Blackstone's Criminal Practice*, 2009 edn, section A5.

6.2.3 Criminal responsibility starts at 10

Historically, a presumption of innocence (or 'incapacity') was applied to juveniles aged 10–13 years. This presumption stated that children were presumed not to know that they were doing wrong, even though they had done an act which constituted a crime. The onus was on the prosecution to rebut this presumption by calling evidence intended to show that the child in question knew that what he or she had done was 'seriously wrong'. The presumption was abolished in 1998 (see CDA 1998, s 34). The rationale for abolition was a concern that the need to call evidence to rebut the presumption 'could lead to real practical difficulties, delaying cases or even making it impossible for the prosecution to proceed' (No *More Excuses*, ch 4; for a contrary perspective, see *Protecting the Rights of Children*, a report by the Howard League for Penal Reform, 1999).

Many other European countries consider their youngsters incapable of bearing criminal responsibility before their fourteenth birthday. The issue of a minimum age was considered by the European Court of Human Rights in *T v UK* (2000) 30 EHRR 121. The Court considered whether the attribution of criminal responsibility for acts done when the defendant was aged 10 might amount to inhuman or degrading treatment, contrary to the European Convention on Human Rights, Article 3. The Court said that:

it did not find that there was any clear common standard amongst the member States of the Council of Europe as to the minimum age of criminal responsibility. While most had adopted an age-limit which was higher than that in force in England and Wales, other States, such as Cyprus, Ireland, Liechtenstein and Switzerland, attributed criminal responsibility from a younger age, and no clear tendency could be ascertained from examination of the relevant international texts and instruments, for example, the United Nations Convention on the Rights of the Child. Even if England and Wales was among the few European jurisdictions to retain a low age of criminal responsibility, the age of ten could not be said to be so young as to differ disproportionately to the age limit followed by other European States. The attribution of criminal responsibility to the applicants did not, therefore, in itself give rise to a breach of Article 3.

In an interesting development, in 2007 the QB Divisional Court suggested (obiter) that s 34 had only abolished the presumption but that the common law defence of *doli incapax* remained: see *Crown Prosecution Service v P* [2007] EWHC 946 (Admin). See Smith LJ at paragraphs [37]–[47], suggesting that a juvenile could still raise the defence that they did not know what they were doing was wrong; if they could discharge an evidential burden, it would fall to the prosecution to prove beyond a reasonable doubt that they did so know. This 'new shoot on a bleak landscape' (see Telford, Child and Family Law Quarterly, 2007) was soon lopped off when the Court of Appeal decided that s 34 had done away with *doli incapax* as both a presumption and a defence; see *R v T* [2008] EWCA Crim 815.

6.2.4 10–17-year-olds

Juveniles between the ages of 10 and 13 inclusive are often described in criminal law statutes as 'children', but this is not a universal usage. Those aged between 14 and 17 years inclusive are usually described as 'young persons'. See the CJA 1991, s 68 and Sch 8. Historically, these two groups have been distinguished for two reasons—sentencing powers, and the presumption of innocence. We looked at that presumption in **6.2.3**.

The sentences which are available for young offenders are dealt with at length in **Chapters 17** and **18**. In summary, the range of sentences available to courts when dealing with juveniles differs significantly from those available for adult offenders. Again, different types of sentence (or different maxima) apply to juveniles of different ages. However, the trend in recent years has been to toughen the sentences available, even when dealing with the youngest offenders. One example is the power to sentence defendants as young as 10 to long-term detention for various grave offences (eg burglary of a house, certain types of arson and criminal damage, and robbery). Another example is the power to make detention and training orders (DTOs). A DTO may be used for 15–17-year-olds who are convicted of any imprisonable offence which is sufficiently serious to cross the custody threshold in the CJA 1991. Twelve to 14-year-olds would be at risk of a DTO when convicted of an imprisonable offence if they have a record of persistent offending.

6.3 The youth court

6.3.1 Youth court—the usual forum for juvenile defendants

The type of court in which a juvenile accused will make his or her first appearance, following charge, is the magistrates' court. If the juvenile is charged alone, or with other juveniles, then this will be the youth court (the branch of magistrates' court which specialises in juvenile justice). If the juvenile is charged with an adult defendant (either on a

Youth court trials

single joint charge or on multiple but related charges), then the first appearance for both accused will be in the adult magistrates' court. The basic aim is that juvenile defendants should be dealt with at summary level unless some exceptional circumstance is present, and that the specialist summary court—the youth court—will be the most appropriate forum. See, for example, *R (H) v Southampton Youth Court* [2004] EWHC 2912 (Admin); and MCA 1980, s 24(1) as substituted by the CJA 2003, Sch 3, para 9.

It may be suggested, on occasion, that even the youth court is unsuitable to try the charge against a particular juvenile. This can occur when the juvenile's development is later or slower than normal. It is clear that a juvenile, like any other defendant, is entitled to receive a fair trial but the lack of sufficient development may hamper this.

In the case of a child, it is essential that he will be dealt with in a manner which takes full account of his age, level of maturity and intellectual and emotional capacities, and that steps are taken to promote his ability to understand and participate in the proceedings, including conducting the hearing in such a way as to reduce as far as possible his feeling of intimidation and inhibition. [However] the trial of a defendant with a mental age of 8 does not necessarily involve a breach of Article 6. What is crucial is whether the tribunal hearing the case . . . is able to adapt its procedures so that the defendant can effectively participate in the proceedings.

Scott Baker LJ in *R (on the application of TP) v West London Youth Court* [2005] EWHC 2583 (Admin), offering his view on the European Court of Human Rights judgment in *SC v UK* (2004) EHRR 10.

Youth courts often sit in the same buildings and rooms that are used by the local adult magistrates' court. However, courts are required to make arrangements so 'that young defendants do not associate with adult defendants whilst awaiting hearing' (see CYPA 1933, s 31).

In some places, mainly inner city areas where the scale of juvenile proceedings justifies the cost, special youth courts have been built to deal with the workload. Adult defendants never appear in these courtrooms.

6.3.2 Inside the youth court

6.3.2.1 The magistrates

In a youth court, the court will usually consist of three lay magistrates (or 'justices of the peace'). They will have been selected from a 'youth court panel' of magistrates who are specially qualified to deal with juveniles and who have also had some additional training for this purpose. Normally, there should be at least one male and one female magistrate present for a hearing in the youth court. If all the magistrates in court are of the same sex, they may only hear cases if:

- this situation could not have been foreseen; and
- having heard representations from the parties in open court, the magistrates do not consider it is expedient to adjourn proceedings to see if a mixed gender bench might be formed.

District judges are professional judges (formerly known as stipendiary magistrates). They usually sit in the adult magistrates' court but are also members of the youth court panel by virtue of their office and may deal with cases in the youth court. If they do so, they will usually sit unaccompanied by lay magistrates. In 1997, a Home Office report (*Review of Delay in the Criminal Justice System*, often known as the Narey Report after its author) recommended that district judges should specialise in the management of particularly complex cases which, when they involve children and young persons, 'can be particularly difficult'.

6.3.2.2 The parents of the juvenile

When a juvenile appears in court, accused of a crime, it is understandable that his or her parents may want to be present to support their child. This is not always the attitude of parents, however, and the trial courts possess the power to compel parents to attend court. If a juvenile is aged 15 or under, the court must order a parent to attend, unless it would be unreasonable to do so. If the juvenile is aged 16 or 17, the court *may* make such an order (see CYPA 1933, s 34A, inserted by the CJA 1991, s 56). When parents attend court, they usually sit next to their child.

Part of the reason for requiring a juvenile's parents to be present in court may be that although '[p]arents of young offenders may not directly be to blame for the crimes of their children, [they] have to be responsible for providing their children with proper care and control' (*No More Excuses*, 1997). Home Office research has shown that inadequate parental supervision is strongly associated with offending; also that the quality of the parent-child relationship is crucial. Bringing the parents to court may bring home to them the need to modify their behaviour as well as that of their child. However, *No More Excuses* also reported that parental firmness was not necessarily the answer: 'We know that parents who are harsh or erratic in disciplining their children are twice as likely to have children who offend.'

Parents may need to be present in court anyway, to represent their own interests. For example—courts are able to make *a parenting order* (see CDA 1998, s 8). This order obliges parents to attend counselling or guidance sessions for a maximum of three months and to comply with any additional requirements for up to one year (for example, ensuring full school attendance by their child). Non-compliance, without reasonable excuse, may result in a conviction and a fine of up to £1,000. In 2004, the Court of Appeal considered the appeal of a man against a compensation order for £1,000. The man had been ordered by a judge to pay this sum to the victim of a robbery committed by the man's 16-year-old son. The judge had the power to make the order but it was set aside by the Court of Appeal as the judge had failed to give the man the chance to be heard on the matter and had not considered whether it would be reasonable to order the man to pay compensation. See *R v JJB* [2004] EWCA Crim 14; PCC(S)A 2000, s 137.

6.3.2.3 The witnesses

As the youth court is a criminal court, all witnesses will usually be kept out of the courtroom until it is their time to give evidence. Once their evidence is concluded, they could stay in the courtroom but in practice there is often nowhere convenient for them to sit.

An adult witness, for example a police officer or store detective, will give their evidence in exactly the same way as they would in any other court proceedings. However, if the witness is a juvenile (perhaps the victim of a mugging), then special provisions become relevant. One simple difference is that the juvenile witness gives a 'promise' to tell the truth, rather than 'swear' to do so. Another difference is that special procedures may be used in order to get the best evidence from the juvenile witness since such a witness is considered to be vulnerable.

The YJCEA 1999 established a coherent set of provisions to deal with all of the so-called 'special measures' which may be used by courts to protect vulnerable (or intimidated) witnesses. In summary, these are:

- the power to clear the public from the courtroom while the witness gives evidence (in trials involving sexual offences or when it appears that someone is trying to intimidate the witness);

- that the lawyers and the judge may remove their wigs and gowns;
- that a screen may be used in court, to shield the witness from the accused;
- that a pre-recorded video may serve as part or all of the evidence of the witness;
- that the witness may give evidence at the trial from a separate room via a live link.

Some of these provisions existed already, either in statute or more informally. The intention of the YJCEA 1999 appears to have been to clarify and strengthen the facilities which are available to aid children (and other vulnerable witnesses). Also, the process of making decisions on which special measures to adopt is put onto a rational basis. In principle, the special measures are available for proceedings in all criminal trial courts. In practice, a specific court will need notice from the Home Secretary that appropriate facilities are available to it, either permanently or temporarily, before it can consider making a special measures order.

Children under the age of 17 at the time of the trial are presumed to be in need of such help. The procedure for determining which special measure to use for a child witness will depend upon which of three categories the witness falls into:

- children testifying in a case involving a sexual offence;
- children testifying in a case involving an offence of violence, abduction or neglect;
- children giving evidence in all other cases.

For most child witnesses, the YJCEA 1999, s 21, creates a presumption (or 'primary rule'; see s 21(3)) that their evidence will be given by pre-recorded video (for evidence-in-chief) and live link (for all other evidence). The appropriate orders for special measures should be made unless the court decides that the measures would not be likely to maximise the quality of the witness's evidence as far as practicable.

A child testifying in a trial for a sexual offence will give evidence-in-chief through a pre-recorded video. Any cross-examination should also take place at a pre-trial hearing and be recorded for playback at the trial unless the witness tells the court that he or she does not want that protection. Video evidence may be excluded in certain circumstances; in particular if the court is of the opinion, having regard to all the circumstances of the case, that it is not in the interests of justice that the recording be used in evidence (YJCEA 1999, s 27(2)). A child witness in a trial for an offence involving violence, abduction or neglect will have his or her examination-in-chief recorded on video for playback at the trial. Any further evidence (including cross-examination and re-examination) will normally be via a live link. The court is not required to take a decision on whether the special measures are likely to maximise the quality of the evidence. ?

Almost all of the special measures provisions in the YJCEA are now in force (the exception is s 28—cross-examination by pre-recorded video). As Baroness Hale has said,

Parliament has decided what is to be the norm when child witnesses give evidence. Hence there will have to be a special reason for departing from it. The fact that there is no particular reason to think that [a specific] child will be upset, traumatised or intimidated by giving evidence in court does not make it unjust for her to give it by live link and video if there is one.

See *R (D) v Camberwell Green Youth Court* [2005] 1 WLR 393.
The House of Lords held that SMDs are compatible with the right to a fair trial under ECHR, Article 6. Although they have sometimes been criticised as being too inflexible, Baroness Hale pointed out that several SMDs may be *disapplied* by exercise of the court's discretion and that this may be used where, for example, 'the child was positively anxious to give evidence in the courtroom and the court considered that it would be contrary to the interests of justice to require her to use the live link'.

138   Youth court trials

The exclusion of juvenile defendants from SMDs has been criticised; see, for example, the commentary by Professor Di Birch to *R (on the application of the DPP) v Acton Youth Court* [2002] Crim LR 75, where she refers to this as an 'almost spiteful' exclusion. This position has been defended by both the Government and the CPS who feel that defendants are already adequately protected by various rules and procedures (see for example, the note by Hoyano in [2005] JoCL 69 6). In D, however, Baroness Hale expressed the view that whilst defendants are properly excluded from the SMD scheme as 'it is clearly inappropriate to apply the whole scheme to [them]', it is also correct to say that courts have inherent powers to ensure that an accused receives a fair trial. This might permit allowing the use of an interpreter to help with communication, allowing a detailed written statement to be read to the jury, and even allowing the use of leading questions based upon such a statement in order to enable the juvenile defendant to give a proper and coherent account. Baroness Hale drew attention to YJCEA s 19(6), which leaves intact any power of a court to make an order 'in relation to a witness who is not an eligible witness . . .' Lord Rodgers noted that in Scotland (since 2006), child defendants are treated mostly in the same way as any other child witness (see Vulnerable Witnesses (Scotland) Act 2004, s 271F) so that 'there are no insuperable difficulties in the way of taking some such step . . .' However, since January 2007, provisions in the Police and Justice Act 2006 allow a vulnerable accused person to give their evidence via a live link instead of from the witness box, so some assistance may now be extended to the juvenile accused. The Ministry of Justice published a consultation paper in June 2007, setting out proposals for changes to the special measures regime, *Improving the Criminal Trial Process for Young Witnesses*, (available at <http://www.cjsonline.gov.uk>). For a thorough review of that paper, what led to it and the current issues in the evidence of children, see Hoyano, *The child witness review: much ado about too little* [2007] Crim LR 849.

A child witness must not be cross-examined by an unrepresented defendant where the trial involves sexual offences. In such cases, the defendant will be given an opportunity to appoint a lawyer specifically to cross-examine the witness. If he or she does not take that opportunity, the court must decide whether it should appoint a cross-examiner in the interests of justice (YJCEA 1999, s 38).

6.3.2.4   The media

Currently there is a ban on the media reporting any details which may identify any child or young person involved in a case in the youth court (whether as a defendant or as a witness; see CYPA 1933, s 49 as substituted by the CJPOA 1994, s 49). Thus,

> no report shall be published which reveals the name, address or school of any child or young person concerned in the proceedings or includes any particulars likely to lead to the identification of [such a person]; [further] no picture shall be published [of any such person].

This ban may be lifted in three situations.

(a) The defence may apply to lift the ban. Publicity must be appropriate for the avoidance of injustice to the juvenile accused (for example, publicising details of the incident to attract the attention of potential defence witnesses).

(b) The prosecution may apply to lift the ban. Publicity may be necessary here if the juvenile accused is 'unlawfully at large' and publicity may assist in his or her recapture. The offence must be either:

   (i)   serious (in that it carries a maximum punishment of 14 years' or more imprisonment for an adult offender); or

(ii) violent or sexual (as defined in Sch 15 CJA 2003; see **Chapter 20** and *Blackstone's Criminal Practice*, 2009 edn, section D23.12).

(c) After the juvenile has been convicted, the youth court itself may consider it to be in the public interest to remove the reporting restrictions. Before doing so, the court should allow the parties to make representations on the matter. The aims here are to disclose the outcome of the case, to show that justice has been done and, perhaps, to shame the individual offender.

The CYPA 1933, s 49 has been amended by the Youth Justice and Criminal Evidence Act 1999 (YJCEA), Sch 2 but that provision is not yet in force. When it is brought into force, the prohibition will read:

No matter relating to any child or young person concerned in proceedings to which this section applies shall while he is under the age of 18 be included in any publication if it is likely to lead members of the public to identify him as someone concerned in the proceedings.

The CYPA 1933, s 49 applies mainly to proceedings in the youth court. A complementary, discretionary, power to prohibit reports on information which may lead to the identification of a defendant, victim or witness under the age of 18 in any other criminal court proceedings now exists but is not yet in force (see YJCEA 1999, s 45). Once this new discretionary power comes into effect, the CYPA 1933, s 39 will continue in force only for non-criminal proceedings.

6.3.2.5 Probation officers

It is quite usual to see probation officers or staff from local authority social services sitting in the youth court. It is sometimes the case that the juvenile defendant is in the care of the local authority; more often, the defendant is already 'known' to these bodies and the personnel may have been involved in preparing a pre-sentence report in a previous hearing or have worked with the defendant on a supervision order, for example. They may be a helpful source of information for a barrister inexperienced in appearing before the youth court.

6.3.2.6 The public

Youth courts operate rather differently from other courts, in that there is no general right to enter a youth courtroom. Attendance is governed by the CYPA 1933, s 47(2), as amended, so that no person shall be present at any sitting of a youth court except:

- the juvenile, his or her parents, the parties' legal representatives and the magistrate(s);
- court officers (the clerk, ushers);
- bona fide media reporters (but not to take photographs or to film);
- witnesses (both during and after giving their evidence);
- anyone else directly concerned in that case (probation officers, social workers, etc);
- such other persons as the court may specially authorise to be present.

In the past, these restrictions on access have usually been enforced strictly. The reason for this limited access was, in part, a desire to protect the juvenile from being (or feeling) stigmatised as a criminal. The effect was to exclude the general public and, not infrequently, the victim of the offence. The victim would enter the courtroom only when and if needed as a witness, where the juvenile pleaded not guilty. In the late 1990s this led to criticism of the youth court system as a 'secret garden', where proceedings took place in private and young offenders were not encouraged to face the consequences of their actions and take steps to change their behaviour. It was suggested that the practice placed too great an emphasis on protecting the identity of young offenders at the expense of victims and the community. In 1998, the former Home Office Minister Alun Michael observed that youth courts:

> . . . have wide discretion about who can attend [their] proceedings . . . We believe that justice is best served in an open court where the criminal process can be scrutinised and the offender cannot hide behind a cloak of anonymity.

Subsequently, the Home Office and Lord Chancellor's Department issued a joint circular which included the following recommendations:

- all victims of juvenile crime should have the opportunity to attend the youth court (for the trial or preceding hearings) unless to do so would not be in the interests of justice;
- greater access should be allowed for the public to attend proceedings in the youth court (an example being a case where the offender's conduct has had an impact on the local community generally).

6.3.2.7 The layout of the youth court

There will not usually be seating provided for members of the public in dedicated youth courtrooms. These courtrooms provide seating only for those people who are specifically allowed to be present during the proceedings (see CYPA 1933, s 47(2)). The magistrates do not sit up on a raised platform, but often are on ordinary chairs behind plain tables. Since the court clerk, lawyers, probation officers and social workers also sit on ordinary chairs behind desks, it is not as obvious as in other courtrooms where one should sit.

As a rule of thumb, the chairs in the centre of the room will be reserved for the juvenile defendant(s) and parents. These chairs will face the desk where the magistrates sit (and the Royal Coat of Arms may be on the wall behind the magistrates). The clerk's desk will be at the side of the one used by the magistrates and, usually, the lawyers' seats and desks will be on the same side of the room as the clerk. These dedicated youth courtrooms do not contain docks to hold a prisoner.

In adult magistrates' courts and the Crown Court, public seating is always provided. When an adult courtroom is used as a youth court, typically the public seating will be left empty. Everyone will sit where they normally would, except that no dock will be used even if there is one. In such cases, the juvenile defendant will sit in front of the dock.

6.3.3 Procedure in the youth court

As the youth court is a special type of magistrates' court, most of what happens in a hearing is the same as for adults in the adult magistrates' court. In particular, a juvenile can be tried summarily, sentenced if found guilty and remanded if a case is adjourned for any reason by the youth court. The youth court can issue a warrant for the arrest of a juvenile defendant who fails to attend the hearing (see BA 1976, s 7; MCA 1980, s 13). There are some differences, however, which are largely semantic. See **Figure 6.1**.

> Name
>
> Juveniles (both defendants and witnesses) are addressed by their first names.
>
> Oath
>
> Juveniles 'promise' to tell the truth. The usual form of oath requires a witness to swear to do so. (Those aged under 14 give evidence *unsworn*: YJCEA 1999, s 55.)
>
> Guilt
>
> A juvenile is never 'convicted' of an offence; the court will simply record a finding of guilt.
>
> The difference is largely cosmetic, presumably to avoid the trauma of conviction.
>
> Sentence
>
> A juvenile is not sentenced to a punishment after the case has been proved, rather the court makes an order upon a finding of guilt. Again, the distinction is semantic.

Figure 6.1

The usual method of classifying offences that we saw in **Chapter 4** (summary, indictment-only, and triable either way) does not of itself determine the mode of trial for juvenile defendants. Indictment-only crimes, such as robbery and rape, need not be sent to Crown Court for trial where the accused is a juvenile (the exception is homicide offences which *must* be sent for trial to Crown Court; see PCC(S)A 2000, s 91 and MCA 1980, s 24). Similarly, just because the juvenile accused faces a crime which is triable either way, it does not follow that the court must work through a mode of trial determination, nor that the accused can choose trial by jury. However, it is quite possible for the youth court to send a juvenile defendant for trial to Crown Court on indictable offences. It is necessary to consider how this may happen.

The current position is quite complicated. In essence, there are two sets of procedures, one of which was intended to succeed the other but which are presently both in force and therefore overlapping. The provisions containing these procedures are the MCA 1980, s 24 and the CDA 1998, s 51A. Both statutes were amended by the CJA 2003 and the two procedures have been described by the Court of Appeal as 'not merely labyrinthine but manifestly inconsistent with each other'; see *Crown Prosecution Service v South East Surrey Youth Court and Ghanbari* [2005] EWHC 2929 (Admin). The Divisional Court endeavoured to take 'as sensible an approach as can be achieved' notwithstanding the temptation to say that 'the Holy Grail of rational interpretation is impossible to find'.

The upshot was that the MCA 1980, s 24 in its present form requires that a juvenile be tried summarily *unless* the offence with which he or she is charged:

(a) is a *grave* one; AND

(b) may require a sentence of long-term detention.

If these two criteria are met, then the first thing that should happen is plea before venue—that is, following the appropriate warnings, the juvenile is asked to indicate what his plea would be (compare **Chapter 4**). If the juvenile indicates a guilty plea, the court proceeds as if he or she has just pleaded guilty and convicts him. The magistrates may then commit the juvenile to Crown Court under PCC(S)A 2000, s 3B, where a possible sentence of long-term detention may then be passed under PCC(S)A, s 91 (or under s 3C, if he or she is a dangerous offender). If he indicates a plea of not guilty, the Youth Court must commit the juvenile to Crown Court for trial if the court considers there is a real prospect (or 'real possibility') of a sentence of two years' or more detention. A *grave* offence is one within PCC(S)A 2000, s 91—one where an adult offender may face 14 or more years' imprisonment, or a variety of offences under the Sexual Offences Act 2003 and Firearms Act 1968.

The circumstances in which a sentence of two or more years' detention will be a 'real prospect' have been considered in many cases. One example is *R (H) v Southampton Youth Court* [2004] EWHC 2912 (Admin). The court said that:

- Crown Court trial should be reserved for the most serious cases;
- usually, first-time offenders aged 12–14 and all offenders aged under 12 should not be detained in custody;
- offenders aged under 15 would rarely require a sentence of detention; such a sentence would be even more exceptional for those under 12;
- if a defendant is under 15 and would not qualify for a detention and training order, the court might ask if there is a real prospect that a sentence of detention shorter than two years is required, but there would need to be some unusual feature in the case to justify such a conclusion.

By way of illustration of the sort of problems that can confront a youth court, one can look at *R (on the application of W) v Brent Youth Court and DPP and others* [2006] EWHC 95 (Admin). The Divisional Court held here that a youth charged with four counts of robbery and two of attempted robbery of mobile phones from young girls, using threats as part of a group did not face a real prospect of more than two years' detention. Meanwhile, a 12-year-old charged with rape could (as here) lead the court to conclude that there was a real prospect that more than two years' detention would be imposed but it was also possible that circumstances might exist where it would be appropriate for a youth court to accept jurisdiction to try a 12-year-old charged with rape.

CDA 1998, s 51 A, in its present form, requires that a juvenile be sent to Crown Court for trial if:

(a) the offence with which he is charged is a *specified* offence (within Sch 15 of the CJA 2003); AND

(b) it appears that if he is convicted, the case satisfies the criteria for either:

   (i) an indeterminate sentence under the CJA 2003, s 226; OR

   (ii) an extended sentence under the CJA 2003, s 228.

Indeterminate sentences under s 226 are detention for life or for public protection passed for *serious* offences; extended sentences of detention under s 228 are passed for certain violent or sexual offences—the extension is aimed at protecting the public from future serious harm. Specified offences within Sch 15 are quite varied—they are all sexual or violent offences but range from manslaughter, infanticide and wounding with intent to assaulting an officer preserving a wreck and assault occasioning actual bodily harm. Likewise, specified sexual offences include rape, incest and sex with under-age girls but also exposure and voyeurism. *Serious* offences are defined in the CJA 2003, s 224, as all those *specified* offences which are punishable by life imprisonment or imprisonment for ten years or more, in the case of an adult offender.

The Divisional Court in *Ghanbari* offered some guidance for magistrates:

- wherever possible, juveniles should be tried in a youth court;
- a *specified* offence may not be *serious* and so not call for consideration under s 226;
- where a non-*serious specified* offence is charged, it will often be unnecessary to assess whether or not the juvenile is *dangerous* (i.e. appears to merit either an indeterminate or an extended sentence) until after conviction; at that stage, a committal for sentence to Crown Court could be used under the PCC(S)A 2000, s 3C;
- there is a need to be rigorous before concluding that the juvenile poses a significant risk of serious harm through future offending; that conclusion is unlikely to be sound unless the court has a pre-sentence report available.

Echoing the exasperation felt by many, the Divisional Court in *Ghanbari* (see above) noted that they were 'faced with a sample of the deeply confusing provisions of the Criminal Justice Act 2003, and the satellite Statutory Instruments to which it is giving stuttering birth'. Rose LJ noted that 'it is not for us to desert our judicial duty, however lamentably others have legislated'.

6.3.4 Sentencing in the youth court

There are many sentences which are used exclusively in relation to juvenile offenders, for example referral orders and detention and training orders. There were provisions in the CJA 2003 to standardise community orders so that the same scheme applies to both adult and older juvenile offenders. However, secondary legislation passed early in 2007 postponed the implementation of youth community sentences for two years; it was later deferred again to 2010. See further **6.1** above, and **Chapter 17** below; community orders for juveniles will instead be combined in a new Youth Rehabilitation Order.

All sentences which can be applied to a juvenile offender are available to the youth court (reflecting the notion that this court should be the usual venue for juvenile justice) with the exception of custody for life and long-term detention, both of which are reserved for the Crown Court's exclusive use. Further information on juvenile sentences can be found in **Chapters 17**, **18** and **20** of this manual, whilst juvenile committals for sentence are dealt with in **5.4**.

We should note that the general purposes of sentencing which are listed in the CJA 2003, s 142, do not apply to offenders who are aged under 18 at the time of conviction. However, the Criminal Justice and Immigration Act 2008, s9, addresses this apparent vacuum. It inserts a new s 142A into the CJA 2003. First, courts are reminded that the principal aim of the youth justice system is to prevent juveniles from offending. Secondly, CYPA 1933, s 44, is reiterated—having regard for the juvenile offender's welfare—but this is explicitly made subordinate to the principal aim. The purposes of sentencing for juveniles are then specified as:

    a. the punishment of offenders,

    b. the reform and rehabilitation of offenders,

    c. the protection of the public, and

    d. the making of reparation by offenders to persons affected by their offences.

144 Youth court trials

(1) Specified indictable-only offences
- Homicide
- Specified firearms offences
- Specified sexual or violent offences warranting extended sentence or sentence of public protection under ss 226 and 228, CJA 2003
- Specified offences against children where notice served under s 51C
- Specified offences of serious or complex fraud where notice served under s 51B

Sent to Crown Court for trial under s 51A, CDA 1998
(1) Any related summary (if punishable with imprisonment or disqualification) or indictable offences may also be sent up at the same time. However, summary offences may not be tried on indictment unless they are specified in s 40, CJA 1988.
(2) Any other 'serious offences' to which D indicated a guilty plea can be committed for sentence under s 4A, PCC(S)A 2000 the Court will be able to sentence to long-term detention under s 91, PCC(S)A 2000. If the court commits under s 4A, it may also commit the youth to the Crown Court for sentence for any offence whatsoever but sentencing powers will be limited to those of the those of the Youth Court (ss 6 and 7, PCC(S)A 2000).

(2) Serious offence (s 91, PCC(S)A 2000)
(ie punishable in the case of an adult with at least 14 years imprisonment; ss 3, 13, 25 and 26, SOA 2003)

PBV → Guilty → Sentence
PBV → Not Guilty → Allocation Decision (ie will sentence be in excess of two years) → Trial in YC

Committal to Crown Court for sentence available (s 3C PCC(S)A 2000) N.B. The court may also commit the youth to the Crown Court for sentence for any offence whatsoever but sentencing powers limited to those of the Youth Court (ss 6 and 7, PCC(S)A 2000).

(3) All other indictable and summary-only offences

Plea entered → Not Guilty → Trial in YC → Acquittal / Conviction → Sentence
Plea entered → Guilty → Sentence

Committal to Crown Court for sentence available ONLY for specified sexual or violent offences warranting extended sentence or sentence of public protection under ss 226 or 228, CJA 2003 (s 3B, PCC(S)A 2000). N.B. the court may also commit the youth to the Crown Court for sentence for any offence whatsoever but sentencing powers limited to those of the Youth Court (ss 6 and 7, PCC(S)A 2000).

Figure 6.2 Procedure in the Youth Court

6.4 Juveniles in the adult courts

6.4.1 Juvenile defendants in the adult magistrates' court

Where a juvenile is charged with an adult defendant (either on a single joint charge or on multiple but related charges), then the first appearance for both accused will be in the adult magistrates' court. There are several possible permutations:

- juvenile and adult face a single joint charge;
- the juvenile is charged with aiding and abetting the adult to commit an offence (or vice versa);
- the juvenile is charged with an offence which arises out of circumstances which are the same as, or connected with, those which have resulted in a charge against the adult.

The offence or offences involved may be summary, indictable or a combination.

The usual classification of offences is of little direct assistance in determining which court will try (or sentence) a juvenile defendant. In particular, we should note that a juvenile defendant never has the right to select jury trial in the Crown Court. Which court tries the juvenile will be dependent largely upon what happens to the adult defendant. The charge against the adult may be for any one of the usual three types of offence.

6.4.1.1 Summary offence alleged against adult

If the adult faces a summary offence, he or she will simply be asked to enter a plea to the charge. If the plea is guilty, there will be no trial of the adult. In this situation, the juvenile will be asked to enter a plea to his or her charge. If the plea is guilty, the juvenile only requires sentencing and so mode of trial has ceased to be an issue (for sentencing decisions, see **6.4.1.2** below). If the juvenile pleads not guilty, then a summary trial is needed. This may take place in the adult magistrates' court but the case may be referred to the youth court for trial there instead. On the other hand, the adult may plead not guilty to the summary offence, thus necessitating a summary trial. Again, the juvenile will then be asked to enter a plea—if it is guilty, then the juvenile will not face trial and requires only sentencing. If the juvenile pleads not guilty, then both he or she and the adult require summary trial. If there is a single joint charge against them, then they *must* be tried together in the adult magistrates' court. If they are not on a single joint charge but instead face two or more related charges, then the justices in the adult magistrates' court must make a decision. Their choice rests between a single trial of both accused (which will take place in the adult court) or to order split trials (with the juvenile being sent to the youth court). If there are close factual connections between the offences and the witnesses will appear in both trials, the likelihood is that the justices will choose a single summary trial (see also on this point *CPS v South East Surrey Youth Court and Ghanbari* [2005] EWHC 2929 (Admin) para 17(v)). We should also note here that an amendment to the *Consolidated Criminal Practice Direction* [2002], introduced in 2007, requires the magistrates in a case management hearing to consider whether the juvenile (as a vulnerable defendant) should be tried on his or her own, apart from the adult defendant. The provision states that the magistrates 'should so order unless of the opinion that a joint trial would be consistent with the overriding objective and is in the interest of justice'. See *Consolidated Criminal Practice Direction* [2002], Part III.30.4.

6.4.1.2 Indictable offence alleged against adult

If the adult faces an indictable offence, then plea before venue and mode of trial are relevant for him. If the outcome is an indicated plea of guilty by the adult, the court will proceed in the same fashion as considered above (under summary offences). Likewise, if the adult indicates a not guilty plea and the mode of trial outcome is a summary trial, the court proceeds in the same way as if it were now handling a summary offence.

If the adult faces an indictable offence and is sent for trial to the Crown Court, the magistrates must now turn their attention to the juvenile. If the juvenile is charged with a separate, summary offence, then he or she will be asked to enter a plea. If the plea is not guilty, the magistrates will choose between summary trial of the juvenile in the adult magistrates' court or in the youth court (the latter is the more likely choice). If the juvenile is charged with the same, or a related, indictable offence as the adult, then the next stage is plea before venue for the juvenile (this assumes that the amendments to relevant provisions in the CDA 1998 and MCA 1980 made by the CJA 2003, Sch 3, are in force).

The court will explain to the juvenile that:

- if he or she pleads guilty, the court will proceed as if this were a summary trial and he or she has pleaded guilty; furthermore (if the offence is one which may attract long-term detention under PCC(S)A 2000, s 91(1)) that he may be committed for sentence to the Crown Court;
- if he or she pleads not guilty, that he or she will be sent forthwith to the Crown Court for trial, if the magistrates consider this necessary in the interests of justice to do so.

See the CDA 1998, s 51(7), as amended by the CJA 2003, Sch 3. This procedure will apply whether the juvenile appears in court together with the adult defendant or subsequently. When a juvenile is sent for trial under s 51(7), the adult magistrates' court may also send him or her for Crown Court trial on any related offence with which he or she is charged, whether indictable or summary.

The normal forum for sentencing a juvenile is the youth court. If a juvenile appears in the adult magistrates' court and pleads guilty, indicates a plea of guilty, or is tried and found guilty, the usual next step is for the magistrates to send the juvenile to youth court for sentence. The adult magistrates' court may only proceed to sentence the juvenile if it is of the opinion that the proper order to make is one of the following:

- an absolute or conditional discharge;
- a fine;
- a parental recognisance to take proper care of, and exercise proper control over, the juvenile;
- a referral order to a youth offender panel.

If none of these applies, the court must remit the juvenile to the youth court (see PCC(S)A 2000, s 8). It is relatively unusual for a juvenile to be committed to Crown Court for sentence.

6.4.2 Crown Court

Trial of juveniles in the Crown Court ought to follow the same basic pattern as the trial of any adult accused (see **Chapter 11**). However, the courts have recognised over recent years that different principles may need to be considered when a juvenile is tried in the Crown Court. This came to a head with the judgment of the European Court of Human

Rights in *T v UK* (2000) 30 EHRR 121, the appeal by Robert Thompson and Jon Venables in connection with their murder trial at Preston Crown Court (see further at **6.4.3** below). The European Court found that the trial had been defective in many respects. As a result, a Practice Direction was published, setting out guidelines for the trial by jury of juvenile defendants. These guidelines were then absorbed into the *Consolidated Criminal Practice Direction* [2002]. Although initially limited to the Crown Court, these guidelines have recently been revised and also extended to cover summary trial as well (see now *Consolidated Criminal Practice Direction* [2002], Part III.30).

Part III.30 applies to *all* vulnerable defendants but this automatically includes any defendant aged under 18 (Part III.30.1). The guidelines state explicitly that their purpose is to apply youth court procedures to the work of the adult courts, by analogy. The overriding principle, according to Part III.30.3, is that all 'possible steps should be taken to assist a vulnerable defendant to understand and participate in [the] proceedings'. It adds that the trial process 'should, so far as necessary, be adapted to meet those ends'. In particular, it will be desirable:

- for all participants to be on the same (or almost the same) level in the courtroom;
- for the vulnerable defendant to be free to sit with family members or others in a supporting role, whilst being able to communicate easily with his or her lawyer(s);
- to explain to the vulnerable defendant at the outset what is about to take place, in terms he or she can understand, and in the Crown Court to explain the role of the jury;
- to operate a timetable which takes account of any inability to concentrate. 'Frequent and regular breaks will often be appropriate';
- to use simple, clear language to aid understanding;
- not to wear robes and wigs (both lawyers and the judge) unless there is some good reason to do so.

6.4.3 Reporting restrictions

The general principle here is that the media can report proceedings unless ordered not to. Under the CYPA 1933, s 39 any court may direct that no newspaper report of its proceedings shall reveal the name, address, school or any particular calculated to lead to the identification of a child or young person in the proceedings, whether involved as accused, witness or victim. Similar powers exist to censor broadcasts in the sound, television and cable media.

One example of the Crown Court using s 39 was at the murder trial at Preston Crown Court of Robert Thompson and Jon Venables in November 1993. The victim was a toddler, James Bulger, who had been abducted and the case had attracted nationwide publicity. The trial judge ordered that the two accused be known simply as 'child A' and 'child B'. The fact that the identities of these children were published subsequently illustrates the fact that such a ban may be temporary. Typically, it will last until the end of the trial. If the verdict is not guilty, the juvenile is acquitted and the ban will continue in force. If the juvenile is convicted, the ban may be removed. It is thought that the public interest served by naming the juvenile offender may outweigh the consequences of publicity for him or her. However, the court should consider the age of the juvenile and the potential damage that he or she may suffer by being publicly identified as a criminal, before lifting the ban. See further *R v Lee (Anthony William) (A Minor)* [1993] 1 WLR 103; *R v Inner London Crown Court, ex p Barnes (Anthony)* [1996] COD 17.

Under the *Consolidated Criminal Practice Direction* [2002], Part III.30.16, a court may limit the number of reporters allowed into the courtroom (and subject of course to any restrictions it has imposed under the CYPA 1933). Where it does so, arrangements may need to be made to relay the proceedings to another part of the building to enable the media to hear, and possibly see, the proceedings.

6.4.4 Public access to adult courts

Both these trial courts operate their usual policy of being open to the general public when hearing a case, whether or not the case involves a juvenile (either as a witness or defendant). These courts have the power to order the public to be cleared from the courtroom if a juvenile witness is to testify in a trial involving offences of indecency or immorality. The possibility also exists for the court to order that a vulnerable witness may, in certain circumstances, give his or her evidence from behind a screen, or through a live television link, or in the form of a pre-recorded video. Under the *Consolidated Criminal Practice Direction* [2002], Part III.30.15, the court may decide to restrict the members of the public allowed into the courtroom in order to further the overriding principle, namely 'to assist a vulnerable defendant to understand and participate in [the] proceedings'. It may be sensible to allow entry only to people with an immediate interest in the proceedings (family of victim, for example).

6.5 Young adults

6.5.1 Defendants aged 18 or over at the start of proceedings

The youth court has no jurisdiction over such defendants. If a defendant was aged under 18 when charged with an offence, but is 18 when the case first comes to court, he or she should appear in the adult magistrates' court. Parents may be charged with offences such as not sending their child to school. This will be a matter for an adult magistrates' court to hear and to determine the appropriate steps to take to ensure the well-being of the juvenile.

6.5.2 Defendants who reach their eighteenth birthday after their case has begun in the youth court

This situation is governed by the CDA 1998, s 47(1)–(4). This provides a youth court with the discretionary power to remit a defendant to an adult magistrates' court either for trial or for sentence. The power is exercisable if the defendant, having appeared initially before the youth court as a juvenile, subsequently has his or her eighteenth birthday. In that situation, the youth court may remit the defendant either:

- before the start of the trial; or
- after conviction and before sentence.

The defendant has no right of appeal against a decision to remit. The adult magistrates' court may proceed as if all previous proceedings relating to the offence had taken place in that court. The intention behind s 47(1) appears to be to enable the courts to deal with young people in the most appropriate way, taking into account their maturity, attitude and offending history.

The youth court has no power to remit a defendant to the Crown Court for trial or sentence, simply because he or she is now aged 18. Some of the defendants who are remitted to the adult magistrates' court will have been awaiting trial for an offence which, for adults, is triable either way (see **4.1**). It is possible that when such defendants appear in the adult magistrates' court, they will now have the opportunity to opt for trial in the Crown Court; case law on the subject prior to s 47 is unhelpful. It is also possible that a remitted defendant will have only a brief stay in the adult magistrates' court. He or she may be charged with an offence which must be tried on indictment, in the case of an adult. That classification was inapplicable only whilst the case was in the youth court. Now that the defendant is appearing in the adult magistrates' court, the magistrates should send the defendant to Crown Court for trial (and see CDA 1998, s 51).

If a defendant reaches the age of 18 before sentence is passed, he or she may be remitted to the adult magistrates' court for sentence (PCC(S)A 2000, s 9). One effect might be to take the offender out of the detention and training order scheme, and make him or her eligible for detention in a young offender institution. Also, if the offence is triable either way, the offender may be remitted from the youth court into the adult magistrates' court and may then even be committed to the Crown Court for sentence (pursuant to the PCC(S)A 2000, s 3). Alternatively, it appears that the youth court can decide to retain jurisdiction over the 18-year-old and sentence him or her as if still a juvenile (CYPA 1963, s 29).

The Court of Appeal has stated that, where a defendant crosses a relevant age threshold between the date of commission of an offence and the date of conviction, the starting point for the court's sentencing powers is the sentence which the defendant would have been likely to receive if sentenced at the date of commission. In practice, this will mean that a juvenile aged 15, who is not a persistent offender, should not receive a custodial sentence (whether of DTO or under PCC(S)A 2000, s 91), if aged 14 at the time of the offence. Likewise, a defendant aged 17 at the time of the offence but 18 when sentenced may expect to receive a custodial sentence of no more than two years, as this is the maximum term of DTO that could have been imposed. See *R v LM* [2002] EWCA Crim 3047; [2003] Crim LR 205; *R v Ghafoor (Imran)* [2003] 1 Cr App R (S) 84, respectively. *Ghafoor* was subsequently approved in *Britton* [2007] 1 Cr App R(S) 121 but in *R v Bowker* [2007] EWCA Crim 1608, the Court of Appeal restated that *Ghafoor* is a starting-point only. It predates the CJA 2003. That Act set out the principles of sentencing (in s 142) and although those principles do not apply to offenders aged under 18 at the time of conviction, they will apply where the offender has his eighteenth birthday between committing the offence and being convicted of it. One example would be the need for deterrence in a case such as the present one where there was violent disorder between two gangs of youths. The Court considered the impact of Article 7 ECHR (no heavier penalty to be imposed than the one which was applicable at the time the offence was committed) but concluded that it was not constrained by Article 7 in any way—there was no change in the law here; all that changed was the penal regime to which the offender would be exposed as the result of his birthday.

6.6 Alternatives to prosecution

6.6.1 The final warning scheme

It has sometimes been thought that juveniles may be damaged by contact with the criminal justice system. Consequently, an alternative method (or diversion) developed where a juvenile was given a *caution*, instead of being prosecuted for an offence. The effect of a caution was believed to be less traumatic for the juvenile since no court appearance was involved. It might be considered that cautions were quite successful in nipping nascent criminal careers in the bud because statistics show that between 70 and 80 per cent of offenders who were cautioned did not re-offend within the next two years. However, there was also a small core of persistent juvenile offenders to whom a caution clearly meant nothing (3 per cent of young offenders were said to be responsible for 25 per cent of crimes, according to a Home Office report published in 1997, *Aspects of Crime Young Offenders 1995*).

Thorough reform of the system took place in 1998, when the CDA 1998 introduced a *final warning scheme* (see ss 65–66). Under these provisions, each offence committed by a young offender is met with a progressive response, designed to prevent further offending. The scheme came into effect nationwide in 2000. In summary, the scheme sets up three levels of response to a first-time offender. He or she may receive a reprimand, or a *final warning*, or be charged with the offence and appear in court. When dealt with by a final warning, the juvenile will be referred to a youth offending team (set up under the CDA 1998, s 39). The youth offending team will assess the juvenile to determine if it is appropriate to use a rehabilitation programme, aimed at preventing re-offending. Referral under the final warning scheme is carried out by the police. A similar power enables youth courts to make a *referral order*, where a first-time offender appears for sentence. The juvenile is referred to a youth offender panel which will decide upon the terms of a programme for behaviour, to be adhered to by the juvenile for a maximum of one year (see PCC(S)A 2000, Part III). For an interesting article on the difficulties caused in practice by the use of referral orders, see Jos Greenhow, *Referral orders: Problems in practice* [2003] Crim LR 266.

6.6.2 Deciding upon the appropriate action

The responsibility for taking decisions under the final warning scheme rests with the police. In exceptional circumstances it will still be possible for the police to take informal action but otherwise the police must choose between a reprimand, a warning or a charge.

In order to impose a reprimand or a warning, the following four criteria must be satisfied:

- there is sufficient admissible, reliable evidence to provide a realistic prospect of conviction, if the juvenile were prosecuted;
- the juvenile admits committing the offence;
- the juvenile has no previous convictions;
- a prosecution is not in the public interest.

Once those criteria are satisfied, the juvenile may be given a *reprimand* if:

- he or she has not previously been reprimanded or warned; *and*
- the offence is not so serious as to require a warning.

The juvenile may receive a *warning* if:

- he or she has not been warned before; or
- there has been one previous warning but it was given more than two years before the date of the present offence; *and*
- the offence is not so serious as to require a charge against the juvenile.

In addition to these criteria, the juvenile must give *informed consent* to the conclusion of the proceedings by way of a final warning or reprimand. If this is not done, the procedure will fall foul of the ECHR, Article 6. Informed consent means that the juvenile must be told of the consequences of this action. In the case of two juveniles involved in alleged indecent assaults, a failure to warn them of the requirement to be placed on the sex offenders register meant that they had not given the requisite informed consent; see *R (on the application of U) v Commissioner of Police for the Metropolis* [2003] 1 Cr App R 29.

Reprimands are thought to be appropriate for most first-time offenders. There can be no repeat reprimands, so a second-time offender should normally expect a warning, unless he or she was previously warned in which case the police officer will normally decide to charge the juvenile. The usual decision for third-time offenders will be to charge them with the offence. Fourth-time (and subsequent) offenders cannot be reprimanded or given a warning in any circumstances; the only decision can be to charge the juvenile with the offence. It must be emphasised that if a juvenile does not make a clear and reliable admission to all elements of the offence, the only choice facing the police officer is whether or not to charge the juvenile with the offence.

It is most unlikely that reprimands and warnings will be used for a very serious, indictable-only offence (eg murder, rape). Other offences may be too serious to be dealt with by a reprimand or warning, depending on their circumstances. It can be seen that the key factors in making a decision under the final warning scheme are therefore:

- the seriousness of the offence; and
- the offending history of the juvenile.

Important factors, when determining the seriousness of an offence, include its impact on the victim. Victims will normally be asked for their views on the offence, information on any loss or harm suffered and the impact of the offence in the light of their circumstances. An important aggravating factor will be if an offence was racially motivated. A general list of aggravating and mitigating factors has been devised by the Association of Chief Police Officers and this is likely to be relied on by police officers when assessing the seriousness of an offence (and whether a prosecution is in the public interest). This list, known as the ACPO Gravity Factors, endeavours to attach a numerical value to many offences. That numerical value may change, depending on the presence of aggravating or mitigating factors. Essentially, what the Gravity Factors do is to rank crimes in an abstract hierarchy of seriousness, and then allow aggravating or mitigating factors to 'fine tune' that ranking to accord with the circumstances of the actual offence which the juvenile committed. This exercise should produce a 'Final Gravity Score' which will work like this:

Final Score	Action
4	Always charge.
3	Normally warn for a first offence. If offender does not qualify for a warning then charge. Only in exceptional circumstances should a reprimand be given. Decision-maker needs to justify reprimand.
2	Normally reprimand for first offence. If offender does not qualify for a reprimand but qualifies for a warning then give warning. If offender does not qualify for a warning then charge.
1	Always the minimum response applicable to the individual offender, ie reprimand, warning or charge.

If the police decision is to charge, rather than to reprimand or issue a final warning, the matter passes into the hands of the Crown Prosecution Service. What action the CPS take is governed by the Code for Crown Prosecutors. The relevant provisions are paras 8.8 and 8.9:

8.8 Crown Prosecutors must consider the interests of a youth when deciding whether it is in the public interest to prosecute. However Crown Prosecutors should not avoid prosecuting simply because of the defendant's age. The seriousness of the offence or the youth's past behaviour is very important.

8.9 Cases involving youths are usually only referred to the Crown Prosecution Service for prosecution if the youth has already received a reprimand and final warning, unless the offence is so serious that neither of these were appropriate or the youth does not admit committing the offence. Reprimands and final warnings are intended to prevent re-offending and the fact that a further offence has occurred indicates that attempts to divert the youth from the court system have not been effective. So the public interest will usually require a prosecution in such cases, unless there are clear public interest factors against prosecution.

See further *Final Warning Scheme—Guidance for the Police and Youth Offending Teams* on <http://www.homeoffice.gov.uk/documents/final-warning-scheme.pdf?View=Binary>.

6.6.3 What happens when a juvenile offender is reprimanded or warned?

A reprimand or warning must be given orally by a police officer in a police station. The officer should normally be in uniform, and should be of inspector rank, although specially trained sergeants and constables may be used. Unless the juvenile is aged 17, an appropriate adult must be present when the reprimand or warning is given (defined in PACE Code of Practice, Code C). The oral action will be supported by written advice, usually in a standard form.

The officer should always specify the offence or offences which have resulted in the reprimand or warning. When giving a reprimand, the officer should also explain that:

- the reprimand is a serious matter;
- any further offences will result in a final warning or prosecution in all but the most exceptional circumstances;
- (if one or more of the offences is recordable) the reprimand constitutes a criminal record and will be cited in any future criminal proceedings.

When giving a warning, the officer should explain that:

- the warning is a serious matter;
- any further offences will result in charges being brought in all but the most exceptional circumstances;
- (if one or more of the offences is recordable) the warning constitutes a criminal record;
- the warning may be cited in any future criminal proceedings;
- in the event of a conviction within the next two years, the sentence of a conditional discharge will only be used in exceptional circumstances; in most cases, the juvenile should expect a more severe sentence (CDA 1998, s 66(4));
- the juvenile will be referred to a local youth offending team;
- the referral will result in contact by the youth offending team within two working days and, in general terms, what will happen thereafter.

A member of the youth offending team may be present to help explain to the juvenile what are the implications of the warning and the nature of the rehabilitation programme that he or she is likely to be placed on.

All reprimands and warnings will be recorded. The record will be kept, in the case of 10 and 11 year olds, until they are 18; in the case of other juveniles, records will be kept for at least five years. Reprimands and warnings may be cited in court, in the same circumstances as convictions. The Criminal Justice and Immigration Act 2008 brings the Final Warning Scheme within the operation of the Rehabilitation of Offenders Act 1974, so that when a warning or reprimand becomes spent, it need not be disclosed by the offender. It is worth noting that simple cautions and conditional cautions (see **6.6.4** below) are also now covered by the Rehabilitation of Offenders Act. See CJIA 2008, Sch 10, inserting a new provision, s8A, into the 1974 Act.

6.6.4 Conditional cautions

The Criminal Justice and Immigration Act 2008 extends the application of the conditional caution scheme to offenders aged 10–17. As with adults, a failure to comply with the conditions will render the individual liable for prosecution for the original offence. See CJIA 2008, Sch 9, inserting ss 66A–H into the Crime and Disorder Act 1998.

7 Sending cases to the Crown Court

7.1 Background

The majority of cases which are dealt with in the Crown Court are dealt with initially by the magistrates' court. That being so, a mechanism of some sort is necessary to remove the matter from the jurisdiction of the magistrates into that of the Crown Court.

For many years a procedure known as Committal Proceedings was used. This procedure has been under considerable scrutiny in recent years, and was replaced by s 51 of the Crime and Disorder Act 1998 (CDA) in relation to indictable only offences. Section 51 has now been extended to deal with all offences, by the CJA 2003, and the CJA 2003 abolishes committal proceedings altogether. References to s 51 in this Chapter are references to the CDA 1998, s 51 unless otherwise indicated.

7.2 Procedure under s 51

Since 15 January 2001, all indictable only offences are sent to the Crown Court for trial, without spending any time in the magistrates' court other than the first hearing. This is designed to reduce delay in the criminal justice process and is consistent with the close management of the case, through the Plea and Directions Hearings that the Crown Court now has.

This procedure has now been extended to cover all cases which are to be heard in the Crown Court, and s 51 has been amended and extended by the CJA 2003, Sch 3.

Under s 51, an adult who appears before a magistrates' court must have the case sent to the Crown Court in the following cases:

1. The offence is triable only on indictment. This reflects the position before the CJA 2003.

2. The offence is triable either way, but the court is required to send it to the Crown Court because either:

    (i) the defendant has elected trial on indictment; or

    (ii) the court has decided the case is not suitable for summary trial; or

    (iii) the court has decided to send a case to the Crown Court from a summary trial that has already commenced.

3 The offence is one for which a notice has been given under s 51B (notices in serious or complex fraud) or s 51C (notices in certain cases involving children) of the CDA 1998. This is broadly similar to the position before the CJA 2003.

4 The offence is an either-way offence, and the adult is jointly charged with a youth who has been sent (or will be sent) to the Crown Court in respect of that matter or that matter is related to an offence already sent in respect to the youth under the CDA 1998, s 51A (sending cases to the Crown Court: children and young persons).

5 The offence is a related summary (punishable by imprisonment or disqualification) or either-way offence. If another adult is jointly charged or is charged with a related offence, he or she shall also be sent to the Crown Court.

Section 51, as amended, provides as follows:

(1) Where an adult appears or is brought before a magistrates' court ('the court') charged with an offence and any of the conditions mentioned in subsection (2) below is satisfied, the court shall send him forthwith to the Crown Court for trial for the offence.

(2) Those conditions are—

(a) that the offence is an offence triable only on indictment other than one in respect of which notice has been given under section 51B or 51C below;

(b) that the offence is an either-way offence and the court is required under section 20(9)(b), 21, 23(4)(b) or (5) or 25(2D) of the Magistrates' Courts Act 1980 to proceed in relation to the offence in accordance with subsection (1) above;

(c) that notice is given to the court under section 51B or 51C below in respect of the offence.

(3) Where the court sends an adult for trial under subsection (1) above, it shall at the same time send him to the Crown Court for trial for any either-way or summary offence with which he or she is charged and which—

(a) (if it is an either-way offence) appears to the court to be related to the offence mentioned in subsection (1) above; or

(b) (if it is a summary offence) appears to the court to be related to the offence mentioned in subsection (1) above or to the either-way offence, and which fulfils the requisite condition (as defined in subsection (11) below).

(4) Where an adult who has been sent for trial under subsection (1) above subsequently appears or is brought before a magistrates' court charged with an either-way or summary offence which—

(a) appears to the court to be related to the offence mentioned in subsection (1) above; and

(b) (in the case of a summary offence) fulfils the requisite condition, the court may send him or her forthwith to the Crown Court for trial for the either-way or summary offence.

(5) Where—

(a) the court sends an adult ('A') for trial under subsection (1) or (3) above;

(b) another adult appears or is brought before the court on the same or a subsequent occasion charged jointly with A with an either-way offence; and

(c) that offence appears to the court to be related to an offence for which A was sent for trial under subsection (1) or (3) above,

the court shall where it is the same occasion, and may where it is a subsequent occasion, send the other adult forthwith to the Crown Court for trial for the either-way offence.

(6) Where the court sends an adult for trial under subsection (5) above, it shall at the same time send him to the Crown Court for trial for any either-way or summary offence with which he is charged and which—

(a) (if it is an either-way offence) appears to the court to be related to the offence for which he is sent for trial; and

(b) *(if it is a summary offence) appears to the court to be related to the offence for which he is sent for trial or to the either-way offence, and which fulfils the requisite condition.*

(7) *Where—*

(a) *the court sends an adult ('A') for trial under subsection (1), (3), or (5) above; and*

(b) *a child or young person appears or is brought before the court on the same or a subsequent occasion charged jointly with A with an indictable offence for which A is sent for trial under subsection (1), (3) or (5) above, or an indictable offence which appears to the Court to be related to that offence,*

the court shall, if it considers it necessary in the interests of justice to do so, send the child or young person forthwith to the Crown Court for trial for the indictable offence.

(8) *Where the court sends a child or young person for trial under subsection (7) above, it may at the same time send him to the Crown Court for trial for any indictable or summary offence with which he or she is charged and which—*

(a) *(if it is an indictable offence) appears to the court to be related to the offence for which he or she is sent for trial; and*

(b) *(if it is a summary offence) appears to the court to be related to the offence for which he or she is sent for trial or to the indictable offence, and which fulfils the requisite condition.*

(9) *Subsections (7) and (8) above are subject to sections 24A and 24B of the Magistrates' Courts Act 1980 (which provide for certain cases involving children and young persons to be tried summarily).*

(10) *The trial of the information charging any summary offence for which a person is sent for trial under this section shall be treated as if the court had adjourned it under section 10 of the 1980 Act and had not fixed the time and place for its resumption.*

(11) *A summary offence fulfils the requisite condition if it is punishable with imprisonment or involves obligatory or discretionary disqualification from driving.*

(12) *In the case of an adult charged with an offence—*

(a) *if the offence satisfies paragraph (c) of subsection (2) above, the offence shall be dealt with under subsection (1) above and not under any other provision of this section or section 51A below;*

(b) *subject to paragraph (a) above, if the offence is one in respect of which the court is required to, or would decide to, send the adult to the Crown Court under—*

(i) *subsection (5) above; or*

(ii) *subsection (6) of section 51A below,*

the offence shall be dealt with under that subsection and not under any other provision of this section or section 51A below.

(13) *The functions of a magistrates' court under this section, and its related functions under section 51D below, may be discharged by a single justice.*

Section 51A makes similar provision for children and young persons.

7.3 Restrictions on reporting

The CDA 1998, s 52A provides for restrictions on the allocation or reporting of allocation proceedings, in certain circumstances and with certain exceptions. These restrictions are similar to the restrictions that had been in place in relation to committal proceedings. Essentially, under the CDA 1998, s 52A(1), publishing any written or broadcast report of the allocation or sending proceedings is unlawful, subject to the following exceptions:

1 The magistrates' court may order that s 51A does not apply (s 51A(2)).

2   The following matters may be published without an order of the court:
    (i)   the identity of the court and the name of the justice or the justices;
    (ii)   the name, age, home address, and occupation of the accused;
    (iii) in the case of an accused who has been charged with an offence in relation to which a notice has been issued under s 51B (serious or complex fraud) any relevant business information. This includes the name and address of the business, and similar information;
    (iv)   the offence or offences, or a summary of them, with which the accused is charged;
    (v)   the names of counsel and solicitors engaged in the proceedings;
    (vi)   the date and place of adjournment, if adjourned;
    (vii) any arrangements as to bail;
    (viii) whether the accused is funded by the Criminal Defence Service.

Reporting or publishing a matter in contravention of s 52A is an offence punishable with a fine at level 5 in the standard scale. See s 52B for details of these offences.

7.4 Effecting the transfer

Once the decision as to the mode of trial has been taken, the magistrates' court issues a notice under s 51D(1), specifying the location of the Crown Court where the defendant is to be tried. In practice, this is the most local court and the parties rarely apply for the case to be heard elsewhere, though such an application is possible in appropriate circumstances.

Section 51D provides as follows:

(1) The court shall specify in a notice—
    (a)   the offence or offences for which a person sent to trial under s 51 or 51A above; and
    (b)   the place at which he is to be tried (which, if a notice has been given under section 51B above, must be the place specified in that notice).

(2) A copy of the notice shall be served on the accused and given to the Crown Court sitting at that place.

(3) In a case where a person is sent for a trial under s 51 or 51A above for more than one offence, the court shall specify in that notice, for each offence—
    (a)   the subsection under which the person is so sent; and
    (b)   if applicable, the offence to which that offence appears to the court to be related.

(4) Where the court selects the place of trial for the purposes of subsection (1) above, it shall have regard to—
    (a)   the convenience of the defence, the prosecution, and the witnesses;
    (b)   the desirability of expediting the trial; and
    (c)   any direction given by or on behalf of the Lord Chief Justice with the concurrence of the Lord Chancellor under s 75(1) of the Supreme Court Act 1981.

If an offence is triable either way, the defence is entitled to request advance disclosure as discussed in **4.6** above.

There are no rules as to when the first appearance at the Crown Court should take place, though both the magistrates' court and the Crown Court have the power to order a preliminary hearing when it considers one necessary. Otherwise, the *Consolidated Criminal Practice Direction* provides that a plea and case management hearing should be held within 14 weeks of the defendant being sent for trial.

7.5 Applications for dismissal

The defendant may apply for the case to be dismissed any time after the date upon which he or she has been served with the documents and before his arraignment, under the CDA 1998, Sch 3, para (2)(1). The judge must dismiss any charge or quash any count if the indictment has already been preferred, if it appears to him that the evidence against the defendant would not be sufficient for him to be properly convicted.

The application is in writing, the power to make an oral application having been removed by the CJA 2003, Sch 3.

If the judge declines to dismiss the application, there is no power to challenge his decision by way of judicial review. If the application is accepted, the prosecution must commence proceedings again with an application for a voluntary bill of indictment (see 7.6 below).

7.6 Voluntary bills of indictment

Under the Administration of Justice (Miscellaneous Provisions) Act 1933, s 2, as amended by the CJA 2003, a High Court judge has the power to prefer a voluntary bill of indictment, that is, he or she may order that the accused be tried on indictment. In making such an order, the case is not sent to the Crown Court in the usual way.

The preferment of a voluntary bill is exceptional, and consent to the preferment should only be given where 'good reason to depart from the normal procedure is clearly shown, and only where the interests of justice, rather than considerations of administrative convenience, require it': *Practice Direction (Criminal: Consolidated)* [2002] 3 All ER 904, para 35.3.

Traditionally, voluntary bills have been sought in two situations:

(a) Where committal proceedings have resulted in the discharge of an accused. Committal proceedings were abolished by the CJA 2003, and this will no longer apply when those changes come into effect.

(b) Where the prosecution case is that an offence was committed jointly by two or more persons, and at least one of them has already been sent for trial, and an indictment signed against him or her. In these circumstances, the prosecution will wish to try all the accused together, but may only do so if a second indictment is signed against all the accused. A voluntary bill of indictment will achieve the desired result.

Under para 35.2 of the Practice Direction, applications for a voluntary bill must not only comply with the 1993 Act and the Indictments (Procedure) Rules 1971, but must also be accompanied by:

(a) a copy of any charges on which the defendant has been sent for trial;

(b) a copy of any existing indictment which has been preferred in consequence of his sending;

(c) a summary of the evidence or other document which:

   (i) identifies the counts in the proposed indictment on which he has been sent for trial (or which are substantially the same as charges on which he has been so sent); and

   (ii) in relation to each other count in the proposed indictment, identifies the pages in the accompanying statements and exhibits where the essential evidence said to support that count is to be found.

(d) Marginal markings of the relevant passages on the pages of the statements and exhibits identified under (c) (ii) above.

The judge will consider the application and any written submission from the defendant and may seek amplification if necessary. He or she may invite oral submissions from either party or accede to a request for the opportunity to make such oral submissions if he or she considers it necessary or desirable in order to make a sound and fair decision. Any such oral submission should be made on notice to the other party (para 35.6 of the Practice Direction).

There is no requirement under either the Act or the Rules that a defendant be notified of the application for a voluntary bill. Paragraph 35.5 of the Practice Direction, however, gives guidance to prosecutors on procedures to be adopted in seeking judicial consent, directing prosecutors:

   (i) on the making of the application, to notify the defendant;

   (ii) at about the same time, serve on the defendant a copy of all the documents delivered to the judge;

   (iii) inform the defendant of his or her right to make written submissions to the judge within nine working days of giving the notice.

These procedures should be followed unless there are good reasons for not doing so, in which case the prosecutor must inform the judge, and ask for leave to dispense with all or any of them. The judge will only give leave if good grounds are shown.

A High Court judge's decision to issue a voluntary bill is subject to review, according to *R v IRC, ex p Dhesi, The Independent,* 14 August 1995, despite other authority to the contrary (*R v Manchester Crown Court, exp Williams* (1990) 154 JP 589). However, given the nature of the voluntary bill, where the application is made *ex parte* and therefore against the rules of natural justice, the courts' jurisdiction in respect of judicial review is limited and could only be exercised in the case of alleged malice on the part of the prosecutor. Once the bill of indictment has been preferred, it is an indictment like any other, and capable of amendment under the Indictments Act 1915, s 5 (*R v Wells* (1995) 159 JP 243).

8 Appeals from decisions of magistrates

There are three ways of appealing against the decision of the magistrates:

- appeal to the Crown Court;
- appeal to the High Court by way of case stated;
- application for judicial review.

Students should also be aware of the power of the magistrates to rectify mistakes under the Magistrates' Courts Act 1980 (MCA), s 142, discussed at **5.2.13**. This may often prove to be a quick and simple way to correct an error.

8.1 Appeal to the Crown Court

The defendant may appeal against conviction and/or sentence to the Crown Court. If the defendant has pleaded guilty, he or she may only appeal against sentence (MCA 1980, s 108) unless he or she can argue that the plea was equivocal (see **5.2.4**).

Note that if the Criminal Cases Review Commission refers a conviction in the magistrates' court to the Crown Court, such a reference is treated as if it had been made by the person under s 108, whether or not he or she pleaded guilty.

8.1.1 Procedure for appealing

See generally on appeals under the MCA 1980, s 108, the Criminal Procedure Rules 2005, Part 63.

(a) Notice of appeal is given in writing to the clerk of the magistrates' court and to the prosecution within 21 days of sentence. The 21 days run from the date of sentence, even if the appeal is against conviction and the appellant was convicted and sentenced on different days.

(b) The notice of appeal must state the grounds of appeal (see CPR 2005, r 63.2(4)). (This represents an apparent change from the previous rule (Crown Court Rules 1982, r 7), which required the notice to specify whether the appeal was against conviction or sentence or both, but did not require any grounds to be given.)

(c) All documents are forwarded to the Crown Court, where the listing officer will place the appeal on the list, and send notice of the time and place to the appellant, the prosecution and the magistrates' court.

(d) The appellant may appeal out of time by applying for leave in writing from the Crown Court. Leave is not otherwise required.

8.1.2 Bail

If the appellant is in custody and gives notice of appeal, the magistrates may grant him or her bail, with a duty to appear at the hearing of the appeal (MCA 1980, s 113). If bail is refused, or unacceptable conditions are imposed, the appellant may appeal against the decision to the Crown Court under the Supreme Court Act 1981 (SCA), s 81. (See further **3.11**.)

The appellant does not have the right to bail, but bail may well be granted if the sentence is likely to have been served before the appeal is heard.

8.1.3 The hearing

At the hearing, the judge (usually a circuit judge or recorder) sits usually with two lay magistrates who have not been concerned with the case in the magistrates' court.

Where the appeal is an appeal against conviction, the hearing itself is a complete re-hearing of the whole case. It is not a review of what happened before the magistrates. Thus, either party may call evidence not called before the magistrates, or omit evidence that was called before the magistrates.

The lay magistrates must accept the law from the judge, but the decision on the appeal itself is a majority decision. Thus, the lay magistrates may outvote the judge. However, if an evenly numbered court is equally divided, the judge has a casting vote.

A Crown Court judge giving the decision of the court must give reasons for its decision, and a refusal to do so might amount to a breach of natural justice. The reasoning required would depend on the circumstances of each case, but should be enough to demonstrate that the court had identified the main contentious issues, and how it had resolved them. An appellant is entitled to know the basis upon which the prosecution case has been accepted by the court. See *R v Harrow Crown Court, ex p Dave* [1994] 1 WLR 98, DC.

Reasons should be given whether the Crown Court accepts or rejects the appeal (*R v Inner London Crown Court, ex p London Borough of Lambeth Council* [2000] Crim LR 303). Failure to do so will usually, but not necessarily, invalidate the decision of the Crown Court. The decision will not be invalidated, for example, if the reasons are obvious as in *R v Kingston Crown Court, ex p Bell* (2000) 164 JP 633.

The reasons should enable the defendant: (i) to see the nature of the criminality found to exist by the court; and (ii) to consider properly whether there are grounds for a further appeal to the Divisional Court by way of case stated (*R v Snaresbrook Crown Court, ex p Input Management Ltd* (1999) 163 JP 533).

Note: In considering the matter, the judge should not act as prosecutor in the absence of the prosecution advocate. This amounts to a procedural irregularity, as the judge is not sufficiently removed from the proceedings to meet the requirement of justice (*R v Wood Green Crown Court, ex p Taylor* [1995] Crim LR 879).

8.1.4 Powers of the Crown Court

Under the SCA 1981, s 48, as amended by the CJA 1988, s 156, the Crown Court may:

(a) Confirm, reverse or vary any part of the decision appealed against. Thus, if the defendant has appealed against only part of the magistrates' decision, the Crown Court is not restricted to reviewing just that part, but may review the whole decision.

(b) Remit the case to the magistrates with its opinion. This will usually be a direction to enter a plea of not guilty and hear the case, if it thinks the plea was equivocal.

(c) Make any such order as it thinks just. This includes a power to increase sentence up to the maximum sentence which was available to the magistrates. This power is rarely exercised, but its existence is a means of discouraging frivolous appeals, bearing in mind that no leave to appeal is required.

8.1.5 Appeal against sentence

The appropriate court to deal with an appeal against sentence is normally the Crown Court, where the case may be appealed by way of rehearing (see **8.2.1(d)**).

8.1.6 Appeals against orders made under the Crime and Disorder Act 1998

The Crown Court has additional powers when dealing with an appeal against the making of an anti-social behaviour order or a sex offender order, created by ss 1 and 2 of the Crime and Disorder Act 1998 respectively. In determining the appeal, the Crown Court may, under s 4(2):

- make such orders as may be necessary to give effect to its determination of the appeal; and
- also make such incidental or consequential orders as appear to it to be just.

Any order so made is treated as if it were an order of the magistrates' court from which the appeal was brought and not an order of the Crown Court.

Note that there is no appeal to the Crown Court against the refusal of the magistrates to make either sort of order.

8.2 Appeals to the High Court by way of case stated

Under the MCA 1980, s 111(1):

any person who was a party to any proceeding before a magistrates' court or is aggrieved by the conviction, order, determination or other proceeding of the court may question the proceeding on the ground that it is wrong in law or in excess of jurisdiction by applying to the justices to state case for the opinion of the High Court on the question of law or jurisdiction involved . . .

Appeals by way of case stated go to the Administrative Court in the High Court (formerly the Divisional Court of the Queen's Bench Division). The procedure is set down in the Criminal Procedure Rules 2005, Part 64; see also the Civil Procedure Rules, Part 52 and PD 52 (in particular, paras 18.1–18.20).

8.2.1 Subsidiary points on appeals by way of case stated

(a) The magistrates have no power to state a case until they have reached a final determination on the matter. Thus, they have no power to state a case during the hearing and must wait until the end. Similarly, it is not an appropriate method of challenging a committal for trial or sentence.

(b) Both the defence and the prosecution have the right to apply for a case to be stated, and so may a third party whose legal rights have been affected. This means that effectively the prosecution can appeal against the defendant's acquittal, and if it is successful the acquittal will be reversed.

(c) The appellant must show that the decision of the magistrates was either wrong in law or in excess of jurisdiction. Questions raised will therefore be questions of jurisdiction, admissibility of evidence and so on. If the appeal is based on the facts of the case, then generally speaking it will be refused (*Oladimeji v DPP* [2006] EWHC Crim 1100) unless the magistrates have made a finding of fact which is totally unsupported by the evidence, or is one which no reasonable tribunal, properly directing itself, could have reached, in which case the High Court may treat it as an error of law. As to where the magistrates are entitled to draw inferences from facts, see *Plowden v DPP* [1991] Crim LR 850.

Where the applicant sought to raise new matters of fact and law, which were not included in the case stated by the justices, in his appeal by way of case stated, the appeal would be dismissed: *Campbell v DPP* [2003] All ER (D) 412.

Appeal by case stated or judicial review is not appropriate unless there are clear and substantial reasons for believing that disposal in such a way is in the interests of the defendant. See *Allen v West Yorkshire Probation Service Community Service Organisation* [2001] EWHC Admin 2.

(d) The statement itself is usually drafted by the clerk of the magistrates' court, and exceptionally by the magistrates themselves. If parties at trial are represented by advocates, the court may invite the advocates to submit a first draft indicating any areas of disagreement, as long as, by the time the case is stated, it is in satisfactory form: *Vehicle and Operator Services Agency v George Jenkins Transport Ltd and others* [2003] EWHC 2879.

(e) Once an application to state a case to the High Court is made, the right to appeal to the Crown Court is lost (MCA 1980, s 111(4)).

(f) If the same point arises in several cases on the same day, the appellants may apply for a collective case to be stated.

8.2.2 Procedure

(a) The application must be made in writing within 21 days of the sentence, and should state the point of law upon which the opinion of the High Court is sought.

(b) The application is sent to the clerk of the convicting magistrates' court.

(c) The magistrates may refuse to state a case, but this decision is reviewable by the High Court on an application for judicial review. For an example of such an application, see *R v Huntingdon Magistrates' Court, ex p Percy* [1994] COD 323. Magistrates may legitimately refuse to state a case in two situations:

   (i) They may refuse to state the case if they consider that the application is frivolous. The test is whether the application raises an arguable point of law (*R v North West Suffolk (Mildenhall) Magistrates' Court, ex p Forest Heath DC* (1997) 161 JP 401 and *R (on the application of Robertson) v South Western Magistrates' Court* [2003] EWHC 63). The magistrates must give the appellant a certificate to that effect, enabling him or her to seek judicial review of the decision not to state a case.

   (ii) They may refuse to state the case unless the appellant enters into a recognisance to prosecute the appeal without delay, and to pay such costs as the High Court may award. Such a condition would be imposed if the magistrates think the appellant is likely to abandon the appeal halfway through, having incurred expense and wasted time.

Where the magistrates refuse to state a case, the appellant should immediately apply for permission to bring judicial review. If the magistrates have already given a reasoned judgment, the single judge should give permission for judicial review of the original order, assuming there is an arguable point, thus avoiding case stated entirely. In any event, the Divisional Court will adopt the shortest, least expensive and swiftest course of action. The same principles apply to the Crown Court when it refuses to state a case. See generally *R v Blackfriars Crown Court, ex p Sunworld Ltd* [2000] 1 WLR 2102.

(d) The statement itself is usually drafted by the clerk of the magistrates' court, and exceptionally by the magistrates themselves. If parties at trial are represented by advocates, the court may invite the advocates to submit a first draft indicating any areas of disagreement, as long as, by the time the case is stated, it is in satisfactory form: *Vehicle and Operator Services Agency v George Jenkins Transport Ltd and others* [2003] EWHC 2879.

Note: It is a part of the procedure for stating a case that if a properly drafted question is to be altered, the party which framed the original question must be allowed to comment on the changes (*Waldie v DPP* (1995) 159 JP 514).

(e) The draft statement is submitted to the parties for their comments, which must be lodged with the court within 21 days. The statement may be adjusted in response. Where it is adjusted, the court will consider only the final statement, and not any earlier variations.

(f) The contents of the statement are:
   (i) The names of the parties and of the court.
   (ii) The charges.
   (iii) The findings of fact, but not the evidence upon which those findings were made, unless the appellant's argument is that, on that evidence, the magistrates could not have come to the conclusion that they did (see *Crompton and Crompton v North Tyneside Metropolitan Borough Council* [1991] COD 52).
   (iv) The points of law involved, and the authorities relied on. This should include the arguments heard by the justices (*DPP v Kirk* [1993] COD 99).
   (v) The decision of the magistrates.
   (vi) A request for the opinion of the High Court, posing the question which the appellant wishes the High Court to answer.

(g) Once the final draft is completed, the magistrates sign it and send it to the appellant.

(h) The appellant then has 10 days in which to lodge the statement at the Crown Office of the High Court, and a further four days to serve notice on the respondent.

Note: All the time limits set out above may be extended except the first limit of 21 days, which is statutory and cannot be varied (see s 111(2), *Michael v Gowland* [1977] 1 WLR 296 and *Reid v DPP* [1993] COD 111, DC, where 'pressure of work' on the part of the solicitor was insufficient reason for extending time).

8.2.3 Bail

Under the MCA 1980, s 113, the appellant may be granted bail pending the outcome of the hearing in the High Court. Bail will be granted on the basis that the appellant returns to the magistrates' court within 10 days of the High Court hearing, unless the conviction is quashed.

8.2.4 The hearing

Under the SCA 1981, s 66(3), the court must consist of at least two judges, though there are usually three. The court acts entirely on the basis of the facts as set out in the case, and no new evidence is adduced. The hearing therefore consists solely of legal argument by counsel.

If only two judges are sitting, and cannot agree, the decision of the judge who agrees with the court below prevails, and thus the appeal will fail.

8.2.5 Powers of the High Court

Under the Summary Jurisdiction Act 1857, s 6, the High Court may affirm, reverse or vary the decision of the court below, make any other order it thinks fit, or remit it back to the original court with its opinion. The High Court decision is enforced as if it were the decision of the court below. Thus, if the High Court thinks that the acquittal is incorrect, it can remit it back to the magistrates with a direction to convict and sentence. Generally speaking, the High Court does not deal with sentence itself, taking the view that it is not the appropriate forum. However, it may deal with sentence if it is obvious what the sentence should be.

The power of the High Court under s 6 includes a power to order a rehearing of the case before the same or a different bench of justices whenever such a course is appropriate (see *Griffith v Jenkins* [1992] AC 76; *R v Farrand and Galland* [1989] Crim LR 573).

8.2.6 Case stated from the Crown Court

Appeal lies to the High Court from the Crown Court on matters not related to a trial on indictment, by way of case stated. Thus, if the defendant has appealed to the Crown Court against conviction or has been committed to the Crown Court for sentence, either party may appeal to the High Court by way of case stated, under the SCA 1981, s 28, on the basis that the final decision was wrong in law or in excess of jurisdiction.

The procedure is much the same as for applications from the magistrates' court, except that it is usually the appellant who drafts the statement. The respondent also has the right to submit a draft. The judge, who was the judge at the hearing of the appeal or the committal, will read the drafts submitted to him and state a case on that basis.

For an example of the High Court hearing cases by way of case stated from the Crown Court, see *R (on the application of Westminster City Council) v Middlesex Crown Court* [2002] EWHC 1104.

Useful article: J Backhouse, 'Rights of appeal by way of case stated—should it be satisfied?' JP 1992, 156(20), 310–11.

8.3 Application for judicial review

Judicial review is the method by which the High Court controls the activities of inferior tribunals, that is, magistrates' courts and the Crown Court, in matters not relating to trial on indictment. The existence of a right of appeal to the Crown Court does not preclude a person convicted by magistrates from seeking relief by way of judicial review where the complaint was of procedural impropriety, unfairness or bias. Application for judicial review is made to the Queen's Bench Division of the High Court, specifically the Administrative Court (older case reports refer to the Divisional Court of the QBD). The Court's permission to proceed is required whenever a claim is made for judicial review. Permission, however, should only be granted where the applicant has an apparently plausible complaint, and immaterial and minor deviations from the rules will not have this effect (*R v Hereford Magistrates' Court, exp Rowlands* [1998] QB 110). In reaching this decision, the Divisional Court considered *R v Peterborough Justices, ex p Dowler* [1996] 2 Cr App R 561, which held that it was unnecessary to grant the defendant judicial review because, on the facts of the case, the procedural irregularity complained of could be rectified on appeal to the Crown Court. The court in *Ex parte Rowlands* did not doubt the correctness of the decision in *Ex parte Dowler* on the facts, but held that it was not authority for the proposition that parties complaining of procedural irregularity or unfairness in the magistrates' court should be denied permission to apply for judicial review. To hold otherwise would be to deprive a defendant of the right to a proper trial before the magistrates with a right of appeal to the Crown Court, and would emasculate the supervisory jurisdiction of the Divisional Court over the decisions of the magistrates.

Note that the right to apply to the Administrative Court from the Crown Court on matters not relating to a trial on indictment includes the right to apply for reviews of the decision of the Crown Court after an appeal to it from a decision of the magistrates. See, for example, *R v Aylesbury Crown Court, ex p Lait* [1998] Crim LR 264. In *R (P) v Liverpool City Magistrates* (2006) 170 JP 453 the High Court held that judicial review was a more appropriate remedy where it was alleged that there had been unfairness in the way that the trial had been conducted. An appeal by way of case stated is more appropriate where it is alleged that the magistrates have made an error of law.

8.3.1 Prerogative orders

The High Court exercises its control by the use of prerogative orders, namely quashing, mandatory and prohibiting orders (previously *certiorari, mandamus* and prohibition).

8.3.1.1 Quashing orders

A quashing order has the effect of quashing the decision appealed against. In addition, the High Court may:

- remit the case to the court concerned with a direction to reconsider it and reach a decision in accordance with the finding of the High Court (SCA 1981, s 31(5)).
- substitute for an unlawful sentence one which the court had the power to pass (SCA 1981, s 43(1)).

It is usually said that a quashing order will be issued in three situations:

(a) There is an error on the face of the record. However in a magistrates' court, the record is brief, and in any event magistrates rarely give full reasons for their decisions. If the magistrates in fact give reasons, or include them in any affidavit they are swearing for consideration of the High Court, the High Court will treat them as part of the record.

(b) The court acts in excess of jurisdiction. See, for example, *R v Tunbridge Wells Justices, exp Tunbridge Wells Borough Council* [1996] 160JP 574, where the justices adjourned the case, part heard, after a submission of no case to answer was made. The High Court set aside the decision to accept the submission, which was subsequently pronounced in open court by a different bench of magistrates, as *ultra vires*. See also *R v Parker and the Barnet Magistrates' Court, ex p DPP* (1994) 158 JP 1061. The High Court may also set aside a sentence if it is one which the magistrates have no power to pass, but such an error is rare. However, in very limited circumstances, the High Court will treat a sentence which is so harsh and oppressive that no reasonable tribunal could have passed it as being in excess of jurisdiction, and quash it accordingly, even though it was in fact within the court's powers (see *R v St Albans Crown Court, ex p Cinnamond* [1981] QB 480). But such a course is exceptional, and should only be followed when an appeal against sentence to the Crown Court has failed (*R v Battle Justices, ex p Shepherd* (1983) 5 Cr App R (S) 124). But see also on this point, *R v Bradford Justices, ex p Wilkinson* [1990] 1 WLR 692 and *R v Truro Crown Court, ex p Adair* [1997] COD 296. The appropriate test for interfering with sentence was set out in *Ex parte Adair* as follows:

> It would perhaps seem more helpful to ask the question whether the sentence or order in question falls clearly outside the broad area of the lower court's sentencing discretion.

(c) Where the court acts in breach of the rules of natural justice. The court is under a duty to act fairly, there being two aspects of this duty:

   (i) No person may be a judge in his or her own cause. See, for example, *Dimes v Grand Junction Canal* (1852) 3 HLC 759 and *R v Altrincham Justices, ex p Pennington* [1975] 1 QB 549.

   (ii) The court must hear both sides of the case. The rule will be relied on where there has been some procedural irregularity which has prejudiced the appellant. The test laid down in *R v Gough* [1993] AC 646, 'Was there a real danger that the appellant did not receive a fair trial?' was considered in *Re Medicaments and Related Cases of Goods (No 2)* [2001] 1 WLR 700. The Court of Appeal reviewed *R v Gough* and all the authorities in the light of the Human Rights Act, and concluded that, once European Convention case law had been taken into account, 'a modest adjustment' to *R v Gough* was required. The approach should be as follows. The court must ascertain all the circumstances having a bearing on the suggestion of bias. It must then ask whether those circumstances would lead a fair-minded and informed observer to conclude that there was a real possibility or a real danger (which were the same thing) of bias. One circumstance will be any explanation offered by the judge. If this explanation is not accepted by one party, it becomes something for the court to take account of from the point of view of a fair-minded observer, thereby avoiding the necessity of the court ruling on whether the explanation should be accepted or rejected.

   There are many and varied examples of the application of this principle to be found in the law reports, and the following are included merely by way of example:

   — *R v Thames Magistrates' Court, ex p Polemis* [1974] 1 WLR 1371 (where the defendant was not given sufficient time to prepare his case);

   — *R v Marylebone Justices, ex p Farrag* [1981] Crim LR 182 (where a verdict of guilty was announced before defence counsel's closing speech);

   — *R v Romsey Justices, ex p Gale* [1992] Crim LR 451 (where one of the magistrates, during the prosecution case, prepared a note of what he proposed the bench should say if it were to convict);

- *R v Ely Justices, ex p Burgess* [1992] Crim LR 888 (where the justices travelled to view the *locus in quo* with the prosecutor, and did not allow the defendant to be present—either or both of these factors would allow the conviction to be quashed);
- *R v Hendon Justices, ex p DPP* [1994] QB 167 (where the magistrates announced an acquittal without hearing prosecution evidence and without having a good reason to refuse to hear witnesses);
- *Vincent v The Queen* [1993] 1 WLR 862, PC (where the fact that the defendant, following normal practice, was not given detailed notice of the evidence against him was not sufficient to establish that he had been denied a fair hearing);
- *R v Newbury Justices, ex p Drake* [1993] COD 24 (where the allegedly partisan demeanour of the clerk was held not to have affected the magistrates' decision);
- *R v Nottingham Justices, ex p Fraser* (1995) 159 JP 612 (where the magistrates took into account the adequacy of the defendant's representation);
- *R v Worcester Justices, ex p Daniels* (1997) 161 JP 121 (where a member of the bench failed to give full attention to the defendant's evidence, and had been reading material unconnected with the trial);
- *Johnson v Leicestershire Constabulary, The Times*, 7 October 1998 (where a magistrate recognised the defendant from his role as a prison visitor, thereby apprising the bench that the defendant had spent some time in prison).

The High Court has on occasion issued a quashing order even though the failure to provide the defence with the necessary information lay with the prosecuting authority and not with the court itself. Consider the following examples:

- *R v Leyland Justices, ex p Hawthorn* [1979] QB 283 (where the defence were not informed of witnesses who could assist their case);
- *R v Knightsbridge Crown Court, ex p Goonatilleke* [1986] QB 1 (where the store detective failed to tell the police that he had a conviction for wasting police time);
- *R v Liverpool Crown Court, ex p Roberts* [1986] Crim LR 622 (where the police did not inform the defence of an additional statement made by the victim which was inconsistent with another statement and with his testimony);
- *R v Bolton Justices, ex p Scally* [1991] 1 QB 537 (where a lack of care meant that medical kits used for testing the level of alcohol in the blood were themselves contaminated with alcohol).

Note: A quashing order to quash an acquittal on the ground that it had been procured by fraud or perjury should seldom if ever be made (*R v Portsmouth Crown Court, ex p DPP* [1994] COD 13, DC).

8.3.1.2 Mandatory orders

A mandatory order compels an inferior tribunal to carry out its duties. It will be ordered when the court refuses to act when it should; not when it has acted and made a mistake. The appropriate remedy in the latter case would be a quashing order. See, for example, *R v Hendon Justices, ex p DPP* [1994] QB 167.

8.3.1.3 Prohibiting orders

A prohibiting order will be made to stop the court acting in excess of its powers. Parties do not have to wait for the final outcome of the hearing, and if there is genuine doubt as to the court's powers, the court will adjourn, so that the opinion of the High Court can be sought.

8.3.2 Discretion

The power to award any of the prerogative orders is entirely discretionary, and even though the appellant has established a prima facie case, the order may still be refused. See, again, *R v Battle Justices, ex p Shepherd* (1983) 5 Cr App R (S) 124.

8.3.3 Procedure

Under the SCA 1981, s 31, the Civil Procedure Rules, Part 54 and PD54, the procedure is as follows:

(a) Within three months of the decision, the applicant must file an application for leave to apply for judicial review, setting out his or her name and address and that of his or her solicitor, the relief sought and the grounds. This application must be supported by affidavit evidence.

(b) The application for leave is heard *ex parte* (ie in the absence of the other side), usually without a hearing. If there is no hearing, the judge will simply read the papers in chambers. If the applicant specifically applies for a hearing, one may be held, and this may be in court.

(c) If leave is refused, the applicant has 10 days in which to renew his or her application before the Divisional Court.

(d) If leave is granted, the application is made by originating motion. Notice of motion must be served on the other side, and on the court below.

(e) The hearing itself consists of affidavit evidence and argument from counsel. Evidence is not usually called, though it may be necessary to establish the error of the court below.

(f) The court will reach a decision, and make any appropriate orders.

8.3.4 Bail

Magistrates have no power to grant bail for an application for judicial review. The application for bail must be made to the High Court judge in chambers under the Criminal Justice Act 1948 s 37(1) (d). However, if the application is from the Crown Court on a matter not relating to trial on indictment, the Crown Court may grant bail.

Further reading: Inigo Bing, 'Curing bias in criminal trials—the consequences of *R v Gough*' [1998] Crim LR 148.

8.3.5 Case stated and judicial review compared

In many situations, the appellant could apply for either a case to be stated or judicial review, and in some respects the two are similar. However, by appealing by way of case stated, the appellant is challenging the actual decision of the court, alleging, for example, that a statute has been misapplied. In some circumstances this may be said of judicial review, but judicial review tends to be directed, not at the decision itself, but more at the decision-making process. It is the legality of the process which is under review, not whether the decision is right or wrong.

If both remedies do apply, the appellant should appeal by way of case stated, as all the facts can then be placed before the High Court (*R v Ipswich Crown Court, ex p Baldwin* [1981] 1 All ER 596 and *R v Oldbury Justices, ex p Smith* (1995) 159 JP 316). See also *R v Ipswich Justices, ex p D* (5 December 1994) and *R v Gloucester Crown Court, ex p Chester* [1998] COD 365.

8.4 Appeal to the House of Lords

A decision of the High Court in a criminal cause or matter is appealed directly to the House of Lords, and there is no right of appeal to the Court of Appeal (Administration of Justice Act 1960, s 1). The appeal will lie if the following conditions are satisfied:

- the High Court certifies that the case involves a point of law of general public importance; and
- leave is granted by either the High Court or the House of Lords.

From October 2009, the House of Lords becomes the UK Supreme Court. This does not affect its appellate jurisdiction.

9

Disclosure

We have already seen that, where the defendant is to be tried in the Crown Court, the process whereby the case is sent to the Crown Court requires the prosecution to serve on the defence copies of the statements of the prosecution witnesses who will be called. In the case of summary and either-way offences, Part 21 of the Criminal Procedure Rules provides that, by no later than the beginning of the day of the first hearing in the case, the prosecutor must provide 'initial details' to the defence. Those 'initial details' must include a summary of the prosecution case or any written statements (or other documents) setting out the facts or matters on which the prosecution case will be based (i.e. written statements of the prosecution witnesses). It should also be noted that, under the Attorney-General's Guidelines on Disclosure, the prosecution should provide the defence with the statements of the prosecution witnesses prior to any summary trial (whether the offence is summary or triable either way).

The Criminal Procedure and Investigations Act 1996 (CPIA) creates additional duties of disclosure. This Act is considered in section D9 of *Blackstone's Criminal Practice*. The Act is supplemented by a Code of Practice issued under the CPIA 1996, by the Attorney-General's Guidelines: Disclosure of Information in Criminal Proceedings, and by *Disclosure: a Protocol for the Control and Management of Unused Material in the Crown Court*, all of which may be found in Appendix 5 of *Blackstone's Criminal Practice*. R v K [2006] EWCA Crim 724 (affirmed in R v L [2007] EWCA Crim 764), emphasised the importance of compliance with the Protocol. Reference should also be made to the draft *Protocol for the Provision of Advance Information, Prosecution Evidence and Disclosure of Unused Material in the Magistrates' Courts* available at <http://www.judiciary.gov.uk/judgment_guidance/protocols/mags_unused_material.htm>.

9.1 The duty of the investigating officer

The investigating officer is under a duty to retain material obtained in a criminal investigation which may be relevant to that investigation. Paragraph 5.4 of the Code of Practice issued under s 23 of the CPIA 1996 provides a non-exhaustive list of the material that should be retained:

(a) Crime reports (including crime report forms, relevant parts of incident report books or police officers' notebooks).

(b) Custody records.

(c) Records derived from tapes of telephone messages (eg 999 calls) containing descriptions of the alleged offence or offender.

(d) Final versions of witness statements (and draft versions where their content differs from the final version).

(e) Interview records.

(f) Communications between police and experts (eg forensic scientists) and reports of work carried out by experts.

(g) Any material casting doubt on the reliability of a confession.

(h) Any material casting doubt on the reliability of a witness.

(i) Any other material that would fall within the test for primary prosecution disclosure (see below).

9.2 Prosecution disclosure

Section 3 of the CPIA 1996 (as amended by the CJA 2003) requires the prosecutor to:

. . . disclose to the accused any prosecution material which might reasonably be considered capable of undermining the case for the prosecution against the accused or of assisting the case for the accused.

This is an objective test, covering a very wide range of material. The Attorney-General's Guidelines on Disclosure of Information in Criminal Proceedings stipulate that the prosecution should disclose any material which:

- casts doubt upon the accuracy of any prosecution evidence;
- may point to another person, whether charged or not (including a co-accused) having involvement in the commission of the offence;
- may cast doubt upon the reliability of a confession;
- might go to the credibility of a prosecution witness;
- might support a defence that is either raised by the defence or apparent from the prosecution papers (if the material might undermine the prosecution case it should be disclosed at this stage even though it suggests a defence inconsistent with or alternative to one already advanced by the accused or his solicitor);
- may have a bearing on the admissibility of any prosecution evidence.

A useful rule-of-thumb test is that material ought to be disclosed if it might give the defence a useful basis for cross-examination of prosecution witnesses or if it would support defence arguments that prosecution evidence is inadmissible or that the proceedings ought to be stayed. See paras 10 and 12 of the Guidelines.

It follows, for example, that the prosecution should inform the defence if any prosecution witnesses have previous convictions (see *R v Vasiliou* [2000] Crim LR 845).

Under s 7A of the 1996 Act (inserted by the CJA 2003), there is a continuing duty on the prosecution to disclose unused material that falls within the ambit of s 3. Section 7A provides as follows:

Continuing duty of prosecutor to disclose

(1) This section applies at all times—

(a) after the prosecutor has complied with section 3 or purported to comply with it, and

(b) before the accused is acquitted or convicted or the prosecutor decides not to proceed with the case concerned.

> (2) The prosecutor must keep under review the question whether at any given time (and, in particular, following the giving of a defence statement) there is prosecution material which—
>
>> (a) might reasonably be considered capable of undermining the case for the prosecution against the accused or of assisting the case for the accused, and
>>
>> (b) has not been disclosed to the accused.
>
> (3) If at any time there is any such material as is mentioned in subsection (2) the prosecutor must disclose it to the accused as soon as is reasonably practicable . . .
>
> (4) In applying subsection (2) by reference to any given time the state of affairs at that time (including the case for the prosecution as it stands at that time) must be taken into account.
>
> (5) Where the accused gives a defence statement [or an updated defence statement],
>
>> (a) if as a result of that statement the prosecutor is required by this section to make any disclosure, or further disclosure, he must do so . . .
>>
>> (b) if the prosecutor considers that he is not so required, he must . . . give to the accused a written statement to that effect.
>
> (6) For the purposes of this section prosecution material is material—
>
>> (a) which is in the prosecutor's possession and came into his possession in connection with the case for the prosecution against the accused, or
>>
>> (b) which . . . he has inspected in connection with the case for the prosecution against the accused.
>
> . . .
>
> (8) Material must not be disclosed under this section to the extent that the court, on an application by the prosecutor, concludes it is not in the public interest to disclose it and orders accordingly.
>
> . . .

9.3 Defence disclosure

Where the case is to be tried in the Crown Court, the defence *must* supply a 'defence statement' to the prosecution (see s 5 of the CPIA 1996); where the case is to be tried in the magistrates' court, the defence *may* supply such a statement (see s 6 of the CPIA 1996).

The content of the defence statement is governed by s 6A of the CPIA 1996. This requires the accused to set out the nature of his defence, including any particular defences on which he intends to rely, and indicate any points of law he wishes to take. Section 6A (as amended by the Criminal Justice and Immigration Act 2008) provides:

> *6A Contents of defence statement*
>
> (1) For the purposes of this Part a defence statement is a written statement—
>
>> (a) setting out the nature of the accused's defence, including any particular defences on which he intends to rely,
>>
>> (b) indicating the matters of fact on which he takes issue with the prosecution,
>>
>> (c) setting out, in the case of each such matter, why he takes issue with the prosecution,

(ca) setting out particulars of the matters of fact on which he intends to rely for the purposes of his defence, and

(d) indicating any point of law (including any point as to the admissibility of evidence or an abuse of process) which he wishes to take, and any authority on which he intends to rely for that purpose.

(2) A defence statement that discloses an alibi must give particulars of it, including—

(a) the name, address and date of birth of any witness the accused believes is able to give evidence in support of the alibi, or as many of those details as are known to the accused when the statement is given;

(b) any information in the accused's possession which might be of material assistance in identifying or finding any such witness in whose case any of the details mentioned in paragraph (a) are not known to the accused when the statement is given.

(3) For the purposes of this section evidence in support of an alibi is evidence tending to show that by reason of the presence of the accused at a particular place or in a particular area at a particular time he was not, or was unlikely to have been, at the place where the offence is alleged to have been committed at the time of its alleged commission.

...

Under s 6B of CPIA 1996 (not in force at the time of writing), the accused, prior to the trial, must provide an updated defence statement, or else a written statement that there are no changes to be made to the defence statement previously served.

Section 6 C of the CPIA 1996 (not in force at the time of writing) requires the defence to identify any witnesses they propose to call. It provides:

6C Notification of intention to call defence witnesses

(1) The accused must give to the court and the prosecutor a notice indicating whether he intends to call any persons (other than himself) as witnesses at his trial and, if so—

(a) giving the name, address and date of birth of each such proposed witness, or as many of those details as are known to the accused when the notice is given;

(b) providing any information in the accused's possession which might be of material assistance in identifying or finding any such proposed witness in whose case any of the details mentioned in paragraph (a) are not known to the accused when the notice is given.

...

(2) If, following the giving of a notice under this section, the accused—

(a) decides to call a person (other than himself) who is not included in the notice as a proposed witness, or decides not to call a person who is so included, or

(b) discovers any information which, under subsection (1), he would have had to include in the notice if he had been aware of it when giving the notice, he must give an appropriately amended notice to the court and the prosecutor.

This was a very controversial proposal. In an attempt to allay fears that people might be put off testifying as defence witnesses, or encouraged to change their evidence, s 21A of the CPIA 1996 requires the Secretary of State to publish a Code of Practice giving guidance to police officers (and others charged with the duty of investigating offences) in relation to the arranging and conducting of interviews of people whose particulars are given to the prosecution because they are alibi witnesses or because they fall within s 6C. Section 21A(2) requires that:

The code must include (in particular) guidance in relation to—

(a) information that should be provided to the interviewee and the accused in relation to such an interview;

(b) the notification of the accused's solicitor of such an interview;

(c) the attendance of the interviewee's solicitor at such an interview;

(d) the attendance of the accused's solicitor at such an interview;

(e) the attendance of any other appropriate person at such an interview taking into account the interviewee's age or any disability of the interviewee.

Because of the potentially damaging effects of failure to comply with the obligations imposed by these provisions, s 6E(2) of the CPIA states that:

If it appears to the judge at a pre-trial hearing that an accused has failed to comply fully with section 5, 6B or 6C, so that there is a possibility of comment being made or inferences drawn under section 11(5), he shall warn the accused accordingly.

The obligations of the defence extend beyond witnesses they propose to call in the case of experts, where there is an obligation to reveal the identity of experts who have been instructed on behalf of the defence, whether or not they are to be called as defence witnesses. This obligation is contained in s 6D of the 1996 Act (not in force at the time of writing), which provides:

6D Notification of names of experts instructed by accused

(1) If the accused instructs a person with a view to his providing any expert opinion for possible use as evidence at the trial of the accused, he must give to the court and the prosecutor a notice specifying the person's name and address.

. . .

Section 5 of the CPIA 1996 makes provision for the service of defence statements on co-defendants, if the court so orders. It provides:

(5A) Where there are other accused in the proceedings and the court so orders, the accused must also give a defence statement to each other accused specified by the court.

(5B) The court may make an order under subsection (5A) either of its own motion or on the application of any party.

. . .

This essentially gives statutory effect of the decision of the Court of Appeal in *R v Cairns* [2003] 1 WLR 796, that the prosecution would sometimes have to disclose the statement of one co-defendant to the other where it might assist the defence of that other defendant.

The defence statement is important because of the adverse inferences that can be drawn under s 11 of the CPIA 1996 (see below). However, s 6E makes it important to take great care in the drafting of defence statements for another reason: it makes provision for the jury to be shown the defence statement (or updated defence statement if there is one). Section 6E provides as follows:

(4) The judge in a trial before a judge and jury—

(a) may direct that the jury be given a copy of any defence statement, and

(b) if he does so, may direct that it be edited so as not to include references to matters evidence of which would be inadmissible.

(5) A direction under subsection (4)—

(a) may be made either of the judge's own motion or on the application of any party;

(b) may be made only if the judge is of the opinion that seeing a copy of the defence statement would help the jury to understand the case or to resolve any issue in the case.

...

The defence statement has to be served within 14 days of the date on which the prosecution comply (or purport to comply) with their duty of disclosure under s 3 of the Act (see reg 2 of the Criminal Procedure and Investigations Act 1996 (Defence Disclosure Time Limits) Regulations 1997 (SI 1997/684)).

To remove any doubt as to whether a defence statement served by the defendant's solicitor is to be regarded as being given on behalf of the defendant, s 6E(1) of the CPIA 1996 provides that where the accused's solicitor 'purports to give on behalf of the accused' a defence statement or an updated defence statement, that statement 'shall, unless the contrary is proved, be deemed to be given with the authority of the accused'.

Defence statements are normally drafted by the accused defendant's solicitor, but counsel may be instructed to draft the defence statement. In the Code of Conduct (available online on the Bar Standards Board Council website), *Section E: Guidance on Preparation of Defence Case Statements* says that where a barrister is instructed to draft a defence statement, he or she must ensure that the accused:

- understands the importance of the accuracy and adequacy of the defence statement, and
- has had the opportunity of carefully considering the statement drafted by counsel and has approved it.

In *R v Wheeler* (2000) 164 JP 565 the defendant was charged with and convicted of an offence contrary to s 170(2) of the Customs and Excise Management Act 1979 following his arrest at Gatwick airport when he was found to be concealing drugs internally. At trial, an inconsistency had become apparent between the defence statement which had been served by his solicitors (in which it was said that the accused knew he was carrying the drugs when he arrived in the UK) and his evidence during cross-examination (in which he maintained that he believed he had regurgitated all of the packets before travelling to the UK). The defence statement had not been signed and the defendant alleged that his solicitor had made a mistake in serving an incorrect statement of his case. Although the trial judge referred to the alleged mistake in his summing up, he did not provide the jury with specific guidance. The Court of Appeal held that the judge had erred in failing to give specific directions as to the inconsistency, given that the jury would be affected by it. The court said that it was advisable that defence statements were signed by a defendant rather than served by solicitors on a defendant's behalf without procedures being followed to verify accuracy. It should be noted, however, that the court has no power to order the defence statement to be signed by the accused (*R (Sullivan) v Maidstone Crown Court* [2002] 1 WLR 2747).

Special provisions apply to alibi evidence, which is defined as:

evidence tending to show that by reason of the presence of the accused at a particular place or in a particular area at a particular time he was not, or was unlikely to have been, at the place where the offence is alleged to have been committed at the time of its alleged commission (s 6A(3)).

Where the accused will be relying on an alibi, the defence statement must include the names and addresses of any witnesses the accused believes are able to give evidence in support of the alibi or (if the accused does not know names or addresses) any information which might be of assistance in finding such witnesses (s 6A(2)).

9.4 Sanctions for non-compliance by the defence

The penalties for non-compliance by the defence with their disclosure obligations under the CPIA 1996 are set out in s 11 (as amended by the CJA 2003). Section 11 applies in three cases:

(a) Where the accused is to be tried in the Crown Court (and so is required by s 5 of the Act to provide a defence statement) and the accused:
  (i) fails to give an initial defence statement under s 5, or
  (ii) provides an initial defence statement but does so late, or
  (iii) fails to provide an updated defence statement (or a statement that there are no changes), or
  (iv) provides an updated statement (or a statement that there are no changes) but does so late, or
  (v) sets out inconsistent defences in the defence statement, or
  (vi) at the trial, puts forward a defence which was not mentioned in his defence statement or which is different from any defence set out in that statement, or
  (vii) at the trial, relies on a matter which was not mentioned in his defence statement but which should have been so mentioned, or
  (viii) at the trial adduces evidence in support of an alibi without having given particulars of the alibi in the defence statement, or
  (ix) at the trial, calls an alibi witness without having given appropriate notice of the alibi, or details of that particular witness, in the defence statement.
(b) Where the accused is to be tried in a magistrates' court and gives an initial defence statement voluntarily but does so late or does any of the things set out in paras (iii) to (ix) in the preceding paragraph.
(c) Where the accused gives a witness notice (under s 6C, when brought into force) but does so late or, at the trial, calls a witness who was not included, or not adequately identified, in a witness notice.

Under s 11(5), where s 11 applies:

(a) the court or any other party may make such comment as appears appropriate;

(b) the court or jury may draw such inferences as appear proper in deciding whether the accused is guilty of the offence concerned.

Section 11(6) provides that where adverse inferences could be drawn for failure to mention a point of law (including any point as to the admissibility of evidence or an abuse of process) or an authority used to support legal argument, comment by another party may be made only with the leave of the court. Similarly, s 11(7) provides that where the failure in question is a failure to comply with the witness notice requirements, comment by another party may only be made with the leave of the court.

Section 11(9) stipulates that where the accused calls a witness whom he has failed to include, or to identify adequately, in a witness notice, the court must have regard to whether there is any justification for the failure.

Under s 11(8), where the accused puts forward a defence which is different from any defence set out in his defence statement, the court must have regard (a) to the extent of the differences in the defences, and (b) to whether there is any justification for it.

Section 11(10), importantly, confirms that 'a person shall not be convicted of an offence solely on an inference drawn under subsection (5)'.

In *Murphy v DPP* [2006] EWHC 1753 (Admin), the Divisional Court said that a defendant does not lose his entitlement to disclosure under the CPIA merely because he serves his defence statement out of time.

9.5 Public interest immunity

Public interest immunity ('PII') enables the prosecution to withhold material that would otherwise have to be disclosed under the CPIA. Material can only be withheld on the basis of PII with the permission of the court. Common examples of cases where PII is raised are where the prosecution wish to protect the identity of an informant whom the prosecutor does not intend to call as a witness at the trial (as in *R v Turner* [1995] 1 WLR 264) or where the police wish to keep secret the location of an observation post from which they were watching the movements of the accused (as in *R v Johnson* [1988] 1 WLR 1377).

Paragraph 20 of the Attorney-General's Guidelines on Disclosure, dealing with applications for non-disclosure in the public interest, states that:

Before making an application to the court to withhold material which would otherwise fall to be disclosed, on the basis that to disclose would give rise to a real risk of serious prejudice to an important public interest, prosecutors should aim to disclose as much of the material as they properly can (for example, by giving the defence redacted or edited copies or summaries). Neutral material or material damaging to the defendant need not be disclosed and must not be brought to the attention of the court. It is only in truly borderline cases that the prosecution should seek a judicial ruling on the disclosability of material in its possession.

Paragraph 21 of the Guidelines states that, prior to or at the hearing, the court must be provided with full and accurate information. The prosecution advocate must examine all material which is the subject matter of the application and make any necessary enquiries of the prosecutor and/or investigator. The prosecutor (or representative) and/or investigator should attend such applications.

In *Rowe and Davis v United Kingdom* (2000) 30 EHRR 1, the European Court held that there is a:

fundamental aspect of the right to a fair trial that criminal proceedings, including the elements of such proceedings which relate to procedure, should be adversarial and that there should be equality of arms between the prosecution and defence. The right to an adversarial trial means, in a criminal case, that both prosecution and defence must be given the opportunity to have knowledge of and comment on the observations filed and the evidence adduced by the other party. In addition Article 6(1) requires, as indeed does English law, that the prosecution authorities should disclose to the defence all material evidence in their possession for or against the accused (para 61).

However, the Court went on to hold that:

the entitlement to disclosure of relevant evidence is not an absolute right. In any criminal proceedings there may be competing interests, such as national security or the need to protect witnesses at risk of reprisals or keep secret police methods of investigation of crime, which must be weighed against the rights of the accused. In some cases it may be necessary to withhold certain evidence from the defence so as to preserve the fundamental rights of another individual or to safeguard an important public interest. However, only such measures restricting the rights of the defence which are strictly necessary are permissible under Article 6(1). Moreover, in order to ensure that the accused receives a fair trial, any difficulties caused to the defence by a limitation on its rights must be sufficiently counterbalanced by the procedures followed by the judicial authorities (para 61).

In *Jasper v United Kingdom* (2000) 30 EHRR 441, where the European Court held (by a bare majority of nine votes to eight) that there was no violation of Article 6, the defence had been informed that a PII application was to be made by the prosecution (although they were not told into which category the material being withheld was said to fall); the defence had thus had the opportunity to make submissions and to participate (albeit to a comparatively limited extent) in the decision-making process. They were given the opportunity to outline the defence case to the trial judge and to ask the judge to order disclosure of any evidence relevant to that case. On this basis, the Court (at para 55) said that it was:

satisfied that the defence were kept informed and permitted to make submissions and participate in the above decision-making process as far as was possible without revealing to them the material which the prosecution sought to keep secret on public interest grounds.

At para 56, the Court said that:

The fact that the need for disclosure was at all times under assessment by the trial judge provided a further, important, safeguard in that it was his duty to monitor throughout the trial the fairness or otherwise of the evidence being withheld . . . He was fully versed in all the evidence and issues in the case and in a position to monitor the relevance to the defence of the withheld information both before and during the trial.

In some cases involving PII, however, the defendant will not have the information that the defence had in *Jasper*. In *R v H; R v C* [2004] UKHL 3, [2004] 2 AC 134, the House of Lords considered the question of public interest immunity and the potential role for 'special independent counsel' in PII hearings. The Court of Appeal had certified two points of law of general public importance were involved in its decision:

(1) Are the procedures for dealing with claims for public interest immunity made on behalf of the prosecution in criminal proceedings compliant with article 6 of the European Convention for the Protection of Human Rights and Fundamental Freedoms?

(2) If not, in what way are the procedures deficient and how might the deficiency be remedied?

The procedure for determining claims of PII had been set out in *R v Ward* [1993] 1 WLR 619 and *R v Davis* [1993] 1 WLR 613 at 617–618. The Court of Appeal had identified three classes of case, which Lord Bingham (in *R v H*) summarised in the following terms:

In the first, comprising most of the cases in which a PII issue arises, the prosecution must give notice to the defence that they are applying for a ruling of the court, and must indicate to the defence at least the category of the material they hold (that is, the broad ground upon which PII is claimed), and the defence must have the opportunity to make representations to the court. There is thus an *inter partes* hearing conducted in open court with reference to at least the category of the material in question. The second class comprises cases in which the prosecution contend that the public interest would be injured if disclosure were made even of the category of the material. In such cases the prosecution must still notify the defence that an application to the court is to be made, but the category of the material need not be specified: the defence will still have an opportunity to address the court on the procedure to be adopted but the application will be made to the court in the absence of the defendant or anyone representing him. If the court considers that the application falls within the first class, it will order that procedure to be followed. Otherwise it will rule. The third class, described as 'highly exceptional', comprises cases where the public interest would be injured even by disclosure that an *ex parte* application is to be made. In such cases application to the court would be made without notice to the defence. But if the court considers that the case should be treated as falling within the second or the first class, it will so order (para 20).

The procedural regime established by *R v Ward* and *R v Davis* is largely replicated in Part 25 of the Criminal Procedure Rules (Applications for Public Interest Immunity and specific disclosure).

Lord Bingham, in *R v H*, went on (at para 36) to give guidance on how the courts should approach PII hearings:

When any issue of derogation from the golden rule of full disclosure comes before it, the court must address a series of questions:

(1) What is the material which the prosecution seek to withhold? This must be considered by the court in detail.

(2) Is the material such as may weaken the prosecution case or strengthen that of the defence? If No, disclosure should not be ordered. If Yes, full disclosure should (subject to (3), (4) and (5) below) be ordered.

(3) Is there a real risk of serious prejudice to an important public interest (and, if so, what) if full disclosure of the material is ordered? If No, full disclosure should be ordered.

(4) If the answer to (2) and (3) is Yes, can the defendant's interest be protected without disclosure or disclosure be ordered to an extent or in a way which will give adequate protection to the public interest in question and also afford adequate protection to the interests of the defence?

This question requires the court to consider, with specific reference to the material which the prosecution seek to withhold and the facts of the case and the defence as disclosed, whether the prosecution should formally admit what the defence seek to establish or whether disclosure short of full disclosure may be ordered. This may be done in appropriate cases by the preparation of summaries or extracts of evidence, or the provision of documents in an edited or anonymised form, provided the documents supplied are in each instance approved by the judge. In appropriate cases the appointment of special counsel may be a necessary step to ensure that the contentions of the prosecution are tested and the interests of the defendant protected (see para 22 above). In cases of exceptional difficulty the court may require the appointment of special counsel to ensure a correct answer to questions (2) and (3) as well as (4).

(5) Do the measures proposed in answer to (4) represent the minimum derogation necessary to protect the public interest in question? If No, the court should order such greater disclosure as will represent the minimum derogation from the golden rule of full disclosure.

(6) If limited disclosure is ordered pursuant to (4) or (5), may the effect be to render the trial process, viewed as a whole, unfair to the defendant? If Yes, then fuller disclosure should be ordered even if this leads or may lead the prosecution to discontinue the proceedings so as to avoid having to make disclosure.

(7) If the answer to (6) when first given is No, does that remain the correct answer as the trial unfolds, evidence is adduced and the defence advanced?

It is important that the answer to (6) should not be treated as a final, once-and-for-all, answer but as a provisional answer which the court must keep under review.

His Lordship continued (at para 37):

Throughout his or her consideration of any disclosure issue the trial judge must bear constantly in mind the overriding principles referred to in this opinion. In applying them, the judge should involve the defence to the maximum extent possible without disclosing that which the general interest requires to be protected but taking full account of the specific defence which is relied on. There will be very few cases indeed in which some measure of disclosure to the defence will not be possible, even if this is confined to the fact that an ex parte application is to be made. If even that information is withheld and if the material to be withheld is of significant help to the defendant, there must be a very serious question whether the prosecution should proceed, since special counsel, even if appointed, cannot then receive any instructions from the defence at all.

Lord Bingham concluded (at para 39) that:

Provided the existing procedures for dealing with claims for public interest immunity made on behalf of the prosecution in criminal proceedings are operated with scrupulous attention to the governing principles referred to and continuing regard to the proper interests of the defendant, there should be no violation of Article 6 of the Convention.

The main focus of *R v H* was the appointment of special independent counsel to represent the interests of the defendant but who is not permitted to disclose to the defendant the secret material that is disclosed to counsel in order to make representations on behalf of the defendant. Such counsel is not, in the ordinary sense, professionally responsible to the defendant. Special counsel may be appointed when it is in the interests of justice to do so. However, the House of Lords said that the need must be shown; such an appointment will 'always be exceptional, never automatic; a course of last and never first resort. It should not be ordered unless and until the trial judge is satisfied that no other course will adequately meet the overriding requirement of fairness to the defendant' (para 22).

The House of Lords in *R v H* also gave general guidance on PII hearings in magistrates' courts. Lord Bingham affirmed the approach taken in *R (DPP) v Acton Youth Court* [2001] EWHC Admin 402, [2001] 1 WLR 1828.

If PII applications are confined, as they should be, to material which undermines the prosecution case or strengthens that of the defence, the bench will not be alerted to material damaging to the defendant. If it is, the principles which should govern the court's decision whether to recuse itself are the same as in the case of any other tribunal of fact, but the court's duty of continuing review ordinarily militates in favour of continuing the proceedings before the court which determines the PII application. If a case raises complex and contentious PII issues, and the court has discretion to send the case to the Crown Court for trial, the magistrates' court should carefully consider whether those issues are best resolved in the Crown Court. The occasions on which it will be appropriate to appoint special counsel in the magistrates' court will be even rarer than in the Crown Court (para 44).

9.6 Third party disclosure

Sometimes material that may weaken the prosecution case or support the defence case is in the hands of a third party. For example, the accused might be charged with a sexual offence involving a child, and the child's school, or the relevant social services department, might have records of false allegations made by the child who is the alleged victim of the offence (as in *R v Brushett* [2001] Crim LR 471). If the material comes into the hands of the police, it should be retained and would fall within the ordinary disclosure regime under the CPIA 1996. Otherwise, if the third party is not prepared to hand over the material needed by the defence, the accused can seek a witness summons (using the procedure laid down by s 2 of the Criminal Procedure (Attendance of Witnesses) Act 1965 in Crown Court cases, or s 97 of the Magistrates' Courts Act 1980 in magistrates' court cases). The accused has to be able to show that the third party is likely to be able to give or produce material evidence in the case, and that it is in the interests of justice to issue a summons. Rule 28.5(3) of the Criminal Procedure Rules requires the applicant to serve the application on the proposed witness (unless the court otherwise directs) and, if the court so directs, on any a person to whom the proposed evidence relates. Under r 28.6(1), a person served with an application for a witness summons requiring production of a document or other evidence may object to its production on the ground that either it is not likely to be material evidence, or that the duties or rights (including rights of confidentiality) of the proposed witness or of any person to whom the document relates outweigh the reasons for issuing a summons. Under r 28.6(2), the court may require the proposed witness to make the document or thing available for the objection to be assessed by the court. In the context of disclosure, a third party would be to able to argue, for example, that the evidence should not be disclosed on grounds of public interest immunity (see above) or because disclosure would infringe the right to privacy under Art 8 of the ECHR.

10

Indictments

10.1 What is an indictment?

The indictment is the formal document which sets out the charge(s) to be tried in the Crown Court. Detailed information on indictments can be found in section D11 of *Blackstone's Criminal Practice*. The key legislative provisions governing the form and content of indictments are to be found in ss 3 and 5 of the Indictments Act 1915, s 2 of the Administration of Justice (Miscellaneous Provisions) Act 1933, and in Part 14 of the Criminal Procedure Rules.

10.1.1 What does an indictment contain?

The indictment begins with a heading, which contains a unique reference number for the case, identifies the location of the Crown Court and the name of the defendant(s).

Each charge faced by the defendant is contained in a separate 'count'.

10.1.2 What does a count contain?

Section 3(1) of the Indictments Act 1915 provides that the indictment must contain 'a statement of the specific offence or offences with which the accused person is charged, together with such particulars as may be necessary for giving reasonable information as to the nature of the charge'. The form and content of the indictment is governed by r 14.2 of the Criminal Procedure Rules. Under r 14.2(1) each count must contain:

  (a) a statement of the offence charged that:
    (i) describes the offence in ordinary language, and
    (ii) identifies any legislation that creates it; and
  (b) such particulars of the conduct constituting the commission of the offence as to make clear what the prosecutor alleges against the defendant.

Each count is therefore divided into two parts:

- the 'Statement of Offence', which sets out the name of the offence (for example, 'theft') and, where the offence is a statutory one, the statutory provision which creates the offence (for example, s 1 of the Theft Act 1968).
- the 'Particulars of Offence', giving factual information about the charge; this must disclose the essential elements of the offence.

Further guidance on drafting indictments can be found in Chapter 24 of the ***Drafting*** manual. Guidance on how to draft counts in respect of particular offences is given in the commentary relating to individual offences in Part B of *Blackstone's Criminal Practice*.

A single count must only allege one offence. If a count alleges more than one offence, it is said to be 'duplicitous' or 'bad for duplicity', and the defence can ask the court to quash the count. For example, a count which alleges that the defendant 'on 16 August 2009 assaulted John Smith and on 17 August 2009 assaulted Peter Jones' is alleging two separate offences and so will be quashed.

It is possible, however, for several acts to constitute a single offence. Rule 14.2(2) of the CPR provides that 'more than one incident of the commission of the offence may be included in a count if those incidents taken together amount to a course of conduct having regard to the time, place or purpose of commission'. It is submitted that this formulation is intended to reflect the practice of the courts under the Indictment Rules 1971 (which were replaced in April 2007 by Part 14 of the Criminal Procedure Rules). In *DPP v Merriman* [1973] AC 584, it was said that a number of acts may properly be said to amount to a single offence if they form part of the 'same transaction'. For example, in *R v Wilson* (1979) 69 Cr App R 83, the defendant was charged in one count with stealing a number of different items from Debenhams (three jumpers, a pair of shorts, two pairs of trousers, four dimmer switches and a cassette tape) and in another count with stealing a number of different items from Boots (eight records and a bottle of aftershave). The defence sought to argue that each count was duplicitous, on the basis that the goods had been stolen from different departments of the stores in question and so there should have been separate counts relating to each department. The Court of Appeal held that where counts in an indictment each charge theft of a number of separate items from different departments of the same store, those counts are not bad for duplicity, since it is legitimate to charge in a single count one activity even though that activity may involve more than one act. The various acts of theft in each store had amounted to a single course of conduct, and so those acts could legitimately be regarded as amounting to a single offence of theft against each store.

Similarly, in *DPP v McCabe* [1992] Crim LR 885, it was held that an allegation that the defendant stole 76 library books between two specified dates was a single offence and so a count alleging this theft was not bad for duplicity. However, a count which alleged that the defendant stole £200 from A one day and £200 from B the next would be duplicitous because there are two separate acts of theft. See also *Barton v DPP* [2001] EWHC Admin 223 (discussed at **14.8**).

If a section of a statute creates one offence which may be committed in a number of ways, the alternatives may properly be charged in a single count. If, however, the section creates more than one offence, each offence the prosecution wish the jury to consider must be put in a separate count. A good example of this principle (in practice, if not in strict legal theory) may be seen in the offence of handling stolen goods (s 22 of the Theft Act 1968). Handling effectively comprises two offences. The first is that of dishonestly receiving stolen goods; the second comprises all the other ways of handling (these ways are all different ways of committing a single offence). The various ways of committing the second form of handling can, and usually will, be charged in a single count. However, a single count which charged both receiving and the other forms of handling together would be regarded as defective.

Thus, there are two basic handling counts; either:

- AB on [date] dishonestly received stolen goods, namely [description of goods], knowing or believing the same to be stolen goods; or
- AB on [date] dishonestly undertook or assisted in the retention, removal, disposal or realisation of stolen goods, namely [description of goods], by or for the benefit of another, or dishonestly arranged to do so, knowing or believing the same to be stolen goods.

If a count is bad for duplicity (in that it charges more than one offence), the defence may make an application to quash the indictment. However, the prosecution may counter this application by asking for leave to amend the indictment under s 5(1) of the Indictments Act 1915, thus splitting the duplicitous count into two separate counts. In *R v Levantiz* [1999] 1 Cr App R 465, several discrete acts of supplying a controlled drug were alleged in a single count in the indictment. The Court of Appeal held that, where a count in an indictment is duplicitous, that count is not void and the conviction is not necessarily unsafe. It follows that an appeal against conviction on that count can be dismissed if the Court of Appeal decides that the conviction is safe despite the irregularity in the indictment. In deciding whether a conviction based on a duplicitous count is safe, it is submitted that the Court should ask itself whether the accused was prejudiced by the duplicitous nature of the count. If it is the case that the defendant must have been guilty of everything alleged in the count—or nothing alleged in the count—it is unlikely that he would have been prejudiced by the duplicity.

Each count in an indictment is a separate entity. In *R v O'Neill* [2003] EWCA Crim 411, the defendant was charged in an indictment which included a count that was defective, in that it was based on a statutory provision which had not been in force at the relevant time. The Court of Appeal confirmed that even if one count charges an offence not known to the law, any other counts in the same indictment can stand and need not be quashed.

EXAMPLE 10.1

This is an example of an indictment containing two counts.

No. 2009/12345

INDICTMENT

THE CROWN COURT AT CROYDON

THE QUEEN v ANDREW JAMES CLARKE

ANDREW JAMES CLARKE is charged as follows:

COUNT 1

Statement of Offence

Burglary, contrary to s 9(1)(b) of the Theft Act 1968

Particulars of Offence

ANDREW JAMES CLARKE, on 3 November 2009, having entered a dwelling, namely 27 Acacia Avenue Croydon, as a trespasser, stole therein a television set and video recorder belonging to John Mark Richardson.

COUNT 2

Statement of Offence

Unlawful wounding, contrary to s 20 of the Offences Against the Person Act 1861

Particulars of Offence

ANDREW JAMES CLARKE, on 3 November 2009, unlawfully and maliciously wounded John Mark Richardson.

10.1.3 Who draws up the indictment?

The indictment is normally drafted by the Crown Prosecution Service. In complex cases, however, counsel may be instructed to advise on evidence and to draft the indictment. The document is then sent to the Crown Court, where it is signed by an officer of the court.

Under r 14.1 of the Criminal Procedure Rules, the prosecutor must serve a draft indictment on the Crown Court officer not more than 28 days after service on the defendant and on the Crown Court (as part of the transfer procedure under s 51 or 51A of the Crime and Disorder Act 1998) of copies of the documents containing the evidence on which the charge or charges are based. The Crown Court may extend this 28-day limit, even after it has expired (see r 14.1(2)). The draft indictment becomes an indictment upon signature by the officer of the Crown Court (see r 14.1(3)(a)).

In *R v Clarke* [2008] UKHL 8; [2008] 1 WLR 338, the ground of appeal was that the indictment upon which the trial proceeded was not signed before the start of the trial and that the trial and conviction was therefore rendered a nullity (an argument based on *R v Morais* [1988] 3 All ER 161). The House of Lords held that without an indictment there cannot be a valid trial, and that the only step which changes a draft indictment into an indictment is the signing of the draft by the proper officer of court; that step is therefore indispensable. The indictment had, in fact, been signed during the course of the trial, but the House ruled that this could not 'throw a blanket of legality over the invalid proceedings already conducted'. Thus, the draft indictment must be signed before the start of the trial.

Where there is more than one defendant, the order in which the names of defendants are placed on an indictment is the responsibility of the prosecutor, who has a discretion as to that order. The mere fact that a co-defendant named later on the indictment might give evidence adverse to a defendant after that defendant has given evidence, provides no basis for regarding the prosecution's exercise of its discretion in drafting the indictment as improper. Nor does it provide grounds for severing the indictment and ordering a separate trial since, in principle, defendants jointly charged should be tried in a single trial: *R v Cairns* [2002] EWCA Crim 2838; [2003] 1 WLR 796.

10.2 Joinder of counts

Rule 14.2(3) of the Criminal Procedure Rules provides that an indictment may contain more than one count if all the offences charged:

(a) are founded on the same facts; or
(b) form or are a part of a series of offences of the same or a similar character.

10.2.1 Founded on the same facts

Two offences are founded on the same facts if they arise from a single incident or are part of the same 'transaction' (e.g. assaulting the householder in the course of a burglary).

One offence can also arise from the same facts as another if one would not have been committed but for the other. For example, in *R v Barrell and Wilson* (1979) 69 Cr App R 250, the indictment charged assault and affray (arising out of a single incident) and attempting to pervert the course of justice (based on attempts to prevent prosecution witnesses from testifying). The defence objected to the joinder of the latter charge. However, it was held by the Court of Appeal that the phrase 'founded on the same facts' does not mean that, for charges to be properly joined in the same indictment, the facts in relation to the respective charges must be identical in substance or virtually contemporaneous; rather, the test is whether the charges have 'a common factual origin'. That test was satisfied in *Barrell and Wilson*: the allegation of attempting to pervert the course of justice would not have arisen but for the allegations of assault and affray, and so it could legitimately be said that the charges had a common factual origin.

In *R v Roberts* [2008] EWCA Crim 1304; [2009] 1 Cr App R 20, police officers searched the defendant's home. A bag containing drugs was found in the kitchen. Two firearms were found in the bedroom. The defendant was charged with unlawful possession of drugs and with firearms offences. He argued that the drugs counts and firearms counts should not appear on the same indictment. The Court of Appeal held that the phrase 'founded on the same facts' in r 14.2 of the Criminal Procedure Rules does not mean that the facts in relation to the respective charges must be identical in substance or virtually contemporaneous. Rather, the test is whether the charges have a common factual origin. In the present case, joinder was proper. At paras 12 and 13, Latham LJ said:

> ... the facts upon which each of the counts was based was the finding in the one premises at the same time of the drugs and the firearms. In our judgment, that ... falls into the category of case where the factual connection is established by the coincidence of time and place ...

10.2.2 Series of similar offences

For two offences to belong to a series of similar offences, there must be a 'nexus' between them. For a nexus to exist, the offences must be similar both legally and factually. The leading case is *Ludlow v Metropolitan Police Commissioner* [1971] AC 29, where the House of Lords upheld the joinder of a count alleging attempted theft at a public house in Acton on 20 August 1968 and a count alleging robbery at a public house in Acton on 5 September 1968.

It should be noted that two offences do not form a series merely because evidence relating to one offence is uncovered during the investigation into the other (see *R v Harward* (1981) 73 Cr App R 168).

Several examples of the operation of the second limb of r 14.2(3) of the Criminal Procedure Rules can be found in para D11.63 of *Blackstone's Criminal Practice*.

10.3 Joinder of defendants

A count in an indictment can name more than one defendant if it is alleged that there was more than one participant in the offence (*DPP v Merriman* [1973] AC 584). Where one person is alleged to have aided and abetted the other, he or she can either be charged specifically with aiding and abetting, or as a principal. In practice, however, secondary participants are usually charged as principal offenders. So, if it is alleged that John Smith carried out a burglary and Jane Jones acted as look-out, the usual practice would be to charge them jointly (in the same count) with burglary.

It is also permissible to join defendants in an indictment even if the defendants are not charged with the same offence (i.e. they are charged in separate counts), provided that the offences are sufficiently linked so that they can properly be joined under r 14.2(3).

188 Indictments

In *R v Assim* [1966] 2 QB 249, for example, there were two defendants. The charges arose out of a fracas at a nightclub. A receptionist at a nightclub (D1) had tried to prevent a customer from leaving without paying and was alleged to have wounded the customer; another customer had intervened and was allegedly assaulted by a doorman (D2). Given the fact that this was effectively a single incident with a number of participants, it was held that there was sufficient nexus for the two separate counts (one against D1 and the other against D2) to be joined in the same indictment.

10.4 Discretion to order separate trials

Section 5(3) of the Indictments Act 1915 provides that where (either before the trial or at any stage of a trial) the court is of the opinion that the defendant may be:

> prejudiced or embarrassed in his defence by reason of being charged with more than one offence in the same indictment, or that for any other reason it is desirable to direct that the person should be tried separately for any one or more offences charged in an indictment, the court may order a separate trial of any count or counts of such indictment.

This power to order separate trials of offences on an indictment is technically known as 'severing the indictment'. It applies both to a defendant who seeks separate trials for a number of offences and to co-defendants seeking separate trials from each other.

This power can only be exercised where joinder of the offences is proper under r 14.2(3) of the Criminal Procedure Rules, and so cannot be used to cure the defect where counts are joined improperly (see *R v Newland* [1988] QB 402).

The power to order separate trials applies where a single trial would prejudice or embarrass the defendant(s) or if there is some other good reason (s 5(3)). In *Ludlow*, the House of Lords said that where counts are properly joined, they should normally be tried together unless the defendant can show a 'special feature' justifying separate trials. In other words, the burden rests on the defendant to show that exceptional circumstances merit separate trials.

Relevant considerations include the following:

(a) How easy or difficult will it be for the jury to disentangle the evidence relating to the different counts?

(b) Is one of the counts likely to arouse hostility in the minds of the jurors, creating a risk that they will not approach the other counts with open minds?

(c) Is the strength of the evidence relating to the counts disproportionate, with the risk that the jury will think that if the defendant is guilty of the charge supported by the stronger evidence, he must also be guilty of the charge in respect of which the evidence is weaker?

(d) Is the evidence on all the counts weak, creating a risk that the jury may convict on the basis of an overview of the case rather than considering the evidence in respect of each count separately?

It has to be borne in mind that the effect of these risks can often be minimised, if not removed altogether, by appropriately worded directions from the judge on how to approach the task of analysing the evidence.

Where there are two defendants and they seek separate trials, it has to be shown that a fair trial cannot be achieved without severance. Judges are generally reluctant to order separate trials of defendants charged with the same offence: if there are separate trials, the cost of the proceedings will be doubled, the witnesses will have to testify twice, and there is a risk of inconsistent verdicts.

In *R v Lake* (1976) 64 Cr App R 172, the prosecution evidence included material which was admissible against D1 but inadmissible against D2. D2 argued that he should be tried separately, since the jury would otherwise hear the inadmissible evidence. The Court of Appeal upheld the judge's refusal to order separate trials, on the basis that the judge's direction to the jury was sufficient to ensure that the jury would disregard evidence that was inadmissible against D2 when considering the case against that defendant even if the same evidence was admissible against D1. Similarly, separate trials were not thought necessary in *R v Grondkowski and Malinowski* [1946] KB 369, even though the defendants were blaming each other (running so-called 'cut-throat' defences).

A defendant who is charged in an indictment containing more than one count may apply for that indictment to be severed, so that particular counts are tried separately. An example of where severance would have been appropriate is *R v Laycock* [2003] EWCA Crim 1477; [2003] Crim LR 803, where the defendant was charged with a number of offences, including possession of a firearm when a prohibited person, namely having been sentenced to imprisonment for more than three years (an offence under the Firearms Act 1968). The very nature of this offence revealed the fact that he had previously been convicted of a serious offence. The Court criticised the number of counts, saying that in formulating an indictment an excessive number of counts should not be included, since this overloads the indictment. Furthermore, the Court went on to say that prosecutors should be careful not to charge counts that would prejudice a defendant unless there is a real purpose to be served. In the present case, the firearms offence should not have been joined in the indictment since it did not give the judge any additional sentencing powers. If the prosecution were determined to seek a conviction for the offence in question, a separate trial of that count would have been fairer.

10.5 Misjoinder

If an indictment contains counts which should not be joined together, because the rules for joinder are not satisfied, there is no power to sever the indictment (i.e. to order separate trials). In *R v Newland* [1988] QB 402, the defendant was charged with a drugs offence and three counts alleging assaults which were wholly unconnected with the drugs charge. The trial judge simply ordered separate trials (purporting to 'sever' the indictment under the Indictments Act 1915, s 5(3)), so that the drugs offence and the assault charges were tried separately. The Court of Appeal held that the judge had no power to 'sever' the indictment under s 5(3), since this power applies only to a valid indictment, and the indictment in the present case was defective because it failed to comply with what is now r 14.2(3) of the Criminal Procedure Rules. The court went on to say that the trial judge should have deleted from the indictment either the drugs charge or the assault charges, and proceeded with the trial on that indictment. The allegations deleted from the indictment could only be proceeded with if the prosecution brought fresh proceedings in the magistrates' court in respect of them or else sought a voluntary bill of indictment.

In *R v Follett* [1989] QB 338, however, a differently constituted Court of Appeal accepted a rather simpler solution. In this case, the indictment was invalid because it contained counts which were not sufficiently linked. The Court of Appeal upheld the decision of the trial judge to stay proceedings on the indictment as drafted and to give the prosecution leave to serve fresh indictments (each complying with r 14.2(3)). The effect of this is that the defective indictment remains in existence but becomes irrelevant. Two or more trials then follow, based on the new indictments.

It follows that, where there has been misjoinder, the situation can be remedied either by:

- deleting one or more counts from the indictment, leaving only counts which can properly be joined under r 14.2(3) (the course of action taken in *Newland*); or
- staying the existing indictment and allowing the prosecution to serve fresh indictments, each indictment containing only counts which can properly be joined under r 14.2(3) (the course of action taken in *R v Follett*).

There was authority to the effect that an indictment containing improperly joined counts was invalid (and so if a defendant was to be convicted on such an indictment, all the convictions would have to be quashed). However, that line of authority was based on a misreading of *Newland*. In *R v Smith* [1997] QB 836, three summary offences were added to an indictment under CJA 1988, s 40; joinder of two of those summary offences was improper because there was no sufficient link with the indictable offence which was also on the indictment. The Court of Appeal held that convictions for offences which are correctly joined are valid convictions. Accordingly, the convictions for the indictable offence and the correctly joined summary offence stood; only the convictions for the two improperly joined summary offences were quashed. Similarly, in *R v Lockley and Sainsbury* [1997] Crim LR 455, the appellants were charged with conspiracy to commit burglary and dangerous driving (the car they used in connection with the burglary was dangerously defective). Both offences are indictable offences and so only r 14.2(3) of the CPR had to be considered. The Court of Appeal held that the dangerous driving charge was improperly joined and confirmed that CJA 1988, s 40 and r 14.2(3) are in all material respects in the same terms (and so the same principles regarding misjoinder and the consequences thereof must apply to both). The court went on to hold that misjoinder does not nullify the whole indictment. It followed that only the conviction(s) on the wrongly joined count(s) should be quashed. It is thus clear that misjoinder of counts does not render the entire indictment invalid.

10.6 Deciding the contents of the indictment

In most cases, the counts on the indictment are the same as the charges which were sent to the Crown Court under s 51 (or 51A) of the Crime and Disorder Act 1998. However, it is possible for the indictment to contain different charges from the original ones. Under s 2(2) of the Administration of Justice (Miscellaneous Provisions) Act 1933 the indictment may contain, as well as or instead of the original charges, any counts which are disclosed in the prosecution witness statements and which can properly be joined in the same indictment.

Rule 14.2(5) of the CPR states that an indictment may contain:

(a) any count charging substantially the same offence as one for which the defendant was sent for trial; and

(b) any other count based on the prosecution evidence already served which the Crown Court may try.

In *R v Lombardi* [1989] 1 WLR 73, the Court of Appeal emphasised that counts for which there is evidence in the prosecution papers, but in respect of which the accused was not sent for trial, can only be added to the indictment if they are in substitution for offences which were sent for trial, or could lawfully be joined in the indictment which results from the sending of the original offence(s) to the Crown Court (on the basis that they arise from the same facts as, or form a series of offences of the same or similar character to, the original charge).

Some examples may help to illustrate the effect of s 2(2) of the 1933 Act.

EXAMPLE 1

The defendant is sent for trial on a charge of burglary. The prosecutor, when drafting the indictment, takes the view that, although there is ample evidence of theft, the evidence relating to the element of trespass is very weak. The prosecutor could draft a count for theft in place of the burglary charge on which the defendant was sent for trial.

EXAMPLE 2

The magistrates send the defendant for trial on a charge of theft but the prosecutor subsequently decide that there is sufficient evidence to prove that the theft was committed in the course of a burglary. The prosecutor could indict the defendant for burglary instead of theft.

EXAMPLE 3

The defendant is sent for trial on a single charge of robbery. The prosecution witness statements include evidence that the defendant was brandishing a gun at the time of the robbery. The allegation of possession of a firearm arises from the same facts as the robbery, so the prosecutor could add a charge alleging a firearms offence even though the defendant was not sent for trial in respect of that offence.

EXAMPLE 4

The defendant is charged with handling stolen goods. In the course of investigating the handling charge, the police search the defendant's home and find a quantity of drugs. The defendant is sent for trial only on the handling offence. The prosecutor cannot add a drugs charge to the handling charge, because the defendant was not sent for trial in respect of it and joinder of the two charges would not be permissible under r 14.2(3), as there is no link between the two charges. The prosecutor cannot put the drugs charge in a separate indictment, because the defendant was not sent for trial in respect of the drugs charge.

In *Lombardi*, Lord Lane CJ also confirmed that, where the magistrates have sent a defendant to the Crown Court on more than one charge, the prosecution may prefer a number of separate indictments if they feel that it is appropriate to do so.

If the magistrates send two or more defendants for trial at the same time, it is open to the prosecution to draft separate indictments against them if the prosecution feel that it would be appropriate to do so. If defendants are not sent for trial at the same time, it is nevertheless open to the prosecution to join those defendants in the same indictment (assuming r 14.2(3) is satisfied); this is so even if an indictment in respect of a defendant who has been sent for trial has already been signed (see *Consolidated Practice Direction*, para IV.34.2).

10.7 Alternative counts

It is possible for counts to appear on an indictment in the alternative. For example, the indictment might contain one count alleging wounding with intent (s 18 of the Offences Against the Person Act 1861) and a separate count alleging unlawful wounding (s 20 of the 1861 Act). This is appropriate where the prosecutor is unsure whether there is sufficient evidence to prove the more serious offence. Nothing on the face of the indictment indicates that the counts are alternatives, so this fact has to be explained to the jury.

10.8 Amending the indictment

Under s 5(1) of the Indictments Act 1915, where, either before the trial or at any stage during the trial, it appears to the court that the indictment is defective, the court is empowered to make such order for the amendment of the indictment as it thinks necessary to meet the circumstances of the case unless, having regard to the merits of the case, the required amendments cannot be made without injustice.

In *R v Pople* [1951] 1 KB 53 it was held that it is not necessary that an indictment, in order to be 'defective' within the meaning of s 5(1), must be bad on its face. On the contrary, said the court, any alteration in matters of description may be made in order to meet the evidence in the case so long as the amendment causes no injustice to the accused. In that case, the Court of Appeal upheld the decision of the trial judge to allow the indictment to be amended at the close of the prosecution case to allege the obtaining by deception of a cheque rather than alleging the obtaining of a sum of money for which the cheque was drawn. The court held that the defendant was not prejudiced, since the substance of the allegation was unaltered.

In *R v Collison* (1980) 71 Cr App R 249, the defendant was charged with one count of wounding with intent (s 18 of the Offences Against the Person Act 1861). The jury was unable to reach either a unanimous or a majority verdict on this count. The judge allowed the prosecution to add a further count of unlawful wounding (contrary to s 20 of the 1861 Act). The Court of Appeal held that no injustice to the defendant had resulted from the amendment since the lesser s 20 offence was effectively already before the jury, since the jury could have acquitted the defendant of the s 18 offence and convicted him of the s 20 offence under s 6(3) of the Criminal Law Act 1967.

The important question in deciding whether or not to allow an amendment once the trial has started is whether the defence case would have been conducted differently had the amendment taken place at the outset. In *R v Harris* (1993) *The Times*, 22 March, the defendant was charged with rape but, at the close of the defence case, the prosecution applied to add an alternative count alleging attempted rape to the indictment. The judge allowed this amendment, but the Court of Appeal held that this decision was wrong, since the defence case would have been put differently (different cross-examination of prosecution witnesses and different defence evidence). Similarly, in *R v Thomas* [1983] Crim LR 619, the Court of Appeal quashed a conviction where a count of receiving stolen property was added to an indictment which hitherto alleged only theft. This amendment took place after the close of the prosecution case and the defence would have cross-examined the prosecution witnesses differently if both allegations had been made at the outset. In *R v Foster* [2007] EWCA Crim 2869; [2008] 1 WLR 1615, Sir Igor Judge P said (at para 65):

> ... it is now common practice to permit amendments to the indictment at any stage of the trial, whether by amending or adding or substituting new counts, provided that these steps may be taken without unfairness to the accused. Whether unfairness results will usually depend on the purpose of the amendment, the stage of the trial at which the amendment is sought, the degree, if any, to which the defendant is required by the amendment to meet a new prosecution case and whether he would be disadvantaged in the presentation of his defence.

The amendment may take the form of inserting a new count in the indictment, whether in addition to, or instead of, the original count (*R v Johal* [1973] QB 475). Where there is no injustice to the defendant, an indictment can even be amended under s 5(1) so as to add a new defendant (*R v Palmer* [2002] EWCA Crim 892; (2002) *The Times*, 18 April).

11

Crown Court trial

11.1 Preliminary hearings

Part 3 of the Criminal Procedure Rules contains general case management powers. Part 3 is supplemented by Part IV.41 of the *Consolidated Criminal Practice Direction*. Para IV.41.3 of the Practice Direction states that a preliminary hearing (PH) is not required in every case sent for trial; rather, a PH should be ordered by the magistrates' court or by the Crown Court only where such a hearing is considered necessary (eg where there are case management issues which call for such a hearing). Where a PH is necessary, it should be held approximately 14 days after the case is sent to the Crown Court. A Case Progression Preliminary Hearing Form has to be completed by the parties, providing an agenda for the PH; the form envisages three possible outcomes, namely a guilty plea (at the PH or a subsequent hearing), directions for a 'plea and case management hearing' (PCMH), or fixing of the trial date.

11.1.1 Plea and case management hearings

Where the magistrates' court does not order a PH, it must order a PCMH to be held within approximately 14 weeks after the case has been sent for trial where the defendant is in custody (within approximately 17 weeks where the defendant is on bail) (para IV.41.5 of the *Consolidated Practice Direction*). In a case where the defendant intends to plea not guilty, it is clear that the effectiveness of the PCMH is dependent on the presence of the trial advocate or of an advocate who is able to make decisions about the conduct of the case and give the court the assistance which the trial advocate could be expected to give (para IV.41.8). Additional pre-trial hearings should be held only for some compelling reason; where necessary, the power to give, vary or revoke a direction without a hearing should be used (para IV.41.11).

Annex E to the *Consolidated Criminal Practice Direction* contains a standard form to be completed for PCMHs. It includes questions such as:

- Has the defendant been advised about credit for pleading guilty?
- Has the defendant been warned that if he is on bail and fails to attend, the proceedings may continue in his absence?
- Might the case against a defendant be resolved by a plea of guilty to some counts on the indictment or to a lesser offence?
- In the case of a guilty plea, is there a written basis of plea? Is the basis of plea acceptable to the prosecution?
- Are there any other matters which should be dealt with at the same time as these proceedings (other offences/TICs)?

- What is the estimated length of the prosecution, defence cases?
- Should the defendant's interview(s) be edited before the trial?
- Has a defence statement been served (under the CPIA 1996)? Is there an issue as to its adequacy? Is the defence alleging that the prosecution has not complied with its obligation to disclose material?
- Have the parties considered formal admissions?
- Is expert evidence likely to be called by either side? Does the court approve of the need for the identified expert evidence? Should the expert evidence be presented in a particular way in order to be more easily understood by the jury? Would it be helpful if the experts produced a written note of points of agreement or disagreement with a summary of reasons?
- Are there any outstanding issues about special measures or live links?
- Are any special arrangements needed for a child defendant?
- Will a defendant be unrepresented at trial?
- Will there be applications regarding hearsay evidence or bad character evidence?
- What are the legal or factual issues which should be resolved before the trial? Do the parties wish to call witnesses to give evidence orally to enable the court to resolve the issues?

The PCMH guidance notes state that the parties must use their best endeavours to reduce the amount of oral evidence given to a minimum, in particular by reducing the number of witnesses who give similar evidence, or by the deletion of challenged passages the omission of which will not materially affect the case for the party calling that witness, or by the use of admissions which make the calling of the witness in person unnecessary.

Under s 40 of the CPIA 1996, the court may make rulings, which have binding effect, as to: (a) any question as to the admissibility of evidence; (b) any other question of law relating to the case. The extent to which courts exercise the power to make these rulings at this hearing is a matter for the court, after considering representations. Such rulings can be varied or discharged, but only if there has been a material change of circumstance since the order was made and if the judge is satisfied that it is in the interests of justice to do so.

To encourage pre-trial resolution of issues, PCMH guidance notes say that the parties should, before the PCMH, agree or try to agree what legal issues are likely to be raised (for example, joinder, severance, admissibility of evidence, abuse of process, issues of substantive law etc) and at what stage they should properly be resolved. Any application to stay an indictment on the ground of abuse of process should be considered at the PCMH.

11.1.2 Preparatory hearings

Under the CPIA 1996, s 29, a Crown Court judge may, 'on an application by one of the parties or of his own motion', order a preparatory hearing to take place if it appears to the judge that the indictment 'reveals a case of such complexity, a case of such seriousness or a case whose trial is likely to be of such length, that substantial benefits are likely to accrue from a hearing . . .'. See also Part 15 of the Criminal Procedure Rules.

Thus a preparatory hearing can be held on the basis that the case appears to be:

- complex; or
- serious; or
- lengthy.

Section 29(2) sets out the purposes of the preparatory hearing. These include:

- *identifying issues which are likely to be material to the determinations and findings which are likely to be required during the trial;*
- *assisting the comprehension by the jury of any such issues;*
- *expediting the proceedings before the jury;*
- *assisting the judge's management of the trial;*
- *considering questions as to the severance or joinder of charges.*

Section 31(3) empowers the judge to make rulings as to:

(a) *any question as to the admissibility of evidence;*

(b) *any other question of law relating to the case;*

(c) *any question as to the severance or joinder of charges.*

In *R v Claydon* [2004] 1 Cr App R 36, the Court of Appeal ruled that applications to exclude evidence (eg under PACE 1984, s 78) should be regarded as being for the purpose of 'expediting the proceedings before the jury', and so within s 29(2).

There are provisions for appeals from rulings made by the judge at a preparatory hearing to the Court of Appeal and, ultimately, the House of Lords. Where leave to appeal has been granted, the preparatory hearing may continue, but the jury trial cannot begin until the appeal has been determined or abandoned.

In *R v H (Interlocutory application: Disclosure)* [2007] UKHL 7; [2007] 2 AC 270, the House of Lords held that a judge who is considering whether to hold a preparatory hearing has only to decide whether a substantial benefit, for one of the purposes listed in the legislation, would arise from determining the relevant issues at a preparatory hearing, rather than after a jury has been empanelled. The judge may determine other interlocutory applications at the same time as the preparatory hearing, but there is no appeal to the Court of Appeal in respect of those issues, since an appeal is available only if the matter for determination relates to one of the statutory purposes. It followed that determination of an application for disclosure under s 8 of the CPIA 1996 would qualify for an appeal only if it involves the determination of a question of law relating to the case. This case was decided under the CJA 1987, but the principles laid down are equally applicable to hearings under s 29 of the CPIA 1996.

Under s 31, the judge may also order the prosecutor to:

- supply to the court and to the accused a written case statement (setting out the principal facts of the case for the prosecution, the witnesses who will give evidence of those facts, any exhibits relevant to those facts, and any proposition of law on which the prosecutor proposes to rely);
- prepare the prosecution evidence and any explanatory material in such a form as appears to the judge to be likely to aid comprehension by the jury;
- give the court and the accused written notice of documents, the truth of the contents of which ought in the prosecutor's view to be admitted, and any other matters which ought to be agreed.

Where a judge has ordered the prosecutor to give a case statement and the prosecutor has complied with the order, the judge may order the accused to:

- provide a written statement setting out (in general terms) the nature of his or her defence and indicating the principal matters on which he or she takes issue with the prosecution;

- give the court and the prosecutor written notice of any objections that he or she has to the case statement;
- give the court and the prosecutor written notice of any point of law (including any point as to the admissibility of evidence) which he or she wishes to take, and any authority on which he or she intends to rely for that purpose.

In *R v K* [2006] EWCA Crim 724; [2006] 2 All ER 552, the Court of Appeal said that the case management powers conferred by the Criminal Procedure Rules mean that a judge dealing with matters preliminary to a trial may, if he or she thinks it right to do so, deal with the issues exclusively by reference to written submissions, or to place a time limit on oral submissions. The judge is not bound to allow oral submissions (or, if oral submissions are permitted, is entitled to place a time limit on them).

In *Kanaris v Governor of Pentonville Prison* [2003] UKHL 2; [2003] 1 WLR 443, the House of Lords held that a Crown Court judge is entitled to hold separate preparatory hearings (under s 29 of the CPIA 1996) in respect of defendants who are charged jointly in the same indictment.

11.1.3 Adjournments

The existence of the various forms of pre-trial hearing should mean that the trial can go ahead on the date that is fixed. However, there may still be occasions when an adjournment is sought. In *R v Chaaban* [2003] EWCA Crim 1012; *The Times*, 8 May 2003, the Court of Appeal said that adjournments must be justified and, if at all possible, should be avoided. However, the Court noted that the decision whether or not to adjourn is pre-eminently a matter for the trial judge, and so the Court of Appeal will not interfere with that decision unless it can be demonstrated that the decision to refuse an adjournment was wholly unreasonable and caused real (as opposed to fanciful) prejudice to the defendant, undermining the safety of the conviction.

11.2 The arraignment

At the arraignment (which should take place at the PCMH), the indictment is 'put' to the defendant, in that he or she is asked to plead guilty or not guilty. The proceedings will go something like this:

Clerk of the Court: 'Are you Michael Smith?'
Smith: 'Yes.'
Clerk: 'Michael Smith, you are charged in an indictment containing one count of robbery contrary to s 8 of the Theft Act 1968. The particulars of the offence are that on 8 December 2009 you robbed Alice Jones of £450 in cash. Michael Smith, to this indictment do you plead guilty or not guilty?'

If the indictment contains more than one count, each count will be put to the defendant separately, so that a separate plea is entered on each. The defendant must enter their plea personally (not through counsel or solicitor).

The defendant must be present at the arraignment in order to enter a plea. If the defendant fails to attend court on the date fixed for the trial, a bench warrant for the defendant's arrest will usually be issued. The court also has a discretion to proceed with the trial in the absence of the defendant. In *R v Jones* [2002] UKHL 5; [2003] 1 AC 1, the defendants had pleaded not guilty on arraignment but absconded before the date fixed for the trial. The judge (after a number of adjournments) decided to try them in their absence. It was held by the House of Lords that the discretion to commence a trial in the absence of the defendant should be exercised with the utmost care and caution, and if the absence is attributable to involuntary illness or incapacity it will very rarely, if ever, be right to do so, at any rate unless the defendant is represented and has asked that the trial should begin (per Lord Bingham at para 13). The House of Lords went on to say that it is generally desirable that a defendant be represented even if he has voluntarily absconded. Trial judges should therefore ask counsel to continue to represent a defendant who has absconded and counsel should normally accede to such an invitation and defend their absent client as best they properly can in the circumstances (para 15). The factors to be considered by the judge in deciding whether or not the defendant should be tried *in absentia* were set out by the Court of Appeal in the same case ([2001] EWCA Crim 168; [2001] QB 862), though Lord Bingham (at para 14) said that the seriousness of the offence should not be considered (since the judge's overriding concern will be to ensure that the trial, if conducted in the absence of the defendant, will be as fair as circumstances permit and lead to a just outcome, and these objects are equally important, whether the offence charged be serious or relatively minor). In *R v O'Hare* [2006] EWCA Crim 471, it was said that it should be made clear to each defendant that if he fails to attend a trial, the trial may well proceed in his absence and without legal representation.

In *R v Kepple* [2007] EWCA Crim 1339, the Court of Appeal said that where the defendant is being tried *in absentia* but counsel continues to act, counsel should conduct the case, on the basis of any instructions already received from the client, as though the client were still present in court but had decided not to give evidence. Counsel is free to use any material contained in the brief, and may cross-examine prosecution witnesses (to put the absent defendant's case to them or to cast doubt upon the coherence or accuracy of their accounts) and may call defence witnesses.

If the defendant pleads guilty to some charges but not guilty to others, the sentencing on the offences to which there was a guilty plea will usually be postponed until the trial of the charges on which there was a not guilty plea has been concluded.

11.2.1 Procedure on a plea of guilty

If the defendant pleads guilty to all the counts on the indictment, the prosecution will summarise the facts of the offence(s) and tell the court about the defendant's antecedents, that is basic details about them (education, employment, income, etc), based on what the defendant has told the police, together with details of any relevant previous convictions. The court will in fact have a complete list of the defendant's previous convictions, but will invite the prosecution to read out only those that are relevant, which will usually mean fairly recent ones. See para III.27 of the *Consolidated Practice Direction*.

11.2.2 The *Newton* hearing

In some cases, the defendant may plead guilty to an offence but on a factual basis that is less serious than the version of events put forward by the prosecution. The procedure to be adopted by the court in such a case was laid down in *R v Newton* (1982) 77 Cr App R 13 (dealt with extensively in paras D19.8–19.29 of *Blackstone's Criminal Practice*).

According to *Newton*, where the defendant pleads guilty but there is a significant difference between the prosecution version and the defence version (significant in the sense of being likely to have an effect on the sentence imposed by the court), the court must either accept the defence version of events or else hear evidence (in a *Newton* hearing) about what happened and then make a finding of fact. In other words, in a case where there is a significant factual dispute, the court cannot accept the prosecution version of events without having first heard evidence to support that version.

For example, in *R v McFarlane* (1995) 16 Cr App R (S) 315, the defendant was charged with assault occasioning actual bodily harm. He pleaded guilty. The prosecution alleged that he had jabbed his wife in the face with a fork and had repeatedly punched her about the face. He admitted assaulting her but claimed that he had not jabbed her in the face with a fork and said that he had slapped her (and not punched her).

The course of action set out in *Newton* should be followed unless the defence story may fairly be described as 'incredible' (*R v Hawkins* (1985) 7 Cr App R (S) 351).

Where a *Newton* hearing takes place, the judge must be satisfied beyond reasonable doubt before accepting the prosecution version of events (*R v Kerrigan* (1993) 14 Cr App R (S) 179).

Where the judge does hold a *Newton* hearing, the Court of Appeal will not interfere with the judge's findings of fact unless no reasonable judge could reach those findings based on the evidence heard (*R v Ahmed* (1984) 80 Cr App R 295; *R v Wood* [1991] Crim LR 926).

If the judge wrongly accepts the prosecution version of events without having held a *Newton* hearing, the Court of Appeal will give the defendant the benefit of the doubt and will replace the sentence imposed by the judge with the sentence that would have been appropriate on the basis of the version of events put forward by the defendant (*R v Mohun* (1993) 14 Cr App R (S) 5).

In *R v Tolera* [1999] 1 Cr App R 29 the Court of Appeal emphasised the responsibility of defence counsel to make sure that the court is alerted to any significant difference between prosecution and defence versions of the facts.

In *Newton*, the Court of Appeal suggested an alternative way of resolving a dispute of fact on a guilty plea—by empanelling a jury to decide the issue. That method is only appropriate where the difference between the prosecution version and the defence version amounts (in effect) to an allegation by the prosecution that the defendant committed an additional offence (which can therefore be added to the indictment). For example, in *R v Gandy* (1989) 11 Cr App R (S) 564 the defendant was charged with violent disorder. The prosecution alleged that he had thrown a glass at someone (who lost an eye as a result). The defendant denied throwing the glass. The Court of Appeal noted that this dispute could (indeed should) have been resolved by adding a count alleging wounding with intent (Offences Against the Person Act 1861, s 18) or a count alleging unlawful wounding (s 20 of the 1861 Act). Another example is *R v Eubank* [2001] EWCA Crim 891; [2002] 1 Cr App R (S) 4. In that case, the defendant was charged with robbery. The prosecution alleged that the accused had brandished a firearm, but he denied this. The judge held a *Newton* hearing to resolve the dispute about whether or not the accused had been in possession of a gun at the time of the robbery. The Court of Appeal held that this dispute should have been resolved by adding a firearms charge to the indictment and empanelling a jury to try that count. Indeed, the failure to do so meant that the accused had been deprived of his right to jury trial in respect of that allegation. An example of a case where it was wrong to empanel a jury is *R v Dowdall* (1992) 13 Cr App R (S) 441. The dispute in that case was whether the theft of a pension book (which the defendant admitted) was theft by finding or theft by taking the book from the victim's bag. The judge resolved the dispute by amending the indictment to contain one count alleging theft by finding and a second count alleging theft from the victim's bag. The Court of Appeal held that this was inappropriate, as both allegations were in law the same, namely theft.

These principles are summarised comprehensively in *R v Underwood* [2004] EWCA Crim 2256; [2005] 1 Cr App R 13. See also **13.4.3**.

11.2.3 Prosecution offering no evidence; leaving counts on the file

If the defendant pleads not guilty to some or all of the counts on the indictment, the next stage (which will take place some time after the PCMH) is to empanel a jury. However, it may be that new evidence has come to light showing that the wrong person has been charged or considerably weakening the case against this defendant, or it may be that a vital witness has refused to testify (and, although a person can be compelled to give evidence, a reluctant witness nearly always does more harm than good). In that case the prosecution will offer no evidence against the defendant, in which case a finding of not guilty is entered under the Criminal Justice Act 1967, s 17. An alternative to offering no evidence is for the prosecution to ask the judge to direct that one or more counts be left on the file marked 'not to be proceeded with without the leave of the Crown Court or the Court of Appeal'.

If the defendant pleads guilty to some counts but not guilty to others, and the prosecution are content for the defendant to be dealt with solely on the basis of the counts to which he has pleaded guilty, prosecuting counsel may agree not to proceed with the counts to which the defendant pleads not guilty (either by offering no evidence in respect of them or asking for them to be left on the file). Leaving a count on the file is not an acquittal, whereas offering no evidence does result in an acquittal. Nonetheless, counts which have been left on the file would not be reactivated save in very unusual circumstances (for example, where the Court of Appeal sets aside the guilty pleas because the pleas were entered under duress).

11.2.4 Plea of guilty to an alternative offence: 'plea bargaining'

The Criminal Law Act 1967 (CLA), s 6(1)(b), provides that the defendant may plead not guilty to the offence on the indictment but guilty to a lesser offence of which the jury would be able to convict him under the CLA 1967, s 6(3). For example, the offence of robbery is committed by a person who commits theft together with actual or threatened violence. If the accused admits the theft but denies the use or threat of violence, a plea of 'not guilty to robbery but guilty to theft' could be offered. In *R v Yeardley* [2000] 1 QB 374 it was held that where the defendant pleads not guilty to the offence on the indictment but guilty to a lesser offence, the guilty plea becomes a nullity if the prosecution choose to proceed with the offence on the indictment. The obvious solution is to add the lesser offence to the indictment (the defendant then pleads guilty to one count and not guilty to the other).

11.2.5 Different pleas from different defendants

If there is more than one defendant and one pleads guilty and the others not guilty, it is a matter for the judge whether to sentence the one who has pleaded guilty immediately or at the end of the trial of the others. The argument in favour of postponing sentence is that, at the end of the trial, the judge will have a much better idea of who did what. However, it is a little more difficult if the defendant who pleads guilty also indicates a willingness to 'turn Queen's evidence', giving evidence against the other accused. This will attract a very substantial discount in sentence, well beyond the one-third normally credited to those who simply plead guilty. Such a person becomes a competent witness for the Crown after pleading guilty. However, if sentence is postponed, it may seem that the sentence imposed after the defendant has given evidence depends more on the quality of the evidence given than on the extent of the defendant's guilt; on the other hand, if the defendant is sentenced before giving evidence but then has a change of mind, the lenient sentence given on the basis of the promised testimony cannot be altered (see *R v Stone* [1970] 1 WLR 1112). The Court of Appeal, in *R v Weekes* (1980) 74 Cr App R 161, said that sentence should normally be postponed until after the trial of the other defendant. However, in *R v Clement*, *The Times*, 12 December 1991 the court observed that it is a matter for the judge whether the defendant is sentenced sooner or later.

If one defendant pleads guilty but another pleads not guilty, the jury should not be told about the guilty plea of the other defendant (unless, of course, that defendant gives evidence for the prosecution). For example, in *R v Manzur and Mahmood* [1997] 1 Cr App R 414, three people had been charged with rape. One defendant pleaded guilty, the other two pleaded not guilty, saying that the victim had consented to sexual intercourse. The judge allowed the jury to be told of the third defendant's plea of guilty. The Court of Appeal accepted the argument that the jury might have taken the view, on the basis of the third defendant's guilty plea, that the two appellants must have known that the victim was not consenting and so might not have given proper consideration to the evidence of the two appellants that they believed the woman to be consenting to intercourse. The admission of the evidence of the plea of the third defendant was therefore unduly prejudicial to the appellants and so a re-trial was ordered.

11.2.6 The ambiguous plea

If the defendant pleads guilty but then advances mitigation which amounts to a defence, then the plea is ambiguous (eg the defendant pleads guilty to theft but then claims mistaken belief that the property was their own). In those circumstances, the law will be explained to the defendant, who will then be asked to plead again. If the plea remains ambiguous, a plea of not guilty will be entered on behalf of the defendant and a trial will take place in the usual way.

Sometimes a defendant will say to counsel, 'I didn't do it but I want to plead guilty to get things over and done with quickly'. In such a case, counsel should try to dissuade the client from pleading guilty to an offence which they deny. In particular, it should be pointed out that nothing can be said in mitigation which suggests innocence (since that would render the plea ambiguous) or even remorse (one cannot be remorseful for something one denies doing).

11.2.7 Seeing the judge in chambers

In *R v Goodyear* [2005] EWCA Crim 888; [2005] 1 WLR 2532, the Court of Appeal reviewed the guidance on advanced indications of sentence in the Crown Court (see *R v Turner* [1970] 2 QB 321 and para IV.45 of the *Consolidated Practice Direction*). In a break with former practice, the Court held that it does not constitute inappropriate judicial pressure on the defendant for the judge to respond to a request, made by or on behalf of the defendant, for an indication of the judge's current view of the maximum sentence which would be imposed on the defendant. Any advance indication of sentence given by the judge should normally be confined to the maximum sentence if a plea of guilty were tendered at the stage at which the indication is sought (not the maximum possible sentence following conviction by the jury). The judge should not give an advance indication of sentence unless one has been sought by the defendant. However, the judge is entitled in an appropriate case to remind the defence advocate (in open court and in the presence of the defendant) that the defendant is entitled to seek such an indication. The judge retains an unfettered discretion to refuse to give an advance indication of sentence or to wait, for example until a pre-sentence report is available, before deciding whether to give one. Once an indication has been given, it is binding on the judge who has given it, and on any other judge who becomes responsible for the case. If, after a reasonable opportunity to consider the indication, the defendant does not plead guilty, the indication ceases to have effect. The defendant's advocate should not seek an indication without written authority, signed by the client, that the client wishes to seek an indication; the advocate is responsible for ensuring that the client fully appreciates that:

(a) he or she should not plead guilty unless in fact guilty;

(b) any sentence indication given by the judge remains subject to the entitlement of the Attorney-General (where it arises) to refer an unduly lenient sentence to the Court of Appeal;

(c) any indication given by the judge reflects the situation at the time when it is given, and that if a guilty plea is not tendered in the light of that indication the indication ceases to have effect.

An indication should not be sought while there is any uncertainty between the prosecution and the defence about an acceptable plea (eg where there is a possibility of the defendant pleading guilty to a lesser offence), or about any factual basis relating to the plea. Any agreed basis should be reduced into writing before an indication is sought. The judge should not be asked to indicate levels of sentence which would vary depending on possible different pleas. If an indication is sought, the prosecution should normally enquire whether the judge is in possession of all the evidence relied on by the prosecution, including any personal impact statement from the victim of the crime, as well as any information of relevant previous convictions recorded against the defendant. Any sentence indication should normally be sought at the PCMH. The hearing should normally take place in open court, with a full recording of the entire proceedings, and both sides represented, in the defendant's presence. Any reference to a request for a sentence indication, or the circumstances in which it was sought, is inadmissible in any subsequent trial (should the defendant maintain a not guilty plea). Reporting restrictions should normally be imposed, to be lifted if and when the defendant pleads or is found guilty.

In *Attorney-General's Reference No 80 of 2005: R v Wedlock-Ward* [2005] EWCA Crim 3367, Rose LJ said (at para 29):

Lest the Court's decision in *Goodyear* be misunderstood . . . we wish to make three matters about that decision plain. First, its purposes was [sic] not to encourage a return to the practice disapproved of in *R v Turner* [1970] 2 QB 321 at 326H of counsel seeing the judge about sentence, privately in his room. On the contrary, . . . hearings involving an indication of sentence 'should normally take place in open court'. There are, of course, exceptions to this principle, for example, where a defendant is unaware that he is terminally ill. Secondly, the principal feature of the new approach to indications of sentence prescribed in *Goodyear* is that advance indications of sentence should be sought by the defence not promulgated by the judge . . . Thirdly, if an indication in such a context is to be made, it is not appropriate . . . for [the judge] to identify, by reference to a trial, the much longer sentence which he would impose compared with the sentence which he proposes if the defendant pleads guilty . . . such a course is likely to apply pressure to a defendant which the judgment in *Goodyear* sought to avoid.

11.2.8 Securing attendance of witnesses

Where the prosecution or defence wish to secure the attendance of a witness, but have reason to believe that the witness will not attend voluntarily, they can apply for a witness summons under the Criminal Procedure (Attendance of Witnesses) Act 1965, ss 2–4. The court may issue a witness summons if it considers it in the interests of justice to do so. The procedure is set out in r 28.3 of the Criminal Procedure Rules.

11.3 The jury

11.3.1 Who can serve?

Under the Juries Act 1974, s 1 (as amended by the CJA 2003), 'every person shall be qualified to serve as a juror in the Crown Court . . . and be liable accordingly to attend for jury service when summoned under this Act' if on the electoral roll and neither mentally disordered or disqualified from jury service because of previous convictions. Everyone, unless mentally disordered or disqualified because of previous convictions, is required to serve when summoned to do so.

R v Abdroikov [2007] UKHL 37; [2007] 1 WLR 2679 concerned three unrelated trials. In two cases, the trial jury had included among its members a serving police officer, and in the third case it included a solicitor employed by the CPS. The House of Lords held (by a 3:2 majority) that the question to be asked was whether, on the particular facts of each of the cases, a fair-minded and informed observer would conclude that there was a real possibility that the jurors in question were biased, having regard to the fact that Parliament had declared that such persons were eligible to sit on juries, envisaging that any objection to their sitting would be the subject of judicial decision. They went on to hold that the convictions should be quashed in the case where one of the jurors was an employee of the CPS (that fact was enough to create a suspicion of bias in a case where the prosecution was brought by the CPS) and the case where one of the jurors was a serving police officer who worked in the same area as police witnesses in the case; however, the conviction should not be quashed in the other case, where the police officer who was on the jury did not work in the same area as the police witnesses. It follows that, if an issue arises as to whether a member of the jury may be unsuitable to sit on that jury, the test in *Porter v Magill* [2002] 2 AC 357, 494 has to be applied in order to determine whether or not the requirements of fairness have been met. The effect of this ruling was considered in *R v Alan I* [2007] EWCA Crim 2999. Nelson J (at para 29) said that, in all cases the test is one of apparent bias. This will depend on the facts. If, for example, a potential juror knows a witness personally, it is common for such a juror to stand down. Where, however, the witness he knows is not contentious and not to be called, but is taken simply as read as an agreed statement, there may well be no possibility of bias. It is therefore necessary for the judge to make all appropriate factual enquiries. Usually, this is by posing questions, either in court or in writing to the potential juror. The manner in which the questions are asked will depend on the circumstances. Sometimes a few questions in open court will suffice. In other cases, where the information might be sensitive, or more detail is required, the matter may have to be dealt with in writing. His Lordship went on to hold (at paras 35 and 36) that any potential juror who knows witnesses who are to be called to give oral evidence should be stood down at the outset, 'unless it can be said with certainty that the evidence of the witnesses who are known will play no contested part in the determination of the matter'. The Court of Appeal gave further guidance in *R v Khan* [2008] EWCA Crim 531; [2008] 3 All ER 502. Lord Phillips CJ said that 'the fact that a police juror may seem likely to favour the evidence of a fellow police officer will not, automatically, lead to the appearance that he favours the prosecution'. It would not do so, for example, if the police evidence is not challenged or does not form an important part of the prosecution case (para 29). Similarly, the 'mere suspicion that a juror might, by reason of having been employed as a prison officer in a prison where the defendant was held, have acquired knowledge of that defendant's bad character could not, of itself, lead an objective observer to conclude that the juror had an appearance of bias' (para 120). Moreover, there can be no objection to a member of the Crown Prosecution Service sitting in a case prosecuted by some other prosecuting authority (para 97).

Disqualification as a result of previous convictions is dealt with by the Juries Act 1974, Sch 1, Part 2. The following people are disqualified from jury service:

- a person who is on bail in criminal proceedings at the relevant time;
- a person who has at any time been sentenced in the United Kingdom to imprisonment or detention for life, to detention during her Majesty's pleasure, to imprisonment or detention for public protection, to an extended sentence under the CJA 2003, s 227 or s 228, or to a term of imprisonment or detention of five years or more;
- a person who at any time in the last ten years has, in the United Kingdom, served any part of a sentence of imprisonment or detention, or has had passed on him a suspended sentence of imprisonment or detention;
- a person who at any time in the last ten years has, in England and Wales, received a community order.

No-one is entitled to refuse to do jury service. However, s 9(2) of the Juries Act 1974 provides that a person who has been summoned for jury service may seek excusal if they can show a 'good reason' for this, and s 9A(1) enables a person summoned for jury service to seek deferral of the summons (and so, if the dates specified in the summons clash with the person's holiday arrangements or business commitments, attendance can be deferred to a later date). The discretion to excuse or defer is exercised by the Jury Central Summoning Bureau (JCSB) which administers the jury summoning system on behalf of the Crown Court. The JCSB works on the basis that deferral is always preferable to excusal.

Section 9B of the Juries Act 1974 enables a person to be excused from jury service because he or she is not capable of acting effectively as a juror because of a physical disability.

Paragraph IV.42.1 of *Consolidated Practice Direction* makes the point that, whether or not an application has already been made to the JCSB for deferral or excusal, it is also open to the person summoned to apply to the court to be excused. Paragraph IV.42.3 deals with the situation where a juror unexpectedly finds him or herself in difficult professional or personal circumstances during the course of the trial: such problems should be raised with the trial judge, who then has to decide whether (assuming the juror has presented a sufficient reason to require action) it would be better to adjourn the trial for a short period or to discharge the juror and continue the trial with a reduced number of jurors.

11.3.2 Empanelling the jury

A number of potential jurors come into the courtroom. The clerk reads out the names of 12 of them, selected randomly from the list of those present. The 12 go into the jury box. The clerk will also explain to the defendant that the list of names about to be called out will form the jury which will try the case and will inform the defendant of the right to challenge jurors before they are sworn.

11.3.3 Challenging potential jurors

There are two main types of challenge.

11.3.3.1 Standby

The first type of challenge is the right of the prosecution to stand a juror by. Just as the juror starts to take the oath, prosecuting counsel says 'Stand by'. The judge will then explain to that juror that he or she cannot sit on this jury but may be required to sit on another one. This challenge is confined to the prosecution, and prosecuting counsel does not have to give any reasons for the challenge. The fact that the prosecution would seem to have an advantage over the defence (who no longer have any right of peremptory challenge) led the Attorney-General to issue guidelines on the related issues of use of the standby and jury vetting (see Appendix 3 to *Blackstone's Criminal Practice* for the full text). In many cases there will be no check at all on potential jurors. However, in ordinary cases the names of the potential jurors may be put through the Police National Computer to see if any have previous convictions which mean that they are disqualified from jury service or are unsuitable to serve on this particular jury. In cases involving national security and terrorism, however, a more thorough check is carried out. Unsuitable jurors can then simply be stood by. Another case where use of the standby is appropriate, according to the Guidelines, is where the person is manifestly unsuitable to sit on this jury, and the defence agrees that he or she should not sit. An example might be the person who is clearly unable to read the words on the card which contains the jury oath and so is unsuitable for a case which involves perusal of documentary evidence.

It should be noted that the judge also has power to stand a juror by, but this power is exercised only very rarely. Some judges had used it (at the request of the defence) to try to secure a racially balanced jury so that some members shared the defendant's ethnic origin. However, in *R v Ford* [1989] QB 868 the Court of Appeal ruled that this practice was unlawful. *Ford* was followed in *R v Smith* [2003] EWCA Crim 283; [2003] 1 WLR 2229, where a black defendant was tried, by an all white jury, with causing serious injury to a white victim. It was held that the jury-summoning procedure in the Juries Act 1974 is not inconsistent with Article 6 of the European Convention on Human Rights. The court said that it is not unfair that a black defendant is tried by a randomly selected all-white jury, nor would a fair-minded and informed observer consider it unfair. The court added that consideration of the evidence in the present case did not require knowledge of the traditions or social circumstances of a particular racial group (even though there was a racial element to the offence); rather it was a common situation of violence outside a club. Similarly, in *R v Tarrant* [1998] Crim LR 342, it was held that the judge cannot use his discretion to discharge individual jurors so as to interfere with the composition of the jury panel by selecting jurors from outside the court's catchment area, in order to minimise the risk of intimidation.

11.3.3.2 Challenge for cause

The other important form of challenge (and the only one open to the defence) is the challenge for cause. This challenge is used in cases where it is suspected that a potential juror might be biased. It should be remembered that although the names of potential jurors are available for inspection by the prosecution and defence, it is unlikely that any checks will have been carried out apart from the check for previous convictions carried out by the prosecution. The defence is unlikely to have information to show that a particular juror is biased (unless the defendant happens to recognise the person in question). Further (and this is different from the position in the United States) no questions may be asked of a potential juror unless the challenging party has already established a prima facie case that the person is likely to be biased (see *R v Chandler* [1964] 2 QB 322). An example of how this operates may be seen in the trial of the Kray brothers, presided over by Lawton J (see *R v Kray* (1969) 53 Cr App R 412). A national newspaper had published a colourful account of the allegations against the Krays. The judge was persuaded that anyone who had read this material might well be biased against the defendants. He therefore allowed the defence to ask each juror whether he or she had read the material in question. If the juror said yes, that person was then successfully challenged. However, a more restrictive view was taken by the Court of Appeal in *R v Andrews* [1999] Crim LR 156. The appellant claimed that her conviction for murder was unsafe because of adverse pre-trial publicity. It was argued on her behalf that potential jurors should have been asked whether they had read or heard the reports in question. It was held that such questioning of jurors (whether done orally or by means of a questionnaire) is of doubtful efficacy and may even be counter-productive (by reminding the jurors of the publicity); it should therefore only be done in the most exceptional circumstances. In *Montgomery v HM Advocate; Coulter v HM Advocate* [2001] 2 WLR 779, the Privy Council (hearing a Scottish appeal) held that where there has been prejudicial pre-trial publicity, the court is entitled to expect the jury to follow the directions which they receive from the trial judge and to return a verdict based only on the evidence they have heard in court. On that basis, a defendant may be regarded as having received a fair trial even if there has been adverse pre-trial publicity. Likewise, in *R v Abu Hamza* [2006] EWCA Crim 2918; [2007] 3 All ER 451, the Court of Appeal observed that the fact that there has been adverse publicity is no reason for not proceeding with the trial if the judge concludes that it will be possible to have a fair trial.

To challenge for cause, counsel merely says 'challenge' before the juror takes the oath. If it is a straightforward case (eg the juror knows the defendant), counsel will simply state that this is the case and the judge will ask that person to leave the jury box. If it is more complicated, the jurors who have already been sworn and the rest of the potential jurors (the 'jury in waiting') will be asked to leave court and counsel will have to explain the basis of the challenge and (if the judge so directs) question the challenged juror.

In *R v Gough* [1993] AC 646 the House of Lords held that the test where bias is alleged is whether there is a 'real danger' that the juror is biased. In *Porter v Magill* [2002] 2 AC 357, the House of Lords said that the test is whether a fair-minded and informed observer would conclude that there was a real possibility of bias on the part of the tribunal. See also *R v Wilson* (1979) 69 Cr App R 83, where convictions were quashed (and retrials ordered) because one of the jurors was the wife of a prison officer serving at the prison where the appellants had been held on remand. The Court of Appeal said that the test is one of *possibility* of bias rather than *probability* of bias and so it was not necessary to inquire into the juror's actual state of mind. There was a real danger that, consciously or not, she may have been biased against the appellants.

11.3.3.3 Replacement of juror after successful challenge

When a juror has been stood by or successfully challenged, he or she is replaced by another member of the jury in waiting.

11.3.4 Discharge of jurors

11.3.4.1 Discharge of individual jurors during the trial

A Crown Court jury always starts off with 12 jurors. However, under the Juries Act 1974, s 16, up to three jurors may be discharged during the course of the trial in case of illness or other necessity (eg bereavement). What constitutes necessity is a matter for the trial judge. In *R v Hanberry* [1977] QB 924 a juror was discharged because the trial went on longer than expected and she would otherwise have had to cancel a holiday.

If more than three jurors can no longer serve, the trial has to be abandoned; a fresh trial will take place later.

11.3.4.2 Discharge of entire jury

The entire jury may be discharged if, for example:

(a) The jury hears evidence that is inadmissible and prejudicial to the defendant: where evidence that is prejudicial to the defendant has inadvertently been adduced, it is not automatically the case that the jury should be discharged, since in some instances a direction to the jury to ignore the inadmissible evidence might be sufficient (*R v Weaver* [1968] 1 QB 353). Whether or not the jury should be discharged is a matter for the discretion of the trial judge. The test to be applied is the test for bias, namely whether there is a real possibility of injustice occurring because the jury, having heard the prejudicial matter, may be biased (*R v Docherty* [1999] 1 Cr App R 274). In *R v Lawson* [2005] EWCA Crim 84; [2007] 1 Cr App R 20, Auld LJ, at para 65 (cited with approval in *R v Mills* [2008] EWCA Crim 3001, per Beatson J, at para 24) said:

Whether or not to discharge the jury is a matter for evaluation by the trial judge on the particular facts and circumstances of the case . . . It follows that every case depends on its own facts and circumstances, including: 1) the important issue or issues in the case; 2) the nature and impact of improperly admitted material on that issue or issues, having regard, inter alia to the respective strengths of the prosecution and defence cases; 3) the manner and circumstances of its admission and whether and to what extent it is potentially unfairly prejudicial to a defendant; 4) the extent to and manner in which it is remediable by judicial direction or otherwise, so as to permit the trial to proceed . . . The test is always the same, whether to continue with the trial would or could, by reason of the admission of the unfairly prejudicial material, result in an unsafe conviction.

(b) The jury cannot agree on a verdict (see **11.13.5** below).

(c) An individual juror has to be discharged and there is a risk that he or she may have contaminated the rest of the jury (eg because he or she knows that the defendant has previous convictions which have not been ruled admissible or that the defendant is facing further trials for other offences—see, for example, *R v Hutton* (1990) Crim LR 875). Where a juror has specialized knowledge of something relevant to the case against the defendant, and has communicated that knowledge to the rest of the jury, who have then come to a verdict, the judge is obliged to discharge the jury since the defendant has had no opportunity to challenge what amounts to new evidence or to put forward their own explanation (*R v Fricker, The Times*, 13 July 1999).

If members of the jury misbehave during the course of the trial, the jury should be discharged if there is a 'real danger of prejudice' to the accused (*R v Spencer* [1987] AC 128). In *R v Sawyer* (1980) 71 Cr App R 283, for example, some jurors were seen in conversation with prosecution witnesses during an adjournment. The trial judge questioned them and it transpired that the conversation had been on subjects unconnected with the trial. The decision of the judge not to discharge the jury was upheld by the Court of Appeal. In *R v Azam* [2006] EWCA Crim 161, the Court of Appeal said that it is open to the judge to exercise the discretionary power to discharge the jury, whichever side invites the making of such an order and even if both sides submit that such an order should not be made.

The judge must make a judgment whether the interests of justice require the discharge of the jury; if the judge concludes that there are 'real grounds for doubting the ability of the jury to bring an objective judgment to bear' on the issues, the jury should be discharged. That decision requires a balanced judgment of the things said to create the risk of bias in the jury, while also taking account of the directions that may be given to the jury to address and extinguish the risk (per Sir Igor Judge P, at para 50).

Where the jury is discharged from giving a verdict, the defendant can be re-tried, as he or she is not regarded as having been acquitted.

11.3.5 Start of the trial

Once the jury has been empanelled, the trial begins with the clerk reading out the indictment and telling the jury that the defendant has pleaded not guilty. The jury is then told, 'It is your charge to say, having heard the evidence, whether he [or she] be guilty or not'.

11.4 Change of plea

The defendant may change plea from not guilty to guilty at any stage of the trial before the jury has returned a verdict. The defence simply asks for the indictment to be put again and then pleads guilty. The jury usually returns a formal verdict of guilty; however, in *R v Poole* [2002] 1 WLR 1528, the Court of Appeal held that where a defendant pleads not guilty but then changes the plea to guilty during the course of the trial, there is no requirement that the judge should ask the jury for a formal verdict of guilty. It is permissible for the judge simply to discharge the jury and proceed to sentencing (though, in fact, many judges still ask the jury for a formal verdict).

The defendant can change plea from guilty to not guilty at any stage of the trial prior to the passing of sentence, but only with the permission of the judge. The judge will want some explanation for the change of heart and may take into account matters such as the legal advice the accused has received, their age and level of intellect, and experience of criminal proceedings. See *R v Dodd* (1981) 74 Cr App R 50; *S v Recorder of Manchester* [1971] AC 481. Permission to withdraw the guilty plea is unlikely to be given unless the defendant did not realise that he had a defence when he pleaded guilty (*R v McNally* [1954] 1 WLR 933). In *R v Drew* [1985] 1 WLR 914, Lord Lane CJ (at p. 923) said that it would be appropriate only in rare cases to allow a defendant to change an unequivocal plea of guilty to one of not guilty. This is particularly so in cases where the accused has been advised by experienced counsel.

In *R v Sheikh* [2004] EWCA Crim 492; [2004] 2 Cr App R 13, the defendants applied to withdraw their pleas of guilty. The basis of their application was that they had not been informed that they could be made the subject of confiscation proceedings in the event of conviction. The trial judge refused to allow a change of plea, and the Court of Appeal upheld the refusal. The Court said that it is well accepted that, quite apart from cases where the plea of guilty is equivocal or ambiguous, the court retains a residual discretion to allow the withdrawal of a guilty plea where not to do so might work an injustice. Examples might be where a defendant has been misinformed about the nature of the charge or the availability of a defence, or where he has been put under pressure to plead guilty in circumstances where he is not truly admitting guilt. Commonly, however, it is reserved for cases where there is doubt that the plea represents a genuine acknowledgment of

Crown Court trial 209

guilt. The possibility of confiscation proceedings taking place could not, of itself, have any bearing upon their acceptance of guilt.

11.5 The prosecution case

After the indictment has been read to the jury, counsel for the prosecution opens the Crown's case:

May it please your Honour [or your Lordship, if a High Court judge or sitting at the Old Bailey], members of the jury, I appear to prosecute and my learned friend Miss Singh appears for the accused.

11.5.1 The opening speech

The purpose of the prosecution opening speech is to give the jury an overview of the prosecution case. The jury will be reminded of the charge(s) which the defendant faces, which should be explained in everyday language. Counsel will probably tell the jury what witnesses will be called by the prosecution and what it is hoped they will establish. Counsel will also mention the burden of proof and the standard of proof, and make it clear that anything said about the law is subject to what the judge will say in the summing-up.

If counsel for the defence takes the view that an objection should be taken to the admissibility of some of the evidence which the prosecution will be calling, but no ruling on admissibility was sought at the PCMH, then he or she should inform counsel for the prosecution. The prosecutor will then omit any reference to the disputed material from the opening speech, and the judge will then be asked to rule on the admissibility of the evidence at the appropriate moment (see **11.5.2.4**). It may be, however, that the disputed evidence is such an important part of the prosecution case that an opening speech would make no sense if no reference were to be made to that evidence (e.g. if the only evidence against the defendant is a confession, the admissibility of which is disputed). In that case, once the jury has been empanelled, the judge will be informed (either by the prosecution or the defence) that a ruling on a matter of law is needed at the outset. The jury will be sent out of the court and counsel will then seek the judge's ruling on the admissibility of the evidence. If the judge rules the evidence inadmissible, the prosecution will almost certainly have little option but to offer no evidence (see **11.2.3** above), in which case the jury will be called back into court and directed to acquit the defendant.

In *R v Lashley* [2005] EWCA Crim 2016; (2005), *The Times*, 28 September 2005, the Court of Appeal said that the presumption should be that an opening address by counsel for the Crown should not address the law, save in cases of real complication and difficulty where counsel believes (and the trial judge agrees) that the jury may be assisted by a brief and well-focused submission (per Judge LJ at para 13).

11.5.2 The prosecution evidence

At the conclusion of the opening speech, prosecuting counsel calls the evidence. It is the rule that the prosecution must call all the witnesses whose evidence was included in the statements on the basis of which the defendant was sent for trial. If one witness is expected to duplicate the evidence of another (eg the second police officer present at an interview with the accused), the prosecution may 'tender' that second witness for cross-examination. This means that the witness is called into the witness box by counsel for the prosecution and, having been identified and their relevance to the case established, he or she will be told to stay there in case the defence has any questions. The only exceptions to the rule that the prosecution must call (or tender for cross-examination) all the witnesses whose evidence was used in the transfer process are those set out in *R v Russell-Jones* [1995] 1 Cr App R 538 at 544:

- the defence has consented to the written statement of that witness being read to the court;
- counsel for the prosecution takes the view that the evidence of that witness is no longer credible; or
- counsel for the prosecution takes the view that the witness would so fundamentally contradict the prosecution case that it would make more sense for that person to be called as a witness by the defence.

The other side of the coin is that the prosecution can *only* call as witnesses people whose evidence was used at the transfer stage or whose statements have been disclosed to the defence by way of a notice of additional evidence. The notice of additional evidence procedure is used wherever the prosecution want to use evidence which was not used as the basis for transferring the case to the Crown Court. A copy of the witness statement is served on the defence along with a notice saying that the prosecution will be adducing the evidence of this witness at trial. The statement can be tendered in evidence (i.e. read to the court) unless the defence objects within seven days of the service of the notice, in which case the prosecution must either abandon that evidence or call the maker of the statement as a witness at the trial. There is no time limit within which a notice of additional evidence must be served, but if it is served just before the trial, so that the defence has had insufficient time to adjust its preparation in the light of the new evidence, then the judge should grant an adjournment.

11.5.2.1 Taking evidence from the witnesses

Each witness called by the prosecution, having taken the oath (or affirmed) to 'tell the truth, the whole truth and nothing but the truth', is examined in chief by counsel for the prosecution (unless that witness is only being tendered for cross-examination) and may produce (i.e. identify) items of real evidence which then become exhibits in the case. In examination-in-chief, counsel must take great care not to lead the witness on matters which are contentious—if in doubt, ask your opponent if you can lead on specified matters.

Each witness is then subject to cross-examination by the defence. Cross-examination is not limited to matters arising from the examination-in-chief, but must be relevant to the issues arising in the case. The cross-examination is followed by re-examination by the prosecution; the rule against leading questions applies to re-examination and the questions must arise out of the cross-examination.

Under the CJA 2003, s 139(1), witnesses may, whilst giving evidence, refresh their memory from documents made or verified by them at an earlier time if they testify that the document records their recollection of the matter at that earlier time, and that their recollection of the matter is likely to have been significantly better at that time than it is at the time of the oral evidence. The CJA 2003, s 139(2), allows a witness to refresh their memory from the transcript of a sound recording in the same circumstances.

11.5.2.2 Formal admissions

If the defendant pleads not guilty, that puts the prosecution to proof of each and every element of the offence(s) on the indictment to which a plea of not guilty has been entered. The only exception to this is where the defence has made a formal admission under the CJA 1967, s 10. This provides that either party in a criminal case (though, in practice, it is usually the defence) may admit any fact which would otherwise be in issue and this admission is conclusive evidence of the fact admitted. This admission may be made orally in court (by counsel) or in writing signed by the person making it, in which case the document will be read to the jury.

11.5.2.3 Reading witness statements

Formal admissions are not very common. Usually, where evidence is not disputed by the defence, they will consent to the prosecution reading out the written statement of the witness who provides the uncontroversial evidence (eg the loser of stolen property where the defence case is not that the property was not stolen but rather that the defendant was not the thief). If a witness says some things which are not disputed by the defence but others which are, that witness will have to give oral evidence (since it would not be appropriate for the written statement to be read to the court) and it will no doubt become apparent from the cross-examination by the defence which parts of that witness's evidence are disputed.

When the written statement of a witness is read to the court with the consent of the defence, the judge should explain to the jury that the contents of the witness statement are not in dispute and so the defence has consented to the statement being read to the jury without the maker having to attend court, thus saving time and money. The jury should be told that the evidence is just as good as evidence given 'live'. Counsel, in reading the statement, must read out the declaration signed by the maker of the statement, that it is true to the best of that person's knowledge and belief and is made knowing that a prosecution may be brought if the statement contains anything which the maker knows or believes to be false.

There are also instances where a statement may be read to the jury without the consent of the defence. These are set out in the CJA 2003, s 116 and include cases where a witness does not testify because of fear. In order to satisfy the requirements of s 116 (2)(e), the court must hear oral evidence (for example, from a police officer) as to the fear of the witness (*R v Belmarsh Magistrates' Court, ex p Gilligan* [1998] 1 Cr App R 14, following *Neill v North Antrim Magistrates' Court* [1992] 4 All ER 846, both decided under earlier but very similar legislation).

Where a statement has been read to the jury without the consent of the defence, the jury must be warned to use particular care when considering that witness statement, since the maker of the statement was not in court to be cross-examined as to its contents. Where the witness statement is vital to the prosecution case, failure to give such a direction will render any subsequent conviction unsafe (*R v Curry*, *The Times*, 23 March 1998). (Hearsay evidence)

11.5.2.4 Defence objections to prosecution evidence

If counsel for the prosecution agrees with the defence suggestion made before the start of the trial that certain evidence is inadmissible, the prosecutor should (via the Crown Prosecution Service representative or the police officer in charge of the case) warn the relevant witness not to give that particular evidence. If this involves evidence which will come into the possession of the jury (eg interview notes, which count as real evidence and may be exhibited and so handed to the jury), this evidence may well have to be edited. In accordance with para III.24 of the *Consolidated Practice Direction*, this should be done after consultation between both counsel and the judge.

If, however, the prosecution do not accept that the evidence in question is inadmissible, the question of admissibility may be dealt with at the PCMH, at which the judge is empowered to give binding rulings on the admissibility of evidence. Otherwise, the objection is made (in the absence of the jury) during the course of the trial. If the objection is made during the course of the trial, the prosecution evidence is called in the usual way until the part of the evidence to which there is objection is reached. At that point the jury is invited to retire to the jury room.

Although s 82 of PACE 1984 expressly preserves the common law rules on the admissibility of evidence, objections to prosecution evidence are usually made under PACE 1984, s 76 (which applies only to confessions) or s 78 (which applies to all prosecution evidence).

Where the defence invoke s 76 and allege that a confession has been obtained by oppression or in circumstances likely to render it unreliable, the prosecution must prove beyond reasonable doubt that the confession was not so obtained. The requirement for the prosecution to prove that the confession was not obtained improperly means that they must call evidence on the point and so a *voir dire* ('trial within a trial') takes place in the absence of the jury. Unless the witness is in the middle of giving (or has already given) evidence in the course of the trial, a witness giving evidence on a *voir dire* takes a special form of oath in which they swear (or affirm) to 'answer truthfully all such questions as the court may ask.' Each prosecution witness called in the *voir dire* may be cross-examined by the defence. When the relevant prosecution witnesses have given evidence, the defence may call evidence (including the evidence of the defendant); each defence witness may be cross-examined by the prosecution.

After the evidence has been called, both counsel may address the judge and the judge then rules on the admissibility of the confession. In *Mitchell v The Queen* [1998] AC 695, it was held by the Privy Council that where a judge conducts a *voir dire* and holds that a confession is admissible, the judge should not tell the jury of the ruling (the trial should simply continue with the prosecution adducing evidence of the confession). If the judge indicates that he has ruled against the accused, this might lead the jury to think that the judge does not believe the accused.

The only question to be determined under s 76 is *how* the confession was obtained. It is wholly irrelevant whether the confession was true or not. If the defence case is simply that the police have fabricated the confession, this is a matter for the jury to decide and not a question of admissibility. However, there are cases where the defence alleges that the confession has been fabricated but also argues that, even if that was not so, the confession is inadmissible anyway. In *Thongjai v The Queen* [1998] AC 54, the Privy Council (following *Ajodha v The State* [1982] AC 204) said that if the defendant denies making an oral admission and also alleges that he was ill-treated by the police before or at the time of the alleged admission, the two issues are not mutually exclusive. The judge has to assume that the admission was made and decide whether it is admissible. If (and only if) the judge decides that the evidence is admissible, it is then for the jury to decide whether the admission was in fact made.

If the objection to the prosecution evidence is brought *solely* on the basis of s 78, that it would be unfair to the defence for the evidence to be admitted, the judge may hold a *voir dire* but is not obliged to do so. Such applications may be dealt with on the basis of submissions by counsel if the factual basis for the submissions is agreed between prosecution and defence (for example, if the custody record discloses breaches of the

Codes of Practice under PACE 1984 and the only question to be determined is whether the evidence thereby obtained should be excluded under s 78). These submissions will, of course, be heard in the absence of the jury. The judge gives a ruling and the trial then proceeds, either with or without the disputed evidence.

It should be noted that if inadmissible evidence is heard by the jury, the judge has to consider whether the prejudicial effect can be cured by an appropriate direction (repeated in the summing-up) or whether the entire jury should be discharged and a new trial take place.

11.5.3 Special measures

Sections 16–33 of the Youth Justice and Criminal Evidence Act 1999 (YJCEA) contain provision for various 'special measures' which the court can direct in respect of certain witnesses:

- screening the witness from the accused (s 23);
- giving evidence by live link (s 24) [note that s 51 of the CJA 2003 enables a court to authorise witnesses, other than the defendant, to give evidence through a live link in criminal proceedings];
- ordering the removal of wigs and gowns while the witness gives evidence (s 25);
- giving evidence in private, in a sexual case or where there is a fear that the witness may be intimidated (s 26);
- video recording of evidence-in-chief (s 27) [note that s 137 of the CJA 2003 extends the circumstances in which evidence-in-chief can take the form of a video-recorded statement];
- video recording of cross-examination and re-examination where the evidence-in-chief of the witness has been video recorded (s 28);
- examination through an intermediary in the case of a young or incapacitated witness (s 29);
- provision of aids to communication for a young or incapacitated witness (s 30).

The procedure for making an application for special measures is contained in Part 29 of the CPR. Rule 29.4 makes provision for applications to vary or discharge a special measures direction; such applications must be based on a material change of circumstances since the direction was made (see s 20 of the 1999 Act). Also, where an application for a special measures direction has been refused by the court, the application may be renewed if there is a material change of circumstances since the court refused the application (r 29.5).

Rule 29.6 deals with applications for special measures directions for witnesses to give evidence by means of a live television link. A party who seeks to oppose an application for a child witness to give evidence by means of a live link must state why, in his view, the giving of a special measures direction would not be likely to maximise the quality of the witness's evidence (unless the application relates to a child witness in need of special protection within the meaning of s 21(1)(b) of the 1999 Act, in which case this provision does not apply). The Rule goes on to state that, where a special measures direction is made enabling a witness to give evidence by means of a live link, the witness must be accompanied at the live link only by persons acceptable to the court.

Rule 29.7 deals with video recording of testimony from witnesses. Where an application is made for a special measures direction enabling a video recording of an interview of a witness to be admitted as evidence-in-chief of the witness, the application must be accompanied by the video recording which it is proposed to tender in evidence and must include full details of the circumstances in which the recording was made. Where a party opposes the use of the video recording, that party must lodge a notice giving reasons why it would not be in the interests of justice for the recording (or part of it) to be admitted.

Section 29 of the YJCEA 1999 allows, as part of the special measures provision, for the use of intermediaries to facilitate communication with witnesses with special communication difficulties. Section 29 states that the function of an intermediary is to communicate (a) to the witness, questions put to the witness, (b) to any persons asking such questions, the answers given by the witness in reply to them, and to explain such questions and answers so far as necessary to enable them to be understood by the witness or person in question. Such intermediaries have to be professionally experienced in their own specialist area of communication, and are subject to a Code of Practice and a Code of Ethics.

Part 8 of the CJA 2003 extends the circumstances where live links can be used. A 'live link' (defined in s 56(2)) will usually mean a closed circuit television link, but could apply to any technology with the same effect, such as video conferencing facilities or the internet. Under the CJA 2003, s 51(4), a direction that a witness may give evidence through a live link may be given if the court is satisfied that it is in the interests of the efficient or effective administration of justice for the person concerned to give evidence in the proceedings through a live link. Under s 51(6) and (7), in deciding whether to give such a direction the court must consider all the circumstances of the case, and in particular: the availability of the witness; the need for the witness to attend in person; the importance of the witness's evidence to the proceedings; the views of the witness; the suitability of the facilities at the place where the witness would give evidence through a live link; whether a direction might tend to inhibit any party to the proceedings from effectively testing the witness's evidence. The CJA 2003, s 54, empowers the judge to give the jury 'such direction as he thinks necessary to ensure that the jury gives the same weight to the evidence as if it had been given by the witness in the courtroom or other place where the proceedings are held'.

The CJA 2003, s 137(1), extends the cases where evidence can be given by means of a video recording. It empowers the court to allow a video recording of an interview with a witness (other than the defendant), or a part of such a recording, to be admitted as evidence-in-chief of the witness (i.e. to replace live evidence-in-chief of that witness) provided that the person is called as a witness in proceedings for an offence which is triable only on indictment, or for an either way offence prescribed in regulations made under the section; and the person claims to have witnessed (whether visually or in any other way) events alleged by the prosecution to include conduct constituting the offence or part of the offence, or events that were closely connected with such events; and that person has previously given an account of the events in question; and that account was given at a time when those events were fresh in the person's memory; and a video recording was made of the account.

Under s 137(3), such a direction may not be made in relation to a recorded account given by the defendant. In respect of any other person, a direction may be made only if it appears to the court that the witness's recollection of the events in question is likely to have been significantly better when they gave the recorded account than it will be when they give oral evidence, and it is in the interests of justice for the recording to be admitted. In deciding whether it is in the interests of justice, the court must have regard (under s 137(4)) to the interval between the time of the events in question and the time when the recorded account was made; any other factors that might affect the reliability of what the witness said in that account; the quality of the recording; and any views of the witness as to whether their evidence-in-chief should be given orally or by means of the recording.

Section 33A of the Youth Justice and Criminal Evidence Act 1999 allows the court, on application by the accused, to direct that any evidence given by him should be given via a 'live link'. Section 33B defines 'live link' very broadly: it encompasses any technology that enables the accused to see and hear a person in the courtroom, and to be seen and heard by the persons listed in s 33B(2), namely the judge and the jury (if there is one), any co-accused, the legal representatives acting in the proceedings and any interpreter or other person appointed by the court to assist the accused. Before giving a live link direction, the court must be satisfied that it would be in the interests of justice to do so, and:

(a) if the accused is under the age of 18, that his ability to participate effectively as a witness giving oral evidence is compromised by his 'level of intellectual ability or social functioning', and that use of a live link would enable him to participate more effectively as a witness, whether by improving the quality of his evidence or otherwise (s 33A(4)); or

(b) if the accused is aged 18 or over, that he is unable to participate effectively in the proceedings effectively as a witness giving oral evidence because he has a mental disorder (within the meaning of the Mental Health Act 1983) or a 'significant impairment of intelligence and social function', and that use of a live link would enable him to participate more effectively as a witness, whether by improving the quality of his evidence or otherwise (s 33A(5)).

There is a presumption that adult defendants should give evidence in court. The criteria set out in s 33A(5) are intended to ensure that the use of live links is reserved for exceptional cases where the accused has a condition that prevents effective participation as a witness and so may prevent a fair trial from taking place. In the case of a juvenile accused, however, the test is less strict (in that there is no reference to a mental disorder or impairment); it is sufficient that the accused's ability to participate is compromised. However, although this lower threshold recognises that it may be more common for juveniles to experience difficulties during the trial through limited intelligence and social development, s 33A(4) is aimed at juvenile defendants with a low level of intelligence or a particular problem in dealing with social situations, and is not intended to operate merely because a juvenile accused is nervous.

Section 46 of the YJCEA 1999 also empowers the court to impose 'reporting directions'. The effect of such directions is that no matter relating to the witness is to be included in any publication during the lifetime of the witness, if that matter is likely to lead members of the public to identify that person as a witness in the proceedings. The procedure is set out in Part 16 of the CPR.

As well as the powers conferred by the YJCEA 1999, the court has power, under the Criminal Evidence (Witness Anonymity) Act 2008, to safeguard the interests of witnesses by ensuring their anonymity. A witness anonymity order may be made only if necessary to protect the safety of the witness or another person, or to prevent any serious damage to property, or to prevent real harm to the public interest; the taking of those measures must be consistent with the right of the accused to a fair trial; and it must be necessary in the interests of justice to make the order because it is important that the witness should testify but he or she will not testify unless the order is made. In *R v Mayers* [2008] EWCA Crim 2989, the Court of Appeal noted (at para 13) that 'nothing in the Act diminishes the overriding responsibility of the trial judge to ensure that the proceedings are conducted fairly'. Moreover, the judge should normally 'reflect both at the close of the prosecution case, and indeed if the defendant has given evidence, when the defence evidence is concluded, whether properly directed, notwithstanding that crucial incriminating evidence was given by an anonymous witness or witnesses, and in the light of the evidence as a whole, the case can safely be left to the jury . . .' The Court added, at para 37, that the court must be satisfied that the conditions set out in the Act are met, and that even if the conditions are established, the order cannot be made unless the court is also satisfied that the trial will be fair.

11.6 Submission of no case to answer

When the prosecution has called all its witnesses, counsel will say, 'That is the case for the prosecution'. At the close of the prosecution case the defence may make a submission that there is no case to answer (colloquially called 'a half-time submission').

This submission is made in the absence of the jury. Counsel for the defence makes the submission and counsel for the prosecution then has the right to reply.

The submission is governed by the principles laid down in *R v Galbraith* [1981] 1 WLR 1039 at 1042 (*per* Lord Lane CJ):

(a) The submission should succeed if the judge comes to the conclusion that the prosecution evidence, taken at its highest, is such that a jury, properly directed, could not properly convict on it. In this case the judge should direct the jury to acquit on the count(s) in respect of which the submission has succeeded. If there are other counts on the indictment and either no submission was made in respect of them or a submission was made but failed, the trial proceeds on those counts.

(b) The submission should fail if the strength or weakness of the prosecution case depends on the view to be taken of the reliability of a witness and, on one possible view, there is evidence on which a reasonable jury, properly directed, could convict. In this case, the matter should be left to the jury and the trial should be allowed to take its course with the jury being left in ignorance about what has happened.

The basis for this distinction is that questions relating to the credibility of witnesses are matters of fact which are within the exclusive province of the jury. However, regard should be had to the ruling of Turner J in *R v Shippey* [1988] Crim LR 767. His Lordship found no case to answer because of 'really significant inherent inconsistencies' in the complainant's evidence, which he found to be 'frankly incredible'. In other words, the judge can have regard to the sheer improbability of what the witness says and to internal inconsistencies in the evidence. If no reasonable jury could believe the witness whose evidence is central to the prosecution case, then the submission of no case to answer should succeed.

Where the only evidence against the accused is identification evidence, the special considerations highlighted in *R v Turnbull* [1977] QB 224 should be borne in mind, and the case withdrawn from the jury if the evidence is weak.

If defence counsel notices a procedural error on the part of the prosecution, he or she should take the point at the outset, and not wait until the close of the prosecution case. For example, in *R v Gleeson* [2003] EWCA Crim 3357; [2004] 1 Cr App R 29, the defendant was charged with common law conspiracy. The charge was inappropriate and the trial judge accepted a submission of no case to answer. However, the judge also gave the prosecution leave to amend the indictment to allege statutory conspiracy. The Court of Appeal held that, just as a defendant should not be penalised for errors on the part of his legal representatives in the conduct of his defence if he is unfairly prejudiced by them, so also the prosecution should not be frustrated by errors on the part of the prosecutor, unless such errors have irremediably rendered a fair trial for the defendant impossible. It is contrary to defence counsel's professional duty, and not in the legitimate interests of the defendant, to take advantage of procedural errors by the prosecution by delaying in identifying those errors as issues in the case until the last possible moment (per Auld LJ at para 35). The point was made that a criminal trial is not a game; its object is to ensure that the guilty are convicted and the innocent acquitted (para 36).

In *R v Powell* [2006] EWCA Crim 685, the Court said that where a submission of no case to answer is made but rejected, the judge should give brief reasons for deciding that there is sufficient evidence to go before a jury (to enable the defence to understand clearly the grounds upon which the application has failed and to demonstrate that the judgment has been made on a rational basis rather than a personal whim).

If the judge wrongly refuses to uphold a submission of no case to answer this constitutes an error of law. Any evidence called afterwards (that is by the defence) is irrelevant on appeal as no evidence would have been called by the defence if the submission had been upheld. So if, in the course of giving evidence, the accused makes damaging admissions, those admissions will have to be ignored by the Court of Appeal: see *R v Smith* [2000] 1 All ER 263.

It should be borne in mind that the Criminal Justice and Public Order Act 1994 (CJPOA), s 34(2)(c) provides that adverse inferences can be drawn from failure to answer police questions when the court is considering a submission of no case to answer. However, s 34(2)(c) can only be relied upon to take the case past half-time if a fact has been relied on by the defence which brings s 34 into play. This would be the case where, for example, the defence cross-examine prosecution witnesses on the basis of facts that were not mentioned by the defendant when he or she was questioned (see *R v Webber* [2004] UKHL 1; [2004] 1 WLR 404).

In *Attorney-General's Reference (No 2 of 2000)* (2001) 165 JP 195, the Court of Appeal held that, where a prosecution has been properly brought (i.e. it is not an abuse of process), a trial judge has no power to prevent the prosecution from calling evidence, nor to direct the jury to acquit, on the basis that he or she thinks a conviction unlikely. However, if the judge, at the conclusion of all the evidence (that is, both the prosecution case and the defence case), is of the view that no reasonable jury could convict, he should raise that view for discussion with counsel (in the absence of the jury), whether or not a submission of no case to answer was made at the close of the prosecution case. If, having heard submissions, the judge remains of the view that there is no case to answer, he should withdraw the case from the jury. However, this power is to be used very sparingly (*R v Brown* [2001] EWCA Crim 961; [2002] 1 Cr App R 5).

Not to be confused with the right of the defence to seek a ruling from the judge that there is no case to answer, the jury themselves have the power to stop the case and acquit the defendant at any time after the close of the prosecution case. In *R v Kemp* [1995] 1 Cr App R 151, the Court of Appeal said that where the judge informs the jury that they may acquit the defendant without hearing further evidence, the direction should not do anything other than merely inform them of their right to stop the case. Thus, the judge should not in effect invite the jury to acquit the defendant. If the judge considers that the case against the defendant is too weak to be left to the jury, then the judge should simply stop the case. In *R v Speechley* [2004] EWCA Crim 3067; [2005] 2 Cr App R (S) 15, the Court of Appeal held that the common law right of the jury to acquit a defendant after the conclusion of the prosecution case is exercisable only where they have been invited to do so by the trial judge. It follows that, if a jury is invited by counsel (or seeks of its own motion) to return a verdict before being asked by the judge to do so, the judge should direct the jury that it is not open to them to return a verdict until the judge has invited them to do so. In *R v Collins* [2007] EWCA Crim 854, the Court of Appeal strongly disapproved of the practice of inviting a jury to acquit.

11.7 The defence case

The defence is under no obligation to call any evidence, and so it would be possible for counsel for the defence to address the jury on the basis that the prosecution evidence has failed to show beyond reasonable doubt that the defendant is guilty. This may be appropriate where there is only just a case to answer. However, the CJPOA 1994, s 35, enables adverse inferences to be drawn by the jury if the accused either fails to give evidence or fails without good cause to answer questions put by the prosecution. It follows that the accused should, in the vast majority of cases, be advised to give evidence. If a defendant decides not to testify, despite advice to the contrary by counsel, that defendant should be asked to endorse a note on counsel's brief confirming that he or she has chosen not to give evidence (see *R v Bevan* (1993) 98 Cr App R 354). Paragraph IV.44 of the *Consolidated Practice Direction* requires the judge to ensure that the defendant is aware of the possible consequences of not testifying.

The defence case may start with an opening speech outlining the evidence the defence will be calling and showing how it will rebut the evidence called by the prosecution. In fact, opening speeches are rarely made by the defence (unless the case is a complex one). In any event, the defence is not allowed to make an opening speech unless it will be calling at least one witness to the facts of the case, in addition to the evidence of the defendant. So, if the only defence evidence is from the accused and/or character witnesses, there can be no opening speech.

11.7.1 The defence evidence

If the defendant does give evidence, then he or she must be called as the first defence witness (unless the judge gives leave to the contrary) (PACE 1984, s 79).

Each defence witness takes the oath (or affirms) and is then examined in chief on behalf of the defendant, cross-examined by the prosecution and (if necessary) re-examined on behalf of the defence.

11.7.1.1 Alibi evidence

If the defendant wishes to adduce evidence in support of an alibi, particulars of that alibi must be given to the prosecution (CPIA 1996, s 6A(2)). Section 6A(3) defines alibi evidence as:

evidence tending to show that by reason of the presence of the defendant at a particular place or in a particular area at a particular time he was not, or was unlikely to have been, at the place where the offence is alleged to have been committed at the time of its alleged commission.

Thus, alibi evidence must show where the defendant was at the time of the offence: evidence which merely shows that the defendant was not present at the scene of the crime does not amount to alibi evidence (*R v Johnson* [1994] Crim LR 949).

Section 6A(2) requires the defence to supply the prosecution with the name and address of any witness the accused believes is able to give evidence in support of the alibi or (where the defendant does not know the name or address) information which may help the prosecution to find the witness.

If the defendant fails to give particulars of the alibi in the defence statement, or calls a witness without having given particulars of that witness to the prosecution, the jury may draw 'adverse inferences' against the defendant (see **9.4**).

11.7.1.2 Expert evidence

The defence may not call any expert witness without leave of the judge if it has not disclosed the expert's written report to the prosecution before the trial. See Part 24 of the Criminal Procedure Rules.

11.8 Closing speeches

At the close of the defence case the prosecution may make a closing speech. However, the prosecution have no right to make a closing speech if the defendant is unrepresented and has called no witnesses as to the facts of the case apart from his or her own testimony. In a fairly straightforward case the prosecution may in any event forgo a closing speech.

The defence always have the right to make a closing speech and this right should never be waived. It is a vital speech, giving counsel the chance to show how reasonable doubt has been cast on the prosecution case.

11.9 Two or more defendants

Where two or more defendants are charged in the same indictment (remember that joinder must satisfy the requirements of rule 14.2(3) of the Criminal Procedure Rules), and those defendants are separately represented (which will be the case where they are putting forward inconsistent defences), their cases will be presented in the order in which their names appear on the indictment. So if the indictment is against D1, D2 and D3, the order is:

D1 opening speech

D1's witnesses (starting with D1)

      Examination-in-chief by D1's counsel

      Cross-examination on behalf of D2

      Cross-examination on behalf of D3

      Cross-examination by prosecution

      Re-examination by D1's counsel (if necessary)

D2 opening speech

D2's witnesses (starting with D2)

      Examination-in-chief by D2's counsel

      Cross-examination on behalf of D1

Cross-examination on behalf of D3

Cross-examination by prosecution

Re-examination by D2's counsel (if necessary) and so on

D3 opening speech, evidence and witnesses

Closing speeches are in the order: prosecution, D1, D2, D3.

If the defendants are jointly represented, they are regarded as putting forward a joint defence. Their counsel may make an opening speech. Then D1 may give evidence, followed by D2, then D3, and then any other witnesses the defence wish to call.

11.10 Unrepresented defendants

Where the defendant is unrepresented:

- the trial judge should ask such questions as he or she sees fit to test the reliability of the prosecution witnesses and may ask the defendant whether there are certain matters he or she wishes to be put to the witnesses;
- the jury should be instructed (at the start of the trial and in the summing-up) that the defendant is entitled to represent himself or herself and the defendant should also be warned of the difficulty of doing so properly;
- the judge should prevent repetitious questioning of prosecution witnesses by the defendant.

It should be borne in mind that the YJCEA 1999, s 34, provides that no person charged with a sexual offence may cross-examine the complainant, either in connection with that offence, or in connection with any other offence (of whatever nature) with which that person is charged in the proceedings. Under s 35, unrepresented defendants are not allowed to cross-examine in person a child who is either the complainant of, or a witness to the commission of, an offence of a sexual offence, kidnapping, false imprisonment or abduction. Section 36 gives courts the power to prohibit unrepresented defendants from cross-examining witnesses in cases where a mandatory ban does not apply under ss 34 and 35, but where the court is satisfied that the circumstances of the witness and the case merit a prohibition, and that it would not be contrary to the interests of justice.

11.11 The summing up

After the prosecution and defence counsel have made their closing speeches, the judge sums the case up to the jury. The judge must do this in all cases, however simple the case may seem. Although traditionally the judge produces the summing up without reference to counsel, in *R v Taylor* [2003] EWCA Crim 2447; *The Times*, 8 October 2003, the Court of Appeal said that, where complex directions are to be given to the jury, counsel in the case should be permitted to consider and comment upon the draft directions before the judge addresses the jury. A summing up should contain the following elements:

(a) *The respective functions of judge and jury.* Questions of law are for the judge and questions of fact are for the jury. The judge is entitled to express a view on the facts but should always make it very clear that if he or she seems to be expressing a view on the facts, then the jury must feel free to disregard that view. See *R v Jackson* [1992] Crim LR 214.

(b) *Burden and standard of proof*. It is for the prosecution to prove the case against the accused, not for the accused to prove his or her innocence. Before convicting, the jury must be 'satisfied so that they are sure' (a preferred formulation to the time-honoured 'beyond reasonable doubt'). The judge should not expand on what is meant by 'sure', as this is likely to generate confusion. See *Ferguson v The Queen* [1979] 1 WLR 94 and *R v McVey* [1988] Crim LR 127. In *R v Stephens* [2002] EWCA Crim 1529 (a case in which the jury sought additional guidance on how sure they had to be before convicting), the Court of Appeal stated that the Judicial Studies Board guideline to direct a jury to be satisfied so that it was sure of guilt is a well-established direction. It is not helpful for a judge to direct a jury to distinguish between being sure and being certain and a judge should avoid doing so. If necessary, a judge should direct a jury that telling them to be sure is the limit of the help that can be given. If the case (exceptionally) involves a burden on the defendant (eg to show lawful authority or reasonable excuse for possession of an offensive weapon: Prevention of Crime Act 1957, s 1) then the jury must be told that the standard is to the balance of probabilities, ie, more likely than not.

(c) *The law and the evidence*. There should be an explanation of the law involved and how it relates to the facts of the case. The judge should remind the jury of the main features of the prosecution and defence evidence, even if the case is a straightforward one (see *R v McVey* [1988] Crim LR 127 and *R v Gregory* [1993] Crim LR 623). In *R v Bowerman* [2002] 2 Cr App R 189, the Court of Appeal emphasised the importance of the summing up as a means of focusing the jury's attention on the issues to be decided. This involves fitting the evidence that has been heard into the legal framework of the charge(s), so that the jury knows what the prosecution must prove and what (if anything) the defence has said in response. In going through the evidence which has been heard, the judge must be careful to present both the prosecution and defence stories even-handedly (*R v Marr* (1989) 90 Cr App R 154). For example, it is important that the defence case is put fully and fairly before the jury (*R v Gaughan* [1990] Crim LR 880). The judge must avoid sarcastic and extravagant language which disparages the defence case (*R v Berrada* (1989) 91 Cr App R 131). If there is an appeal, the Court of Appeal will look at the overall effect of the summing-up (*R v Berrada* (1989) 91 Cr App R 131). In *R v Spencer* [1995] Crim LR 235, the defendant's conviction was held to be unsafe as a result of excessive and largely one-sided comments made by the judge when directing the jury. It was said by Henry LJ that some comment is permissible, but not to the extent that the rehearsal of the evidence is interrupted and the jury's task made more difficult. See also *R v Farr* (1999) 163 JP 193, where a conviction was quashed, and a retrial ordered, because the summing-up failed to refer to a number of the key features of the defence case and, instead of being fair and balanced, resembled a speech for the prosecution. Indeed, where the case against the defendant is strong, and the defence correspondingly weak, the judge has to be scrupulous to ensure that the defendant's defence is presented to the jury in an even-handed and impartial manner (*R v Reid, The Times*, 17 August 1999).

(d) *Identification evidence*. If the case against the accused depends on identification evidence, there should be a warning about the special need for care when examining identification evidence, as a witness may appear convincing yet also be mistaken. The factors which should be taken into account in assessing the quality of the evidence should be set out: see *R v Turnbull* [1977] QB 224.

(e) *More than one count or defendant.* If there is more than one count or more than one defendant, a warning must be given that each count and each defendant must be considered separately. Where evidence is admissible against one defendant but not the other (eg a police interview in which a defendant implicates both himself and a co-accused), the judge must instruct the jury to disregard the evidence in so far as it relates to the other defendant. In a case where there are co-defendants and each defendant denies responsibility for the alleged crime, the jury should be directed that: (i) the case for and against each defendant should be considered separately; (ii) the case should be decided on all of the evidence, including the evidence of the co-defendant(s) and the defendant whose case they are considering; (iii) when considering a co-defendant's evidence against the particular defendant whose case they are considering, they should bear in mind that he or she may have an interest to serve; (iv) they should assess the evidence of a co-defendant in the same way as any other witness in the case (see *R v Jones and Jenkins* [2003] EWCA Crim 1966; [2004] 1 Cr App R 5).

(f) *Previous convictions.* The judge's summing up must reflect the principles governing the admissibility of previous convictions under ss 98–112 of the Criminal Justice Act 2003. The jury should be told that they may take the defendant's record into account when deciding whether or not the evidence was truthful (since a person with a bad character may be less likely to tell the truth) and that they may, if they think it right to do so, take the defendant's record into account when deciding whether or not he or she committed the offence(s) charged. However, the jury must also be warned that bad character cannot by itself prove the defendant's guilt (and so it would be wrong to jump to the conclusion that a defendant is guilty just because of his or her bad character). See *R v Hanson* [2005] EWCA Crim 824; [2005] 1 WLR 3169; *R v Highton* [2005] EWCA Crim 1985; [2005] 1 WLR 3472; and *R v Campbell* [2007] EWCA Crim 1472; [2007] 1 WLR 2798.

Where the defendant has no previous convictions, the jury should be directed that this is relevant both to the credibility of the defendant as a witness (a person of good character is more likely to be truthful) and to the likelihood that he or she committed the offence (a person with good character is less likely to commit a crime) (*R v Vye* [1993] 1 WLR 471, *R v Teasdale* [1993] 4 All ER 290, *R v Aziz* [1996] AC 41 and *Teeluck v State of Trinidad and Tobago* [2005] UKPC 14; [2005] 1 WLR 2421). However, it should be noted that in *Barrow v The Queen* [1998] 2 WLR 957 (followed in *Teeluck*), it was held by the Privy Council that the judge ought only to direct the jury on the relevance of the good character of the accused if the matter is raised by the defence either calling evidence or questioning prosecution witnesses with a view to establishing the defendant's good character. In *R v Gray* [2004] EWCA Crim 1074; [2004] 2 Cr App R 30, Rix LJ (at para 57) summarised the law on good character directions:

(i) The primary rule is that a person of previous good character must be given a full direction covering both credibility and propensity. Where there are no further facts to complicate the position, such a direction is mandatory and should be unqualified. (ii) If a defendant has a previous conviction which, either because of its age or its nature, may entitle him to be treated as of effective good character, the trial judge has a discretion so to treat him, and if he does so the defendant is entitled to a *Vye* direction. (iii) Where the previous conviction can only be regarded as irrelevant or of no significance in relation to the offence charged, that discretion ought to be exercised in favour of treating the defendant as of good character. In such a case the defendant is entitled to a *Vye* direction. Where there is room for uncertainty as to how a defendant of effective good character should be treated, a judge is entitled to give an appropriately modified *Vye* direction. (iv) Where a defendant of previous good character, whether absolute or effective, has been shown at trial, whether by admission or otherwise, to be guilty of criminal conduct, the prima facie rule of practice is to deal with this by qualifying a *Vye* direction rather than by withholding it. However, in such a case, there remains a narrowly circumscribed residual discretion to withhold a good character direction in whole, or in part, where it would make no sense, or would be meaningless or absurd or an insult to common sense, to do otherwise. (v) A direction should never be misleading. Therefore, where a defendant has withheld something of his record so that otherwise a trial judge is not in a position to refer to it, the defendant may forfeit the more ample, if qualified, direction which the judge might otherwise have been able to give.

(g) *Failure by accused to testify.* In *R v Cowan* [1996] QB 373 the Court of Appeal considered what should be said in the summing-up if the defendant decides not to testify. The judge must remind the jury that the burden of proof remains on the prosecution. The jury must also be directed that:

(i) an inference from failure to give evidence cannot on its own prove guilt (CJPOA, s 38(3));

(ii) they must be satisfied (on the basis of the evidence called by the prosecution) that the prosecution have established a case to answer before inferences can be drawn from the accused's silence; and

(iii) they can draw an adverse inference from the accused's silence only if they conclude that the silence can only sensibly be attributed to the accused having no answer to the charge or none that stands up to cross-examination.

In *R v Birchall* [1999] Crim LR 311, the Court of Appeal emphasised that where the defendant fails to testify, the trial judge must tell the jury that it should not start to consider whether to draw adverse inferences from the failure to testify until it has concluded that the Crown's case against the defendant is sufficiently compelling to call for an answer.

Thus, there are two key steps before adverse inferences can be drawn under s 35:

(i) Is the jury satisfied that the prosecution have established a case to answer against the defendant?

(ii) Have the jury rejected any explanation put forward by the defendant for his refusal to give evidence?

If the answer to these questions is 'yes', the jury may draw adverse inferences from the defendant's silence.

(h) *Failure to answer police questions.* In *R v Condron* [1997] 1 WLR 827, the Court of Appeal said that the guidelines set out in *R v Cowan* [1996] QB 373 regarding the drawing of adverse inferences where the accused fails to testify are equally applicable where the accused fails to answer questions when being interviewed by the police. Detailed guidance was given in *R v Argent* [1997] 2 Cr App R 27, where the Court of Appeal set out the conditions which have to be satisfied before adverse inferences can be drawn from a person's failure to answer police questions (CJPOA 1994, s 34). The conditions include:

(i) the alleged failure must take place before the person has been charged;

(ii) the alleged failure must occur during questioning under caution;

(iii) the questioning must be directed at trying to discover whether and by whom the alleged offence has been committed;

(iv) the alleged failure must be a failure to mention a fact relied on by the defendant in his or her defence;

(v) the fact must be one which this particular defendant (not some hypothetical reasonable accused) could reasonably be expected to have mentioned when being questioned, taking account of all the circumstances existing at that time (for example, the time of day, the defendant's age, experience, mental capacity, state of health, sobriety, personality and access to legal advice).

It should be borne in mind that a defendant may rely on a fact even if that defendant does not give evidence of that fact. In *R v Webber* [2004] UKHL 1; [2004] 1 WLR 404, the House of Lords confirmed that s 34 might apply if a defendant fails to mention when questioned by the police a significant matter on which he seeks to rely in his defence at trial (a) by giving evidence of it, (b) by adducing evidence of it from another witness, or (c) by putting it to a prosecution witness. Thus, adverse inferences can be drawn under s 34 even if the accused does not testify at the trial. Where the judge decides that it is not appropriate for the jury to draw adverse inferences from the defendant's silence, the jury should be specifically directed not to draw adverse inferences (*R v McGarry* [1999] 1 Cr App R 377). In *R v Betts and Hall* [2001] 2 Cr App R 257, the Court of Appeal considered the effect of the Human Rights Act 1998. The defendants had elected to remain silent in interviews with the police following legal advice. The judge directed the jury that they were entitled to draw adverse inference from the defendants' silence. The Court of Appeal held that any direction that left the jury at liberty to draw an adverse inference from a defendant's failure to answer questions in police interview, notwithstanding that they might have been satisfied as to the plausibility of the explanation for not so doing, amounts to a breach of the right to a fair trial under Article 6(1) of the European Convention on Human Rights. If it was a plausible explanation that the reason for not mentioning facts when interviewed was that the particular defendant had acted on the advice of his or her solicitor, and not because the defendant had no satisfactory answer to give, then no inference could be drawn. It must be made clear to the jury that it can only draw adverse inferences if sure that the accused had no explanation to offer, or none that the accused believed would stand up to questioning or investigating. The approach taken by the Court of Appeal in this case was approved by the European Court of Human Rights in *Beckles v UK* (2003) 36 EHRR 13.

In *R v Beckles* [2004] EWCA Crim 2766; [2005] 1 WLR 2829, the Court of Appeal re-visited the effect of legal advice not to answer questions, holding that where a defendant relies on a solicitor's advice as an explanation for having failed to mention in interview any fact relied on at trial, the ultimate question for the jury under s 34 remains whether the facts relied on at trial were facts which the defendant could reasonably have been expected to mention when interviewed. If they were not, that is the end of the matter. If the jury consider that the defendant genuinely relied on the advice, that is not necessarily the end of the matter; if it is possible to say that the defendant genuinely acted upon the advice but did so because it suited his purpose, that might mean he was not acting reasonably in failing to mention the facts. Reasonableness in not mentioning the facts remains to be determined by the jury: if they conclude the accused was acting unreasonably, they can draw an adverse inference from the failure to mention the facts. In

R v Essa [2009] EWCA Crim 43, Hughes LJ (at para 15) said that it is important to remember that the significance of s 34 does not lie in silence in interview; rather, it lies in reliance at trial on something that should have been said in interview. It is also important to remember that the 'acid question' in any s 34 case is not: 'was it reasonable to rely on the solicitor's advice?' Rather it is: 'could the appellant reasonably have been expected to say what he now relies upon at trial?'

(i) *Adverse inferences under the CPIA.* Where the defendant fails to provide a defence statement setting out the defence case, or does so late, or sets out inconsistent defences in the defence statement, or presents to the court a defence which is inconsistent with the defence statement, or presents alibi evidence without having given details of the alibi to the prosecution, adverse inferences may be drawn by the jury (see s 11). The judge must therefore give an appropriate direction to the jury.

(j) *Lies by defendant.* Where there is evidence before the jury that the defendant has lied about something, and there is a risk of the jury thinking that, because the defendant has lied, he or she must therefore be guilty of the offence charged, they should be directed that proof of lying is not proof of guilt, and that an innocent defendant might lie (*R v Lucas* [1981] 1 QB 720).

(k) *Alibi.* Where the defendant has relied on an alibi and the prosecution have sought to prove that the alibi was false, the judge should direct the jury to the effect that 'even if you conclude that the alibi was false, that does not entitle you to convict the defendant. The Crown must still make you sure of his guilt. An alibi is sometimes invented to bolster a genuine defence'. A failure to give such a direction does not, however, automatically render a conviction unsafe. The Court of Appeal will consider whether the jury might have come to a different conclusion had the direction been given (*R v Harron* [1996] 2 Cr App R 457 and *R v Lesley* [1996] 1 Cr App R 39).

(l) *Corroboration.* Where an accomplice testifies as a prosecution witness against a defendant, there is no duty to warn the jury about the dangers of convicting on the basis of that evidence (CJPOA 1994, s 32). However, the trial judge nevertheless has a discretion to give such a warning (*R v Makanjuola; R v Easton* [1995] 1 WLR 1348). The Court of Appeal will only rarely interfere with the exercise of this discretion.

(m) *Expert witness.* Where there has been evidence from an expert witness, the jury should be directed that it is not bound by the opinion of the expert witness (*R v Stockwell* (1993) 97 Cr App R 260; *R v Fitzpatrick* [1999] Crim LR 832).

(n) *Failure to call defence witness.* It should be noted that it is generally inappropriate for the judge to comment on the failure of the defence to call a particular witness, as such comment can easily detract from what is said about the burden of proof (see *R v Wheeler* [1967] 1 WLR 1531, 1535; *R v Wright* [2000] Crim LR 510).

(o) *Reaching a verdict.* Finally, the judge will tell the jury that, at this stage at least, only a unanimous verdict is acceptable (and that the jury should not at this stage concern itself with the possibility of a majority verdict) and the judge will suggest that the jury elects a foreman to chair their discussions. So that the jury does not get distracted by the possibility of a verdict other than a unanimous verdict, para IV.46.1 of *Consolidated Practice Direction* suggests that, before the jury retires, the judge should direct them as follows:

As you may know, the law permits me, in certain circumstances, to accept a verdict which is not the verdict of you all. Those circumstances have not as yet arisen, so that when you retire I must ask you to reach a verdict upon which each one of you is agreed. Should, however, the time come when it is possible for me to accept a majority verdict, I will give you a further direction.

In *R v Hastings* [2003] EWCA Crim 3730; *The Times*, 12 December 2003, the Court of Appeal reiterated that it is extremely important that the judge warns the jury not to deliberate on their verdict until all jury members are present.

In *R v Mirza* [2004] 1 AC 1118, the House of Lords confirmed that the Court of Appeal is not entitled to enquire what happened in the jury room while the jury was considering its verdict. In an attempt to make sure that any problems come to light before the verdict has been delivered (so that the judge can investigate and take appropriate action), para IV.42.6–9 of the *Consolidated Practice Direction* requires judges to ensure that jurors are alerted to the need to bring any concerns about fellow jurors to the attention of the judge at the time, and not to wait until the case is concluded. Judges should therefore take the opportunity, when warning the jury of the importance of not discussing the case with anyone outside the jury, to add a further warning, to the effect that it is the duty of jurors to bring to the judge's attention any behaviour among the jurors, or by others affecting the jurors, that causes concern. The point should be made that, unless that is done while the case is continuing, it may be impossible to put matters right. Particularly in the case of a longer trial, the judge should consider whether this should also be said prior to the retirement of the jury.

Where the judge fails to direct the jury adequately on a particular point, and that failure appears to provide a ground of appeal, defence counsel should not remain silent but should draw the matter to the attention of the judge. The duty to assist the judge rests upon both the prosecution and the defence (*R v Langford*, *The Times*, 12 January 2001).

In *R v Wang* [2005] UKHL 9; [2005] 1 All ER 782, the House of Lords held that there are no circumstances in which a judge is entitled to direct a jury to return a verdict of guilty.

A very useful resource is the *Criminal Bench Book* published by the Judicial Studies Board. It contains a set of 'specimen directions' which cover all the major matters which have to be covered in a summing-up. These specimen directions are freely available on the web at <http://www.jsboard.co.uk/criminal_law/index.htm>.

11.12 Bail

In *R v Central Criminal Court, ex p Guney* [1996] AC 616, the House of Lords held that when a defendant who has not previously surrendered to the custody of the court is arraigned, he or she thereby surrenders to the custody of the court at that moment. The result is that the Crown Court judge then has to decide whether or not to grant bail; unless the judge grants bail, the defendant will remain in custody pending and during the trial.

In *R v Maidstone Crown Court, ex p Jodka* (1997) 161 JP 638, the Divisional Court went further and held that bail granted by magistrates ceases when the defendant surrenders to the custody of the Crown Court, whether or not the defendant is arraigned at the hearing at which he or she surrenders. Where the magistrates grant bail subject to a surety, the responsibility of that surety under the magistrates' court order ceases once the defendant surrenders to the custody of the Crown Court. If the Crown Court wishes to grant bail subject to the same surety, the court must consider the position of that surety before imposing such a condition.

It follows from this that the question of bail will have to be considered at the PCMH. In any event, if the defendant is on bail before the trial, this bail effectively expires at the start of the trial. Therefore, once a defendant who was on bail before the trial has surrendered to the custody of the court at the start of the trial, he or she will only be released from custody if the judge grants bail. So a very brief bail application has to be made at the lunchtime adjournment and the end of each day. Such applications should be made in the absence of the jury (as refusal might prejudice them against the accused). Some judges will withhold bail at lunchtime (eg where there is a risk that the defendant might come into contact with jurors); others grant bail but forbid the defendant to leave the court building or require the defendant to remain in the company of their solicitor. Paragraph III.25.3 of *Consolidated Practice Direction* states that an accused who was on bail while on remand should not be refused overnight bail during the trial unless the judge is of the opinion that there are positive reasons to justify this refusal. The *Practice Direction* suggests that such reasons are likely to be: (a) that a point has been reached where there is a real danger that the accused will abscond, either because the case is going badly for him, or for any other reason; (b) that there is a real danger that the accused may interfere with witnesses or jurors. Paragraph III.25.4 goes on to state that there is no universal rule of practice that bail shall not be renewed once the summing-up has begun: it is for the judge to assess the risks involved in granting bail at this stage. Finally, para III.25.5 points out that once the jury has returned a verdict, a further renewal of bail should be decided in the light of the gravity of the offence and the likely sentence.

11.13 The verdict

11.13.1 The jury's retirement

The jury is put in the charge of a jury bailiff, who takes an oath to take the jurors to a private place and not to allow anyone to speak to them. The jurors then go off to the retiring room to consider their verdict.

Section 13 of the Juries Act 1974 enables the court to allow the jury to separate after (as well as before) it has been sent out to consider its verdict. Formerly, separation was only permitted before the jury had been sent out to consider its verdict. In *R v Oliver* [1996] 2 Cr App R 514, the Court of Appeal gave guidance on the directions which should be given to a jury which is allowed to separate before delivering its verdict. The jury must be warned that:

- it may only decide the case on the basis of the evidence it has heard in court; and

- jurors must not talk to anyone about the case except other jurors and even discussions with other jurors may only take place while they are deliberating in the retiring room.

Where a jury is sent to an hotel overnight, it must be told not to continue its deliberations in the hotel but only to discuss the case when it has returned to court the following day (otherwise, discussions might take place without all jurors being present) (*R v Tharakan* [1995] 2 Cr App R 368).

When deliberating, the jury is allowed to have with it any exhibit in the case. In *R v Tonge* (1993) 157 JP 1137 the Court of Appeal considered what should be done if the jury (after it has retired) asks to hear the tape recording of the defendant's interview at the police station. It was said that if the tape recording has not been played in open court during the trial and the jury asks to hear the tape, it should usually be played in open court. However, if the tape has already been played in court, the jury may be allowed to hear it again in the jury room.

Once the jury has retired, any communication between the judge and jury has to take place in open court in the presence of the entire jury, both counsel and the defendant (*Ramstead v The Queen* [1999] 2 AC 92). Where the judge receives a note from the jury, the procedure laid down in *R v Gorman* [1987] 1 WLR 545 should be followed: unless the note has nothing to do with the trial, the judge should, in open court (but in the absence of the jury), state the contents of the note and seek submissions from both counsel. The judge should then send for the jury and deal with the query in open court.

Once the jury has retired to consider its verdict, no further evidence can be adduced before them (*R v Owen* [1952] 2 QB 362). In *Owen*, the jury came out of retirement to ask whether the premises where a sexual assault was alleged to have taken place would have been occupied or not at the relevant time. The Court of Appeal held that no further evidence can be called after the jury has retired to consider its verdict. However, in *R v Hallam* [2007] EWCA Crim 1495, Toulson LJ said (at para 22) that there is no longer an absolute rule to the effect that evidence cannot be admitted after the retirement of the jury; rather, the question is what justice requires. The same view was expressed by Gage LJ in *R v Khan* [2008] EWCA Crim 1112 (at para 39), where his Lordship said that, although historically there was an absolute principle that no further evidence should be given after the judge's summing-up has been concluded and the jury has retired, in recent years this principle has been subject to some relaxation.

Each time the jury comes into court, it is asked by the clerk, 'Have you reached a verdict upon which you are all agreed?' If it has come back with a query, the answer will of course be 'no'. If it has come back with a verdict, the answer will be 'yes'. A verdict must be taken on each count of the indictment separately. However, if two counts were in the alternative and the jury convicts on the first (and most serious) count, it will be discharged from giving a verdict on the second.

11.13.2 Alternative verdicts

It is possible for the jury to acquit the defendant of the count on the indictment but to convict of another offence, sometimes known as a 'lesser included offence'. This is only possible if the Criminal Justice Act 1967, s 6 applies. This provides that where allegations in an indictment amount to or include, whether expressly or by implication, an allegation of another offence which may be tried on indictment, then the jury may acquit of the offence charged and convict of that other offence.

'Express inclusion' means that if certain words are deleted, the allegation of another offence remains. For example, if the indictment alleges that 'AB on 1st December 2009 entered 4 Gray's Inn Place as a trespasser and stole therein a laptop computer, the property of City University London', and the words 'entered 4 Gray's Inn Place as a trespasser and' are deleted, that leaves a valid count alleging theft. So if the jury feel that the prosecution have failed to prove trespass, an essential ingredient of burglary, but none the less find that the defendant stole the goods in question, they can convict of theft. See, for example, *R v Lillis* [1972] 2 QB 236.

'Implied inclusion' means that the lesser offence is either a necessary step towards committing the offence charged on the indictment or else is an offence which, in the vast majority of cases, is a step on the road to committing the offence charged. See *Metropolitan Police Commission v Wilson* [1984] AC 242. So, for example, theft is a valid alternative verdict to a charge of robbery (where the jury decides there was no assault);

sexual assault is a valid alternative to rape. Section 47 of the Offences Against the Person Act 1861 is a valid alternative to s 20 of that Act (*R v Savage* [1992] 1 AC 714); s 20 is a valid alternative to s 18 of the Act (*R v Mandair* [1995] 1 AC 208).

Under s 6(3A) of the Criminal Law Act 1967, an offence falls within the jurisdiction of the Crown Court for these purposes if it is an offence to which s 40 of the CJA 1988 applies, even if a count charging the offence is not included in the indictment. Thus, the jury may acquit the accused of the offence on the indictment but convict of an offence under s 40 of the 1988 Act, even though that offence is a summary offence (provided, of course, that it is expressly or impliedly included in the offence that does appear on the indictment). For example, if the accused is charged with assault occasioning actual bodily harm (s 47 of the Offences Against the Person Act 1861) but the jury find that no actual bodily harm was caused, they may acquit of that charge but convict of common assault (to which s 40 of the 1988 Act applies) even though that charge does not appear on the indictment. Under s 6(3B), a person convicted of an offence by virtue of s 6(3A) may only be dealt with for it in a manner in which a magistrates' court could have dealt with him.

There are, in any event, some specific statutory provisions which enable the jury to convict the defendant of a summary offence if they acquit the defendant of an indictable offence. The Theft Act 1968, s 12(4) provides that taking a conveyance without the owner's consent is a valid alternative verdict to a charge of theft, and the Road Traffic Offenders Act 1988, s 24 provides that careless driving is a valid alternative verdict to a charge of dangerous driving or causing death by dangerous driving.

Of course a jury will only be aware of its power to convict of a lesser included offence if it is told that it can do so; and even if the possibility is raised by counsel, the judge can decide to direct the jury not to consider that possibility. In *R v Fairbanks* [1986] 1 WLR 1202 the Court of Appeal said that if there was an alternative and less serious offence to that charged, the judge should put the alternative offence to the jury if it is necessary in the interests of justice to do so. The court seemed to create a presumption in favour of leaving the lesser offence to the jury. The defence might argue that the jury might think that the defendant was innocent of the offence charged but guilty of something and so convict as charged to prevent the defendant getting off scot-free; the prosecution might argue that if the jury took the view that the defendant was guilty of something, albeit not the offence on the indictment, it would be wrong for him or her to be acquitted altogether.

However, in *R v Maxwell* [1990] 1 WLR 401 the House of Lords took a more restrictive view. In that case, the defendant was charged with robbery but would have been willing to plead guilty to burglary. The prosecution declined to add a plea of burglary to the indictment and to accept the defendant's plea to that rather than to robbery. Defence counsel asked the judge to leave theft to the jury as an alternative to robbery. The judge refused and his refusal was ultimately upheld by the House of Lords. It was said that, in view of the way the prosecution had presented the case, the essential issue was whether or not violence had been used; the theft was trivial in comparison. To have left theft to the jury would have been to distract them from the main issue in the case. It therefore represented an unnecessary and undesirable complication. This decision appears to say that the judge should give great weight to the view of the prosecution before letting the jury consider a lesser offence. Similarly, in *R v Hussain* [2004] EWCA Crim 325, where the defendant was charged with causing death by dangerous driving, the trial judge rejected an application to leave the alternative offence of careless driving to the jury. The Court of Appeal confirmed that the test to be applied when considering whether to leave an alternative offence to the jury is: (i) whether there is any sensible basis on which the jury might convict of the more serious offence; (ii) whether leaving an alternative charge might compromise the jury's consideration and lead to an element of confusion; and (iii) in circumstances where the criminality is graver than the alternative offence and the judge concludes that the lesser charge is not what the case is all about, whether it is undesirable to leave an alternative to the jury, even if that leaves the jury with the stark choice between convicting of the full offence or acquitting altogether. Where an alternative offence is not left to the jury, a conviction might be rendered unsafe, said the Court, if the jury convicted the defendant out of reluctance to see an acquittal where they had found some misconduct. In those circumstances, it is incumbent on the judge to direct the jury exactly as to what they have to find in order to convict. On the facts of the present case, it was open to the judge not to leave the alternative to the jury, and the direction to the jury was clearly designed to ensure that the jury only convicted the defendant if the offence on the indictment was made out; the conviction was therefore safe.

In *R v Coutts* [2006] UKHL 39; [2006] 1 WLR 2154, it was said that an alternative verdict should be left to the jury only if it is 'obviously raised by the evidence'. In *R v Foster* [2007] EWCA Crim 2869; [2008] 1 WLR 1615, the Court of Appeal had to consider the effect of *Coutts*. Sir Igor Judge P said (at para 61):

not every alternative verdict must be left to the jury. In addition to any specific issues of fairness, there is . . . a proportionality consideration. The judge is not in error if he decides that a lesser alternative verdict should not be left to the jury if that verdict can properly be described in its legal and factual context as trivial, or insubstantial, or where any possible compromise verdict would not reflect the real issues in the case. He must, of course, reconsider any decision he may have reached about alternative verdicts in the light of any question which the jury may see fit to ask . . . However when the defence to a specific charge amounts to the admission or assertion of a lesser offence, the primary obligation of the judge is to ensure that the defence is left to the jury . . . the judge must examine whether the absence of a direction about a lesser alternative verdict or verdicts would oblige the jury to make an unrealistic choice between the serious charge and complete acquittal which would unfairly disadvantage the defendant . . .

Allowing the jury to consider an alternative verdict will only be in the interests of justice as far as the accused is concerned if he or she has had the opportunity of fully meeting the alternative charge in the course of presenting the defence case. Would the cross-examination of prosecution witnesses have been different? Would the defence have called different witnesses or presented its case differently? In other words, it is the same test as that applied if the court is asked to add a count to an indictment during the course of the trial. See, for example, *R v Banton* [2007] EWCA Crim 1847. It would of course be inappropriate to leave a lesser offence to the jury if it is inappropriate to the way in which the defence has been conducted, eg if the defence is one of alibi.

In *R v Lahaye* [2005] EWCA Crim 2847; [2006] 1 Cr App R 11, the Court of Appeal said that it is better if the availability of the alternative charge appears on the face of the indictment. This removes the need for the judge to exercise discretion as to whether or not the jury can consider a lesser offence.

Note that a verdict on a lesser offence is only possible if the jury acquits of the offence actually on the indictment. In *R v Collison* (1980) 71 Cr App R 249, for example, the jury was unable to agree on an acquittal. To enable it to convict of a lesser offence, that offence had to be added to the indictment as a new count (and the decision to do this, even though the jury had been considering its verdict for some time, was upheld on appeal as the defence would not have been conducted any differently). Similarly, in *R v Khela* [2006] 1 Cr App R 23, the Court of Appeal said that where a jury has been discharged from returning a verdict (eg after a successful application to stay the proceedings for abuse of process, or because the jury were unable to reach a verdict), the jury cannot then proceed to return a verdict of guilty to a lesser offence where the relevant statute provides that they can convict of the lesser offence only if the defendant has been found not guilty of the more serious offence. However, in *R v Livesey* [2006] EWCA Civ 3344; [2007] 1 Cr App R 35, the Court of Appeal said that, where the judge allows a submission of no case to answer to an offence with a statutory alternative verdict, he or she may allow that offence to remain on the indictment to enable the jury to consider the alternative verdict.

11.13.3 Majority verdicts

The Juries Act 1974, s 17, provides that a majority verdict may be accepted after the jury have been considering their verdict for two hours, or such longer time as the judge thinks appropriate given the nature and complexity of the case. As a matter of practice, the jury is given a further 10 minutes in which to settle into the retiring room and elect a foreman. The procedure to be adopted is set out in para IV.46 of the *Consolidated Practice Direction*.

Should the jury return before a period of two hours and ten minutes (or such longer time as the judge thinks reasonable) has elapsed since the jury retired to consider its verdict, the foreman should be asked, 'Have you reached a verdict upon which you are all agreed? Please answer "Yes" or "No"'. If the jury have reached a unanimous verdict, the foreman should be asked, 'What is your verdict?' If the jury have not reached a unanimous verdict, they should be sent out again for further deliberation with a direction to arrive, if possible, at a unanimous verdict.

When the judge decides that (subject to the two hour, 10 minute minimum) the jury have had long enough to reach a verdict, they will be called back into court. Again, the foreman will be asked if they have reached a unanimous verdict. If they have not, the judge will direct them to retire once more and will direct them that they should continue to endeavour to reach a unanimous verdict but that, if they cannot, a majority verdict will be accepted.

The only permissible majorities (bearing in mind that up to three jurors may be discharged during the course of the trial due to illness or other necessity) are:

12 jurors: 11–1 or 10–2
11 jurors: 10–1
10 jurors: 9–1

If the jury has been reduced to nine jurors, only a unanimous verdict is acceptable.

When the jury returns into court after the majority verdict direction has been given, the foreman will be asked, 'Have at least 10 [or nine as the case may be] of you agreed on your verdict?' If the answer is 'Yes', the foreman will be asked 'What is your verdict? Please only answer "guilty" or "not guilty"'. If the verdict is 'not guilty', that is the end of the matter. If the verdict is 'guilty', the foreman will be asked, 'Is that the verdict of you all or by a majority?' If the answer is that it was a majority verdict, the foreman will be asked, 'How many of you agreed to the verdict and how many dissented?'

The reason for this slightly complicated procedure is to prevent it being known that a verdict of 'not guilty' was a majority verdict, and to ensure that a verdict of 'guilty' was that of a permissible majority.

Under s 17(3) of the Juries Act 1974, the foreman must state in open court the number of jurors who respectively agreed to and dissented from the verdict before the judge can accept a majority verdict of guilty. In *R v Austin* [2003] Crim LR 426, the court confirmed that a majority verdict of guilty will be a nullity if the words used by the clerk of the court and the foreman are not such that it would be clear to an ordinary person how the jury was divided.

11.13.4 Reaching a verdict

No pressure should be put on the jury to reach a verdict (*R v Duggan* [1992] Crim LR 513). However, the judge can inquire whether there is a reasonable prospect of a verdict being reached; the judge may tell the jury that if there is no reasonable prospect of them reaching a verdict they will be discharged and if there is, then they can have as much time as they need (*R v Modeste* [1983] Crim LR 746).

In *R v Watson* [1988] QB 690, the Court of Appeal provided a model direction to be given to a jury which is having trouble reaching a verdict:

Each of you has taken an oath to return a true verdict according to the evidence. No one must be false to that oath, but you have a duty not only as individuals but collectively. That is the strength of the jury system. Each of you takes into the jury box with you your individual experience and wisdom. Your task is to pool that experience and wisdom. You do that by giving your views and listening to the views of the others. There must necessarily be discussion, argument and give and take within the scope of your oath. That is the way in which agreement is reached. If, unhappily, [10 of] you cannot reach agreement you must say so.

The *Watson* direction was considered in *R v Buono* (1992) 95 Cr App R 338. It was held that there should rarely be any need for a *Watson* direction, but if one has to be given it should be given either during the summing-up (which the present writer thinks unlikely ever to be justified) or after the jury have been given a reasonable time to consider a majority verdict direction. It was said that the *Watson* direction should never be given at the same time as a majority verdict direction.

The judge should not alter the words of the model direction given by the Court of Appeal in *Watson*. In *R v Atlan* [2004] EWCA Crim 1798; [2005] Crim LR 63, the jury sent a note to the judge saying that they were unanimous on all counts except for one, and that they wanted assistance. The judge gave a modified *Watson* direction, telling the jury that they had to try harder as it was not yet time to allow a majority verdict, but that 'there might have to be a bit of give and take in your deliberations and your thoughts'. Shortly afterwards, the jury convicted the defendant under the count in question. The Court of Appeal said that a *Watson* direction has to make it clear that any 'give and take' should be within the scope of the juror's oath. It is, said the court, just as dangerous to omit words from the *Watson* direction as to add them. Moreover, such a direction should not be given after the jury have retired unless a majority verdict is to be permitted. In the present case, the direction might have put undue pressure on the jury to compromise, and so the subsequent conviction was unsafe.

Where the defendant is charged with a number of offences and the jury indicates that it has agreed on verdicts on some, but not all, of the offences, it is good practice to take the verdicts on those counts upon which the jury is agreed before it carries on to consider the other counts (*R v F* [1994] Crim LR 377).

11.13.5 Discharge of the jury

If the jury cannot reach a verdict within what the judge holds to be a reasonable time, the jury will be discharged. This does not count as an acquittal and there is every chance that there will be a re-trial. In the event of the second jury also being 'hung', the prosecution is likely to let the matter rest.

11.14 Sentence

If the defendant is convicted of some or all of the counts on the indictment, the judge will proceed to hear the defendant's antecedents (including any relevant previous convictions) from prosecuting counsel, just as on a plea of guilty (see **11.2.1** above). Obviously, there is no need for the prosecution to summarise the facts as the judge has just presided over the trial.

In most instances, the case will have to be adjourned (with the presumption in favour of bail created by the Bail Act 1976, s 4 still applying to the defendant) for the preparation of a pre-sentence report, although the court may dispense with a report if it takes the view that a report is unnecessary. Once a report is available, counsel for the defence makes a plea in mitigation in the usual way.

11.15 The effect of the European Convention on Human Rights

Article 6 of the Convention guarantees the right to a fair trial. Under Article 6(1) this is a right to a fair and public hearing, within a reasonable time, by an independent and impartial tribunal. Article 6(1) goes on to provide that judgment shall be pronounced publicly but the press and public may be excluded from all or part of the trial in the interest of morals, public order or national security in a democratic society, where the interests of juveniles or the protection of the private life of the parties so require, or to the extent strictly necessary in the opinion of the court in special circumstances where publicity would prejudice the interests of justice.

Article 6(2) enshrines the presumption of innocence.

Article 6(3) confers a number of 'minimum rights', for example, for the accused to examine, or have examined, witnesses against him or her and to obtain the attendance and examination of witnesses on his or her behalf under the same conditions as witnesses against him or her.

It has been held by the European Court of Human Rights that Article 6 does not apply to preliminary hearings concerning trial arrangements (*X v UK* (1978) 5 EHRR 273).

An important aspect of the operation of Article 6 is the principle of 'equality of arms'. This requires that the defendant should have a reasonable opportunity of presenting his or her case to the court under 'conditions which do not place him at a substantial disadvantage vis-à-vis his opponent' (*Foucher v France* (1998) 25 EHRR 234). For example, handcuffing the accused during the trial may violate Article 6 (*Kaj Raninen v Finland* [1998] EHRLR 344).

The trial must take place before an unbiased tribunal. In the case of trial on indictment, that requirement applies to both the judge and the jury. There is a presumption that the court has acted impartially (*Hauschildt v Denmark* (1990) 12 EHRR 266; compare the UK case of *Locabail (UK) Ltd v Bayfield* [2000] QB 451). The test applied by the European Court of Human Rights is whether a legitimate doubt as to the impartiality of the tribunal can be objectively justified (*Hauschildt v Denmark*). This seems very similar to the test applied by UK courts ('a real danger or possibility of bias': see *R v Gough* [1993] AC 646 and *Porter v Magill* [2002] 2 AC 357).

11.16 Less common pleas

Most of this chapter has been devoted to cases which involve straightforward pleas of guilty or not guilty. Other situations are sometimes encountered, for example, where the defendant is unfit to enter a plea, or where he or she seeks to rely on the 'double jeopardy' rule.

11.16.1 Fitness to plead

A person is unfit to plead if incapable of understanding the proceedings and so unable to put forward any defence, challenge any juror for cause, give proper instructions to defence counsel, or follow the evidence (see *R v Podola* [1960] 1 QB 325). The issue of fitness to plead can be raised by the prosecution or the defence. The procedure to be followed is contained in s 4 of the Criminal Procedure (Insanity) Act 1964. The court may postpone consideration of the question of fitness to plead until any time up to the opening of the defence case if this is in the defendant's interests (s 4(2) of the 1964 Act). This enables a submission of no case to answer to be made before the question of fitness has to be determined. Under s 4(5) the question of fitness is to be determined 'by the court without a jury'.

If the defendant is found fit to plead, the trial takes its normal course. If, however, the defendant is found unfit to plead, a jury has to decide whether the defendant committed the *actus reus* of the offence. The procedure for this is governed by s 4A of the 1964 Act. If the question of fitness was determined at the start of the trial, a jury must be empanelled to determine whether the defendant committed the *actus reus*. If determination of the question was postponed and the defendant is found unfit to plead, the jury trying the substantive offence must determine whether the defendant committed the *actus reus* (s 4A(5)). If it is found that the defendant did not commit the *actus reus*, he or she is acquitted. If it is found that the defendant is not fit to plead, a hospital order (with or without a restriction order) or a supervision order may be made or the court may grant an absolute discharge (s 5). The procedure to be followed is summarised by Thomas LJ in *R v Norman* [2008] EWCA Crim 1810; [2009] 1 Cr App R 13 (at para 34).

In *R v H* [2003] UKHL 1; [2003] 1 All ER 497 the House of Lords held that the procedure laid down by the 1964 Act for determining whether the accused has done the act or omission charged against him does not involve the determination of a criminal charge but is, in any event, compatible with the rights of the accused under Article 6 of the European Convention on Human Rights.

11.16.2 Double jeopardy: *autrefois acquit* and *autrefois convict*

The principle of autrefois acquit and convict, sometimes known as the rule against 'double jeopardy', comprises the following elements (derived from *Connelly v DPP* [1964] AC 1254):

(a) A person should not be tried for a crime in respect of which he has previously been acquitted or convicted.

(b) A person should not be tried for a crime of which he could on some previous occasion have been convicted by way of an alternative verdict under s 6(3) of the Criminal Law Act 1967. For example, where the defendant was tried for rape, the jury could, if it acquitted him of rape, convict him instead of the lesser offence of sexual assault; it follows that the defendant should not be tried, on a later occasion, for sexual assault arising out of that incident.

(c) A person should not be tried for a crime, proof of which would necessarily entail proof of a crime of which he has previously been acquitted. In *R v Forest of Dean Justices, ex p Farley* [1990] RTR 228 it was said that there is an almost invariable rule that a person who has been tried for a lesser offence should not be tried again on the same facts for a more serious offence (eg a person acquitted of theft should not be tried for robbery, of which theft is an essential ingredient, arising out of the same incident).

(d) The defendant cannot be tried for a crime which is in effect the same, or substantially the same, as one of which he has previously been acquitted or convicted (or of which he could have been convicted by way of alternative verdict).

In *R v Beedie* [1998] QB 356, the Court of Appeal held that, in all cases except the first, the court has a discretion whether or not to strike out the later prosecution.

In *R v Dabhade* [1993] QB 329, it was held that where a charge is dismissed (without a hearing on the merits) on the ground that it is defective as a matter of law or because the evidence available to the prosecution is insufficient to sustain a conviction on the charge as laid, it cannot properly be said that the defendant was ever in jeopardy of conviction, and so the *autrefois* principle does not apply. This is particularly the case where the prosecution substitutes a new charge which is regarded as more appropriate to the facts. The consensual dismissal of the original charge does not give rise to the application of the doctrine of *autrefois acquit*.

However, in *R v G* [2001] 1 WLR 1727 it was held that, where the prosecution offer no evidence against a defendant and a verdict of not guilty is entered, the prosecution cannot then proceed against the defendant on a charge alleging a more serious offence based on the same facts, as the defendant is entitled to rely on the defence of *autrefois acquit*.

The *autrefois* principle does not apply where the defendant is re-prosecuted following the quashing of an indictment; where the prosecution serves a notice of discontinuance but reserves the right to institute proceedings at a later date under the Prosecution of Offences Act 1985, s 23(9); where the first jury was discharged from giving a verdict; or where the High Court quashes an acquittal where, under the Criminal Procedure and Investigations Act 1996, ss 54–57, someone has been convicted of interfering with, or intimidating, a juror or witness in the original trial.

Part 10 of the CJA 2003 provides, by way of exception to the normal rule against 'double jeopardy', for retrials in certain cases. CJA 2003, s 75, restricts the possibility of re-trial following acquittal to 'qualifying offences' (listed in Part 1 of Sch 5). Under s 76, the prosecution may apply to the Court of Appeal for an order quashing the defendant's acquittal and ordering him to be re-tried for the qualifying offence. Such an application may only be made with the written consent of the DPP. Only one application for an acquittal to be quashed may be made in respect of any acquittal, giving the prosecution only one further 'bite at the cherry'. The Court of Appeal can only order a re-trial where the requirements of ss 78 and 79 are satisfied. Section 78 requires there to be 'new and compelling evidence against the acquitted person in relation to the qualifying offence'. Under s 78(2), evidence is 'new' if it was not adduced in the proceedings in which the person was acquitted; and evidence is 'compelling' if it is 'reliable', 'substantial', and 'appears highly probative of the case against the acquitted person'. Under s 79, an order for re-trial can only be made if, in all the circumstances, it is in the interests of justice for the court to make such an order. Section 79(2) provides that this question is to be determined having regard to whether existing circumstances make a fair trial unlikely (having regard to the length of time since the qualifying offence was allegedly committed); whether it is likely that the new evidence would have been adduced in the earlier proceedings against the acquitted person but for a failure by an officer or by a prosecutor to act with due diligence or expedition; and whether, since those proceedings, any officer or prosecutor has failed to act with due diligence or expedition. Thus, s 78 requires the Court to make a decision on the strength of the new evidence and the impact it would have had if it had been adduced at the original trial. In considering the interests of justice, the Court will have regard to factors such as whether a fair trial would be made more difficult because of, for example, adverse publicity about the case or the length of time that has elapsed since the original trial. The Court is specifically required to consider whether the police and prosecution acted with due diligence and expedition in relation to both the original trial and the new evidence that has come to light.

11.17 Trial by judge alone

Part 7 of the CJA 2003 makes provision for trial by judge alone in complex fraud cases and in cases where there is a danger of jury tampering.

Section 43 of the 2003 Act enables an application to be made by the prosecution for certain fraud trials to be conducted without a jury. Such an order can only be made with the approval of the Lord Chief Justice or a judge nominated for this purpose by the Lord Chief Justice (s 43(4)). It only applies where notice has been given under s 51B of the Crime and Disorder Act 1998 (notices in serious or complex fraud cases) in respect of the offence(s) (s 43(1)(b)), and (under s 43(5)) the judge can only accede to the request if:

the complexity of the trial or the length of the trial (or both) is likely to make the trial so burdensome to the members of a jury hearing the trial that the interests of justice require that serious consideration should be given to the question of whether the trial should be conducted without a jury.

In deciding whether or not he is satisfied that this condition is fulfilled, the judge must have regard to any steps which might reasonably be taken to reduce the complexity or length of the trial (s 43(6)); in other words, a trial without a jury is very much a last resort. However, under s 43(7), 'a step is not to be regarded as reasonable if it would significantly disadvantage the prosecution'.

Section 44 of the Act enables an application to be made by the prosecution for a trial to be conducted without a jury where there is a danger of jury tampering. The judge may only make such an order if two conditions are satisfied: the first condition is that 'there is evidence of a real and present danger that jury tampering would take place' (s 44(4)) and the second condition is that 'notwithstanding any steps (including the provision of police protection) which might reasonably be taken to prevent jury tampering, the likelihood that it would take place would be so substantial as to make it necessary in the interests of justice for the trial to be conducted without a jury' (s 44(5)). Section 44(6) gives some examples of cases where there may be evidence of a real and present danger that jury tampering would take place:

- a case where the trial is a retrial and the jury in the previous trial was discharged because jury tampering had taken place;
- a case where jury tampering has taken place in previous criminal proceedings involving the defendant or any of the defendants;

- a case where there has been intimidation, or attempted intimidation, of any person who is likely to be a witness in the trial.

The word 'examples' indicates that this is not intended to be an exhaustive list of the cases where s 44 may apply.

Under the CJA 2003, s 45, an application for an order under s 43 or s 44 must be made at a preparatory hearing; all parties must be given an opportunity to make representations about the application.

Section 46 of the CJA 2003 makes provision for the discharge of a jury because of jury tampering. Before discharging the jury in such a case, the judge must allow the parties an opportunity to make representations. The judge may then make an order that the trial is to continue without a jury if satisfied that jury tampering has taken place, and that to continue the trial without a jury would be fair to the defendant(s). Under s 46(4), if the judge considers that it is necessary in the interests of justice for the trial to be terminated, he or she must terminate the trial; in such a case the judge may (under subs (5)) order that any new trial must be conducted without a jury.

Section 17 of the Domestic Violence, Crime and Victims Act 2004 makes further provision for Crown Court trial without a jury. It permits a judge, on application by the prosecution, to order such trial of some, but not all, of the counts on the indictment if three conditions are satisfied, namely:

- the number of counts included in the indictment is likely to mean that a trial by jury involving all of those counts would be impracticable;
- each count or group of counts which would be tried with a jury can be regarded as a sample of counts which could be tried without a jury;
- it is in the interests of justice for an order to be made.

In deciding whether or not to make an order, the judge must have regard to any steps which might reasonably be taken to facilitate a trial by jury, but a step is not to be regarded as reasonable if it could lead to the possibility of a defendant receiving a lesser sentence than would be the case if that step were not taken.

Section 19 sets out the effect of an order under s 17(2): where, in the course of the proceedings to which the order relates, a defendant is found guilty by a jury on a count which can be regarded as a sample of other counts to be tried in those proceedings, those other counts may be tried without a jury in those proceedings. Where the defendant is subsequently found guilty, the judge must give a judgment which states the reasons for the conviction.

Section 18 requires that applications under s 17 must be determined at a preparatory hearing (under s 29 of the Criminal Procedure and Investigations Act 1996); s 18(5) makes provision for appeal (under s 35 of the 1996 Act) to the Court of Appeal from the determination by a judge of an application under s 17.

12

Appeals to the Court of Appeal

12.1 The Criminal Division of the Court of Appeal

Traditionally, the Criminal Division of the Court of Appeal has entertained appeals from the Crown Court on all matters relating to a trial on indictment, and appeals against any sentence imposed by the Crown Court following a committal for sentence. Appeals on matters not relating to a trial on indictment, such as when the Crown Court hears an appeal from a decision of the magistrates, have been heard in the High Court, either on appeal by way of case stated, or on an application for judicial review.

The following have all been held to be matters relating to a trial on indictment, and hence not susceptible to appeal in the High Court:

- a ruling given at a pre-trial hearing (*R v Southwark Crown Court, ex p Johnson* [1992] COD 364, DC);
- an order staying the whole or part of an indictment (*R v Manchester Crown Court, ex p DPP* [1993] 2 WLR 846, HL);
- a decision, after argument, as to the date of the trial (*R v Southwark Crown Court, ex p Ward* [1995] COD 140).

This position has been altered by the CJA 2003 s 58, which allows the prosecution to appeal against the trial judge's rulings, in certain circumstances discussed in **12.2** below.

12.1.1 Composition of the court

If the Court of Appeal is hearing an appeal against conviction, the court must comprise at least three judges. Very occasionally, if the court is dealing with a case of exceptional difficulty, the court will consist of five judges. If the court is dealing with an appeal against sentence, it is usual for two judges only to sit. However, it is rare to have more than one judgment delivered, in order to make for certainty of the law.

The Court of Appeal itself consists of 32 Lords Justices of Appeal, and a number of ex-officio judges including the Lord Chief Justice. In addition, the Lord Chief Justice may ask either of the following to sit in the Criminal Division:

- any High Court judge, who may deal with any case that comes before the Court of Appeal, except a case in which he was either the trial judge or passed sentence; but see *R v Sampson* (unreported, 24 October 2006, CA) where the defendant was sentenced to life imprisonment with a minimum recommendation of 12 years. The defendant appealed against the recommendation, as it happened, to the same High Court judge, now elevated, who had imposed the original tariff. Dismissing the appeal it was held that the crucial point was that the judiciary, and not the executive, should set the tariff; or

- in certain circumstances, circuit judges, who may sit in appeals specified as suitable by the Lord Chancellor, except that they may not sit on any appeal from the decision of a High Court judge (s 9(1) of the Supreme Court Act 1981, as amended by s 52 of the Criminal Justice and Public Order Act 1994).

12.1.2 The Court's Registrar

The administrative work of the Criminal Division is carried out by the Registrar of Criminal Appeals, who receives all notices and applications, and in turn serves all relevant notices on the parties to the appeal. In addition, the Registrar will obtain necessary transcripts, exhibits or other material.

Under the Criminal Procedure Rules Part 65.2(2), the registrar:

(a) must fulfil the duty of active case management under rule 3.2;

(b) in fulfilling that duty may exercise any of the powers of case management under—

   (i) rule 3.5 (the court's general powers of case management);

   (ii) rule 3.9(3) (requiring a certificate of readiness); and

   (iii) rule 3.10 (requiring a party to identify intentions and anticipated requirements),

subject to the directions of the court.

Certain additional powers have been conferred on him by virtue of the Criminal Appeal Act 1995 and the Criminal Procedure Rules. See **12.7.1** below.

12.1.3 The right of appeal

The statute governing the right to appeal is the Criminal Appeal Act 1968, as amended by the Criminal Appeal Act 1995, referred to in this chapter as the CAA 1968 and the CAA 1995 respectively. The changes effected by the CAA 1995 came into effect on 1 January 1996, unless otherwise indicated. Students should also refer to the Criminal Procedure Rules Part 65.

12.2 The appeal against a ruling

Sections 57–74 of the CJA 2003 permit the prosecution to appeal against certain of the trial judge's rulings, namely a 'termination ruling' or an 'evidentiary ruling'. A termination ruling is one that has the effect of stopping the case such as a ruling that there is no case to answer or that the proceedings should be stayed. An evidentiary ruling is one which relates to matters such as the inclusion or exclusion of evidence. Such rulings may have a serious and detrimental effect on the way the prosecution develops its case. It seems inevitable that some evidentiary rulings will form part of an appeal against a termination ruling.

An appeal against a ruling only lies with leave of the trial judge or the Court of Appeal (s 57(4)).

12.2.1 The general right of appeal in respect of rulings

The procedure for appeal is fairly complex, but in essence is as follows, under the CJA 2003 ss 58–61 and the Criminal Procedure Rules Part 66:

(a) Following the ruling, the prosecution informs the court that it intends to appeal or requests an adjournment to consider whether to appeal. It must also inform the court that it agrees that, if leave to appeal is not granted or the appeal is abandoned, the defendant should be acquitted.

(b) The trial judge may agree to or refuse the request for an adjournment. If an adjournment is granted and the prosecution decide to appeal, it must inform the court at the adjourned hearing. If an adjournment is refused, the prosecution must decide either to continue with the appeal, or lose the right to do so.

(c) Where there are two or more offences, the prosecution must indicate which offence is the subject of the appeal.

(d) Where the trial judge has ruled that there is no case to answer, and the prosecution has informed the court that it intends to appeal, it may also nominate other rulings made in the course of the trial.

(e) The trial judge must decide whether to:
  (i) adjourn the case and expedite the appeal. The Court of Appeal may reverse the order to expedite.
  (ii) adjourn the case and not order that the appeal is expedited;
  (iii) discharge the jury and not order that the appeal is expedited.

(f) Once the prosecution has informed the court that it intends to appeal the ruling, the ruling has no effect whilst the appeal is pursued. Any consequences of the ruling equally have no effect, and no steps should be taken in consequence of the ruling. Such a consequence seems to include that a defendant who has been detained in custody prior to and during the trial will continue to be detained, even though the trial judge has decided that there is no case to answer. One can envisage conflict between the application of the defence for bail, which the trial judge is minded to give, and the clear wording of the section.

12.2.2 Power of the Court of Appeal for an appeal under s 58

On hearing an appeal under s 58, the Court of Appeal may either:

(a) Where the challenged ruling is no case to answer and the Court of Appeal confirms the ruling, the defendant is acquitted of that offence.

(b) Where the challenged ruling is no case to answer and the Court of Appeal reverses or varies the ruling, it must consider the following rulings:
  (i) an order that proceedings are resumed in the Crown Court, if necessary in the interests of justice;
  (ii) an order that a fresh trial should commence in the Crown Court, if necessary in the interests of justice;
  (iii) order that the defendant be acquitted of that offence.

The Criminal Justice and Immigration Act 2008 s 44 does not limit the discretion of a court considering an application by the Crown for leave to appeal from a ruling of a trial judge in the Crown Court. Rather than merely asking whether the Crown's case was arguable or had some reasonable prospect of success, the test to be applied was a broad "interests of justice test": *R v Al-Ali* The Times 3 October 2008. For a recent example of an appeal against a termination ruling see *R v NW and Others* [2008] EWCA Crim 2, where the prosecution appealed against the judge's acceptance of a submission of no case to answer.

12.2.3 The right of appeal in respect of evidentiary rulings

A separate set of provisions, the CJA 2003, s 62 and 63, applies to evidentiary rulings. Nothing in these sections affects the right of the prosecution to appeal under s 58 (s 62(11)). The ruling must be one which significantly weakens the prosecution case (s 63(2)).

In order to come within these sections, the ruling must:

- be made before the close of the prosecution case (s 62(2)); and
- relate to one of the qualifying offences in Sch 4 (s 62(9)). These are the most serious offences and include murder, manslaughter, rape, arson, endangering life, and war crimes.

In order to appeal against the trial judge's evidentiary ruling, the following procedure is followed:

(a) The prosecution inform the court, before the opening of the defence case, that it intends to appeal against the ruling, and specifies to which ruling or rulings the appeal relates.

(b) For the avoidance of doubt, s 62(8) defines the opening of the defence case as the earliest of the following events:

  (i) evidence begins to be adduced on behalf of the defendant;

  (ii) it is indicated to the court that no evidence will be adduced on behalf of the defendant; or

  (iii) the defence make an opening speech.

(c) Leave of the trial judge or the Court of Appeal must be obtained. This will only be given if the court is satisfied that the ruling significantly weakens the prosecution case (s 63(l)).

Note that a ruling which was an 'evidentiary ruling' within the meaning of s 62(9) could also be a ruling within s 58(1): *R v Y* [2008] EWCA Crim 10, where it was held that since the appealed ruling was a ruling about what evidence the Crown would be permitted to adduce in its attempt to prove the offences for which the defendant had been indicted, the judge's ruling fell within s 58(1) notwithstanding that it was also an evidentiary ruling.

12.2.4 Power of the Court of Appeal for an appeal under s 62

On hearing an appeal under s 62, the Court of Appeal may, by virtue of s 66:

(a) Confirm, reverse or vary any ruling to which the appeal relates.

(b) In addition, the Court of Appeal must, in respect of each offence, make one of the following orders:

  (i) an order that the proceedings be resumed in the Court of Appeal;

  (ii) an order that a fresh trial take place in the Crown Court;

(iii) an order that the defendant be acquitted of that offence, if the prosecution indicates that it does not intend to continue with the prosecution of the offence.

Under s 63, the Court of Appeal may not reverse a ruling unless it is satisfied that:

- the ruling is wrong in law; or
- the ruling involved an error of law or principle; or
- the ruling was a ruling that it was not reasonable for the judge to have made.

Section 64 permits a further appeal to the House of Lords.

12.3 The appeal against conviction

By virtue of the CAA 1968, s 2, as substituted by the CAA 1995, s 2, a person convicted on indictment may appeal on the single ground that the conviction is 'unsafe' (see **12.3.2**). Leave to appeal is always required (see **12.3.5**).

12.3.1 Grounds of appeal: the 1968 Act

Prior to 1996, the Court of Appeal would allow an appeal if one of the three grounds of appeal, set out below, were made out. The proviso to this was that the Court of Appeal could dismiss the appeal if no miscarriage of justice had actually occurred. This was known as 'exercising' or 'applying' the proviso. In this situation the Court of Appeal in effect agreed that a ground of appeal had been made out but that the ground was so trivial that the jury would inevitably come to the same conclusion. The grounds were as follows:

(a) *The conviction was unsafe or unsatisfactory.* In deciding whether the conviction was unsafe or unsatisfactory, the Court of Appeal considered the case as a whole and asked itself the subjective question 'whether we are content to let the matter stand as it is, or whether there is not some lurking doubt in our minds which makes us wonder whether an injustice has been done'. See *R v Cooper* [1969] 1 QB 267 *per* Widgery LJ, applied in *R v O'Leary* (1988) 87 Cr App R 387.

(b) *The trial judge made a wrong decision on a question of law.* If an appeal was on the basis of a wrong decision by the trial judge on a question of law, even if this could be demonstrated, the Court of Appeal still had to consider whether the judgment of the trial court should be set aside on that account. In effect, it considered the proviso. See *R v Moghal* (1977) 65 Cr App R 56.

(c) *There was a material irregularity in the course of the trial.* An appeal on the basis that there was a material irregularity succeeded if there had been a procedural error during the trial. But the irregularity had to be major and material, ie serious enough to have affected the course of the trial.

12.3.2 Grounds of appeal: the 1995 Act

The CAA 1995 abolished the three grounds of appeal and the proviso, replacing them with the single test of the safety of the conviction.

The CAA 1995, s 2 provides as follows:

2.—In section 2 of the 1968 Act (disposal of appeal against conviction), for subsection (1) (grounds on which Court of Appeal are to allow or dismiss appeal including the proviso) substitute—

(1) Subject to the provisions of this Act, the Court of Appeal—

(a) shall allow an appeal against conviction if they think that the conviction is unsafe; and

(b) shall dismiss such an appeal in any other case.

The Act does not contain any definition of the word 'unsafe'. The meaning of the word has, however, been considered by the Court of Appeal in the following cases.

In *R v Chalkley* [1998] QB 848, it was described as 'in essence much the same as the intertwined and overlapping provisions of the old test, as was intended by the Royal Commission in recommending it, the Government in promoting it, the senior judiciary in supporting its parliamentary passage and Parliament in enacting it'.

At one time, it was thought that the 'lurking doubt' test had been swept away by the amendments to s 2—see, for example, *R v Farrow* (1998), *The Times*, 20 October 1998 (reported as *R v F* [1999] Crim LR 306), where the Court of Appeal described the 'new' test as simple and clear and one upon which it was undesirable to impose any gloss, in particular, that of 'lurking doubt'. However, the Court in many subsequent cases has continued to ask itself whether it was left with a lurking doubt. See, for example, *R v Conley* [2005] EWCA Crim 63, where Auld LJ said that the 'lurking doubt' test continued to be a tool available to the Courts Martial Appeal Court as an application of the test of unsafety of a conviction in s 2, as amended. If the Court 'has a lurking doubt, or feels unease, about the safety of a conviction, then, in the words of section 2(1)(a) of [the] Act, it "thinks that the conviction is unsafe", and is bound to quash it'.

The modern approach

The traditional approach of the Court of Appeal when dealing with misdirections of law, inadmissible material placed before the jury, or a failure to direct a jury on a material point due to oversight or error, was frequently to quash the conviction. A new approach was set out in *R v Lambert* [2006] EWCA Crim 827. The correct approach was to decide whether the defendant's trial had been so prejudiced as a result that it would have called for the discharge of the jury or the conviction being quashed. The starting point was not to assume that the trial process had been vitiated as a result of the error(s).

A similar new approach can be seen in relation to procedural failures. In *R v Sekhon* [2002] EWCA Crim 2954 the Court of Appeal held that 'the purpose of rules of procedure is not usually to give or take away a court's jurisdiction'; rather, procedural requirements 'provide a convenient and just machinery enabling the court to exercise its jurisdiction'.

In *R v Soneji* [2005] UKHL 49, the House of Lords rejected a distinction between rules of procedure which were mandatory or directory. 'Instead [. . .] the emphasis ought to be on the consequences of non-compliance, and posing the question whether Parliament can fairly be taken to have intended total invalidity'. At para [23] in dealing with the interests of justice in that case, Lord Steyn concluded '. . . that the rigid mandatory and directory distinction, and its many artificial refinements, have outlived their usefulness'.

In *R v Ashton* [2006] EWCA Crim 794, Lord Woolf CJ stated:

4. [. . .] in our judgment it is now wholly clear that whenever a court is confronted by failure to take a required step, properly or at all, before a power is exercised ('a procedural failure'), the court should first ask itself whether the intention of the legislature was that any act done following that procedural failure should be invalid. If the answer to that question is no, then the court should go on to consider the interests of justice generally, and most

particularly whether there is a real possibility that either the prosecution or the defence may suffer prejudice on account of the procedural failure. If there is such a risk, the court must decide whether it is just to allow the proceedings to continue.

5. On the other hand, if a court acts without jurisdiction—if, for instance, a magistrates' court purports to try a defendant on a charge of homicide—then the proceedings will usually be invalid.

12.3.3 The Criminal Appeal Act 1968 and the Human Rights Act 1998

The power of the Court of Appeal to uphold a conviction of an appellant if it is 'safe' must now be read in the light of Article 6 of the European Convention on Human Rights, which confers on the defendant the right to a fair trial. The relationship between the safety of the conviction and the fairness of the trial has been the subject of some discussion in the Court of Appeal. On one hand, the Court of Appeal may find that the conviction is safe even though there has been some irregularity or misdirection in the trial that would render it 'unfair', ie the defendant is guilty. On the other hand, a conviction may be quashed because the trial was unfair even though the defendant is clearly guilty, ie the conviction would be 'safe'.

A review of all the cases in which the Court of Appeal has dealt with these different approaches is beyond the scope of this Manual, but the following cases are worthy of note: *Condron v United Kingdom* [2000] Crim LR 679, *R v Francom* [2001] 1 Cr App R 237, *R v Davis* [2001] 1 Cr App R 115 and *R v Togher* [2001] 3 All ER 463.

In *Condron* the European Court of Human Rights stressed the need for the Court of Appeal to examine the fairness of the trial, rather than the safety of conviction, stating: 'The question whether or not the rights of the defence guaranteed to an accused under Article 6 of the Convention were secured in any given case cannot be assimilated to a finding that his conviction was safe in the absence of any enquiry into the issue of fairness'.

In *Francom*, where the trial judge had failed to direct the jury at all, the Court of Appeal accepted that the term 'unfair' in the context of Article 6 had to be given a broad meaning favourable to the accused. It was not limited to the safety of the conviction itself, but encompassed the entire prosecution process. Lord Woolf went on to say:

A misdirection of the jury could result in a breach of Article 6. But it may not do so. In the same way it may not make a conviction unsafe. It all depends on the circumstances of the case. In a case such as the present, we would expect this court to approach the issue of lack of safety in exactly the same way as the [European Court of Human Rights] approaches the lack of fairness. The directions which a judge gives at trial are designed to achieve the very fairness required by Article 6(1). As we understand the jurisprudence of the ECHR, that court does not adopt a technical approach to the question of fairness. The European Court is interested . . . in requiring fairness of the trial in all circumstances.

Later he continued:

The test which we have to apply before upholding the conviction is whether, notwithstanding the non-direction, we are satisfied that no reasonable jury could have come to a different conclusion from that which was reached by the jury, if they were properly directed. That approach not only means there must not be a lack of safety, it also means there must be no unfairness because the non-direction or misdirection must not affect the accused's right to a fair trial.

In *Davis*, the European Court of Human Rights decided that there had been a violation of the appellant's right, which was not cured by the appeal process. Mantell LJ stated that:

The court is concerned with the safety of the conviction. A conviction can never be safe if there is doubt about guilt. However the converse is not true. A conviction may be unsafe even where there is no doubt about guilt, but the trial process has been vitiated by serious unfairness or significant legal misdirection. That being so, there is no tension between s 2(1)(a) of the Criminal Appeal Act 1968 and s 3(1) of the Human Rights Act 1998.

Later he said:

[W]e are satisfied that the two questions (ie safety and fairness) must be kept separate and apart. The European Court of Human Rights is charged with enquiring into whether there has been a breach of a Convention right. This court is concerned with the safety of the conviction. That the first question may intrude upon the second is obvious. To what extent it does so will depend upon the circumstances of the particular case.

In *Togher*, an appeal following a plea of guilty, Lord Woolf CJ said, after discussing *Condron*:

Now that the Convention is part of our domestic law, it would be most unfortunate if the approach identified by the European Court and the approach of this court continued to differ unless this is inevitable because of provisions contained in this country's legislation or the state of our case law.

Moreover, in *Togher* Lord Woolf said, 'We would expect . . . that the approach of this court applying the test of lack of safety would produce the same result as the approach of the European Court applying the test of lack of fairness'.

Note that in the view of the editors of *Blackstone's Criminal Practice*, there is no insuperable problem in interpreting the requirement under the CAA 1968 that the conviction is safe in such a way as to encompass the Convention right that the trial is fair. If this is done, then the two requirements are not incompatible.

12.3.4 Errors commonly before the Court of Appeal

Some errors occur commonly and the following cases are intended to illustrate the way the Court of Appeal approaches such errors. This list includes cases decided both before and after the CAA 1995, and it may be that some of the pre-1995 cases would now be decided differently, particularly in view of the Human Rights Act 1998 (HRA) and the Criminal Procedure Rules. This list is not intended to be exhaustive.

(a) *The wrongful admission or exclusion of evidence.* If the wrongful admission or exclusion of evidence renders the conviction unsafe, the Court of Appeal will quash the conviction.

(b) *Defects in the indictment.* For example, the indictment is bad for duplicity or falls foul of r 9 of the Indictments (Procedure) Rules 1971, SI 1971/1253. Before 1995, the Court of Appeal would only quash the conviction if the defect was serious. Applying the new test in the light of the HRA 1998, the Court of Appeal may now come to a different conclusion.

(c) *The absence of corroboration.* If there was no corroboration when it was required, the Court of Appeal will usually quash the conviction.

(d) *Failure or misdirection by the trial judge on the burden or standard of proof.* Such a non-direction or misdirection will often lead to the quashing of the conviction, but see *R v Edwards* (1983) 77 Cr App R 5, where the trial judge did not direct the jury as to the standard of proof. The conviction was upheld because the evidence against the defendant was overwhelming and the jury had been reminded of the standard by both counsel in any event.

(e) *A wrong rejection of no case to answer.* Prior to 1995, if the trial judge wrongly rejected a submission of no case to answer, the appeal succeeded and the proviso was not applied. Had the trial judge not erred in law, the defendant would have been acquitted and no matter what evidence was adduced in the trial subsequently, the acquittal would not have been affected (*R v Cockley* (1984) 79 Cr App R 181). In *R v Smith* [1999] 2 Cr App R 238, the Court of Appeal reached the same conclusion applying the new test, even though, in this case, the defendant admitted guilt during cross-examination. See also *R v Broadhead* [2006] EWCA Crim 1705, where it was held that the application of S2 did not apply to this situation.

(f) *Interventions by the trial judge.* If there are a large number of interventions by the trial judge, which effectively prevent the proper development of the defence case, then the conviction is likely to be quashed (see *R v Matthews and Matthews* (1984) 78 Cr App R 23, *R v Whybrow*, The Times, 14 February 1994 and *R v Ahmed*, The Times, 9 March 1995). In *R v Cameron* [2001] Crim LR 587 the Court of Appeal upheld the actions of the trial judge who conducted the cross-examination of the 14-year-old complainant in a rape case after she refused to respond to questions put by defence counsel. For a recent example, see *R v Marsh* [2002] EWCA 1497.

See also *R v Garrett* [2005] EWCA Crim 1169, where the conviction was quashed due, *inter alia*, to the cumulative effect of the trial judge's questions to the jury in a short and straightforward case.

(g) *Failure or misdirection by the trial judge on law.* This will usually lead to the quashing of the conviction. See, for example, *R v Jones* [1997] Crim LR 598 where, on a charge of robbery, the trial judge did not direct the jury that the use of force had to be with the intention of stealing. The Court of Appeal quashed the conviction, holding that it was crucial to direct the jury on this element as well as the theft element. In *R v Clarke* [2006] EWCA Crim 3427 the convictions for murder and manslaughter were quashed due to errors in the summing up in relation to these offences and inadequate directions in relation to evidence of bad character. The CA observed:

> It is commonplace and much to be recommended that the judge, however experienced, should pass their written directions to the jury on issues such as the distinction between murder and manslaughter, so long as they are couched in clear terms, shown to counsel in advance and are not too lengthy.

(h) *Failure to deal with the essential thrust of the defence case.* For an example, see *R v Osborn* [2002] All ER (D) 320, where the Court of Appeal quashed the conviction of a defendant charged with causing grievous bodily harm where the possibility of accident, raised at the trial, was not mentioned in the summing-up.

In *R v Stephenson* [2005] EWCA Crim 3111, the conviction for possession with intent to supply was quashed because the trial judge introduced a new factual basis for the commission of the offence in his summing up to the jury.

(i) *Errors by defence counsel.* The Court of Appeal will not allow an appeal on the basis that defence counsel's actions were mistaken or unwise, though in the case of 'flagrantly incompetent advocacy' it will quash the conviction (*R v Ensor* [1989] 1 WLR 497). In *R v Clinton* [1993] 1 WLR 1181, the appeal was on the basis that the appellant was not advised to give evidence but should have been. The Court of Appeal said that the crucial issue was not counsel's incompetence, but the effect on the trial and the verdict, and quashed the conviction. The test of flagrantly incompetent advocacy has been doubted in subsequent cases, for example *R v Chatterjee* [1996] Crim LR 801 where the conviction was quashed because impressive expert evidence available to defence counsel was not properly put before the jury, and *R v Scollan* [1999] Crim LR 566 where defence counsel did not properly follow the accused's instructions as to crucial details of the defence. In *R v Nangle* [2001] Crim LR 506, and *R v Thakrar* [2001] 1 All ER (D) 103, the Court of Appeal said that if the failures of defence counsel mean that the defendant has been deprived of his right to a fair trial, it may be compelled to intervene. In *R v Doherty* [1997] 2 Cr App R 218, the Court of Appeal set out the guidance and procedure to be followed where the appeal involves criticism of trial counsel. Guidance issued in December 1995 by the Bar Council was quoted with approval by the Lord Chief Justice. In particular, an appeal on this basis should not be pursued unless 'it can be demonstrated that in the light of the information available to him at the time, no reasonably competent counsel would sensibly have adopted the course taken by him at the time when he took it'. In *R v Pluck* [2002] All ER (D) 281, where the Court of Appeal held that decisions made by defence counsel in good faith after proper consideration of the arguments, and after discussion with the defendant if appropriate, did not render the conviction unsafe. See also *R v Hobson* [1998] 1 Cr App R 31, *R v Nasser*, *The Times*, 19 February 1998 and *Boodram v Trinidad and Tobago* [2002] 1 Cr App R 12.

The point arose again in slightly unusual contexts in *R v Shatwell and Lea* [2002] EWCA Crim 215 and *R v Hall* [2002] EWCA Crim 1881. In the first case, the defendants' appeal was rejected, as the fact that prosecution were represented by Queen's Counsel did not mean that the defendants had been deprived of their right to a fair trial on the basis of an inequality of arms. What was required was that the chosen advocate had competently presented the defence, and in this case, no valid criticism could be made. In the second case, leading counsel had been diagnosed with a terminal illness just before the trial, and the defendant argued that he had not received a fair trial, as the illness may have affected counsel's ability to make decisions regarding his defence. The Court of Appeal dismissed the appeal, holding that the question was whether the conduct of the case fell below the proper standard so that the defendant did not receive a fair trial. In this case, the decisions made by counsel were within the range of decisions which competent counsel could have made. In *R v Kamar*, *The Times*, 5 November 2002, the Court of Appeal held that, where credibility is an issue of central importance, the failure of defence counsel to raise the issue of the defendant's good character rendered the trial defective.

The test when assessing if the conduct of a legal adviser had been such as to render a defendant's trial unfair was whether the conduct of the legal adviser had been unreasonable in the *Wednesbury* sense and whether as such it had had an actual affect on the fairness of the trial: *R v Bolivar, R v Lee* [2003] EWCA Crim 1167.

(j) *A refusal by the trial judge to exercise a discretion in favour of the defence.* The Court of Appeal is generally reluctant to interfere with the exercise of the trial judge's discretion, and will usually do so only if the discretion was exercised on the wrong basis (eg *R v Morris* [1991] Crim LR 385) or if the discretion was not exercised at all (eg *R v Dubarry* (1976) 64 Cr App R 7). Where the trial judge is exercising a discretion under PACE 1984, s 78, however, the Court of Appeal is much more willing to interfere. See *Blackstone's Criminal Practice* 2006, D24.20, F17.13.

(k) *A failure by the trial judge to direct the jury to ignore his views.* In *R v Dow* [2003] EWCA Crim 3621, the trial judge's failure to direct the jury, *inter alia*, that they should ignore his views unless they coincided with the jury's own was not enough to lead to the quashing of the conviction.

(l) *The residual discretion of the CA.* Even where the trial process cannot be faulted, there remains in the Court of Appeal a residual discretion to set aside a conviction where it is felt it would be unsafe or unfair to allow it to stand: *R v B* [2003] All ER (D) 67, where the defendant was put in an impossible position to defend himself, having regard to the 30-year delay, even though the judge had warned the jury fairly and carefully with ample warning of the difficulties faced by the defendant, and the very limited evidence which was available. This was one of the residual cases where, in the interests of justice, the conviction had to be set aside. In *R v A and Others* [2007] EWCA Crim 2485 the trial lasted approximately 11 months but was very disrupted with an inadequate summing up. The strong prosecution evidence was hardly challenged but nevertheless there were issues which the jury had to decide and the CA came to the conclusion that the jury were 'deprived of the fair opportunity to reach rational conclusions . . . [T]he trial process was so defective and the failure of the summing up to cure those defects so great that the verdicts were unsafe'.

(m) *Inconsistencies in the verdicts.* Where the verdict of guilty is inconsistent with the verdict of not guilty, the conviction may be quashed. See for example *R v Loi* [2003] EWCA 801.

(n) *Witness known to the trial judge.* Even though the witness was withdrawn and replaced by another who could give the same evidence, there were clear dangers of bias: *AWG Group v Morrison* (unreported 1 December 2005).

(o) *Bias:* a number of cases have attempted to define the test to apply when looking at whether the court is biased. In *In re Medicaments and Related Classes of Goods (No 2)* [2001] 1 WLR 700, Lord Phillips of Worth Matravers MR summarised the court's conclusions, at pp 726–7: '85. . . . *The court must first ascertain all the circumstances which have a bearing on the suggestion that the judge was biased. It must then ask whether those circumstances would lead a fair-minded and informed observer to conclude that there was a real possibility, or a real danger, the two being the same, that the tribunal was biased.*' This was approved by Lord Hope of Craighead in *Porter v McGill* [2002] 2 AC 357, who added that *'I would however delete from it the reference to "a real danger". Those words no longer serve a useful purpose here, and they are not used in the jurisprudence of the Strasbourg court. The question is whether the fair-minded and informed observer, having considered the facts, would conclude that there was a real possibility that the tribunal was biased.'*

For examples of alleged bias see *R v C* [2005] EWCA Crim 2170, where the trial judge said to Defence counsel: 'I am not having the jury misled by you', 'are you content with half-truths', 'you cannot have your cake and eat it' and 'do you take any notice of anything that anybody says to you?' These remarks were unwarranted and so prejudicial that the conviction was quashed. See also *R v Cordingley* [2007] EWCA Crim 2174.

(p) *Composition of the jury*: Traditionally, people involved in the administration of justice, such as police officers, crown prosecutors, barristers and judges have been excluded from sitting on a jury. This exclusion was removed by the Criminal Justice Act 2003 s321 and Schedule 33. There have, as a result, been a number of cases in which the defendant has appealed on the basis that, by virtue of the presence of a member of the previously excluded category on his jury, the jury has been biased. In *R v Abdroikov, Green and Wilkinson* [2007] UKHL 37 the HL repeated that justice should not only be done, but should manifestly and undoubtedly be seen to be done, which now equates with the right to a fair trial under Article 6 of the European Convention. The appellants argued that, though there was no actual bias, justice is not seen to be done where one of those charged to decide whether the appellant was guilty or not, is employed full-time by a body dedicated to promoting the success of one side in the adversarial trial process. Lord Bingham said: *'It must in my view be accepted that most adult human beings, as a result of their background, education and experience, harbour certain prejudices and predilections of which they may be conscious or unconscious. I would also, for my part, accept that the safeguards established to protect the impartiality of the jury, when properly operated, do all that can reasonably be done to neutralise the ordinary prejudices and predilections to which we are all prone. But this does not meet the central thrust of the case made. . . for the appellants: that these cases do not involve the ordinary prejudices and predilections to which we are all prone but the possibility of bias (possibly unconscious) which, as he submits, inevitably flows from the presence on a jury of persons professionally committed to one side only of an adversarial trial process, not merely (as the Court of Appeal put it) "involved in some capacity or other in the administration of justice". [The] expectation that each doubtful case would be resolved by the judge on a case by case basis is not, he pointed out, met if neither the judge nor counsel know of the identity of a police officer or the juror, as appears to be the present practice.'*

This case led to a number of other appeals, for example *R v Khan* [2008] EWCA Crim 531 where Lord Phillips CJ said: *"Where an impartial juror is shown to have had reason to favour a particular witness, this will not necessarily result in the quashing of a conviction. It will only do so if this has rendered the trial unfair, or given it an appearance of unfairness. To decide this it is necessary to consider two questions:*

(i) *would the fair minded observer consider that partiality of the juror to the witness may have caused the jury to accept the evidence of that witness? If so,*

(ii) *would the fair minded observer consider that this may have affected the outcome of the trial?*

If the answer to both questions is in the affirmative, then the trial will not have the appearance of fairness. If the answer to the first or the second question is in the negative, then the partiality of the juror to the witness will not have affected the safety of the verdict and there will be no reason to consider the trial unfair." The mere fact that a member of the jury is a member of the police or a CPS employee will not of itself justify quashing the conviction. Witnesses who fall into this category should be identified at the outset so that if necessary that juror could be stood down.

See also R v GC [2008] EWCA Crim 1033.

(q) *Unduly long trials:* In *R v A and Others* [2007] EWCA 2845 Crim, the trial was estimated to last 4 months but lasted for 11 months and was very disrupted, with an inadequate summing up. The CA held that the verdicts were unsafe and quashed the convictions.

In *R v Owens and Another* (unreported, 6 September 2006), the Crown and the defence reached an agreement as to the disposal of the appeals. This was unacceptable.

[. . .] *such a compromise was in the court's experience unprecedented, and they were unable to proceed on that basis. Of course, there are occasions, for instance where new evidence comes forward on appeal, where the Crown indicates that it is not minded to resist an appeal. Even in such* circumstances, however, the matter is fully opened to the court, so that the court can form its own view of the situation and resolve the matter for itself. In the present case, however, the suggested compromise had no logical or intellectual basis in the appeal, and simply represented a 'deal'. It was described by counsel as a 'compromise'. It was unacceptable. It showed a fundamental misunderstanding of the function of the court in determining appeals in accordance with section 2 of the Criminal Appeal Act 1968, namely to allow an appeal against conviction if the court considers the conviction unsafe, and to dismiss the appeal in any other case.

Where a trial judge removes a defence from a jury's consideration, the prosecution must still prove an affirmative case and it remains for the jury to return its own voluntary verdict. It is never right for the trial judge to direct the jury to convict in terms: *R v Kelleher* [2003] EWCA 2846 where the defence was self-defence, and on the evidence, the only proper verdict was guilty and the conviction was safe.

The deliberations of the jury are immune from examination, and the Court of Appeal will not intervene where, after an unambiguous verdict, a juror subsequently alleges that the verdict was not unanimous. As a matter of policy, the verdict is final. Further, jurors should be protected from pressure or inducement to alter their views. This position is not altered by the HRA 1998. See *R v Millward* [1999] 1 Cr App R 61, and *R v Lewis* (26 April 2001). Note also *R v Young* [1995] QB 324, where the use, by some members of the jury, of a ouija board during the overnight adjournment to determine the defendant's guilt was held to be outside the course of the jury deliberations and therefore reviewable by the Court of Appeal.

12.3.5 Leave to appeal

By virtue of the CAA 1968, as amended, leave to appeal against conviction is always required. Leave may be given either by the trial judge, or by the Court of Appeal itself.

The CAA 1968, s 1 provides as follows:

> (2) An appeal under this section lies only—
>
> (a) with the leave of the Court of Appeal; or
>
> (b) if the judge of the court of trial grants a certificate that the case is fit for appeal.

The certificate may be granted either:

- on the judge's own initiative, in which case the judge drafts the question which he or she considers ought to be raised (it is then read to counsel for their comment); or
- on counsel's application (in which case counsel normally drafts the question and the application itself is made in chambers with a shorthand writer present).

See generally *Practice Direction (criminal: consolidated)* [2002] 3 All ER 904, para 50.

It will be rare for the defendant to ask the trial judge for a certificate that the case is fit for appeal. Such a certificate should only be sought in exceptional circumstances, and the normal rule is that it should be left to the Court of Appeal, whether as the single judge or the full court, to consider when a case is suitable for the granting of leave to appeal: *R v Inskip* [2005] EWCA Crim 3372. The mere fact that a judge has a difficult exercise of evaluation before reaching a conclusion that a case should go to the jury is plainly an insufficient reason for the grant of a trial judge's certificate.

There must be a particular and cogent ground of appeal on which the appellant will have a substantial chance of succeeding (*R v Bansal* [1999] Crim LR 484). See also *Practice Direction (criminal: consolidated)*, para 50 and, in particular, see para 50.4:

> The first question for the judge is then whether there exists a particular and cogent ground of appeal. If there is no such ground there can be no certificate, and if there is no certificate there

can be no bail. A judge should not grant a certificate with regard to sentence merely in the light of mitigation to which he has, in his opinion, given due weight, nor in regard to conviction on a ground where he considers the chance of a successful appeal is not substantial. The judge should bear in mind that, where a certificate is refused, application may be made to the Court of Appeal for leave to appeal and for bail.

Under the Proceeds of Crime Act 2002, the person (designated by the statute) who has applied for a restraint order under ss 40–41 (prohibiting the person specified in the order from dealing with any 'realisable property'), or the person affected by the order may appeal against the decision of the Crown Court with leave of the Court of Appeal. A further appeal may be made to the House of Lords, but a certificate from the Court of Appeal that the case involves a point of law of general public importance is not required, nor is leave to appeal from either the Court of Appeal or the House of Lords.

12.3.6 Appeals after a plea of guilty

The defendant may appeal against conviction after a plea of guilty but only in exceptional circumstances. These are:

(a) Where the defendant did not appreciate the nature of the charge (*R v Forde* [1923] 2 KB 400).

(b) Where the defendant did not intend to admit that he or she was guilty of the charge (*Forde*). This would include cases where pressure was put on the defendant to plead guilty by either counsel or the trial judge.

(c) Where on the admitted facts the defendant could not in law have been convicted of the offence charged (*Forde*).

(d) In exceptional circumstances where the defendant knew what he was doing when he pleaded guilty, intended to plead guilty and did so unequivocally after having taken legal advice (*R v Lee* [1984] 1 WLR 578).

(e) Where the plea was founded on an incorrect ruling of law on admitted facts which left an accused with no legal escape from a verdict of guilty (*R v Chalkley* [1998] QB 848). If, on the other hand, the defendant pleaded guilty because he realised that as a result of the ruling the evidence against him was so strong that his case was hopeless, no appeal against conviction would apply. In such cases, the accused should plead not guilty and appeal in the normal way. *Chalkley* was followed in *R v Rajcoomar* [1999] Crim LR 728.

The second, wider, approach was preferred in *R v Togher* [2001] 3 All ER 463, to the effect that a plea of guilty following a material irregularity could also found an appeal. In particular, the word 'unsafe' should be applied in a way compatible with the European Convention on Human Rights. Fairness of the trial and the safety of conviction went together. Denial of a fair trial almost inevitably rendered the conviction unsafe. See **12.3.2**.

Note that where the appellant appeals after a plea of guilty, there is no power to substitute a verdict of guilty of an alternative offence under CAA 1968, s 3.

12.3.7 Single right of appeal

Under the CAA 1968, the appellant has the right to bring an appeal before the Court of Appeal. If that appeal is dismissed, he or she has no right to bring a second appeal on the

252 Appeals to the Court of Appeal

same matter (see *R v Pinfold* [1988] QB 462). Two apparent exceptions were recognised in *Pinfold*:

- where an appellant seeks to revive an abandoned appeal;
- where, owing to some defect in the procedure, the appellant has, on the first appeal being dismissed, suffered an injustice, such as where he or she was not notified of a hearing date.

In *R v Thomas* [2002] EWCA 941, the Court of Appeal held that it was not bound by the rule in *Pinfold* when dealing with a case which had been referred to it by the Criminal Cases Review Commission (see **12.13**). The power to make such a re-determination, however, should be limited to 'exceptional circumstances'. The court found it difficult to envisage such exceptional circumstances, but concluded that they would have to be such as to convince the court that if the case had been argued in that way on the previous occasion, it would, not might, have quashed the conviction. In any event, the court should be very slow to differ from the earlier judgment.

It appears that the appellant has a separate right of appeal on the basis that the proceedings were a nullity, as the powers of the Court of Appeal to issue a *venire de novo* (an order returning the proceedings to the point immediately before the error, so that it can be corrected) exist independently of CAA 1968. See also *R v Lamming* (1989) 90 Cr App R 450.

12.3.8 Appeals in the case of death

Prior to the CAA 1995, there was no procedure whereby the conviction of a deceased person could be challenged on appeal. The CAA 1995, s 7 inserts an entirely new provision into the CAA 1968. Section 44A now gives a person approved by the Court of Appeal the right to begin or continue an appeal after the death of the deceased.

The persons approved by the Court of Appeal under s 44A(3) must be one of the following:

- the widow or widower of the deceased;
- his or her personal representatives;
- any other person who, by family or other similar relationship with the deceased, has a substantial financial or other interest in the determining of the appeal.

The application for approval must be made within one year of death (s 44A(4)).

R v Whelan [1997] Crim LR 659, is believed to be the first application under this section. A widow was held to be entitled to continue her deceased husband's appeal against conviction for assault on his daughter, where only death had prevented him from pursuing the appeal himself.

12.4 Evidence

Under the CAA 1968, as amended by the CAA 1995, s 4, the Court of Appeal may receive any evidence if it considers that it is necessary or expedient in the interests of justice.

The CAA 1968, s 23, as amended, provides as follows:

(1) *For purposes of an appeal under this part of this Act [appeals against conviction and/or sentence and references to the Court of Appeal by the Home Secretary] the Court of Appeal may, if they think it necessary or expedient in the interests of justice—*

(a) order *the production of any document, exhibit or other thing connected with the proceedings, the production of which appears to them necessary for the determination of the case;*

(b) *order any witness who would have been a compellable witness in the proceedings from which the appeal lies to attend for examination and be examined before the court, whether or not he was called in those proceedings; and*

(c) *receive any evidence which was not adduced in the proceedings from which the appeal lies.*

(2) The Court of Appeal shall, in considering whether to receive any evidence, have regard in particular to—

   (a) whether the evidence appears to the Court to be capable of belief;

   (b) whether it appears to the Court that the evidence may afford any ground for allowing the appeal;

   (c) whether the evidence would have been admissible in the proceedings from which the appeal lies on an issue which is the subject of the appeal; and

   (d) whether there is a reasonable explanation for the failure to adduce the evidence in those proceedings.

(3) Subsection (1)(c) above applies to any evidence of a witness (including the appellant) who is competent but not compellable.

(4) For purposes of an appeal under this Part of this Act, the Court of Appeal may, if they think it necessary or expedient in the interests of justice, order the examination of any witness whose attendance might be required under subsection (1)(b) above to be conducted, in a manner provided by rules of court, before any judge or officer of the Court or other person appointed by the Court for the purpose, and allow the admission of any depositions so taken as evidence before the Court.

In *R v Pendleton* [2002] 1 WLR 72, the House of Lords considered that the correct test to be applied, where fresh evidence was to be admitted, was whether the conviction was safe, and not whether the accused was guilty. This was a matter for the judgment of the Court of Appeal, which should apply the test from the viewpoint of the effect of the fresh evidence on the minds of members of the court, and not the presumed effect on the minds of the trial jury. However, it would usually be appropriate for the court to ask itself the question, to test its provisional view, whether the evidence, if given at the trial, might reasonably have affected the decision of the trial jury to convict. If so, the conviction should be regarded as unsafe.

In *R v Hanratty* [2002] EWCA 1141, the Court of Appeal held that the overriding consideration in deciding whether fresh evidence should be admitted was whether the evidence would assist the Court to achieve justice, which may either be by upholding a conviction which was safe or setting it aside if it was unsafe. Fresh evidence may be admitted where, though not relevant to a specific ground of appeal, it was relevant to the overall question of the guilt or innocence of the appellant. Where the issue before the court was the safety of the conviction, ie the guilt of the appellant, fresh evidence would usually be admitted. Where the issue before the court was the fairness of the proceedings, fresh evidence would not usually be admissible because it did not deal with the defect at the trial, unless it placed the defect in its context. This approach was particularly important where the Court was dealing with old cases where standards have changed over the years. The Court would be expected to enforce standards, but this did not apply where the rule was not in force at the time of the trial.

For recent examples see *R v Winzar* [2002] EWCA 2950, *R v Jacques* [2003] All ER (D) 26 and *R v Mynott* [2003] All ER (D) 39.

The following points may be noted about s 23 of the CAA 1968:

(a) The test for receiving evidence is that of the interests of justice. See *R v Jones*, *The Times*, 23 July 1996, where the court received fresh medical evidence, even though there was no strong argument to do so, holding that it was expedient in the interests of justice.

(b) The section permits any evidence to be called before the Court of Appeal, whether or not it was called at the trial (*R v Mercer* [2001] All ER (D) 187).

(c) If evidence is to be received, the matters contained in s 23(2) are important. These points, however, are merely matters to which the court should have regard and not conditions for the admissibility of the evidence namely:

   (i)   whether the evidence appears to be capable of belief;

   (ii) whether the evidence affords any ground for allowing the appeal;

   (iii) whether the evidence would have been admissible;

   (iv) where there is a reasonable explanation for not calling the evidence at trial.

(d) Section 23(2)(a) provides that the evidence must be 'capable of belief', replacing the old test of 'likely to be credible'. In *R v Parks* [1961] 1 WLR 1484, it was held that 'likely to be credible' meant whether the witness's proof of evidence was intrinsically credible, and whether it fitted in with at least some of the other evidence in the case.

(e) As to whether there is a 'reasonable explanation' for the failure to adduce evidence at the trial, the case of *R v Beresford* (1971) 56 Cr App R 143, on precisely similar words, decided that the test was whether the evidence could have been obtained with 'reasonable diligence'.

(f) Rules on the receipt of fresh evidence have more relevance to factual evidence than to expert evidence, as experts are interchangeable to a certain extent, and if there is only one expert, and that expert is unavailable, the case may be postponed. See *R v Jones* [1997] 1 Cr App R 86. Fresh expert evidence will be received in appropriate circumstances, however. In *R v Latte* (1996), fresh expert evidence was called and the Court of Appeal accepted that there was a reasonable explanation for not adducing the evidence at trial because the field of expertise (lighting and facial recognition) was highly specialised and not well known.

(g) The role of the Court of Appeal is not to make a finding of fact but to assess new evidence that has become available since the trial and to make a decision on the safety of the earlier conviction (*R v Twitchell* [2000] 1 Cr App R 373).

(h) *R v Guppy* (1995) 16 Cr App R (S) 25, a decision on the old law, held that on a true construction of ss 11(3) and 23(1)(c), the Court of Appeal is empowered to receive fresh evidence of any witness, including the appellant, on an appeal against sentence. It would seem that this decision will be followed under the new formulation of s 23(1)(c).

(i) In *R v Ahluwalia* [1992] 4 All ER 889, the fresh evidence which the appellant wished to adduce raised a defence which was not raised at the trial (psychiatric reports as to the appellant's diminished responsibility). The Court of Appeal admitted the reports as fresh evidence, concluding that there may have been an arguable defence which, for some unexplained reason, was not raised at the trial.

See also *R v Moringiello* [1997] Crim LR 902, where the Court of Appeal did not allow fresh evidence to be called by the appellant's solicitor that the trial judge had fallen asleep during part of the evidence. Such an allegation had to be made at the time so that it could be known which parts of the evidence the judge was supposed to have missed.

12.5 Appeal against sentence

The right of appeal against sentence after conviction on indictment is found in CAA 1968, s 9. However, the Court of Appeal has always recognised that judges approach the question of sentencing in different ways, and must be allowed a measure of discretion in their approach. Thus, the court will not interfere merely because it would have passed a somewhat different sentence in a particular case.

The following are the most widely accepted grounds of appeal:

(a) *The sentence is wrong in law.* Where the judge passes a sentence which he has no jurisdiction to pass, such as a sentence of imprisonment on someone under the age of 21 years, the Court of Appeal will interfere. However, appeals on such grounds are rare.

(b) *The sentence is wrong in principle.* This contention covers two situations:
   (i) Where the appellant argues that entirely the wrong type of sentence was imposed, such as a sentence of custody when non-custodial measures were appropriate.
   (ii) Where the judge combines two sentences which are inconsistent with each other, such as a sentence of imprisonment and a probation order.

(c) *The sentence is manifestly excessive.* Here the appellant is arguing that the right type of sentence has been imposed, but that in the circumstances it is too severe.

(d) *The judge took the wrong approach to sentencing.* If the trial judge, in passing sentence, has taken into account an irrelevant consideration, such as the fact that the appellant has alleged that the police officers had fabricated their evidence, the sentence is likely to be reduced.

(e) *The judge followed the wrong procedure prior to sentence.* If, following a plea of guilty, there has been a dispute as to the facts of the case, and the judge accepts the prosecution version without any inquiry or investigation, then the Court of Appeal may feel obliged to reduce the sentence. See *R v Newton* (1982) 77 Cr App R 13 and, generally, **11.2.2** above and **13.4.2** below.

(f) *Disparity.* Any disparity between the sentence imposed on co-defendants is probably best seen as merely a factor that the Court of Appeal will take into account when considering an appeal against sentence. It is unlikely, on its own, to support a successful appeal against sentence, but the view of the court has been inconsistent. On the one hand, the court says that if the disparity is so marked that one of the former co-defendants is left with a burning sense of grievance, then it would be right to interfere (see *R v Dickinson* [1977] Crim LR 303). On the other hand, the court has also expressed the view that the mere fact that one sentence is wrong (the lighter sentence) is no reason for altering the right sentence and making two wrong sentences (see *R v Stroud* (1977) 65 Cr App R 150).

(g) *Sense of grievance.* If the sentencing procedure and the actual sentence, taken together, leave the offender with a justifiable sense of grievance, then the Court of Appeal may interfere, notwithstanding that the sentence is not in itself too severe, for example where the offender is sentenced to custody after reports have been ordered, leading him actually and legitimately to expect a non-custodial sentence if the reports are good, and the reports are good (see *R v Gillam* (1980) 2 Cr App R (S) 267, *R v Ward* (1982) 4 Cr App R (S) 103, *R v Jackson* [1996] Crim LR 355 and *R v Horton* (1985) 7 Cr App R (S) 299).

12.6 Procedure for appeal

Preliminary notes: The procedure is the same whether the appeal is against conviction or sentence. The procedure is governed by the CAA 1968, the Criminal Appeal Rules 1968 (SI 1968/1262) and 'the Guide', namely 'A Guide to Proceedings in the Court of Appeal Criminal Division', produced by the Registrar of Criminal Appeals. The latest version of the Guide was produced in 1997. Students should also be familiar with *Practice Direction (criminal: consolidated)* [2002] 3 All ER 904.

Within 28 days of conviction (or sentence if the appeal is against sentence) notice of application for leave to appeal should be served on the Crown Court at which the proceedings took place. If appealing against conviction, counsel should observe the 28-day limit, even if there are practical difficulties, if there has been a delay between conviction and sentence.

The notice of application for leave to appeal is in a standard form (form 2), which includes:

- the name and address of the appellant;
- the name of the court where he or she was tried, the name of the judge and the dates of his or her appearances;
- the offences of which he or she was convicted and the sentence imposed; and
- the application being made.

This will include not only the application for leave but also, where appropriate:

- leave to appeal out of time;
- legal aid;
- bail pending determination of the appeal;
- leave to be present at the hearing; or
- leave to call witnesses.

Another standard form (form 3) sets out the grounds of appeal (see **12.6.2** below). The forms are served on the Crown Court where the proceedings took place, and are then forwarded to the Criminal Appeal Office by the Crown Court.

The notice and grounds must be signed either by the appellant or by someone on his or her behalf.

12.6.1 Transcripts

Once the Registrar at the Criminal Appeal Office has the notice and grounds, he or she may then order a transcript of any necessary part of the trial or summing-up as specified by counsel in the grounds of appeal. It is rare to request a transcript of the entire case and counsel should not do so unless it is essential.

12.6.2 Grounds of appeal

Once counsel has received a copy of the transcript, the grounds of appeal can be set out in full, or 'perfected', as counsel will now have, for example, the exact words with which the judge directed the jury. Counsel has 14 days to perfect the grounds of appeal.

No particular form of words is required when settling the grounds of appeal, but each point on which appeal is being made should be clearly identified, and set out in sufficient detail for the court to identify clearly the matters relied on. It is often convenient to make these points in chronological order. The grounds should refer to the transcript by page and paragraph number, and should cite any authorities upon which counsel proposes to rely. If counsel wishes to call a witness at the appeal, the reason why such a course is necessary should be explained fully. Further, any document referred to should be clearly identified.

Paragraphs 15.1 and 15.2 of *Practice Direction (Criminal: Consolidated)* [2002] 3 All ER 904 provide as follows:

15.1 Advocates should not settle grounds or support them with written advice unless they consider that they are properly arguable. Grounds should be carefully drafted and properly particularised. Advocates should not assume that the court will entertain any ground of appeal not set out and properly particularised. Should leave to amend the grounds be granted it is most unlikely that further grounds will be entertained.

15.2 A copy of the advocate's positive advice about the merits should be attached as part of the grounds.

In appeals against conviction, counsel should send the court a document expanding the grounds of appeal and outlining the arguments he or she intends to place before the court (known as a 'skeleton argument'). This saves time and therefore expense at the hearing of the appeal itself. *Practice Direction (criminal: consolidated)* [2002] 3 All ER 904, paras 17.1 and 17.5 provide as follows:

17.1 In all appeals against conviction a skeleton argument from the advocate for the appellant is to be lodged with the Registrar of Criminal Appeals and served on the prosecuting authority within 14 days of receipt by the advocate of the notification of the grant of leave to appeal against conviction or such longer period as the registrar or the court may direct. The skeleton may refer to an advice, which should be annexed with an indication of which parts of it are relied upon, and should include any additional arguments to be advanced.

17.5 A skeleton argument should contain a numbered list of the points the advocate intends to argue, grouped under each ground of appeal, and stated in no more than one or two sentences. It should be as succinct as possible, the object being to identify each point, not to argue it or elaborate on it. Each listed point should be followed by full references to the material to which the advocate will refer in support of it, ie, the relevant passages in the transcript, authorities etc. It should also contain anything which the advocate would expect to be taken down by the court during the hearing, such as propositions of law, chronologies etc. If more convenient, these can be annexed to the skeletons rather than included in it. For points of law, the skeleton should state the point and cite the principal authority or authorities in support with reference to the passages where the principle is enunciated. Chronologies should, if possible, be agreed with the opposing advocate before the hearing. Respondents' skeletons should follow the same principles.

In order to assist the court, the Criminal Appeal Office prepares a summary of the cases coming before it, once the single judge gives leave to appeal. The summary is entirely objective and does not contain any advice about how the court should deal with the case or any view about its merits. *Practice Direction (criminal: consolidated)* [2002] 3 All ER 904, para 18.1.

The summary consists of two parts. Part I is provided to all advocates in the case (para 18.2), and to unrepresented appellants, unless a judge of the High Court or the Registrar directs to the contrary in a case involving material of an explicitly salacious or sadistic nature (para 18.5). Part I generally contains, according to para 18.2:

- particulars of the proceedings before the Crown Court;
- particulars of the proceedings before the Court of Appeal;

- the facts of the case as drawn from the transcripts, advice of the advocates, witness statements and/or exhibits (if an advocate does not want any factual material in his or her advice to be taken into account, this should be stated in his or her advice);
- the submissions and rulings, summing-up and sentencing remarks.

The contents of the summary are a matter for the writer, but if an advocate wishes to suggest any significant alteration, he or she should write to the Registrar. If the writer does not agree, the summary and the letter are put before the court.

Part II is for the court alone, and contains:

- a summary of the grounds of appeal;
- in appeals against sentence (and applications for leave) summaries of the antecedent histories of the parties and any relevant pre-sentence medical or other reports.

12.6.3 The single judge

The application for leave to appeal, and any other applications (see **12.6**), is placed before the single judge. No oral submission or arguments are heard by the single judge, who decides the matter on the basis of the papers before him or her.

If the single judge refuses to grant leave, the appellant has 14 days to renew the application before the full court, whose decision is final. When applying for leave to the single judge, or to the full court, the appellant should bear in mind the court's power to order 'loss of time' (see **12.8.1**).

The court has power to extend the 14-day time limit, but very rarely does so (see *R v Dixon* [2000] 1 WLR 782).

Where the single judge grants leave in respect of certain grounds of appeal, but expressly refuses leave in respect of others, the latter grounds may only be argued on appeal with leave of the full court (*R v Jackson* [1999] 1 All ER 572). Further guidance on this issue was given in *R v Cox and Thomas* [1999] 2 Cr App R 6.

12.7 Powers of the single judge

Most of the powers of the Court of Appeal, short of deciding the appeal itself, are exercised by the single judge of the court under the CAA 1968, s 31. The single judge has power to:

(a) Grant leave to appeal.

(b) Allow the appellant to be present at the hearing of the appeal. Under the CAA 1968, s 22(1), the appellant is entitled to be present at the hearing of an appeal even if he or she is in custody. However, if the appellant is in custody, he or she is not entitled to be present if the appeal is on the ground of law alone, nor on any preliminary application, without leave.

(c) Order a witness to attend for examination. The court may order a witness to appear before it, in pursuance of an appeal under the CAA 1968, s 23. This has the advantage of allowing both parties to the appeal to cross-examine.

(d) Allow bail pending the appeal hearing. Under the CAA 1968, s 19, the court has the power to grant bail to an appellant pending the hearing of the appeal.

Appeals to the Court of Appeal

However, bail is granted only rarely, and only where it appears that the appeal is likely to be successful; or where the sentence is so short that it is likely to have been served before the appeal can be heard. In deciding whether to grant bail, the true test is, 'are there exceptional circumstances which would drive the court to the conclusion that justice can only be done by the granting of bail?' (*per* Geoffrey Lane LJ in *R v Watton* (1978) 68 Cr App R 293).

(e) Make, vary or discharge orders, for example, as to whether the appellant is in custody or on bail pending retrial.

(f) Make orders as to the costs of the appeal, including legal aid.

(g) Give directions for loss of time (see **12.8.1**).

12.7.1 Powers of the Registrar

By virtue of the CAA 1968, s 31A, inserted by the CAA 1995, s 6, certain of these powers may be exercised by the Registrar. These are:

- to extend the time within which notice of application for leave to appeal may be given;
- to order a witness to attend for examination;
- to vary the conditions of bail granted by either the Court of Appeal or the Crown Court. However, he or she may not do so unless satisfied that the prosecution does not object to the variation (s 31A(3)).

If the Registrar refuses any of these applications, the appellant may apply to the single judge.

12.8 Powers of the Court of Appeal

12.8.1 Following appeal against conviction

Having heard the appeal against conviction the Court of Appeal may do any of the following:

(a) Dismiss the appeal.

(b) Allow the appeal and quash the conviction.

(c) Allow part of the appeal and dismiss the other part. If it does this, the court may pass a new sentence on the remaining conviction, but this must not be greater than the sentence as a whole passed by the convicting court (CAA 1968, s 4(3)). For example, the defendant is convicted of two offences and sentenced to one year's imprisonment on each to run consecutively. On appeal, one conviction is quashed. The Court of Appeal may increase the sentence on the remaining conviction to up to two years, this being the total imposed by the convicting court.

(d) Find the appellant guilty of an alternative offence. Under the CAA 1968, s 3, if the appellant has been convicted of one offence, but the jury, under the Criminal Law Act 1967, s 6, could have found him or her guilty of another offence, then the court may substitute a conviction for that other offence. Thus, if the jury has convicted of murder, the court may substitute a verdict of guilty of manslaughter. Further, if the defendant is charged with two counts in the alternative, and is convicted on one but the jury is discharged from giving a verdict on the other, the court may reverse the verdicts. The court must consider that the jury was satisfied of facts which proved him or her guilty of the other offence. See *R v Spratt* [1980] 1 WLR 554 and *R v Peterson* [1997] Crim LR 339. Section 4(3) of the CAA 1968 applies. The power under s 3 to find the appellant guilty of an alternative offence only applies where the appellant pleaded not guilty at the trial (*R v Horsman* [1998] QB 531).

The CJA 2003 s 316, however, creates a new s 3A, under which a defendant who has pleaded guilty may be found guilty of an alternative offence. This will apply where the defendant has been convicted of an offence to which he has pleaded guilty; if he has not so pleaded, he could have pleaded guilty to or been found guilty of another offence, and it appears to the Court of Appeal that the original plea of guilty indicates an admission by the appellant of facts which prove him guilty of the other offence. In these circumstances, the Court of Appeal may, instead of allowing or dismissing the appeal, substitute for the appellant's plea of guilty a plea of guilty to the other offence. It may also pass sentence on the substitute offence, but not of greater severity than the sentence imposed by the original court.

(e) Determine the appeal summarily under the CAA 1968, s 20. If the Registrar considers that an appeal has no real merit, he or she may put it before the Court for 'summary determination'. The Court may, if it is of the same opinion, simply dismiss it without a full hearing and without hearing argument from either side. This process is to discourage vexatious or frivolous appeals, and applies to all appeals, whether on points of pure law, fact, or mixed fact and law.

(f) Order a retrial. Under the CAA 1968, s 7, the court may order a retrial if it considers that a retrial is required in the interests of justice. The power to order a retrial is generally available, whether the appeal is on the basis of fresh evidence, or because of some irregularity or misdirection in the trial.

(g) Make an order for loss of time. Under the CAA 1968, s 29(1), any time spent in custody pending the determination of the appeal is to be reckoned as part of the term of any custody sentence which has been imposed, subject to any directions to the contrary that the Court may give. Such directions may be given where either the single judge or the full Court refuse leave to appeal.

Practice Direction (crime: consolidated) [2002] 3 All ER 904, para 16.1 provides:

16.1 Both the court and the single judge have power in their discretion to direct that part of the time during which an applicant is in custody after putting in his notice of application for leave to appeal should not count towards sentence. Those who contemplate putting in such a notice and their legal advisers should bear this in mind. It is important that those contemplating an appeal should ask advice and should remember that it was useless to appeal without grounds and that grounds should be substantial and particularised and not a mere formula. Where an application devoid of merit has been refused by the single judge and a direction for loss of time has been made, the full court, on renewal of the application, may direct that additional time shall be lost if it, once again, thinks it right so to exercise its discretion in all the circumstances of the case.

See *R v Hart* [2006] EWCA Crim 3239 for a discussion of s 29 and the Consolidated Criminal Practice Direction.

In addition, the Court of Appeal has inherent powers, independent of the CAA 1968, to issue a writ of *venire de novo*. If there has been such an irregularity at the trial that the trial can be said to have been a nullity, and the appellant was never in danger of a valid conviction, then the court may order the writ of *venire de novo* to be issued and the appellant may be retried. The irregularity has to be so fundamental that there could not be said to have been a trial (*R v Rose* [1982] AC 822, followed in *R v Booth, Holland and Wood* [1999] 1 Cr App R 457).

See also Patrick O'Connor, 'The Court of Appeal Retrials and Tribulations' [1990] Crim LR 615.

12.8.2 Following appeal against sentence

Having heard the appeal against sentence the court may:

- Quash any sentence or order which is the subject of the appeal.
- Impose any sentence that was available to the Crown Court, except that it may not deal with the appellant, taking the sentence as a whole, more severely than he or she was originally dealt with.

12.8.3 Following an appeal against sentence after summary conviction

Under the CAA 1968, s 10, the Court of Appeal also has the power to deal with an appeal against a sentence imposed by the Crown Court after the defendant has been convicted summarily. Section 10 covers two separate situations:

(a) *After committal for sentence*. A defendant who has been summarily convicted and committed to the Crown Court for sentence may appeal against that sentence if:
   (i) the sentence was to imprisonment or detention in a young offenders institution for a term of six months or more; or
   (ii) the sentence was one which the magistrates did not have power to pass; or
   (iii) the sentence included disqualification from driving, a recommendation for deportation, or activation of a suspended sentence.
(b) *Breach of a community order or conditional discharge*. A defendant who has been summarily convicted of an offence which puts him or her in breach of a community order or conditional discharge, and who is sentenced by the Crown Court for the original offence, may appeal against that sentence in the same circumstances as set out in (a) above.

12.8.4 The Human Rights Act 1998

The Human Rights Act 1998, s 4, provides the Court of Appeal (together with the other superior courts) with the power to make a declaration of incompatibility, ie that a provision of primary legislation is incompatible with Convention rights. Section 5 further provides that if the Court is considering making such a declaration, the Crown is entitled to notice in accordance with rules of court. The Criminal Appeal (Amendment) Rules 2000 (SI 2000 No. 2036) amend the Criminal Appeal Rules 1968 accordingly.

Section 5(2) of the 1998 Act entitles a Minister of the Crown (or person nominated by him or her), a member of the Scottish Executive, a Northern Ireland Minister or a Northern Ireland department, on giving notice, to be joined as a party to the proceedings.

12.9 The appeal against acquittal and order for retrial

12.9.1 The right to appeal

Since 2004, the prosecution may appeal against the acquittal of the defendant by the Crown Court, if certain conditions are satisfied, by virtue of CJA 2003 ss 75–97. It also applies to acquittals following a successful appeal against conviction.

The right to appeal under this section is not available for every offence, but only for the offences listed in Sch 5 to the Act. These are the most serious offences and include murder, manslaughter, rape, arson endangering life, and war crimes. There is no appeal under these sections where the defendant was found guilty or found not guilty either by reason of insanity or in respect of which he has been found to be under a disability (CJA 2003, s 75(a), (b) and (c)).

Note that s 75(4) makes provision for the retrial of offences where the offender was acquitted outside the UK.

In order to take advantage of this right to appeal, under the CJA 2003, s 76, a prosecutor applies to the Court of Appeal for an order:

- quashing a person's acquittal; and
- ordering his retrial for the offence.

12.9.2 Procedure

There is a two-stage procedure in applying for the above order.

(a) The order may only be applied for with the consent of the Director of Public Prosecutions (s 76). Such consent will only be given if:
   (i) there is new and compelling evidence (see below);
   (ii) it is in the public interest for the application to proceed; and
   (iii) it does not conflict with the treaty obligations under Article 31 or 34 of the Treaty on European Union (the Articles essentially prevent the bringing of new proceedings as opposed to opening up old proceedings).

(b) The prosecutor must seek the leave of the Court of Appeal. The basic steps are as follows, as set out by the CJA 2003, s 80:
   (i) the prosecution must give notice of application to the Court of Appeal;
   (ii) within two days of such notice, the prosecutor must give notice to the person affected. This time limit may be extended if the person affected is outside the UK;
   (iii) the Court of Appeal must consider the application at a hearing;
   (iv) the person is entitled to be present at the hearing, and whether or not he is present, he is entitled to be represented;
   (v) the Court of Appeal may, if it thinks it necessary in the interests of justice, order the production of any document or exhibit or the appearance of any compellable witness;
   (vi) the Court of Appeal may hear more than one application at one hearing but only if the matters could be tried together on the same indictment.

12.9.3 New and compelling evidence

Section 78 of the CJA 2003 provides that there must be new and compelling evidence against the acquitted person. Under s 78(2), evidence is new if it was not adduced in the proceedings in which the person was acquitted, or from which he appealed. An example of such evidence is new testing techniques.

Under s 78(3), evidence is compelling if:

- it is reliable;
- it is substantial; and
- in the context of the outstanding issues, it appears highly probative of the case against the acquitted person. The outstanding issues are the issues in dispute in the proceedings in which the person was acquitted and, if those were appeal proceedings, any other issues remaining in dispute from earlier proceedings to which the appeal related.

12.9.4 Determination by the Court of Appeal

If the Court of Appeal is dealing with an appeal against acquittal, it must make the order applied for and if not, must dismiss the application, if the requirements under the CJA 2003, ss 78 and 79 are met (see above).

In addition, the Court of Appeal must be satisfied, under s 9, that it is in the interests of justice for the court to make the order. In determining this issue, the Court of Appeal will have regard, under s 79, to:

(a) whether existing circumstances make a fair trial unlikely;

(b) for the purposes of that question and otherwise, the length of time since the offence was committed;

(c) whether it is likely that the new evidence would have been adduced in the earlier proceedings against the acquitted person but for the failure by an officer or by a prosecutor to act with due diligence;

(d) whether since those proceedings (or since the commencement of this part of the Act, if later) any officer or prosecutor has failed to act with due diligence.

See by way of example, *R v Dunlop* [2006] EWCA Crim 1354, the first instance of this power being used. The defendant had been acquitted of murder but subsequently informally admitted the offences, and was recharged. At the retrial, he pleaded guilty to murder. See also *R v Miell* [2007] EWCA Crim 3130 where the CA had to form its own view as to whether the acquitted person's subsequent plea of guilty to perjury at his trial constituted compelling evidence that he had committed the offence charged (murder).

12.10 Other methods of appeal

12.10.1 The Attorney-General's reference

Under the Criminal Justice Act 1972, s 36(1), where a defendant has been acquitted following a trial on indictment, the Attorney-General may refer any point of law that arose in the case to the Court of Appeal for its opinion. The purpose is to prevent potentially false decisions becoming too widely accepted. Whatever conclusion the Court of Appeal reaches on the point of law, the acquittal is not affected.

In order to bring proceedings under s 36, the Attorney-General serves a notice on the defendant within 28 days, containing the point of law to be argued, a summary of the argument, and the authorities the Attorney-General relies on. The Court of Appeal must hear the argument from the Attorney-General or his representative, and may hear submissions from the defence.

Under s 36(3), the Court of Appeal may refer the point to the House of Lords, either on its own initiative or following an application from either party. The House of Lords then considers the matter and gives its opinion.

12.10.2 Reference by the Attorney-General on a matter of sentence

Under the CJA 1988, ss 35 and 36, the Attorney-General may refer a sentence, which includes any order made by a court when dealing with an offender, to the Court of Appeal for review if:

(a) he or she considers that the sentence was 'unduly lenient' (this may, but need not, be because the Attorney-General considers that the judge erred in law as to his powers of sentence);

(b) leave of the Court of Appeal is granted; and

(c) the offence was triable only on indictment, or was triable either way but specified as reviewable in an order made by the Home Secretary.

By the Criminal Justice Act 1988 (Reviews of Sentencing) Order 1994 (SI 1994/119), indecent assault, threats to kill, cruelty to a person under 16, and attempts or incitement to commit any of these offences are specified as reviewable.

If an offender is sentenced for two separate matters, only one of which is triable only on indictment or specified as reviewable, they are to be treated as having been passed in the same proceeding if they are passed on the same day, or passed on different days but ordered to be treated as one sentence by the sentencing court. Thus, sentences may be reviewed by the Court of Appeal even though they do not fall within (c) above.

The procedure for bringing a sentencing reference is the same as for bringing an appeal against sentence (see **12.6**). The Court of Appeal may quash any sentence, and impose such a sentence as it thinks appropriate, provided it is a sentence which the Crown Court had power to pass.

The correct approach to sentencing references was set out by the Court of Appeal in *Attorney-General's Reference (No 4 of 1989)* [1990] 1 WLR 41:

- the sentence must be *unduly* lenient, that is it must fall out of the range of sentences which the judge could reasonably consider appropriate;
- assuming that it is unduly lenient, the court still has a discretion as to whether to exercise its powers;
- the court's powers are not confined to increasing the sentence.

According to *R v Krivee* [2007] *The Times* 24 April, mitigation might well justify a subsequent departure from established sentencing guidelines and trial judges should not hesitate to impose the right sentence merely because they fear a reference by the AG. Nor should the AG ignore the fact that a substantial departure from the guidelines will not automatically justify intervening.

For examples, see *R v Shaw, Attorney-General's Reference (No 28 of 1996)* and *R v Harnett, Attorney-General's Reference (No 60 of 1996)*, both reported in *The Times*, 27 January 1997 and *Attorney-General's Reference (No 110 of 2002)* [2003] EWCA Crim 540.

Further reading: Ralph Henham, '*Attorney-General's Reference* Revisited' (1998) 62(5) JCL 468.

12.11 Appeal to the House of Lords

Under the CAA 1968, s 33, either the prosecution or defendant may appeal from any decision of the Court of Appeal to the House of Lords if:

- leave is granted by either the Court of Appeal or the House of Lords; and
- the Court of Appeal certifies that the case raises a point of law of general public importance which ought to be considered by the House of Lords. There is no appeal against the court's refusal to grant a certificate. See *R v Tang, The Times*, 23 May 1995.

One of the effects of s 33 is that the prosecutor may appeal to the House of Lords against the order of the Court of Appeal quashing the appellant's conviction. If the prosecutor is successful in the House of Lords, the conviction will be restored.

Students are also referred to Criminal Procedure Rules Part 74.

12.12 Reference to the European Court of Justice

Under the Criminal Procedure Rules 2005, Part 75, the Court of Appeal has power to refer a case to the European Court of Justice at any time before the determination of the appeal (see *Archbold*, 2008 edn, paras 7–315 to 7–318 and *Blackstone's Criminal Practice*, 2008 edn, para D29.3 for details).

12.13 The Criminal Cases Review Commission

Prior to 1997, the Home Secretary had the power to refer a case, or any point arising in it, to the Court of Appeal (CAA 1968, s 17). The reference was made in the exercise of the Home Secretary's discretion and could be made whether or not the defendant had made an application to the Home Secretary for the reference to be made. In any event the defendant could not be prejudiced by the reference as the Court of Appeal had no power to order loss of time in these circumstances.

If the whole case was referred, it was treated as if it were an appeal to the Court of Appeal by the defendant, who was then able to raise any questions of law, fact or mixed law and fact.

However, it became clear that the power was not satisfactory. In practice, the Home Secretary only referred cases to the Court of Appeal where there was fresh evidence, or some other significant matter arose which had not been investigated at the trial. In 1991, the then Home Secretary announced the creation of a Royal Commission on Criminal

Justice to examine the ways in which alleged miscarriages of justice were dealt with. As a result of the recommendations of the Royal Commission, the Criminal Cases Review Commission (the Commission) was established by the CAA 1995, replacing the Home Secretary's power to refer matters to the Court of Appeal. The Commission started work on 1 April 1997. See the website at <http://www.ccrc.gov.uk>.

What follows is a general outline of the work of the Commission. A full discussion is beyond the scope of this manual.

12.13.1 Membership of the Commission

The Commission is a body corporate and is intended to be independent of government and the courts. It must consist of at least 11 members, appointed by Her Majesty on the recommendation of the Prime Minister. At least one-third must be legally qualified. At least two-thirds must be persons who have knowledge or experience of any aspect of the criminal justice system, and at least one of them should have such knowledge in relation to Northern Ireland. It may be noted that no specific requirement is made as to any representation from ethnic minorities, or of any technical or forensic expertise. Fourteen members have initially been appointed, under the chairmanship of Sir Frederick Crawford.

12.13.2 Making the reference

The Commission may refer to the Court of Appeal any conviction or sentence following a trial on indictment, such a reference being treated as an appeal by the person concerned, under the CAA 1968, s 1 (CAA 1995, s 9). Section 11 makes similar provisions in relation to a person convicted in a magistrates' court, referring the matter to the Crown Court.

Under the CAA 1995, s 13, three conditions must be fulfilled before any matter will be referred to the Court of Appeal:

(a) The Commission must consider that there is a 'real possibility that the conviction, verdict, finding or sentence would not be upheld were the reference to be made'.

(b) The Commission must consider this:

   (i) in the case of a conviction, on the basis of an argument or evidence not raised in the trial *or* there must be exceptional circumstances which justify the reference;

   (ii) in the case of a sentence, on the basis of an argument on a point of law, or information not raised in the proceedings.

(c) The appeal procedure has been followed without success or leave to appeal has been refused *or* there are exceptional circumstances which justify a reference.

The result of these conditions is that in general a reference will only be made if there is fresh evidence leading to a real possibility that the conviction will be quashed. It remains to be seen whether the Commission will exercise its power to refer a matter in exceptional circumstances in situations where there is no fresh evidence, but the existing evidence is weak and unsatisfactory.

In deciding whether to make a reference, the Commission should also have regard, under s 14(2) and (3), to the following:

(a) Any application or representations made to the Commission by or on behalf of the person to whom it relates. Note that the reference may be made without any application being made to it by the person to whom it relates (s 14(1)).

(b) Any other representations made to the Commission in relation to it.

(c) Any point on which it desires the assistance of the Court of Appeal.

(d) Any other matters which appear to the Commission to be relevant.

Since there is no mention of a time limit in the CAA 1995 and given the retrospectivity of the HRA 1998, s 22(4), the Commission is entitled to refer a case to the Court of Appeal no matter how old the conviction. The only question for the Court of Appeal when hearing an appeal against conviction in these circumstances is whether the conviction was unsafe. See *R v Kansal* [2001] 3 WLR 751.

For an example of a reference by the Commission to the Court of Appeal, see *R v Bentley* [2001] 1 Cr App R 21.

12.13.3 Information to the parties

Where the Commission decides to refer the matter to the court, it shall inform the court, and any likely party to the proceedings, of its reasons for making the reference (s 14(4)). Further, where the Commission decides not to make a reference after an application has been made to it, the Commission must give the applicant the reasons for not so doing.

12.13.4 Investigations

The Commission has no power to carry out investigations into alleged miscarriages of justice. Instead, the police will be asked to carry out investigations for them, acting in a manner which is similar to the Police Complaints Authority. The Commission may require an appropriate person from the body which carried out the original investigation to appoint someone to make enquiries and report back to the Commission (CAA 1995, s 19(1)). In the majority of cases this will be a police force, and the appropriate person will be the Chief Constable. The Chief Constable may be required to appoint someone from his own force or another force. See also *Boyle v Criminal Cases Review Commission* [2007] EWHC 8 (Admin) (7 March 2007) for a discussion of the CCRC.

12.13.5 Relationship with the Court of Appeal

For a discussion of the relationship between the Commission and the Court of Appeal, see *R v Criminal Cases Review Commission, ex p Pearson* [1999] 3 All ER 498, where the appellant was convicted of murder and wished the Commission to refer her case to the Court of Appeal. The Commission refused to do so, on the basis that there was no likelihood that the Court of Appeal would receive the fresh evidence that the appellant wished to adduce, and there was therefore no real possibility that the conviction would be quashed. The appellant sought judicial review, in which the following principles were set out:

(a) The role of the Commission was to try to predict the response of the Court of Appeal, and it could only do this by making its own assessment based on the same process of reasoning that the Court of Appeal might follow. To do so was not to usurp the function of the Court of Appeal.

(b) The Commission's reasoning did not include any defects which would allow the court to interfere, and the conclusion of the Commission was not irrational and not legally misdirected. The issue was within the Commission's discretion and the only role for the court in such cases was to ensure that the Commission had acted lawfully.

Three final points may be made about the Commission:

(a) The Court of Appeal is not restricted to dealing with the matter on the point referred to, but may examine the case as a whole (s 14(5)).

(b) The Court of Appeal has the discretionary power, if practical considerations so demand, to adjourn an appeal referred to it by the Commission (see *R v Smith* [1999] 2 Cr App R 444).

(c) Once a reference has been made to the Court of Appeal on whatever grounds, an appellant may put forward additional grounds of appeal that he or she has been advised could be pursued, arising from the original trial, despite the fact that the Commission has previously rejected them. The Commission does not act in the same way as the 'single judge'. See *R v Smith* [2002] EWCA Crim 2907.

13

Procedure between conviction and sentence

13.1 Advance indications of the sentence

The traditional position has been that, if he or she wished to do so, a Crown Court judge may—prior to the indictment being put to the accused for plea—indicate that the sentence either will or will not take a particular form, regardless of how the accused pleads (see *R v Turner* [1970] 2 QB 321 at 327). Such indications would usually be given to counsel privately in the judge's room, and then communicated to the accused by defence counsel. The Court of Appeal for many years took the view that such visits by counsel to the judge should be extremely rare. Their concerns were twofold. First, a pre-trial promise of this nature would restrict the court's freedom of action if and when the time eventually came to pass sentence. The court would be bound by the judge's indication, even if there was an adjournment prior to sentence and a different judge eventually dealt with the accused (see *R v Moss* (1984) 5 Cr App R (S) 209). Second, and of greater significance, was the fear that defendants would plead guilty, be sentenced and then appeal against their conviction on the ground that they had been pressured into pleading guilty, in the knowledge of the indication of sentence. For that reason, the Court in *Turner* said that indications of sentence had to be made *regardless of plea*. If a judge fell into the trap of differentiating between sentences on the basis of different pleas, the Court of Appeal would treat any guilty plea as a nullity, quash the conviction and order a re-arraignment. Nevertheless, such indications were often seen by defence counsel as valuable—in cases where defence counsel suspects that the defendant is saying he or she is not guilty but really wants to plead guilty and is being prevented from doing so by the fear that he or she will be sent to prison. An indication from the judge can save court time in these situations and can be good for the defendant as the eventual sentence will reflect some credit for the guilty plea.

Recently, there have been some developments affecting both magistrates' courts and the Crown Court. Advance indications may now be given in the magistrates' court but only as part of a mode of trial determination and are therefore intended to assist the accused in choosing between the magistrates' court and Crown Court as the trial venue (see MCA 1980, s 20A, inserted by the CJA 2003; and **4.2.2**). For the Crown Court, the Court of Appeal has had a partial change of opinion. In *R v Goodyear* [2005] ECWA Crim 888, the Court stated that the time had come to revisit the applicability of the *Turner* practice and convened a five-judge court to do so. Having reminded itself that the Runciman Royal Commission on Criminal Justice had recommended modification of the *Turner* practice in its 1993 Report, and that further suggestions for change had been made by Auld LJ in his Review of the Criminal Courts in 2001, the court said that there was now a very different culture from that pertaining when *Turner* was decided. The court felt that a significant distinction could be made between:

(a) indicating sentence to a defendant who had deliberately chosen to seek it from the judge; and

(b) an unsolicited indication directed to him from the judge via defence counsel.

The latter was simply the defendant's attempt to substitute his 'legitimate reliance on [defence] counsel's assessment of the likely sentence with the more accurate indication provided by the judge himself'. It emphasised that its aim was not to water down the 'essential principle that the defendant's plea must always be made voluntarily and free from any improper pressure'.

The court laid down the following guidance (and to the extent that it runs counter to *Turner*, the previous practice need no longer be followed):

- A judge should only give an advance indication of sentence when a defendant seeks one. However, the judge can remind defence counsel that the defendant is entitled to seek such an indication. The normal stage to seek an indication would be at the plea-and-case-management hearing.

- Any indication of sentence by a judge should normally be confined to a statement of the maximum sentence if a plea of guilty were to be tendered at the stage of proceedings when the indication is sought. Nothing should be said about possible sentence following a trial, unless the judge indicates that the sentence will or will not take a particular form regardless of plea (the old *Turner* exception).

- The judge retains an unfettered discretion to refuse to give an indication. That discretion may be exercised where, perhaps, the judge feels that the defendant is already under considerable pressure (for example, because of his or her age) and does not wish to add to it. It would remain open to the defendant to ask again at a later stage.

- The judge may also postpone an indication until such time as he or she feels able to give one, for example, once reports on the defendant become available.

- There is no obligation on a judge to give reasons for refusing or postponing an indication of sentence.

- Once an indication is given, if the defendant pleads guilty, it is binding both on that judge and any subsequent judge who assumes responsibility for that case. If, following a fair chance to consider his or her position, the defendant does not plead guilty, then the indication will cease to have effect (and any reference to this process would be inadmissible in a subsequent trial).

- Defence counsel should not seek an indication without signed, written authority from the defendant that he or she wishes an indication to be sought. Defence counsel remains under an obligation to advise the defendant professionally on his or her plea; for example, that he or she should not plead guilty unless he or she is guilty; also that the Attorney General may refer any sentence to the Court of Appeal if he or she feels it to be unduly lenient.

- In order to seek an indication, the factual basis of the plea must be agreed between prosecution and defence and put in writing. Where there is a disputed fact which defence counsel feels is immaterial to sentence, that difference should be recorded as well to enable the judge to make up his or her own mind. If defence counsel seeks an indication in the absence of agreement on the basis of plea, prosecuting counsel should remind the judge of this guidance in *Goodyear*.

- The judge should not become, or be asked to become, involved with any plea bargaining. He or she should not be asked to indicate levels of sentence dependent upon possible different pleas.

- Once an indication is sought, the prosecution should enquire if the judge has access to all of the evidence relied upon by the prosecution, including the defendant's criminal record and any victim impact statements. It may also be appropriate for the prosecution to invite the judge to allow him or her to refer the judge to relevant guidelines from the Court of Appeal or Sentencing Guidelines Council, and to draw attention to any mandatory or minimum sentence requirements. Prosecution counsel should avoid saying anything which may imply that an indication of sentence has the support of the prosecution.

- The defendant would retain the right to appeal against sentence where, for example, it was suggested that the judge had made insufficient allowance for defence mitigation. Likewise, the Attorney General would retain the power to refer unduly lenient sentences to the Court of Appeal under the CJA 1988, s 36.

- In complicated or difficult cases, it would be appropriate to give seven days' written notice to the prosecution and court of an intention to seek an indication. The hearing itself should normally be held in open court, with a record of the proceedings kept, both sides represented, and the defendant present. However, reporting restrictions should normally be imposed for the 'indication' hearing, to be lifted if and when the defendant either pleads guilty or is found guilty.

- This practice is, for the time being, confined to the Crown Court whilst its effects can be considered.

13.2 Advising on sentence

Counsel has to rely upon knowledge of the tariff for the offence in question and on prior experience (if any) of the judge. There are suggestions (see *R v Cain* [1976] Crim LR 464) that, when completely unsure as to what the penalty is likely to be, counsel can ask the judge for a private *and confidential* indication of what the latter has in mind. In basing advice on such an indication, counsel would not reveal to the accused that he or she had seen the judge. In the light of *R v Turner*, however, it is highly unlikely that this procedure would now be approved by the Court of Appeal, and it is rarely, if at all, resorted to in practice. Either the judge gives a *'Turner-type'* indication which can be passed on openly to the accused, or he or she tells counsel nothing at all about the probable sentence.

An accused should always be told, assuming he or she does not know it already, that credit is given to an offender who pleads guilty. He or she receives a lighter sentence than he or she would have done had he or she pleaded not guilty and been found guilty by a jury. Strong advice, stressing the advantage of a guilty plea from the point of view of the eventual sentence, is permissible (*R v Peace* [1976] Crim LR 119), but it must not be so strong as effectively to deprive the accused of his or her free choice as to how he or she pleads (*R v Inns* (1975) 60 Cr App R 231). See also *R v Keily* [1990] Crim LR 204, *R v Smith* [1990] 1 WLR 1311, *R v Pitman* [1991] 1 All ER 468, CA and *R v Thompson* (1995) 159 JP 568.

13.3 Adjournments

The court does not necessarily sentence the offender on the day on which he or she pleads guilty or is found guilty. It has power to adjourn prior to passing sentence. The Crown Court's power to adjourn is one which it possesses at common law; a magistrates' court's power to do so is governed by the Magistrates' Courts Act 1980 (MCA). During the period of an adjournment before sentence, the offender is remanded in custody or on bail. He or she has a prima facie right to bail by reason of the Bail Act 1976 (BA), s 4, but bail may be refused, not only on the grounds which apply before conviction, but also on the ground that the adjournment is for the purpose of preparing a report and it would be impracticable to do that if the offender were at liberty (see BA 1976, Sch 1, Pt I, para 7). Where an offender remanded for reports is granted bail the court may, at its discretion, include a condition that he or she must be available for interview, etc, so that the report can be compiled (BA 1976, s 3(6)(d)).

13.3.1 Adjournments for reports

Independent reports on offenders are often a vital factor in the sentencing decision, coming from sources such as probation officers and social workers producing pre-sentence reports, or from doctors and psychiatrists producing medical reports. Where an accused intimates an intention to plead guilty and it seems likely that the court will need reports before sentencing, the reports are prepared before the hearing if that is at all possible. If, however, the accused is pleading not guilty, it is unlikely that reports will be prepared. Even if pleading guilty, reports are not prepared automatically. Sometimes the court can properly proceed without reports, but in many cases the sentencer's provisional view of the proper sentence will be such that to pass it without consulting a report would either be positively unlawful or at least bad sentencing practice. The court must then adjourn for reports. Two or three weeks will probably be sufficient, although the Crown Court could in theory adjourn for any period. Section 10(3) of the MCA 1980 provides that when magistrates adjourn for reports it must be for not more than four weeks if the offender is remanded on bail, and for not more than three weeks if he or she is in custody.

Section 10(3) of the MCA 1980, which applies to adjournments for any type of report, is supplemented by the Powers of Criminal Courts (Sentencing) Act 2000 (PCC(S)A), s 11, which applies only to medical reports. The main difference between the two sections is that under s 11 the magistrates can adjourn for a medical report even before convicting the accused, provided they are satisfied that the accused committed the *actus reus* of the offence charged. This may enable them to make a *hospital* order without finding the accused guilty. Adjournments under the MCA 1980, s 10(3), on the other hand, presuppose that the magistrates have convicted the accused. In addition, provisions under ss 35 and 36 of the Mental Health Act (MHA) 1983, allow both the Crown Court and magistrates' courts to remand offenders to a hospital for the preparation of reports.

13.3.2 Adjournments where there are several accused

Sentencing joint offenders together should ensure consistent treatment for them all, with any disparity in sentence being justified by the differing degrees to which they were involved in the criminal conduct or by differences in their records.

If there are consistent pleas by the accused, there should be no problem. But, if one accused (A1) pleads guilty and another accused (A2) pleads not guilty, then difficulties arise. A2 obviously cannot be sentenced unless and until he or she is convicted by a jury. The desirability of dealing with A1 and (if convicted) A2 together has led to a general rule that sentence on A1 should be postponed until after the trial of A2. This has the additional advantage of allowing the judge to hear the evidence called at A2's trial, and proportion his or her sentence according to which, if either, of the accused apparently played the leading role in the offence(s) (see *R v Payne* [1950] 1 All ER 102).

However, a special problem arises if A1 is going to be called by the prosecution at the trial of A2, since he or she might be tempted to give false evidence minimising his or her own part in the crime. For this reason, it used to be the practice in such cases to depart from the general rule and sentence A1 before A2's trial (*Payne*). More recently, the Court of Appeal has indicated strongly that the general rule should always be followed, notwithstanding that Al will be a prosecution witness (see *R v Weekes* (1982) 74 Cr App R 161). Perhaps, though, the matter should be left to the discretion of the trial judge, who is in the best position to balance the interests of the co-accused (that the accomplice, when he or she testifies, should have no motive for giving false evidence) against the wider interests of justice (that confederates in crime should be sentenced together so as to avoid unjustified differences in sentence).

If the accomplice is sentenced before testifying for the prosecution, defence counsel in mitigation may outline the evidence his or her client proposes to give. This will no doubt secure a significant reduction in sentence. Should the accomplice fail to give the evidence thus foreshadowed, his or her sentence may *not* be increased (*R v Stone* [1970] 1 WLR 1112).

The desirability of sentencing confederates in crime together applies when they are to be dealt with in the magistrates' court just as much as when they are to be dealt with in the Crown Court.

13.3.3 Adjournments where there are outstanding charges

It is desirable that an accused with several charges outstanding against him or her should be sentenced on one occasion for all matters in respect of which he or she is ultimately convicted. If he or she is sentenced piecemeal by different judges (or even by the same judge on different occasions) there is a danger that the aggregate sentence will be out of proportion to the overall gravity of his or her conduct. There is also a danger that the first judge, dealing perhaps with the less serious offences, will pass a non-custodial sentence and thus create a dilemma for the second judge. The latter may feel that a custodial sentence is necessary for the offences with which he or she is dealing, but to pass such a sentence might prevent the earlier non-custodial sentence running its natural course. To avoid such difficulties, it is **better that one sentencer should deal with everything on one occasion, even if this means adjournments and some extra administrative work behind the scenes.**

Much will depend on whether or not the offences have been joined in the indictment, under r. 14.2(3) Crim PR 2005. A court and jury can try only one indictment at a time, so sentence on one indictment where the accused is found guilty may have to be postponed until trial on a second indictment. Furthermore, where an accused has indictments outstanding against him or her at different locations of the Crown Court, it will be necessary for the Crown Court at one location to transfer its indictment to the Crown Court at the second location (see *R v Bennett* (1980) 2 Cr App R (S) 96).

13.4 The facts of the offence

If the accused pleads guilty, the first stage in the procedure (before sentence is passed) is for the prosecution to present the brief facts of the offence. In the Crown Court this is always the task of counsel, or solicitor with rights of audience in the Crown Court, for the prosecution must be legally represented for proceedings on indictment (*R v George Maxwell Developments Ltd* [1980] 2 All ER 99).

In the magistrates' court, the prosecution case will be presented by a Crown Prosecutor (or by an agent instructed by the CPS). The procedure before sentence is passed is essentially the same in both the Crown Court and magistrates' courts, but it is less formal in the latter.

13.4.1 Presenting the facts

The prosecuting advocate in the Crown Court has the benefit of the statements from the committal proceedings. Counsel summarises the prosecution case based on these statements. He or she will probably describe in sequence: (i) the circumstances, method and gravity of the offence; (ii) the manner in which the offender was arrested; and (iii) his or her questioning at the police station.

Concerning the advocate's account of the offence itself, details which should be included will obviously vary according to the nature of the offence. The degree of planning which apparently preceded the commission of the offence is always a relevant factor, as is any other aggravating factor, eg breach of trust in an offence involving dishonesty committed by an employee against his or her employer.

As to the arrest and questioning of the offender, the judge will want to know whether the offender was frank and co-operative with the police. If he or she was, that is useful mitigation. Also, what the offender said to the police may foreshadow what defence counsel will say in his or her speech in mitigation about the way the offence was committed, the motive for it, and the offender's degree of involvement if it was a joint offence. Where the offender followed up verbal admissions by making a written statement under caution, the advocate can either read it out in full or give the gist of it, whichever seems more convenient.

When presenting the facts, the prosecuting advocate should not try to make the offence seem as serious as possible so as to obtain a heavy sentence. Traditionally, the prosecution has taken a neutral attitude to the sentence which ought to be passed, not asking for any particular sentence. So, the advocate must present the facts fairly in the light of the prosecution evidence contained in the committal statements, conceding to the defence those points in mitigation which are apparent from the statements, but equally giving full weight to any aggravating factors which make the offence a serious one of its type. In particular, if the offender (in his or her statements to the police) or defence advocate (in mitigation) puts forward a version of the facts of the offence which does not accord with the evidence the prosecution has available, the advocate should indicate that he or she cannot accept what the defence is saying about the offence.

Two further points should be made:

(a) The prosecuting advocate should apply for compensation, confiscation or forfeiture if appropriate.

(b) Both prosecuting and defence advocates should draw the court's attention to any limits on its sentencing powers (*R v Komsta* [1990] 12 Cr App R (S) 63). In addition, prosecuting advocate should also mention guideline cases (*R v Panayioutou* [1989] 11 Cr App R (S) 535). See also *R v Hartrey* (1993) 14 Cr App R (S) 507.

It is often appropriate for the judge to receive factual information as to the effect of the offence on the victim, a 'victim personal statement'. *Practice Direction (Criminal: Consolidated)* [2002] 3 All ER 904, para 28, sets out the approach the court should take when dealing with a victim personal statement:

28.1 This section draws attention to a scheme which started on 1 October 2001, to give victims a more formal opportunity to say how a crime has affected them. It may help to identify whether they have a particular need for information, support and protection. It will also enable the court to take the statement into account when determining sentence.

28.2 When a police officer takes a statement from a victim the victim will be told about the scheme and given the chance to make a victim personal statement. A victim personal statement may be made or updated at any time prior to the disposal of the case. The decision about whether or not to make a victim personal statement is entirely for the victim. If the court is presented with a victim personal statement the following approach should be adopted.

(a) The victim personal statement and any evidence in support should be considered and taken into account by the court prior to passing sentence.

(b) Evidence of the effects of an offence on the victim contained in the victim personal statement or other statement, must be in proper form, that is a witness' statement under [s 9 of the Criminal Justice Act 1967] or an expert's report, and served upon the defendant's solicitor or the defendant, if he is not represented, prior to sentence. Except where inferences can properly be drawn from the nature of or circumstances surrounding the offence, a sentencer must not make assumptions unsupported by evidence about the effects of an offence on the victim.

(c) The court must pass what it judges to be the appropriate sentence having regard to the circumstances of the offence and of the offender, taking into account, so far as the court considers it appropriate, the consequences to the victim. The opinions of the victim or the victim's close relatives as to what the sentence should be are therefore not relevant, unlike the consequence of the offence on them. Victims should be advised of this. If, despite this advice, opinions as to sentence are included in the statement, the court should pay no attention to them.

(d) The court should consider whether it is desirable in its sentencing remarks to refer to the evidence provided on behalf of the victim.

13.4.2 Disputes about the facts after a guilty plea

By pleading guilty an offender does not necessarily concede that the prosecution case against him or her is correct in its entirety. He or she admits, of course, that he or she committed the offence described in each of the counts of the indictment to which he or she enters a guilty plea, and if the defence advocate says anything in mitigation which is inconsistent with the pleas the judge will ignore that part of the mitigation or invite the defence to consider a change of plea. But the particulars about an offence given in a count of an indictment are so basic that they only partially reveal whether the offence is a serious or trivial one of its type. Thus, it occasionally happens that an offender quite properly pleads guilty and then, after the facts have been presented by the prosecuting advocate, denies that his or her crime is as grave as has been alleged. However, the sentence can be significantly affected by whether the judge accepts the prosecution statement of facts or the defence mitigation.

Guidance in these circumstances is given by *R v Newton* (1982) 77 Cr App R 13, followed in *R v Costley* (1989) 11 Cr App R (S) 357. After the guilty plea, the judge may either:

- hear whatever evidence the parties wish to call on the disputed issue, and come down on one side or the other (this is usually referred to as a '*Newton* hearing'); or
- act merely on the basis of counsels' respective submissions, in which case he or she must accept the defence version as far as possible; or
- empanel a jury to decide the issue (in such a case a count will be added to the indictment by way of amendment and a trial on that count will ensue, see *R v Eubank* [2001] Crim LR 495).

There have been a considerable number of cases on this area since *Newton*, and the cases considered below are merely examples of the issues which have arisen. Students are referred to *Blackstone's Criminal Practice*, para D18.2 et seq for a full discussion.

Defence solicitor and counsel have a duty to notify the Crown that a guilty plea will be put forward, but that the prosecution version of the facts will be contested, so that the prosecution can ensure the presence of any necessary witnesses to enable a *Newton* hearing to proceed (*R v Mohun* [1992] Crim LR 598, CA; *R v Gardener* [1994] Crim LR 301).

When the judge conducts a *Newton* hearing, the rules of evidence should be strictly followed, and the judge should give himself or herself the same directions which he or she would give to a jury, for example, in accordance with the guidelines in *R v Turnbull* [1977] QB 224 (*R v Gandy* (1989) 11 Cr App R (S) 564). Further the judge should openly direct himself or herself that the facts have to be proved to the criminal standard, though failure to do so will not necessarily be fatal (*Rv Kerrigan* (1992) 156 JP 889, CA).

The fact that the judge knows of the defendant's antecedents does not preclude him from conducting a *Newton* hearing, but, where the offence is a serious one, it is preferable to have the benefit of a jury verdict (*R v Eubank* [2002] 1 Cr App R (S) 4).

It is not right, on a *Newton* hearing, to sentence the defendant on the basis of a more serious offence than charged. In *R v Druce* (1993) 14 Cr App R (S) 691, CA, the prosecution alleged rape although the charges were unlawful sexual intercourse and indecent assault. The Court of Appeal held that if that was the prosecution case, the defendant should have been so charged. The judge had no alternative but to deal with the case by giving the defendant the benefit of the doubt, and proceed on the basis that the complainant had consented (cf *R v Nottingham Crown Court, ex p DPP* [1995] Crim LR 902).

It should be noted that the defence cannot frustrate the *Newton* inquiry procedure by declining to give evidence. In these circumstances, where the basic facts are not in dispute, the judge is entitled to draw inferences from these undisputed facts (*R v Mirza* (1992) 14 Cr App R (S) 64, CA).

Where the alleged facts relied upon by the offender to reduce the gravity of the offence are exclusively within his or her knowledge, so that the prosecution cannot reasonably be expected to call evidence in rebuttal, the judge is entitled to reject the offender's evidence of what happened as unbelievable, notwithstanding that it is the only evidence there is (*R v Kerr* (1980) 2 Cr App R (S) 54); and see *R v Hawkins* (1985) 7 Cr App R (S) 351 where it was said that the judge is entitled to reject the defence version without hearing evidence if the story is 'incredible'.

Occasionally, a defendant will decide to change his or her plea halfway through the trial, after at least some evidence has been given for the prosecution. In these circumstances, the judge should hear evidence from the defendant and then decide upon the version of facts upon which he or she is going to sentence, forming his or her view on the whole of the evidence that was given. See *R v Mottram* [1981] 3 Cr App R (S) 123 and *R v Archer* [1994] Crim LR 80.

Section 80(2)(b) of the PCC(S)A 2000 provides for the imposition of longer than normal sentences where the offence is of a violent or sexual nature and the court is of the opinion that it is necessary in order to protect the public from harm from the offender. In such a situation, the court must hold a *Newton* hearing to resolve any important issue relevant to sentence. See *R v Oudkerk* [1994] Crim LR 700.

Credit should be given for a plea of guilty, since court time has been saved, even if the judge rejects the version of the facts put forward by the defendant, taking the view that the plea was put forward on a false basis (*R v Williams* (1990) 12 Cr App R (S) 415).

If the judge wrongly fails to hold a *Newton* hearing, the Court of Appeal may vary the sentence to one which is appropriate on the basis that the defendant's version of events is correct (*R v Mohun* (1993) 14 Cr App R (S) 5).

See *R v Cranston* (1993) 14 Cr App R (S) 103, CA, for a recent example and note that further guidance has been provided by the Court of Appeal in *R v Beswick* (1996) 160 JP 33. See *R v Tolera* [1999] 1 Cr App R (S) 25 where the Court of Appeal clarified the practice to be followed where the defendant pleaded guilty but sought to be sentenced on a factual basis other than that which was advanced by the prosecution.

In *R v Underwood* [2005] 1 Cr App R (S) 90, the court heard a number of appeals together to set out guidelines to re-emphasise the procedure to be adopted when dealing with a *Newton* hearing. These are, in brief:

1. The essential principle was that the sentencing judge must do justice. As far as possible, the offender should be sentenced on the basis which accurately reflects the facts of the individual case.

2. The starting point is the defendant's instructions. If the dispute as to facts is such that it may affect the sentence, the defence should take the initiative and alert the prosecution. The prosecution should not be taken by surprise, and should, if necessary, take time for proper reflection and consultation to consider its position and the interests of justice.

3. Whatever the view formed by the prosecution, it is deemed to be conditional on the judge's acceptance of it.

4. The Crown may accept the defendant's account of the facts. If so, the agreement should be reduced into writing and signed by both advocates. It should then be made available to the judge before the start of the Crown's opening. If the agreement is not signed or is illegible, the judge is entitled to ignore it.

5. If the Crown rejects the defendant's version the areas should be identified in writing and the document should focus the court's attention on the precise fact or facts which are in dispute.

6. Where the Crown lacks the evidence positively to dispute the defendant's account, it should not normally agree the defendant's account unless it is supported by other material. Neither the Crown nor the Court is bound to agree facts merely because they cannot be refuted. The points in issue should be set out in writing and made available to the judge.

7. Even if the facts are agreed, the judge is not bound to accept them and is entitled to insist that any relevant evidence is called, as he or she is the one who is responsible for the sentencing decision.

8. Both parties should call and test appropriate evidence. The defence should be prepared to call the defendant to give evidence if there are facts which are within his or her exclusive knowledge, and he or she is willing. If he or she does not, in the absence of any explanation, the court may draw such inferences as it thinks fit.

9 An adjournment may, but will not usually, be necessary.

10 The judge must then make up his or her mind as to the facts in dispute, directing him or herself in accordance with ordinary principles.

11 The following limitations exist with the *Newton* hearing:

 (a) There will be some cases when the hearing will be inappropriate and the matter should be resolved by a jury, for example whether any necessary intent has been proved.

 (b) The judge cannot make findings of fact which are inconsistent with the pleas that have already been accepted by the Crown.

 (c) Where a number of defendants are charged with a joint enterprise, the judge should bear in mind both the seriousness and context of the joint enterprise.

 (d) Generally speaking, mitigation is rarely dealt with in a *Newton* hearing, but the court may always allow a defendant to give evidence of matters of mitigation within his or her own knowledge.

 (e) Where the impact of the dispute on the eventual sentencing decision is minimal, a *Newton* hearing is usually unnecessary. The judge is rarely likely to be concerned with minute differences about events on the periphery.

 (f) The judge is entitled to decline to hear evidence about disputed facts if the case advanced by the defence is to be regarded, for whatever reason, as absurd or obviously untenable. In such circumstances, he or she should explain his or her decision.

12 If the issues raised at the *Newton* hearing are resolved in the defendant's favour, he or she should not lose the credit for a guilty plea. On the other hand, however, if he or she is disbelieved and obliges the prosecution to call evidence from a victim, who is then subjected to cross-examination, which, because it is unfounded, causes unnecessary and inappropriate distress, or if he or she conveys to the judge that he or she has no insight into the consequences of his or her actions and no remorse for it, then the judge may reduce the discount which would otherwise be available. In exceptional cases, the entitlement to a discount may be wholly dissipated, in which case the judge should explain his or her reasons.

The Court of Appeal may interfere with the decision of the sentencing judge after a *Newton* hearing (*Attorney-General's References (Nos 3 and 4 of 1996)* [1997] 1 Cr App R (S) 29). Any interference, however, is likely to be only in exceptional cases, where the judge has reached a decision which no reasonable jury, properly directed, could have reached.

13.4.3 Disputes about the facts after a not guilty plea

Post-conviction disputes about the circumstances of the offence are not limited to cases where the offender pleaded guilty, for a jury's verdict of guilty after a not guilty plea is not necessarily a total vindication of the prosecution's case. In such cases, it is for the judge to form a personal view of the evidence adduced before the jury, and decide what the facts of the offence were. He or she should not ask the jury the reasons for its verdict or what facts it found proved (*per* Humphreys J in *R v Larkin* [1943] KB 174, although that case recognised an exception to the rule where the jury finds the accused not guilty of murder but guilty of manslaughter, and may be asked whether the verdict was on the basis of provocation, diminished responsibility or something else). The judge is not obliged to adopt as a basis for sentencing the least serious version of events consistent with the jury's verdict (*R v Solomon* (1984) 6 Cr App R (S) 120), but should be 'extremely astute' in giving the benefit of any doubt to the offender (*per* Watkins LJ in *R v Stosiek* (1982) 4 Cr App R (S) 205). In *R v Wood* (1991) 13 Cr App R (S) 207, the Court of Appeal said that it would only interfere with the finding of fact by a judge after hearing evidence in exceptional circumstances.

The view the judge takes of the facts must naturally be consistent with the jury's verdict. Thus, if the jury refuses to find the accused guilty as charged but only convicts him or her of a lesser offence, the sentence must be appropriate to the lesser offence, notwithstanding that the judge is convinced there should have been a conviction for the more serious offence (*R v Hazelwood* (1984) 6 Cr App R (S) 52 and *R v Dowdall* (1992) 13 Cr App R (S) 441, CA).

13.5 Character and antecedents evidence

After the prosecution summary of the facts or, in the case of a not guilty plea, immediately after the guilty verdict, the Crown Prosecutor in the magistrates' court or prosecuting counsel in the Crown Court provides the court with information about the character and antecedents of the offender. Information about the character of the offender will be wholly or principally concerned with the matter of his or her previous convictions, if any. Information about antecedents deals with the offender's general background and circumstances.

13.5.1 The antecedents

Practice Direction (Criminal: Consolidated) [2002] 3 All ER 904, Part III.27 sets out the procedure for the provision of antecedents in magistrates' courts and in the Crown Court.

Antecedents evidence is usually provided by prosecution counsel, provided that defence counsel has agreed that they are not in dispute.

Should the defence challenge anything in the antecedents, the antecedents officer and any other witnesses may have to be called, as the prosecution is expected to provide proper proof of what it has alleged, ie evidence of a type which would be admissible in a trial of a not guilty plea. If it fails to provide such proof, the judge should ignore the challenged allegation, and state that he or she is ignoring it (*R v Campbell* (1911) 6 Cr App R 131). It follows that where the prosecution does not have proper proof of an allegation prejudicial to the offender, it should not make the allegation in the first place (see *R v Van Pelz* [1943] KB 157 and *R v Wilkins* (1977) 66 Cr App R 49). Where the prosecution does propose to adduce first-hand antecedents evidence of a factual nature, but it realises that the facts may well be challenged by the defence, it should give notice of the proposed evidence (*R v Robinson* (1969) 53 Cr App R 314). It is not entirely clear whether the prosecution is ever entitled to refer to the offender as having criminal associates. In *R v Bibby* [1972] Crim LR 513 it was held that it was unfair of the antecedents officer to say that B mixed with criminals, but in *R v Crabtree* [1952] 2 All ER 974 Lord Goddard CJ held such evidence to be acceptable provided the officer could speak from his personal knowledge. In the light of these cases, the safest rule for a police officer giving antecedents evidence must be to restrict himself or herself to what is on the antecedents form, and not make additional allegations likely to be disputed by the defence.

13.5.2 Previous convictions

Section 51(1) of the PCC(S)A 2000 provides that when considering the seriousness of any offence, the court may take into account any previous convictions or any failure of the offender to respond to previous sentences. Prosecutors therefore make available to the court a list of any previous convictions of the offender in accordance with the *Practice Direction*.

Practice Direction (criminal: consolidated) [2002] 3 All ER 904, Part III.27 provides guidance for the provision of information of antecedents in the Crown Court and magistrates' courts:

27.1 In the Crown Court the police will provide brief details of the circumstances of the last three similar convictions and/or of convictions likely to be of interest to the court, the latter being judged on a case by case basis. This information should be provided separately and attached to the antecedents as set out below.

27.2 Where the current alleged offence could constitute a breach of an existing community order, eg community rehabilitation order, and it is known that that order is still in force then, to enable the court to consider the possibility of revoking that order, details of the circumstances of the offence leading to the community order should be included in the antecedents as set out below.

27.3 [standard formats]

Provision of antecedents to the court and parties

Crown Court

27.4 The Crown Court antecedents will be prepared by the police immediately following committal proceedings, including committals for sentence, transfers under section 4 of the Criminal Justice Act 1987 or section 53 of the Criminal Justice Act 1991, or upon receipt of a notice of appeal, excluding non-imprisonable motoring offences.

. . .

Magistrates' court

27.8 The magistrates' court antecedents will be prepared by the police and submitted to the CPS with the case file.

. . .

27.10 In instances where antecedents have been provided to the court some time before the hearing the police will, if requested to do so by the CPS, check the record of convictions. Details of any additional convictions will be provided using the standard format above. These will be provided as above and attached to the documents already supplied. Details of any additional outstanding cases will also be provided at this stage.

. . .

13.5.3 Spent convictions

The Rehabilitation of Offenders Act 1974 (ROA) was passed with the aim of helping criminals who had decided to 'go straight' to live down their past. Its main effect is that, once a certain time (the 'rehabilitation period') has elapsed from the date of an offender's conviction, the conviction becomes spent and the offender, in respect of that conviction, is a rehabilitated person. As a rehabilitated person he or she is, for most purposes, treated as if he or she had never committed or been convicted of the offence.

Whether a conviction is capable of becoming spent depends upon the length of the sentence imposed for the offence. The length of the sentence, assuming that it is within the limit, also governs the length of the rehabilitation period.

Section 7 of the ROA 1974 provides that the ban on revealing or asking questions about spent convictions does *not* apply in criminal proceedings. However, *Practice Direction (criminal: consolidated)* [2002] 3 All ER 904, para 6, provides that neither judge

Procedure between conviction and sentence 281

nor counsel should refer to a spent conviction where 'such reference can be reasonably avoided'. Mention of a spent conviction always requires the judge's authority, that authority being given only where the interests of justice so require. At the sentencing stage, the list of previous convictions given to the court should mark those which are spent. When passing sentence the judge should say nothing about spent convictions unless it is vital to do so to explain the penalty he or she has decided upon.

[Margin note: Should the judge take spent convictions into account when sentencing?]

13.5.4 Defence questions

If a police officer has testified about the offender's antecedents and previous convictions, defence counsel can ask him or her questions. The questioning is unlikely to be hostile in nature, but counsel might wish to confirm that his or her client was co-operative when questioned about the offence or showed signs of genuine remorse. If there has been a change in the offender's circumstances since the antecedents were prepared the officer can be asked if he or she knows anything about that. Upon the officer leaving the witness box the prosecution case is closed.

13.6 Reports

After information as to character and antecedents has been presented to the court, the judge—if he or she has not already done so before court—reads any reports which have been prepared about the offender. Sometimes sentence may properly be passed without the benefit of reports, but there are many occasions when the court must have them either because there is a statutory provision to that effect or because good sentencing practice demands it.

13.6.1 The necessity for pre-sentence reports

A pre-sentence report is defined by s 162 of the PCC(S)A 2000 as a report in writing which is made or submitted by a probation officer or social worker or member of a youth offending team with a view to assisting the court to reach the most suitable method of dealing with the offender, and contains such information as may be specified by the Secretary of State.

Under s 81(1) of the PCC(S)A 2000, when a court is forming any necessary opinion under s 79(2) or s 80(2) of that Act (whether a custodial sentence should be imposed and the length of that order), the court is under a duty to obtain and consider a pre-sentence report. Section 81(1) does not apply, however, if the offender is aged 18 or over, and in the circumstances of the case, the court is of the opinion that it is unnecessary to obtain a pre-sentence report (s 81(2)). This would apply where the sentence was clear, and the report would, in practice, make no difference.

Failure to obtain a report does not invalidate a sentence, but any court sitting on appeal against sentence must obtain one and consider it, unless it is of the opinion that it is unnecessary (s 81(5) and (6)).

Where the offender is aged under 18, by virtue of s 81(3), the court must obtain and consider a report unless either:

- the offence is triable only on indictment, and the court is of the opinion that it is unnecessary to obtain one; or
- there already exists a report, and the court has considered the information. If more than one report exists, the court should consider the most recent.

When making any of the following orders, the court, under s 36, is under a duty to obtain and consider a pre-sentence report, unless it considers it unnecessary (s 36(5)):

- a community rehabilitation order which includes additional requirements authorised by the PCC(S)A 2000, Sch 2;
- a community punishment order;
- a community punishment and rehabilitation order;
- a drug treatment and testing order; and
- a supervision order which includes requirements authorised by Sch 6.

Section 36 contains provisions relating to failure to obtain a report, and offenders under 18 which are parallel to those in s 81 above.

A probation officer writing a report will draw upon many sources. Of prime importance is the interview with the accused. He or she may also visit the accused's home and speak with members of the family. With permission, he or she might talk to the accused's employer, although great care would obviously have to be taken not to jeopardise continued employment. He or she will also have access to background sources of information such as police antecedents and any records the probation service has of previous contact with the accused. If the accused has recently been released from a custodial sentence, the probation officer could consult the authorities at the relevant establishment to see what effect the sentence apparently had on him or her. Where medical or psychiatric reasons seem to have contributed to the offence, assistance might be sought from the accused's doctor, and the report might suggest the preparation of full medical reports.

13.6.2 Contents of a pre-sentence report

By s 162(1) and (2) a pre-sentence report is defined as a report in writing which:

- with a view to assisting the court in determining the most suitable method of dealing with an offender, is made or submitted by a probation officer or by a social worker of a local authority social services department or a member of a youth offending team; and
- contains information as to such matters, presented in such manner, as may be prescribed by rules made by the Secretary of State.

In the White Paper, 'Punishment and Supervision in the Community' (paras 3.10 and 3.11) the government outlined the purpose of the pre-sentence report:

The purpose of requiring the courts to consider a report by the probation service when a custodial sentence is contemplated will be to provide the court with detailed information about how the offender could be punished in the community, so that option can be fully considered. Its purpose will not be to make recommendations about sentencing or to be a plea in mitigation.

In addition, the Green Paper entitled 'Punishment and Supervision in the Community' described (at para 9.6) what such a report should contain:

The reports should include: information about the offence and the offender's attitude towards it, background information about the offender, an assessment of the offender's ability and willingness to stop committing crimes, and a detailed programme of supervision to achieve this. Preparing a report of this sort needs skill in assessing the likely outcome of various sentencing options; these assessments can be made only against a background of detailed knowledge about court practice, about the resources available for supervising offenders together with knowledge and understanding of offending; judgements involving issues of public safety have to be made; and those preparing the reports exercise their discretion in ways which can have serious and lasting consequences for offenders under sentence.

Reports do not contain recommendations, made by the probation officer or social worker involved, as to the appropriate sentence. On the other hand, the contents of reports will need to reflect a clear understanding of sentencing principles and practice. Reports have to deal with the various factors in the commission of the crime that may or may not make it 'serious' for the purposes of s 79(2)(a).

13.6.3 The presentation of pre-sentence reports

A representative of the probation service should always be available at court to hand in reports and assist the court in any other way he or she can (eg by interviewing an offender so as to bring an old report up to date). Unless required to do so by the defence, the probation officer who prepared a report need not attend when its subject appears to be sentenced, although may choose to do so if, for instance, the offence was committed while on probation. Such a practice is confirmed by s 162(1) which indicates that the report is 'made or submitted' by a probation officer, social worker or member of a youth offending team. The report would then be presented by a liaison officer. It is clear from s 162(1) that the pre-sentence reports must be in writing. This ends the occasional practice of probation officers or social workers giving their report orally in court.

A copy of the report must be given to the offender or his or her legal representative, except that in cases of unrepresented juveniles it should be given to their parents (s 156(3)). It is considered bad practice to read out the whole of a pre-sentence report in open court since it may well contain matters which, in the offender's best interests, should not be publicly emphasised. The defence, in mitigation, may, however, refer the sentencer to passages in the report or perhaps read isolated sentences which are especially favourable. The defence can challenge allegations made in the report by requiring the probation officer concerned to attend for questioning in open court.

Particular care must be taken where the allegations in the report contain an admission of the full facts of the offence, not formally accepted in court. In *R v Cunnah* [1996] 1 Cr App R (S) 393, the report contained details of the defendant's admission to the full seriousness of the offences as alleged by the victims, but pleas of guilty had been accepted by the prosecution on a more limited basis. There was no discussion of the implications of this with counsel and, on appeal, the sentence was reduced to the level which was appropriate to the pleas given and accepted.

13.6.4 Other reports

In addition to pre-sentence reports, the court may be assisted by the following types of report:

(a) *Medical reports*. These may concern the offender's physical condition or his or her mental condition or both. If an offender is remanded on bail, it may be made a condition of bail that he or she attend a hospital, etc, for the preparation of medical reports (BA 1976, s 3(6)(d) and PCC(S)A 2000, s 11(3)). If remanded in custody, he or she may be examined by the prison medical officers. Also, there is now the possibility under the Mental Health Act (MHA) 1983 of a remand to a mental hospital for reports in cases where the court is considering a hospital order under s 37 of the MHA 1983. A hospital order can only be made on the basis of reports from two doctors, one of whom must be a psychiatrist.

A copy of a report on an offender's mental condition must be given to his or her counsel or solicitor, but the offender personally is not entitled to a copy. If unrepresented, he or she should be told the gist of what is in the report (MHA 1983, s 54(3)). The psychiatrist who prepared the report may be required to attend court to give oral evidence.

(b) *Reports on juveniles*. Having found a juvenile guilty, the youth court sometimes remands him or her to local authority accommodation for two or three weeks so that a detailed report can be prepared. Such a report will deal with intelligence, aptitudes, attitudes to those in authority, relationships with peers and many other matters. The school he or she attends (or fails to attend) may also submit a report, together with a record of attendance.

(c) *Remand centre reports*. There is nothing to stop the court adjourning for a remand centre report on a young offender (under the age of 21), if it considers that that would be helpful. Generally, reports on the behaviour of offenders held at custodial institutions are more likely to be prepared for the assistance of the Court of Appeal than for sentencers at first instance. In determining an appeal against a custodial sentence, the Court of Appeal is quite often given information about the appellant's progress in prison, young offenders institution, etc, during the period between the passing of the sentence and the hearing of the appeal.

13.7 Defence mitigation

After the judge has read the reports the defence has the opportunity to present mitigation on behalf of the offender. If he or she wishes, defence counsel may call character witnesses. The offender will not be called personally unless either there is a dispute about the facts of the offence, or it is a road traffic case and he or she would be liable to mandatory disqualification unless he or she can show special reasons for not disqualifying. In most cases there will not be any character witnesses, and defence counsel will proceed immediately to make a plea in mitigation. (See the **Advocacy** manual, Chapter 41.)

There is no set pattern for mitigation, and what ought to be said will obviously vary from case to case. However, a plea in mitigation will usually include a discussion of the facts of the offence, the circumstances which led up to it, and the offender's personal circumstances. As regards the potential sentence, one possible approach is to discuss all the available sentences, explaining why they would not be appropriate in this case, concluding with the sentence that is thought appropriate. However, counsel should bear in mind the seriousness of the offence in deciding what is appropriate. If the offence is so serious that only a custodial sentence would be justified, the judge's patience should not be tried by discussing non-custodial sentences at length. Conversely, counsel will look foolish if he or she virtually concedes that the offender must go to prison, and then the judge imposes a community sentence.

The fact that the defendant has pleaded guilty has always been seen as an important point in mitigation, and has been said to reduce the sentence by as much as a third. Section 152 of the PCC(S)A 2000 provides as follows:

(1) In determining what sentence to pass on an offender who has pleaded guilty to an offence in proceedings before that or another court, a court shall take into account—

   (a) the stage in the proceedings for the offence at which the offender indicated his intention to plead guilty, and

   (b) the circumstances in which this indication was given.

> (2) If, as a result of taking into account any matter referred to in subsection (1) above, the court imposes a punishment on the offender which is less severe than the punishment it would otherwise have imposed, it shall state in open court that it has done so.

It should be noted, however, that the section does not go on to provide that failure to comply invalidates the sentence.

Other matters which are generally accepted as being good mitigation include the youth of the offender or his or her age; previous good character; that the offender had assisted the police; that the offender has expressed genuine remorse or made attempts to compensate the victim; that the offender was under some sort of particular stress at the time of the offence; and the potential effect on the offender's family in the event, for example, of a custodial sentence. For a more detailed discussion on mitigation, see the later chapters of this manual, and the *Advocacy* manual.

One important point to bear in mind is that counsel almost always has the most up-to-date information on the offender. The antecedents are taken at the time of the arrest, which may have been some considerable time before the trial, and in any event are only an outline of the offender's circumstances. There is not always a pre-sentence report, and even if there is, it may also be out of date, or may not contain the information that is required. Consequently, courts increasingly look to counsel to provide accurate, detailed, up-to-date information concerning the offender.

The Code of Conduct of the Bar, para 610(e), provides that defence counsel must not make statements or ask questions which are merely scandalous or intended or calculated only to vilify, insult or annoy. If the defence asserts facts which the prosecution disputes, this should be drawn to the attention of the defence, and if necessary a *Newton* hearing will be held.

The Criminal Procedure and Investigations Act 1996 (CPIA), ss 58–61, allows the judge to impose reporting restrictions where, under s 58(4), there are substantial grounds for believing that:

- the assertion is derogatory to a person's character, and
- the assertion is false or irrelevant to sentence.

Any order made will not apply to an assertion previously made at trial or during any other proceedings relating to the offence (s 58(5)).

The order may be revoked by the court and if not so revoked will cease to have effect after a period of one year (s 58(8)).

It is an offence to publish material in breach of an order under s 58, the sentence being a fine on summary conviction not exceeding level 5 on the standard scale.

Sometimes, when counsel has concluded his or her mitigation, the judge asks the offender whether he or she personally has anything to say. After that it is for the judge to pronounce sentence.

13.8 Pronouncing sentence

A Crown Court judge sitting alone will normally pronounce sentence immediately after defence mitigation (or after giving the offender the opportunity to make a personal statement). If he or she is sitting with lay magistrates and the decision is a difficult one, they sometimes retire to consider it. Similarly, a lay bench of magistrates may wish to retire to consider sentence, and they may also ask their clerk to retire with them to advise on their sentencing powers. In the magistrates' court, the decision on sentence may be taken by a majority but it is pronounced by the chairman of the bench.

Under the CJA 2003 s 174, the judge or magistrates must explain in open court, and in words that the defendant will understand, why a particular sentence has been imposed. Section 174 provides as follows:

(1) Subject to subsections (3) [where the sentence is fixed by law] and (4) [power of the Secretary of State to prescribe cases to which the section does not apply], any court passing a sentence on an offender—

    (a) must state in open court, in ordinary language and in general terms, its reasons for deciding on the sentence passed, and

    (b) must explain to the offender in ordinary language—

        (i) the effect of the sentence;

        (ii) where the offender is required to comply with any order of the court forming part of the sentence, the effects of non-compliance with the order;

        (iii) any power of the court, on the application of the offender or any other person, to vary or review any order of the court forming part of the sentence; and

        (iv) where the sentence consists of or includes a fine, the effects of failure to pay the fine.

The remainder of the section includes a number of supplementary provisions.

In a few other cases, statute obliges the court to give reasons for its decisions. For instance, both the magistrates' court and the Crown Court must explain a decision not to activate a suspended sentence if they are dealing with an offender who is in breach of such a sentence. In other cases (notably the making of a probation order with a requirement for treatment for mental disorder or for treatment for drug or alcohol dependency) the offender's willingness to comply with such requirement must be sought by the court. In yet other cases (eg suspended sentences) the effect of the sentence must be explained to him or her by the court. See the later chapters of this manual for details.

The Crown Court may vary or rescind a sentence within 28 days of its being passed (if the offender was jointly indicted with other accused, the period is 56 days from the passing of the sentence or 28 days from the conclusion of the joint trial, whichever expires sooner). The variation must be made by the Crown Court judge who originally passed the sentence, but if he or she was then sitting with lay justices they need not be present for the variation. It is clear that the power to vary may be used to correct technical errors in the original sentence or to alter it in the offender's favour. The extent to which a sentence may be fundamentally varied to the offender's detriment is unclear. The Crown Court's power to vary sentence is now contained in s 155 of the PCC(S)A 2000.

Once the statutory period for variation has expired a court may *not* vary its sentence even if, through inadvertence, it failed to consider including in the sentence an order which really ought to have been included.

Magistrates' courts may also vary or rescind a sentence at any time if it is considered to be in the interest of justice to do so (MCA 1980, s 142) (see **5.2.13**).

13.9 Taking other offences into consideration

An offender is sentenced for the offences to which he or she pleads guilty or of which he or she is found guilty. In deciding on sentence, the judge or magistrates must not be influenced by any circumstances which lead them to think that the offender may also have committed other offences with which he or she has not been charged (eg *R v Courtie* [1984] AC 463). There is one major exception to this rule, namely the practice of taking other offences into consideration.

Other offences taken into consideration when sentence is passed (or TICs as they are colloquially known) are offences of which the offender is never convicted, but which are admitted by him or her in court and, at his or her request, are borne in mind by the judge when passing sentence for the offences in respect of which there is a conviction ('conviction offences'). The sequence of events leading up to offences being 'TIC'ed will vary from case to case. Typically it will involve a suspect who has been arrested on suspicion of one or more crimes admitting at the police station that he or she committed those crimes, and making it obvious that he or she is going to plead guilty. The police may then ask him or her about other similar offences which they believe he or she may have committed, but which, in the absence of an admission from him or her, they will find it difficult to prove. Since he or she is resigned to having to plead guilty to the offences for which he or she was arrested, the suspect often decides to make a clean breast of everything on the understanding that some or all the offences he or she is now being asked about will not be the subject of separate charges but will merely be taken into consideration. A list is then drawn up of the offences to be 'TIC'ed and the suspect signs the list. The offences for which he or she was arrested and with which he or she was charged are then prosecuted in the normal way, and, if the matter is to be dealt with in the Crown Court, appear as counts on the indictment. He or she duly pleads guilty. Then at some convenient stage during the procedure before sentence is passed, prosecuting counsel mentions to the judge that the offender wants other matters considered. The judge is handed the list of offences signed by the offender at the police station, and he or she (or the court clerk) asks whether he or she admits committing them and whether he or she wants them taken into consideration. Assuming the offender answers 'yes' to both questions, the judge may, at his or her discretion, comply with the request. Prosecuting counsel should be in a position to give the judge brief details of the nature of the offences. The sentence the judge eventually passes for the conviction offences will no doubt be somewhat more severe than it would have been in the absence of TICs, but the addition to the sentence will almost certainly not be as great as the penalty for the offences had they been prosecuted separately. Thus, the system of taking offences into consideration has advantages for offenders. It also has advantages for the police, because they clear up offences which might otherwise have remained unsolved. This is why the system flourishes even though it has no solid basis in law.

The following points about taking offences into consideration should be noted:

(a) The sentence the court may pass is restricted to the maximum permissible for the offence(s) of which the offender has been convicted. This does not in practice deter the courts from 'TIC'ing offences because maximum penalties are usually far higher than a sentencer would wish to impose even for a grave instance of the offence in question. It is thus possible to add something to the sentence to reflect the TICs without exceeding the maximum penalty.

(b) Which offences to charge and which to refrain from charging in anticipation of their eventually being taken into consideration is essentially a matter for the police and the prosecution. Sometimes the most serious offences are charged and later appear on the indictment, while other less grave but broadly similar crimes are taken into consideration. Or perhaps the most recent offences will be charged and the remainder 'TIC'ed. On occasions, the TICs vastly outnumber the conviction offences (see, eg *R v Sequeira* (1982) 4 Cr App R (S) 65).

(c) Offences should not be taken into consideration unless the offender clearly requests the sentencer to do so. The offender should also admit in open court that he or she committed the offences (*R v Griffiths* (1932) 23 Cr App R 153). It is not, however, necessary to put the particulars of each offence to the offender one by one. Usually the offender is asked whether he or she signed at the police station the list of other offences, whether he or she admits committing those offences, and whether he or she wants them considered.

(d) Since the taking of an offence into consideration does not, as a matter of strict law, amount to a conviction, the offender is unable to bar a subsequent prosecution for the offence by reliance on a plea of autrefois convict (*R v Nicholson* [1947] 2 All ER 535). However, the police do not in practice prosecute for matters which have already been 'TIC'ed because to do so would undermine a system which they themselves find very convenient. If a prosecution were to be brought, the court would almost certainly pass a nominal sentence such as an absolute discharge.

(e) Although the TIC system is geared to offenders pleading guilty, there is nothing to stop the prosecution using a short adjournment after the accused has been found guilty on a not guilty plea to ask him or her whether, given the outcome of the trial, he or she would now like other offences considered.

(f) The court is not obliged to comply with a request to take offences into consideration. It is generally bad practice to TIC offences of a different type from the conviction offences, and the court should never consider offences which carry endorsement of the driving licence and disqualification if the conviction offences are not so punishable (*R v Collins* [1947] KB 560). The reason for this is that taking endorsable offences into consideration will not entitle the court to endorse the licence or disqualify if the conviction offences are non-endorsable, whereas if the offences are prosecuted in the normal way endorsement would be virtually certain and disqualification a possibility.

(g) The practice of taking offences into consideration is as common in the magistrates' courts as it is in the Crown Court. However, magistrates should not TIC offences which are triable only on indictment (see *R v Simons* [1953] 1 WLR 1014).

(h) The court should state when passing sentence how many other offences it has taken into consideration.

(i) TICs can establish or assist in the establishment of a criminal lifestyle as defined by the Proceeds of Crime Act 2002, s 75.

The court gave practical guidance as to the use of TICs in *R v Miles* [2006] EWCA Crim 256. See **14.9**.

13.10 Sample offences

From time to time, the prosecution may invite the judge to treat the offences on which he or she is now passing sentence as samples of a continuing course of conduct over a period of time. This is a convenient way of proceeding if the offences are numerous and were committed over a long period. It would be possible to include all the offences as TICs but this may result in an over-long list, as in *R v Sequeira* (1982) 4 Cr App R (S) 65, where the defendant admitted 150 offences.

The problem for the court is how such sample offences should be sentenced. Recent authorities take the view that the defendant should not be sentenced for offences for which he or she has not pleaded guilty or been found guilty. Thus the fact that the offences are described as 'specimens' does not entitle the court to sentence him or her as if he or she had been found guilty of offences not included in the indictment (*R v Burfoot* (1990) 12 Cr App R (S) 252), unless the offender admitted them (*R v Clark* [1996] 2 Cr App R (S) 351 and *R v Canavan* [1998] 1 Cr App R 79). Previous authority to the contrary (*R v Mills* (1979) 68 Cr App R 154; *R v Singh* (1981) 3 Cr App R (S) 90; and *R v Bradshaw* [1997] 2 Cr App R (S) 128) was rejected.

Two further points should be made:

(a) Prosecutors should ensure that offenders are charged with sufficient offences to reflect the overall criminality involved.

(b) The PCC(S)A 2000, s 80(2) (a), provides that the sentence shall be 'commensurate with the seriousness of the offence, or the combination of the offence and one or more offences associated with it'. Included in the definition of an associated offence is where the offender has admitted the offence and 'requests the court to take it into consideration in sentencing him for that offence' (s 161). It would seem that the court is therefore precluded from sentencing on any other offences.

13.11 Legal representation

The offender can, of course, represent himself or herself if he or she so wishes, and present his or her own mitigation. If the offence is a trivial one, for which the offender is obviously only going to be fined, he or she would be well advised not to employ a lawyer because his or her solicitor's bill would exceed any slight reduction in the fine which might be achieved by eloquent mitigation. In more serious cases, especially where the offender's liberty is at stake, legal representation is desirable.

Legal representation not only assists the offender but it should assist the court, in that the lawyer can clarify the issues, highlight those matters which are in the offender's favour and remind the judge that although the offender might qualify for a custodial sentence, the court is still under a duty to consider whether such sentence is appropriate having regard to the mitigating factors available and relevant to the offender (see *R v Cox* [1993] 1 WLR 188). The court will not want to resort to the drastic expedient of prison unless there is really no alternative. The same applies whenever a custodial sentence of any description is contemplated for a young offender. So, in these types of cases the offender is not merely allowed to have legal representation, but is positively encouraged to have it by the grant of the right to funded representation as part of the Criminal Defence Service.

The general effect of the relevant legislation is that, when dealing with an offender who is not legally represented in court, the court *must* give him or her an opportunity to apply for funded representation before doing any of the following:

- passing a sentence of imprisonment if the offender has never previously been sentenced to imprisonment (PCC(S)A 2000, s 83(1));
- passing a sentence of detention in a young offenders institution, custody for life, detention during Her Majesty's pleasure or making a detention and training order (PCC(S)A 2000, s 83(2));
- making an order for detention under the PCC(S)A 2000, s 91.

The first situation applies both to the passing of an immediate sentence of imprisonment and to the passing of a suspended sentence, but in deciding whether an offender has previously been sentenced to imprisonment, a suspended sentence which has not been brought into effect must be ignored. Points two and three apply irrespective of whether the offender has previously received the sentence in question.

The court must not pass the relevant sentence on an unrepresented offender unless either:

- he or she was granted a right to funded representation as part of the Criminal Defence Service but the right was withdrawn because of his or her conduct; or
- having been informed of his or her right to apply for funded representation and having had the opportunity to do so, he or she refused or failed to apply (PCC(S)A 2000, s 83(3)).

The effect of the legislation is that, if the court is considering a first sentence of imprisonment, etc, for an unrepresented offender, it must (if it has not been done already) tell him or her that he or she can apply for funded representation as part of the Criminal Defence Service and grant him or her an adjournment of sufficient length to make the application and instruct solicitors. If the offender fails to use the adjournment for the purpose for which it was granted, that is his or her fault, and the court at the resumed hearing can pass whatever sentence it considers appropriate even if the offender is still unrepresented.

If s 83 of the PCC(S)A 2000 is not complied with, but a sentence of imprisonment is nonetheless passed on an offender who has not previously been so sentenced, it would seem that the consequences of the error depend on which court makes it. If it was a magistrates' court which failed to comply with s 83, the Crown Court (which hears appeals against sentences passed in the magistrates' courts) must replace the sentence of imprisonment with a sentence the magistrates could lawfully have passed on the occasion on which they dealt with the offender. So the replacement sentence cannot be a sentence of imprisonment (*R v Birmingham Justices, ex p Wyatt* [1976] 1 WLR 260). If it was the Crown Court which failed to comply with s 83, the Court of Appeal can uphold the lower court's sentence if, notwithstanding the procedural irregularity, it considers that the sentence was the appropriate one for the offender (*R v McGinlay* (1976) 52 Cr App R 156). Presumably the same consequences will flow from breach of any of the other sections requiring the court to allow time for an application for funded representation to be made.

13.12 Differences between sentencing procedure in the Crown Court and in the magistrates' courts

The procedure before sentence is passed is essentially the same whatever the court. The practice of taking other offences into consideration and the power to defer sentence are equally applicable to both the Crown Court and the magistrates' courts. For minor driving matters, the court relies merely on the endorsements, if any, on the offender's licence.

14

The principles of sentencing

14.1 Introduction

Chapter 13 sets out the procedure to be followed prior to passing sentence. In brief, the prosecutor provides a summary of the facts of the case (unless sentence is being passed immediately after the trial has taken place) and the defence advocate makes a plea in mitigation.

In many cases, there will be an adjournment prior to the passing of sentence. The most common reason for such an adjournment is where the court requires a pre-sentence report before passing sentence. In the magistrates' court, adjournments after conviction must not exceed four weeks where the offender is granted bail or three weeks if the offender is remanded in custody (see s 10(3) of the MCA 1980). The Crown Court normally adopts the same periods.

Where the court adjourns between conviction and sentence, it has to be made clear to the offender that all sentencing options remain open to the court when sentence is passed if that is the intention of the court. If the offender is led to believe that a particular type of disposal—for example, custody or, where the offender has been convicted of an either-way offence in the magistrates' court, committal for sentence—will not be used, the sentencer has to abide by this indication. See, for example, *Gillam* (1980) 2 Cr App R (S) 267 and *Moss* (1984) 5 Cr App R (S) 209.

In *R v Cain* [2006] EWCA Crim 3233, the Court of Appeal emphasised that it is the responsibility of both counsel (prosecution and defence) to ensure that the judge does not pass an unlawful sentence.

14.2 Sentencing Guidelines Council

Section 167 of the CJA 2003 establishes the Sentencing Guidelines Council ('SGC'), chaired by the Lord Chief Justice. One of the main objectives of the SGC (which is assisted by the Sentencing Advisory Panel under s 169 of the Act) is to promote consistency in sentencing (see s 170(5)(a)). Under the CJA 2003, s 172(1),

every court must—

(a) *in sentencing an offender, have regard to any guidelines which are relevant to the offender's case, and*

(b) *in exercising any other function relating to the sentencing of offenders, have regard to any guidelines which are relevant to the exercise of the function.*

14.3 Purposes of sentencing

The CJA 2003, s 142(1), sets out the objectives of sentencing, to which the courts are required to have regard when dealing with offenders. Those objectives are:

- punishment of offenders;
- reduction of crime (including reduction by deterrence);
- reform and rehabilitation of offenders;
- protection of the public;
- making of reparation by offenders to persons affected by their offences.

14.4 The sentencing process

The sentencing process requires consideration of both aggravating and mitigating factors. At its most basic, it involves considering:

- What sentence does the seriousness of the offence itself merit?
- Can that sentence be reduced in light of mitigation relating to the offender?

14.5 The concept of seriousness

Seriousness determines whether either of the sentencing thresholds has been crossed (see below); indicates whether a custodial, community or other sentence is the most appropriate; and is the key factor in deciding the length of a custodial sentence, the onerousness of requirements to be incorporated in a community sentence and the amount of any fine imposed.

The concept of 'thresholds' is exemplified by two provisions in the CJA 2003. As regards custodial sentences, s 152(2) provides that:

The court must not pass a custodial sentence unless it is of the opinion that the offence, or the combination of the offence and one or more offences associated with it, was so serious that neither a fine alone nor a community sentence can be justified for the offence.

As regards community orders, s 148(1) provides that:

A court must not pass a community sentence on an offender unless it is of the opinion that the offence, or the combination of the offence and one or more offences associated with it, was serious enough to warrant such a sentence.

14.5.1 Seriousness according to type of offence

As well as the general guidance issued by the SGC, there are guidelines on particular factors which may make specific offences more, or less, serious. These guidelines can be found in *Blackstone's Criminal Practice*, *Archbold*, and *Current Sentencing Practice*. Guideline judgments of the Court of Appeal in respect of specific offences are gradually being superseded by SGC Guidelines.

It must be borne in mind that guidelines, whether laid down by the Court of Appeal or the Sentencing Guidelines Council, are only guidelines. There will be cases where there is good reason to depart significantly from the guidelines. In particular, this might be appropriate where the facts of the offence diminish its seriousness in comparison to the norm, or where there is particularly powerful personal mitigation (*R v Krivec (Attorney-General's Reference No 8 of 2007)* [2007] EWCA Crim 922; [2008] 1 Cr App R (S) 1 per Lord Phillips CJ at para 16). Moreover, as the Court of Appeal pointed out in *R v Martin* [2006] EWCA Crim 1035; [2007] 1 Cr App R (S) 3, sentencing is not a mathematical exercise. It involves the weighing up of sometimes conflicting mitigating and aggravating factors. Although the court has a duty to consider 'definitive' guidelines under s 172 of the Criminal Justice Act 2003, the guidelines of the Sentencing Guidelines Council remain guidelines. For those purposes, the term 'definitive guidelines' means simply guidelines that have been through the process outlined in s 170 of the Act.

14.5.2 General factors affecting seriousness

The CJA 2003, s 143(1) provides that:

the offender's culpability in committing the offence and any harm which the offence caused, was intended to cause or might foreseeably have caused.

Thus, 'culpability' is the initial factor in determining the seriousness of an offence. The SGC Guidance on Seriousness identifies four levels of culpability:

(a) *Intention* to cause harm: highest culpability when an offence is planned; the worse the harm intended, the greater the seriousness.

(b) *Recklessness* as to whether harm is caused (appreciates some harm would be caused but proceeds, giving no thought to consequences even though extent of risk would be obvious to most people).

(c) *Knowledge* of specific risks entailed by actions but does not intend to cause the harm that results.

(d) *Negligence*.

The SGC guidance also notes that culpability is greater if:

- the offender deliberately causes more harm than is necessary for the commission of the offence; or
- the offender targets a victim who is vulnerable (because of old age or youth, disability or by virtue of the job they do).

The SGC suggests a number of general factors which are relevant to assessing the seriousness of an offence. This guidance lists a number of factors that indicate **higher culpability**:

- Offence committed whilst on bail for other offences. This is a statutory aggravating factor—see s 143(3) of the CJA 2003, which provides that if the offence was committed while the offender was on bail, the court must treat that as an aggravating factor.
- Failure to respond to previous sentences.

- Offence was racially or religiously aggravated. Racial or religious aggravation is a statutory aggravating factor under s 145 of the CJA 2003, which provides that if the offence was racially or religiously aggravated, the court must treat this as an aggravating factor.
- Offence motivated by, or demonstrating, hostility to the victim based on his or her sexual orientation (or presumed sexual orientation) or disability (or presumed disability). Again, these are statutory aggravating features. Section 146(2) of the CJA 2003 provides that the court must treat circumstances as aggravating where (a) at the time of committing the offence, or immediately before or after doing so, the offender demonstrated towards the victim of the offence hostility based on (i) the sexual orientation (or presumed sexual orientation) of the victim, or (ii) a disability (or presumed disability) of the victim, or (b) the offence is motivated (wholly or partly) (i) by hostility towards persons who are of a particular sexual orientation, or (ii) by hostility towards persons who have a disability or a particular disability. Under s 146(4), it is immaterial whether or not the offender's hostility is also based, to any extent, on any other factors. For these purposes 'disability' means any physical or mental impairment: s 146(5).
- Previous conviction(s), particularly where a pattern of repeat offending is disclosed. The effect of previous convictions is dealt with by s 143(2) of the CJA 2003 (see below).
- Planning of an offence.
- An intention to commit more serious harm than actually resulted from the offence.
- Offenders operating in groups or gangs.
- 'Professional' offending.
- Commission of the offence for financial gain (where this is not inherent in the offence itself).
- High level of profit from the offence.
- An attempt to conceal or dispose of evidence.
- Failure to respond to warnings or concerns expressed by others about the offender's behaviour.
- Offence committed whilst on licence (ie following release from a custodial sentence).
- Offence motivated by hostility towards a minority group, or a member or members of it.
- Deliberate targeting of vulnerable victim(s).
- Commission of an offence while under the influence of alcohol or drugs.
- Use of a weapon to frighten or injure victim.
- Deliberate and gratuitous violence or damage to property, over and above what is needed to carry out the offence.
- Abuse of power.
- Abuse of a position of trust.

The SGC guidance goes on to identify factors that indicate a **more than usually serious degree of harm**:

- Multiple victims.

- An especially serious physical or psychological effect on the victim, even if unintended (on the use of 'victim person statements' see para III.28 of the *Consolidated Practice Direction*).
- A sustained assault or repeated assaults on the same victim.
- Victim is particularly vulnerable.
- Location of the offence (for example, in an isolated place).
- Offence is committed against those working in the public sector or providing a service to the public.
- Presence of others eg relatives, especially children or partner of the victim.
- Additional degradation of the victim (eg taking photographs of a victim as part of a sexual offence).
- In property offences, high value (including sentimental value) of property to the victim, or substantial consequential loss (eg where the theft of equipment causes serious disruption to a victim's life or business).

Paragraph 1.39 of the SGC guidance says that there may be exceptional local circumstances which may lead a court to decide that the prevalence of the offence should influence sentencing levels: this is only appropriate where there is appropriate evidence of prevalence and where there is a compelling need to treat the offence more seriously than elsewhere. In *R v Oosthuizen* [2005] EWCA Crim 1978; [2006] 1 Cr App R (S) 73, the Court of Appeal emphasised that if, in any particular city or town, statistics are available to CPS or the local Criminal Justice Board which demonstrate a prevalence of a particular offence greater than that at a national level, those statistics should be made available to the sentencing court. In the absence of such statistics or other evidence identifying particular prevalence in a particular area, a judge, however experienced in a particular area, should not make the assumption that prevalence of that offence is more marked in the area with which he is familiar than it is nationally.

The list of factors identified by the SGC as indicating **significantly lower culpability** is somewhat shorter:

- A greater degree of provocation than normally expected.
- Mental illness or disability.
- Youth or age, where it affects the responsibility of the individual defendant.
- The fact that the offender played only a minor role in the offence.

14.6 Credit for guilty plea

Pleading guilty is, in itself, good mitigation. Section 144(1) of the CJA 2003 requires the sentencer to have regard to the fact that the offender pleaded guilty and to take into account (a) the stage of the proceedings at which the offender indicated an intention to plead guilty and (b) the circumstances in which that indication was given.

Cases such as *Buffery* (1993) 14 Cr App R (S) 511 and *Costen* (1989) 11 Cr App R (S) 511 had established that an offender should receive a one-third discount if the guilty plea is entered at the earliest opportunity. In *R v Rafferty* (1999) 1 Cr App R 235 and *R v Barber* [2002] 1 Cr App R (S) 130, the Court of Appeal emphasised that the earliest opportunity in 'either way' cases is at the 'plea before venue' hearing, where the defendant is asked to indicate his intention as regards plea (and is regarded as having pleaded guilty if he or she indicates an intention to plead guilty). The SGC guidelines on guilty pleas confirm that this is so.

The SGC guidance on guilty pleas points out that a reduction in sentence as a result of a guilty plea is appropriate because that plea avoids the need for a trial (enabling other cases to be disposed of more expeditiously); shortens the gap between charge and sentence; saves considerable cost; and saves victims and witnesses from having to give evidence.

A guilty plea was traditionally regarded as evidence of remorse on the part of the offender. However, para 2.4 of the SGC guidance says that the sentencer should address remorse separately, and so should decide the appropriate length of sentence before calculating the reduction for the guilty plea.

The SGC guidance also points out that the giving of a discount for pleading guilty is not relevant only to the length of any custodial sentence to be passed. Where the offence crosses the threshold for the imposition of a community or a custodial sentence, application of the reduction principle may properly form the basis for imposing a non-custodial sentence even though the custody threshold has been passed, or a fine or discharge rather than a community sentence. Where the reduction is applied in this way, the actual sentence imposed incorporates the reduction and so no further discount is appropriate (see para 2.3).

The SGC guidelines provide that discount for pleading guilty should be based on a sliding scale, so that the offender gets more credit for pleading guilty at the earliest opportunity (and less credit for pleading guilty at a later stage). Under that sliding scale, the offender receives:

- the [normal] maximum of one third where the guilty plea was entered at the first reasonable opportunity;
- a maximum of one quarter where a trial date has been set;
- a maximum of one tenth for a guilty plea entered at the 'door of the court' or after the trial has begun.

The guidelines summarise the effect of this sliding scale:

- The maximum reduction (of one third) is to be given only where the offender indicated willingness to admit guilt at the first reasonable opportunity.
- Where the admission of guilt comes later than the first reasonable opportunity, the reduction will be less than one third.
- Where the plea of guilty comes very late, it is still appropriate to give some reduction (albeit much reduced).
- If the 'not guilty' plea was entered and maintained for tactical reasons, a late guilty plea should attract very little, if any, discount.

The SGC guidance also makes it clear that where there is a *Newton* hearing (because the defendant puts forward a version of events that differs significantly from the prosecution version, and the court is not willing simply to accept the defendant's version), and the defendant's version of events is rejected, this should be taken into account in determining the level of reduction in sentence. In other words, the defendant will lose some of the discount for pleading guilty in such a case.

It is also worthy of note that in *Landy* (1995) 16 Cr App R (S) 908, it had been held that the discount for pleading guilty should be withheld if the offender had been caught 'red-handed'. However, the first edition of the SGC guidelines on guilty pleas stated that, 'Since the purpose of giving credit is to encourage those who are guilty to plead at the earliest opportunity, there is no reason why credit should be withheld or reduced on these grounds alone. The normal sliding scale should apply'. This proved very controversial, and in the amended version of the Guidelines, published in 2007, said that

5.2 The purpose of giving credit is to encourage those who are guilty to plead at the earliest opportunity. Any defendant is entitled to put the prosecution to proof and so every defendant who is guilty should be encouraged to indicate that guilt at the first reasonable opportunity.

5.3 Where the prosecution case is overwhelming, it may not be appropriate to give the full reduction that would otherwise be given. Whilst there is a presumption in favour of the full reduction being given where a plea has been indicated at the first reasonable opportunity, the fact that the prosecution case is overwhelming without relying on admissions from the defendant may be a reason justifying departure from the guideline.

5.4 Where a court is satisfied that a lower reduction should be given for this reason, a recommended reduction of 20% is likely to be appropriate where the guilty plea was indicated at the first reasonable opportunity.

14.7 Effect of previous convictions

The CJA 2003, s 143(2), provides that:

... the court must treat each previous conviction as an aggravating factor if (in the case of that conviction) the court considers that it can reasonably be so treated having regard, in particular, to

(a) the nature of the offence to which the conviction relates and its relevance to the current offence, and

(b) the time that has elapsed since the conviction.

In other words, an offence is to be regarded as more serious if committed by someone with relevant previous convictions (relevance depending on how old the previous convictions are, and how similar in type they are to the present offence).

The approach prior to the implementation of the CJA 2003 was to regard the existence of relevant previous convictions as resulting in a 'progressive loss' of 'good character mitigation' (see, for example, *Carlton* (1994) 15 Cr App R(S) 335). This meant that an offender without relevant previous convictions would receive a discount in the sentence to reflect previous good character. The more relevant previous convictions recorded against the offender, the more discount was lost. Under the CJA 2003, however, the court should increase the sentence imposed on the offender in order to reflect previous convictions (on the basis that an offence is to be regarded as more serious if committed by someone with relevant previous convictions).

It remains the case that a custodial sentence may be imposed because of previous failures to respond to non-custodial sentences. For example, where the offence crosses the custody threshold but the defence argue that mitigating circumstances justify the imposition of a community order instead, the court may reject the suggestion of a community order on the basis that such sentences have been tried previously but the offender has nonetheless committed further offences (see, for example, *Oliver & Little* [1993] 2 All ER 9). It should be borne in mind, however, that even if the offender has a very bad record, the defence may argue for a non-custodial sentence to give the offender 'one last chance' to break the cycle of offending (see, for example, *Bowles* [1996] 2 Cr App R (S) 248).

14.8 Specimen/sample counts

It used to be the practice, where the defendant was alleged to have committed a large number of offences, to charge 'sample' or 'specimen' charges/counts. This practice was effectively outlawed by the Court of Appeal in a series of cases: *Clark* [1996] 2 Cr App R (S) 351; *Kidd* [1998] 1 All ER 42; and *Rosenburg* [1999] 1 Cr App R(S) 365. These cases emphasise that an offender is to be sentenced only for offences to which he or she has pleaded guilty or been found guilty or has admitted by asking the court to take them into consideration (see below). In *R v Smith; R v Tovey* [2005] EWCA Crim 530; [2005] 2 Cr App R (S) 100, the Court of Appeal repeated that an offender should only be sentenced for an offence which has either been proved against him or admitted by him. Where, however, an offender pleads guilty to conduct on a basis wider than that specifically charged, doing so is the equivalent of an informal invitation to the court to take into consideration other offences and a sentencing judge can properly proceed to pass sentence on the wider basis admitted. The Court added that where the evidence of the prosecution and defence does not raise different issues in respect of all the acts said to be part of the same activity, it is perfectly acceptable to charge the defendant with the single activity in order to represent more than one act, provided that there is no unfairness caused to the defendant. The Court approved *Barton v DPP* [2001] EWHC Admin 223; (2001) 165 JP 779 (where there were 94 takings from a cash register, each of about £15, over a period of years; the Divisional Court concluded that it was permissible to charge the whole course of conduct as a continuous offence because the defendant had no specific explanation for the individual takings and put forward the same defence for all the takings). The Court added that, in preparing the indictment in a situation of multiple offending, the prosecution should always have in mind the need to provide the sentencing judge with sufficient examples (and no more) of the offending, to enable the judge to impose a sentence which properly reflects the offender's criminal behaviour. It is also important to draft counts in a way that establishes the period during which the offending occurred (eg whether the offences occurred regularly over a significant period). With offences involving money, for example, the period over which offences occurred can be as significant as the total sum involved.

14.9 'TICs' (offences 'taken into consideration')

An offender who pleads guilty to one or more charges can also ask for other offences to be 'taken into consideration'. These offences are not the subject of separate charges (and so no plea is entered in respect of them) but the court will take account of them when passing sentence for the offence(s) to which the offender has pleaded guilty. This is advantageous to the offender because (despite a small increase in sentence to reflect the admission of guilt of other crimes) the agreement to 'wipe the slate clean' is good evidence of remorse (a mitigating factor which serves to reduce the sentence); also, as a matter of practice, where offences have been taken into consideration, they will not be the subject of separate prosecution (and the small increase in sentence that results from such offences being taken into consideration is considerably less than the sentence that would be imposed if the offender were to be convicted—and sentenced separately—for those offences).

In *R v Miles* [2006] EWCA Crim 256, the Court of Appeal made some observations about offences taken into consideration: the sentence passed by the court is intended to reflect the defendant's overall criminality. Offences cannot be taken into consideration without the express agreement of the offender. If they are to be taken into account (and the court is not obliged to take them into account), they have relevance to the overall criminality. When assessing the significance of TICs, the court is likely to attach weight to the demonstrable fact that the offender has assisted the police, particularly if they are enabled to clear up offences which might not otherwise be brought to justice. Co-operative behaviour of that kind will often provide its own very early indication of guilt, and usually means that no further proceedings at all need be started. They may also serve to demonstrate a genuine determination by the offender to wipe the slate clean, so that when he emerges from whatever sentence is imposed, he can put his past completely behind him, without having concern that he will be returned to court for the other offences. In some cases, TICs add little or nothing to the sentence which the court would otherwise impose. However, TICs may lead to a substantial increase in the sentence—for example, where the offences show a pattern of criminal activity which suggests careful planning or deliberate rather than casual involvement in a crime; or offences committed on bail; or a return to crime immediately after the offender has been before the court and been given a chance that, by committing the crime, he or she has immediately rejected. One advantage to the defendant, said the Court, is that once an offence is taken into consideration, there is no likely risk of any further prosecution for it (per Sir Igor Judge P, at paras 10 and 11). In *R v Lavery* [2008] EWCA Crim 2499, Owen J (at para 14) said that it is not appropriate for offences which are 'substantially more serious' to be taken into consideration. Moreover, it will be open to a judge to refuse to take an offence into consideration if he forms the view that to do so would be to distort the sentencing exercise and lead to an unjust result or that the public interest requires that the offence be charged (at para 16).

See also **13.9**.

15

Non-custodial sentences in the magistrates' court

In this chapter we look at the various non-custodial sentences that may be imposed by a magistrates' court.

Most of the law relating to non-custodial sentences can be found in the Powers of Criminal Courts (Sentencing) Act 2000 (PCC(S)A).

15.1 Absolute discharge

An absolute discharge (PCC(S)A 2000, s 12(1)(a)) is ordered where the court decides that it is inappropriate to inflict any punishment. Such an order may be appropriate where the circumstances of the offence disclose little or no blame on the part of the offender (for example, *R v O'Toole* (1971) 55 Cr App R 206, where an ambulance driver collided with another vehicle while responding to an emergency call).

15.2 Conditional discharge

Where a conditional discharge is imposed (PCC(S)A, s 12(1)(b)), the offender is discharged on condition that he or she does not commit a further offence during the period specified by the court (which can be up to three years). An offender who commits a further offence during the period of the conditional discharge can be re-sentenced for the offence in respect of which the conditional discharge was imposed, as well as being sentenced for the later offence.

One magistrates' court can deal with the breach of a conditional discharge imposed by another magistrates' court, but only with the consent of that court (s 13(8)). If the Crown Court is dealing with the breach of a conditional discharge imposed by a magistrates' court, the powers of the Crown Court when re-sentencing are limited to those of a magistrates' court (s 13(7)). If the conditional discharge was imposed by the Crown Court, only the Crown Court can re-sentence; so if a magistrates' court convicts someone of an offence committed in breach of a conditional discharge imposed by the Crown Court, the magistrates are empowered to commit the offender to the Crown Court to be dealt with for the breach of the conditional discharge (s 13(5)).

The court which re-sentences the offender for the original offence can impose any sentence which could have been passed when the conditional discharge was ordered (PCC(S)A 2000, s 13(6)).

See *Blackstone's Criminal Practice*, E12.

15.3 Fines

More offenders are dealt with by means of a fine than by means of any other sentence.

15.3.1 The maximum fine

For summary offences, fines are expressed in terms of a standard scale containing five 'levels' (Criminal Justice Act 1982, s 37(2), as amended):

Level	Maximum fine
1	£200
2	£500
3	£1,000
4	£2,500
5	£5,000

[handwritten note: Fine is for each individual offence.]

For offences that are triable either way, the maximum fine is £5,000 (a figure sometimes referred to as the 'statutory maximum'), unless the statute creating the offence prescribes a larger maximum fine (Magistrates' Courts Act 1980 (MCA), s 32).

These limits apply to the fine for each individual offence. So if, for example, the offender is being dealt with for five either way offences, he could be fined a total of £25,000.

15.3.2 Fixing the amount of the fine

The procedure for fixing the amount of a fine is set out in the CJA 2003, s 162. There are three stages:

(a) The court begins by deciding what fine is appropriate in light of the seriousness of the offence.

(b) Next, the court considers whether the fine should be reduced on the basis of any mitigating circumstances relating to the offender. The fine should also be reduced to reflect an early plea of guilty.

(c) Finally, the court takes account of the financial circumstances of the offender. The means of the offender can operate to increase or decrease the amount of the fine.

Under the CJA 2003, s 162, the court can make a 'financial circumstances order' against the offender, requiring the offender to provide a statement of means within the period specified in the order.

If the offender spent time remanded in custody but subsequently receives a fine rather than a custodial sentence for the offence, the fine should be reduced to reflect the time spent in custody (*R v Warden* [1996] 2 Cr App R 269).

The Magistrates' Courts Sentencing Guidelines produced by the Sentencing Guidelines Council provide detailed guidance on fines.

15.3.3 Enforcement of fines

Where a fine is imposed, payment is due immediately. However, where the offender does not have the means to pay the fine forthwith, the magistrates are empowered to allow time for payment or to order payment by instalments (MCA 1980, s 75(1)). Where payment by instalments is ordered, the total fine should usually be one that the offender will be able to pay off within 12 months.

A magistrates' court, when it imposes a fine, may only fix a term of imprisonment in default if either the offence is punishable with imprisonment and it appears to the court that the offender has sufficient means to pay the fine immediately, or if it appears to the court that the offender is unlikely to remain long enough at an address where he can be found (so that enforcement of the fine by other methods is likely to be impossible) (MCA 1980, s 82(1)).

Enforcement of fines is carried out by the offender's local magistrates' court. If the offender fails to pay the fine (or fails to pay the instalments as ordered), the magistrates' court can issue a summons requiring the offender to attend court (or the court can issue a warrant for the offender's arrest) (MCA 1980, s 83). At the hearing, the court will investigate the offender's means (and the offender can be required to produce evidence of income and outgoings).

Under s 85(1) of the Magistrates' Courts Act 1980, where a fine has been imposed by a magistrates' court, the court may at any time remit the whole or any part of the fine, but only 'if it thinks it just to do so having regard to a change of circumstances'. Under subs (2), where the court remits the whole or part of the fine after a term of imprisonment has been fixed (as will always be the case with Crown Court fines), it must also reduce the term by a proportionate amount (or remit the whole term if the whole fine is cancelled). It should be noted that the power to remit is restricted to fines; there is no equivalent power in respect of compensation orders (s 85(4)).

Assuming that the fine is not remitted, the court has at its disposal a wide array of enforcement mechanisms to ensure that fines are paid:

(a) A 'distress warrant' authorising seizure and sale of goods owned by the offender. These warrants are re-named 'warrants of control' by s 62 of the Tribunals, Courts and Enforcement Act 2007.

(b) An 'attachment of earnings order', so that money is deducted from the offender's wages (Attachment of Earnings Act 1971).

(c) An order for deduction of money from the offender's income support or income-based job-seeker's allowance (Fines (Deductions from Income Support) Regulations 1992 (SI 1992/2182)).

(d) An attendance centre order, but only if the offender is under 25 (MCA 1980, s 82(4A)).

(e) Under the CJA 2003, s 300(2), where a court has the power to commit an offender to prison in default of payment of a fine (see below), the court may instead order the offender to comply with an unpaid work or curfew requirement.

(f) Under the CJA 2003, s 301, instead of committing an offender to custody in default of payment of a sum, the court may disqualify the offender from driving for a period of up to 12 months (this provision is based on s 40 of the Crime (Sentences) Act 1997).

(g) Imprisonment, but only if either (a) the offence for which the fine was imposed is imprisonable and the offender has sufficient means to pay forthwith, or (b) the court is satisfied that the offender's failure to pay the fine is due to 'wilful refusal' or 'culpable neglect' and the court has considered or tried all other methods of enforcement but it appears to the court that they are inappropriate or have been unsuccessful (MCA 1980, s 82(4)).

Schedule 5 to the Courts Act 2003 puts in place an additional set of powers to aid the enforcement of fines. It complements (rather than replacing) the other mechanisms for enforcement. There is provision for fines to be increased in the event of non-payment. The Act also enables the offender's vehicle to be clamped, and then sold, if a fine remains unpaid. Schedule 6 enables the court to allow an offender over the age of 18 to discharge a fine by means of unpaid work (under a 'work order').

See *Blackstone's Criminal Practice*, section **E15**.

15.4 Community sentences under the Criminal Justice Act 2003

The CJA 2003 effectively gives the court a 'pick-and-mix' menu to enable it to construct a community order that is appropriate to the particular offender.

The term 'community order' is defined by s 177(1) of the Act. This provides that where a person aged 18 or over is convicted of an offence, the court may make an order (a 'community order') imposing on him any one or more of the following requirements:

- an unpaid work requirement;
- an activity requirement;
- a programme requirement;
- a prohibited activity requirement;
- a curfew requirement;
- an exclusion requirement;
- a residence requirement;
- a mental health treatment requirement;
- a drug rehabilitation requirement;
- an alcohol treatment requirement;
- a supervision requirement; and
- in a case where the offender is aged under 25, an attendance centre requirement.

Under s 177(3), where the court makes a community order imposing a curfew requirement or an exclusion requirement, it must normally impose an electronic monitoring requirement as well; under s 177(4), the court may impose an electronic monitoring requirement when it makes a community order containing any of the other requirements.

Under s 177(6), before making a community order imposing two or more different requirements, the court must consider whether, in the circumstances of the case, the requirements are compatible with each other. Moreover, s 217 requires the court to ensure, as far as practicable, that any requirement imposed by the order avoid any conflict with the offender's religious beliefs or with the requirements of any other relevant order to which he may be subject, and avoids any interference with the times, if any, at which he normally works or attends any educational establishment.

The maximum duration of a community order is 3 years (s 177(5)).

15.4.1 Restrictions on imposing community sentences

Under s 148(1) of the CJA 2003, the community sentence 'threshold' has to be crossed before a community sentence can be imposed. In other words, the offence must be sufficiently serious to justify a community order:

A court must not pass a community sentence on an offender unless it is of the opinion that the offence, or the combination of the offence and one or more offences associated with it, was serious enough to warrant such a sentence.

Moreover, under s 148(2), the court must ensure that the order is both suitable for the offender and commensurate with the seriousness of the offence:

Where a court passes a community sentence which consists of or includes a community order—

(a) the particular requirement or requirements forming part of the community order . . . must be such as, in the opinion of the court, is, or taken together are, the most suitable for the offender, and

(b) the restrictions on liberty imposed by the order must be such as in the opinion of the court are commensurate with the seriousness of the offence, or the combination of the offence and one or more offences associated with it.

Under s 150A, a community sentence can only be imposed if the offence is punishable with imprisonment, unless s 151(2) is applicable (this enables a community order to be made if the offender has previously been fined three or more times, even if the current offence does not justify a community sentence).

Section 166(2) makes it clear that a court is not prevented, after taking into account any mitigating matters that are relevant, from passing a community sentence even though it is of the opinion that the offence(s) is/are so serious that a community sentence could not normally be justified for the offence(s). In other words, the fact the case crosses the custody threshold does not mean that custody is inevitable. If there is sufficient mitigation, it is open to the court to impose a community sentence instead. Similarly, s 148(5) provides that the fact that a community sentence may be passed on the offender does not require a court to pass such a sentence.

15.4.2 Procedural requirements

Before deciding that the offence is sufficiently serious to merit a community sentence and before deciding what restrictions on the offender's liberty would be commensurate with the seriousness of the offence, and whether the offender is suitable for the imposition of particular requirements, the court must obtain and consider a pre-sentence report (unless, in the case of an offender who has attained the age of 18, the court takes the view that such a report is unnecessary): see s 156 of the CJA 2003.

15.4.3 Requirements that may be imposed under a community order

The requirements that may be imposed as part of a community order are listed in the CJA 2003, s 177(1).

15.4.3.1 Unpaid work requirement (ss 199, 200)

This is a requirement that the offender must perform unpaid work in accordance with the CJA 2003, s 200. The number of hours' work that may be required under an unpaid work requirement must be specified in the order and must be between 40 and 300. The court may only impose an unpaid work requirement if satisfied that the offender is a suitable person to perform work under such a requirement. Under s 200(2), the work should normally be performed during a period of 12 months. However, under subsection (3), unless it is revoked, a community order imposing an unpaid work requirement remains in force until the offender has completed the number of hours specified.

15.4.3.2 Activity requirement (s 201)

This is a requirement that the offender must:

- present himself to a specified person, at a specified place, for a specified number of days; and/or
- participate in specified activities for a specified number of days.

The specified activities may include activities whose purpose is reparation (including activities involving contact between the offender and people affected by the offence(s)). A requirement may only be added if the court is satisfied that it is feasible to secure compliance. The aggregate of the number of days specified must not exceed 60. The place specified in the order will usually be a 'community rehabilitation centre' (that is, premises at which non-residential facilities are provided for use in connection with the rehabilitation of offenders).

15.4.3.3 Programme requirement (s 202)

This is a requirement that the offender must participate in an accredited programme (comprising a systematic set of activities) for the number of days specified in the order. The court can only include such a requirement if the programme has been recommended to the court as being suitable for the offender by the probation service.

15.4.3.4 Prohibited activity requirement (s 203)

This is a requirement that the offender must refrain from participating in specified activities on specified days or for a specified period. Before including such a requirement, the court must consult a probation officer.

15.4.3.5 Curfew requirement (s 204)

This is a requirement that the offender must remain at a specified place for specified periods. The order may specify different places or different periods for different days, but may not specify periods which amount to less than two hours or more than 12 hours in any day. The order may only specify periods that fall within six months from the date when the order was made.

15.4.3.6 Exclusion requirement (s 205)

This has the effect of prohibiting the offender from entering a specified place for a specified period (which cannot be for more than two years). An exclusion requirement may provide for the prohibition to operate only during specified periods, and the order may specify different places for different periods or days.

15.4.3.7 Residence requirement (s 206)

This is a requirement that, during a period specified in the order, the offender must reside at a specified place. Before imposing such a requirement, the court must consider the home surroundings of the offender. The court cannot specify a hostel or other institution as the place where the offender must reside, except on the recommendation of a probation officer.

15.4.3.8 Mental health treatment requirement (s 207)

This is a requirement that the offender must submit, during the period(s) specified in the order, to treatment by a registered medical practitioner or a chartered psychologist with a view to the improvement of the offender's mental condition. The treatment may be on an in-patient or out-patient basis. The court may only impose such a requirement if satisfied, on the evidence of a registered medical practitioner, that the mental condition of the offender is such as requires (and may be susceptible to) treatment, but is not such as to warrant the making of a hospital order or guardianship order under the Mental Health Act 1983 and that the offender has expressed his willingness to comply with such a requirement.

15.4.3.9 Drug rehabilitation requirement (s 209)

This is a requirement that, during the period specified in the order ('the treatment and testing period'), the offender must submit to treatment by an appropriately qualified person with a view to the reduction or elimination of the offender's dependency on or propensity to misuse drugs; the order also requires that, for the purpose of ascertaining whether he has any drug in his body during that period, the offender must provide samples for testing. Such a requirement can only be imposed if the court is satisfied that the offender is dependent on, or has a propensity to misuse, drugs, and that his dependency or propensity is such as requires and may be susceptible to treatment. Also, the requirement must have been recommended to the court as being suitable for the offender by a probation officer, and the offender must have expressed willingness to comply with the requirement. The treatment and testing period must be at least six months. The treatment required under the order can be on an in-patient or out-patient basis.

Sections 210 and 211 provide for review by the court where a drug rehabilitation requirement has been imposed. Under s 210, a community order imposing a drug rehabilitation requirement may (or must if the treatment and testing period is more than 12 months) provide for the requirement to be reviewed periodically at intervals of not less than one month, at a 'review hearing' convened by the court. Under s 211, at a review hearing, the court may, after considering the responsible officer's report, amend the drug rehabilitation requirement. Such an amendment can only be made if the offender expresses willingness to comply with the requirement as amended. If the offender withholds consent to the amendment, the court may revoke the community order and re-sentence him for the offence in respect of which the order was made, dealing with the offender in any way in which he could have been dealt with for that offence by the court which made the order. If the offender is re-sentenced, the court must take into account the extent to which the offender has complied with the requirements of the order; the court can impose a custodial sentence even if the offence did not cross the custody threshold. If, at a review hearing, the court is of the opinion that the offender's progress under the requirement is satisfactory, the court may amend the order to provide for subsequent reviews to be without a hearing. If at a review without a hearing, the court is of the opinion that the offender's progress under the requirement is no longer satisfactory, it may require the offender to attend a hearing at the court, and the court may order that subsequent reviews are carried out at review hearings.

15.4.3.10 Alcohol treatment requirement (s 212)

This is a requirement that the offender must submit, during a specified period, to treatment by a suitably qualified person with a view to the reduction or elimination of the offender's dependency on alcohol. Such a requirement may only be imposed if the court is satisfied that the offender is dependent on alcohol, and that this dependency is such as requires (and may be susceptible to) treatment. The court may not impose an alcohol treatment requirement unless the offender expresses willingness to comply with its requirements. The period for which the alcohol treatment requirement has effect must be not less than six months. The treatment can be on an in-patient or out-patient basis.

15.4.3.11 Supervision requirement (s 213)

This is a requirement that, during the time that the community order remains in force, the offender must attend appointments with the assigned probation officer at times and places determined by the officer. The purpose for which a supervision requirement may be imposed is that of promoting the offender's rehabilitation.

15.4.3.12 Attendance centre requirement (s 214)

Section 221(2) defines an 'attendance centre' as 'a place at which offenders aged under 25 may be required to attend and be given under supervision appropriate occupation or instruction'. Section 214 defines an attendance centre requirement as a requirement that the offender must attend an attendance centre for the specified number of hours, and must engage in occupation, or receive instruction, under the supervision of (and in accordance with instructions given by) the person in charge of the centre. The maximum total number of hours must be between 12 and 36. The offender cannot be required to attend an attendance centre on more than one occasion on any day, or for more than three hours on any occasion.

15.4.3.13 Electronic monitoring requirement (s 215)

Under s 215, an electronic monitoring requirement is a requirement for securing the electronic monitoring of the offender's compliance with other requirements under a community order.

15.4.3.14 Other duties of offenders subject to community orders

Section 220 imposes a duty on the offender to keep in touch with the assigned probation officer in accordance with such instructions as he may from time to time be given by that officer, and to notify any change of address.

15.5 Persistent offenders

The CJA 2003, s 151, provides the court with an additional (discretionary) power for dealing with persistent petty offenders. Where an offender aged 18 or over has been sentenced to a fine on at least three previous occasions, the court may impose a community sentence, instead of a fine, even if the current offence does not cross the community sentence threshold. It does not matter whether the offender has on previous sentencing occasions received community or custodial sentences.

The SGC guidance on community sentences under the CJA 2003 makes the point that the:

> ... justification for imposing a community sentence in response to persistent petty offending is the persistence of the offending behaviour rather than the seriousness of the offences being committed. The requirements imposed should ensure that the restriction on liberty is proportionate to the seriousness of the offending, to reflect the fact that the offences, of themselves, are not sufficiently serious to merit a community sentence.

The guidance suggests that such offenders would merit a 'light touch' approach, for example, a single requirement such as a short period of unpaid work, or a curfew, or a prohibited activity requirement or an exclusion requirement (where the circumstances of the case mean that this would be an appropriate disposal without electronic monitoring).

15.6 Credit for time spent on remand

Section 149(1) of the CJA 2003 provides that:

In determining the restrictions on liberty to be imposed by a community order . . . the court may have regard to any period for which the offender has been remanded in custody in connection with the offence . . .

The SGC guidance says that the court should seek to give credit for time spent on remand in all cases where the offender was remanded in custody prior to conviction/sentence. Thus, the offender may receive a more lenient community sentence to reflect the fact that he or she has already spent some time in custody in connection with the offence(s) for which sentence is now being passed.

The guidance adds that the court should make clear, when announcing sentence, whether or not credit for time on remand has been given and should explain its reasons for not giving credit when it considers that this is not justified, would not be practical, or would not be in the best interests of the offender.

15.7 Breach of community orders under the Criminal Justice Act 2003

Schedule 8 of the CJA 2003 deals with breach, revocation and amendment of community orders.

Under para 5(1), if the probation officer who is supervising the offender is of the opinion that the offender has failed, without reasonable excuse, to comply with any of the requirements of a community order, the officer must give him a warning unless the offender has received such a warning during the last 12 months or the responsible officer decides to refer the matter back to the court. If a warning is given, it must inform the offender that if, within the next 12 months, he again fails to comply with any requirement of the order, he will be liable to be brought before the court (para 5(2)).

Paragraph 6(1), which deals with further non-compliance after a warning, is cast in mandatory terms. It provides that if the responsible officer has given the offender a warning under para 5 and, during the next 12 months, the offender again fails (without reasonable excuse) to comply with any of the requirements of the order, the officer *must* refer the case back to the court. Under para 7, the court can issue a summons, or an arrest warrant, to secure the offender's attendance.

Under para 9(1), if it is proved to the satisfaction of the court that the offender has failed without reasonable excuse to comply with any of the requirements of the community order, the court must deal with him in any one of the following ways:

(a) by amending the terms of the community order so as to impose more onerous requirements which the court could include if it were then making the order;

(b) where the community order was made by a magistrates' court, by dealing with him, for the offence in respect of which the order was made, in any way in which the court could deal with him if he had just been convicted by it of the offence;

(c) where—

    (i) the community order was made by a magistrates' court,

    (ii) the offence in respect of which the order was made was not an offence punishable by imprisonment,

    (iii) the offender is aged 18 or over, and

    (iv) the offender has wilfully and persistently failed to comply with the requirements of the order,

    by dealing with him, in respect of that offence, by imposing a sentence of imprisonment for a term not exceeding 51 weeks.

Option (a) would, for example, empower the court to extend the duration of a particular requirement, but not beyond the maximum duration applicable to that requirement and not beyond the three-year limit applicable to the duration of a community order (para 9(3)).

Option (b) involves revocation of the order (if it is still in force at the date of the hearing) and then re-sentencing (subject to the limitation on the court's sentencing powers when it was first dealing with the offender). Paragraph 9(4) empowers the court to impose a custodial sentence even if the offence did not cross the custody threshold.

Option (c) enables the court to punish wilful and persistent non-compliance with a custodial sentence even though the offence for which the order was made was non-imprisonable (where the offender was sentenced under s 151). As with (b), the community order is revoked if this option is chosen.

When dealing with the non-compliance, the court must take into account the extent to which the offender has complied with the order (para 9(2)). If the offender is re-sentenced by a magistrates' court, he can appeal to the Crown Court against the new sentence (para 9(8)).

Where the order was made by the Crown Court, the magistrates' court dealing with the breach can commit him, in custody or on bail, to be dealt with by the Crown Court (para 9(6)). The options available to the Crown Court, set out in para 10, mirror those available to the magistrates' court.

The SGC guidance on community sentences gives the following guidance on sentencing for breach of a community order:

- The primary objective is to ensure that the requirements of the community sentence are completed.

- A court sentencing for breach must take account of the extent to which the offender has complied with the requirements of the community order, the reasons for breach and the point at which the breach has occurred.

- Custody should be the last resort, reserved for those cases of deliberate and repeated breach where all reasonable efforts to ensure that the offender complies have failed.

- Before increasing the onerousness of the requirements of a community sentence, the sentencer should take account of the offender's ability to comply and should avoid precipitating further breach by overloading the offender with too many or conflicting requirements.

- It may be necessary to consider re-sentencing to a differently constructed community sentence in order to secure compliance with the purposes of the original sentence.

From this it is clear that the emphasis is on achieving the objectives of the original sentence rather than punishing the offender for failure to comply with the terms of that original sentence.

In *West Yorkshire Probation Board v Boulter* [2005] EWHC 2342; [2006] 1 WLR 232, it was held that a breach of a community order has to be proved to the criminal standard (namely, beyond reasonable doubt).

In *Greater Manchester Probation Committee v Bent* (1996) 160 JP Rep 297, it was held that the fact that an appeal had been lodged did not prevent the probation service from instituting proceedings for breach of the order which was under appeal. The same approach was adopted in *West Midlands Probation Board v Sutton Coldfield Magistrates' Court* [2008] EWHC 15 (Admin). Dyson LJ said (at para 13) that,

> like any other sentence, a community order takes effect when it is imposed and it remains in full force and effect until and unless it is quashed on appeal or revoked or amended by order of the court. The lodging of an appeal does not of itself have any effect on the enforceability of the order.

His Lordship continued (at para 15):

> Although the concept of 'reasonable excuse' is broad, I do not consider that it can have been intended by Parliament to be stretched to include the mere fact that the defendant has lodged an appeal against the community order or the conviction on which it is based. To do that would be to undermine the general principle that community orders take effect from the date on which they are made and remain in force until and unless they are quashed on appeal or revoked or amended by order of the court. To accept non-compliance with a community order as a reasonable excuse merely because the defendant is appealing would amount to an acknowledgement that defendants may pick and choose whether and in what circumstances they will comply. That is wrong in principle.

15.7.1 Revocation of community orders other than for breach

Part 3 of Sch 8 deals with the revocation of community orders other than in the case of a breach of the requirement of the order. Paragraph 13 states that (provided the order is still in force) either the offender or the responsible officer may apply to the magistrates' court for the revocation of the order, or for the offender to be dealt with in some other way for the offence in respect of which the order was made, if—having regard to circumstances which have arisen since the order was made—it would be in the interests of justice to do so.

Under para 13(3), the circumstances in which a community order may be revoked include the fact that the offender is making good progress or is responding satisfactorily to supervision or treatment under the order. The revocation of the order may also be appropriate if, for example, the offender is taken ill or becomes disabled, and so becomes unable to complete the requirements of the order.

If the court re-sentences the offender, it must take into account the extent to which the offender complied with the original order (para 13(4)). If a new sentence is passed, the offender can appeal against that sentence (para 13(5)).

15.8 Amendment of community orders

Part 4 of Sch 8 to the Criminal Justice Act 2003 deals with the amendment of community orders.

Paragraph 16 deals with amendments made necessary because the offender has changed residence and is living in a different area (and so should be supervised by a different magistrates' court).

Under para 17(1), the court may, on the application of the offender or the responsible officer, amend a community order by cancelling any of the requirements of the order, or by replacing any of those requirements with a requirement of the same kind, which the court could include if it were then making the order.

The court cannot add a wholly new requirement or substitute a different requirement for one that was originally specified in the order. However, the court can cancel a requirement or adjust it (for example, changing the hours of a curfew or substituting one specified activity for another). The court is also empowered to add electronic monitoring to any of the original requirements under the order.

The court cannot amend a drug rehabilitation, alcohol treatment or mental health treatment requirement without the offender's consent. If the offender withholds consent, the court can revoke the order and re-sentence him; if it re-sentences him it must take into account the extent to which he has complied with the requirements of the community order. The court can impose a custodial sentence if the original offence was punishable with imprisonment.

Paragraph 18 provides that, where a community order includes a drug rehabilitation, alcohol treatment or mental health treatment requirement, and the medical practitioner (or other person responsible for the treatment) is of the opinion that the treatment of the offender should be continued beyond the period specified on that behalf in the order, or the offender needs different treatment, or the offender is not susceptible to treatment, or the offender does not require further treatment, or the doctor is for any reason unwilling to continue to treat or direct the treatment of the offender, then he must make a written report to that effect to the responsible officer; the responsible officer must then apply (under para 17) to the court for the variation or cancellation of the requirement.

Paragraph 20 provides that, on the application of the offender or the responsible officer, the court may extend an unpaid work requirement beyond the 12-month limit (specified in s 200(2)) if it believes it to be in the interests of justice to do so having regard to circumstances which have arisen since the order was made.

15.9 Commission of subsequent offences

Part 5 of Sch 8 deals with the powers of the court in relation to a community order where the offender is subsequently convicted for another offence.

Paragraph 21 provides that where an offender in respect of whom a community order made by a magistrates' court is in force is convicted of another offence by a magistrates' court, and it appears to the court that it would be in the interests of justice to do so, the magistrates' court may either (a) revoke the order, or (b) revoke the order and re-sentence the offender for the offence in respect of which the order was made, dealing with him in any way in which he could have been dealt with for that offence by the court which made the order. If it re-sentences him, the court must take into account the extent to which he complied with the order (para 21(3)), and the offender has a right of appeal to the Crown Court (para 21(4)).

If the magistrates' court is dealing with the later offence but the community order was made in the Crown Court, the magistrates may commit the offender, in custody or on bail, to appear at the Crown Court (para 22(1)). The options open to the Crown Court, set out in para 23, mirror the options available to the magistrates' court.

312 Non-custodial sentences in the magistrates' court

15.10 Disqualification under PCC(S)A 2000, s 146

Section 146 of the PCC(S)A 2000 provides that, in addition to or instead of dealing with an offender in any other way, a court may disqualify him from driving for such period as it thinks fit. In *R v Cliff* [2004] EWCA Crim 3139; [2005] 2 Cr App R (S) 22, it was held that it is not necessary that the offence should be connected in any way with the use of a motor vehicle. The Court said that the Act provides an additional form of punishment where a person might be disqualified from driving notwithstanding that the offence of which he has been convicted was not connected with the use of a vehicle.

[Handwritten margin note: Court may disqualify offender from driving regardless of whether the offence had anything to do with driving.]

15.11 Surcharges

Section 161A of the Criminal Justice Act 2003 provides that when a court is sentencing an offender for one or more offences it must also order him to pay a 'surcharge' unless the court considers that it would be appropriate to make a compensation order, but the offender has insufficient means to pay both the surcharge and appropriate compensation, in which case the court must reduce the surcharge accordingly, if necessary to nil. This provision does not apply if the court grants an absolute discharge. Under para 3 of the Criminal Justice Act 2003 (Surcharge) (No 2) Order 2007 (SI 2007/1079), the duty to order the offender to pay a surcharge applies only where he is ordered to pay a fine (whether or not any other penalty is also imposed). Under para 4, the amount of the surcharge is £15.

The Government's intention (*Hansard* 20 April 2007: Column 827W, John Reid, then Home Secretary) is that money raised by the surcharge system will be spent on a range of services for victims of crime and witnesses, such as witness care units and services to victims of domestic violence and sexual violence (through the Victims' Fund, which supports the development of community-based services for victims of sexual offending).

15.12 Anti-social behaviour orders (ASBOs)

The Crime and Disorder Act 1998 makes provision for ASBOs in two circumstances. The first is what may be termed a 'civil' ASBO (under s 1 of the 1998 Act), made on the application of a 'relevant authority' (eg a local authority or the police); the second (under s 1C of the 1998 Act) is where the defendant has been convicted of an offence.

In both cases, the grounds for making the order are that the defendant has acted in an anti-social manner (that is, 'in a manner that caused or was likely to cause harassment, alarm, or distress to one or more persons not of the same household as himself'), and that such an order is 'necessary to protect persons from further anti-social acts by him'.

The ASBO prohibits the defendant from doing anything described in the order. The prohibitions that may be imposed under an ASBO are those necessary for protecting persons from further anti-social acts by the defendant.

In *R (McCann) v Crown Court at Manchester* [2003] 1 AC 787, the House of Lords held that applications for ASBOs under s 1 of the 1998 Act are civil (not criminal) in nature (indeed, the behaviour which prompts the application for an ASBO need not amount to a criminal offence) but that the court should apply the criminal standard of proof. Proceedings under s 1C are also regarded as civil, not criminal, in nature (*R (W) v Acton*

Youth Court [2005] EWHC 954 (Admin); (2006) 170 JP 31), but again the criminal standard of proof is applied.

An ASBO may be made following conviction either at the request of the prosecution or at the volition of the court. However, s 1C(4) provides that an ASBO can be made only in addition to a sentence imposed in respect of the offence of which the offender has been convicted, or in addition to an order for a conditional discharge.

An ASBO has effect for the period specified in the order (which must be at least two years) or until further order of the court (s 1(7)).

In *R v P (Shane Tony)* [2004] EWCA Crim 287; [2004] 2 Cr App R (S) 343, at para 34, Henriques J said that the test for making an order is one of necessity to protect the public from further anti-social acts by the offender, and the terms of the order must be precise and capable of being understood by the offender. In *R v McGrath* [2005] EWCA Crim 353; [2005] 2 Cr App R (S) 85, it was said that the terms of an ASBO must be clear and commensurate with the risk they seek to guard against. For an example of an ASBO which was too wide in its application, see *W v DPP* [2005] EWHC 1333; (2005) 169 JP 435, where the ASBO contained a clause which prohibited the defendant from committing any criminal offence; it was held that this clause was plainly too wide, since a person subject to a restraining order is entitled to know what he can and cannot do.

In *R v Boness* [2005] EWCA Crim 2395; [2006] 1 Cr App R (S) 120, the Court of Appeal gave detailed guidance on the use of ASBOs:

(1) An ASBO must be precise and capable of being understood by the offender. It follows that the court should ask itself before making an order: 'Are the terms of this order clear so that the offender will know precisely what it is that he is prohibited from doing?'

(2) Following a finding that the defendant has acted in an anti-social manner (whether or not the act constituted a criminal offence), the test for making an order that prohibits the offender from doing something is one of necessity. Each separate order prohibiting a person from doing a specified thing has to be necessary to protect persons from further anti-social acts by him. Accordingly, any order has to be tailor-made for the individual defendant.

(3) Given the requirement that the order has to be necessary to protect persons from further anti-social acts by the defendant, the purpose of an ASBO is not to punish. It follows that the use of an ASBO to punish a defendant is unlawful. A court should not impose an ASBO as an alternative to prison or other sanction; rather, the court should decide the appropriate sentence and then move on to consider whether an ASBO should be made after sentence has been passed.

(4) It also follows from the requirement that the order has to be necessary to protect persons from further anti-social acts by him, that the court should not impose an order which prohibits a defendant from committing a specified criminal offence, if the sentence which can be passed following conviction for the offence should be a sufficient deterrent. An ASBO should not be used merely to increase the sentence of imprisonment which a defendant is liable to receive.

(5) As well as considering whether an order is necessary to protect persons from further anti-social acts by him, the court must ensure that the terms of the order are proportionate, in the sense that they must be commensurate with the risk to be guarded against.

The principles were repeated by the Court of Appeal in *R v Wadmore* [2006] EWCA Crim 686; [2007] 1 WLR 339 (per Aikens J at para 41), where the court stressed that the test of 'necessity' requires the exercise of judgment or evaluation but does not require proof beyond reasonable doubt that the order is 'necessary'; the terms of the order made must be precise and capable of being understood by the offender; the conditions in the order must be enforceable in the sense that the conditions should allow a breach to be identified readily and capable of being proved (and so should not impose generic prohibitions, but should identify and prohibit the particular type of anti-social behaviour that gives rise to the necessity for an ASBO); each separate order within the ASBO must be necessary to protect persons from anti-social behaviour by the offender (and so must be specifically fashioned to deal with the offender concerned); the court should not impose an order which prohibits an offender from committing specified criminal offences if the sentence which could be passed following conviction for the offence should be a sufficient deterrent; and an ASBO must not be used merely to increase the sentence of imprisonment that the offender is to receive.

The appropriateness of arguing about validity in the context of proceedings for breach (rather than on appeal from the making of the order) was considered in *DPP v T* [2006] EWHC 728 (Admin); [2007] 1 WLR 209. The Court held that an order of the court must be treated as valid and to be obeyed unless and until it is set aside. Even if the order should not have been made in the first place, a person may be liable for any breach of it committed before it is set aside. The person against whom an ASBO is made has a full opportunity to challenge that order on appeal, or to apply to vary it; accordingly, in so far as any question does arise as to the validity of such an order, there is no obvious reason why the person against whom the order was made should be allowed to raise that issue as a defence in subsequent breach proceedings rather than by way of appeal against the original order, or possibly an application for judicial review (*per* Richards LJ at paras 27 and 34).

At para 35, his Lordship went on to say that it is doubtful that the suggestion that a provision of the ASBO is unduly wide, uncertain, or unnecessary for the purpose of protecting against further anti-social acts could be said to go to the validity of the order. If the order itself was within the court's jurisdiction, it would remain valid even if there were errors in it that were open to correction on appeal. His Lordship (at para 37) went on to suggest that, where a court is concerned that one or more of the terms of an ASBO is drafted too widely, the court may 'consider whether the relevant provision lacked sufficient clarity to warrant a finding that the respondent's conduct amounted to a breach of the order; whether the lack of clarity provided a reasonable excuse for non-compliance with the order; and whether, if a breach was established, it was appropriate in the circumstances to impose any penalty for the breach'.

Under r 50.2(1) of the Criminal Procedure Rules, the court must not make a 'behaviour order' (which includes an ASBO) unless the person to whom it is directed has had an opportunity to consider what order is proposed and why, and to make representations at a hearing (whether or not that person in fact attends). This does not apply to an interim behaviour order, but such an order has no effect unless the person to whom it is directed is either present when it is made, or handed a document recording the order not more than 7 days after it is made (r 50.2(2) and (3)). Under r 50.3(2), where a prosecutor wants the court to make an ASBO (but not an interim ASBO), if the defendant is convicted, the prosecutor must, as soon as practicable (and without waiting for the verdict), serve a notice of intention to apply for such an order on the court and on the defendant. The notice must summarise the relevant facts; identify the evidence on which the prosecutor relies in support; attach any written statement that has not already been served; and specify the order that the prosecutor wants the court to make (r 50.3(3)). The defendant must then serve on the court and on the prosecutor written notice of any evidence on which he or she relies, and must identify that evidence and attach any written statement that has not already been served (r 50.3(4)).

Practice Direction (Magistrates' Courts: Anti-Social Behaviour Orders: Composition of Benches) (2006) 170 JP 173 stipulates that where there is an application to a magistrates' court for an ASBO, or an application for an ASBO to be varied or discharged, and the person against whom the order is sought is under 18, the justices constituting the court should normally be qualified to sit in the youth court.

Under s 1(10) of the 1998 Act, a person who, without reasonable excuse, does anything that he is prohibited from doing by an ASBO, commits an offence. The maximum penalty is six months' imprisonment and/or a fine of up to £5,000 following summary conviction or up to five years' imprisonment and/or an unlimited fine following conviction in the Crown Court.

In *R v Stevens* [2006] EWCA Crim 255; [2006] 2 Cr App R (S) 68, the Court of Appeal said that the sentence for breach of an ASBO must be proportionate, or 'commensurate'. Where conduct constituting breach of the ASBO is also a distinct criminal offence, the maximum sentence for that offence is a factor to be borne in mind when considering proportionality. However, the court said that it cannot be right for the court's power to be limited to that maximum sentence, as breach of an ASBO is an offence in its own right. Accordingly, it is not wrong in principle for the judge to impose a custodial sentence for breach of an ASBO even if the maximum sentence for the offence is a fine (or to pass a prison sentence greater than the maximum for that offence). However, the court added that it should not be taken as suggesting that ASBOs should be imposed as a device to circumvent a maximum penalty for an offence which might be believed to be too modest. That, said the court, relates to whether it is proper to make an order, not to the consequences which follow breach of an order properly made.

See generally Chapter D24 of *Blackstone's Criminal Practice*.

16

Custodial sentences in the magistrates' court

16.1 Introduction

[margin note: Different powers for offenders aged 18-20 and those over 21]

In this chapter, we examine the custodial powers of the magistrates' court. These powers differ according to whether the offender is aged 18–20 or has attained the age of 21.

16.2 Magistrates' powers of custodial sentencing

Under provisions of the CJA 2003 which were not in force at the time of writing, for imprisonable summary offences, the maximum sentence can be up to 51 weeks. The CJA 2003, Sch 26, lists a large number of summary offences for which this is the maximum penalty. For summary offences not listed in this schedule, the maximum (assuming the offence carries a custodial sentence—many summary offences do not) is specified by the statute which creates the offence. For either way offences, the magistrates' court can impose up to 12 months for a single offence (s 282 of the CJA 2003). Where the magistrates are dealing with an offender for two or more offences (whether triable either way or summarily only), the maximum aggregate sentence is 65 weeks (see s 155 of the CJA 2003).

Until those provisions come into force, if a summary offence is an imprisonable offence, the maximum sentence is six months or that prescribed by the statute which creates the offence, whichever is less (s 78(1) of the Powers of Criminal Courts (Sentencing) Act 2000). If an offence is triable either way because it is listed in Sch 1 to the Magistrates' Courts Act 1980, the maximum sentence is six months' imprisonment (s 32(1) of the MCA 1980); if the offence is triable either way because the statute creating it gives alternative penalties for summary conviction and conviction on indictment, the maximum penalty is six months' imprisonment or the term specified in the statute creating the offence, whichever is the less (s 78(1) of the Powers of Criminal Courts (Sentencing) Act 2000). Section 133(1) of the Magistrates' Courts Act 1980 empowers a magistrates' court to order custodial sentences to run consecutively. However, the maximum aggregate sentence which may be imposed is six months (s 133(1)) unless the court is dealing with the offender for two or more offences which are triable either way, in which case the maximum aggregate sentence is 12 months (s 133(2)).

16.3 Imprisonment

Before a custodial sentence can be imposed, the case has to be regarded as sufficiently serious to cross the custody threshold.

16.3.1 The custody threshold

Section 152(2) of the CJA 2003 provides that:

The court must not pass a custodial sentence unless it is of the opinion that the offence, or the combination of the offence and one or more offences associated with it, was so serious that neither a fine alone nor a community sentence can be justified for the offence.

The SGC guidance on seriousness emphasises two key points about the custody threshold:

- Parliament's clear intention is to reserve imprisonment as a punishment for the most serious offences;
- passing the custody threshold does **not** mean that a custodial sentence should be regarded as inevitable: custody can still be avoided in light of personal mitigation or where there is a suitable community order which provides sufficient restriction (by way of punishment) while addressing the rehabilitation of the offender to prevent future crime.

The custody threshold under the legislation that preceded the CJA 2003 had been considered in *R v Cox* [1993] 1 WLR 188. It was held that an offence is 'so serious that only a custodial sentence can be justified' (the test then applicable) if it is such as to make all right-thinking members of the public, knowing all the facts, feel that justice would not be done by the passing of anything other than a custodial sentence. In *R v Howells* [1999] 1 WLR 307, the Court of Appeal expressed the view that this test was not particularly helpful. The court chose not to replace the test with a different form of words, but did set out some factors that could make the difference between a custodial or non-custodial sentence. Lord Bingham CJ said that:

. . . in approaching cases which are on or near the custody threshold courts will usually find it helpful to begin by considering the nature and extent of the defendant's criminal intention and the nature and extent of any injury or damage caused to the victim. Other things being equal, an offence which is deliberate and premeditated will usually be more serious than one which is spontaneous and unpremeditated or which involves an excessive response to provocation; an offence which inflicts personal injury or mental trauma, particularly if permanent, will usually be more serious than one which inflicts financial loss only. In considering the seriousness of any offence the court may take into account any previous convictions of the offender or any failure to respond to previous sentences . . . and must treat it as an aggravating factor if the offence was committed while the offender was on bail. . . .

In deciding whether to impose a custodial sentence in borderline cases the sentencing court will ordinarily take account of matters relating to the offender.

(a) The court will have regard to an offender's admission of responsibility for the offence, particularly if reflected in a plea of guilty tendered at the earliest opportunity and accompanied by hard evidence of genuine remorse, as shown (for example) by an expression of regret to the victim and an offer of compensation . . .

(b) Where offending has been fuelled by addiction to drink or drugs, the court will be inclined to look more favourably on an offender who has already demonstrated (by taking practical steps to that end) a genuine, self-motivated determination to address his addiction.

(c) Youth and immaturity, while affording no defence, will often justify a less rigorous penalty than would be appropriate for an adult.

(d) Some measure of leniency will ordinarily be extended to offenders of previous good character, the more so if there is evidence of positive good character (such as a solid employment record or faithful discharge of family duties) as opposed to a mere absence of previous convictions. It will sometimes be appropriate to take account of family responsibilities, or physical or mental disability.

(e) While the court will never impose a custodial sentence unless satisfied that it is necessary to do so, there will be even greater reluctance to impose a custodial sentence on an offender who has never before served such a sentence.

One issue is the extent to which the prevalence of an offence can affect its seriousness. The SGC notes that the key factor in determining whether sentencing levels should be enhanced in response to the prevalence of the particular offence is the level of harm that is being caused in the locality. The guidance emphasises that 'enhanced' sentences should be exceptional and in response only to exceptional circumstances, and that sentencers must sentence within the sentencing guidelines once prevalence has been addressed.

The Court of Appeal has encouraged sentencers to consider sentences other than custody—for example, imposing a fine instead. See, for example, *R v Kefford* [2002] EWCA Crim 519; [2002] 2 Cr App R (S) 106, and *R v Baldwin* [2002] EWCA Crim 2647; *The Times*, 22 November 2002. In *Attorney-General's Reference (No 11 of 2006)* [2006] EWCA Crim 856; [2006] 2 Cr App R (S) 108, the Court of Appeal commented that, when prisons are overcrowded, the result is to hinder or prevent the valuable work of rehabilitation that a prison should normally provide. The fact that prisons are overcrowded may, for this reason, be a relevant factor where the sentencer's decision is 'on the cusp', so that there is a real issue as to whether a community sentence can be justified rather than a custodial sentence (per Lord Phillips CJ, at para 20). This point was re-emphasised in *R v Seed* [2007] EWCA Crim 254; [2007] 2 Cr App R (S) 69, when the Court of Appeal revisited the question of the custody threshold because of prison overcrowding. Lord Phillips CJ said that judges were, once again, confronted with the fact that the prisons are full. When considering the length of a custodial sentence, the court should bear in mind that the prison regime is likely to be more punitive as a result of prison overcrowding (para 5). His Lordship added (at para 6) that:

Unless imprisonment is necessary for the protection of the public the court should always give consideration to the question of whether the aims of rehabilitation and thus the reduction of crime cannot better be achieved by a fine or community sentence rather than by imprisonment and whether punishment cannot adequately be achieved by such a sentence. We believe that there may have been a reluctance to impose fines because fines were often not enforced. Enforcement of fines is now rigorous and effective and, where the offender has the means, a heavy fine can often be an adequate and appropriate punishment. If so, the 2003 Act requires a fine to be imposed rather than a community sentence.

Particular care should be exercised before imposing a custodial sentence on a first offender. Association with seasoned criminals may make re-offending more likely rather than deter it, particularly where the offender is young. A clean record can be important personal mitigation and may make a custodial sentence inappropriate, notwithstanding that the custodial threshold is crossed (para 7).

16.3.2 Proviso to the custody threshold

Section 152(3) of the CJA 2003 contains a proviso to s 152(2), that:

Nothing in subsection (2) prevents the court from passing a custodial sentence on the offender if—

(a) he fails to express his willingness to comply with a requirement which is proposed by the court to be included in a community order and which requires an expression of such willingness . . .

16.3.3 Length of sentence

Section 153(2) of the CJA 2003 provides that (apart from mandatory minimum sentence cases (see **Chapter 19**)) the custodial sentence 'must be for the shortest term (not exceeding the permitted maximum) that in the opinion of the court is commensurate with the seriousness' of the offence(s).

In *R v Howells* [1999] 1 WLR 307 (following such cases as *R v Ollerenshaw* [1999] 1 Cr App R (S) 65), Lord Bingham said that 'the sentence imposed should be no longer than is necessary to meet the penal purpose which the court has in mind'.

This is particularly so in the case of the offender who has not previously served a custodial sentence. For that offender, the effect of the 'clang of the prison gates' is spent after a comparatively short time in custody.

Where the offender is being sentenced for two or more offences, the court can make the terms run concurrently or consecutively. Essentially, this will depend on whether the offences constitute a single series of incidents (in which case, concurrent terms would be appropriate) or unrelated offences (in which case, consecutive terms would be appropriate). CJA 2003, s 166(3)(b), preserves the 'totality' principle, which requires that where consecutive sentences are imposed, the court must ensure that the total time to be served is commensurate with the seriousness of the overall course of offending that is being dealt with.

In calculating the time to be served, account has to be taken of any time spent on remand prior to conviction/sentence (see s 240 of the CJA 2003). Section 240A of the 2003 Act also makes provision, where the offender was on bail subject to a curfew condition and an electronic monitoring condition, for half of the number of days spent subject to those conditions to count as time served by the offender as part of the sentence.

Section I.7.2 of the *Consolidated Practice Direction* stipulates that whenever a custodial sentence is imposed on an offender, the court should explain the practical effect of the sentence in addition to complying with existing statutory requirements. Section I.8.1 goes on to stipulate that where a court passes more than one term of imprisonment, the court should state in the presence of the defendant whether the terms are to be concurrent or consecutive.

16.3.4 Procedure

Section 156 of the CJA 2003 requires the court to obtain and consider a pre-sentence report in order to decide whether the case is sufficiently serious for a custodial sentence and, if so, what length of sentence would be commensurate with the seriousness of the offence. However, if the offender has attained the age of 18, the court may refrain from seeking a report on the basis that it is unnecessary to obtain one.

In *Gillette*, *The Times*, 3 December 1999, the Court of Appeal said that the court should always seek a pre-sentence report before passing a custodial sentence on someone who has not previously served a custodial sentence. However, in *Armsaramah* (2000) 164 JP 709, the Court of Appeal accepted that there may be cases where it is open to court to pass a custodial sentence without seeking a pre-sentence report even where the offender has not served a custodial sentence before.

16.3.5 Custody options in the magistrates' court

Under the CJA 2003, custodial sentences of under 12 months (or 65 weeks where the offender is being sentenced for more than one offence) may take one of three forms:

- 'custody plus' (not yet in force);

- intermittent custody (however, use of this form of custody was suspended in late 2006);
- a suspended sentence.

The SGC has given guidance on the order in which those alternatives should be considered (assuming that the case is one where the custody threshold has been crossed):

(a) has the custody threshold been passed?

(b) if so, is a custodial sentence unavoidable?

(c) if so, can the sentence be suspended?

(d) if not, can the sentence be served intermittently? [this question has to be disregarded, given the withdrawal of intermittent custody as an option]

(e) if not, impose a sentence which takes immediate effect for a term commensurate with seriousness of the offence.

16.4 Prison sentences of less than 12 months: 'custody plus'

The objectives of 'custody plus' are twofold:

- to make short prison sentences more onerous, and
- to make sure that the offender receives supervision after release from prison (rather than simply being released on licence and left to their own devices).

When the relevant provisions of the CJA 2003 come into force, a 'custody plus' sentence will comprise a custodial period (time spent behind bars) and licence period (time spent in the community).

Under s 181(2) of the CJA 2003, the 'term' of the sentence must be between 28 and 51 weeks. The 'custodial period' has to be between two and 13 weeks (s 181(5)), and the licence period has to be at least 26 weeks (s 181(6)).

Where the court is dealing with two or more offences and imposes consecutive prison sentences, the aggregate length of the terms of imprisonment must not be more than 65 weeks, and the aggregate length of the custodial periods must not be more than 26 weeks (s 181(7)).

During the licence period, the offender can be made subject to a number of requirements (effectively combining the custodial sentence with a community sentence). The requirements that can be specified are set out in s 182(1) of the CJA 2003:

- an unpaid work requirement;
- an activity requirement;
- a programme requirement;
- a prohibited activity requirement;
- a curfew requirement;
- an exclusion requirement;
- a supervision requirement;
- an attendance centre requirement (provided that the offender is under 25).

16.5 Suspended sentences

Suspended sentences of imprisonment are governed by ss 189–191 of the CJA 2003.

Where the custodial term is between 28 and 51 weeks (prior to the implementation of changes to the sentencing powers of magistrates' courts, at least 14 days but not more than twelve months, or in the case of a magistrates' court, at least 14 days but not more than six months) or between 28 and 65 weeks if the court is imposing consecutive sentences for more than one offence (prior to the implementation of changes to the sentencing powers of magistrates' courts, twelve months, or in the case of a magistrates' court, six months), the court may suspend that sentence, ordering that the sentence of imprisonment is not to take effect unless either (i) during the 'supervision period', the offender fails to comply with a requirement imposed under the order, or (ii) during the 'operational period', the offender commits another offence (whether or not punishable with imprisonment): s 189(1)(b).

Thus, where the court passes a suspended sentence it must specify an 'operational period' (the time for which the sentence is suspended) and a 'supervision period' (the time during which the offender has to comply with community sentence requirements). The 'supervision period' and the 'operational period' both have to be between six months and two years (s 189(3)). The 'supervision period' must end not later than the operational period (s 189(4)).

During the supervision period, the offender can be required to comply with additional requirements which are the same as those which comprise a community order: s 190 of the CJA 2003, namely:

(a) an unpaid work requirement,
(b) an activity requirement,
(c) a programme requirement,
(d) a prohibited activity requirement,
(e) a curfew requirement,
(f) an exclusion requirement,
(g) a residence requirement,
(h) a mental health treatment requirement,
(i) a drug rehabilitation requirement,
(j) an alcohol treatment requirement,
(k) a supervision requirement, or
(l) in a case where the offender is aged under 25, an attendance centre requirement.

Sections 191 and 192 provide for periodic reviews by the court of the offender's progress in complying with the requirements of the sentence; these reviews will be informed by a report from the appointed probation officer who is supervising the offender during the 'supervision period'.

It should be emphasised that a suspended sentence counts as a custodial sentence and so is appropriate only for an offence that passes the custody threshold and for which imprisonment is the only option.

The SGC guidance points out that the operational period should reflect the length of sentence being suspended. For example, an operational period of up to 18 months might be appropriate for a suspended sentence of up to 12 months.

The SGC also gives guidance on the imposition of requirements during the supervision period. To ensure that the overall terms of the sentence are commensurate with the seriousness of the offence, the requirements to be undertaken during the supervision period should usually be less onerous than if a community sentence had been imposed (because of the clear deterrent threat involved in a suspended sentence). A court wishing to impose onerous community requirements on an offender should therefore consider whether a community sentence might be more appropriate than a suspended sentence. Any community requirements should address those factors that are most likely to reduce the risk of re-offending.

16.5.1 Breach of suspended sentence requirements or re-offending during the operational period

This is governed by Sch 12 to the CJA 2003.

Where an offender has breached any of the requirements without reasonable excuse for the first time, the responsible officer must either give a warning or initiate breach proceedings (para 4). Where there is a further breach within a 12-month period, breach proceedings must be initiated (para 5).

Under para 8, if the offender is brought to court because he or she:

- has failed, without reasonable excuse, to comply with any of the community requirements of the suspended sentence order, or
- is convicted of an offence committed during the operational period of a suspended sentence,

then the court has three options:

1. order that the suspended sentence take effect with its original custodial period unaltered (this is sometimes known as 'activating' the suspended sentence); or
2. order that the sentence take effect but with a shorter period of custody (ie activating the suspended sentence only in part); or
3. amend the order by:
    - imposing more onerous community requirements
    - extending the supervision period, or
    - extending the operational period.

There is a presumption (under para 8(3)) that the suspended prison sentence will be activated, either with its original custodial term or a lesser term, unless the court takes the view that this would, in all the circumstances, be unjust. In reaching this decision, the court may take into account both the extent to which the offender has complied with the requirements and the facts of the new offence.

The SGC has given guidance on the action to be taken where the offender commits a further offence during the operational period of the suspended sentence:

- If the new offence is committed near the end of the operational period (the offender having complied with the requirements imposed), it may be more appropriate to amend the order rather than activate the custodial term.
- If the new offence is of a less serious nature than the offence for which the suspended sentence was passed, this may justify activating the suspended sentence with a reduced term or amending the terms of the order.
- It is expected that any activated suspended sentence will be consecutive to the sentence imposed for the new offence.

- If the new offence is non-imprisonable, the sentencer should consider whether it is appropriate to activate the suspended sentence at all (the implication being that it would generally not be appropriate).
- Where the court decides to amend a suspended sentence order rather than activate the custodial sentence, it should give serious consideration to extending the supervision or operational periods (within statutory limits) rather than making the requirements more onerous.

16.6 Intermittent custody

This sentence (which is governed by s 183 of the CJA 2003) applies to sentences of under 12 months. The court specifies a number of 'custodial days', but these are not served all in one go. Rather, the offender is released on temporary licence at set intervals throughout the sentence. The court may only impose intermittent custody if the offender consents to serving the custodial part of the sentence intermittently.

Under s 183(4), the term of the sentence must be at least 28 weeks, and must not be more than 51 weeks in respect of any one offence. Under s 183(5), the 'custodial days' have to number between 14 and 90 (unless the offender is being dealt with for two or more offences, in which case the maximum is 180 custodial days). Where the court is sentencing for two or more offences and imposes consecutive terms of imprisonment, the aggregate length of the terms of imprisonment must not be more than 65 weeks, and the aggregate of the numbers of custodial days must not be more than 180 (see s 183(7)).

SGC guidance suggested that suitable candidates for weekend custody might include offenders who are: full-time carers; employed; or in education. However, the Home Office announced that Intermittent Custody was to be withdrawn with effect from 20 November 2006. The relevant provisions remain on the statute book, however, and so this form of custodial order may be re-introduced at some stage.

16.7 Offenders aged 18–20: detention in a young offender institution

Under s 96 of the PCC(S)A 2000, the custodial sentence applicable to an offender who is aged 18, 19 or 20 at the date of conviction is 'detention in a young offender institution'.

The maximum term of such detention is the same as the maximum term of imprisonment that the court may impose on an adult for that offence.

Under s 189(1) of the Criminal Justice Act 2003, a sentence of detention in a young offender institution may be suspended in the same way that a sentence of imprisonment can. The discussion of suspended sentences (see above) is therefore equally applicable to detention in a young offender institution.

This sentence is due to be abolished (so that offenders aged 18–20 would be sentenced to the custodial sentences that are currently available in the case of offenders who have attained the age of 21). However, the provision that repeals s 96 of the 2000 Act (s 61 of the Criminal Justice and Court Services Act 2000) has not yet been brought into force.

17

Non-custodial sentences in the youth court

17.1 Introduction

In this chapter, we look at the non-custodial sentences available where the offender is under the age of 18. Offenders under the age of 18 are subject to a different range of non-custodial sentences to adult offenders (see **Chapter 15**).

17.1.1 The aims of sentencing young offenders

The Criminal Justice and Immigration Act 2008 inserts a new section, s 142A, into the Criminal Justice Act 2003, setting out the purposes of sentencing offenders aged under 18. It provides as follows:

> (1) This section applies where a court is dealing with an offender aged under 18 in respect of an offence.
>
> (2) The court must have regard primarily to the principal aim of the youth justice system, that is, to prevent offending by children and other persons aged under 18.
>
> (3) The court must also—
>
> > (a) have regard to the purposes of sentencing mentioned in subsection (4), so far as it is not required to do so by subsection (2), and
> >
> > (b) in accordance with section 44 of the Children and Young Persons Act 1933, have regard to the welfare of the offender.
>
> (4) Those purposes of sentencing are—
>
> > (a) the punishment of offenders,
> >
> > (b) the reform and rehabilitation of offenders,
> >
> > (c) the protection of the public, and
> >
> > (d) the making of reparation by offenders to persons affected by their offences.

The 2008 Act also amends s 142 of the 2003 Act to make it clear that where a young defendant reaches his 18th birthday before being sentenced, the court must have regard to the adult purposes of sentencing in s 142 (not s 142A).

17.2 Fines and discharges

Young offenders may be dealt with by means of a fine or an absolute or conditional discharge.

17.2.1 Absolute discharge

See **15.1**.

17.2.2 Conditional discharge

See **15.2**. In the case of young offenders, it should be noted that s 66(4) of the Crime and Disorder Act 1998 provides that where a juvenile who has received a warning under s 65 is convicted of an offence committed within two years of the warning, the court is not permitted to order a conditional discharge in respect of the offence unless it is of the opinion that there are exceptional circumstances relating to the offence or the offender which justify its doing so.

17.2.3 Fines

Where the offender is aged 15, 16 or 17, the maximum fine that may be imposed is £1,000. Where the offender is aged between 10 and 14, the maximum fine is £250.

Where the offender is under 16, the court *must* order that the fine is paid by the offender's parents (and so the means of the parents have to be taken into account in assessing the amount of the fine). If the offender is aged 16 or 17, the court *may* order the parents to pay the fine. See s 137 of the PCC(S)A 2000; **6.3.2.2**.

17.2.4 Binding over

Where the offender is under the age of 16, the court must consider binding over the parents to take proper care of, and exercise proper control over, the offender. See s 150 of the PCC(S)A 2000. In fact, such orders are comparatively rare.

17.3 Referral order

Provision for referral orders is made by ss 16–18 of the PCC(S)A 2000.

Under s 17(1), the making of a referral order is *mandatory* (unless the court is considering either an absolute discharge or the imposition of a custodial sentence) if the offender pleads guilty to an imprisonable offence and has not previously been convicted of any offence.

Under s 17(2), the making of a referral order is *discretionary* if (a) the offender is being dealt with for two or more connected offences, pleads guilty to at least one of them and has not previously been convicted of any offence, or (b) the offender has one previous finding of guilt but was not referred to a youth offender panel under s 16 on that occasion, or (c) the offender has one or more previous findings of guilt and has been referred to a youth offender panel under s 16 on only one previous occasion, an appropriate officer recommends a referral order, and the court considers that there are exceptional circumstances which justify a referral order.

Under s 19(4), where the court makes a referral order, it cannot also impose a community sentence, a fine, a reparation order, or a conditional discharge, nor can it bind the offender's parents over.

As part of complying with the referral order, the offender has to attend meetings with a 'youth offender panel', over a period of between three and 12 months.

In addition, the offender can be required to comply with additional requirements (see s 23), such as:

- making reparation;
- undergoing mediation;
- carrying out unpaid work;
- taking part in specified activities;
- refraining from taking part in specified activities;
- staying away from specified places and/or people.

17.4 Pre-sentence reports on young offenders

Section 156 of the CJA 2003 requires the court to obtain a pre-sentence report before deciding that an offence is sufficiently serious to merit a community sentence and before deciding what restrictions on the offender's liberty are commensurate with the seriousness of the offence. Where the offender has attained the age of 18, the court can take the view that a report is unnecessary. However, under s 156(5), if the offender is under the age of 18, the court cannot dispense with a pre-sentence report unless there exists a previous pre-sentence report obtained in respect of the offender, and the court has had regard to the information contained in that report (or, if there is more than one such report, the most recent report).

17.5 Youth Rehabilitation Order under the Criminal Justice and Immigration Act 2008

17.5.1 Youth rehabilitation orders

Section 1 of the Criminal Justice and Immigration Act 2008 creates a new generic community sentence – the 'youth rehabilitation order' – for children and young people, mirroring the generic community order for adults established by the Criminal Justice Act 2003. As a consequence of the new sentencing regime for young offenders, the Act also makes provision for the abolition of certain existing youth orders which could be made under the Powers of Criminal Courts (Sentencing) Act 2000, namely curfew orders, exclusion orders, attendance centre orders, supervision orders and action plan orders.

The 2008 Act provides that, where a person aged under 18 is convicted of an offence, the court may make a youth rehabilitation order imposing any one or more of the following requirements (the detailed description of which is set out in Sch 1 of the Act):

(a) an 'activity requirement': this requires the offender to participate in specified activities for a total of up to 90 days;

(b) a 'supervision requirement': this requires the offender to attend appointments with their supervisor;

(c) in a case where the offender is aged 16 or 17 at the time of the conviction, an 'unpaid work requirement': the number of hours must be between 40 and 240, and the work should be completed within 12 months;

(d) a 'programme requirement': this requires participation in a systematic set of activities (designed to allow juvenile offenders to engage in programmes that will address their offending behaviour, teach life-skills and engage in other positive interventions to prevent re-offending);

(e) an 'attendance centre requirement': up to a maximum of 12 hours for an offender aged under 14, between 12 and 24 hours for an offender aged 14 or 15, and between 12 and 36 hours if the offender is aged 16 or over (an offender cannot be required to attend at an attendance centre on more than one occasion on any day, or for more than three hours on any occasion; whilst at the attendance centre, the offender is required to engage in occupation, or receive instruction, under the supervision of and in accordance with instructions given by the officer in charge of the centre);

(f) a 'prohibited activity requirement': this requires the offender to refrain from participating in specified activities for a specified period;

(g) a 'curfew requirement': this requires the offender to remain, for specified periods, at a specified place for between 2 and 12 hours in any given day over a period of up to 6 months;

(h) an 'exclusion requirement': this prohibits the offender from entering a specified place for a specified period of up to 3 months;

(i) a 'residence requirement': this requires the offender to reside with a specified individual or, if the offender was aged 16 or over at the time of conviction, at a specified place;

(j) a 'local authority residence requirement': this requires the offender to reside, for up to 6 months, in accommodation provided by the local authority; this requirement can only be imposed if the court is satisfied that the behaviour which constituted the offence was due to a significant extent to the circumstances in which the offender was living, and that the imposition of the requirement will assist in the offender's rehabilitation;

(k) a 'mental health treatment requirement': this requires the offender to undergo mental health treatment, as an in-patient or out-patient, by a registered medical practitioner and/or chartered psychologist; such a requirement may be imposed only if the mental condition of the offender is such as requires and may be susceptible to treatment, but is not such as to warrant the making of a hospital order or guardianship order under the Mental Health Act 1983; the consent of the offender is also required;

(l) a 'drug treatment requirement': this requires the offender to undergo drug treatment, as an in-patient or out-patient, by a specified person with the necessary qualifications; this requirement may be imposed only if the court is satisfied that the offender is dependent on or has a propensity to misuse any drug, and requires and may be susceptible to treatment; the consent of the offender is also required;

(m) a 'drug testing requirement': this requires the offender to provide samples for drug-testing purposes; such a requirement may only be imposed with a drug treatment requirement and with the consent of the offender;

(n) an 'intoxicating substance treatment' requirement: this requires the offender to undergo treatment, as an in-patient or out-patient, but may only be imposed if the offender is dependent on, or has a propensity to misuse, intoxicating substances, and this dependency or propensity is such as requires and may be susceptible to treatment; the consent of the offender is also required; and

(o) an 'education requirement': this requires the offender to comply with approved education arrangements, namely those made by the offender's parent or guardian and approved by the local authority; such a requirement may be imposed only if the court is satisfied that it is necessary for the offender's future good conduct or prevention of further offending.

The Act enables the court to impose an electronic monitoring requirement as part of a youth rehabilitation order (s 1(2)).

Under s 1(3), a youth rehabilitation order may be a 'youth rehabilitation order with intensive supervision and surveillance' (this is an 'extended activity requirement' for between a total of 90 and 180 days, together with a supervision requirement, a curfew requirement and an electronic monitoring requirement) or a 'youth rehabilitation order with fostering' (this is a requirement that the offender must reside with a local authority foster parent for up to 12 months; such a requirement can only be imposed if the court is satisfied that the behaviour which constituted the offence was due to a significant extent to the circumstances in which the offender was living, and that the imposition of a fostering requirement would assist in the offender's rehabilitation). An order may only take one of these forms if the offence for which the juvenile is being sentenced is punishable with imprisonment in the case of an adult offender, and the court is of the opinion that the offence(s) are so serious that a custodial sentence would otherwise be appropriate. Moreover, if the offender was aged under 15 at the time of conviction, the court must also be of the opinion that he is a persistent offender.

Section 1(6) of the Act makes it clear that the power to impose a youth rehabilitation order is subject to ss 148 and 150 of the Criminal Justice Act 2003 (restrictions on community sentences), and so a youth rehabilitation order may be imposed only if the seriousness of the offence merits it, and the requirements imposed must be commensurate with the seriousness of the offence.

Schedule 2 to the Act makes detailed provision about failures to comply with the requirements of youth rehabilitation orders and about the revocation or amendment of such orders.

18

Custodial sentences in the youth court

18.1 Introduction

In this chapter, we look at the detention and training order, which is the custodial sentence applicable to offenders who fall within the jurisdiction of the youth court.

18.2 Detention and training orders

Under the PCC(S)A 2000, s 100, an offender aged under 18 at the date of conviction may be sentenced to a detention and training order ('DTO').

The minimum age for such a sentence is 12 (although the Secretary of State has power under the Act to include 10 and 11 year olds).

If the offender was under 15 at the date of conviction, a DTO may be imposed only if the juvenile is a 'persistent offender'. Surprisingly, this term is not defined in the legislation. Normally, a juvenile will be regarded as a persistent offender because of the number of previous findings of guilt. However, a juvenile may also be regarded as a persistent offender on the basis that he or she is currently being dealt with for several offences (see *R v Charlton* (2000) 164 JP 685).

A sentence of DTO is a custodial sentence (and so the custody 'threshold' criteria have to be met).

The total length of the DTO has to be 4, 6, 8, 10, 12, 18 or 24 months (s 101(1)). It follows that a DTO cannot be imposed where the maximum sentence in the case of an adult offender is less than four months. Accordingly, it is unlawful for a youth court to impose a detention and training order for an offence of criminal damage in respect of an offender under the age of 18 where the value of the damage is less than £5,000 (since the maximum sentence for an adult in such a case is three months but the minimum DTO is four): (*Pye v Leeds Youth Court* [2006] EWHC 2527). For summary offences, the length of the DTO must not exceed 6 months (s 101(2A)).

An offender who receives a DTO is placed in detention for half of the term of the order. On release, the juvenile is then placed under supervision for the rest of the order (supervision being provided by a probation officer, social worker or member of youth offending team).

It should be noted that, as regards the DTOs, the powers of the youth court and the Crown Court are identical, as neither court can exceed the maximum duration of 24 months.

If the juvenile fails to comply with the supervision requirement under the DTO, the court can (under s 104(3)) either:

- order that the offender must return to custody (for three months or for the remainder of the order, whichever is less); or
- impose a fine of up to £1,000.

If the juvenile re-offends during the second half of the DTO, the court may (as well as dealing with the juvenile offender for the later offence) order that he or she return to custody for the length of time between the date of the offence and the expiry of the original order (s 105).

18.3 More serious offences

If the juvenile is charged with an offence which falls within the scope of s 91 of the PCC(S)A 2000 (see **Chapter 20**) and indicates an intention to plead not guilty, the youth court has to decide whether to try the case or to send the juvenile to the Crown Court for trial. Where the juvenile indicates a guilty plea to an offence to which s 91 applies, the youth court has to decide whether to pass sentence itself (bearing in mind the limitations on both the length of the DTO and the offenders who can be made subject to a DTO) or to commit the juvenile to the Crown Court for sentence. The Crown Court may then pass a sentence under s 91.

18.4 Summary: custodial sentences available according to age

- 10–11: the only custodial sentence available is detention under s 91 of the PCC(S)A 2000 (and only the Crown Court can impose such a sentence);
- 12, 13 or 14: a 'DTO' is available, provided that the juvenile is a 'persistent offender'; detention under s 91 of the 2000 Act is also available in appropriate cases;
- 15, 16 or 17: a 'DTO' is available; detention under s 91 is also available in appropriate cases.

19

Non-custodial sentences in the Crown Court

Apart from the amount of any fine, the powers of the Crown Court to impose non-custodial sentences are identical to those of the magistrates' court, set out in **Chapter 15** of this manual. This chapter will therefore simply summarise some of the key points.

19.1 Fines

The Crown Court is empowered to impose a fine instead of, or in addition to, dealing with the offender in any other way (the CJA 2003, s 163). This is so whether the offender was convicted in the Crown Court or was committed to the Crown Court for sentence under the PCC(S)A 2000, s 3.

There is no statutory limit on the amount of a fine imposed by the Crown Court.

Where the Crown Court imposes a fine it must fix a term of imprisonment (if the offender is aged 21 or over) or detention in a young offenders institution (if the offender is aged between 18 and 20) in default. The maximum term set in default depends on the amount of the fine (see PCC(S)A 2000, s 139(4)):

Fine (£)	Term (maximum)
1–200	7 days
201–500	14 days
501–1,000	28 days
1,001–2,500	45 days
2,501–5,000	3 months
5,001–10,000	6 months
10,001–20,000	12 months
20,001–50,000	18 months
50,001–100,000	2 years
100,001–250,000	3 years
250,001–1,000,000	5 years
over 1,000,000	10 years

19.2 Other non-custodial sentences

Like a magistrates' court, the Crown Court is empowered to impose any of the following:

- absolute discharge;
- conditional discharge (1–3 years);
- community order.

Where the Crown Court is dealing with a juvenile (for example, where the juvenile was charged alongside an adult and the magistrates decided that it was necessary in the interests of justice for the juvenile to be sent to the Crown Court to be tried with the adult), there is a statutory presumption that the Crown Court should remit the juvenile to the youth court for sentence. Section 8(2) of the PCC(S)A 2000 provides that in such a case the court shall, unless satisfied that it would be undesirable to do so, remit the case to the youth court. However, in *R v Lewis* (1984) 79 Cr App R 94, Lord Lane CJ pointed out that declining to remit to the youth court could be justified for a number of reasons (for example, the Crown Court judge will, after the trial, be better informed about the facts of the offence and general nature of the case than the youth court could hope to be; sentencing the juvenile in the Crown Court will avoid the risk of unjustifiable disparity in sentencing that could otherwise arise if the juvenile and adult are sentenced by separate courts; and remitting the case would cause delay, unnecessary duplication of proceedings and extra expense). Where the Crown Court does pass sentence on the juvenile, all the non-custodial options available to a youth court are equally available to the Crown Court (see **Chapter 17**).

19.3 Breach of community order imposed by the Crown Court

Where the Crown Court imposes a community order, it can include in the order a direction that any failure to comply with the requirements of the order is to be dealt with by a magistrates' court. Where the order does not contain such a stipulation and the offender breaches the order, he or she will be brought before the Crown Court pursuant to para 8(2) of Sch 8 to the CJA 2003, which provides that, if it appears to the Crown Court that the offender has failed to comply with any of the requirements of the order, it may issue a summons (or an arrest warrant) to secure the offender's attendance. Under para 8(4), if a summons is issued but the offender fails to appear before the Crown Court, an arrest warrant may be issued.

Under para 9(6), where a community order was made by the Crown Court and the order provided that any failure to comply could be dealt with by a magistrates' court, and the offender is brought before the magistrates for non-compliance with the order, the magistrates have a discretion to commit the offender (in custody or on bail) to the Crown Court to be dealt with for the breach.

Paragraph 10(1) sets out the powers of the Crown Court where it is dealing with an offender for breach of a community order. If it is proved to the satisfaction of the court that the offender has failed, without reasonable excuse, to comply with any of the requirements of the community order, the Crown Court *must* deal with the offender in one of the following ways:

(a) *by amending the terms of the community order so as to impose more onerous requirements which the Crown Court could impose if it were then making the order;*

(b) *by dealing with him, for the offence in respect of which the order was made, in any way in which he could have been dealt with for that offence by the court which made the order if the order had not been made;*

(c) *where—*
   (i) *the offence in respect of which the order was made was not an offence punishable by imprisonment,*
   (ii) *the offender is aged 18 or over,*
   (iii) *the offender has wilfully and persistently failed to comply with the requirements of the order,*

by dealing with him, in respect of that offence, by imposing a sentence of imprisonment for a term not exceeding 51 weeks [6 months until the relevant provisions of the CJA 2003 come into force].

Paragraph 10(2) requires the Crown Court to take account of the extent to which the offender has complied with the requirements of the community order.

Paragraph 10(3) makes it clear that, if the Crown Court adopts the option set out in para 10(1)(a), it may extend the duration of particular requirements under the community order, but not beyond the three-year maximum duration of community order fixed by s 177(5) of the Act.

Paragraph 10(4) goes on to provide that where the Crown Court adopts the option set out in para 10(1)(b) in the case of an offender who has wilfully and persistently failed to comply with the requirements of the community order, it may impose a custodial sentence (provided the offence for which the community order was imposed was an imprisonable offence) whether or not the original offence crossed the custody threshold contained in s 152(2) of the Act.

Under para 10(5), if the Crown Court chooses either of the options set out in para 10(1)(b) or (c), it must also revoke the community order if it is still in force.

Finally, para 10(6) makes it clear that the question whether the offender has complied with the requirements of the community order is to be determined by a Crown Court judge sitting alone (without a jury).

19.4 Revocation of Crown Court community orders other than for breach

Under para 14(1) of Schedule 8 to the CJA 2003, where the community order was made by the Crown Court and does not include a direction that any failure to comply with the requirements of the order is to be dealt with by a magistrates' court, any application by the offender or by the 'responsible officer' for the order to be revoked, or for the offender to be dealt with in some other way for the original offence, has to be made to the Crown Court.

Where such an application is made, para 14(2) empowers the Crown Court, if it takes the view that it is in the interests of justice to do so (having regard to circumstances which have arisen since the order was made), either to revoke the order or else both to revoke the order and re-sentence the offender for the original offence.

Para 14(3) provides that the circumstances in which a community order may be revoked include the fact that the offender is making good progress or is responding satisfactorily to supervision or treatment.

If the court re-sentences the offender for the original offence, it must take into account the extent to which the offender has complied with the requirements of the community order (para 14(4)).

19.5 Commission of subsequent offences

Paragraph 22(1) of Sch 8 to the CJA 2003 provides that where an offender is subject to a community order made by the Crown Court and is convicted of an offence by a magistrates' court, the magistrates' court may commit the offender (in custody or on bail) to the Crown Court.

Under para 23(1) and (2), where an offender in respect of whom a community order is in force is either convicted of an offence by the Crown Court, or sent to the Crown Court under para 22, the Crown Court may either revoke the order or else both revoke the order and re-sentence the offender for the original offence.

Paragraph 23(1)(b) stipulates that the Crown Court may only exercise the power conferred by para 23 if it would be in the interests of justice to do so, having regard to circumstances which have arisen since the community order was made.

If the court re-sentences the offender for the original offence, it must take into account the extent to which the offender has complied with the requirements of the community order (para 23(3)).

20

Custodial sentences in the Crown Court

20.1 Introduction

In this chapter we consider the custodial sentences that can be imposed by the Crown Court on offenders who have attained the age of 18.

Where the offender is aged 18–20 (inclusive) the appropriate custodial sentence is 'detention in a young offender institution' (see **Chapter 16**). The maximum sentence is the same as that applicable to offenders who have attained the age of 21.

Where the offender has attained the age of 21, the custodial sentences available to the Crown Court are:

(a) Sentences of less than 12 months, including:
 (i) custody plus (when the relevant provisions are brought into force);
 (ii) suspended sentence;
 (iii) intermittent custody (although this form of sentence is not currently in use).
(b) Sentences of over 12 months.

Sentences of less than 12 months are considered in **Chapter 16**.

20.2 Sentences over 12 months—release on licence

Prisoners serving sentences of 12 months or more (apart from dangerous offenders and life sentence prisoners, for whom there is separate provision) must be released on licence after serving half of their sentence. This release is subject to 'standard' and 'prescribed' conditions (and so, in effect, the second half of the sentence is 'served in the community').

The SGC Guidance on the sentences created by the CJA 2003 Act says that:

- A court may sensibly suggest interventions that could be useful when passing sentence, but should only make specific recommendations about the requirements to be imposed on licence when announcing short sentences and where it is reasonable to anticipate their relevance at the point of release. The Governor and Probation

Service should have due regard to any recommendations made by the sentencing court but the final decision should be contingent upon any changed circumstances during the custodial period.

- The court should make it clear, at the point of sentence, that the requirements to be imposed on licence will ultimately be the responsibility of the Governor and Probation Service and that they are entitled to review any recommendations made by the court in the light of any changed circumstances.

The *Criminal Justice (Sentencing) (Licence Conditions) Order 2005* (SI 2005/648) sets out conditions of licences upon release from prison under s 250 of the Criminal Justice Act 2003: there are standard conditions and additional conditions that may be imposed. The standard conditions of licence (under para 2) include requirements that the prisoner must keep in touch with the responsible officer, permanently reside at an address approved by the responsible officer (and obtain the prior permission for any stay of one or more nights at a different address), undertake work only with the prior approval of the responsible officer, not travel outside the UK without prior permission, be of good behaviour, and not commit any offence. Other conditions of licence that may be imposed on a prisoner (under para 3) include residence at a certain place, a restriction relating to making or maintaining contact with a specified person, a restriction on participation in a specified activity, participation in a programme or set of activities designed to further certain objectives (namely the protection of the public, the prevention of reoffending, and securing the successful reintegration of the prisoner into the community), compliance with a curfew, restrictions on the prisoner's freedom of movement, or a requirement relating to supervision in the community by a responsible officer, a restriction on his or her participation in, or undertaking of, an activity, compliance with a curfew, and supervision in the community by a responsible officer.

20.3 Life sentences—murder

An offender aged 21 or over who is convicted of murder must be sentenced to imprisonment for life. In fact, as is well known, life generally does not mean life. The offender will be eligible for release after serving a specified minimum period of detention. The setting of the 'tariff' for such cases is governed in part by Sch 21 to the CJA 2003. However, in *R v Last* [2005] EWCA Crim 106; [2005] 2 Cr App R (S) 64, the Court of Appeal said that judges are free to depart from the guidelines contained in Sch 21 (and guidance issued by the Sentencing Guidelines Council), provided that valid reasons are given for doing so.

20.4 Mandatory minimum sentences

Under the PCC(S)A 2000, s 110, the court must impose a mandatory minimum sentence of at least seven years' custody where the offender is convicted for the third time of trafficking in class A drugs unless 'particular circumstances' (relating to the offences or the offender) make this 'unjust'.

Under s 111 of the 2000 Act, the court must impose a sentence of at least three years' custody where the offender is convicted for the third time of domestic burglary unless 'particular circumstances' (relating to the offences or the offender) make this 'unjust'.

Finally, s 51A of the Firearms Act 1968 lays down mandatory minimum sentences for certain firearms offences: a minimum term of five years in the case of an offender who was aged 18 or over when he committed the offence or three years in the case of an offender who was under 18 at that time. The court has to impose a sentence of not less than this minimum term unless it is of the opinion that there are exceptional circumstances relating to the offence or to the offender which justify not doing so. In *R v Redfern* [2004] EWCA Crim 3291; [2005] 2 Cr App R (S) 44, the Court of Appeal expressed the view that cases where there are exceptional circumstances will be rare.

20.5 Dangerous offenders

Sections 224–236 of the CJA 2003 deal with dangerous offenders. These complex provisions apply only to certain offences. Section 224 defines the key terms. A 'specified offence' means a violent offence specified in Part 1 of Sch 15 to the Act or a sexual offence specified in Part 2 of that Schedule. A 'serious offence' means a violent or sexual offence specified in Sch 15 and punishable with life imprisonment or a determinate sentence of at least ten years' imprisonment. The phrase 'serious harm' means death or serious personal injury (whether physical or psychological).

Section 225 enables the court to impose imprisonment for public protection where an offender aged 18 or over is convicted of a 'serious offence' and the court is of the opinion that there is a significant risk to members of the public of serious harm occasioned by him of further specified offences (i.e. offences specified in Sch 15). Under s 225(2), if the offence is punishable with life imprisonment and the court considers the seriousness of the offence(s) to be such as to justify the imposition of a life sentence, then the court must impose a life sentence. In all other cases which fall within s 225 but not within s 225(2), the court (under s 225(3)) may impose a sentence of imprisonment for public protection if either (a) at the time the offence was committed, the offender had one or more previous convictions for offences specified in Sch 15A (s 225(3A)) or (b) the minimum term appropriate for the present offence is at least two years (s 225(3B)). Under s 225(4), a sentence of imprisonment for public protection is a sentence of imprisonment for an indeterminate period.

Section 226 applies similar principles to offenders under the age of 18.

Section 227 enables the court to impose an 'extended sentence' where the offender has attained the age of 18 and is convicted of a specified violent or sexual offence, and the court considers that there is a significant risk to members of the public of serious harm, caused by the offender committing further specified offences (ie offences specified in Sch 15), but the court is not required by s 225(2) to impose a life sentence. The court may impose an extended sentence if either (a) at the time the offence was committed, the offender had one or more previous convictions for offences specified in Sch 15A (s 227(2A) or, if the court were to impose an extended sentence, the term that it would specify as the appropriate custodial term would be at least four years (s 227(2B)).

Section 227(2C) defines an 'extended sentence' as a sentence of imprisonment the term of which is equal to the aggregate of (a) the appropriate custodial term (defined in s 227(3) as the term that is commensurate with the seriousness of the offence), and (b) a further period ('the extension period') for which the offender is to be subject to a licence and which is 'of such length as the court considers necessary for the purpose of protecting members of the public from serious harm occasioned by the commission by him of further specified offences'. Section 227(4) provides that the extension period must not exceed five years in the case of a specified violent offence, and eight years in the case of a specified sexual offence. In any event, the term of an extended sentence of imprisonment must not exceed the maximum term permitted for the offence (s 227(5)).

Section 228 applies similar provisions to offenders under the age of 18.

Section 229(2) provides that, when assessing dangerousness, the court must take into account all available information about the nature and circumstances of the present offence, and may take into account any available information about the nature and circumstances of any previous convictions and any information about any pattern of behaviour of which the present and/or previous convictions form part, and may take into account any other information about the offender which is before it.

In *R v Lang* [2005] EWCA Crim 2864; [2006] 2 Cr App R (S) 3, the Court of Appeal gave detailed guidance on these provisions:

(a) 'Significant risk to members of the public' requires significant risk to be shown in relation to two matters: the commission of further specified, but not necessarily serious, offences; and the causing thereby of serious harm to members of the public. The risk must be significant, meaning 'noteworthy, of considerable amount or importance'.

(b) In assessing the risk of further offences being committed, the court must take into account the nature and circumstances of the present offence, the defendant's history of offending (including the kind of offence, its circumstances, and the sentence passed, and whether the defendant demonstrated any pattern), social and economic factors in relation to the defendant (including accommodation, employability, education, associates, relationships, and drug or alcohol abuse), and the defendant's attitude towards offending.

(c) A pre-sentence report should usually be obtained before any sentence is passed which is based upon significant risk of harm. The court will be guided, but not bound by, the assessment of risk in such reports; if the judge contemplates differing from the assessment, counsel should be given the opportunity of addressing the point.

(d) The court should guard against assuming that there is a significant risk of serious harm merely because the foreseen specified offence is serious. Where the foreseen specified offence is not serious, there will be comparatively few cases in which a risk of serious harm can properly be regarded as significant.

(e) In relation to particularly young offenders, an indeterminate sentence might be inappropriate even where a serious offence has been committed and there is a significant risk of serious harm from further offences.

(f) Escalation of risk of serious harm can, in appropriate cases, properly be inferred from a multiplicity of relatively minor offences.

(g) Where defendants are to be sentenced for several offences, only some of which were serious or specified, a court which imposes an indeterminate sentence under ss 225 or 226, or an extended sentence under ss 227 or 228 for the principal offences, should generally impose a shorter concurrent term for the other offences.

In *R v Johnson* [2006] EWCA Crim 2486; [2007] 1 WLR 585, the Court of Appeal observed that previous convictions for offences which are not specified offences may be relevant (a pattern of minor previous offences of gradually escalating seriousness may be significant). In *R v Reynolds* [2007] EWCA Crim 538; [2007] 2 Cr App R (S) 87, the Court of Appeal observed that the 'dangerous offender' regime requires the court to carry out a careful step-by-step evaluation of the sentencing consequences of the type of offence, the age of the offender and the assessment of dangerousness.

The Sentencing Guidelines Council has issued guidance entitled *Dangerous Offenders: Guide for Sentencers and Practitioners* (available on their website at <http://www.sentencing-guidelines.gov.uk/docs/Dangerous%20Offenders%20%E2%80%93%20Guide%20for%20Sentencers%20and%20Practitioners.pdf>). Annex A contains useful flow charts for both adult offenders and young offenders.

20.6 Young offenders—long-term detention under PCC(S)A 2000, s 91

Under s 91 of the PCC(S)A 2000, the Crown Court may impose a sentence of long-term detention (the maximum length of the sentence being the same as for an adult offender) where an offender under the age of 18 is being dealt with for an offence which is punishable (in the case of an adult offender) with 14 years' imprisonment or more (or the offence is one of those specified in s 91 itself, such as sexual assault).

This power is available in two circumstances:

(a) where the offender pleads guilty in the youth court and the youth court decides that the case is too serious for them to deal with, the offender may be committed to the Crown Court to be sentenced; or

(b) where the accused indicates an intention to plead not guilty and the youth court, having heard a summary of the case from the prosecution (and any representations from the defence) decide that, in the event of conviction, a sentence of detention under s 91 of the 2000 Act ought to be available, the accused is sent to the Crown Court for trial.

Section 91 has two important effects:

(a) it enables the Crown Court to impose a sentence of detention that is longer than a detention and training order (which is limited to a total of no more than 24 months, of which half is spent in custody and half is spent, under supervision, in the community: see **Chapter 18**); and

(b) it enables the Crown Court to impose a custodial sentence on young offenders for whom a detention and training order is not available (namely (i) those aged 10 and 11, and (ii) those aged 12–14 and who are not 'persistent offenders').

In *R (C) v Balham Youth Court* [2003] EWHC (Admin) 1332; [2004] 1 Cr App R (S) 22, Scott Baker LJ (at para 33) said that 'the fact that an offender . . . does not qualify for a detention and training order because he is only 14 and not a persistent offender is not an exceptional circumstance to justify passing a sentence of less than two years under s 91 of the 2000 Act'. At para 34, his Lordship said that the relevant question in that case was whether it was such a serious case that detention above two years would or might realistically be required. In *R (M and W) v West London Youth Court* [2004] EWHC (Admin) 1144, Leveson J (at para 16) put the same question in slightly different terms:

Whether there is a real prospect that a custodial sentence of, or in excess of, two years might be required, or is there any unusual feature of this case which might justify a sentence of less than two years, pursuant to s 91(3), for which purpose the absence of a power to impose a detention and training order because the offender is under the age of 15 is not an unusual feature.

In *R (H) v Southampton Youth Court* [2004] EWHC 2912 (Admin); [2005] 2 Cr App R (S) 30, it was emphasised that offenders under 18, and in particular those under 15, should be tried in the youth court, with Crown Court jurisdiction being reserved for the most serious crimes. It would, said the Court, only be in exceptional cases that an offender aged 12–14 should be sent for trial to the Crown Court. Leveson J summarised the relevant principles as follows (paras 33–35):

33. The general policy of the legislature is that those who are under 18 years of age, and in particular children of under 15 years of age, should, wherever possible, be tried in the youth court. It is that court which is best designed to meet their specific needs. A trial in the Crown Court with the inevitably greater formality and greatly increased number of people involved (including a jury and the public) should be reserved for the most serious cases.

34. It is a further policy of the legislature that, generally speaking, first-time offenders aged 12 to 14 and all offenders under 12 should not be detained in custody and decisions as to jurisdiction should have regard to the fact that the exceptional power to detain for grave offences should not be used to water down the general principle. Those under 15 will rarely attract a period of detention and, even more rarely, those who are under 12.

35. In each case the court should ask itself whether there is a real prospect, having regard to his or her age, that this defendant whose case they are considering might require a sentence of, or in excess of, two years or, alternatively, whether although the sentence might be less than two years, there is some unusual feature of the case which justifies declining jurisdiction, bearing in mind that the absence of a power to impose a detention and training order because the defendant is under 15 is not an unusual feature.

A useful summary of the approach to be taken in cases which fall within the ambit of s 91 may be found in *R (CPS) v Redbridge Youth Court* [2005] EWHC 1390 (Admin); (2005) 169 JP 393, at para 11.

An extended sentence under s 228 of the CJA 2003 cannot be added to a detention and training order under s 85 of the Powers of Criminal Court (Sentencing) Act 2000 (*R v B (Sentence: Detention and training orders)* [2005] EWCA Crim 312; [2005] 2 Cr App R (S) 87.

APPENDIX 1
TRIABLE EITHER WAY OFFENCES—DETERMINING THE MODE OF TRIAL (SS 17A–23, MCA 1980)

1 The usual procedure (ss 17A–21 and 23, MCA 1980)

If someone aged 18 or over appears or is brought before a magistrates' court on an information charging him or her with an offence triable either way, the magistrate (or magistrates) must determine the mode of trial: s 17A(1) and s 18(5). (A single lay justice may do this but it is unusual for this to happen.) See Figure A1.

2 Preliminary procedure for charges of criminal damage (s 22, MCA 1980)

For offences under the Criminal Damage Act 1971, s 1 (ie, destroying or damaging property), other than those involving arson, the following preliminary procedure must be used. This applies also to charges alleging that the accused attempted to commit such offence, or incited, aided, abetted, counselled or procured its commission (MCA 1980, s 22 sch 2).

Cross-refer to **Chapter 4** (Allocation), where offences which are triable either way are considered in more detail.

For charges involving allegations of criminal damage, there is a preliminary procedure which must be followed: MCA 1980, s 22.

Note that:

(a) The value involved is measured in accordance with the MCA 1980, Sch 2. Simply, it is the cost of repair (if possible) or replacement, whichever is the less, at the time the offence was committed.

(b) Where two or more criminal damage offences are alleged against the accused on the same occasion **and** they form a series (or part-series) of offences of the same or a similar character, then the value of the damage/destruction which is used by the court is the aggregate for all the offences: s 22(11).

(c) The court must treat the offence initially as triable either way, and work through the 'plea before venue' procedure (see MCA 1980, s 17A; **Chapter 4**) with the accused. If the accused either indicates a plea of *not guilty*, or makes no indication as to plea, the procedure set out above will be followed in order to determine where the accused will be tried.

If the accused indicates a plea of *guilty*, there is currently some doubt as to whether he or she may then be committed to the Crown Court for sentence if the value of the criminal

342 Appendix 1

```
┌─────────────────────────────────────────────────────────────────────┐
│ Clerk reads charge: s 17A(3). The court explains to D that D may    │
│ indicate whether, if the offence were to proceed to trial, D would  │
│ plead guilty or not guilty and that if D indicates that he or she   │
│ would plead guilty, the proceedings will be treated as a summary    │
│ trial at which a guilty plea has been entered and he or she may be  │
│ committed to the Crown Court for sentence: s 17A(4). The court      │
│ then asks D whether he or she would plead guilty or not guilty:     │
│ s 17A(5).                                                            │
└─────────────────────────────────────────────────────────────────────┘
             │                                    │
             ▼                                    ▼
   ┌──────────────────┐                  ┌──────────────────┐
   │ D indicates a not│                  │ D indicates a    │
   │ guilty plea.     │                  │ guilty plea.     │
   └──────────────────┘                  └──────────────────┘
             │                                    │
             │                                    ▼
             │                          ┌──────────────────────┐
             │                          │ Court proceeds as if │
             │                          │ D had pleaded guilty │
             │                          │ at a summary trial:  │
             │                          │ s 17A(6).            │
             │                          └──────────────────────┘
             ▼
┌─────────────────────────────────────────────────────────────────────┐
│ Prosecution given opportunity to make representations on the more   │
│ suitable mode of trial: s 19(2)(b).                                 │
└─────────────────────────────────────────────────────────────────────┘
             │
             ▼
┌─────────────────────────────────────────────────────────────────────┐
│ Defence given similar opportunity: s 19(2)(b).                      │
└─────────────────────────────────────────────────────────────────────┘
             │
             ▼
┌─────────────────────────────────────────────────────────────────────┐
│ Magistrates consider which mode more suitable having regard to      │
│ (i) any representations made; (ii) the nature of the case;          │
│ (iii) whether the circumstances make the offence one of a serious   │
│ character; (iv) whether they would have adequate sentencing powers; │
│ and (v) any other circumstances relevant to the decision: s 19(1)   │
│ and (3). See also the National Mode of Trial Guidelines.            │
└─────────────────────────────────────────────────────────────────────┘
             │                                    │
             ▼                                    ▼
   ┌──────────────────────────┐        ┌──────────────────────────┐
   │ Magistrates consider     │        │ Magistrates consider     │
   │ summary trial more       │        │ trial on indictment      │
   │ suitable.                │        │ more suitable.           │
   └──────────────────────────┘        └──────────────────────────┘
             │                                    │
             ▼                                    ▼
┌──────────────────────────────────────────┐  ┌──────────────────────┐
│ Clerk tells D of the decision and (i)    │  │ Court tells D trial  │
│ informs D that he or she may, if he or   │  │ on indictment is     │
│ she consents, be tried by magistrates or │  │ more suitable: s 21. │
│ may choose to be tried by jury; (ii)     │  └──────────────────────┘
│ informs D that if he or she chooses      │              │
│ summary trial and is found guilty, may   │              │
│ be committed to the Crown Court for      │              │
│ sentence; and (iii) puts D to his or her │              │
│ election: s 20.                          │              │
└──────────────────────────────────────────┘              │
             │                                            │
             ▼                                            │
┌──────────────────────────────────────────┐              │
│ D may seek an indication of sentence. If │              │
│ given one, D may ask to reconsider his   │              │
│ plea. If D changes to a guilty plea,     │              │
│ court proceeds in accordance with that.  │              │
│ Otherwise, mode of trial process         │              │
│ continues: s 20(3)–(7).                  │              │
└──────────────────────────────────────────┘              │
             │                                            │
    ┌────────┴────────┐                                   │
    ▼                 ▼                                   │
┌─────────────┐  ┌────────────────────────────────────┐   │
│ D consents  │  │ D does not consent to summary      │   │
│ to summary  │  │ trial: s 20(3)(b). Note: where Ds  │   │
│ trial:      │  │ are jointly charged with an        │   │
│ s 20(3)(a). │  │ offence and one elects trial on    │   │
└─────────────┘  │ indictment, it does not follow     │   │
    │            │ that all must be committed for     │   │
    ▼            │ trial. The right of election is    │   │
┌─────────────┐  │ given to each D individually, and  │   │
│ SUMMARY     │  │ not to all Ds collectively:        │   │
│ TRIAL       │  │ R v Brentwood JJ, ex parte         │   │
└─────────────┘  │ Nicholls [1991] 3 WLR 201 (HL).    │   │
                 └────────────────────────────────────┘   │
                              │                           │
                              ▼                           │
                 ┌────────────────────────┐               │
                 │ 'SENDING TO CROWN      │◄──────────────┘
                 │ COURT' PROCEEDINGS     │
                 └────────────────────────┘
```

Figure A1

damage is £5,000 or less (see, for example, *Blackstones' Criminal Practice*, 2009 edn, para D6.32). The offence is, of course, triable either way for purposes other than determining the mode of trial. It seems likely, though, that the procedure set out above will be followed up to the point where the value of the criminal damage is established. If the value of the criminal damage is found to be £5,000 or less, then the offence will continue to be regarded as summary only and there can be no committal for sentence under the Powers of Criminal Courts (Sentencing) Act 2000, s 3; see MCA 1980, s 33 (as amended). Conversely, if the value clearly exceeds £5,000, then the defendant may be committed for sentence and appropriate representations should be made to the magistrates on that topic. One suggestion is that the magistrates' court should determine the value of a criminal damage charge before it does anything else. If the value is £5,000 or less, then mode of trial procedure would not apply, neither would committal for sentence nor plea before venue. See Figure A2.

```
┌─────────────────────────────────────────────────────────────────────────┐
│ Court clerk indicates the offence is subject to the s 22 procedure.     │
└─────────────────────────────────────────────────────────────────────────┘
                                    │
                                    ▼
┌─────────────────────────────────────────────────────────────────────────┐
│ Prosecution given opportunity to make representations to the court on   │
│ whether the value of the damage/destruction exceeds the relevant sum    │
│ (currently £5,000): s 22(1).                                            │
└─────────────────────────────────────────────────────────────────────────┘
                                    │
                                    ▼
              ┌──────────────────────────────────────────┐
              │ Accused given similar opportunity: s 22(1). │
              └──────────────────────────────────────────┘
                                    │
      ┌─────────────────────────────┼─────────────────────────────┐
      ▼                             ▼                             ▼
┌──────────────────┐    ┌──────────────────┐    ┌──────────────────┐
│ It appears to    │    │ It appears to    │    │ It appears to    │
│ the court clear  │    │ the court unclear│    │ the court clear  │
│ that the value   │    │ whether the value│    │ that the value   │
│ involved is      │    │ involved         │    │ involved         │
│ £5,000 or less.  │    │ does/does not    │    │ exceeds £5,000.  │
│ The court        │    │ exceed £5,000:   │    │ The court then   │
│ proceeds as if   │    │ s 22(4).         │    │ proceeds as if   │
│ the offence were │    └──────────────────┘    │ it was an offence│
│ triable only     │                            │ triable either   │
│ summarily;       │                            │ way: s 22(3).    │
│ ss 19–21 do not  │                            └──────────────────┘
│ apply: s 22(2).  │
└──────────────────┘
         │                          │                          │
         ▼                          ▼                          ▼
┌──────────────────┐   ┌──────────────────────┐   ┌──────────────────┐
│ SUMMARY TRIAL    │   │ Clerk writes         │   │ MODE OF TRIAL    │
└──────────────────┘   │ charge(s) down,      │   │ DETERMINATION —  │
                       │ reads charge(s) to   │   │ ss 19–21         │
                       │ accused and explains:│   └──────────────────┘
                       │ (i) if he or she     │            │
                       │ wishes, the accused  │      ┌─────┴─────┐
                       │ can consent to       │      ▼           ▼
                       │ summary trial; (ii)  │  ┌────────┐ ┌────────┐
                       │ if tried summarily   │  │SUMMARY │ │CASE    │
                       │ and convicted, he or │  │TRIAL   │ │SENT TO │
                       │ she may be fined up  │  └────────┘ │CROWN   │
                       │ to £2,500 or         │             │COURT   │
                       │ imprisoned for up to │             │FOR     │
                       │ 3 months: s 22(5);   │             │TRIAL   │
                       │ s 33.                │             └────────┘
                       └──────────────────────┘
                                  │
                                  ▼
                       ┌──────────────────────┐
                       │ Clerk asks accused if│
                       │ he or she consents to│
                       │ summary trial or not.│
                       └──────────────────────┘
                                  │
                      ┌───────────┴───────────┐
                      ▼                       ▼
            ┌──────────────────┐   ┌──────────────────────┐
            │ Accused consents.│   │ Accused does not     │
            │ Court proceeds as│   │ consent. Court       │
            │ if offence was   │   │ proceeds as if       │
            │ triable only     │   │ offence was triable  │
            │ summarily:       │   │ either way: s 22(6)b.│
            │ s 22(6)a.        │   └──────────────────────┘
            └──────────────────┘              │
                      │                       ▼
                      ▼            ┌──────────────────────┐
            ┌──────────────────┐   │ MODE OF TRIAL        │
            │ SUMMARY TRIAL    │   │ DETERMINATION —      │
            └──────────────────┘   │ ss 19–21             │
                                   └──────────────────────┘
                                              │
                                        ┌─────┴─────┐
                                        ▼           ▼
                                   ┌────────┐ ┌────────┐
                                   │SUMMARY │ │CASE    │
                                   │TRIAL   │ │SENT TO │
                                   └────────┘ │CROWN   │
                                              │COURT   │
                                              │FOR     │
                                              │TRIAL   │
                                              └────────┘
```

Figure A2

APPENDIX 2
VICTIMS AND OTHER WITNESSES

The purpose of this section is to alert you to the very particular and special problems faced by the victims and witnesses of crime, especially those who appear as witnesses in any criminal proceedings. It is a large and complex area, and this section can do little more than draw your attention to the issues involved. While it is intended as background reading only, you should not underestimate its importance in your professional life.

The word 'victim' is technically correct only after a verdict of guilt has been recorded. Until then, the word 'complainant' is probably more accurate. For the sake of simplicity, however, the word 'victim' is used throughout this section.

Much of what is said in this section relates to many witnesses, not just the victim, and this section should be read with that in mind.

History and background

Until the middle of the nineteenth century, the person primarily responsible for the prosecution of offences was the victim himself. Consequently he played a central role in the criminal justice system. With the introduction of efficient police forces, which took over the prosecuting role, the victim's main involvement in the criminal justice system was as (usually the chief) prosecution witness. Over time many rights he may have had came to be sidelined by the criminal justice system. Indeed, many victims found in the past that the criminal justice system has served them so badly that it was more traumatic than the original offence. Some say that they would never report an offence and face the system a second time.

In recent years, a number of steps have been taken to redress the balance.

(a) The year 1964 saw the introduction of the Criminal Injuries Compensation Board (CICB), now the Criminal Injuries Compensation Authority (CICA), which has the power to make payments to victims of crime following an application made to them by the victim. Many victims, however, neither knew of the scheme nor how to access it. A recent decision by the European Court of Human Rights decided, *inter alia*, that the Criminal Injuries Compensation Scheme was not an *ex gratia* scheme.

(b) In 1972, the court was given, for the first time, the power to make compensation orders to benefit the victim in suitable cases. Similar problems of ignorance existed as with the CICB. This power has been extended by the CJA 1988, and further amended by the Powers of Criminal Courts (Sentencing) Act 2000, and students should refer to the sentencing section of this manual for details, and see below, for a further discussion.

(c) In 1974, the first Victim Support scheme was established in Bristol. It is a national independent charity for people affected by crime. It provides a service in each community across England and Wales. It provides a free and confidential service, whether or not a crime has been reported, and regardless of when it happened. Trained staff and volunteers at affiliated local charities offer information, support and practical help to victims, witnesses, their families and friends. Victim Support works to increase awareness of the effects of crime and to achieve greater recognition of victims' and witnesses' rights. The organisation receives funding from the Home Office but also receives outside support. Each year Victim Support contacts over one million victims and works with over 300,000 witnesses. Particular skills have been developed to deal with more sensitive cases, such as cases involving racial harassment, the families of murder victims and child victims of offences. Research undertaken by Victim Support has established that those who have been contacted by Victim Support made a better recovery from the offence than those who did not.

(d) In 1988, a working party under the chairmanship of Lady Ralphs, CBE, JP, DL examined how a court appearance could be made less of an ordeal for the victim, and reported its findings under the title 'The Victim in Court'. Following this, in 1990, the government introduced the 'Victim's Charter: A Statement of the Rights of Victims of Crime'. In 1995 Victim Support published 'The Rights of Victims of Crime', which called for greater recognition of victim's rights. It stated five basic rights for victims:

1. The victim should not bear the burden of dealing with the offender.
2. The victim should receive information about their case, and be able to provide information for use in the criminal justice process.
3. The victim should be protected.
4. The victim should receive compensation.
5. The victim should receive respect, recognition and support.

The last version of the Charter entitled *'Victim's Charter: Statement on the Treatment of Victims and Witnesses'* was issued in 1996.

(e) Since then, a number of steps have been taken, the most important of which are set out in detail below.

The Code of Practice for Victims of Crime

The Code of Practice for victims came into force on 3 April 2006, replacing the Victim's Charter. The Code of Practice sets out the services that victims can expect to receive from the criminal justice system including:

- A right to information about their crime within specified time scales including the right to be notified of arrests and court cases.
- A dedicated family liaison police officer to be assigned to bereaved relatives.
- Clear information from the Criminal Injuries Compensation Authority (CICA) on eligibility for compensation under the scheme.

- All victims to be told about Victim Support and either referred on to them or offered their service.
- An enhanced service in cases of vulnerable or intimidated victims.
- Flexibility with regard to opting in or out of receiving services to ensure victims receive the level of service they want.

The Code is too long to be included here and the following are merely some of the key points. Students should refer to the complete Code for details. It can be found at <http://press.homeoffice.gov.uk/documents/victims-code-of-practice>.

Victim

In the Code, the word 'victim' is defined as a person entitled to receive services under the Code. In addition, the Code also speaks of vulnerable and intimidated victims. The police are under an obligation to identify vulnerable or intimidated witnesses.

A **vulnerable victim** is one who is vulnerable by virtue of their personal circumstances, or the circumstances of the offence, namely that the victim:

- was under the age of 17 at the time of the offence; or
- is suffering from a mental disorder within the meaning of the Mental Health Act 1973; or
- has a significant impairment of intelligence and social functioning; or
- has a physical disability or is suffering from a physical disorder.

An **intimidated victim** is one the quality of whose evidence is likely to be diminished by fear or distress on the part of the victim in connection with testifying. In deciding this, the following matters should be taken into account:

(a) the nature and alleged circumstances of the offence to which the proceedings relate;
(b) the age of the victim;
(c) any of the following which appear relevant:
    (i) the social, cultural background and ethnic origin of the victim,
    (ii) the domestic and employment circumstances of the victim, and
    (iii) any religious beliefs or political opinions of the victim;
(d) any behaviour toward the victim on the part of:
    (i) the accused,
    (ii) members of the family or associates of the accused, or
    (iii) any other person who is likely to be an accused or a witness in the proceedings.

Obligations of service providers

There has long been a concern that victims of crime have not been properly involved in the proceedings in court—they are given very little information about the case and its progress; they have very limited opportunities to find out more for themselves; and usually they cannot make representations to the court prior to decisions being taken (for example, whether to accept a defendant's plea of guilty to an alternative and less serious form of the offence; or whether particular bail conditions are necessary).

The Code deals with these concerns by imposing obligations on a number of criminal justice bodies including the police, the CPS, the Court Service, and the Probation Service and the Prison Service. It represents a minimum level of service which victims of crime can expect.

The obligations of the police include, some of them in conjunction with the CPS, explanation and information. Explanation is required about such matters as special measures provisions. Information must be given about each stage of the process such as any decision to charge or not to charge, bail, the outcome of any trial, and the process of any appeal.

The obligations of the courts include liaising with both the police and CPS to ensure that information is passed on to victims promptly, that victims have a separate waiting room from the defendant and defence witnesses, that special measures are available if required.

The obligations of the CICA include processing efficiently and sensitively all applications made to them, giving explanations for refusal or reduction of compensation, and informing the applicant of the right to apply for review if the application is refused.

The obligations of the prison service include maintaining a telephone helpline which can be used by victims if they receive unwanted contact from a prisoner who had been convicted or remanded in custody in respect of relevant criminal conduct or have any concern about the prisoner's temporary or final release, and consider whether to impose additional conditions requested by the Probation Service or recommended by the Parole Board as a result of information offered by the victim.

The obligations of the Criminal Cases Review Commission include considering whether, during the course of a review of a case, contact with the victim should be made if there is a likelihood of the review coming to the victim's attention, and the result of any decision to refer the case to the Court of Appeal, unless the victim has made it clear that they do not wish to be informed or there is no identifiable victim.

All the obligations set out above carry strict time limits within which the information must be conveyed.

Failure to comply with these obligations does not render any individual liable for any offence, but may be taken into account in any proceedings where relevant.

The DVCVA 2004, s 47 enables the Parliamentary Commissioner for Administration (who investigates complaints about poor administration by Government departments and agencies) to investigate breaches of the *Code of Practice*. Victims will need to make a written complaint to their Member of Parliament who will then refer the complaint to the Parliamentary Commissioner for investigation. There is no date yet for implementation of this provision.

In addition, in sexual and violent offences where the offender is sentenced to at least one year in prison (or where the court orders that the defendant be diverted to the mental health system in equivalent cases), the victim has certain rights to provide and receive information relating to the management of the offender (Chapter 2 of the DVCVA 2004).

A Commissioner for Victims and Witnesses

Sections 48 to 53 of the DVCVA create the position of Commissioner for Victims and Witnesses—a champion for victims' interests across government. His or her remit extends beyond criminal justice to include departments such as Work and Pensions,

Health, and Education and Skills. He or she is involved in promoting victim and witness rights at a general rather than individual level.

The Witness Service, run by Victim Support, provides a free and confidential service in every criminal court in England and Wales. It aims to provide emotional support and practical information about court proceedings to both prosecution and defence witnesses. Further it provides a range of services including someone to talk to in confidence, a visit to the court centre, if possible a look round the courtroom before the witness is called, someone to accompany the witness into the courtroom when giving evidence, and a chance to talk over the case when it has ended and get more help and information.

The Witness Service produces a leaflet entitled 'Going to Court', which is information for witnesses and victims in either the magistrates' court or the Crown Court.

Victim personal statements

Victims have expressed considerable concern in the past that the court, when dealing with the offender, has not heard anything from the victim on how the crime has affected him, nor has any opportunity to do so been available. After a good deal of debate, victim personal statements (VPS) are now accepted in court. A VPS adds to the information the victim has already given to the police about the crime. It enables the victim to explain how the crime has affected him, whether physically, emotionally or financially. The VPS then becomes part of the case papers and is seen by everyone involved with the case, including the CPS, the defence and the relevant court.

In the VPS, the victim may give any information that is not included in the evidential statement. It may include anything the victim thinks might be helpful or relevant, including, for example, that the crime has caused or made worse, any medical or social problems (such as marital problems), that the victim feels vulnerable or intimidated and that the victim is worried about the offender being given bail.

The VPS is not a victim impact statement and it was never the Government's intention to create a means by which the victim can influence a sentence. The VPS should not, therefore, include an opinion as to how the court should punish the offender, as this is a matter for the court, but the court will take into account how the victim has been affected. In addition, the court may use the VPS to decide matters such as bail.

The VPS also offers a means to record information in relation to the victim's needs and interests. As the VPS travels with the case papers, all agencies can respond to these needs. For example, the VPS may record the fact that the victim seeks a compensation order if the defendant is convicted. The VPS may also highlight the victim's vulnerability, prompting an application for special measures under the Youth Justice and Criminal Evidence Act 1999.

The *Consolidated Criminal Practice Direction*, issued on 29 July 2004, Part 3, para 28 provides as follows:

1. This part of the Practice Direction draws attention to a scheme which started on 1st October 2001 to give victims a more formal opportunity to say how a crime has affected them. It may help to identity whether they have a particular need for information, support and protection. It will also enable the court to take the statement into account in determining sentence.

2. When a police officer takes a statement from a victim the victim will be told about the scheme and given the chance to make a victim personal statement. A victim personal

statement may be made or updated at any time prior to the disposal of the case. The decision about whether or not to make a victim personal statement is entirely for the victim. If the court is presented with a victim personal statement the following approach should be adopted:

(a) The victim personal statement and any evidence in support should be considered and taken into account by the court prior to passing sentence.

(b) Evidence of the effects of an offence on the victim contained in the victim personal statement or other statement must be in proper form, that is a witness statement made under s 9 CJA 1967 or an expert's report and served upon the defendant's solicitor, or the defendant if he is not represented, prior to sentence. Except where inferences can be properly drawn from the nature of or circumstances surrounding the offence, a sentence must not make assumptions unsupported by evidence about the effects of an offence on the victim.

(c) The court must pass what it judges to be the appropriate sentence having regard to the circumstances of the offence and of the offender, taking into account, so far as the court considers appropriate, the consequences to the victim. The opinions of the victim or the victim's close relatives as to what the sentence should be are therefore not relevant, unlike the consequence of the offence on them. Victims should be advised of this. If despite the advice, opinions as to sentence are included in a statement, the court should pay no attention to them.

(d) The court should consider whether it is desirable in its sentencing remarks to refer to the evidence provided on behalf of the victim.

Compensation

There are two separate considerations when dealing with the issue of compensation:

1 The making of a compensation order should be at the forefront of the court's mind when dealing with an offender. The Powers of Criminal Courts (Sentencing) Act 2000, s 1 provides that the court may impose a compensation order on an offender 'instead of or in addition to dealing with him in any other way'. This order may be made whether or not an application is made for it. The Act requires that the court should give its reasons if it decides not to make a compensation order.

In the absence of an application, however, the court may not make an order. Prosecution counsel, therefore, may need to consider in advance of sentencing whether such an order should be applied for. This may involve discussion with the police who are likely to have had the closest contact with the victim, to discover whether such an application would be desirable.

2 A victim of crime may apply to the CICA for compensation for the crime to which he has been subject. Although an application may be made before trial, CICA will not make a decision until the trial has concluded. It may be appropriate to question a witness about any payment that has been made or promised to him, as it is relevant to the credibility of the witness. It is suggested, however, that great care should be taken when the victim of a violent or sexual offence is asked about any compensation that she or he has received. While it is known that allegations of rape are made for a variety of reasons, it is thought unlikely that it is in order for an application for compensation to be made. In some cases, the trial judge has intervened to stop this line of questioning, and prosecuting counsel may consider it appropriate to themselves challenge the questions or at least explain to the jury that the complainant has a right to compensation whether or not the defendant is even identified.

Reparation

Under the CDA 1998, the courts may pass two new sentences: the action plan order and the reparation order. The action plan order requires the offender to partake in specific activities, or to desist from specific activities, designed to achieve the offender's rehabilitation. The order may also specify that reparation is made to the victim of the offence (with his consent) or to the community.

The reparation order requires the offender to undertake certain work for the victim, provided that the victim agrees. This will be a maximum of 24 hours' work to be undertaken within a period of three months from the making of the order.

The existence of such order may be very beneficial to victims. Reparation may include writing a letter of apology to the victim or apologising in person, cleaning graffiti or repairing criminal damage. Any one of these may help the victim put the crime behind him or her. However, it is seen as very important that the reparation is something which is commensurate with the seriousness of the offence, is something to which the victim agrees and finally is tailor made for this offender, this crime and this victim, rather than a standard response to the type of crime.

See **Chapters 15** and **17** of this manual for fuller discussion of these orders.

Conduct in court

It is important to be aware of the recent changes to the law which govern the way in which the witness may be cross-examined. Students are referred to the *Evidence* manual for full details, but some of the most important are:

(a) The CJA 2003, s 51 enables witnesses to give evidence from a location outside the court where it is in the interests of justice to do so.

(b) The CJA 2003, s 116 allows for a witness's statement to be admitted as evidence where the witness is too frightened to give live evidence. The Act stipulates that the court should interpret 'fear' widely and consider whether admitting the statement as evidence is in the interests of justice.

(c) The CJA 2003, s 137 provides for video recording of interviews with witnesses to be admissible where the witness's recollection of events is likely to be significantly better at the time of the recording than at the trial, and where this is in the interests of justice.

(d) The CJA 2003, s 100 provides that witnesses other than the defendant may only be asked about previous character with the agreement of the parties or with the leave of the court and then only in specified circumstances.

(e) The YJCEA 1999, s 41 restricted circumstances under which a victim's previous sexual history may be adduced as evidence.

It is also important to be aware of the provisions of the Code of Conduct. A barrister's first duties are to his client and to the court. See paras 302 and 303 of the Code of Conduct:

302 A barrister has an overriding duty to the Court to act with independence in the interests of justice: he must assist the Court in the administration of justice and must not deceive or knowingly or recklessly mislead the Court.

303 A barrister:

(a) must promote and protect fearlessly and by all proper and lawful means the lay client's best interests and do so without regard to his own interests or to any consequences to himself or to any other person (including any professional client or other intermediary or another barrister);

While bearing these two duties in mind, a barrister must also act with sensitivity towards the victims of crime and other vulnerable witnesses. The Code gives some guidance in para 708 which provides:

708 A barrister when conducting proceedings in Court:

(g) must not make statements or ask questions which are merely scandalous or intended or calculated only to vilify, insult or annoy either a witness or some other person;

(h) must if possible avoid the naming in open Court of third parties whose character would thereby be impugned;

(i) must not by assertion in a speech impugn a witness whom he has had an opportunity to cross-examine unless in cross-examination he has given the witness an opportunity to answer the allegation;

(j) must not suggest that a victim, witness or other person is guilty of crime, fraud or misconduct or make any defamatory aspersion on the conduct of any other person or attribute to another person the crime or conduct of which his lay client is accused unless such allegations go to a matter in issue (including the credibility of the witness) which is material to the lay client's case and appear to him to be supported by reasonable grounds.

These are reproduced in the Written Standards for the Conduct of Professional Work issued on 31 October 2004.

These separate principles may cause some difficulty when making a plea in mitigation. The barrister acting for the defence must be careful that any plea in mitigation does not make defamatory aspersions on the conduct of the victim, which is very distressing to the victim, and in cases where the offence is murder, is very distressing to the family. A barrister acting for the prosecution must be alert to the mitigation which is being put forward, and correct any matters if necessary.

INDEX

A

abbreviations 9
absence of defendants 95
   mode of trial determination 99–100
   summary trial 115–17
absence of prosecution 117
absolute discharge 300, 325, 331
accused persons *see* defendants
acquittal
   appeal against 262–3
action plan orders 131
active case management 17–18
activities
   as condition in community sentences 305
   as requirement in youth rehabilitation orders 327
adjournment 89, 95
   for preliminary hearings 197
   for sentencing 233, 272–3
   see also remand
admissions 211
advance indication of sentence 103–4, 201–2, 269–71
advice and assistance
   public funding 48–9
advocacy assistance 49
aggravated vehicle taking
   mode of trial guidelines 113
alcohol treatment requirement
   in community sentences 306–7
alibi evidence 176–7, 218–19, 225
allocation *see* mode of trial
alternative counts 192
alternative offences
   alternative verdicts 228–31, 259–60
   guilty plea to alternative offence 200
ambiguous pleas 201
antecedents 233, 279
   previous convictions 222–3, 233, 280, 297
anti-social behaviour orders 312–15
   appeal against 162, 314
appeals
   after plea of guilty 251
   against acquittal 262–3
   against committal for sentence 129
   against conviction 242–52, 259–61
   against grant of bail 85–7
   against refusal of bail 65–6
   against refusal of public funding 50–1
   against ruling 239–42
   against sentence 51, 162, 255, 261
   Attorney-General's reference 263–5
   in case of death 252
   common errors 245–50
   Criminal Cases Review Commission 265–8
   European Court of Justice reference 265
   evidence 252–4
      new and compelling 263
   from magistrates' court
      application for judicial review 165–70
      Crown Court 160–2
      to High Court by way of case stated 162–5
   grounds 242–4, 255, 256–8
   human rights issues 244–5, 261
   leave to appeal 250–1, 256
   powers of Court of Appeal 240–2, 259–61
   powers of single judge 258–9
   procedure
      case stated appeal 163–4
      Court of Appeal 256–8, 262
      Crown Court appeal from magistrates' court 160–2
   public funding and 50–1
   right to appeal 251–2, 262–3
   to House of Lords 6, 7, 170, 265
appropriate adult
   presence at interviews 33–4
arraignment 197–203
   ambiguous pleas 201
   different pleas from different defendants 200–1
   guilty plea to alternative offence 200
   leaving counts on file 200
   Newton hearing 198–9
   plea bargaining 200
   procedure on plea of guilty 198
   prosecution offering no evidence 200
   securing attendance of witnesses 202–3
arrest 21–5
   caution 29–31
   detention of arrested person at police station 25–8
   effecting 24–5
   indictable offences 23–4
   interviews of arrested person 31–3
      caution before 29–31
      persons at risk 27, 33–5
      risk assessment 29
   powers of arrest without warrant 21–3
   rights of suspect 35–8
   warrant for 45–6, 96
attachment of earnings order 302
attendance centres
   attendance centre orders 302
   requirement in community sentences 307
   requirement in youth rehabilitation order 327
Attorney-General's reference 263–5
authorised person
   conditional cautions 41–3
autrefois acquit and autrefois convict 234–6

B

bail 57–96
   appeal against refusal 65–6, 85–7
   application for 66–7

bail (cont.)
    legal representation 87–8
    renewing 83–5
  certificate of full argument 65, 85
  conditions of 40, 72–6
    changing 76–7
    common conditions 75
    conditional police bail 76
    non-compliance 78–9
    security 74
    surety 73–4, 82–3
  Crown Court appeal from magistrates' court 161
  Crown Court trial 226–7
  decision on
    certificate of full argument 65, 85
    how taken 64
    reasons for 64–5
    record of 64
    when taken 63–4
  duty to surrender to custody 58–9
  failure to surrender 77–8
    penalties 80–2
    prosecution for 79–80
  general right to 57–8
  High Court case stated appeal 164–5
  as human right 60–2
  judicial review 169
  juvenile 88–9
  no right to 59–60
  objections to release on 66
    overcoming 72
  obligation to consider 83–5
  police 40, 73, 92
    conditional 76
    failure to surrender to custody 78–9
  refusal
    appeal against 65–6, 85–7
    considerations for court 70–1
    imprisonable offences 67–70
    non-imprisonable offences 71–2
  security 74
  street bail 25, 59–60, 92
  surety 73–4
    forfeiture 82–3
  unconditional 58–9
  warrant for arrest backed for 46, 77–8, 96
bench warrants 46, 77–8, 96
bias 248
binding over 325
body samples 26
burglary
  mode of trial 106–7, 111

C

case management 5–6
  active 17–18
  CJSSS 20
  Criminal Procedure Rules 16–20
  Plea and Case Management Hearings 194–5
case management hearings 114–15
case stated appeal 162–5
  bail 164–5
  compared with judicial review 169–70
  from Crown Court 165
  hearing 165

  powers of High Court 165
  procedure 163–4
caution
  arrested person 29–31
  conditional 41–3
  formal 41
challenging potential jurors
  for cause 205–6
  replacement of juror after successful challenge 206
  stand by 205
changing plea 117, 208–9
character and antecedents evidence 279–81
charge
  alternatives to 41–3
  charging suspects 38–9
  dismissal of 96
  written charge and requisition 43–4
    amendment 44
    duplicity 44
    two or more charges 44
  see also **indictment**
children and young people
  in adult courts
    Crown Court 146–7
    magistrates' courts 145–6
    public access 148
    reporting restrictions 147–8
  bail and 88–9
  categories of juvenile defendants 133–4
  committal to Crown Court for sentence 127–8
  conditional cautions 153
  criminal responsibility 133–4
  criminality 131
  detention in young offender institution 323
  final warning scheme 132, 149–50, 152, 153
  interviews at police station 27, 33–5
  persistent young offenders 88, 329
  pre-sentence reports 326
  presumption of innocence 133
  protection for young witnesses 136–8, 213–16
  reoffending 132
  reports on 284
  reprimands 150–3
  sentencing 131, 134
    aims 324
    custodial sentences 323, 329–30, 339–40
    non-custodial sentences 131, 324–30
    pre-sentence reports 326
  serious offences 330
  special measures 136–7, 213–16
  young adults 148–9
  see also **youth court**
clerk to justices see **justices' clerk**
clients
  duty of confidentiality 52
  duty to protect interests of 51–2
closing speeches
  Crown Court trial 219
  summary trial 120
Commissioner for Victims and Witnesses 347–8
committal proceedings 91
  procedure under CDA 1998 s51 154–6
    applications for dismissal 158
    effecting transfer 157–8
    restrictions on reporting 156–7
Community Legal Service 46

community punishment orders 302
community sentences 303–7
 amendment 310–11
 breach 308–10, 332–3
 credit for time spent on remand 308
 persistent offenders 307–8
 procedural requirements 304
 requirements imposed under 304–7
 restrictions on imposition of 304
 revocation 310, 333
 subsequent offences and 311, 333–4
 threshold 292, 304
 see also individual orders
compensation orders 349
conditional cautions 41–3
 children and young people 153
conditional discharge 300–1, 325, 331
confidentiality
 duty of 52
convictions
 previous convictions 222–3, 233, 280, 297
 spent convictions 280–1
Coroners and Justice Bill 2009 8
corroboration 225, 245
costs 52–4
 making order for 53–4
counsel
 advising on sentence 271
  public funding and 51
counts 183–5, 190–1
 alternative 192
 duplicity 44, 185
 joinder 186–7, 222
  misjoinder 189–90
  separate trials 188–9
 leaving counts on file 200
 misjoinder 189–90
Court of Appeal 6, 7, 238
 appeal after plea of guilty 251
 appeal against acquittal 262–3
 appeal against conviction 242–52, 259–61
 appeal against ruling 239–42
 appeal against sentence 255, 261
 appeal in case of death 252
 common errors 245–50
 composition 238–9
 Criminal Cases Review Commission and 267–8
 evidence 252–4
  new and compelling 263
 grounds for appeal 242–4, 255
 human rights issues 244–5, 261
 leave to appeal 250–1, 256
 powers of court 240–2, 259–61
 powers of single judge 258–9
 procedure 256–8, 262
 Registrar 239, 259
 residual discretion 248
 right to appeal 239, 251–2, 262–3
court legal adviser 125–6
courts
 bail imposed by 40
 choice of, costs and 54
 reducing delay in legal process 54–6
 structure and relationship 6, 7
 see also individual courts and remand
Criminal Cases Review Commission 265–8

 information to parties 267
 investigations 267
 making reference to 266–7
 membership 266
criminal damage
 mode of trial and 105–6, 113, 341–3
Criminal Defence Service 46–8
 purpose and objectives 47–8
Criminal Evidence (Witness Anonymity) Act 2008 8
Criminal Injuries Compensation Authority 344, 349
Criminal Justice: Simple, Speedy, Summary 20
Criminal Justice Act 2003 8–9
 provisions in force 10–15
Criminal Justice and Immigration Act 2008 6–8, 326–8
Criminal Procedure Rules 2005 4–6, 16–20
 active case management 17–18
 case management powers 5–6
 duties of participants 18
 overriding objective 4–5
 progressing the case 18–20
 sanctions 20
Crown Court 6, 7
 advance indication of sentence 269–70
 appeal against refusal of bail in magistrates' court 85–6
 appeal by way of case stated to High Court 165
 appeal from magistrates' court 160–2
  against sentence 162
  bail 161
  hearing 161
  powers of Crown Court 161–2
  procedure 160
 committal for sentence from magistrates' court 126–9
 committal to trial from magistrates' court 91
 custodial sentences 335–40
 custody time limits 63
 failure to surrender to custody 79, 80
 juveniles in 141–3, 332
  media reporting 138–9
  public attendance 139–40
 mode of trial determination *see* **mode of trial**
 non-custodial sentences 331–4
 procedure under CDA 1998 s51 154–6
  applications for dismissal 158
  effecting transfer 157–8
  restrictions on reporting 156–7
 remands in 92, 95
 sentencing procedure 290
 trial
  arraignment 197–203
  bail 226–7
  by judge alone 236–7
  changing plea 208–9
  closing speeches 219
  defence case 218–19
  effect of European Convention on Human Rights 233
  judge's summing up 220–6
  jury *see* **juries**
  no case to answer submission 216–18, 245–6
  preliminary hearings 194–7
  prosecution case 209–16
  sentence 233
  summing up 220–6
  two or more defendants 219–20
  unrepresented defendants 220, 289–90
  verdict 225–6, 227–32
 voluntary bills of indictment 158–9

Crown Prosecution Service (CPS)
  appeal against grant of bail by 86–7
curfew 131, 302, 305
  as bail condition 75
  in youth rehabilitation order 327
custodial sentences
  children and young people 323, 329–30, 339–40
  Crown Court 335–40
  custody plus 320
  dangerous offenders 337–9
  detention in young offender institution 323
  enforcement of fines and 302–3
  imprisonment 316–20
  intermittent custody 323
  length of sentence 319
  life sentences 336
  magistrates' court 316–23
  minimum sentences 336–7
  release on licence 335–6
  suspended sentences 321–3
    breach of 322–3
  thresholds 292, 316–18
  unrepresented defendants 289–90
custody
  custody record 25–6
  detention periods 28
  duty to surrender to 58–9
  failure to surrender to 77–8
    penalties 80–2
    prosecution for 79–80
  remand to local authority care 88–9
  review 26–7
  time limits 62–3
custody officer 25–6
custody plus 320

D

dangerous driving
  mode of trial guidelines 113
dangerous offenders 337–9
death
  appeal against conviction after death of accused 252
defence side
  Crown Court trial
    closing speech 219
    evidence 218–19
    no case to answer submission 216–18, 245–6
    objection to prosecution evidence 211–13
  disclosure of information 173–7
    sanctions for non-disclosure 177–8
  errors by 246–7
  failure to deal with 246
  mitigation 284–5
  summary trial
    closing speech 120
    no case to answer submission 119–20
    presentation of case 120
defendants
  absence of 95
    mode of trial determination 99–100
    summary trial 115–17
  appeal against conviction after death of 252
  bail *see* **bail**
  change of mode of trial and 104–5
  children and young people 133–4

costs against 53–4
defendant's cost order 52–3
disorderly 99–100, 117
failure to answer police questions 223–5
failure to testify 223
joinder 187–8, 219–20, 222
  different pleas from different defendants 200–1
lies 225
pleas from *see* **pleas**
previous convictions 222–3, 233, 280, 297
remand *see* **remand**
unrepresented 220, 289–90
see also **defence side**
delay in legal process
  reduction of 54–6
detention at police station 25–8
  see also **interviews of arrested person**
detention and training orders 131, 134, 329–30
directions to juries 232, 247
  misdirections 245, 246
discharge
  absolute 300, 325, 331
  conditional 300–1, 325, 331
discharge of jurors
  entire jury 207–8
  individual jurors during trial 206–7
disclosure of information
  defence side 173–7
    sanctions for non-disclosure 177–8
  duty of investigating officer 171–2
  investigating officer's duty 171–2
  mode of trial and 108, 109
  pre-sentence reports 281–3
  prosecution side 172–3
  public interest immunity 178–81
  third party 181–2
dismissal of case 96
disqualification from driving 302, 312
disqualification from juries 204
distress warrant 302
district judges 135–6
double jeopardy 234–6
driving
  disqualification from 302, 312
drug offences
  mode of trial guidelines 113
drug rehabilitation
  requirement in community sentences 306
  requirement in youth rehabilitation order 327–8
drug testing requirement
  in youth rehabilitation order 328
duplicity 44
  indictment 185
duty solicitor schemes 50

E

Early Administrative Hearings (EAHs) 55
education requirement
  in youth rehabilitation order 328
either way offences 91, 97, 341–3
electronic tagging 75, 307, 328
empanelling juries 204
enforcement
  fines 301–3
equivocal pleas 118

European Court of Justice reference 265
evidence
    alibi evidence 176–7, 218–19, 225
    appeal in respect of evidentiary rulings 241
    appeals 252–4
        against acquittal 263
    Crown Court trial
        alibi evidence 218–19, 225
        character and antecedents 279–81
        defence side 218–19
        expert evidence 219, 225
        identification evidence 221–2
        judge's summing up 220–6
        objections to 211–13
        previous convictions 222–3, 233
        prosecution evidence 209–13
        special measures 213–16
        spent convictions 280–1
    disclosure of *see* **disclosure of information**
    Newton hearing 198–9
    prosecution offering no evidence 200
    summary trial 119
    wrongful admission or exclusion of 245
exclusion requirement
    in community sentences 305
    in youth rehabilitation order 327
expert witnesses 175, 219, 225
extended sentences 337–9, 340

F

facts
    disputes
        after guilty plea 275–8
        after not guilty plea 278–9
    presentation of facts 274–5
fair trial right 233, 244–5
family
    right to be informed of detention 37–8
final warning scheme 132, 149–50, 152, 153
fines 301–3, 325, 331
    surcharges and 312
fingerprints 26
fitness to plead 234
forfeiture of surety 82–3
formal admissions 211
formal caution 41
fraud
    mode of trial guidelines 112
    trial by judge alone 236–7
friends
    right to be informed of detention 37–8

G

General Criminal Contract 47, 49, 50, 51–2
guilty plea
    ambiguous plea 201
    appeals against conviction after 251
    arraignment procedure on plea of guilty 198
    change of plea 208–9
    disputes about facts after 275–8
    Newton hearing 198–9
    postal 116–17
    reduction in sentence for 271, 284–5, 295–7
    to alternative offence 200

H

half-time submission *see* **no case to answer submission**
handling
    mode of trial guidelines 112
High Court 6, 7
    appeal against refusal of bail in magistrates' court 86
    appeal by way of case stated 162–5
        bail 165
        compared with judicial review 169–70
        hearing 165
        powers of High Court 165
        procedure 163–4
    appeal to House of Lords 170
    judicial review 165–70
        bail 169
        compared with case stated appeal 169–70
        prerogative orders 166–9
        procedure 169
House of Lords 6, 7, 170
    appeal to 265
human rights issues
    appeals 244–5, 261
    bail and 60–2
    Crown Court trial and 233

I

identification evidence 221–2
immunity from prosecution 16
imprisonment 302–3, 316–20
indication of sentence 103–4, 201–2, 269–71
indictable offences 23–4
indictment
    amendment 192–3
    counts 183–5, 190–1
        alternative 192
        joinder 186–7, 222
        leaving counts on file 200
        misjoinder 189–90
    deciding contents 190–1
    defects in 245
    drawing up 186
    duplicity 44, 185
    joinder of counts 186–7, 222
        misjoinder 189–90
        separate trials 188–9
    joinder of defendants 187–8, 219–20, 222
        different pleas from different
            defendants 200–1
    meaning 183–6
    offences triable on 97
        linked summary and indictable offences 107–8
    severing 188–9
    voluntary bills of indictment 158–9
informal warning 41
information
    disclosure of *see* **disclosure of information**
    laying 43, 44
innocence
    presumption of 133
instituting proceedings
    amendment 44
    duplicity 44, 185
    two or more charges 44
    written charge and requisition 43–4

intensive supervision and surveillance order 328
interests of client
    duty to protect 51–2
intermediaries
    communication with witnesses and 214
intermittent custody 323
interviews of arrested person 31–3
    caution before 29–31
    failure to answer police questions 223–5
    outside police station 32
    persons at risk 27, 33–5
    risk assessment 29
investigating officer
    duty of disclosure of information 171–2

J

joinder of counts 186–7, 222
    misjoinder 189–90
    separate trials 188–9
joinder of defendants 187–8, 219–20, 222
    different pleas from different defendants 200–1
judges
    Crown Court trial 201–2
        challenge to jurors 205
        directions to jury 232, 247
        interventions by 246
        misdirections 245, 246
        summing up 220–6
        trial by judge alone 236–7
    district judges 135–6
    powers of single judge in Court of Appeal 258–9
    wrong decisions 242
judicial review 165–70
    bail 169
    compared with case stated appeal 169–70
    discretion of court 169
    prerogative orders 166–9
    procedure 169
juries
    challenging potential jurors
        for cause 205–6
        replacement of juror after successful challenge 206
        stand by 205
    discharge of jurors
        entire jury 207–8
        individual jurors during trial 206–7
        unable to reach verdict 232
    disqualification 204
    empanelling 204
    functions of 220–1
    judge's directions to 232, 247
        misdirections 245, 246
    retirement 227–8
    start of trial 208
    tampering 236–7
    who can serve 203–4, 248–9
    see also **verdict**
jurisdiction 16
    court acting in excess of 166–7
    to try offences 46
justices' clerk 55
    summary trial and 123–6
justices of the peace *see* **magistrates' court**
juveniles *see* **children and young people**

L

laying an information 43, 44
leave to appeal 250–1, 256
legal aid *see* **public funding**
legal representation *see* **solicitor(s)**
Legal Services Commission (LSC) 46–7
lesser offences
    alternative verdicts 228–31, 259–60
    guilty plea to alternative offence 200
licence
    conditions on early release 335–6
lies 225
life sentences 336
local authority care
    remand to 88–9

M

magistrates' court 6, 7
    advance indication of sentence 269–70
    appeals from
        application for judicial review 165–70
        Crown Court 160–2
        to High Court by way of case stated 162–5
    certificate of full argument 65, 85
    committal to Crown Court for trial *see* **committal proceedings**
    custodial sentences 316–23
        custody plus 320
        detention in young offender institution 323
        imprisonment 316–20
        length of sentence 319
        procedure 319
        sentencing powers 316
    custody options 319–20
    custody time limits 62–3
    deferring sentence 92
    duty solicitor scheme 50
    Early Administrative Hearings (EAHs) 55
    failure to surrender to custody 79
    jurisdiction 46
    juveniles in 134–5
        media reporting 138–9
        public attendance 139–40
    mode of trial determination *see* **mode of trial**
    powers exercised by single justice 55
    remands in 92
        alternatives to 95–6
        duration of 92–4
    sentencing powers 122
        custodial sentences 316
        non-custodial sentences 300–15
    sentencing procedure 290
    summary trial in *see* **summary trial**
    suspended sentences 321–3
        breach of 322–3
    warrant for further detention 28
    youth court in *see* **youth court**
    see also **youth court**
majority verdicts 231–2
mandatory orders 168
media, reporting restrictions
    juvenile defendants 138–9
    in adult courts 147–8
    under CDA 1998 s51 procedure 156–7

medical reports 283–4
mental health treatment requirement
　in community sentences 306
　in youth rehabilitation order 327
mentally vulnerable people
　interviews at police station 27, 33–5
minimum sentences 336–7
misjoinder of counts 189–90
mitigation 284–5
　guilty plea and 271, 284–5, 295–7
mode of trial 97–113
　advance information 109
　advantages/disadvantages of each mode 108–9
　burglary 106–7, 111
　classification of offences 97–9, 141
　criminal damage cases 105–6, 113, 341–3
　linked summary and indictable offences 107–8
　national guidelines 110–13
　procedure for determination 99–105, 341–3
　　absence of defendant 99–100
　　changing mode of trial 104–5
　　criminal damage cases 105–6, 113, 341–3
　　failure to comply with procedure 104
　series of offences 106
　standard 100–4

N

National mode of trial Guidelines 110–13
natural justice 167–8
neglect of children
　mode of trial guidelines 112
Newton hearing 198–9
no case to answer submission
　Crown Court trial 216–18, 245–6
　summary trial 119–20
non-custodial sentences 300–15
　children and young people 131, 324–30
　community sentences 303–7
　　amendment 310–11
　　breach 308–10, 332–3
　　credit for time spent on remand 308
　　persistent offenders 307–8
　　procedural requirements 304
　　requirements imposed under 304–7
　　restrictions on imposition of 304
　　revocation 310, 333
　　subsequent offences and 311, 333–4
　　threshold 292, 304
　　see also individual orders
　Crown Court 331–4
　discharge
　　absolute 300, 325, 331
　　conditional 300–1, 325, 331
　fines 301–3, 325, 331
　　surcharges and 312
　youth court 324–30
not-guilty plea
　change of plea 208–9
　disputes about facts after 278–9

O

offences
　classification of 97–9, 141
　disputes about facts

　　after guilty plea 275–8
　　after not guilty plea 278–9
　indictable offences 23–4
　on indictment *see* counts
　jurisdiction to try 46
　presentation of facts 274–5
　sample offences 288–9, 298
　seriousness 292–5
　taking into consideration 286–8, 298–9
opening speech, prosecution side
　Crown Court trial 209
　summary trial 119
organised crime 55–6

P

parenting orders 131, 136
parents of young offenders 136
particulars of offence 183
persistent offenders
　community sentences and 307–8
　young offenders 88, 329
plea bargaining 200
Plea and Case Management Hearings 194–5
pleas
　ambiguous 201
　changing plea 118, 208–9
　costs order and 54
　different pleas from different defendants 200–1
　equivocal plea 118
　fitness to plead 234
　guilty plea *see* guilty plea
　indication of 101
　less common pleas 234–6
　plea bargaining 200
　summary trial
　　changing plea 118
　　equivocal plea 118
police
　bail 40, 73, 92
　　conditional 76
　　failure to surrender to custody 78–9
　custody officer 25–6
　investigating officer's duty of disclosure of information 171–2
police station
　caution of arrested person 29–31
　charging suspects 38–9
　Code of Practice, right to consult 38
　detention of arrested person 25–8
　duty solicitor scheme 50
　interviews 31–3
　　caution before 29–31
　　failure to answer police questions 223–5
　　persons at risk 27, 33–5
　　risk assessment 29
　reporting to, as condition of bail 75
　rights of suspect 35–8
Policing and Crime Bill 2008-9 8
pre-sentence reports
　adjournment for 233, 272
　children and young people 326
pre-trial reviews 114–15
preliminary hearings 194–7
　adjournment for 197
　Newton hearing 198–9

preliminary hearings (*cont.*)
  Plea and Case Management Hearings 194–5
  preparatory hearings 195–7
preparatory hearings 195–7
prerogative orders 166–9
press *see* **media**
presumption of innocence 133
previous convictions 222–3, 233, 280, 297
prison sentences 302–3, 316–20
private prosecutions 43
probation officers 139
proceedings *see* **instituting proceedings**
programme requirement
  in community sentences 305
  in youth rehabilitation orders 327
prohibited activity requirement
  in community sentences 305
  in youth rehabilitation order 327
prohibiting orders 169
proof
  burden and standard of 221, 245
prosecution of offences
  immunity from 16
  right to 16
prosecution side
  appeal against acquittal 262–3
  costs of 53
  Crown Court trial
    challenge to jurors 205
    closing speech 219
    evidence 209–13
    opening speech 209
  disclosure of information 172–3
  objections to release on bail 66
    overcoming 72
  offering no evidence 200
  summary trial
    absence of 117
    evidence 119
    opening speech 119
public funding 46–52
  advice and assistance 48–9
  advocacy assistance 49
  appeals against conviction/sentence and 51
  appeals against refusal of 50–1
  bail applications 87–8
  duty solicitor schemes 50
  General Criminal Contract 47, 49, 50, 51–2
  representation 49–50, 87–8
  use of counsel 51
public interest immunity 178–81
public order offences
  mode of trial guidelines 112
public prosecutors 43–4
publicity *see* **media**

Q

quashing orders 166–8
questioning *see* **interviews of arrested person**

R

referral orders 132, 325–6
Registrar of Criminal Appeals 239, 259
release on licence 335–6
remand
  alternatives to 95–6
  duration 92–4
  meaning 89
  weekly, avoidance 94–5
  when case will be remanded 89–92
  who can remand a case 92
  see also **bail**; **custody**
remand centre reports 284
reparation orders 131, 132, 350
reporting restrictions
  juvenile defendants 138–9
    in adult courts 147–8
  under CDA 1998 s51 procedure 156–7
reports
  other reports 283–4
  pre-sentence reports 281–3
    adjournment for 233, 272
    children and young people 326
representation orders 49–50
reprimands 150–3
residence requirement
  in community sentences 305
  in youth rehabilitation order 327
retrial
  order for 260
risk assessment
  interviews at police stations 29

S

sample offences 288–9, 298
security for bail 74
sentence(s)
  adjournment for sentencing 233, 272–3
  advance indication of 103–4, 201–2, 269–71
  advising on 271
  appeals against 51, 162, 255, 261
  Attorney-General's reference and 264–5
  children and young people 131, 134
    custodial sentences 323, 329–30, 339–40
    non-custodial sentences 131, 324–30
  committal for sentence from magistrates' court 126–9
  costs order and 54
  Crown Court trial 233
  custodial *see* **custodial sentences**
  deferring 92
  guilty plea and 271, 284–5, 295–7
  indication of 103–4, 201–2, 269–71
  legal representation and 289–90
  magistrates' powers 122
    custodial sentences 316
    non-custodial sentences 300–15
  mitigation 284–6
    guilty plea and 271, 284–5, 295–7
  non-custodial 300–15
    children and young people 131, 324–30
    community sentences 303–7, 331
    Crown Court 331–4
  pre-sentence reports 281–3
    adjournment for 233, 272
    children and young people 326
  previous convictions and 297
  process of sentencing 292
  pronouncing 285–6
  purpose of sentencing 292
  rectifying mistakes 123
  sample offences 288–9, 298

Sentencing Guidelines Council (SGC) 291–2
  seriousness of offence and 292–5
  summary trial 122
    committal to Crown Court for 126–9
  suspended sentences 321–3
    breach of 322–3
  taking into consideration 286–8, 298–9
Sentencing Guidelines Council (SGC) 291–2
Serious Fraud Office 21
Serious Organised Crime Agency (SOCA) 55–6
seriousness of offence
  sentencing and 292–5
sexual offences
  extended sentences for 337–9
  mode of trial guidelines 112–13
  protection for young witnesses and 136, 137, 138
silence
  failure to answer police questions 223–5
  failure to testify 223
social security fraud
  mode of trial guidelines 112
solicitor(s)
  bail applications and 87–8
  public funding and 50, 87–8
    advice and assistance 48–9
    advocacy assistance 49
    duty solicitor schemes 50
    General Criminal Contract 47, 50, 51–2
  right of suspect to 35–7
  sentencing and 289–90
special measures
  Crown Court trial 213–16
  youth courts 136–7
spent convictions 280–1
stand by challenge to potential jurors 205
statement of offence 183
street bail 25, 59–60, 92
subsequent offences
  community sentences and 311, 333–4
summary offences 91, 97
  linked summary and indictable offences 107–8
summary trial
  absence of defendant 115–17
  clerk to justices and 123–6
  court legal adviser 125–6
  Criminal Procedure Rules 122
  defence
    closing speech 120
    no case to answer submission 119–20
    presentation of case 120
  power to rectify mistakes 123
  private representations 117–18
  procedure 115, 122
  prosecution
    evidence 119
    opening speech 119
  sentence 122
    committal to Crown Court for 126–9
  taking plea 118–19
  verdict 121
summing up 220–6
summons 43, 44
  witnesses 202–3
supervision
  requirement in community sentences 307
  requirement in youth rehabilitation orders 327

suspended sentences 321–2
surcharges 312
surety
  as condition of bail 73–4
  forfeiture 82–3
suspects
  caution 29–31
  charging 38–9
  detention at police station 25–8
  interviews 31–3
    caution before 29–31
    persons at risk 27, 33–5
    risk assessment 29
  release decision 39–41
  rights of 35–8
  see also **defendants**
suspended sentences 321–3
  breach of 322–3

T

tagging 75, 307, 328
taking into consideration 286–8, 298–9
tape recording of interviews 32
television link
  protection for young witnesses and 137, 213, 214, 215
theft
  mode of trial guidelines 112
third parties
  disclosure 181–2
time limits
  custody 62–3
  power to rectify mistakes 123
transcripts 256
trial
  Crown Court
    arraignment 197–203
    bail 226–7
    by judge alone 236–7
    changing plea 208–9
    closing speeches 219
    defence case 218–19
    effect of European Convention on Human Rights 233
    jury *see* **juries**
    no case to answer submission 216–18, 245–6
    preliminary hearings 194–7
    sentence 233
    summing up 220–6
    two or more defendants 219–20
    unrepresented defendants 220, 289–90
    verdict 225–6, 227–32
  mode of trial 97–113
    advance information 109
    advantages/disadvantages of each mode 108–9
    classification of offences 97–9, 141
    criminal damage cases 105–6, 113, 341–3
    linked summary and indictable offences 107–8
    national guidelines 110–13
    procedure for determination 99–105, 341–3
  pre-trial reviews 114–15
  summary trial
    absence of defendant 115–17
    clerk to justices and 123–6
    Criminal Procedure Rules 122
    power to rectify mistakes 123

preliminary hearings (*cont.*)
    private representations 117–18
    procedure 115, 122
    prosecution 119
    sentence 122
    taking plea 118–19
    verdict 121
  unduly long 249
trigger offences 26

U

unconditional bail 58–9
unpaid work
  as condition in community sentences 304–5
  as requirement in youth rehabilitation orders 327
unrepresented defendants 220, 289–90

V

venire de novo **writ** 261
verdict
  alternative 228–31
  Crown Court trial 225–6, 227–32
  discharge of jury 232
  failure to reach 232
  inconsistencies 248
  majority verdicts 231–2
  reaching a verdict 232
  retirement of jury 227–8
  summary trial 121
victims 344–51
  Code of Practice 345–6
  Commissioner for Victims and Witnesses 347–8
  compensation orders 349
  conduct in court 350–1
  intimidated 346
  obligations of service providers 346–7
  personal statement 348–9
  reparation 131, 350
  services to 345–6
  Victim's Charter 345
  vulnerable 346
video recording
  evidence given by 137, 213–15
violent offences
  extended sentences for 337–9
  mode of trial guidelines 112
  protection for young witnesses and 137
voluntary bills of indictment 158–9

W

warnings
  final warning scheme 132, 149–50, 152, 153
  informal 41
warrant for arrest 45–6, 96
witnesses
  Commissioner for Victims and Witnesses 347–8
  Crown Court trial 210
    special measures 213–16
    statements 211
  expert 175, 219, 225
  failure to call 225
  intention to call 174–5
  known to judge 248
  protection for young witnesses 136–8, 213–16
  securing attendance of 202–3
  special measures 136–7, 213–16
  summons 202–3
  Witness Service 348
  Youth Court 136–8
written charge and requisition 43–4
  amendment 44
  duplicity 44
  two or more charges 44

Y

young adults 148–9
young people *see* **children and young people**
Youth Court 6, 7, 130–53
  custodial sentences 329–30
  hearing procedure 142–3, 144
  layout 140
  non-custodial sentences 131, 324–30
  persons in court
    district judges 135–6
    magistrates 135–6
    media reporting 138–9
    parents 136
    probation officers 139
    public attendance 139–40
    witnesses 136–8
  reforms in youth justice system 130–2
  seating 140
  sentencing 143
  special measures 136–7
  as usual forum for juvenile defendants 134–5
youth offending teams 131
youth rehabilitation order 132, 326–8